THE DYSLEXIA DEBATE REVISITED

T0384596

In every country, and in every language, a significant proportion of children struggle to master the skill of reading. In 2014, *The Dyslexia Debate* examined the problematic interpretation of the term "dyslexia" as well as questioning its efficacy as a diagnosis. *The Dyslexia Debate Revisited* reflects on the changes in dyslexia assessment and treatment in the decade since then, including the introduction of dyslexia legislation in many US states. Addressing the critical responses to their original challenge of the dyslexia construct, Julian G. Elliott and Elena L. Grigorenko also consider why, despite scientific critiques, existing dyslexia conceptions and assessment practices continue to be highly attractive to many professionals, individuals, and families. Based on current scientific knowledge, the authors strive to promote a shared understanding of reading difficulties and emphasize the importance of providing timely and appropriate intervention and support to anyone who faces difficulties with learning to read.

JULIAN G. ELLIOTT is Principal of Collingwood College and Professor of Educational Psychology at the University of Durham. He is a Fellow of the Academy of Social Sciences, a Fellow of the British Psychological Society, and has been a teacher of children with learning difficulties and chartered educational psychologist.

ELENA L. GRIGORENKO is Professor of Psychology at the University of Houston and Human and Molecular Genetics at Baylor College of Medicine. She received doctorates in general (cognitive) psychology from Moscow State University and developmental psychology and genetics from Yale University before re-specializing in clinical psychology at Fielding University. She has published more than 600 peer-reviewed articles, book chapters, and books.

THE DYSLEXIA
DEBATE REVISITED

JULIAN G. ELLIOTT

Durham University

ELENA L. GRIGORENKO

University of Houston

Shaftesbury Road, Cambridge CB2 8EA, United Kingdom

One Liberty Plaza, 20th Floor, New York, NY 10006, USA

477 Williamstown Road, Port Melbourne, VIC 3207, Australia

314–321, 3rd Floor, Plot 3, Splendor Forum, Jasola District Centre,
New Delhi – 110025, India

103 Penang Road, #05–06/07, Visioncrest Commercial, Singapore 238467

Cambridge University Press is part of Cambridge University Press & Assessment,
a department of the University of Cambridge.

We share the University's mission to contribute to society through the pursuit of
education, learning and research at the highest international levels of excellence.

www.cambridge.org
Information on this title: www.cambridge.org/9781316514443

DOI: 10.1017/9781009083140

© Julian G. Elliott and Elena L. Grigorenko 2024

This publication is in copyright. Subject to statutory exception and to the provisions
of relevant collective licensing agreements, no reproduction of any part may take
place without the written permission of Cambridge University Press & Assessment.

First published 2024

Printed in the United Kingdom by CPI Group Ltd, Croydon CR0 4YY

A catalogue record for this publication is available from the British Library

Library of Congress Cataloging-in-Publication Data
NAMES: Elliott, Julian G., 1955– author. | Grigorenko, Elena L., author.
TITLE: The dyslexia debate revisited / Julian G. Elliott,
Durham University, Elena L. Grigorenko, University of Houston.
DESCRIPTION: Cambridge, United Kingdom ; New York, NY :
Cambridge University Press, 2024. | Includes bibliographical references and index.
IDENTIFIERS: LCCN 2023045131 | ISBN 9781316514443 (hardback) | ISBN 9781009078665
(paperback) | ISBN 9781009083140 (ebook)
SUBJECTS: LCSH: Dyslexia. | Dyslexia – Psychological aspects.
CLASSIFICATION: LCC RJ496.A5 E523 2024 | DDC 616.85/53–dc23/eng/20231221
LC record available at https://lccn.loc.gov/2023045131

ISBN 978-1-316-51444-3 Hardback
ISBN 978-1-009-07866-5 Paperback

Cambridge University Press & Assessment has no responsibility for the persistence
or accuracy of URLs for external or third-party internet websites referred to in this
publication and does not guarantee that any content on such websites is, or will
remain, accurate or appropriate.

Contents

Figures

Table

Foreword

Jack M. Fletcher
University of Houston

The Dyslexia Debate Revisited marks a return to the issues and recommendations first presented in Elliott and Grigorenko's *The Dyslexia Debate* (2014). The dyslexia debate refers to questions about the validity and utility of the dyslexia label, a debate that has been active for at least fifty years. In addition to reviewing the evidence on both sides of the dyslexia debate, the book provides a detailed update of the scientific evidence on the cognitive and neurobiological correlates of dyslexia, and its assessment and instruction. It is a scholarly and eminently practical review of scientific evidence and its application to practical issues related to dyslexia.

The book is organized as six chapters, starting with the dyslexia debate (Chapter 1) and then chapters on cognitive explanations (Chapter 2), neurobiology (Chapter 3), and assessment, instruction, and intervention (Chapter 4). The fifth chapter returns to the dyslexia debate and the positive and negative consequences of the label. The final chapter provides a set of well-reasoned conclusions and recommendations that are different from *The Dyslexia Debate* (2014). In this foreword, I will first discuss the issues that made their earlier book unnecessarily controversial and then turn to what makes it a truly excellent contribution to the field – the reviews of the research base on assessment and identification, cognitive and neurobiological correlates, and intervention.

The scientific contributions of the 2014 book were not sufficiently appreciated because of the provocative title and the overt questioning of the validity and utility of the dyslexia label. This questioning of the value of dyslexia as a diagnostic label seemed to surprise professional and advocacy groups despite the thorough grounding in the scientific literature and the long history of concern about the label in the scientific community. As the authors note in the present volume, they did not question whether there was a subgroup of individuals with learning disabilities who have significant problems with basic reading and spelling skills. Rather, they questioned whether this subgroup was adequately captured by the dyslexia label because it is hard to define this subgroup consistently. In addition, there is a lack of evidence for a subgroup of individuals with basic reading and spelling problems that are unique and separate from other individuals with basic reading and spelling skill deficits who should not be called dyslexic. In both 2014 and the present text, Elliott and Grigorenko systematically review different hypotheses about how dyslexia might be differentiated into subgroups of children with basic reading and spelling skill deficits. They examine hypotheses related to intelligence, cognitive strengths and weaknesses, socioeconomic status and other so-called exclusions, and instructional response, just to highlight some of the major hypotheses.

Even in this new volume, Elliott and Grigorenko find little evidence to support these hypothetical differentiations. To make this conclusion plainer, ideas that dyslexia is present only in individuals with high intelligence quotient (IQ) scores or cognitive strengths are debunked. Efforts to explain away reading problems in relation to socioeconomic status or lack of opportunity to learn are also identified as unsupported by evidence. They give a nod to the hypothesis that inadequate response to instruction may have some viability but note the practicality of implementing the multi-tiered service delivery systems needed to implement response to intervention methods. More broadly, Elliott and Grigorenko address in uncomfortable detail the social and economic inequities associated with efforts to make dyslexia a unique disorder requiring specialized assessment and intervention available only to families with means. As they note, presently there is no basis for differentiating individuals with dyslexia from slow learners, backward readers, garden-variety poor readers, and other similar labels if the definitional criterion is poor word reading and spelling skills. And even if these different subgroups could be differentiated, there is little evidence that it makes a difference in assessment and instruction.

There is no question that children and adults who have word reading and spelling problems exist and are distinct from individuals with reading problems primarily in comprehension, with primary learning disabilities in math or writing, or comorbid conditions like ADHD. It is also clear that these children are under-identified in schools. Quinn and Wagner (2015) reported that schools identified only one in four boys and one in seven girls as learning disabled when they met research-based criteria for reading difficulties. Part of the problem is that if the label is used with all these children and adults, the prevalence is very high and resources would be strained. But as Elliott and Grigorenko suggest, this problem is partly due to inadequate instruction and the idea that dyslexia requires highly specialized assessment programs from a remedial model where only certain types of "dyslexia-specific" methods are appropriate. Not only is this view inaccurate, it also prevents access to effective instruction for many children.

In 1977, the National Institute of Mental Health convened a meeting that was summarized by a series of chapters and critiques in seven areas of dyslexia research (Benton & Pearl, 1978): nature and prevalence, psychological factors, neurobehavioral research, encephalographic and neurophysiological studies, genetic factors, early detection and prevention, and remediation. The dyslexia debate echoed throughout the conference and the book, with the opening chapter (Rutter, 1978) reviewing different hypotheses about how a specific dyslexia syndrome could be identified that was different from other kinds of reading problems. In particular, Rutter noted that it was not possible to differentiate individuals with reading problems according to whether the problems were genetic, brain-related, or environmental. Elliott and Grigorenko echo these conclusions almost fifty years later. Rutter observed that dyslexia was not obviously a qualitative variation, but a quantitative differentiation – a matter of degree – and the dimensionality of the attributes of dyslexia is now widely accepted by the scientific community. Rutter concluded that "Although the term 'dyslexia' has been used repeatedly throughout the paper, it does not refer to any well-defined group of disorders" (Rutter, 1978: 27). In the incisive and integrative summary at the end of the book, Benton noted that dyslexia research, active since the beginning of the twentieth century, had been particularly prolific in the most recent fifteen years. Nevertheless:

> It might be assumed that, after 70 years of scientific study of developmental dyslexia, a clinical description of the qualitative features of the reading performances of an individual child would provide the basis for investigations of dyslexic children. In fact, this is far from being the case. (Benton & Pearl, 1978: 475)

A central recommendation of the conference was to consider dyslexia as multifactorial, likely manifesting as a set of syndromes. This led to a decade of searching for subtypes of dyslexia throughout the 1980s that produced few reliable findings with clinical significance. This was partly a result of the same problem that had frustrated participants in the 1977 NIMH conference – the heterogeneity of children and adults with dyslexia. Elliott and Grigorenko's new book helps us to understand that this heterogeneity results partly from comorbidity, the multiple cognitive factors associated with reading development and difficulties, and the complex patterns of heritability and environment that lead to brains that struggle to mediate reading skills.

Here we turn to the chapters in the present text on scientific research, where progress since the 1977 conference (and *The Dyslexia Debate*, 2014) is so clearly apparent. In Chapter 2, the authors thoroughly review different competing cognitive explanations of dyslexia, noting the strong support for links with phonological processing and the weaker evidence for other correlates, especially outside the language domain. In the 1977 NIMH conference, Doehring (1978) referred to behavioral research on dyslexia as a "tangled web." He attributed the web to the focus on trying to associate dyslexia with unitary deficits, which he characterized as a problem given the multifactorial nature of dyslexia, suggesting the need for a multivariate approach. Elliott and Grigorenko echo this notion, critiquing what is still a tendency to identify and compare isolated skills in individuals with basic reading problems and typically developing individuals. Since these skills are generally correlated and the groups are sampled from different parts of the normal distribution, these comparisons will yield a significant difference on that skill and often lead to a "theory" of dyslexia. The question is the size of the difference and its uniqueness in an ocean of correlated deficits. The authors note that no single skill deficit explains all cases of dyslexia and nicely summarize the overriding consensus of the scientific community for multiple deficit conceptualizations of cognitive deficits in dyslexia. At the same time, the authors argue that the evidence for some cognitive explanations is stronger than others, with phonological processing standing out as a robust and unique correlate, especially in a multivariate context. The research on phonological processing represents real advances in dyslexia research over the past fifty years. However, the unitary deficit approach persists to the detriment of the field.

Chapter 3 is a masterful review of genetic and neural research findings on the heritability of dyslexia and the role of the brain. A particular strength is the careful explanation of the different research paradigms used to study neurobiological factors, which makes the chapter consumable by the general population of individuals interested in dyslexia. Here we learn about candidate genes, genome-wide searches, and behavioral genetic research on dyslexia. The section on genetics is very thorough and illuminating: while we are not yet able to map out the genetic contributions to dyslexia, Elliott and Grigorenko show that the field has progressed far beyond the review of the heritability of dyslexia in the 1977 NIMH conference, which was mostly based on demonstration that familial patterns of association-reading problems run in families.

The material on the role of the brain in reading and dyslexia is similarly strong. Elliott and Grigorenko again help the reader understand different paradigms and what we know about brain mechanisms in reading and dyslexia. This area has also progressed considerably since 1977 because of new technology and more rigorous studies. There is quite a contrast with the almost apologetic conclusions on the role of endogenous factors in dyslexia at the 1977 conference. The authors balance this evidence with attention to environmental and instructional factors in dyslexia, which clearly have endogenous and exogenous causes that vary across individuals in ways we cannot yet define.

In Chapter 4 on assessment and intervention, Elliott and Grigorenko make a strong case for assessments that are straightforward, simpler than many current approaches, and directly linked to intervention. They review the role of cognitive factors and conclude that the primary focus should be on the assessment of reading and writing skills, especially since the extensive "dyslexia" batteries used to identify dyslexia are neither strongly supported by research nor related to treatment. These assessments are also inequitable because they are typically only available to individuals with economic means and may deprive many children and adults of access to resources that would address their reading and spelling difficulties. In intervention, the authors support the implementation of evidence-based instruction based on what I have often termed "the science of reading." In intervention, they summarize the features of effective intervention, noting that there is little evidence for treatment programs specific to children with dyslexia that are not appropriate for the broader population of individuals with basic reading and spelling problems. They also identify approaches to intervention with limited evidence for effectiveness. This chapter is practical and eminently readable by the spectrum of parents, professionals, and researchers interested in dyslexia.

Chapter 5 is really a return to the dyslexia debate and expansion of the themes introduced in Chapter 1. Here Elliott and Grigorenko explore in depth policy at national levels that affects how dyslexia is identified and served. They evaluate positive and negative consequences of the dyslexia label, including its role in access to services. But resources are finite and the dyslexia label has created an industry built upon defining who, among poor readers, has dyslexia and who does not. This false differentiation leads to inequities because in many cases access is only possible for economically advantaged families. At the end of the chapter the authors review many fallacies about the dyslexia label that are popular, but not supported by scientific evidence.

In the final chapter, Elliott and Grigorenko reach a conclusion not present in *The Dyslexia Debate*. Instead of recommending that the dyslexia label be abandoned, and that the term reading disability be used instead, they suggest maintaining the use of the term dyslexia so long as it is not used as a diagnosable condition intended to refer to or support identification of a unique group of individuals with a qualitatively different reading problem from others who have difficulties with word reading and spelling. They recognize the value of the label, its entrenchment in educational parlance, and its positive consequences. This conclusion is more than reasonable – it is supported by the evidence in the book. Part of the tangled web described by Doehring (1978) occurs because of the mixing of features that describe the reading problem with cognitive level explanations and factors that reflect comorbidity. This differentiation is responsible for much of the progress in the last thirty years. If we focus on a subgroup of children with basic reading and spelling problems, explanations at a cognitive and neurobiological level begin to align and we see more replication across laboratories across these domains. What the 1977 conference did not recognize, and which is clearly laid out in the conclusions of Elliott and Grigorenko, is the importance of beginning by identifying individuals with basic reading problems. For Elliott and Grigorenko and many others, all of these children display the defining characteristics of dyslexia – word reading and spelling difficulties. They will vary in the cognitive and neurobiological correlates, but not in ways that are obviously relevant to assessment and intervention. Such an approach creates a large population of individuals with dyslexia who vary across levels of intelligence, socioeconomic class, and instructional opportunity. But we do know how to screen for risk in these children, introduce early intervention that may prevent the reading problem, and make the resources associated with the identification and treatment of dyslexia available to many more individuals than is currently the case. It is hard not to agree with this conclusion from Elliott and Grigorenko.

Not all will agree with the dyslexia nihilism in the authors' interpretation of the dyslexia debate. But their reasoning and support from the scientific literature is strong, and consistent with the scientific consensus around dyslexia. Translating this consensus to everyday school environments will continue to be difficult, but this book is a good place for the curious to start. It is certainly appropriate for graduate and undergraduate instruction. It is equally important for professionals who focus on dyslexia and learning disabilities. Parents may especially find the book helpful as they advocate for their children and address the barriers that prevent children with basic reading and spelling problems (i.e., dyslexia) accessing services. In the end, it is important for the reader to understand that *The Dyslexia Debate Revisited* is not about "dyslexia as it should be," but rather "dyslexia as it is."

Preface

In every country, and in every language, a significant proportion of children struggle to master the skill of reading. Although many young people gradually overcome their initial difficulty and acquire functional literacy, there is a significant proportion who continue to encounter difficulties that persist throughout childhood into adulthood. As these individuals struggle to cope with the changing demands of school and wider life, the hardship and difficulties that typically result are often incapacitating, undermining, and distressing. Given such a scenario, it is hardly surprising that there is often a strong desire on the part of these individuals, their families, and their teachers, for some form of clinical diagnosis that can help to explain the reasons underpinning these problems and which can indicate, and secure, effective forms of intervention.

For such reasons, one can understand why the term most frequently used to describe this phenomenon – dyslexia – has such strong resonance. However, as Jack M. Fletcher notes in the Foreword to this book, challenge to the scientific rigor and educational utility of this term has been evident since the middle of the last century. In seeking a resolution to this, our book, *The Dyslexia Debate* (Elliott & Grigorenko, 2014) represented an attempt to draw upon contemporary research findings to inform and resolve differing scientific and practitioner understandings which could underpin recommendations for policy and practice. Our central conclusion – that the term "dyslexia" was unhelpful and operated to the disadvantage of many struggling learners – led to our recommendation that its use should be discontinued. As expected, this met with strong responses, supportive and critical, from multiple stakeholders.

Ten years later, much has been learned and we consider it timely to revisit the debate – hence this present volume. This book follows a structure that closely follows that of *The Dyslexia Debate*. As before, it explores the history and evolution of the term prior to examining the contribution to the debate of each of the core disciplines – genetics, neuroscience, cognitive science, and psychology. It then examines educational issues concerning the assessment, prevention, and treatment of reading disability. A key issue that is explored is whether there is value in assessing and addressing underlying cognitive processes widely considered to be markers of dyslexia, or alternatively, whether it is preferable to focus primarily upon core academic skills.

The present text departs from the structure of the 2014 book by adding a new chapter that considers why, despite critiques based upon the scientific literature, existing dyslexia conceptions and assessment practices continue to be highly attractive to many professionals and the lay public. Critical responses to our earlier challenge to the construct, and to our recommendation that the use of the term dyslexia should be discontinued, are examined and analysed. The significant expansion of the dyslexia construct, in some cases ranging far beyond reading, and the growing importance and contribution of neurodiverse understandings, emphasizing difference rather than disability, are examined, and their contribution to the dyslexia debate is evaluated.

Finally, in the light of our examination of all of these issues, we revisit and reflect upon our earlier position concerning the value of the dyslexia construct. Recognizing the resilience of the label, and perhaps a more nuanced understanding of exactly which aspects are most problematic, we recommend a new solution. Our recommended approach, while different to that offered in *The Dyslexia Debate,* is designed to achieve exactly the same primary goals as before: to ensure a commonality of understanding based upon current scientific knowledge and to concentrate attention and resources upon the provision of appropriate and timely intervention and support for all who struggle to learn to read.

Many of the specific disciplinary issues discussed in this book are complex and draw upon rather specialized language and technical terminology. For this reason, most readers will encounter work in one or more disciplines which, initially at least, is likely to prove challenging. This may be exacerbated, or perhaps aided, by our very deliberate decision to offer a comprehensive set of references that provides an encyclopedic overview of the available literature. However, although gaining a full and detailed grasp of all the issues is likely to require further independent reading, it is hoped that the contents of this book will enable the reader to grasp key issues in the dyslexia debate.

In preparing this book, we have sought advice and guidance from many scholars. We wish to thank them all for their help and guidance, particularly to Joni Holmes, Jessica Church-Lang, Kelly Mahaffy, and

Deny Menghini. We also thank colleagues at Cambridge University Press for their support, faith, and patience and wish to acknowledge Janet Croog's talent and skill in preparing the figures. We owe a particular debt to Gordon Lee, our outstanding copy editor. Of course, all remaining errors and misunderstandings are our own.

Finally, we would like to express our heartfelt gratitude to Jack M. Fletcher, not only for providing the Foreword but, more importantly, for his immense contribution to the field over a period of more than four decades.

Abbreviations

ADHD	attention deficit hyperactivity disorder
aMRI	anatomical magnetic resonance imaging
BOLD	blood oxygenation-level-dependent
DD	double deficit
DEST	*Dyslexia Early Screening Test*
DIBELS	*Dynamic Indicators of Basic Early Literacy Skills*
DLD	developmental language disorder
DSM	*Diagnostic and Statistical Manual*
DSR	dyslexic struggling reader
DTI	diffusion tensor imaging
EEG	electroencephalography
EF	executive functioning
ERF	event-related field
ERP	event-related potentials
fMRI	functional magnetic resonance imaging
fNIRS	functional near-infrared spectroscopy
GRB	genomic regulatory block
GWAS	genome-wide association studies
IC	inhibitory control
ICD	*International Classification of Diseases*
IDA	International Dyslexia Association
IOR	inhibition of return
IQ	intelligence quotient
LC	language comprehension
LD	learning disability
MEG	magnetoencephalography
MMF	mismatch field
MMN	mismatch negativity
MRI	magnetic resonance imaging
MRS	magnetic resonance spectroscopy

MTSS	multi-tiered systems of support
NDSR	non-dyslexic struggling reader
NIBS	noninvasive brain stimulation
OG	Orton-Gillingham approach
PA	phonological awareness
PET	positron emission tomography
PHAST	Phonological and Strategy Training
PRS	polygenetic risk scores
RAN	rapid automatized naming
RAVE-O	*Retrieval, Automaticity, Vocabulary Elaboration, Orthography*
RC	reading comprehension
RSFC	resting-state functional connectivity
RTI	response to intervention
SAS	sluggish attentional shifting
SBM	surface-based morphometry
SD	standard deviation
SES	socioeconomic status
SLD	specific learning difficulty
SNP	single-nucleotide polymorphism
SoR	science of reading
SSD	speech sound disorder
tACS	transcranial alternating current stimulation
tDCS	transcranial direct current stimulation
TMS	transcranial magnetic stimulation
tRNS	transcranial random noise stimulation
TS	temporal sampling
VAS	visual attention span
VBM	voxel-based morphometry
WM	working memory

CHAPTER I

What Is Dyslexia?

Introduction

One type of learning disability, formally described more than a century ago, has been estimated as being currently experienced by a billion people across the world.[1] Its nature, and the best ways for it to be tackled, have been scientifically examined for decades by researchers working in the fields of genetics, neuroscience, cognitive science, psychology, education, sociology, and social policy, leading to the publication of many thousands of research papers, books, monographs, manuals, academic theses, and technical reports. It is now one of the major areas of professional focus of educational (school) and clinical psychologists, speech and language therapists, and teachers of children with learning difficulties. Its formal diagnosis often results in more favorable educational resourcing, special accommodations for examinations, classwork, and other activities in educational and vocational settings, and more responsive and sympathetic understanding from friends, family, colleagues, and the general public. Its assessment and intervention have become a multimillion dollar industry attracting the interest of parents, teachers, lecturers, clinicians, politicians, and the general public with claims of expert analyses and wonder cures. Reference to this disability is ubiquitous within most industrialized societies and its salience has been increased by frequent reference to famous figures from history, politics, the arts, and commerce who have achieved greatly in their specialist fields despite struggles with this problem. Some have argued that this is not a disability but a difference, and, for some, it can be considered as a gift that offers many compensatory strengths and advantages. Nevertheless, its legacy in terms of social and emotional trauma and its challenge to the individual's prospects of educational and vocational success are substantial.

---

[1] https://dyslexiaida.org/times-square; accessed November 16, 2023.

Indeed, it is widely accepted that its prevalence severely undermines society's ability to grow and prosper.

Given the above scenario, one might expect that science would be able to provide a clear conceptualization, describe its fundamental nature and causal biological and cognitive processes, articulate how it should be assessed, highlight effective evidence-based forms of intervention, and ensure that unsubstantiated programs lacking strong empirical support were avoided or challenged. Educationalists and clinicians would ensure that not only were they familiar with this knowledge base but they would also act accordingly. Based upon the scientific literature, there would be clear and consistent criteria for its diagnosis, and the basis for clinical judgements would not differ significantly from one assessor to another. Clinical judgements would in no way be inappropriately influenced by political, economic, or client pressures. It would be questionable for professionals to persevere in the use of a diagnostic label that has been criticized for being amorphous, nebulous, variously understood and operationalized, and thus scientifically flawed. Neither would it be appropriate to offer justification on the grounds that, although these criticisms are valid, its use can nevertheless prove helpful for those so labeled. Such a stance might seem unacceptable where there is a split between diagnosed dyslexic "winners" and other poor reader "losers" that, to a significant degree, reflects existing social inequities.

Unfortunately, the scenario above describes science, policy, and practice in the field of dyslexia. Despite the phenomenal degree of attention it has attracted for decades, dyslexia remains a "very hot" topic in the scientific literature on literacy, with seemingly little resolution of a number of fundamental areas of debate (Cassidy, Ortlieb, & Grote-Garcia, 2022; Grote-Garcia & Ortlieb, 2023).

Although the first account of "word-blindness" was produced in 1676 by the physician John Schmidt, much of the early published work appeared in the latter part of the nineteenth century, a time when an inability to learn to read first became a medical concern (Kirby, 2020a). Early investigations were largely concerned to examine difficulties that had been acquired as a result of some form of brain trauma. In 1872, Sir William Broadbent reported the case of a man who, following head injury lost the capacity to read, despite being able to write with little difficulty. Although he had good conversational skills and extensive vocabulary, he struggled to name objects presented to him. Broadbent asserted that the reading failure was a result of this more general difficulty in naming objects. Five years later Kussmaul (1877) reported on the case of an adult patient with no apparent disabilities other than severe reading difficulties. Kussmaul coined the term "word-blindness" to describe the inability to read text despite sound eyesight, intelligence, and speech.

The term "dyslexia" was first used in 1887 by Rudolf Berlin, a German opthalmologist, to describe a particular form of word-blindness found in adults that, he argued, was caused by brain lesions. Berlin contended that severe damage would result in alexia, a total inability to read, whereas, partial damage would most likely result in dyslexia, a significant difficulty in decoding written symbols. Here, the focus was upon the effect of a physical trauma of some kind, "acquired dyslexia," rather than that which develops naturally from a young age, "developmental dyslexia," the focus of almost all of the dyslexia literature.

The idea that "word-blindness" could be a developmental, as well as an acquired condition, came somewhat later. As Shaywitz and Shaywitz (2020b) note, this is unsurprising as the suddenness of an acquired loss is considerably more salient than the more subtle picture of unfolding developmental difficulties. In 1896, a paper on "Congenital Word Blindness" by a British physician, W. Pringle Morgan, described a child of fourteen years of age who had failed to learn to read despite normal intelligence and good eyesight. Noting the boy's other abilities, he observed that, "The schoolmaster who has taught him for some years says that he would be the smartest lad in the school life if the instruction were entirely oral" (Pringle Morgan, 1896: 1378). Pringle Morgan described two generations of one family with six cases that had strikingly similar symptoms and opined that the problem was congenital, involving a defective ability to store visual impressions of words.

Pringle Morgan's paper acted as a stimulus for a flurry of case studies, most notably by a Scottish ophthalmologist, James Hinshelwood, who gathered data on several cases involving both acquired and congenital word-blindness. The children he reported upon in a classic text, *Congenital Word-Blindness* (Hinshelwood, 1917) were typically male (as were the majority of similar cases of this period [Stephenson, 1904]), intelligent, had sound eyesight, and performed well on oral tasks.

Following an autopsy upon a patient whose progress he had monitored for several years, Hinshelwood (1902) attributed the cause of reading disability to the angular gyrus. He suggested that the primary disability was visual memory for words and letters and, advocated one-to-one training designed to increase visual memory as the preferred form of intervention. Noting the embarrassment and ridicule often experienced by poor readers in the classroom, he commented:

> It is a matter of the highest importance to recognize as early as possible the true nature of this defect, when it is met with in a child. It may prevent

much waste of valuable time and may save the child from suffering and
cruel treatment. When a child manifests great difficulty in learning to read
and is unable to keep up in progress with its fellows, the cause is generally
assigned to stupidity or laziness, and no systematized method is directed to
the training of such a child. A little knowledge and careful analysis of the
child's case would soon make it clear that the difficulty experienced was
due to a defect in the visual memory of words and letters; the child would
then be regarded in the proper light as one with a congenital defect in a
particular area of the brain, a defect which, however, can often be remedied
by persevering and persistent training. The sooner the true nature of the
defect is realised, the better are the chances of the child's improvement.
(Hinshelwood, 1902, cited in Shaywitz & Shaywitz, 2020b: 22)

In their historical account of learning disabilities, a term that includes a
number of specific areas of problematic functioning, including reading disability, Hallahan and Mercer (2001) observed that groundbreaking work
largely shifted from Europe to the USA during the 1920s. With the increasing trend towards mass education and the issues that resulted in conjunction with the dissemination of the idea of universal literacy (Grigorenko,
2011), many researchers found themselves with the responsibility not only
of understanding and explaining children's academic and behavioral difficulties, but also of taking a lead in assessment and remediation techniques,
particularly in relation to reading disabilities (Hallahan & Mock, 2003).

Leading clinical researchers at this time were Samuel Orton and
Grace Fernald. Fernald was a psychologist who employed a multisensory
approach for those with reading difficulties and sought to evaluate the success or otherwise of her techniques by maintaining detailed case records of
her clients' progress. Despite the rather anecdotal mode of evaluation, still
largely the case for multisensory approaches today (see Chapter 4), such
techniques have an intuitive appeal and continue to be popular among
specialist dyslexia teachers. Such professionals are typically qualified by
accrediting bodies to conduct informal curriculum-based assessments and
deliver specialist teaching programs to those with dyslexia.

Orton, Fernald's contemporary, was a neurologist who became best
known for his work on educational intervention, in particular multisensory approaches and an emphasis upon phonics. Orton attempted to
understand the origins of reading difficulties, introducing a number of
ideas that added to contemporary understandings. Like his intellectual
predecessor, Hinshelwood, he was interested in areas of the brain that
might be influential but believed those other than the angular gyrus were
involved. He suggested that reading difficulties were primarily the result
of poor cerebral dominance in which the nondominant hemisphere stored

a different representation from that of the dominant one. This explained the common tendency for cases to exhibit letter and word reversals, and the use of mirror reading and writing. To reflect a shift from an emphasis upon purely visual deficits, Orton recommended that the term "word-blindness" should be replaced by "strephosymbolia" which in Greek means twisted. His work proved highly influential and promoted much theorizing on various visual mechanisms held to be responsible for reading difficulties (see Kirby & Snowling, 2022, for further detail).

These early pioneers sought to understand a condition that continues to pose significant problems for many individuals, and challenges to those who seek to help them. Their puzzlement over the particular problems encountered by a small number of children would appear sufficient to refute any suggestion that dyslexia or reading disability is merely the consequence of poor teaching. Since then, more than a century of research activity has provided incontrovertible evidence that some children experience particular difficulties that render the reading process highly problematic. The original belief of these early clinicians that the difficulty was caused by a visual pathology has now been largely rejected in favor of language-based origins (see Chirkina & Grigorenko, 2014, for details of similar conclusions that were reached rather earlier in the Soviet Union). Nevertheless, a conception of dyslexia as essentially a visual problem is still widely held by the general public (Johnston & Scanlon, 2021) and the role of visual factors in reading difficulty has attracted greater researcher attention, particularly as the primary focus has moved from visual processing to visual attention (see Chapter 2).

Given all of the above, it may seem incomprehensible that some have claimed that dyslexia does not actually exist (Hitchens, 2014; Schwartz, 2019); that it is a concocted invention that serves to exculpate those who are responsible for the delivery of inadequate education. As discussed throughout the present text, it is clear that there are many children who struggle to learn to read for reasons other than poor-quality schooling.

Other critics contend that the term is little more than a confected prop that largely meets the needs of the middle classes, particularly the "worried mothers" of struggling learners (see Kirby, 2019, 2020b). Such arguments have tended to be promoted by political or social commentators with an insufficient understanding of the science involved.

In many ways, the question "Does dyslexia exist?" is both unhelpful and misleading. It typically leads to the answer that, of course "it" exists because the severity of problems that some children encounter with reading are surely all too real. However, the primary issue here is not whether biologically based reading difficulties exist (the answer is an unequivocal "yes," although these are intertwined with environmental factors) but rather, how we should best understand and address literacy problems across clinical, educational, occupational, and social policy contexts. Essentially, what is sometimes known as "the dyslexia debate" has centered upon the extent to which this construct operates as a rigorous scientific construct that adds to, rather than reduces, our capacity to identify and help those who struggle to learn to read. Allied to this is disagreement as to whether dyslexia should be employed to describe difficulties that range far beyond literacy. To achieve any meaningful resolution of the debate we need a consensual understanding of how to define and operationalize the term, and it is here that fundamental problems first arise.

Definitions of Dyslexia

> Without an agreed-on definition that can be implemented reliably and validly, understanding the nature, causes, and best treatments for reading disability is unlikely. Similarly, an agreed-on definition is essential for practice.
>
> (Brown Waesche et al., 2011: 296)

Somewhat paradoxically, defining dyslexia is seemingly both very easy and very difficult. It is easy, largely because most parties are agreed that the definition should principally concern the inherent and particular difficulties that are encountered by those who struggle to learn how to read. It is difficult because the field has been unable to produce a universally accepted definition (Helland, 2022). As noted in the above extract, without a universally agreed operational definition, we cannot be sure that assessments are measuring the same thing, and as a result, there are likely to be serious doubts about any resultant diagnosis or classification.

One of the particular difficulties concerning definitions of dyslexia is that the term has variously been seen as different from, or synonymous to, several other labels that involve problems with literacy. These include specific reading retardation, reading difficulties, specific reading difficulties, reading disability, learning disability, unexpected reading difficulty, and specific learning difficulties. These terms overlap substantially and vary according to causal assumptions (Rice & Brooks, 2004), thus compounding the confusions that abound.

Irrespective of the specifics of the definition, it is generally agreed that the core problem of dyslexia is difficulty in accurately and fluently reading text; this is why it is sometimes also known as a word-level reading disorder (Miciak & Fletcher, 2023). Single word reading is seen as important for studying word recognition skill as, presented in isolation, words are unable to offer any semantic or syntactic cues that could assist word identification.

Many writers use the term "decoding" as synonymous with "word recognition" (e.g., Hoover & Gough, 1990). Here the former term reflects the notion that print effectively operates as a code that needs to be deciphered in order to convert printed text into language. On the grounds that words like "yacht" and "does" cannot be decoded using knowledge of letter–sound relationships, others tend to use "decoding" in a narrower manner. While reading irregular words places significant emphasis upon sight-word recognition, and the distinction between these two terms is important for instructional purposes, it should be noted that there is a strong relationship between phonological decoding and sight-word reading (Aaron et al., 1999). In order to avoid potential misunderstandings resulting from different usage in the literature, the terms "word recognition" and "decoding" are largely used interchangeably throughout this book.

Word recognition and decoding can be contrasted with the ultimate goal of reading – taking meaning from the written word (Nation & Snowling, 1998). While decoding skill and reading comprehension are highly related (Fletcher et al., 2019; Georgiou et al., 2022), the overlap should not be overestimated. Some people can understand considerably more of a passage of text than one would expect on the basis of their reading skills; others may read the words without apparent difficulty but derive little meaning from them. Unsurprisingly, however, those who experience severe difficulties with word recognition will usually experience associated problems of reading comprehension, in part because the effort that must be expended upon decoding is likely to result in heavy cognitive load demands that detract from their capacity to focus upon deriving meaning.

The issue as to whether spelling difficulty should be seen as a core component of dyslexia has been subject to varying opinion. Although most definitions of dyslexia focus upon reading difficulty, problems with spelling are often identified as key symptoms. While word reading and spelling skills are closely related processes (in their meta-analysis, Kim, Wolters, and Lee (2023) reports a high correlation of r = 0.82), they are far from identical skills. In order to understand and address literacy problems, it is important to differentiate clearly between them (see Kim & Petscher, 2023, for a detailed discussion).

In reconciling debate about the use and value of the term "dyslexia," it is first helpful to have a clear understanding of the different ways that this term has been conceptualized, understood, and operationalized. In an attempt to highlight some key distinctions, Elliott (2020) identified four broad categories:

- Dyslexia 1: a synonym for reading disability (i.e., a significant problem with the accuracy and/or fluency of single-word decoding which affects word reading in isolation or in text);
- Dyslexia 2: a condition manifested by a clinically derived subgroup of poor decoders;
- Dyslexia 3: a condition manifested by persistent intractability to high-quality reading intervention;
- Dyslexia 4: a neurodiverse condition that involves a range of cognitive problems, one of which may be a difficulty in decoding.

Each of these is now considered in turn.

Dyslexia 1: A Synonym for Reading Disability

There is an important distinction between defining dyslexia as an end state represented by word reading deficits and basing the definition upon the supposed causes of such deficits (Catts & Petscher, 2022). The former represents the approach that is typically employed by researchers (Elliott, 2020; Odegard, Farris, & Washington, 2022) who largely use the terms reading disability and dyslexia as synonyms to describe a single-word-level reading difficulty that may involve either or both reading accuracy and reading fluency (Fletcher et al., 2019; Lopes et al., 2020; Pennington, McGrath, & Peterson, 2019). Reading fluency concerns the ability to read text both accurately and speedily. It is often considered to demonstrate the extent to which word reading has achieved a level of automaticity such that it has become instantaneous and effortless (LaBerge & Samuels, 1974).

Underpinning a Dyslexia 1 conception is a recognition that reading is a skill that is normally distributed in the population with no clear boundary existing between so-called "normal" and "disabled" performance.

> Dyslexia is mainly defined as the low end of a normal distribution of word reading ability (Rodgers, 1983; Shaywitz et al., 1992). Thus, in order to diagnose the disorder, a somewhat arbitrary cutoff must be set on a continuous variable. (Peterson & Pennington, 2015: 285)
>
> Dyslexics are children (and later adults) whose reading is at the low end of a normal distribution. Reading skill results from a combination of dimensional factors (that is, ones that vary in degree), yielding a bell-shaped curve. The reading difficulties of the children in the lower tail are severe and require special attention. Dyslexia refers to these children. Viewed this way,

dyslexia is on a continuum with normal reading. All children face the same challenges in learning to read but dyslexics have more difficulty with the essential components. (Seidenberg, 2017: 156–157)

There is no doubt that dyslexia exists as the lower part of a continuous distribution of basic reading skills. (Miciak & Fletcher, 2020: 346)

Such difficulties would typically be present from an early age and prove difficult to remedy even by high-quality teaching (Snowling, Hulme, & Nation, 2020).

Lopes et al. (2020) analysed 800 dyslexia studies across a range of scientific disciplines (genetics, neuroscience, psychology, education) that had been undertaken over the previous two decades. While clear criteria for participant recruitment were rarely made explicit, the use of the term dyslexia was typically employed to describe poor readers in general (and sometimes spellers). An attempt to identify dyslexic groups, as distinct from other poor readers, was found in only about six percent of the studies.

Dyslexia 2: A Condition Manifested by a Clinically Derived Subgroup of Poor Decoders

Much of the fuel for the dyslexia debate lies in the fact that the use of the terms "dyslexic" or "with dyslexia" to describe all those operating at the lower extreme of reading ability is far less common in educational, clinical, and occupational professional practice. Deeming a Dyslexia 1 conception to be overly inclusive, a significant proportion of psychologists, educators, medical practitioners, and members of the lay public reserve its use to describe a subgroup existing within a larger pool of poor decoders. Here, not all of those with word-level reading difficulties are considered to be dyslexic, and the relative influence of nature (their biological features) and nurture (their home environments and instructional histories) is generally perceived to be an important discriminating factor.

In recent years, dyslexia has become a high profile issue in the United States where extensive lobbying from support groups has resulted in the introduction of federal and state legislation for dyslexia identification and intervention that is largely independent of the existing framework for children with learning difficulties (Gabriel, 2020a; Miciak & Fletcher, 2020). Such developments are prompted by a belief that the needs of the dyslexic child often go unrecognized:

> Despite the prevalence of dyslexia, many Americans remain undiagnosed, untreated and silently struggle at school or work. (Lamar Smith,

Chairman of the US Science, Space, and Technology Committee, quoted in Richardson, 2016)

It is a matter for debate whether Smith's observation should be interpreted as suggesting that US schools are failing to identify and cater for large numbers of struggling readers (i.e., Dyslexia 1) or, alternatively, that there is a large unrecognized pool of dyslexic people, with very particular needs, who are failing to be differentiated from other poor readers (Dyslexia 2). Reflecting the confusions that result from the use of these contrasting understandings, Rice and Brooks (2004) offer clarification:

> The critical question in dyslexia research is not whether dyslexic people in particular differ from normal readers. It is *whether dyslexic people differ from other poor readers*. (Rice & Brooks, 2004: 33, emphasis as in original)

One of the key difficulties for those who have tried to produce a definition of dyslexia in which dyslexia is differentiated from others with poor word recognition skills is that providing a scientifically acceptable version that can reflect this distinction has proven elusive. Popular definitions tend not to permit clear differentiation of this kind. For example, the British Psychological Society's, Division of Educational and Child Psychology's operational definition (1999) states that:

> Dyslexia is evident when accurate and fluent word reading and/or spelling develops very incompletely or with great difficulty. This focuses on literacy learning at the word level and implies that the problem is severe and persistent despite appropriate learning opportunities. (1999: 64)

Based largely upon the severity of the reading difficulty, this appears to reflect a Dyslexia 1 understanding. However, somewhat puzzlingly, some diagnosticians appear not to find any dissonance in citing this definition as justification for their use of a Dyslexia 2 approach.

A Dyslexia 2 definition would seem to need to be framed in a fashion that embodies either symptoms, causality or prognosis (Tønnessen, 1995). Symptoms refer to, "… observable and/or measurable signs of underlying conditions and processes. When we describe reading behavior or reading achievement without reference to their underlying causes, then we are at the symptom level" (Tønnessen, 1997: 80). Symptom-based definitions of dyslexia may be inclusionary or exclusionary; the condition may be signaled by the absence of certain factors or symptoms, or by the presence of others.

An early example of a definition that utilizes exclusionary factors is that offered by the World Federation of Neurology in 1968. This states that dyslexia is:

... a disorder manifested by difficulties in learning to read despite conventional instruction, adequate intelligence, and socioeconomic opportunity. It is dependent upon fundamental cognitive disabilities that are frequently of constitutional origin. (cited in Critchley, 1970: 11)

Here can be found two of the most commonly employed exclusionary factors – intelligence and socioeconomic disadvantage.

Within the field of psychiatric classification, there was much debate about the use of the term dyslexia prior to the final production of the American Psychiatric Association's *Diagnostic and Statistical Manual – Fifth Edition* (DSM-5) (APA, 2013). An earlier draft version had removed reference to dyslexia on the grounds that the differing conceptions and understandings of this term rendered the construct scientifically problematic; however, following vigorous and sustained lobbying, it later appeared in the final version.

The overarching term *Specific Learning Disorder* was introduced to describe a type of neurodevelopmental condition that impedes the ability to learn or employ academic skills. Clinicians are required to specify for a given individual any particular domains of academic difficulty, together with their subskills, that might be impaired. One specific learning disorder category concerns *impairment in reading*, with the particular skills identified as word reading accuracy, fluency, and reading comprehension. *Dyslexia* can be employed here as a "specifier," "... an alternative term used to reflect a pattern of learning difficulties characterized by problems with accurate or fluent word recognition, poor decoding, and poor spelling abilities" (APA, 2013: DSM-5, Diagnostic Code 315). While its inclusion into DSM-5 largely satisfied dyslexia advocacy groups, the term appears not to offer any additional diagnostic information.

A second literacy-related category, entitled *written expression*, includes spelling, grammar and punctuation, and clarity or organization of written expression. Learning problems should be "unexpected" when considered in relation to other areas of development and, "... must have persisted for at least six months despite the provision of interventions that target those difficulties" (APA, 2013: 66).

The other major psychiatric classification system, the International Classification of Diseases (ICD)-11 (World Health Organization, 2023), locates dyslexia within the overarching category of "Developmental Learning Disorder." This refers to a group of neurologically-based developmental disorders characterized by significant and persistent difficulties in learning academic skills such as reading, written expression, and arithmetic. In respect of reading, ICD-11 states:

> Developmental learning disorder with impairment in reading is characterised by significant and persistent difficulties in learning academic skills related to reading, such as word reading accuracy, reading fluency, and reading comprehension. The individual's performance in reading is markedly below what would be expected for chronological age and level of intellectual functioning and results in significant impairment in the individual's academic or occupational functioning. Developmental learning disorder with impairment in reading is not due to a disorder of intellectual development, sensory impairment (vision or hearing), neurological disorder, lack of availability of education, lack of proficiency in the language of academic instruction, or psychosocial adversity. (World Health Organization, 2023: Section Code 6A03.0)

ICD-11 shares many of the same characteristics of DSM-5 including the notion of unexpectedness. However, in ICD-11, unlike for DSM-5, unexpectedness may be based upon a discrepancy between reading and intellectual ability, a notion that is now widely discredited (Fletcher et al., 2019). Unlike DSM-5, it does not employ the criterion of an insufficient response to appropriate forms of intervention.

Arguably, the most widely cited current definition is that developed by a research group convened by the International Dyslexia Association (IDA) and subsequently adopted by its Board in 2002:

> Dyslexia is a specific learning disability that is neurobiological in origin. It is characterized by difficulties with accurate and/or fluent word recognition and by poor spelling and decoding abilities. These difficulties typically result from a deficit in the phonological component of language that is often unexpected in relation to other cognitive abilities and the provision of effective classroom instruction. Secondary consequences may include problems in reading comprehension and reduced reading experience that can impede growth of vocabulary and background knowledge. (Lyon, Shaywitz, & Shaywitz, 2003: 2)

This definition has been endorsed by many leading international researchers Dickman (2017) although more recently has been subject to criticism (Brady, 2019; Elliott, 2020). Intensive lobbying by dyslexia advocacy groups over the past decade has seen it adopted widely in US legislation and taken up in many other countries. While the definition works adequately where the term dyslexia is used to describe reading disability in line with a Dyslexia 1 conception, it quickly unravels when employed to differentiate dyslexic from non-dyslexic poor readers (Dyslexia 2).

Similar to the World Federation of Neurology's definition, there is a reference to a biological component although the descriptor "neurobiological" is preferred to "constitutional," perhaps reflecting increasing emphasis upon advances in neuroscience (see Chapter 3). Neurobiological factors apply across all domains of human performance (Protopapas & Parrila, 2018), however, and with reference to reading, the term "neurobiological" neither offers explanatory power nor serves a meaningful diagnostic function (Sand & Bolger, 2019). Reference to phonological ability in the definition reflects its important role in reading development although its portrayal as a unitary causal explanation is likely to decline with increased recognition of multifactorial accounts of reading disability in which no single process is necessary or sufficient to cause reading disability (Compton, 2021; Fletcher et al., 2019; Pennington, McGrath & Peterson, 2019). While secondary consequences of dyslexia are listed in the definition, such outcomes are typically found for the great majority of struggling readers and thus these hardly offer additional diagnostic power. Cognitive functioning and a lack of access to appropriate schooling both appear to be exclusionary, but here they are couched within an inclusionary notion of unexpectedness.

What Might Be Indicators of Unexpected Performance?
The notion of dyslexia as *unexpected* poor performance in reading, writing, or spelling is a uniquely North American conception that reflects the earlier work of Kirk (1963) in the field of specific learning disability (Miciak & Fletcher, 2020). In 2018, the notion of unexpected underachievement was codified in US federal law (First Step Act of 2018: 115–391). It is widely employed as a key criterion in the diagnosis of broader learning disability but is also used to differentiate between dyslexic and other struggling readers (Wagner & Lonigan, 2022). Indeed, in the opinion of S. Shaywitz and J. Shaywitz (2020: 456), unexpected underachievement has been shown by research to be the "… most consistent and enduring core" of the definition of dyslexia for more than one hundred years. More recently, this term has begun to gain some traction in the UK. Nevertheless, used in this way, the term is highly problematic (Elliott, 2020).

> Developmental dyslexia or reading disability refers to unexpected poor performance in reading. Poor performance in reading typically is defined as performance markedly below that of one's peers or expectations based on some form of standards. What constitutes an unexpected level of poor performance in reading has been more difficult to define. (Wagner, 2008: 174)

At one level, a failure on the part of an individual to make age-related progress in reading, given a standard educational diet, could be deemed to be unexpected (Lachmann & Bergström, 2023). Such a judgement would not require a psychometrically based differentiation between dyslexic and other poor readers derived in clinical assessment contexts. Unsurprisingly, perhaps, dyslexia advocates, assessors, and lobbyists have tended to look elsewhere for the unexpected components.

DSM-5 lists a number of factors that could reduce the likelihood of a diagnosis of Specific Learning Disorder, a category which, as noted above, includes the terms word-reading accuracy and reading fluency as types of learning disability. Not only should the individual's performance in culturally and linguistically appropriate tests of the requisite academic skill (reading, writing, mathematics) be well below the average range, but their difficulties should not be better explained by developmental, neurological, sensory (vision or hearing), or motor disorders (APA, 2013).

A child who is severely visually, hearing, or neurologically impaired, or for whom the text is not in their first language, might understandably struggle to learn to read. It is not in these areas of challenge, however, that the dyslexia debate is meaningfully situated, although the needs of second language learners who also have a reading disability can often be particularly complex and difficult to resolve (Vaughn, Martinez, et al., 2019). Rather, argumentation concerning the expected versus unexpected nature of reading difficulties is more commonly centered elsewhere. It is often argued that a reading difficulty would not be unexpected in cases where the individual demonstrates one or more of the following:

• low intelligence (involving a discrepancy between measured intelligence and reading performance and/or a mixed profile of cognitive strengths and weaknesses)
• socioeconomic disadvantage
• a history of inadequate schooling
• emotional and behavioral factors that might affect attention, concentration, and responsiveness to teacher direction.

i. Intelligence
In considering the role of intelligence in understanding why someone might be struggling to learn, it is often thought important to differentiate between children with or without an intellectual disability. In the USA, the presence of an intellectual disability is generally considered to be an exclusionary criterion for determining a learning or reading disability.

A diagnosis of intellectual disability (or its equivalent term in the UK, learning disability) was historically marked by an IQ score below the second percentile. However, this is an overly narrow conception of intelligence and diagnosing this condition on the basis of a single test score is no longer considered advisable. It is generally considered that, for a diagnosis of intellectual disability, consideration should go beyond IQ and include a range of adaptive, functional behaviors (Elliott & Resing, 2019).

In contrast with intellectual disability, learning disability in the USA has historically been signaled by the presence of a discrepancy between a person's IQ score and an area of academic performance; such a discrepancy, therefore, can be considered to operate as an inclusionary criterion (Grigorenko et al., 2019). In diagnosing dyslexia, the "two-group" hypothesis approach contends that poor readers with high IQs (so-called "dyslexics") can be differentiated from non-dyslexics ("garden-variety" poor readers) whose difficulties are considered more likely to result from a more global cognitive weakness (Stanovich, 1991).

It is not difficult to allocate a poor reader to one of these two groups although there are significant problems of reliability (Fletcher et al., 2019: 38–89). However, even if methodological problems were overcome, for such a distinction to have any direct utility for tackling reading difficulties, derived IQ-discrepant groups and non-discrepant groups would need to show meaningful differences in one or more of the following:

a. differences on the basis of academic and/or cognitive factors that underlie reading performance;
b. differences in response to reading instruction;
c. differences in the nature and content of effective forms of intervention;
d. differences in prognosis.

IQ has proven to be unable to make meaningful differentiations on any of these bases. Meta-analyses and scorecard reviews (Fletcher et al., 2007; Hoskyn & Swanson, 2000; Stuebing et al., 2002, 2009) have yielded little evidence to support the suggestion that IQ-achievement discrepancy is an important predictor of decoding-related differences between the two groups. In summarizing the current state of knowledge, Fletcher et al. (2019) note that studies have clearly shown that IQ discrepant and non-discrepant low achiever groups, "… do not differ practically in behavior, achievement, cognitive skills, response to instruction, and neurobiological correlates once definitional variability is controlled …. The classification lacks validity" (Fletcher et al., 2019: 52).

Studies have repeatedly shown that IQ scores are poor predictors of those who can be successfully remediated compared with those who are likely to be more resistant to intervention (Gresham & Vellutino, 2010). On the basis of a meta-analysis of twenty-two studies, Stuebing and colleagues (2009) concluded that IQ predicted only one to three percent of the variance in children's response to reading intervention. Noting that a small effect might still be relevant, particularly where any costs involved are minor, they pointed out that in comparison with relatively expensive IQ procedures, baseline assessment of word reading skills had proven to be a much stronger predictor. For this reason, the authors queried why anyone would choose to use IQ rather than "… a shorter task with a much stronger relation with outcome" (Stuebing et al., 2009: 45).

There is no evidence that IQ discrepancy categories can be used to determine differing forms of intervention (i.e., an aptitude–treatment interaction) for word decoding difficulties (Elliott & Resing, 2015; Kearns & Fuchs, 2013).

Finally, studies undertaken in which students were repeatedly tested over many years (Francis et al., 1996; Flowers et al., 2001; Vellutino, Scanlon, & Lyon, 2000) have shown that IQ discrepancy offers little prognostic information about future reading performance. Peng et al. (2019) assessed the performance of children at risk of reading difficulties over a four-year period from grade one to grade four. Nonverbal reasoning failed to predict word reading growth over this period although it did predict reading comprehension growth.

To date, there is no significant neurophysiological evidence of different etiologies for discrepant and nondiscrepant groups (Fletcher et al., 2007; Tanaka et al., 2011; Simos et al., 2014). However, there is some evidence for a stronger genetic contribution to reading difficulty for those with high IQ (Wadsworth, Olson, & DeFries, 2010) perhaps because of an association between higher IQ and a more supportive educational environment for reading (Olson et al., 2019).

Stanovich and Stanovich (1997) argue that if there is no empirical evidence to support the suggestion that we should make separate classifications and treatments for discrepant and nondiscrepant groups, such a step would need to be based upon a social policy decision arising from notions of social justice in relation to the fulfillment of the child's educational potential. The argument that children with high IQs have a greater severity of need (Ashton, 1996, 1997) because the realization of their supposedly higher potential is undermined by their reading difficulties does not stand up to scrutiny (Siegel & Hurford, 2019; Siegel et al., 2022).

The notion that IQ tests provide a picture of fixed potential that places a limit on academic achievement has a long tradition. As Sir Cyril Burt, England's first school psychologist, noted, "Capacity must obviously limit content. It is impossible for a pint jug to hold more than a pint of milk and it is equally impossible for a child's educational attainment to rise higher than his educable capacity" (1937: 477). Given that IQ was designed originally to predict subsequent educational achievement, a task in which it is relatively successful (Sternberg & Grigorenko, 2002a), it seems plausible to argue that poor readers with high IQs are particularly likely to benefit from additional assistance. If this were true, providing greater help to such children might seem to be a logical way of gaining most benefit from the distribution of limited resources. However, in addition to the ethical issues this raises, the proposition can also be challenged on scientific grounds; IQ was always meant to function as a general predictor across the curriculum, not as a means to make focused predictions in specific curricular areas. Furthermore, reliance on such measures is problematic because the use of the IQ test as a proxy for cognitive potential is itself highly contested (Lidz & Elliott, 2000; Sternberg & Grigorenko, 2002a; Sternberg, 2021).

Reading and IQ test performance have a reciprocal influence. Reading less (and less well) not only affects reading development but also undermines performance on IQ tests (Ferrer et al., 2010). Good readers not only become more competent in reading by applying and practicing their reading skills, but these also help them to develop their cognitive skills and subsequently perform more highly on IQ tests. The opposite outcome applies to poor readers (Fletcher et al., 2019). This phenomenon is an exemplar of the "Matthew effect" (Stanovich, 1986) that can lead to an underestimation of the potential of those with reading difficulties. However, despite this reciprocity, there is some evidence that reading ability has greater influence upon the time spent on reading activity than vice versa (Van Bergen et al., 2018).

A related argument with important implications for policy concerns the use of the discrepancy model to identify those children whose reading is poorer than their cognitive ability, but whose literacy difficulties are not sufficiently low to be normally deemed eligible for additional educational support (such students are sometimes known as "twice exceptional"). In a longitudinal study undertaken in Connecticut (Shaywitz, Morris, & Shaywitz, 2008), it was found that seventy-five percent of children identified by discrepancy criteria also met low achievement reading criteria. These researchers suggest that the remaining twenty-five percent may still be struggling with their reading but not to a level that is recognized on the basis of comparisons with peers using norm referenced measures.

For some (B. Shaywitz & S. Shaywitz, 2020; S. Shaywitz & J. Shaywitz, 2020; Thomson, 2009), such children merit additional assistance; others disagree on the grounds that finite resources should be targeted towards those whose absolute levels of literacy performance are weakest.

In the light of the wealth of research on the limited role of IQ in relation to dyslexia, Vellutino and colleagues concluded that "… intelligence tests have little utility for diagnosing specific reading disability" (Vellutino et al., 2004: 29). Practitioners were advised to:

> … shift the focus of their clinical activities away from emphasis on psychometric assessment to detect cognitive and biological causes of a child's reading difficulties for purposes of categorical labelling in favour of assessment that would eventuate in educational and remedial activities tailored to the child's individual needs. (Vellutino et al., 2004: 31)

The demise of the IQ discrepancy model has done much to undermine the clinical utility of the dyslexia construct. From an original position where it was believed that IQ testing could identify a dyslexic subgroup with genuinely different abilities and needs, the finding that such measures had little to offer diagnosis or intervention in respect of problems of accurate and fluent reading was a massive challenge to existing practice. As noted below, some have merely ignored or discounted this finding even though a positive practical consequence of the demise of the discrepancy approach is that the needs of many more struggling readers could potentially be identified and addressed (Di Folco et al., 2022; Snowling et al., 2020)

a. Profiles of Cognitive Strengths and Weaknesses Some have argued that while global IQ and other cognitive test scores may lack diagnostic or clinical utility for dyslexia, various combinations of subtests from such measures may yield more helpful information. Although sometimes perceived as a modern approach, cognitive profiling of this kind has had a long history (Fletcher et al., 2019).

One approach, particularly popular during the 1980s and 1990s, was to focus upon particular clusters of IQ subtests. For example, low scores on the so-called ACID profile, derived from the Arithmetic, Coding, Information and Digit Span subtests in the Wechsler Intelligence Scales for Children, were considered to be indicative of dyslexia (Vargo, Grossner, & Spafford, 1995). A popular procedure was to compare the child's scores on the ACID profile with their performance on the other subtests that together make up the full IQ score. If each of the four ACID subtest scores proved to be equal to, or lower than, the lowest score on the other subtests, the individual was considered to have a positive ACID profile.[2]

While children with reading difficulties often score poorly on these subtests, the incidence of the overall ACID profile is typically low, generally between four and five percent in samples of learning disabled children (Prifitera & Dersch, 1993; Ward et al., 1995; Watkins, Kush, & Glutting, 1997). Ward et al., 1995 examined a subset of children with marked IQ-reading discrepancies but found the incidence even lower at 3.9 percent. Such incidence levels do not result in useful clinical information for diagnosis and intervention. Somewhat puzzlingly, Thomson (2003), an advocate of psychometric testing for poor readers, found a much higher rate of forty percent in a sample of children at a special school for dyslexic children where he was employed. It is possible that this finding, remarkably different to other major studies, may merely reflect local education authority diagnostic practices and referral patterns. In Thomson's (2003) study, particular weaknesses were found on Digit Span, Coding, and Symbol Search; poor performance on Arithmetic and Information subtests was also noted. Subsequently, using a later version of the Wechsler Scales (WISC-IV), arithmetic was substituted by a new subtest, letter-number sequencing (Thomson, 2009). The subtests in both studies generally tap those cognitive processes (working memory, rapid naming) that are widely agreed to be problematic for poor readers (see Chapter 2), and weaknesses in these areas are unsurprising.[3]

Analyses of this kind have long been criticized on the grounds that subtest scores from IQ tests such as the Wechsler Scales (the most recent being the WISC-V) have questionable reliability and validity (de Jong, 2023; Dombrowski, McGill, Watkins et al., 2022; Watkins et al., 2022). For this reason, leading professional bodies have stated that the potential of subtests "… for accurate prediction of criteria, for beneficial examinee diagnosis, and for wise decision-making is limited" (American Educational Research Association (AERA), American Psychological Association (APA), & National Council on Measurement in Education (NCME), 2014: 35).

An alternative approach seeks to identify an individual's unexpected difficulty in academic areas on the basis of an uneven pattern of strengths

---

[2] Kaufman (1994) suggested a rather different subtest cluster (SCAD) in which the Information measure was replaced by the Symbol Search subtest.

[3] The Information subtest seemingly taps a different set of skills. Low scores on this subtest, a measure of general knowledge, most likely will reflect, in part, reduced opportunity to gain information from reading.

and weaknesses (PSW) in their cognitive functioning. While this can be seen as an extension of the traditional IQ-aptitude discrepancy approach, the key difference here is that a combination of both intellectual strengths and weaknesses is required.

In addition to the use of the commonly employed Wechsler Scales (see Watkins & Canivez, 2021, for a critique of profiling with the WISC-IV) several more specialized measures have proven popular for diagnosing learning disability. These include the Dual/Discrepancy Consistency Model (D/DC; Flanagan et al., 2018), formerly known as the XBA cross-battery assessment method, the Concordance/Discordance Model (C/DM; Hale & Fiorello, 2004) and the Discrepancy/Consistency Model (D/CM; Naglieri, 2011; Naglieri & Feifer, 2018). For proponents of cognitive test profiling, these tools can be used not only to identify a learning disability, but also to provide valuable information for the individualization of tailored interventions. However, a number of problems have been identified in the literature concerning accurate identification, an (in)ability to inform intervention, and poor prognostic prediction.

Problems of accurate identification. PSW approaches have been heavily criticized on psychometric grounds, particularly in relation to their reliability (Beaujean et al., 2018; Fletcher et al., 2019; Miciak, Taylor et al., 2018). This problem appears to be little improved by the use of supplementary assessment data or the application of clinical judgement (Maki, Kranzler, & Moody, 2022). Pennington, McGrath, and Peterson (2019) note that PSW is an intuitively appealing notion but caution against its use. In so doing, they reference the significant difficulties that emerge when employing a single cut-off point on a continuous distribution of an academic or cognitive skill. The PSW approach massively increases this problem because it involves the setting of cut-off points on multiple continuous measures. As a result:

> … the majority of students with clinically impairing literacy problems do not meet PSW criteria, and even a relatively small change in diagnostic criteria results in a large shift in which specific children are identified (Miciak, Fletcher, Stuebing, Vaughn, & Tolar, 2014; Stuebing et al., 2012). These problems make using the PSW for individual diagnosis impractical and potentially harmful. (Pennington, McGrath, & Peterson, 2019: 75)

Others have emphasized the tendency of PSW to produce an undesirable number of false positives (Kranzler et al., 2016a; 2019). This outcome is hardly surprising because, at the level of the individual, significant variability across cognitive processes is commonplace. Thus, in an examination of a large simulated dataset, McGill and Busse (2017) found that employment of one of the PSW models resulted in more than half of 9–13 year olds presenting with at least one cognitive weakness, with a quarter of the sample presenting with two or more weaknesses.

A further threat to reliability and validity results from the finding that comparison of different PSW methods results in little agreement about who should be identified as learning disabled (Taylor et al., 2017). In a study of fourth-graders, Miciak et al. (2016) found agreement levels derived from the XBA and C/DM were little better than chance (see also, Miciak et al., 2014). Where models fail to identify the same students as learning disabled, their joint validity is necessarily low.

Problems in informing intervention. Proponents of the PSW approach argue that it is helpful for drawing up bespoke forms of individualized intervention:

> One of the major purposes of a comprehensive assessment is to derive hypotheses emerging from a student's cognitive profile that would allow the derivation of different and more effective instruction. By eliminating an evaluation of cognitive abilities and psychological processes, we revert to a one-size-fits-all mentality where it is naively assumed that all children fail for the same reason …. At the current stage of scientific knowledge, it is only through a comprehensive evaluation of a student's cognitive and psychological abilities that we can gain insights into the underlying proximal and varied root causes of reading difficulties and then provide specific interventions that are targeted to each student's individual needs. (Reynolds & Shaywitz, 2009a: 46–47)

These confident assertions were challenged on the grounds that supportive evidence was lacking. Thus, Fletcher (2009) argued:

> Despite claims to the contrary (Hale et al., 2008) there is little evidence of Aptitude × Treatment interactions for cognitive/neuropsychological skills at the level of treatment or aptitude (Reschly & Tilley, 1999: 28–29). The strongest evidence of Aptitude × Treatment interactions is when strengths and weaknesses in academic skills are used to provide differential instruction (Connor et al., 2007). (Fletcher, 2009: 6)

Along similar lines, Gresham (2009) expressed concern that no data-based studies (other than individual case studies) had been cited to support the claims of PSW proponents, while hundreds of studies in a variety of different areas of learning had failed to show such a phenomenon (Cronbach, 1975; Cronbach & Snow, 1977; Pashler et al., 2008). According to critics (Fletcher & Vaughn, 2009; Gresham, 2009), those advocating the value of cognitive and neuropsychological data for formulating differentiated interventions have a responsibility to provide empirical evidence to support such claims.

In response to such criticisms a White Paper by fifty-eight leading scholars in the USA (Hale et al., 2010), many closely associated with the psychometric tradition, contended that evidence indicating the value of cognitive
and neuropsychological assessment for determining potential responsiveness to academic and behavioral intervention was only just beginning to
emerge, and further research was needed. However, such optimism appears
to have been misplaced as the ability of cognitive profiles of this kind to
determine effective interventions has not been supported by scientific investigations (McGill, Dombrowski, & Canivez, 2018; Kranzler et al., 2016b).
Burns et al. (2016) conducted a meta-analysis of studies that have sought to
use neuropsychological data to inform interventions in reading and mathematics. The data included measures of cognitive functioning involving
intelligence, rapid naming, verbal memory, executive function, and attention. Also included in the analysis were studies involving phonological or
phonemic awareness and reading fluency. Effect sizes varied considerably
from $g = 0.17$ for measures of cognitive functioning to $g = 0.43$ for reading
fluency and $g = 0.50$ for phonological/phonemic awareness. In reflecting
on these results, the authors concluded that measures of cognitive abilities have little to no utility in screening or planning reading interventions.
It is important to note that the authors challenged the application of the
descriptor "neuropsychological" to phonological/phonemic assessment as
this relates to skills that are proximal, can be directly instructed, and appear
to have a moderate effect on learning (see Chapter 4).

Some leading proponents of PSW approaches have come to accept that
the basis for claims concerning the aptitude × treatment efficacy of the
approach is flawed. Schneider and Kaufman (2017), for example, acknowledged that:

> After rereading dozens of papers defending such assertions, including our
> own, we can say that this position is mostly backed by rhetoric in which
> assertions are backed by citations of other scholars making assertions
> backed by citations of still other scholars making assertions. (Schneider &
> Kaufman, 2017: 8)

Nevertheless, they tempered this seeming volte-face by noting that such
assertions are often backed by "… deep ethical intuitions, fine-tuned professional insights, vivid personal experiences, and a large body of indirect
scientific evidence" (Schneider & Kaufman, 2017: 8). However, similar
justifications could equally be applied to many other popular educational
approaches that have been subjected to systematic scientific research and
subsequently found to be ineffective.

Problems in informing prediction of who will make progress. A further argument for cognitive profiling is that it may be able to point to a struggling learner's likely progress when provided with appropriate intervention. Fletcher and colleagues (2011), for example, found that cognitive processes were able to differentiate subgroups defined on the basis of poor response and low achievement after a small group work intervention. However, they noted that this seemed to reflect the severity of impairment in reading skills rather than qualitatively distinct differences in the cognitive profiles of these groups. As a result, they concluded that the assessment of cognitive processes failed to provide sufficient value-added benefit to justify their use. Miciak et al. (2016) similarly sought to measure the extent to which PSW approaches could predict who would or would not respond to an intervention. Crucially, what was of interest here was the additional predictive capacity over and above that based upon baseline measures of reading. The authors' data simulations indicated that, in the most positive scenarios, an improvement in predictive accuracy was found in approximately five–ten students for every 1,000 students assessed. Most of the comparisons undertaken resulted in no statistically significant or educationally meaningful improvement in prediction.

Two meta-analytic studies (Stuebing et al., 2009, 2015) indicated that cognitive skills (e.g., attention, nonverbal reasoning, and working memory) were weak predictors of response to intervention. Similarly, Peng et al. (2020) demonstrated that following a program of reading instruction with first-grade at-risk readers, neither initial working memory nor nonverbal reasoning scores predicted their responsiveness immediately afterwards, nor in the following year in second grade. In contrast, domain specific reading skills, particularly letter knowledge, proved to be valuable predictors.

In summarizing their revised perspective on the PSW approach, Schneider and Kaufman (2017) acknowledged that:

> The existing evidence base that demonstrates the value of comprehensive cognitive assessments for this purpose is not nearly as strong as it needs to be. Proponents of comprehensive cognitive assessments for learning disability identification must do more to rigorously evaluate their beliefs or else concede the argument to those with better evidence. (Schneider & Kaufman, 2017: 8)

Siegel and Hurford (2019) argue that the use of the PSW approach in dyslexia assessment is:

> Expensive and time-consuming, does not have predictive validity, does not specifically or necessarily highlight the difficulties that the student is

encountering, provides no insight as to remediation, is convoluted, esoteric and unnecessary …. There is little to no evidence that models of patterns of strengths and weaknesses will provide accurate identification of students in need of intervention, while simply assessing the areas in which the student is struggling is considerably more likely to result in academic benefits. Patterns of strengths and weaknesses models are not only unnecessary for the identification and remediation of dyslexia, but should be avoided. (Siegel & Hurford, 2019: 27)

On the basis of overwhelming scientific evidence, unexpectedness on the basis of IQ and cognitive measures, whether involving total scores, or profiles of cognitive strengths and weaknesses, should no longer be used for diagnosing dyslexia or a broader category of (specific) learning disability (Fletcher et al., 2019; Fletcher & Miciak, 2017; McGill, Dombrowski, & Canivez, 2018). Even if more informative forms of profiling could be developed, it would still be necessary to demonstrate that any additional benefits could justify the high costs involved (Fletcher & Miciak, 2017).

At the turn of the century, Watkins (2000) described cognitive profiling as a shared professional myth, yet its continuing popularity led Fletcher and colleagues to comment that: "It is ironic that methods of this sort continue to be proposed when the basic psychometric issues are well understood and have been documented for many years" (Fletcher, Stuebing, Morris & Lyon, 2013: 40). More than a decade later, it remains a puzzle why IQ testing and cognitive profiling approaches are still widely employed by school psychologists for diagnosing learning disability in general and dyslexia more specifically (Al Dahhan et al., 2021; Benson et al., 2019, 2020; Farmer et al., 2021; Kranzler et al., 2020; Lockwood & Farmer, 2020; Lockwood, Benson, et al., 2022; Maki & Adams, 2019; Sadusky, Berger, Reupert, & Freeman, 2022).

b.   The Continuing Popularity of Intelligence for Diagnosing Dyslexia   The dissociation between reading disability and intelligence is now recognized by many dyslexia associations. The website of the International Dyslexia Association, for example, states:

Research indicates that dyslexia has no relationship to intelligence. Individuals with dyslexia are neither more nor less intelligent than the general population.[4]

4 https://dyslexiaida.org/dyslexia-at-a-glance; accessed November 17, 2023.

Despite this, many members of these associations appear to disregard this statement in their assessment practices. Reasons for this include the following:

a.   Average or above intelligence has long been a defining feature of dyslexia; this association, steeped in everyday understandings, has proven difficult to break.

b.   There is a longstanding tendency for popular clinical practices to be passed down across generations, "… through clinical lore and become almost immune to self-correction" (Farmer et al., 2021: 108).

c.   Psychologists can often downplay scientific knowledge where this runs counter to practice habit and existing beliefs and instead prioritize personal intuition and observations (so-called "gut feelings") (Dombrowski, McGill, Farmer, et al., 2022 Dombrowski et al., 2021; Vanderheyden, 2018).

d.   School psychologists' assessment practices in the USA are heavily influenced by the particular frameworks permitted by individual state regulations (Benson et al., 2020).

e.   Such practices persist in the production and delivery of clinical instructional resources and school psychology training programs (Farmer et al., 2021; Lockwood & Farmer, 2020), despite some signs of a gradual decrease (Lockwood, Benson, et al., 2022). The continuing emphasis upon IQ-reading discrepancy undermines the take-up of emerging evidence-based, professional understandings (Dombrowski, McGill, Farmer, et al., 2022 Dombrowski et al., 2021; Farmer et al., 2021).

f.   In many middle- and high-income countries across the world, IQ tests continue to have a role in determining eligibility for additional education services (Elbeheri & Siang, 2023). Policy and legislation are often slow to adapt to advances in scientific understanding and can be greatly influenced by lobby groups.

g.   Some prominent researchers have given credence to discrepancy approaches by continuing to argue that developmental dyslexia concerns an unexpected difficulty in learning to read for those with average or above average intelligence (e.g., Nicolson & Fawcett, 2007). The location of the lower endpoint of the "average" range may vary or is not always made explicit.

h.   Dyslexia as an unexpected condition is difficult to operationalize if IQ, or another measure of cognitive ability, is ruled out as a key indicator.

i.   Practice can be influenced by suggestions that the weighting of genetic and environmental risk factors for dyslexia appears to vary between children with high or low IQs (Wadsworth, Olson, & DeFries, 2010). However, this distinction currently has no practical relevance for differential assessment and intervention (Pennington, McGrath, & Peterson, 2019).

j.   IQ is sometimes used as a criterion in the selection of participants for dyslexia research studies (Lopes et al., 2020; Rice & Brooks, 2004). This has been justified on the grounds that studying poor readers with normal range IQs, may help to shed greater light on key underlying cognitive mechanisms.

k.   For some, the continued use of IQ in the assessment of dyslexia reflects the perceived absence of appropriate alternatives. In putting forward such a position, Elbeheri and Everatt (2009) argue that positive (inclusive) diagnostic indicators are still not sufficiently robust and until these "… are fully explored and reliably measured, the arguments for using IQ tests as a basis of indication will be difficult to refute" (2009: 30).

l.   The IQ discrepancy model is retained in the 11th edition International Classification of Diseases (ICD-11) (World Health Organization, 2023).

m.   IQ tests may help to identify intellectually able children whose reading levels, while depressed, are not so poor that they would typically be identified as requiring special services (Mather & Schneider, 2023; B. Shaywitz & S. Shaywitz, 2020; S. Shaywitz & J. Shaywitz, 2020). As a result, some highly able children may not receive additional literacy support. This argument runs counter to the notion that finite resources should be prioritized for those who experience the greatest literacy difficulties. There is an associated risk that the application of an IQ-achievement model could serve to exclude less intellectually able children from specialized literacy-related intervention (Huettig & Ferreira, 2022; Siegel & Hurford, 2019).

n.   Some psychologists believe that cognitive discrepancy approaches, while currently flawed, may ultimately evolve to produce more meaningful results (Schneider & Kaufman, 2017; VanDerHeyden, 2018).

o.   IQ may be seen as the most suitable alternative by psychologists in countries where systematic response to intervention, RTI models have not been implemented (Sadusky et al., 2022).

p.   There is a relationship between IQ and higher order reading skills. Cognitive tests may help to shed light upon the specific nature of a child's higher-order reading comprehension difficulties involving such processes as reasoning, inferencing, and logical deduction (Cain, Oakhill, & Bryant, 2004; Fletcher et al., 2019; Christopher et al., 2012; Peng et al., 2019; Vellutino et al., 2004).

q. The IQ test is an instrument whose usage is restricted to those with appropriate qualifications and thus it serves as a means of garnering, signaling, and maintaining professional influence and status. Thus, with some evident frustration, Stanovich (2005) cites a comment in the house journal of the American Psychological Association that provides an analogy with an iconic tool of medicine: "… the intelligence test is our stethoscope, like it or not" (Kersting, 2004: 54).

r. Resistance to change by practitioners does not merely reflect a lack of engagement with current scientific knowledge. It would be a mistake to consider professional practice as a purely scientific pursuit devoid of political, social, and personal concerns. To accept the admonitions of Vellutino and colleagues (2004) that practitioners should change the focus of assessment from cognitive testing to reading-related behaviors is to introduce a potential threat to those professionals schooled in the psychometric tradition who may lack high-level expertise in curricular and pedagogic practices in the field of literacy.

s. A populist emphasis upon identifying and celebrating the intellectual and creative strengths of those with "dyslexic brains" has been spurred by powerful media campaigns backed by the endorsement of respected high-profile individuals and public bodies. The conception offered in these accounts involves a substantial reframing of a dyslexia construct that bears little relationship to findings from scientific research.

t. For many poor readers, and their families, there is an understandable desire to ensure that their reading difficulties are not perceived by others as indicative of low intelligence.

ii. Socioeconomic Disadvantage and Psychosocial Adversity

The view that adverse economic and environmental disadvantage can rule out unexpectedness as an explanatory criterion for a given individual (Hammill & Allen, 2020) is highly problematic. This would likely reduce the possibility of a diagnosis of dyslexia in poor readers from impoverished backgrounds (Rutter, 1978) and constrain their access to any benefits that may accrue from the label. Such a phenomenon is exemplified in studies in the USA (Odegard et al., 2020) and the UK, where the results of a large cohort study indicated that teachers were more likely to label as dyslexic those children with greater socioeconomic and cultural capital (Knight & Crick, 2021).

An educational achievement gap between advantaged and disadvantaged backgrounds has been found in most societies (Liu et al., 2022). Highly negative environmental circumstances, in particular, disruptive early life experiences resulting from extreme poverty, and low levels of parental education, are likely to have a significant effect upon the development of children's language and literacy (Hartas, 2011; Herbers et al., 2012; Lervåg et al., 2019). Lurie et al. (2021), for example, employed a longitudinal design that showed that cognitive stimulation, involving elements such as language exposure, access to learning materials, caregiver involvement in children's learning, and variety of enriching experiences, operates as an environmental mechanism linking socioeconomic status and academic achievement through children's receptive and expressive language.

Concern about social class differences in the home language experience of infants was fueled by a study of an impoverished Californian community (Hart & Risley, 2003). Here it was reported that, by the age of five, some of the children studied had heard 32 million fewer words spoken to them than the average middle-class child. While concerns have been expressed about the methodology employed in this study (Sperry, Sperry, & Miller, 2019), and Hart and Risley's "30 Million Word Gap," headline is now considered to represent a considerable overestimate, a recent meta-analysis of studies (Dailey & Bergelson, 2022) has shown that a significant, albeit far smaller, socioeconomic difference does exist, particularly in relation to levels of child-directed speech in the home.

Socially disadvantaged children are also less likely to have high levels of print exposure in the home. While important for all children, such experience appears to be particularly valuable for low ability readers (Mol & Bus, 2011). Outside the home, opportunity to learn, defined in terms of student curricular experience, has also been shown to be significantly poorer in schools serving disadvantaged communities (Schmidt et al., 2015). Accordingly, a student's reading achievement is predicted not only by their socioeconomic status (SES), but also, and more powerfully, by the average SES of their school. Indeed, in comparison with their peers, not only are socioeconomically disadvantaged children more likely to experience less developmentally favorable environments at home and at school, a "double dose of disadvantage" (Neuman, Kaefer, & Pinkham, 2018: 102), they are also likely to be more adversely affected by them (Buckingham, Wheldall, & Beaman-Wheldall, 2013). Nevertheless, where it is provided, high-quality instruction can reduce the negative impact of socioeconomic disadvantage upon reading achievement (Romeo et al., 2018).

DSM-5 and ICD-11 both identify psychosocial adversity as an exclusionary factor for learning and reading disability. How to operationalize this construct is left unclear and understandings vary greatly. De Jong and van Bergen refer to "… educational disadvantages which, for example result in school absenteeism" (2017: 358). Here, they may be referring to the higher levels of truancy typically found in disadvantaged communities but avoidance of school can also be a consequence of reading disability leading to a variety of adverse schooling experiences (Elliott & Place, 2019). In a rare attempt to operationalize the construct, Di Folco et al. (2022) employed "children in care" as a proxy for the exclusionary criterion of psychosocial adversity in their large epidemiological study comparing the prevalence of dyslexia using DSM-5 and ICD-11. These researchers appeared to recognize the conceptual difficulty noting that there were no other available indicators. The obvious fact that this is inappropriate as a basis for a clinical judgement throws up the difficult question of what factors might be drawn upon and the concomitant need for close consideration as to how to avoid bias against certain social and minority groups (B. Shaywitz & S. Shaywitz, 2020).

Dyslexia lobby groups and education policymakers tend to avoid definitions that make direct reference to social or economic disadvantage. It would surely be incongruous and unfair if distinctions between dyslexic and non-dyslexic poor readers and the contrasting perceptions, expectations, and access to additional support that can result, were predicated on the basis of judgements about children's life experiences. All too easily a situation could emerge where inappropriate genetic or neurobiological (dyslexic) or environmental (non-dyslexic) explanations for a reading difficulty are ascribed to an individual on the basis of their socioeconomic circumstances. However, biology and environment cannot be disaggregated in such fashion (Becker al., 2017; Gotlieb et al., 2022; Mascheretti et al., 2017). To illustrate, parents with a family history of reading difficulties living in disadvantaged communities may be less able to provide high-quality language and literacy experiences for their children (van Bergen et al., 2017) with one influential factor being parental linguistic ability (Puglisi et al., 2017).

The quality of adult-child interaction has an important effect upon the developing brain. For example, studies indicate that the quality of the home language and literacy environment is associated with brain structure and later linguistic, cognitive, or behavioral measures (Hutton et al. 2020; Merz et al., 2020). Controlling for socioeconomic status and age, early parent-child shared reading experience was shown to be associated with changes in brain structure, one area of which was found to mediate the relationship between shared reading time and subsequent reading outcomes (Davison et al., 2023). For such reasons, the home literacy environment cannot be considered to be a purely environmental measure (Snowling & Hulme, 2021). Multiple other environmental factors will also affect the infant's physical development. Hoeft and Bouhali (2022) list a range of environmental factors that can influence reading and math outcomes including high concentrations of heavy metals such as lead and methylmercury, and chemicals such as polybrominated diphenyl ethers. Factors that can affect pre- and postnatal development include maternal physical and mental health and substance use. Chronic exposure to high levels of infant stress, can lead to altered brain structure, function, and connectivity and affect academic performance (Burenkova, Naumova, & Grigorenko, 2021). Such factors are not unique to socioeconomically disadvantaged communities, of course.

How could a diagnostician working with a poor reader differentiate a genetic etiology from alternative environmental explanations? Might a family history of reading difficulty be seen as an indicator that the child's problem is gene-based and thus an indicator of "true" dyslexia? Could a home environment that is perceived to be less than optimal be considered to be an exclusionary factor that would rule out a diagnosis? Such questions are oversimplified to the point of meaninglessness and attempting to distinguish between children in this way for clinical purposes is both scientifically impossible and ethically unacceptable. Nevertheless, it is possible that such considerations may sometimes play a subliminal role in determining whether a child's reading difficulties are deemed to be unexpected.

As is typically the case for most aspects of human development (Petrill et al., 2010), a reciprocal interaction between multiple biological and environmental risk and protective factors operates in the development of reading disability (Theodoridou et al., 2021; Turesky et al., 2022) with genetic predispositions changing as a consequence of the particular environmental context environment (see Little & Hart, 2022, for further discussion of these issues).

Given the complexities involved, it is unsurprising that behavior-genetic studies have yet to enable any specification of the balance of genetic and environmental influences for a given individual with a reading disability. These:

> … only provide estimates for the average influence from genes and environment in the sampled population, and for the average influence of

moderating variables such as SES on the balance of genetic and environmental influences across the dyslexic sample. (Olson et al., 2019: 404)

In summary, it is important that clinicians and assessors not only understand that it is not currently possible to offer a dyslexia diagnosis on the basis of genetic/neurobiological (versus environmental) explanations (Fletcher et al., 2019; Protopapas & Parrila, 2019), but also ensure that such ideas do not influence decision-making, even at a tacit or subliminal level.

> The idea that people are born with dyslexia because they have bad genes and bad brains is an outmoded notion that should be replaced with concepts of risk and malleability that are dependent on instruction and early intervention. (Miciak & Fletcher, 2020: 7)

iii.   *Inadequate Schooling and Educational Deprivation*

Dickman's (2017) assertion that a definition of dyslexia that fails to exclude reading difficulties resulting from "educational deprivation" would be too broad might appear to have a certain logic but, on closer analysis, this soon becomes problematic.

One obvious explanation for poor reading is where the child has never attended school or received an appropriate alternative form of education. More challenging is where there is a history of school absenteeism. As noted earlier, school refusal may be an understandable consequence of the experience of learning difficulty (Elliott & Place, 2019). How this should affect a diagnosis of dyslexia is a concern that has caused considerable confusion and uncertainty amongst professionals (Nag, 2022; Sprick et al., 2020). For children who are attending school regularly, determining whether a reading difficulty is a consequence of inadequate schooling is also problematic. How might an assessor operationalize "inadequacy" in order to inform their clinical judgement? Should any determination about the adequacy of schooling be based upon the nature of the reading (or wider) curriculum? the approaches to teaching and learning employed? the perceived skills of the teaching staff? the quality of the classroom learning environment? or the extent to which parents actively support and reinforce the school's work? To what extent could responses to these questions ensure intra- and inter-assessor reliability in decision-making?

As is noted in Chapter 4, there has been an increasing tendency to explain many reading problems on the basis of a failure to apply scientific approaches to the teaching of reading (Hanford, 2018; Seidenberg, 2017). However, while the use of much criticized whole language approaches in isolation is likely to be suboptimal (Tunmer, Greaney, & Prochnow, 2015), most children will become accomplished readers whatever the balance of instructional approaches employed. In contrast, it is the child who is at risk of developing reading difficulties who will most likely be adversely affected by the absence of structured, systematic approaches to instruction. Even in those schools where whole language approaches predominate, one cannot rule out the possibility that a given struggling reader would have experienced a significant reading disability even if an optimal approach to instruction had been employed.

Nevertheless, one might argue that significant reading improvement that follows on from the provision of high-quality intervention may indicate that the original problem was primarily a consequence of poor instruction. However, because of changing classroom, developmental, maturational, and motivational factors it would be difficult to move beyond reasonable speculation to a clear determination. Whether this distinction would still matter anyway in cases where sound progress was being made, is a moot question. To add to this complicated scenario, it is likely that some struggling readers and their families would be discomfited by suggestions that improvements in their reading ability to an adequate level indicated that they should be perceived as "instructional casualties" rather than "compensated dyslexics" (Cavalli et al., 2017).

In summary, differentiating between dyslexic and other poor readers on the grounds of educational deprivation or inadequate schooling is difficult to justify (de Jong & van Bergen, 2017).

iv.   Emotional and Behavioral Factors

Experience of reading difficulty can be traumatic (Edwards, 1994), stigmatizing (Riddick, 2000; Livingston, Siegel, & Ribary, 2018; Haft, Greiner de Magalhães, & Hoeft, 2023) and impact negatively upon self-concept and self-esteem (McArthur et al., 2020; McNulty, 2003) (see Chapter 5 for further discussion). It is unsurprising, therefore, that resultant emotional problems can continue into adulthood (Alexander-Passe, 2015; Cederlöf et al., 2017). A relationship between emotional-behavioral problems and reading difficulties has been reported for both internalizing (e.g., anxiety and depression) and externalizing (conduct disorders) problems (Aro et al., 2022; Cederlöf et al., 2017; Donolato et al., 2022; Francis et al., 2019; Giovagnoli et al., 2020; Grills et al., 2022; Grills-Taquechel et al., 2012; Mugnaini et al., 2009; Ramirez et al., 2019; Visser et al., 2020; Xiao et al., 2023; Zuppardo et al., 2023). There is some evidence that comorbidity between dyslexia and emotional and behavioral problems is greatest at potentially stressful times, such as when children transfer from kindergarten to elementary school, or from primary to secondary school (Horbach et al., 2020).

Ramirez et al. (2019) observed an association between reading anxiety and achievement in first and second-grade students, with a stronger relationship for boys. In contrast, the influence of reading anxiety and general anxiety upon reading accuracy was both found to be marginal in a cross-sectional study of fourth- and fifth-grade struggling readers, with this being rather greater upon reading fluency than untimed single word reading (Macdonald et al., 2021). In a study of early elementary school-children, Grills et al. (2022) found that, contrary to expectation, struggling and typical readers failed to show differences in anxiety levels at the beginning of the school year, perhaps because they had not yet experienced significant difficulties with reading. However, by the end of the year, those who continued to struggle with reading showed greater levels of anxiety and depression than peers who had met reading benchmarks. Supporting Horbach et al.'s (2020) suggestion that the effect of reading difficulty upon anxiety may take some time to develop, McArthur et al. (2022) found that across four large longitudinal databases, emotional health (rated by parents) at age five was unrelated to reading at age seven. In contrast, reading at age seven was related to emotional health at age eleven. In the light of their findings, these researchers suggested that poor reading is likely to impact emotional health rather more than the other way around. This concurs with the finding of Ramirez et al. (2019) that, while reading anxiety appears to be both a cause and outcome of poor reading achievement, the effect of achievement upon anxiety was the greater.

It may be helpful to know if there are any particular cognitive factors that might lead to an increased risk of anxiety for those with reading disability. While evidence suggests a modest relationship between weaknesses in domain general cognitive abilities (such as processing speed and executive functions) and comorbid anxiety and word reading difficulties (Anderson et al., 2023), research in this area is still in its infancy.

There is a long history of studies showing that poor readers are more likely to present with higher levels of problematic externalizing behavior than typical readers. Lin et al. (2013) found that poor readers in third grade were more likely than their peers to demonstrate behavioral difficulties in fifth grade. Similarly, Morgan, Farkas, et al. (2008) found that reading problems in first grade increased the likelihood of problem behavior in third grade even after controlling for prior behavior and potential demographic-related confounds. Noting that early behavioral problems also predicted subsequent reading difficulties, the authors suggested a bidirectional causal model in which initial difficulties create a negative feedback cycle that results in disengagement from academic activity and increasingly problematic behavior (see also McGee et al., 1986; McArthur et al., 2022).

Drawing upon a large data set from seven independent studies, van Dijk et al. (2023) reported that poor readers with significant behavioral problems in kindergarten through third grade, K-3, were less likely to profit from reading instruction and intervention. However, this finding contrasts with the results of a meta-analysis of intervention studies involving students with co-occurring reading and behavior difficulties across grades K-12 (Roberts et al., 2020). Here it was found that small group reading interventions could improve reading achievement; however, this was not associated with an improvement in behavior, neither did a behavioral intervention appear to lead to improved reading outcomes. This led Morgan and colleagues (2008) to question the validity of the argument that behavior and reading difficulties have a reciprocal relationship, although the strength of any interaction is likely to vary according to the child's age and development.

Reading difficulties have been associated with a greater risk of criminality (Cederlöf et al., 2017; Grigorenko et al., 2019) and a high proportion of struggling readers is commonly found in incarcerated settings (Cassidy et al., 2021; Grigorenko et al., 2015; Kirk & Reid, 2001; Lindgren et al., 2002; Morken, Jones, & Helland, 2021).

Attentional difficulties are commonly found in struggling readers, with strong evidence arising from studies employing both clinical (Aro et al., 2022; Cheung et al., 2012 Mayes & Calhoun, 2006) and epidemiological samples (Brimo et al., 2021; Gilger, Pennington, & DeFries, 1992). While comorbid reading disability and attention deficit hyperactivity disorder (ADHD) occurs in approximately 5 percent of the population, between 25 and 40 percent of children with one of these disorders also meet the criteria for the other (McGrath et al., 2011). There is a strong likelihood that the association is genetically mediated (Brimo et al., 2021; Mascheretti et al., 2017). It is estimated that approximately 20 percent of children with the inattentive type of ADHD struggle with reading difficulties (Wadsworth et al., 2015), a far stronger association than is the case for the hyperactive dimension (Pham, 2016). In the search for shared cognitive deficits, processing speed has emerged as an important factor in explaining comorbidity between reading disability and the inattentive component of ADHD (McGrath et al., 2011; Peterson et al., 2017).

It appears likely that the relationship between emotional and behavioral problems and reading difficulties is linked to the comorbid presence of ADHD. (Horbach et al., 2020; Willcutt & Pennington, 2000; Carroll et al., 2005). Horbach et al. (2020) conducted a longitudinal study of children from kindergarten to fifth grade. Parents of children, either with or without reading and spelling difficulties, were asked to rate their child's behavior using the *Child Behavior Checklist*. On the children's entry to school, parental ratings did not differ between the two groups. However, in first grade externalizing and attention problems had become more evident in the struggling reader/speller group. Higher levels of internalizing difficulties emerged later for this group and by fourth grade these had become prominent (see a similar finding by Ackerman et al., 2007) before declining somewhat the following year. This rise and subsequent decline were considered to be most likely a consequence of additional stressors relating to the children's imminent transfer to secondary schooling.

The most significant aspect of this study is that the researchers found that the relationship between reading/spelling and behavior difficulties disappeared when ADHD was taken into account. This outcome largely replicated a similar finding by Willcutt and Pennington (2000) although in this earlier study, internalizing problems were found to be independently related to reading disabilities in girls. As a possible explanation, Horbach et al. (2020) suggested that the difference in the two sets of findings may result from the greater predominance of boys participating in their study.

Given that struggling readers tend to experience higher levels of anxiety, depression, attentional difficulty, and conduct disorder, it is hard to understand how such problems might be employed as exclusionary factors for a diagnosis of dyslexia. Rather than excluding children with emotional and behavioral problems from a label that can provide many benefits, early recognition of the complex nature of these difficulties is required (Livingston, Siegel, & Ribary, 2018), together with multi-component forms of intervention targeted to address both academic and health needs (Hendren et al., 2018; Vaughn et al., 2022).

Inclusionary Approaches: The Search for Marker Variables

Definitions of learning disabilities have tended to move away from the use of exclusionary criteria, indicating what dyslexia is not, towards identifying key marker variables (Fletcher et al., 2019; Helland, 2022). In clinical practice, a dyslexia diagnosis is often based upon the observed presence of various symptoms: high IQ, difficulties in phonological awareness, poor short-term (or working) verbal memory, poor ordering and sequencing, weak spelling, morphological awareness deficits, clumsiness, a poor sense of rhythm, difficulty with rapid information processing, weak executive functioning, poor concentration, inconsistent hand preference, impaired verbal fluency (typically measured by the production of as many words as possible from a particular category in a given time), limited vocabulary, poor phonic skills, frequent letter reversals, poor capacity for mental calculation, difficulties with speech and language, low self-image, and, in one checklist, anxiety when asked to read aloud. Other potential indicators of reading disability, for example, poor sleep patterns (Joyce & Breadmore, 2022) can be found in the literature. Critics of such lists (Elliott & Gibbs, 2008; Rice & Brooks, 2004) note that none of these elements are necessary or sufficient for a dyslexia diagnosis. Commonly reported "signs of dyslexia" can be regularly found in poor readers who may not be considered to be dyslexic, and in others without reading difficulties. Some difficulties seen as indicative of dyslexia, for example, letter reversals, are also commonly found in younger typical readers (Cassar et al., 2005). Similarly, while dyslexic children appear to be more likely than typical readers to demonstrate morphological awareness deficits (i.e., reduced awareness of the smallest units of meaning within any given word), their performance is not significantly different to that of younger children reading at the same level. It appears that the growth rate of morphological awareness is a consequence of phonological awareness and letter knowledge Inoue, Georgiou, and Parrila (2023) and morphological difficulties are more likely to be a consequence than a cause of reading difficulties (Georgiou et al., 2023). Finally, symptoms commonly employed as indicators of dyslexia vary greatly amongst those so diagnosed, and many are commonly found across other diagnosed developmental disorders such as ADHD, dyscalculia and dyspraxia (Astle et al. 2019, 2022; Brimo et al., 2021; Elliott & Place, 2021). Indeed, it has been shown that the same child can often be diagnosed with a different disorder depending upon the disciplinary specialism of the assessor (Bishop et al., 2017). This, together with significant heterogeneity within categories, renders a particular diagnosis highly questionable (Astle et al., 2019; 2022; Mareva et al., 2023; Peters & Ansari, 2019). Accordingly, Astle et al. (2022: 411) consider that "… diagnostic taxonomies that classify individuals in terms of discrete categories are ill-suited" for identifying and catering for individual needs. Instead, when intervening for neurodevelopmental difficulties, it may be preferable to operate a flexible approach that relates to the child's individual needs rather than be guided by a particular primary diagnosis (Finlay-Jones et al., 2019; Mareva et al., 2023).

Protopapas (2019: 4) comments that drawing upon lists of symptoms to conceptualize dyslexia is a "feature of the past" that has largely been abandoned. While this is largely true in relation to research, it is unfortunate that this is unlikely to be a wholly accurate account of current assessor practice.

One of the paradoxes of dyslexia assessment is that certain processes can be held to be indicators of the condition irrespective of whether these are found to be strengths or weaknesses on the part of the individual concerned. S. Shaywitz & J. Shaywitz, (2020), for example, suggest that unexpectedness is revealed by an uneven profile in which a decoding weakness is typically surrounded by a "sea of strengths" (2020b: 56) involving such elements as reasoning, problem solving, empathy, critical thinking, vocabulary, comprehension, and general knowledge. The authors' suggestion that vocabulary may be a particular strength of dyslexic children needs to be set against the finding that weaker vocabulary is a common characteristic of struggling readers and thus, a potential symptom of dyslexia. Snowling et al. (2020), for example, found that approximately a third of their sample of eight- and nine-year old dyslexic children demonstrated lower levels of vocabulary, particularly those who also experienced developmental language disorder. The idea that superior vocabulary may indicate dyslexia runs counter to the observation that weakness in this area is a likely secondary outcome resulting from the reduced reading experience of those who struggle with literacy (Fletcher et al., 2019).

In line with the notion of "set for variability" (Wegener et al., 2022), children will attempt to draw upon their existing vocabulary to guide them in identifying and correcting mispronouncements while reading aloud (Dyson et al., 2017). Poor vocabulary is also likely to impair the young child's capacity to read unknown words, particularly where these can be partially decoded or are irregularly spelled, so hampering the further development of the child's phonological recoding skills (Lawrence et al., 2018; Tunmer & Greaney, 2010). In line with mutualism theory (Kievit, 2020; Kievit et al., 2019; Peng & Kievit, 2020), reading and vocabulary appear to contribute reciprocally to each other's growth (Lervåg & Aukrust, 2010), although, in comparison with reading comprehension, the evidence for a reciprocal relationship between vocabulary and word reading is weaker (Verhoeven, van Leeuwe, & Vermeer, 2011). Georgiou, Inoue, and Parrila (2023), for example, found a unidirectional effect of word reading to vocabulary only in very young children.

There is considerable evidence that exposure to books in the home is important for vocabulary development (Georgiou, Inoue, & Parrila, 2021; Zhang et al., 2020) with greatest impact on those already at risk of reading disability (Caglar-Ryeng, Eklund, & Nergård-Nilssen, 2020). Accordingly, one might anticipate that citing a strong vocabulary as an indicator of dyslexia is likely to be unhelpful for poor readers from disadvantaged backgrounds. A similar argument can also apply to the possible diagnostic value of sound general knowledge.

The co-occurrence of reading and mathematical difficulties (particularly arithmetical problems with higher verbal content) is consistently reported in the literature (Daucourt et al., 2020; De Clercq-Quaegebeur et al., 2018; Landerl & Moll, 2010; Moll et al., 2014, 2019; Joyner & Wagner, 2020; Raddatz et al., 2017) although estimates vary considerably. It has been found that problems co-occur in 30 to 70 percent of individuals with either reading or math disorder (Kovas, Haworth, Harlaar, et al., 2007; Landerl & Moll, 2010; Moll et al., 2014) and that individuals with a math disorder are more than twice as likely to also have a reading disability (Joyner & Wagner, 2020). In part, comorbidity levels are affected by decisions concerning cut-off points. Dirks et al. (2008), for example, found that comorbidity between arithmetic and reading difficulties declined sharply as selection criteria became more stringent. Indeed, for those scoring below the tenth percentile, comorbidity was a mere one percent, a level that might be expected by chance. A similar finding was found in a large population study (Landerl & Moll, 2010) when the cut-off was reduced from a standard deviation of -1 SD to -1.5 SD.

The reasons for comorbidity between reading disability and difficulties in math, and whether there is a common underlying deficit, remain unclear. Moll et al. (2019) suggest that higher comorbidity is found when using math tasks that place greater reliance upon language skills, with language difficulties appearing to be a shared risk factor for both conditions (Snowling, Moll, & Hulme, 2021). Suggestions of other possible deficits include phonological processing (Amland, Lervåg, & Melby-Lervåg, 2021) and working memory (De Weerdt, Desoete, & Roeyers, 2013).

Unsurprisingly, the presence of math difficulties is often listed as a symptom in dyslexia checklists. Somewhat paradoxically, competence in math could also be taken as an indicator of dyslexia as, in line with S. Shaywitz and J. Shaywitz's (2020) notion of a sea of strengths, one could argue that a comparative strength in this area demonstrated the unexpected nature of a child's reading problem. Thus, irrespective of a struggling reader's performance in math, it would still be possible to justify the outcome as an indicator of dyslexia on the grounds of either comorbidity (weak math performance) or unexpectedness (strong math performance).

The idea that seemingly "unexpected" high performance on one or more components listed in the sea of strengths could help to identify dyslexia markedly disadvantages struggling readers from socioeconomically disadvantaged backgrounds. Such a profile is likely to be more commonly found in children assessed by privately funded assessors and dyslexia clinics as such services are more likely to be taken up by families enjoying higher levels of cultural, social, and linguistic capital. It also raises the related question of how we might best represent the needs of those children whose cognitive profiles are relatively flat (Fletcher et al., 2013). Excluding formal recognition of such children's learning disabilities and additional services on such grounds is quite rightly considered to be "absurd" (Fletcher, Morris, & Lyon, 2003: 52) (see also Peterson et al., 2021, for a similar conclusion).

Dyslexia and Language Disorders

Oral language deficits have a critical role in both word reading and reading comprehension difficulties (Catts, 2021; Snowling & Hulme, 2021) although relationships are complex and not easily disentangled. There is strong evidence that reading disability and developmental language disorder (DLD) (Bishop et al., 2017), a difficulty that concerns impaired receptive or expressive language, should best be considered as separate disorders (Adlof, 2020) although in both cases, problems are likely to have a basis in early language difficulties albeit with different developmental trajectories (Snowling et al., 2019; Snowling & Hulme, 2021).

Research suggests that language problems in young children can affect the development of a number of pre-literacy skills, such as letter knowledge and phonological awareness, which have been shown to be important for the acquisition of word reading (Caravolas et al., 2012; van Viersen et al., 2018) although studies have shown mixed results. Significant associations have been found in some studies (e.g., Lyytinen, Eklund, & Lyytinen, 2005; Preston et al., 2010; Price, Wigg, Misener et al., 2022) but absent in others (Rescorla, 2009; Duff et al., 2015). Such inconsistencies may be best explained by the differing degrees of language deficit or reading levels sampled and by the tendency of some young children with early language problems to catch up by the age of five to seven years (Price, Wigg, Misener et al., 2022).

For older children, research has consistently supported a relationship between reading disability and language impairment although the reported overlap varies greatly across studies. Using a clinical sample, Bishop et al. (2017) observed that 50 percent of children diagnosed with dyslexia also fulfilled criteria for DLD, and about 50 percent of children with DLD evidenced significant reading impairments. Findings from epidemiological studies, however, are suggestive of a smaller overlap. Catts et al. (2005), for example, reported that approximately 30 percent of their sample met the criteria for both language impairment and dyslexia.

Children with reading disability and those with DLD typically share some similar features although the latter often experience a broader range of language problems (Snowling et al., 2019; Snowling & Hulme, 2021). While reading-disabled children can also experience a variety of language difficulties (Adlof & Hogan, 2018; Snowling & Melby-Lervåg, 2016), particular difficulty is experienced in the area of phonological processing and the consequent problems this causes for the acquisition of literacy skills (Snowling et al., 2019). Phonological difficulties are particularly severe in children with comorbid reading disability and DLD. Children with DLD but not reading disability may also experience phonological problems but these tend to decrease over time (Snowling et al., 2019). Studies comparing phonological processing in language-impaired and reading-disabled groups have not always yielded a consistent picture, however, and differentiating between the two groups on this basis is not recommended (Adlof, 2020).

The changing demands of the reading process over time help to explain why the composition of poor reader groups is often far from stable as children gravitate from elementary to high school (Adlof, Catts, & Lee, 2010), and offer pointers as to why some children with specific language impairment who demonstrate reading difficulties in the later school years may not be identified as poor readers at a younger age. In the early years of school, an ability to decode simple words may be sufficient for such children to cope with non-complex narratives of commonly used words. In later years, as texts become more syntactically and semantically complex, language-based weaknesses are likely to become more problematic for reading, particularly in relation to comprehension (Snowling & Hulme, 2021).

Some children with reading disability present with speech production deficits that can range from relatively mild problems of mispronunciation to the more serious clinically diagnosed speech sound disorder (SSD). A relationship between speech production problems in young children and subsequent reading difficulties has been consistently shown in the literature (Burgoyne et al., 2019; Hayiou-Thomas et al., 2017; Tambyraja, Farquharson, & Justice, 2020; Mues et al., 2021) and the more severe or persistent the speech production disorder, the more likely the child will experience difficulties in reading (Cabbage et al., 2018). Thus, it has been argued that young children with speech difficulties should be monitored for later language and reading difficulties (Mues et al., 2021; Snowling & Hulme, 2021).

In line with what has been termed the simple view of reading, which differentiates word recognition from language comprehension (LC) (Gough & Tunmer, 1986) it has been suggested that the individual with dyslexia typically struggles with word recognition but has little difficulty in understanding meaning when text is read aloud for them (Tunmer, 2008). From this perspective, reading comprehension (RC) difficulties may result from an inability to decode, an inability to comprehend language, or difficulties with both of these skills. This distinction has substantial evidential support (Sleeman et al., 2022a). It has also proven popular with dyslexia assessors, although Tunmer and colleagues (Chapman & Tunmer, 2019a) have changed their position and now caution against the use of dyslexia as a diagnostic label on the grounds of the social and educational inequities that often result.

Reading disability is associated with both RC and LC although the difference between struggling and typical readers is greater for RC (Georgiou et al., 2022). The suggestion that dyslexia may be marked by an observed discrepancy between LC and RC has risen in prominence recently although this is not a new idea (Odegard, Farris, & Washington, 2022). As long ago as 1991, Stanovich dismissed this and other discrepancy-based approaches, in part on technical grounds (see also Fletcher et al., 2019: 204), but, more importantly, for failing to provide an educationally meaningful distinction between so-called dyslexic and "garden-variety" poor readers. More recently, a higher LC versus lower RC discrepancy, forming part of a hybrid model of dyslexia that includes poor academic achievement and poor response to instruction, has been proposed by Wagner and colleagues (2019, 2020). Its primary purpose is not to help diagnose dyslexia in an individual but, rather, to serve as a proxy in estimating the prevalence of dyslexia in a given population. As part of this formulation, dyslexic individuals are considered to differ from other poor readers on the basis that any LC–RC discrepancy is seemingly unexpected. Simulations using their Listening Comprehension–Reading Comprehension discrepancy index have indicated that only a minority of cases of struggling readers demonstrated such a discrepancy. However, listening comprehension:

> … is a language-specific measure of a child's amassed vocabulary and background knowledge based on prior experiences and educational opportunities. As such, LC [listening comprehension] serves as a proxy measure of a child's exposure to social determinants of language development, promotive factors that foster language development, and vulnerability factors that hinder language development. (Odegard, Farris, & Washington, 2022: 304)

Such exposure is likely to be less favorable for children from disadvantaged communities (Catts & Petscher, 2022; Pace et al., 2017). Such children may also experience less frequent use of academic words by the teachers in their classrooms (Wanzek, Wood, & Schatschneider, 2022). Given the inherent difficulties, Catts (2021) cautions against the use of a word recognition–language comprehension distinction to characterize struggling readers for diagnostic purposes.

This approach runs similar risks to that of the IQ discrepancy model. It provides a seemingly straightforward means of operationalizing "unexpectedness" enabling a distinction to be drawn between dyslexic and non-dyslexic struggling readers, yet its relevance for educational intervention is unclear (Middleton et al., 2022) and any benefits that accrue from receipt of the dyslexia label will be disproportionately absent for children from minority and disadvantaged backgrounds (Odegard, Farris, & Washington, 2022). This does not mean that comparison of performance on LC and RC has no practical utility for, as noted by Wagner and Lonigan (2022), significantly poorer performance on the latter may be helpfully addressed by assistive technology. Additionally, Middleton et al. (2022) argue that the presence of strong oral skills may serve as a protective factor in reading development and, for this reason, the use of LC–RC discrepancy as an indicator may help predict a struggling reader's intervention response. However, any suggestion that strong LC offers a better prognosis, all else being equal, is not easy to align with Wagner et al.'s (2019, 2020) contention that strength in this area can serve as an indicator of dyslexia, a condition that, as is noted in the following section, is often considered to be signaled by a poor response to intervention.

Dyslexia 3: Intractability to High Quality Intervention

It is an unfortunate reality that some struggling readers fail to make sound progress even when provided with high-quality intervention. Accordingly, some contend that a particular characteristic of dyslexia is its persistence, despite appropriate intervention (Miciak & Fletcher, 2020; Snowling, Hulme, & Nation, 2020). However, the notion of intractability and how it should be operationalized is complex and fraught with difficulties (Odegard et al., 2020). Nor is it clear how extensive the period of intractability would need to be before such a diagnosis could be made. Nevertheless, a response to intervention (RTI) approach to diagnosis and intervention is increasingly being seen as preferable to the now discredited discrepancy formulae approaches that have featured in traditional psychometric assessment practices. The service delivery model is now commonly viewed as operating within multi-tiered systems of support (MTSS) that are often broader than those used for earlier RTI conceptions and designed to address academic and behavioral needs and broader physical, emotional, and mental health (Charlton et al., 2020).

In the USA, the use of RTI, both to guide educational intervention in schools and as a means of identifying or diagnosing learning disability that may assist in determining eligibility for special education (Gartland & Strosnider, 2020), has gained considerable support since its incorporation in the Individuals with Disabilities Education Improvement Act of 2004 (US Department of Education, 2004). Discussion and debate about the operation of RTI and MTSS in the USA have largely played out in relation to the classification of specific learning disability (SLD) rather than reading disability/dyslexia, its most common component.

Although models of RTI and MTSS vary, they all share a similar basic structure in which widespread screening of relevant skills is undertaken, problems are identified, appropriate intervention is provided, and close monitoring and examination of the individual's ongoing progress is undertaken (Jimerson, Burns, & VanDerHayden, 2016). While this would not seem dissimilar to many traditional remedial approaches to children's learning difficulties, it is its highly structured and systematic nature that renders it rather different. The approach incorporates the use of (usually, three) tiers or levels (Berkeley et al., 2020) in which the level and nature of support provided is a function of the child's response to earlier intervention. Initially, at Tier 1, a universal process of screening in the relevant domains (e.g., reading or math) operates. A child deemed to be particularly at risk of academic failure would subsequently receive specialized intervention and regular monitoring (Tier 2). Should the child concerned continue to make insufficient progress, input would become gradually more intense and more individualized (Tier 3). Monitoring of academic progress largely involves the use of curriculum-based measures.

The terminology employed can be confusing as the use of the terms RTI and MTSS has been rendered more complex by the absence of consistent language and practices. Thus, in a national survey of practice in the USA, Berkeley et al. (2020) reported that while the majority of states explicitly contrasted RTI with MTSS, others subsumed RTI within MTSS, here used as an umbrella term, and yet others either treated the terms as synonymous or developed their own terminology. Interestingly, the different names employed by the states appeared not to reflect similarities or differences between them in practice reliably. Nevertheless, in relation to dyslexia, it is argued that:

> … dyslexia identification and treatment processes should be built within well-implemented multitier systems of support (MTSS) that include universal screening, evidence-based Tier 1 instruction, preventive intervention, ongoing progress monitoring for high-risk students, and mechanisms to intensify interventions for students who demonstrate inadequate response to quality instruction similar to those that occur with other SLDs. (Miciak & Fletcher, 2020: 343)

Crucially, with this approach, the unexpected component is no longer related to variable levels of functioning in relation to an individual's current strengths and weaknesses, but instead, is determined on the basis of the child's failure to respond to standard and validated instruction (Fletcher et al., 2019). An "inadequate instructional response" therefore becomes an essential inclusionary criterion, unlike the presence of "inadequate instruction," which is identified as an exclusionary criterion by cognitive discrepancy approaches (Fletcher et al., 2019). In RTI, a discrepancy is similarly emphasized but the focus here is on within-individual discrepancies relative to age-based expectations and instruction. This conception is believed by its advocates to have more utility for determining the nature of appropriate intervention than that offered by cognitive discrepancy approaches (Fletcher & Miciak, 2017).

Despite the growing popularity of RTI (Berkeley et al., 2020), there remain a number of difficulties in both how it can best be designed and structured and how to ensure that it operates in practice as intended.

In relation to design and structure, problems result from there being several different RTI models with no single agreed method of determining how best to measure response to intervention, and these are not consistent in identifying poor responders (Fletcher et al., 2014). In general, approaches vary on whether they emphasize rate of growth or a cut-off score of some kind. Fletcher et al. (2019) suggest that growth may be important for informing instruction but is less necessary for identification of a learning disability. Another difficulty concerns the use of a bifurcated responder categorization (responders–non responders), which can be problematic as this fails to capture the range of response accurately (Peng et al., 2020). Finally, there is a risk that assessors may focus unduly upon personal achievement-related characteristics (e.g., effort, motivation) leading to less attention upon actual progress rates (Barrett et al., 2022). These problems are likely to have significant implications for children who require additional services, although differences between leading RTI models tend to be smaller than when compared with the traditional discrepancy approach (Brown Waesche et al., 2011).

The RTI approach has been particularly criticized by those with an allegiance to traditional psychometric approaches. For critics, it cuts at the central component of the traditional conception of learning disability – an unexpected difficulty in relation to ability (based upon comparison of the individual's strengths and weaknesses). A further problem, it is argued, is that bright children, performing below their potential but at a level commensurate with less able peers might fail to be identified. This argument has been supported by a small-scale study reporting that, for a sample of high IQ, age-appropriate readers, reduced brain activity occurred in the same regions as for struggling readers (Hancock, Gabrieli, & Hoeft, 2016). It has been suggested (Tanaka & Hoeft, 2017) that such children may benefit from additional accommodations and interventions. Finally, the common focus of the approach upon specific academic domains may result in a failure to spot other underlying conditions such as autism, ADHD, or a psychiatric disorder until the child has progressed through several tiers (Pennington, McGrath, & Peterson, 2019). To address this last concern, Miciak and Fletcher (2020) suggest a hybrid model of dyslexia which includes three components:

a. low achievement in reading, particularly in relation to accurate and fluent word reading and spelling;
b. poor response to RTI tiers despite effective instruction;
c. consideration of a small number of influential exclusionary factors such as severe visual or hearing impairment or second-language acquisition.

As part of the RTI or MTSS process, they emphasize the need to ensure early identification and treatment of such other conditions.

As noted above, the design of a sound, rigorous RTI or MTSS model is of little value if its subsequent operation within education systems is suboptimal. For this reason, it is difficult to evaluate the value of RTI independently of the level of energy and funding that any society is prepared to provide to ensure its effective operation. Unfortunately, operationalization in school systems has proven problematic with evidence of a significant research to practice gap (D. Fuchs & Fuchs, 2017; Sanetti & Luh, 2019; Savitz, Allen & Brown, 2021).

Two critics of RTI, B. Shaywitz and S. Shaywitz, (2020), have claimed that their longstanding criticisms (Reynolds & Shaywitz, 2009a, 2009b) have been "validated" (B. Shaywitz & S. Shaywitz, 2020: 463) by findings from a large-scale national study in the USA (Balu et al., 2015). This found that first-grade children placed on Tiers 2 or 3 subsequently performed more poorly on reading outcomes than comparison children, with non-significant impacts at Grades 2 and 3. B. Shaywitz and S. Shaywitz, (2020) state:

> Despite the evidence of its ineffectiveness, many schools and school districts seem to remain blithely unaware of this evidence and the majority of schools in the US continue to use RTI as the primary intervention method of educating children with dyslexia. (B. Shaywitz & S. Shaywitz, 2020: 463)

However, based solely upon the findings of Balu et al. (2015), dismissal of the potential of RTI appears unjustified. Methodological considerations (the focus here was upon comparison of students at the cusp of the cut-off point for selection), and problematic practices in the schools studied, may help to explain the results obtained (Gersten, Jayanthi, & Dimino, 2017; D. Fuchs & Fuchs, 2017). There is some competing evidence that where instructional intensity is implemented with consistency and fidelity, positive effects of supplemental small group instruction can result (Coyne et al., 2018; Smith et al., 2016).

Miciak and Fletcher (2020) acknowledge that effective operation of school-wide RTI or MTSS systems will require substantial technical assistance and professional development. In particular, classteachers at Tier 1 must have the requisite skills to deliver the explicit phonics tuition that is particularly needed for struggling readers in the early grades. Despite the challenges inherent in such a large-scale, comprehensive approach, these authors argue that, because of the underpinning principles, it is one worth pursuing:

> A dyslexia identification approach that relies on achievement and instructional data generated within MTSS is dynamic, treatment oriented, preventive, and less likely to result in diagnostic problems because of its recursive and sequential nature. (Miciak & Fletcher, 2020: 350)

The RTI or MTSS model is designed to operate as an organizational framework within which can be provided a high-quality, evidence-based intervention appropriate to the child's needs. To argue that an RTI program needs to be replaced by interventions more appropriately attuned to the needs of dyslexic children is to conflate educational architecture with pedagogic approaches (Gibbs & Elliott, 2020). If RTI is operating appropriately, an alternative, more effective form of instruction or different content should not be required – it should already be being delivered as part of the RTI program. Unfortunately, inappropriate forms of reading intervention, delivered by ill-prepared teachers will undermine progress and, in some cases, this will inflate the number of children progressing to Tier 2 (Moats, 2017). As is discussed in Chapter 4, evidence-based interventions are required that can be increasingly individualized, explicit, comprehensive, and intense, should the child continue to make insufficient progress (Al Otaiba, Russell-Freudenthal, & Zaru, 2024; Grigorenko et al., 2019). If these are not being provided, one cannot conclude that RTI as a general approach is wrong; rather, the problem would be that it is not being implemented as intended.

Of course, this distinction is likely to be of little interest to parents who are anxiously seeking help and support. It is understandable that fears that their child's needs are being overlooked, or that their school is delivering ineffective instruction, may lead them, sometimes with teacher support, to seek a formal diagnosis of dyslexia in the hope that this will lead to a superior outcome (Odegard, Hutchings, Farris, & Oslund, 2021). Such concerns may accurately reflect the reality that, in some school systems, the existence of a high proportion of struggling readers, together with limited resources, cannot enable an RTI or MTSS model to operate effectively.

B. Shaywitz and S. Shaywitz (2020) note that effective interventions for those with dyslexia are expensive and are often unavailable in schools. While this observation may be accurate, their preferred approach, advocating formal diagnosis, and championing the role of both private and public special schools for dyslexia, means that only a very small proportion of struggling readers could receive the help they require (Elliott, 2020). Thus, an understandable tension exists between the use of a traditional diagnostic approach that, because of its nature, typically enables allocation of scarce resources to a "dyslexic" minority (resulting in a form of bottleneck), and an approach that has the potential to identify so many genuinely struggling readers that the quality and level of individual support available is likely to prove insufficient.

Unfortunately, resources available to public education systems are typically overstretched and, in relation to reading disability (and, indeed, learning difficulties more widely), hard decisions must often be taken about which children should have priority access to additional assistance. Whatever approach is taken, the basis for decision-making should be seen to be fair and equitable. It should not be derived from scientifically questionable practices that confer built-in advantage to those who already enjoy higher levels of social and cultural capital.

A further dilemma concerns how best to help those who continue to make minimal progress despite receipt of high-quality intervention in the highest tiers. In the USA, this may be used as evidence to determine eligibility for special education (on the grounds of specific learning disability) thus freeing up additional resources, although such provision may still be provided within an existing RTI or MTSS program.

The use of the dyslexia label could perhaps be meaningfully employed where persistent intractability of this kind has been demonstrated. Elliott and Gibbs (2008) for example, suggested that a dyslexia diagnosis might be restricted to that small proportion of poor readers who, despite having received extensive high-level, high-quality intervention, appear unlikely ever to become functionally literate. For such individuals, the dyslexia label could be employed to determine a need for assistive technology that can help them navigate the literacy demands of adult life (de Beer et al., 2022; Wood et al., 2018). To date, this suggestion has not achieved any significant traction, perhaps because this would mean that dyslexia diagnoses would no longer be required or available at scale.

Dyslexia 4: A Neurodiverse Profile

This conception differs from the other three listed above because here, reading disability is typically considered to be but one possible component of a broader neurodiverse dyslexic condition. Such a perspective, very different to dominant conceptions in the scientific literature, has largely arisen from practitioner concern about comorbid cognitive difficulties often found in poor readers. Many of these are considered in Chapter 2 and include difficulties with working memory, processing speed, attention and concentration, planning, physical coordination, time management, self-organization, and the capacity to express oneself orally (Asghar et al., 2018, 2019). While the cognitive processes considered important for a Dyslexia 4 conception are similar to those used for Dyslexia 2, in the former case, the presence of a severe reading difficulty is neither an essential criterion (Ryder & Norwich, 2018) nor necessarily the primary focus for specialist intervention and assistance.

While neurodiverse perspectives can provide a number of important theoretical insights, with some valuable practical implications (see Chapter 5), these do not justify the reframing of dyslexia into a much expanded and more nebulous construct. The use of the dyslexia label as an umbrella term encompassing a wide range of difficulties cannot be justified simply on the basis that such problems are more commonly found in poor readers. This growing practice seemingly reflects the immense power and leverage of the dyslexia label, in particular, its ability to garner institutional support for a wide variety of cognitive and linguistic difficulties that might otherwise be neglected or discounted.

According to accounts widely promulgated in the media, and supported by dyslexia lobby groups, dyslexia's neurodiverse profile may also include associated gifts (both cognitive and conative) that can help those so affected to thrive (Davis, 1997; Eide & Eide, 2011; West, 2022), such that the condition might be perceived as a desirable difficulty (Gladwell, 2013). Characters from history such as Leonardo da Vinci and Albert Einsten, have been cited as dyslexic (despite an absence of supportive evidence). Celebrated contemporary public figures have outlined how their dyslexic strengths have helped them achieve success despite many challenges. This perspective appears to have some resonance with official bodies. For example, it has been stated by the UK Intelligence Analyst agency (GCHQ) that the enhanced abilities of dyslexic people make them ideal analysts. This organization's website boldly states that "Dyslexic thinking skills are mission critical for protecting the country." Particular strengths of dyslexics according to this organization include "pattern recognition when dealing with big data, seeing the bigger picture when considering complex future scenarios and finding solutions to novel and challenging problems"[5]

In similar vein, a widely publicized 2018 report produced by one of the world's leading management consultant companies (EY, formerly known as Ernst and Young), and produced in conjunction with *Made by Dyslexia*, a dyslexia advocacy group, argued that those with dyslexia often have talents that offer much to business:

> Our research shows that dyslexic strengths provide a significant opportunity for organizations to harness a different, and widely untapped, pool of talent. Dyslexia influences at least 1 in 10 people and is a genetic difference in an individual's ability to learn and process information. As a result, dyslexic individuals have differing abilities, with strengths in creative, problem solving and communication skills and challenges with spelling, reading and memorizing facts. Generally, a dyslexic cognitive profile will be uneven when compared to a neuro-typical cognitive profile. This means that dyslexic individuals really do think differently. What does this mean in work? These varied cognitive profiles give dyslexic individuals natural abilities to form alternative views and solve problems creatively. Heightened cognitive abilities in certain areas, such as visualisation and logical reasoning skills and natural entrepreneurial traits can bring a fresh, often intuitive perspective. (EY, formerly known as Ernst and Young: 5)

As is demonstrated throughout this book, such claims have little or no support in the scientific literature. Nevertheless, *Made by Dyslexia*, backed

[5] www.gchq.gov.uk/news/dyslexic-thinking-skills; accessed November 17, 2023.

by high profile figures interviewed in the UK national media, offer what is described as a "twenty-first century definition of dyslexia":

> Dyslexia influences as many as 1 in 5 people and is a genetic difference in an individual's ability to learn and process information. As a result, dyslexic individuals have differing abilities, with strengths in creative, problem-solving and communication skills and challenges with spelling, reading and memorising facts.
>
> Generally, a dyslexic cognitive profile will be uneven when compared to a neurotypical cognitive profile. This means that dyslexic individuals really do think differently.
>
> Traditional benchmarking disadvantages dyslexics, measuring them against the very things they find challenging. (www.madebydyslexia.org)[6]

Dyslexia 4 conceptions have tended to be most popular in adult settings where it is easier to decouple this wide-ranging, multifaceted conception from its original use to describe severe and persistent reading difficulty. Its popularity in the adult sector rests in part upon its potential to provide various educational accommodations and resources (Asghar et al., 2018, 2019) and to offer employers greater insight into various cognitive difficulties that can prove professionally challenging for those so labeled (e.g., Locke et al., 2017). Commercially, this conception offers a number of attractions. By employing a wide range of tests, assessors are likely to encounter little difficulty in finding strengths, weaknesses and discrepancies which can then form the basis for their diagnosis. Unsurprisingly, however, the high level of heterogeneity in assessor practices adds to the inconsistency and questionable reliability of this approach (Ryder & Norwich, 2018). Further discussion of the inherent difficulties of this conception are outlined in Chapter 5.

The Prevalence of Dyslexia

Given the lack of current consensus about what exactly is meant by the term dyslexia, it is hardly surprising that estimates of its prevalence vary substantially. This problem is by no means new; almost a century ago Hinshelwood (1917) disparagingly commented that some educationalists considered congenital word-blindness to be very common, involving as many as one in a thousand. He noted that such estimates often included cases where there were "... slight degrees of defect in the visual word

---

[6] Accessed May 4, 2023.

centre, while the early writers had reserved it for only those grave cases which could be regarded as pathological" (1917: 82). Two decades later, Orton (1939) suggested that just over ten percent of the school-aged population had reading disabilities. He also introduced the notion of a continuum of disabilities, rather than clear pathological categories, arguing that experience of work with hundreds of cases indicated that clear divisions did not reflect the gradations of difficulty that he had encountered.

As noted above, reading ability is a continuous variable, and dyslexia/reading disability is typically defined by researchers on the basis of an individual's performance at the low end of a normal distribution of reading test scores. Where exactly any diagnostic cut-off should be located is essentially an arbitrary decision (Brady, 2019; Snowling, 2019) although it is widely considered that the reading difficulties should be sufficiently severe as to have clinical implications (Pennington, McGrath, & Peterson, 2019) and not be primarily explained by severe intellectual or sensory disability. However, there is no clear scientific basis to the argument that individuals with intellectual disability would not also have a reading disability, so excluding this group is questionable (Wagner & Lonigan, 2022). In the case of second-language speakers it is important to consider whether any observed reading difficulties also occur in their native language (Fletcher et al., 2019).

Prevalence estimates are affected by whether dyslexia is treated as a synonym for reading disability (Dyslexia 1) or is used to refer to a smaller subgroup consisting of only some individuals with a word reading difficulty (Dyslexia 2). Either way, it is important to be cautious of published estimates which can sometimes provide an inappropriately confident picture:

> Prevalence estimates are often mentioned in the dyslexia literature, giving the false impression that there are absolute criteria on the basis of which dyslexia is defined, further giving rise to the expectation that such criteria might be linked to specific, potentially identifiable causal factors, whereas in fact there is nothing but a continuous distribution of reading skill, with an enormous range of individual differences. (Protopapas & Parilla, 2018: n.p.)

Estimates have tended to range from approximately 5 percent to 20 percent. The lower figure is usually derived from the deployment of a cut-off point of approximately one and a half standard deviations below the mean. Similarly, leading researchers at the influential Florida Center for Reading Research (Catts et al., 2024) argue that the term dyslexia should describe a severe reading difficulty, and suggest a prevalence rate of 5–10%. Snowling (2013) suggests the deployment of two cut-off points, one at 1.5 standard deviations (SDs), and another at two SDs, below the mean, representing moderate and severe reading difficulty respectively.

Research studies have tended to cluster around the 1.5 SD cut-off figure. Yang et al. (2022) undertook a comprehensive systematic review and meta-analysis that sought to estimate the worldwide prevalence of developmental dyslexia in primary school children. This involved the final inclusion of fifty-six studies undertaken between the 1950s and 2021. The results indicated an overall prevalence rate of 7.10 percent. Somewhat surprisingly, they found no significant difference between logographic (6.97%), and alphabetic writing systems (7.26%), or between alphabetic scripts with different orthographic depths (shallow = 7.13%; deep = 7.55%).[7]

Yang et al. (2022) noted that there was no consensus as to diagnostic criteria and this resulted in definitional confusion. In their opinion, a clear operational definition is urgently needed.

Others have suggested a much higher prevalence rate, even as large as 25 percent (Pennington et al., 2019). The Yale Center for Dyslexia and Creativity suggests a dyslexia rate of 20 percent.[8] This likely reflects Shaywitz's influential longitudinal study in Connecticut (Shaywitz, 2005) which identified approximately 17.5 percent of the sample as having a reading disability, defined on the basis of reading performance that was below age, grade, or level of intellectual ability. In citing this figure, it would appear that the term "reading-disabled" was seen as synonymous with "dyslexic" as, in Shaywitz's text, the terms are employed interchangeably:

> The apparent large-scale underidentification of reading-disabled children is particularly worrisome because even when school identification takes place, it occurs relatively late – often past the optimal age for intervention. Dyslexic children are generally in the third grade or above when they are first identified by their schools; reading disabilities diagnosed after third grade are much more difficult to remediate. (Shaywitz, 2005: 30)

Interestingly, in the second edition of this text (S. Shaywitz & J. Shaywitz, 2020: 30) the term "reading-disabled" was replaced by "dyslexic," although the meaning of the passage remains unchanged.

In an earlier, highly influential article, Shaywitz claimed that "… dyslexia affects a full 20 percent of schoolchildren" (Shaywitz, 1996: 100). This estimate was also provided in the revision of her earlier 2005 text (S. Shaywitz & J. Shaywitz, 2020) in which it was stated that dyslexia affected ten million children in America alone.

[7] Orthographies are described as shallow or transparent when the degree of grapheme–phoneme mapping of the language is highly consistent. Where consistency is low, the orthography is described as deep or opaque (Frost et al., 1987; Seymour et al., 2003).
[8] https://dyslexia.yale.edu; accessed November 17, 2023.

Shaywitz and Shaywitz's position reflects the understanding that reading difficulties are dimensional – they lie along a continuum with no clearcut distinction between good and poor readers. Citing the words of Kendell (1975), "Classification is the art of carving nature at the joints; it should indeed imply that there is indeed a joint there, that one is not sawing through bone" (Kendell, 1975: 65), S. Shaywitz & J. Shaywitz (2020) argue that although there is no natural joint separating dyslexic and good readers, "… a gap of nature" (S. Shaywitz & J. Shaywitz, 2020: 27), the provision of educational services has often been based upon just such a belief and, as a result, many struggling readers have failed to receive adequate support.

The prevalence rates for dyslexia provided by national support groups can vary widely. The British Dyslexia Association states that it "… is the voice for the 10% of the population that are dyslexic."[9] The Dyslexia Foundation of New Zealand (2008) similarly claims that 10 percent of children in that country are dyslexic. The International Dyslexia Association avoids specifying a precise figure, but its factsheet suggests that as many as 15–20 percent of the population as a whole may have some of the symptoms of dyslexia.[10]

Females have been shown to score more highly in reading skill across multiple countries, education systems, and orthographies (OECD, 2015). Males are more likely to be identified as having a reading disability with the ratio of males to females so identified ranging from a low of 1.2:1 to a high of 6.8:1 (Quinn, 2018). This variation reflects the use of differing definitions and measures, and differences between clinical and epidemiological samples. A view that males have been disproportionally identified as reading-disabled was spurred by findings from Shaywitz's longitudinal Connecticut study. This reported that school identification procedures resulted in three to four times as many boys as girls being identified as reading-disabled, whereas her research team's own testing programme indicated comparable figures for males and females (B. Shaywitz & S. Shaywitz, 2020). S. Shaywitz's primary explanation for the "myth" of male vulnerability to reading disability (Shaywitz, 1996: 98) was that girls, who tend to be less obtrusive and attention seeking, are more likely to be overlooked for further clinical evaluation. Boys with reading difficulties are more likely to present with comorbid externalizing disorders and the hyperactive-impulsive form of ADHD (Barkley, 2015), whereas girls are more likely to present with internalizing problems (Pennington, 2009). As schools tend to refer to clinical services children with conduct rather than internalizing disorders (Bramlett et al.,

---

[9] www.bdadyslexia.org.uk; accessed July 3, 2022.
[10] www.dyslexiaida.org; accessed July 3, 2022.

2002), disproportionate referral rates of boys and girls for reading related problems are an inevitable outcome. While biased referral rates are likely to be a contributory factor, epidemiological studies indicate that the male incidence of reading disability nevertheless remains higher with studies suggesting a ratio of approximately 1.5:1 (Brimo et al., 2021; Flannery et al., 2000; Flynn & Rahbar, 1994).

In a large international meta-analytic review of dyslexia prevalence, Yang et al. (2022) reported a 2:1 male to female ratio (boys = 9.22%; girls = 4.66%). Quinn's (2018) meta-analysis found a relatively similar figure; males were 1.83 times more likely than females to be identified as having a reading problem regardless of method of identification, reading measure, publication year, and age of the participant. Additionally, it was found that the more severe the level of the reading difficulty, the more likely it would be that males would be identified relative to females. This accords with Arnett et al. (2017) who found a gender discrepancy at the low tail of the distribution, and Quinn and Wagner (2015) who reported male to female ratios of 1.3:1 and 2.0:1 at the thirtieth and third percentiles respectively.

The reasons for meaningful male–female differences remain unclear although there is evidence of greater male difficulty with phonological awareness Lundberg, Larsman and Strid (2012) and also the apparent mediating effects of poorer processing speed and inhibitory control (Arnett et al., 2017).

The Difficulty of Bridging Science and Practice: The Rose Report

Many of the difficulties involved in attempting to provide a sound approach to the understanding and assessment of dyslexia, while attending to political and other external pressures, can be illustrated by reference to the UK Government sponsored Rose Report (2009). While the Report's scientific basis and desire to increase support for struggling readers are generally laudable, its recommendations appear to maintain diagnostic practices that are questionable and fail to work to the advantage of many children.

The Report stated that, as a developmental disorder, the difficulties experienced by the dyslexic child would likely change as he or she passes through school and progresses through adulthood. According to the Report, at the preschool stage, signs of dyslexia are most likely to be delayed or problematic speech, poor expressive language, poor rhyming skills and little interest in or difficulty with learning letters. In the early school years, problems are most likely to include poor letter–sound knowledge, poor phoneme awareness, poor word attack skills, idiosyncratic spelling, and difficulties in copying. In the middle school years, typical difficulties will include slow reading speed, poor decoding skills when confronted by new words, and difficulties with spelling. In adolescence and adulthood, principal difficulties will most likely be poor reading fluency, slow speed of writing, and poor organization and expression in work. While the Report refers to dyslexia, it should be noted that such difficulties are common features of all struggling readers.

The Rose Report identified three characteristic features of dyslexia: weaknesses in: phonological awareness, verbal memory and verbal processing speed. Each of these is examined in greater detail in Chapter 2. Of central importance was the statement that none of these markers was considered to be necessary for a diagnosis. Similarly, problems of language, mental calculation, motor coordination, concentration, and personal organization, while often comorbid, could not, by themselves, be recognized as markers of dyslexia.

In respect of diagnosis, the Rose Report was somewhat confusing. Recognizing that reading disability/dyslexia reflects a dimension, rather than a categorical diagnosis (Pennington & Bishop, 2009; Snowling, 2008), it stated that

> … dyslexia is best thought of as a continuum, not a distinct category, and there are no clear cut-off points …. Until recently, a child was deemed to either have or not have dyslexia. It is now recognised that there is no sharp dividing line between having a learning difficulty such as dyslexia and not having it. (Rose, 2009: 33)

Despite this claim, the Report suggested that an accurate diagnosis could be made by specialists. To many diagnosticians, such a perspective seemed to signal a belief that the use of a categorical label – dyslexia – was more helpful than a dimensional account for communicating the nature of reading difficulty, a position that has been criticized for glossing over the practical realities of identification and resourcing of children with special educational needs (Norwich, 2010). To be in any way effective, such an approach requires consensual understandings as to the meaning of the categorical term concerned. A particular problem for dyslexia is that this is evidently not the case.

The Rose Report appeared to conflate these differing understandings. It endorsed the construct of dyslexia, argued that it was at the more severe end of a reading performance continuum, and appeared to support a medical model in which experts retain a role in determining who is, and who is not, dyslexic. The Report set out a three-level model for assessment and diagnosis. At Level 1, class teachers "… will be aware of the possibility that some children may have dyslexia. However, they will not declare that a particular child has dyslexia" (Rose, 2009: 53). By Level 3, appropriately qualified specialists "… would make a decision on whether or not the child has dyslexia, and with what severity" (Rose, 2009: 53). How exactly such a determination might be arrived at was rendered rather less clear. Such phrasing seems inconsistent with the claims of a member of the Rose Expert Advisory Group that: "… it was not a question of dyslexia, yes or no" (Reason & Stothard, 2013: 12), and seems to strike a dissonant chord with the Report's other remarks about dividing lines. This apparent tension reinforces a perception that influential professional and other lobby groups had exercised pressure to ensure the continuation of what has been sometimes described as the dyslexia industry (Gabriel, 2020a: Holmqvist, 2020).[11]

The Rose Report illustrates the confusions and compromises that can result when sound research is translated into educational policy and practice. Its scientific basis lies in the groundbreaking work of Snowling and others who, as noted above, largely employ the term dyslexia as a synonym for a severe reading (decoding) difficulty that is generally resistant to evidence-based forms of intervention (i.e., approximating to Elliott's (2020) notions of Dyslexia 1 and Dyslexia 3). However, poor response to "well-founded intervention" appears not to be an essential criterion in the Rose Report as it merely describes this element as "… a good indication of the severity and persistence of dyslexic difficulties." By couching the definition of dyslexia in this way, it remains possible for a diagnosis to be provided following a one-off clinical assessment.

In outlining in detail many of the difficulties experienced by those who struggle with reading, and recommending a key role for expert diagnosis, a symptom-driven version of Dyslexia 2 is likely to become dominant. (There is also the potential for a Dyslexia 4 conception although, as noted above, Rose de-emphasizes the diagnostic role of most comorbid features). Through this approach, assessors can undertake a clinical interview, identify a number of particular literacy and cognitive difficulties, and then conclude that their poor reader client is dyslexic. That it is highly unlikely that any child with a serious reading disability would fail to present with some of these difficulties is generally not explicitly recognized.

The inherent confusions in such an approach were highlighted by a UK Government investigation into dyslexia in 2009. In interviews with expert

---

[11] See also the House of Commons, Science and Technology Committee (2009) for criticism of the influence of dyslexia lobby groups on the UK Government.

witnesses and dyslexia lobbyists, members of the House of Commons, Science and Technology Select Committee (House of Commons, 2009) repeatedly sought guidance on how the contents of the Rose Report might help assessors to differentiate between dyslexic and non-dyslexic poor readers, and how this distinction could be used to inform practical educational guidance that would differ for members of these two groups. Scrutiny of the discussion (see, in particular, Q96–Q102) demonstrates a degree of frustration on the part of Committee members that these questions were being insufficiently answered. The resultant Select Committee Report concluded that:

> The Rose Report's definition of dyslexia is … so broad and blurred at the edges that it is difficult to see how it could be useful in any diagnostic sense. (House of Commons, 2009: 26, para. 71)

And added that it:

> … is not useful from an educational point of view… (House of Commons, 2009: 28, para. 77)

Understandings and Definitions of Dyslexia: A Summary

It is incontrovertible that there is a significant number of individuals who struggle to learn to read despite receiving instruction in formal education settings. While word recognition difficulty is widely known as dyslexia, others hold alternative views, and gaining a clear, scientific, and consensual understanding of this term has proven elusive. Table 1.1 outlines some of the many different, often overlapping, understandings that continue to be promoted.

Table 1.1 *Differing understandings of who may be considered to experience dyslexia*

- anyone who struggles with accurate single word decoding;
- anyone who struggles with accurate and/or fluent decoding;
- those who score at the lower end of the normal distribution on an appropriate test of reading accuracy or fluency. Cut-off points vary but are typically either 1, 1.5, or 2 standard deviations below the test's population mean;
- those whose decoding difficulties cannot be explained in alternative ways (e.g., because of severe intellectual or sensory impairment, socioeconomic disadvantage, poor schooling, or emotional/behavioral difficulty);
- those poor decoders who present with a range of symptoms commonly found in those with dyslexia (e.g., poor motor, arithmetical, or language skills, visual difficulties, attentional and organizational problems and low self-esteem);
- those for whom there is a significant discrepancy between decoding performance and IQ;
- those whose decoding difficulty is deemed to be unexpected;

Table 1.1 (cont.)

- those whose poor decoding skills contrast with strengths in other intellectual and academic domains;
- those whose decoding problems are deemed to be biologically determined;
- those whose decoding problems are marked by certain associated cognitive difficulties (in particular, phonological, rapid naming, and verbal short-term or working memory deficits);
- those with a history of very poor spelling;
- those who demonstrate a discrepancy between decoding/reading comprehension and listening comprehension;
- those who fail to make meaningful progress in decoding even when provided with high-quality, evidence-based forms of intervention.
- those for whom decoding is merely one element of a more pervasive dyslexic condition marked by a variety of cognitive strengths and weaknesses. This may include "compensated dyslexics" who no longer present with a reading difficulty.

Reading Disability as a Multifactorial, Heterogeneous Syndrome

One of the factors that has complicated our understanding of reading difficulties in general, and dyslexia in particular, is that researchers tend to operate at differing levels of analysis, depending upon their particular perspectives, disciplines, and specialisms. Frith (1997), for example, contends that the examination of reading difficulties can take place at the level of the biological, the cognitive, and the behavioral.

Perusal of media or professional accounts might lead one to assume that a diagnosis could draw upon data obtained from the direct assessment of an individual's genetic, neuropsychological, or cognitive profiles. However:

> … there is currently no consistent basis – biological, cognitive, behavioral, or academic – for distinguishing those who might be identified as dyslexic from others experiencing difficulty learning to decode words. In the end, determining whether or not someone is dyslexic amounts to deciding where on the normal distribution to draw a line …. There is no agreement about where to draw the line(s), and there is no evidence that instructional response should be different for those above or below the line(s). (Johnston & Scanlon, 2021: 70–71)

Research has demonstrated that single deficit understandings of dyslexia/reading disability, cannot explain the significant variability in underlying causal factors (O'Brien & Yeatman, 2021; Pennington et al., 2019; Rakhlin et al., 2022; van Bergen, van der Leij, & de Jong, 2014). The belief that single cognitive deficits could explain dyslexia (or, indeed, other neurodevelopmental disorders) failed for both theoretical and empirical reasons (McGrath, Peterson, & Pennington, 2020). It failed theoretically because the suggestion that there were innate, localized cognitive modules located in the brain, each of which could be linked to a specific disorder, was ultimately shown to be erroneous. Specialized processing areas emerge developmentally and interactively and their brain substrates change accordingly. It failed empirically, because, as is subsequently detailed in Chapter 2, no specific deficit can be found in all children with a particular neurodevelopmental disorder, and some children without the disorder can present with the deficit.

Surprisingly, perhaps, such understanding, often unreflected by current dyslexia assessment procedures, is not a recent phenomenon. Indeed, almost two decades ago, a seminal publication put the case for a multiple deficit model (Pennington, 2006) operating at a number of levels. In a subsequent text, Pennington (2009) stated:

> (1) The etiology of complex behavioral disorders is multifactorial and involves the interaction of multiple risk and protective factors which can be either genetic or environmental; (2) these risk and protective factors alter the development of the neural systems that mediate cognitive functions necessary for normal development, thus producing the behavioral symptoms that define these disorders; (3) no single etiological factor is sufficient for a disorder and few may be necessary; (4) consequently, comorbidity among complex behavioral disorders is expected because of shared etiological and cognitive risk factors; and (5) the liability distribution for a given disease is often continuous and quantitative rather than discrete and categorical. (Pennington, 2009: 6)

The multifactorial nature of reading disability which sees risk factors as acting probabilistically rather than deterministically with different developmental pathways to reading disability is now widely accepted by leading researchers. However, the development of specific models is still in its infancy and most research activity is currently focusing upon the neuropsychological level of analysis (McGrath, Peterson, & Pennington, 2020).

Understanding of the nature and impact of resilience, a term that concerns better than expected outcomes despite the presence of risk (Luthar et al., 2000; Masten, 2001), is also still relatively rudimentary. The operationalization of resilience is inconsistent across studies but is generally seen to involve relationships between individual, environmental, and sociocultural factors (Lavin Venegas et al., 2019). Resilience typically benefits from the presence of promotive and protective factors (Slomowitz et al., 2021). Promotive factors are associated with positive outcomes irrespective of the presence of risk; however, they are only associated with resilience when they occur in a high-risk context. A high-quality diet and sound sleep patterns, for example, will be valuable for all children, regardless of their risk status. In contrast, protective factors reduce risk and are particularly important for high-risk groups. Examples might be possession of social skills that can help to reduce the likelihood of peer admonishment about one's poor reading, lower personal sensitivity to reading-related stigmatization (Daley & Rappolt-Schlichtmann, 2018), and regular access to teachers highly skilled in the teaching of language and reading. Unlike promotive factors, protective factors can reduce the gaps between differing risk groups because they are likely to offer greater benefit to high-risk groups. High-quality parenting is likely to be a promotive factor for all individuals but this may have the greatest protective role for those most at risk (Catts & Petscher, 2022; Masten & Barnes, 2018).

Recognition has been slow on the part of many assessors and diagnosticians that there is no single cognitive deficit (or group of deficits) that is sufficient to warrant a diagnosis of dyslexia (Catts & Petscher, 2022). The persistent attraction of unitary understandings in diagnostic settings may be partly a consequence of the fact that multifactorial models largely rule out the use of a binary dyslexic/non-dyslexic poor reader distinction (at least, at the current time). Until greater understanding of the relationships and connections between different levels of analysis can be developed (Compton, 2021), attempts to provide differential diagnosis within the population of struggling readers (beyond ascertaining the level of severity and response to intervention) offer little for the purposes of intervention. In line with Vellutino et al. (2004), we should therefore dispense with the search for categorical labels for reading difficulties and, instead, focus assessment upon language and component reading skills together with consideration of relevant behavioral issues (Fletcher & Miciak, 2017).

In relation to the advancement of theory, we would wish to restate a recommendation offered in *The Dyslexia Debate*, and note the relatively slow progress that has been made since that time:

> … in order to derive sophisticated understandings of reading disability/ dyslexia, there is a clear need to derive complex multifactorial models operating at biological, cognitive, and behavioral levels that interact with one another and with the environment …. Such an enterprise will, perhaps, be the key task for the next decade. (Elliott & Grigorenko, 2014: 379–380)

A Note on the Terminology Employed in This Book

As this chapter has demonstrated, the use of the terms *dyslexia, reading disability, reading difficulty* and other closely related constructs varies greatly, with these often being employed interchangeably. This discrepancy renders problematic the use of such terms in this book where a key aim is to achieve greater conceptual clarity. Our solution to this conundrum is, wherever possible, to use the particular constructs that are employed in the publications that are cited. In the case of more general discussion and reflection, the terms *dyslexia* and *reading disability* are used interchangeably to refer to a difficulty concerning the accurate and fluent reading of words and connected text. Where appropriate, however, the distinction between reading accuracy and fluency is highlighted and examined.

Where a categorical distinction between dyslexic and other poor readers is suggested or explored, we have employed the acronyms *DSR* (Dyslexic Struggling Reader) and *NDSR* (Non-Dyslexic Struggling Reader) as a shorthand form to aid the reader.

The distinction between dyslexia/reading disability and the closely related process of reading comprehension is recognized in the text. Throughout, the broader term *reading difficulties* is employed where reference is made to a group of reading problems that will typically include accurate and fluent decoding and reading comprehension.

CHAPTER 2

Explanations at the Cognitive Level

Introduction

This chapter will examine the evidence concerning the nature and role of a number of cognitive and perceptual processes that have been proposed as influential in dyslexia/reading disability: phonological awareness, rapid naming, short-term or working memory, low level sensory auditory and visual processing, scotopic sensitivity, attentional factors, and motor processing. In each case the implications of the available research evidence for clinical and educational intervention will also be considered. As the chapter will demonstrate, this highly complex field is rendered additionally problematic by often contrasting and inconsistent research findings that have resulted in much debate and little consensus, beyond widespread agreement that multiple deficits are evident in reading disability.

From Single to Multiple Deficits

Single deficit causal models are considered to be inadequate in explaining reading disability/dyslexia (O'Brien & Yeatman, 2021; Pennington et al., 2019; Rakhlin et al., 2022). These have now been largely replaced by multifactorial risk and resilience models in which factors at different levels (biological, environmental, and cognitive) combine and interact in the development of reading problems (Catts et al., 2017; Catts & Petscher, 2022; McGrath, Peterson, & Pennington, 2020). Risk factors are not considered to cause the disorder in a simple deterministic fashion; rather, by increasing the likelihood of problems albeit in different ways and to different degrees for different individuals, they are essentially probabilistic. Helping to reduce these risks are a range of moderating promotive and protective (resilience) factors (Masten & Barnes, 2018).

The Phonological Deficit Hypothesis

The suggestion that difficulties of some kind with auditory discrimination, or the analysis of sounds, might have an important role in reading difficulties has been longstanding although, prior to the final decades of the twentieth century, this was little more than a hunch without a theoretical foundation (Share, 2021a). Since this time, the phonological deficit hypothesis (Stanovich, 1988; Stanovich & Siegel, 1994) (or phonological deficit theory; see Zoccolotti, 2022 for a critique) has become the dominant cognitive explanation such that, "… no behavioral or brain-imaging investigation of dyslexia can afford to neglect the assessment of phonological skills in either the definition or the validation of their dyslexic sample" (Share, 2021a: 2). The seeming success of the theory is such that there are few new studies of phonological processing in groups of dyslexics because "… there is nothing new or disputed here" (Share, 2021a: 5). This has led some assessors to hold the erroneous belief that the presence of a phonological difficulty should serve as the crucial diagnostic symptom that enables confirmation of the condition (e.g., see Ottosen et al., 2022 for discussion of the implications of this perspective for diagnosis and resourcing in Denmark). This may have serious implications for those struggling readers who do not present with a phonological problem and, as a result, could be excluded from special accommodations and resources (Brady, 2019; Pennington et al., 2012; Pennington, McGrath, & Peterson, 2019; Protopapas & Parrila, 2018; Ring & Black, 2018).

Studies of cognitive functioning in children with reading problems consistently found three processes (phonological processing, short-term or working memory, and phonological processing speed) that appeared to be particularly significant when comparisons are made with typically achieving readers. For each of these processes, there appears to be a phonological component that is particularly important for reading. According to some, the phonological deficit incorporates processes that concern all three major dimensions: phonological awareness, verbal short-term memory, and slow retrieval of phonological information stored in long-term memory, as exemplified in rapid automatic naming tasks (Wagner & Torgesen, 1987). However, the inclusion of memory and processing speed under a phonological deficit umbrella is controversial and some contend that it is not helpful to conceive of verbal short-term or working memory and naming speed as core elements of phonology (Nicolson & Fawcett, 2008). Noting that these, and several other deficits that appear to be important for the development of dyslexia, involve phonology in some way, Seidenberg

(2017) questions whether they are best considered as multiple kinds of deficits or, alternatively, as multiple manifestations of one or more phonological impairments. His conclusion is that the answer remains unclear:

> There may be several types of phonological deficits, and dyslexia may have other nonphonological causes as well. But phonology is a big umbrella covering all of the ways in which knowledge derived from pronunciation and sound is used in reading, speaking, and other tasks. Impaired phonology jeopardizes performance on all of them. (Seidenberg, 2017: 178)

Tunmer (2011) lists a number of aspects of phonological processing. These include:

> … encoding phonological information (phonetic perception), gaining access to and performing mental operations on phonological information (phonological awareness), retrieving phonological information from semantic memory (lexical retrieval), retaining phonological information in working memory (short-term verbal recall), and translating letters and letter patterns into phonological forms (phonological recoding). (Tunmer, 2011: x)

Confusingly, phonological awareness is sometimes employed as the superordinate construct. Thus, Duff, Hayiou-Thomas, and Hulme (2012) include measures of phoneme awareness, short-term memory, and rapid automatized naming as measures of phonological awareness. For the purposes of the following section, however, we have treated these as separate constructs.

An important distinction that has been drawn is that between implicit and explicit phonological processing (Melby-Lervåg, Lyster, & Hulme, 2012). Tasks involving verbal short-term memory or rapid automatized naming are deemed to involve implicit phonological processing because they do not involve any conscious awareness of, or reflection upon, the sound structure of spoken words. In contrast, phonological awareness, largely understood as the ability to detect and manipulate the sounds of spoken language (Liberman & Shankweiler, 1985) involves metacognitive grasp of the relationship between words and sounds, activity which is different from merely processing the perceptual features of speech (Fletcher et al., 2019).

Phonological decoding is important because it enables the reader to map speech sounds onto orthographic patterns (letters) and thus decode unfamiliar words (Share, 1995, 1999, 2004). Phonological awareness operates at both the phoneme (the most basic elements of speech) and syllable levels within words (Bryant et al., 1990). It appears to follow a developmental sequence with awareness of the larger segments, syllables, and rimes preceding that of smaller segments, phonemes (Carroll et al., 2003). Phonemic awareness (the ability to segment spoken words into phonemic elements) appears to be a particularly important factor for reading. To develop this ability, children must learn to attend to meaningless phonemes rather than the more recognizable morphemes and words. For most children, this skill is necessarily advanced by tuition in learning to read. Where phonemic awareness is poor, children are likely to struggle to acquire the ability to discover spelling to sound relationships and, as a consequence, fail to develop adequate alphabetic coding skills and automatically recognize patterns of letters. Such difficulty, in turn, renders reading a laborious and unfulfilling experience that impairs motivation to learn to read and reading for pleasure.

According to the phonological deficit perspective, children with dyslexia are hindered by faulty representation of speech sounds, which leads to problems involving the precise processing of spoken words. These representations become degraded (more fuzzy, noisy, less specified, or with a lower resolution) and as a result, the child struggles to acquire a range of phonological skills such as phonological awareness, alphabetic mapping, and letter–sound decoding, leading to a deficit in orthographic knowledge (Georgiou et al., 2021). Weak phonological coding may render it difficult for the child to establish strong links between the visual and verbal counterparts of printed words. This is likely to impair the ability to store high-quality representations of word spellings thus constraining rapid word identification and reading fluency. The theory gained prominence in the light of findings from studies of preschool children that sought to ascertain which pre-reading skills were the best predictors of later reading and writing ability. Phonological awareness emerged as an important factor (Bradley & Bryant, 1983) as poor performance on measures of this skill helped to identify children who were later to struggle with reading. Other studies comparing older poor readers with younger children without difficulties, reading at the same level, showed significant phonological deficits for the older groups (Olson, 1985; Rack, Snowling, & Olson, 1992).

Since the ground-breaking work of the 1980s a vast number of studies have pointed to the importance of phonological awareness for reading development although prediction appears to be strongest in the early years where an emphasis upon sequential letter-to-sound decoding, rather than upon automatic word recognition, is likely to be greatest (Lervåg, Bråten, & Hulme, 2009; Vaessen & Blomert, 2010).

Although awareness at the phonemic level is generally considered to be more influential than that of larger units, at least for alphabetic languages

(Verhoeven & Perfetti, 2022), it is likely that all levels are important for reading acquisition (Verhoeven, Perfetti, & Pugh, 2019). However, to the consternation of some speech scientists, an undue focus upon phonemic awareness (Pennington et al., 2019) has not helped to resolve uncertainty and controversy about the role of larger units (Share, 2021a).

Nevertheless, the evidence for the influence of phonemic awareness is persuasive. A large-scale meta-analysis of studies reporting correlations between early skills and subsequent reading performance (National Early Literacy Panel, 2008) found that for decoding, the average correlation with phoneme awareness was somewhat higher than awareness at the subphonemic level (e.g., syllable awareness) (0.42 and 0.36 respectively) but that this difference was not significant. Composite measures of phonological awareness proved to be the best predictors (average correlation = 0.47). Phonological tasks that involved analysis of sounds (i.e., deleting, counting, substituting sound units) were better predictors of decoding and reading comprehension than those that involved judgements involving synthesis (i.e., combining sound units) or identification (i.e., matching initial sounds in words). Of the various phonological measures, rhyming tasks provided the weakest correlations with reading.

A meta-analytic review of the relationships between phonemic awareness, rime awareness, and verbal short-term memory, with children's word reading skills (Melby-Lervåg, Lyster, & Hulme, 2012) established phonemic awareness as the strongest predictor. The authors concluded that these findings lend support to the "pivotal role of phonemic awareness as a predictor of individual differences in reading development" (Melby-Lervåg, Lyster, & Hulme, 2012: 322).

Phonological awareness seems to be a predictor across alphabetic writing systems, although the picture is inconsistent in studies involving transparent languages (Landerl et al., 2019; Landerl, Castles, & Parrila, 2022; Parrila et al., 2020) particularly in relation to the later stages of literacy development (Arnoutse, van Leeuwe, & Verhoeven, 2005; Furnes & Samuelsson, 2010; Landerl & Wimmer, 2000; Ziegler, Bertrand, et al., 2010).

Prediction can involve many different outcome criteria and vary across methods and contexts. The focus employed in research studies may variously be upon predicting reading outcomes in all children, solely those struggling to learn to read, or the reading gains that will be made by those with difficulties once high-quality interventions are put into place. Middleton et al. (2022), for example, found that the predictive power of phonological awareness was low in relation to the progress of dyslexic elementary-age children receiving a long-term comprehensive reading intervention. In seeking to explain this finding, the authors suggest that intensive, targeted instruction in phonological awareness (PA) skill and its application to reading and spelling may reduce its power as a predictor of future progress.

The predictive power of phonological awareness (and, indeed, other reading-related cognitive skills) also appears to vary on the basis of the research design, the operationalization of phonological awareness, the type of tasks used, which may vary by response format, memory load, time constraint and metalinguistic demand, whether measures assess reading accuracy, fluency, or comprehension, and whether an opaque (e.g., English) or transparent (e.g., Italian) language is under consideration (Mundy & Hannant, 2020; Parrila et al., 2020). Additionally, there is some evidence to suggest that when phonological processing (and also the capacity for rapid naming) falls below a critical cut-off point, the relationship between letter knowledge and word reading develops unpredictable patterns with uncertain impact upon the nature of longitudinal reading outcomes (Ozernov-Palchik, Sideridis et al., 2022).

Studies in which phonological deficits have been linked to reading difficulties have generally been correlational or cross-sectional in nature and thus have been unable to resolve issues of causality. More recently, longitudinal studies have added to the picture (e.g., Lefèvre et al., 2023), but as the children involved at the outset are typically very young, additional methodological complexities are introduced. On the basis of the current literature, it appears that the relationship is bidirectional and the development of reading skill can also improve phonemic awareness (Landerl, Castles, & Parrila, 2022; Clayton et al., 2020; Ehri, 1999). However, the balance here is unclear and some doubts have been expressed as to whether the direct causal contribution of phonological awareness may have been overstated (Landerl et al., 2019). Huettig et al. (2018), for example, accept that there is likely to be a reciprocal relationship but argue that the presence of phonological deficits and other cognitive impairments implicated in dyslexia may largely be a consequence of reduced or suboptimal reading experience.

To establish cause and effect, studies need to assess the relevant cognitive processes before any reading skills are developed. Some support using this approach is provided by Zugarramurdi et al. (2022) who, in a longitudinal design in prereaders in Spanish (which has a transparent orthography), assessed the contribution of phonological awareness to subsequent reading acquisition. Phonological awareness appeared not to contribute to the prediction of reading acquisition above and beyond other key literacy skills, in particular, letter knowledge. In similar vein, Peng et al. (2019) studied growth in word reading in children considered to be at risk of reading disability. They found that, unlike letter knowledge, phonological awareness failed to predict growth from first to fourth grade. In contrast, Powell and Atkinson (2021) examined both phonological awareness and rapid naming in a sample of English speaking nursery school (kindergarten) children (mean age 3 years 11 months). The children were tested eighteen and thirty months later on both measures and on various reading tasks. Phonological awareness was found to be a sound predictor of future nonword reading accuracy but not for exception (sight) word accuracy or word or nonword decoding fluency. Powell and Atkinson suggest that this supports a view that phonological awareness has a role in the establishment of alphabetic coding mechanisms but less importance for lexical, orthographic processes that enable one to read exceptional words (e.g., yacht, cough or enough) (Powell & Atkinson, 2021). In a German longitudinal study commencing in kindergarten, Ehm et al. (2023) found phonemic awareness and letter knowledge to be strong predictors of the initial level of word decoding.

Bishop (2006) has outlined three lines of research evidence that suggest that literacy skills can impact performance on phonological tasks. Firstly, orthographic knowledge about how a word is written can influence phonological judgements. Secondly, those who have significant literacy difficulties because of reduced opportunity to learn to read tend to perform more poorly on phonological tasks than normal readers. Finally, children who have had no exposure to reading instruction also tend to perform poorly on such measures yet often make rapid progress once introduced to print, a finding that supports the argument that poor phonemic awareness may sometimes reflect children's early experiences at home and in preschool (Corriveau, Goswami, & Thomson, 2010).

Theoretical difficulties have resulted from findings that reading-disabled children can perform normally on tasks and in conditions where the phonological deficit theory would be expected to predict poor performance (Ramus & Ahissar, 2012). One possible explanation for this is that the underlying problem may not, in actuality, concern the quality of the phonological representations. On the basis of a series of experiments with young adult poor readers (Ramus & Szenkovits, 2008; Soroli, Szenkovits, & Ramus, 2010; Szenkovits & Ramus, 2005; Szenkovits et al., 2016) it was suggested that rather than being degraded in some way, phonological representations generally appeared to be normal (although these may be problematic for a very small minority). However, the existence of a phonological deficit was not questioned; the participants in the studies showed clear weaknesses on phonological measures. Noting that it was the tasks that made significant demands upon short-term memory and retrieval speed that appeared to cause the greatest problems, Ramus and Szenkovits (2008) hypothesized that the core phonological deficit may involve not the quality of the phonological representations but, rather, the ability to access these. Similar ideas, they pointed out, were earlier put forward by Shankweiler and Crain (1986) in their processing limitation hypothesis, and also have parallels with Hulme and Snowling's (1992) conception of an output deficit. Further support for Ramus's hypothesis has been provided by a number of experimental studies (e.g., Berent et al., 2012; Boets et al., 2013; Mengisidou & Marshall, 2019; Mundy & Carroll, 2012) although it is possible that the nature of an earlier degraded phonological representation changes during the course of development to adulthood (Boets, 2014; Vandermosten et al., 2020).

Despite the popularity of phonological explanations for dyslexia, there continue to be a number of difficulties. Relatively simple single causal understandings have been challenged by findings that not all children with reading disabilities demonstrate a phonological deficit (Carroll, Solity, & Shapiro, 2016; Mundy & Hannant, 2020; White et al., 2006) and that children with poor phonological abilities can nevertheless develop good reading skills (Catts et al., 2017; Ring & Black, 2018). Studies of children with speech and language difficulties have also shown that phonological awareness deficits failed to lead to literacy problems in many cases (Bishop et al., 2009; Peterson et al., 2009).

Catts et al. (2017) administered multiple measures of phonological awareness, oral language, and rapid automatized naming to children approximately six weeks into their kindergarten year. Reading skills were assessed at the end of second grade. It was found that those children who demonstrated a deficit in phonological awareness in kindergarten were five times more likely to have dyslexia (operationalized as a score below the tenth percentile on a composite word reading measure). The likelihood was substantially greater for those children who also demonstrated deficits in both oral language and rapid naming but not when only one of these was combined with a phonological deficit (although this may be a consequence of small subgroup sizes). Nevertheless, a significant proportion of children with phonological deficits later proved to be adequate or better readers. Indeed, only approximately one third of those with a phonological deficit alone was found to read at a level indicative of dyslexia at the end of second grade. Similarly, 27 percent of the children found to be dyslexic did not meet the criteria for an earlier deficit in phonological awareness, oral language, or rapid naming, although this number reduced when cut-off points were relaxed. Other studies involving various languages have also shown that a significant proportion of children with reading/dyslexia do not present with a phonological impairment (Dębska et al., 2022; Carroll, Solity, & Shapiro, 2016; O'Brien & Yeatman, 2021; Pennington et al., 2012; Valdois et al., 2021).

Studies of adults with reading disabilities suggest that phonological awareness appears to be less important for older poor readers than for children, with other processes such as verbal memory, vocabulary and naming speed playing an equally significant role in differentiating between those with and without reading disability (Swanson & Hsieh, 2009). It is also possible that, particularly for older children and adults, a phonological deficit is in part a consequence of reading failure (Clayton et al., 2020; Peterson et al., 2018).

To add to the complexity, some researchers (Nicolson & Fawcett, 2008) suggest that a weakness of the phonological theory stems from the observation that deficits in this area are not specific to those with dyslexia (as they understand this term) but appear to be characteristic of all poor readers. Of course, this argument does not sit easily with definitions of dyslexia in which phonological difficulties are presented as a major diagnostic criterion, or those where a dyslexic subgroup is not distinguished from other poor decoders (see Chapter 1 for discussion of this definitional complexity).

Despite overwhelming evidence from both behavioral and neuroimaging studies pointing to the importance of phonological awareness in reading, theoretical understanding continues to be unclear:

> While it is almost universally agreed that a phonological deficit is a key factor for most children with reading disability, there continues to be significant debate as to its precise nature and role. Despite more than thirty years of research into the phonological deficit, … we still don't know what it is. (Ramus & Szenkovits, 2008: 165)

Many years later, this situation remains largely unchanged. As noted above, recognition of the centrality of phonological deficits in dyslexia persists, but equally, we are still far from a sound theoretical understanding, and debates about whether primary auditory deficits underlie these deficits (Goswami, 2015; Goswami et al., 2021) are unresolved. Zoccolotti (2022) provides a detailed critique in which he suggests that the phonological deficit hypothesis has yet to achieve the status of being a theory. Arguing that a theory should provide a formulation that should be testable, he contends that this is not yet possible for the phonological deficit theory as it is under-specified and does not easily permit predictions that can be experimentally tested.

Snowling (2008; Moll, Loff, & Snowling, 2013) has suggested that, rather than being conceived of as a direct marker of reading difficulties, various phonological (and other) deficits may be better conceptualized as endophenotypes, heritable processes that operate between the genotype and the behavioral phenotype. Endophenotypes are considered to be state-independent, that is, they are manifest in an individual, albeit often in a less pronounced fashion, whether or not the particular condition (e.g., reading disability) is present. The suggestion that phonological awareness deficits may be endophenotypes for reading disability has been strengthened by studies demonstrating that family members of those with reading difficulties, but who are typically developing readers themselves, tend to show lower performance on phonological tasks than do controls (Boets et al., 2010; van Bergen et al., 2012).

Research into phonological deficits has resulted in the development of a range of related interventions for at risk and struggling readers that have generally been shown to improve these skills and, consequently, reading performance (Suggate, 2016). Nevertheless, progress has proven to be relatively modest and intervention may vary in its effectiveness according to the quality and timing of its implementation (Kjeldsen et al., 2019) and the particular language and educational system in which it operates (Pfost et al., 2019; Wolff & Gustafsson, 2022). Doubts have also been expressed about long-term effectiveness (Olson, 2011) with the relatively few studies that cover a period of five years or more providing "equivocal" results, particularly in relation to the ultimate goal of reading comprehension (Kjeldsen et al., 2019: 367).

In summary, deficits in phonological awareness have repeatedly been shown to have a significant relationship to the development of reading disability/dyslexia, although questions remain in respect of some non-alphabetic orthographies such as Japanese and Chinese (Perfetti, Pugh, & Verhoeven, 2019). Indeed, even across alphabetic languages, it is possible that the dominance of English orthography in studies of reading may have led to an overestimation of its relevance (Landerl, 2019).

Despite its primacy in explanatory accounts, an overly-simplistic causal association has now been largely rejected "… because a single phonological deficit is neither necessary or sufficient to cause the (reading) disorder" (Pennington et al., 2019: 167). Consideration of phonological deficits needs to operate within a multifactorial framework of dyslexia in which multiple factors act probabilistically in different ways for different people.

While the presence of a phonological deficit should not be employed as an essential diagnostic criterion that indicates dyslexia, phonological awareness is one of a small number of items that appear to be valuable when screening for the potential risk of reading failure in young children (Fletcher et al., 2021).

Rapid Naming and the Double Deficit

A longstanding finding in the dyslexia literature is that a significant proportion of children with reading difficulties are less able to rapidly name visual stimuli that are already well known to them (a process often termed rapid automatized naming [RAN]). Typically, measures of RAN (Denckla & Rudel, 1976a, 1976b) assess the speed in which the individual can name a series of familiar items (letters, numbers, colors, or objects) placed before them. Using such measures, Denckla and colleagues (Denckla, 1972; Denckla & Rudel, 1974) found positive associations between naming speed and reading performance, and this was followed up by the influential work of Wolf, Bowers, and colleagues (Bowers & Wolf, 1993; Norton & Wolf, 2012; Wolf & Bowers, 1999). According to these researchers, fluent reading requires the ability to integrate a range of perceptual, attentional, and naming mechanisms that enable the matching of visual representations to phonological codes, precisely, and at speed. Thus, problems of rapid naming appear not to concern a single isolated deficit but rather a number of difficulties involving several high and low-level processes.

Naming speed appears to be related to almost all aspects of the reading process (J. R. Kirby et al., 2010). While a relationship between RAN and general reading ability has typically been found in studies, the size of correlations has varied greatly (Araújo et al., 2015) as has its predictive importance in comparison with phonological awareness across different orthographies (Zugarramurdi et al., 2022). Its predictive power appears to be higher when the naming task involves letters and numbers rather than pictures or colors in both alphabetic (Araújo et al., 2015; McWeeny et al., 2022) and nonalphabetic orthographies (Song et al., 2016), possibly, in part, because the increased semantic load involved with objects adds noise to the RAN-decoding relationship. (Poulsen, Protopapas, & Juul, 2023). The RAN-reading relationship is usually higher for reading fluency compared with accuracy (Araújo et al., 2015; Meisinger, Breazeale, & Davis, 2022; but cf. McWeeny et al., 2022). It appears that the link with reading fluency is strongest when the naming task requires serial rather than discrete processing, that is, where stimuli are presented in a series of rows, rather than singly, one after the other, typically via a computer screen (Araújo & Faísca, 2019), and when oral production of the names of the stimuli is required, rather than a non-verbal paper and pencil response (Georgiou et al., 2013).

In a large-scale meta-analysis of early skills that might predict later reading, writing or spelling, rapid naming was shown to be moderately correlated with reading (National Early Literacy Panel, 2008). Rapid naming of letters and digits demonstrated an average correlation of $r = 0.40$ for decoding and $r = 0.43$ for reading comprehension, with correlations of $r = 0.32$ and $r = 0.42$ in the case of objects and colors. Such results are not dissimilar to findings from a subsequent meta-analytic review of 137 studies (Araújo et al., 2015) involving different orthographies, which reported an overall moderate to strong relationship of $r = 0.43$. Similar findings were reported in an earlier, more restricted meta-analysis by Swanson et al. (2003) and more recently, by McWeeny et al. (2022) in a meta-analysis involving sixty independent samples where RAN measures were employed with 10,513 English speaking prereaders. The predictive relationships in this latter study were as follows: single word reading ($r = -0.38$), reading fluency ($r = -0.35$) and reading comprehension ($r = -0.38$), indicating that children with faster RAN time before commencing grade school subsequently demonstrated stronger school reading performance.

It has been generally considered that RAN plays a greater role in transparent languages. This reflects the observation that for such orthographies the primary difficulty after the first two years at school is typically slow, laborious reading rather than specific decoding errors (Klicpera & Schabmann, 1993). However, research findings on this issue have been inconsistent and more recent reviews and meta-analyses have led to the view that differences for RAN between opaque and transparent alphabetic orthographies may be relatively small. Rather unexpectedly, Araújo et al.'s (2015) meta-analysis found a stronger association for RAN in English than for a variety of transparent European languages, although a follow-up meta-analysis by the same lead author (Araújo & Faísca, 2019) found no significant differences in effect sizes between opaque, intermediate, and transparent orthographies. In line with the earlier of these two meta-analyses, a comparative study across several European languages also found a stronger RAN association in English for both typical (Moll et al., 2014) and dyslexic (Landerl et al., 2013) readers. In reviewing the literature, Landerl, Castles, and Parrila (2022) argue that differences in such analyses likely reflect differing selection criteria and study designs and conclude that differences between alphabetic orthographies concerning the extent to which RAN predicts reading are "probably minor" (2022: 118).

Research has consistently shown that struggling readers tend to score poorly on measures of RAN. Araújo and Faísca's (2019)'s meta-analytic review of studies comparing individuals with dyslexia with typical readers found a large RAN impairment in the former group. Additionally, the greater the severity of the reading problem, the poorer was the performance on RAN measures. However, it is important to note that this pattern is not consistently reported in the literature and differences between poor and typical readers have sometimes been found to be modest (see, for example, an earlier meta-analysis undertaken by Araújo et al., 2015).

Naming speed appears to be most predictive of future reading difficulties in the case of younger children. Its effects on reading accuracy tend to decline as children pass through school, although its relationship with reading fluency appears to remain relatively stable (Araújo et al., 2015; Araújo & Faísca, 2019). There is some evidence to suggest that, as for phonological abilities, RAN exerts a non-linear effect upon the association between letter knowledge and word-reading skill in young readers, a phenomenon that may explain inconsistent results across studies (Ozernov-Palchik, Sideridis et al., 2022). RAN deficits can also be found in adult poor readers (Reis et al., 2020) and in compensated adult readers; those who have subsequently acquired satisfactory literacy skills (Silva et al., 2016).

According to Wolf's double deficit (DD) hypothesis model (Wolf & Bowers, 1999), those with dyslexia can be subdivided into three groups: those with phonological difficulties but with average naming speed ability, those with a rapid naming deficit but average phonological skills, and those with both phonological and rapid naming difficulties. According to this model, those with the double deficit would be likely to have the most severe form of reading difficulties, a suggestion that has largely been supported in empirical studies in both opaque (Wolf, Bowers, & Biddle, 2000; Steacy et al., 2014) and transparent (Torppa et al., 2013; De la Calle et al., 2021) languages[12] although findings showing no differences between children with a double or single deficit have also been reported (Ackerman et al., 2001; Vaessen et al., 2009).

Evidence to support the suggestion that there exists a subgroup of poor readers with naming speed deficits but no phonological deficits (a single naming speed deficit) has been described as "mixed" (Vaessen et al.,

[12]   See also Furnes et al., 2019 for similar findings across English and Scandinavian samples.

2009: 204). While Wolf, Bowers and Biddle (2000) reported a number of studies in which a significant number of poor readers exhibited a single naming speed deficit, not all studies have found this. In a review of three cross-sectional studies (Badian, 1997; Morris et al., 1998; Pennington et al., 2001) Vukovic and Siegel (2006) concluded that most of the children who had naming speed difficulties also demonstrated phonological processing deficits. While it appeared that those with both naming speed and phonological problems tended to have the most severe reading difficulties, there were relatively few who had rapid naming problems but intact phonological skills.

Younger and Meisinger (2020) examined the double deficit hypothesis in a clinical sample of children attending the first five grades of a private special school catering for dyslexia. Tests were undertaken in early August and late May in the same academic year and children were allocated to groups according to the hypothesis. At the two testing sessions, the categories that resulted in the fall and spring were as follows: typically developing (35%/51%), phonological deficit (16%/17%), naming speed deficit (25%/14%), and double deficit (25%/18%). Although it was found that children categorized in the DD groups performed more poorly on tasks involving text reading accuracy, fluency, and comprehension on both occasions, the temporal stability of the groups across these time points was weak with almost half the children transitioning into a different group at the end of the school year. The authors concluded that if such instability were to be consistently demonstrated in subsequent studies, the value of such categorizations for informing assessment and intervention would become questionable.[13]

In a study of second-grade US children, Catts et al. (2017) concluded that a deficit in rapid naming in isolation was associated with a relatively low probability of dyslexia but added that it may serve as an additive factor to phonological awareness where oral language deficit is also present.[14] Catts et al. (2017) noted, however, that their small subgroup size may have impacted on this latter finding.

Valdois et al. (2021) found a unique RAN deficit of 15.5 percent, compared with a single PA deficit and PA/RAN double deficit of 20 percent and 7.3 percent, in their French poor reader sample. Overall, 31 percent

---

[13] See also two studies of children deemed to be at risk for dyslexia; Spector (2005), which reported similar instability, and Steacy et al. (2014), which found moderate stability in kindergarten to first grade, and greater stability afterwards.

[14] See also Dębska et al., 2022 for a similar suggestion of an additive relationship in a transparent orthography.

of the sample demonstrated a RAN disorder (either isolated or alongside a PA or visual attention disorder). Also diminishing the perceived importance of RAN for identifying dyslexia, Vaessen, Gerretsen, and Blomert (2009) found that 10.5 percent of their sample of dyslexic primary school children demonstrated a single naming speed deficit and noted that there was little difference on literacy performance between this group and the other children in the sample. In a study of Polish children with reading impairment, Dębska et al. (2022) found a RAN deficit in 26 percent of their sample with 14 percent demonstrating both a RAN and a phonological awareness deficit.

Contradictory findings across research studies may stem from differences in orthographies and in the nature of study samples (see Georgiou & Parrila, 2013). Some studies use typically developing readers; others, those with reading disabilities. Arbitrary cut-off points and age groupings vary substantially. J. R. Kirby et al. (2010) suggest that given significant difficulties of group stability over even short periods, a "purer test" (p. 350) of the hypothesis might involve adolescents or adults, although there appear to be no longitudinal studies involving the former and conflicting evidence from the latter.

As is the case for much research work in dyslexia, it has proven more difficult to arrive at a widely agreed-upon theoretical explanation for the nature and role of rapid naming than it has been to demonstrate an association between this process and reading disability (Georgiou & Parrila, 2013; Perfetti, Pugh, & Verhoeven, 2019). Neither a clear consensus upon an operational definition of rapid naming, nor a clear account as to how exactly this relates to reading, have been achieved (Lervåg, Bråten, & Hulme, 2009; Vukovic & Siegel, 2006). Achieving such an understanding has been rendered particularly complex because, rather than being a measure of a single skill, RAN is an activity that requires the efficient coordination of a number of processes (Araújo et al., 2015; Protopapas, 2014).

> Naming speed is conceptualized as a complex ensemble of attentional, perceptual, conceptual, memory, phonological, semantic, and motoric subprocesses that places heavy emphasis upon precise timing requirements within each component and across all components. (Wolf, Bowers, & Biddle, 2000: 395)

The role and balance of the mechanisms underlying the RAN-reading association are disputed (Jones, Snowling, & Moll, 2016; Protopapas, Altani, & Georgiou, 2013). Some have emphasized various executive processes including attention, working memory and inhibition that together ensure skilled performance (Amtmann, Abbott, & Berninger, 2007). For others, naming speed reflects a general processing speed deficit (Kail & Hall, 1994) that may disrupt the temporal integration of visual and phonological information and also timing-related deficits outside of the language domain (Bowers, Sunseth, & Golden, 1999; Farmer & Klein, 1995).

RAN requires phonological skills; for example, naming speed tasks tap rapid access to and retrieval of phonological information from long-term memory. For this reason, some contend that rapid naming deficits are best conceived as reflecting an underlying deficit in phonological representations (Snowling & Hulme, 1994; Wagner & Torgesen, 1987). Wolf and her colleagues (Wolf et al., 2002; Wolf & Bowers, 1999) disagree, arguing that these processes are more related to underlying timing problems and should therefore be considered as independent.[15] For some, "naming speed is phonological, but not only phonological" (J. R. Kirby et al., 2010: 356).

An alternative theory is that poor naming speed disrupts skilled orthographic processing, the mechanism by which words seen frequently come to be speedily recognized as sight words (Bowers, Sunseth, & Golden, 1999; Bowers & Wolf, 1993; Georgiou, Parrila, & Kirby, 2009). A potential weakness with this account is that naming speed has been found to be equally strongly related to the speed of reading pseudowords as real words (Moll et al., 2009). As pseudowords cannot have been stored already, and thus cannot be familiar to the reader, this would appear to rule out the orthographic hypothesis. However, as pseudowords often contain familiar clusters of letters some form of orthographic processing may still be operating, albeit not at the word level (J. R. Kirby et al., 2010). In a longitudinal study, Powell and Atkinson (2021) found that RAN was strongly related to both alphabetic decoding and lexical, orthographic aspects of reading; a finding that suggests that both theoretical accounts have some explanatory power. This possibility is supported by a meta-analysis of sixty-eight studies which found that individuals with dyslexia demonstrated an orthographic knowledge deficit as large as that reported in meta-analyses of phonological awareness and RAN (Georgiou et al., 2021). However, studies by the same team (Georgiou et al., 2016; Martinez et al., 2021) have concluded that orthographic knowledge cannot serve as a viable explanation for the RAN-reading relationship.

RAN measures have been found to be independent predictors of reading skill even when controlling for phonological awareness, memory,

---

[15] See also Nicolson and Fawcett (2006: 260) for criticism of the *ad hoc* lumping together of different processes under the phonology category.

letter knowledge, and IQ (Georgiou, Parrila, & Kirby, 2009; Powell et al., 2007), with the relationship being stronger for measures of orthographic choice and exception word reading than nonword reading, and this latter measure being more closely linked to phonological ability. Powell and colleagues (2007) surveyed a sample of British children aged 7–9 years and found a pattern that supported the double deficit theory. Factor analysis and structural equation modelling of the data led to the conclusion that while phonological processes played a part in RAN performance, other processes, beyond generalized processing speed, also seemed to be important. Moreover, in a large family study of reading skills (Naples et al., 2009) phonemic awareness and RAN were found to be distinct constructs that could not be substituted by each other. Each appeared to be heritable; there were indicators of genetic forces operating in both shared (i.e., contributing to both indicators) and unique (i.e., contributing to each indicator separately) fashion. Also, it was shown that, for each indicator, a number of genes were involved, which were revealed to be both pleiotropic (i.e., contributing to both indicators) and unique (i.e., contributing to each indicator separately). Ozernov-Palchik, Sideridis, et al. (2022) studied two large samples of pre-kindergarten and kindergarten children, with a follow-up examination of reading scores for one of the samples in second grade. It appeared that while phonological ability and RAN influenced reading, independently and in combination, there was no evidence of interactive effects that improved prediction. The researchers concluded that the data indicated that, in line with the double-deficit hypothesis, the two constructs operate independently.[16]

Taking an opposing position, Ziegler, Bertrand, and colleagues consider it "probably misleading" (2010: 557) to conceive of RAN as an independent nonphonological component. They point to a study by Chiappe et al. (2002) showing that while 25 percent of unique variance in reading was explained by naming speed, 75 percent was shared with phonological awareness. Ziegler, Bertrand, et al., (2010) suggest that while RAN tasks may incorporate only a relatively minor phonological component, it is this particular element that appears to be the best predictor of reading performance (Vaessen et al., 2009). Where measures of phonological awareness are insufficiently sensitive or reach a ceiling (as may often be the case in studies of transparent languages), most of the shared variance will be left to RAN and this will become the key predictor.

---

[16] See also Sideridis et al. (2019) for broadly similar findings in relation to RAN, but also referencing the potentially disruptive moderating effects of motivational and affective factors.

The notion of rapid naming as a subcomponent of general processing speed (Johnson et al., 2010) has been challenged by findings that RAN accounts for variance even after global processing has been controlled for (Cutting & Denckla, 2001; Powell et al., 2007; cf. Catts, Gillispie, et al., 2002, for a contradictory finding). Christopher et al. (2012) found that, for a large sample of children, 26 percent of whom had a history of reading disability, naming speed for digits and letters independently predicted word reading after processing speed was controlled for, but this was not similarly the case for nonalphanumeric stimuli. In the light of their finding that speed of processing correlated with RAN but not with reading, Poulsen, Juul, and Elbro (2015) tentatively concluded that speed of processing was unlikely to be an explanation for the relationship between RAN and reading. In line with this view, Araújo and colleagues' meta-analytic review (2015) found correlations of 0.49 for reading fluency and 0.42 for reading accuracy. They argued that processing speed is unlikely to be the primary explanation for the relationship between RAN and reading on the grounds that if this were the case, the figure for accuracy should be considerably lower than that for fluency. These authors concluded that "… whatever RAN taps into, it is beyond letter knowledge and speed of processing" (Araújo et al., 2015: 881).

Gerst et al. (2021) note that while most studies of processing speed in poor readers are conducted through a RAN lens, such a focus may obscure other important relationships. Those studies that have considered RAN and processing speed separately have produced contrasting findings. One research team (Georgiou, Parrila, & Papadopolos, 2016; Papadopoulos, Spanoudis, & Georgiou, 2016) found that RAN had stronger direct effects upon reading while, in contrast, Christopher et al. (2012) found that processing speed had the stronger effect. McGrath et al. (2011) and Peterson et al. (2017) found direct effects for both.

To clarify the structure of processing speed in children, and relate this to reading performance, Gerst et al. (2021) administered a large battery of processing, reading, and language measures to children between third and fifth grades. The authors found that a two-factor model, consisting of simple and complex processing, best fitted the data. Simple processing tasks largely involved perceptual identification where, because very few errors are anticipated, speed rather than accuracy differentiates respondents. This process approximates to other terms found in the psychological literature such as reaction time or perceptual speed. In contrast, complex processing tasks require a greater level of reasoning. These are elsewhere described as measures of information processing or cognitive processing speed. The authors found that simple processing speed demonstrated little predictive value for key reading skills, but prediction improved when more complex measures were employed. In this latter case, performance on the measures was predictive of single word reading, reading fluency and reading comprehension, although the unique variance of processing speed across each of the three measures was found to be low. One difficulty acknowledged by the authors is that the more cognitively complex the measures, the more they overlap with measures of executive functioning. Where processing speed may "end" and executive functioning may "begin" remains unclear.

Stainthorp et al. (2010) found that children with slow RAN performance appeared to have difficulties on visual (but not auditory) discrimination tasks that could not be explained by either general processing speed or word reading ability. Although there was no significant difference between slow and normal RAN groups on accuracy, the former group took longer to make the discriminations, even after controlling for simple reaction times. The authors suggest that a general focus upon accuracy, rather than upon speed, may help to explain the widely held view (Vellutino, 1979) that visuo-perceptual difficulties are not significant in dyslexia. Despite the fact that their low RAN group did not have significant reading problems, Stainthorp and colleagues (Stainthorp et al., 2010) offer a number of possible explanations for the relationship between RAN and reading difficulty involving an underlying visual discrimination problem. However, they accept that without detailed longitudinal studies causal explanations are merely speculative.

The potential role of visual processing and visual attention in RAN has been assisted by eye tracking research. Gordon and Hoedmaker (2016) argue that that in serial naming tasks, eye movement and attention need to be smoothly coordinated with vocalization; the eyes need to be just far enough ahead of the voice. Such processes are seemingly poorer in dyslexic individuals. Although performance on discrete naming tasks is less affected than for serial naming, the observation that those with dyslexia tend to experience difficulty with both types of task is indicative of an underlying naming problem that cannot be wholly explained by visual factors in serial performance (Araújo & Faísca, 2019).

Despite disagreement about rapid naming's underlying mechanisms, it can be generally agreed that:

> The different perspectives largely converge in assuming that sequential naming mimics the timely integration of visual and verbal skills required during efficient word recognition and allows simultaneous processing of multiple stimuli presented serially which explains why RAN exerts its strongest effects on reading fluency. (Landerl, Castles, & Parrila, 2022: 118)

As is the case for phonological awareness, it has been suggested that there may be an interactive relationship between reading and RAN, such that rapid naming performance may be impaired by limited reading experience (Clayton et al., 2020; Huettig et al., 2018; Peterson et al., 2017). However, the methodological challenges involved in undertaking longitudinal studies with very young children (Araújo & Faísca, 2019) are significant and there appears to be insufficient evidence to refute a unidirectional effect (Landerl, Castles, & Parrila, 2022).

Unlike phonological processing deficits, where there is evidence supporting the value of targeted interventions, there remains significant doubt as to whether naming speed can be increased and, if so, whether this would result in improved reading (Gerst et al., 2021). J. R. Kirby and colleagues (2010) outline two alternative scenarios that differ in the extent to which direct intervention is likely to prove valuable for improving reading. In one, naming speed operates as a distal predictor of reading; it is seen as relatively stable and not easily improved by intervention. Given this situation, it may be wiser to follow the lead of Wolf and colleagues (2009) and introduce multicomponential reading skill interventions. An alternative scenario is to conceive of naming speed as having more proximal effects upon reading. Here, interventions would be geared to improving speed directly, and reading performance would be expected to improve as a consequence. The evidence in support of this latter approach is minimal, although one intervention study has reported both RAN and reading gains in a small dyslexic sample (Vander Stappen, Dricot, & Van Reybroeck, 2020). This intervention was relatively demanding, involving 16 × 45-minute sessions, and there was no comparison intervention group or other means to assess the opportunity costs that resulted from a focus upon RAN tasks rather than upon an alternative educational intervention.

The value of work in this area for informing the content of effective educational intervention programs has not been established. Progress has been hindered by the difficulty of providing a full and detailed account of the cognitive components that underpin the RAN-reading relationship, (Poulsen, Juul, & Elbro, 2015; Sideridis et al., 2019). Irrespective of this, given the substantial body of evidence showing limited transfer of gains from general cognitive skills training to academic skill areas, it seems unlikely that dedicated processing speed interventions will prove to be helpful for struggling readers (Gerst et al., 2021).

Rather than being seen as a skill that should be explicitly taught, RAN assessment is more likely to be helpful in the identification of potential reading difficulties (Wolf et al., 2024). Promoting such a view, McWeeny and colleagues suggest that measuring RAN with pre- and beginning readers may offer an easily accessed indicator of future reading problems, "… akin to a 'check engine light' that signals the need for further assessment and monitoring" (McWeeny et al., 2022: 20).

Short-Term and Working Memory

It is unsurprising that memory is associated with the development of reading and reading difficulties (Cunningham et al., 2021; Ober et al., 2020; Peng et al., 2018, 2022; Spiegel et al., 2021) as key processes involve the coding, storage, and retrieval of stable associations between speech and written language.

Crucially important is the lexical retrieval process that requires visual recognition of an array of letters as forming a particular word and subsequent retrieval of its name and meaning from memory. Long-term memory is important here for consolidating sequence regularities in both phonological and orthographic information resulting in stable representations that enable faster and more accurate word recognition. There is some evidence that both verbal and visual long-term memory capacities tend to be weaker in poor readers (Bogaerts et al., 2015, 2016; Menghini et al., 2010; Swanson, 1999), although findings have tended to be inconsistent. Lazzaro et al. (2021c), for example, found this to be true for verbal but not visual measures.

In relation to dyslexia, the great majority of studies of memory processes have focused upon short-term and working memory, both of which involve limited capacity to hold information for a brief period of time. They differ insofar that short-term memory relates to the passive temporary storage of information, whereas working memory (WM) involves both storage and processing and draws upon more executively-demanding and attentional processes.

Multiple models of WM feature in the literature (Cowan, 2017), the most widely cited being those of Engle and colleagues (Engle, 2002), Cowan et al. (2005), and Baddeley (2000). Originally conceived by Baddeley and Hitch (1974), Baddeley's (2000) model conceives of a modality-free central executive responsible for controlling and regulating the flow of information through working memory. This is supplemented by two domain-specific stores, the phonological loop (for verbal material) and the visuospatial sketchpad (for visual information). A fourth component, the episodic buffer, is responsible for binding information across informational domains and memory sub-systems into integrated chunks.

Cowan's and Engle's models place greater emphasis upon working memory as part of a larger more unitary construct that emphasizes focused attention. However, it appears that recognition of the commonalities between working memory models has led to an emphasis upon achieving a consensus as to what their key components should be (Gray et al., 2017).

Short-term and working memory are assessed using simple and complex span tasks respectively, in both verbal and visuospatial domains. While simple span tasks require temporary storage, complex span tasks typically introduce distractions between successive memory items. To succeed on each item, the participant must work out how best to protect the memory representation from interference or decay.

In the verbal domain, relevant tasks often involve the recall of digits or word sequences. A widely used approach involves asking the participant to repeat digits both forwards and backwards. Repetition of digits in the same order represents a simple span measure of short-term memory whereas tasks that require the participant to reverse the series of numbers is generally considered to be a test of WM. There are some doubts, however, as to the value of digit span tasks as the particular strategies involved may not generalize well to tasks such as reading (Swanson, Zheng, & Jerman, 2009) and some consider that these may not be a true measure of WM (Rosen & Engle, 1997). Other WM tasks involve recalling mixed sequences of letters and numbers according to a required order such as the alphabetic sequence. Digit span and letter-number sequencing are both included as WM subtests in the widely employed Wechsler Intelligence Scale for Children (WISC-V; Wechsler, 2014). In experimental work, a popular memory task involves the use of nonwords, although the two main types of measure, nonword repetition and nonword matching, appear not to share common processing demands (Savage, Lavers, & Pillay, 2007). Another commonly used task requires participants to listen to a sequence of sentences and then indicate whether each statement is true or false. They are then asked to provide the final word of each sentence in the order in which they were presented. Memory span is assessed by increasing the number of sentences included for each task item.

Compared with verbal items, the processes involved in visuospatial serial recall are less well understood (Gathercole et al., 2019). Simple span measures utilize a variety of stimulus forms including spatial locations, static patterns, continuous movements, scenes, and unfamiliar objects. One subtest from the Automated Working Memory Assessment (Alloway, 2007), for example, requires the child to examine a maze with a red path drawn through it for three seconds. They are then required to trace the same path on a blank maze presented on the computer screen. Complex span visuospatial measures also vary considerably. Typical tasks require the participant to consider objects that have been presented sequentially on a screen, make a judgement in response to related questions (the distractor activity), and then recall the spatial locations of particular items.

It seems likely that short-term and working memory have particular influence in the early stages of reading when children most need to hold and rehearse information about sounds and letters temporarily and blend them sequentially in order to decode. Through repeated exposure, and as reading expertise builds, readers come to rely increasingly upon direct retrieval of lexical and verbal knowledge from long-term memory (Ordonez Magro et al., 2020; Peng et al., 2018). The nature of the relationship between WM and long-term memory in the process of reading remains unclear (see, for example, Miller-Cotto & Byrnes, 2020; Feldon & Litson, 2021 for contrasting accounts).

As is the case for rapid naming processes, there is disagreement as to whether short-term verbal memory difficulties should be incorporated within the phonological deficit model or considered separately within a broader conception of poor WM. The phonological deficit case is prompted by findings that problems appear to be particularly related to the storage of verbal input (Siegel & Ryan, 1989; Swanson et al., 2009) and conventional tests of phonological processing are highly correlated with measures of verbal short-term memory. It is difficult to conceive of any measure of phonological awareness that does not involve some component of verbal WM, and this probably explains why phonological memory tasks often fail to contribute independent variability in multivariate studies (Fletcher et al., 2007).

> … large-scale studies indicate that measures of phonological memory and phonological awareness measure nearly the same thing at the preschool level, and very highly related things thereafter …. Simply treating them as two completely distinct constructs flies in the face of compelling data. (Wagner & Muse, 2006: 53)

Children with WM difficulties tend to perform poorly on a variety of cognitive, academic, and behavioral measures (Alloway et al., 2009; Banai & Ahissar, 2004, 2010). Similarly, a large proportion of those identified as having learning difficulties also demonstrate WM problems (Astle et al., 2019; Gathercole et al., 2016). However, as appears to be the case for other underlying cognitive processes in dyslexia, memory deficits are not found in all struggling readers (De Clercq-Quaegebeur et al., 2010; Gray et al., 2019) and some typical readers can have significant WM problems. Additionally, the proportion of poor readers with WM difficulties can vary significantly across studies (Swanson, Zheng, & Jerman, 2009), most likely reflecting the nature and complexity of the memory tasks involved (Ramus & Ahissar, 2012). WM appears to be particularly impaired in those children who present with a combination of academic difficulties such as reading, spelling, and mathematics (Maehler & Schuchardt, 2009, 2011; Peng & Fuchs, 2016). It may have a more disruptive role in the acquisition of literacy in cases of greater severity (Nevo & Breznitz, 2011) although this has not been a consistent finding (Swanson, Zheng, & Jerman, 2009; Peng & Fuchs, 2016).

There remains continuing uncertainty as to the unique contribution of short-term and working memory difficulties to reading disability. A five year longitudinal study of children from kindergarten to fourth grade (Wagner et al., 1997), for example, found that while individual differences in phonological awareness exerted a causal influence on word-level reading, there were no independent causal influences for phonological memory. Wagner later noted (Wagner & Muse, 2006) that the apparent irrelevance of phonological memory in this study may have been a statistical arte-fact resulting from a strong correlation between measures of phonological memory and phonological awareness. In a wide-ranging review of the relationship between WM and reading difficulties, Savage, Lavers, and Pillay (2007) examined the unique contribution of phonological memory (and other WM) measures for later reading acquisition. When these were entered into regression equations with other accepted predictors of word reading, little evidence was found that the memory measures added to pre-diction for word reading. In a meta-analysis of studies of those with dys-lexia and controls, where differences between phonemic awareness, rime awareness, and verbal short-term memory were examined, Melby-Lervåg, Lyster, and Hulme (2012), also found only a limited role for verbal short-term memory, with most of the variance apparently explained by phone-mic awareness.

In a more recent meta-analytic review of associations between cogni-tive processes and reading difficulties, in which difficulties of decoding and reading comprehension were included together as one grouping, Peng et al. (2022) found that the poor reading group displayed deficits in short-term and working memory as well as a range of other processes. Problems tended to be more severe with age and for lower reading scores. However, similar to findings from a meta-analysis of typical readers (Peng et al., 2018), the memory measures did not make a unique contribution to reading after controlling for language scores. This was taken to support the contention that the memory-reading difficulty relationship depends heavily upon accessing and using such processes as phonological processing and vocabulary.

Investigations into the relationship of visuospatial short-term or visuospatial WM to reading disability are fewer in number. Although findings have proven to be inconsistent, the bulk of evidence suggests that, in relation to memory, visuospatial factors have a role, albeit one that is less influential than that for verbal measures (Gathercole et al., 2016; Johnson et al., 2010; Kudo, Lussier, & Swanson, 2015; Peng et al., 2022; Swanson, Zheng, & Jerman, 2009; although cf. Booth, Boyle, & Kelly, 2014; Pham & Hasson, 2014). Contrasting findings may, in part, be explained by differences in the nature of the samples, methods, and tasks employed and the extent to which demands are placed upon attentional control (Menghini et al., 2011; Provazza et al., 2019) as visuospatial tasks may sometimes place a greater requirement upon attentional resources than their verbal equivalents (Alloway, Gathercole, & Pickering, 2006). It is also likely that performance will be affected by the extent to which the visual stimuli can be phonologically recoded (Macaruso et al., 1995), a factor that might explain Alt et al.'s, (2021) finding that typical versus dyslexic group differences on visual WM measures disappeared when nonverbal intelligence and language were accounted for.

Studies examining the relationship between deficits in central executive processes of WM and reading difficulties have produced inconsistent findings (Alt et al., 2021; Berninger et al., 2008; Brandenburg et al., 2015; Gray et al., 2019) perhaps in part because of the comorbid presence of other conditions (e.g., attention deficit disorders) in some of those studied (Alt et al., 2021).

Kudo, Lussier, and Swanson (2015) undertook a research synthesis of forty-eight studies comparing children with reading disabilities with typically developing children. It is important to note that their reading-disabled group was selected on the basis of deficits in word recognition or reading comprehension; this may have presented a different picture than if poor decoders had been selected in isolation. The authors reported that the reading-disabled children performed more poorly on a range of cognitive measures. Effect sizes were as follows: verbal WM (–0.79), verbal short-term memory (–0.56), visuospatial WM (–0.48), and executive processing (–0.67). The effect sizes were somewhat smaller than those for phonological awareness (–1.0) and rapid naming (–0.89). Each of these made a unique contribution to the overall effect size differences between the groups.

Indications are that the short-term and working memory problems of struggling readers do not improve with age and, indeed, may be more severe in older poor readers (Cohen-Mimran & Sapir, 2007; Peng et al. 2022; Rose & Rouhani, 2012; Swanson, Zheng, & Jerman, 2009; Swanson & Hsieh, 2009), perhaps because the nature of the relationship and the demands placed upon WM change as students' reading skills develop (Peng et al., 2018). As is the case for other key cognitive processes examined in this chapter, it has been suggested that the relationship between memory and decoding is not unidirectional but, rather, reciprocal and mutualistic (Lazzaro et al., 2021c; Ober et al., 2020; Peng & Kievit, 2020; Peng et al., 2022; Smalle et al., 2019). It is possible that reciprocity may be stronger in some contexts and populations than others. Zhang and Peng (2023) for example, found a reciprocal relationship between reading and a measure of executive functioning, comprised of WM and switching, for high performing students but not for those with a reading disability.

Studies of short-term and working memory in those with dyslexia have not proven greatly helpful for guiding targeted intervention. Gathercole et al. (2016) suggest that WM is best conceived not as a stand-alone element but, rather, as one component of an interrelated and integrated network of cognitive abilities that impact upon learning. As such, targeting improvements in WM (or other cognitive deficits) as a discrete process in isolation is unlikely to prove effective.

Progress has been hampered by limited understanding of the cognitive factors involved in applying gains in particular cognitive processes and, in specific contexts, to other domains. It appears that cognitive training can result in improvements on trained tasks and untrained tasks when these are similar to the trained tasks (near transfer), but such gains are likely to have little impact upon activities that have less overlap (far transfer), and those effects that are witnessed tend not to be sustained over time or have meaningful educational value (Melby-Lervåg & Hulme, 2013; Melby-Lervåg, Redick, & Hulme, 2016; Redick et al., 2015; Randall & Tyldesley, 2016; Sala & Gobet, 2020a; Schwaighofer, Fischer, & Bühner, 2015; Shipstead, Redick, & Engle, 2012; Simons et al., 2016). Some have argued that employing training in natural environments, rather than laboratories, may prove more effective, although studies have yet to provide evidence of resultant far transfer (Rowe et al., 2019).

A helpful theoretical analysis of the issue of transfer in WM training issue is provided by Gathercole and colleagues (2019) who suggest that the nature of WM training should be closely mapped to the key skills relevant to whatever particular academic or other domain progress is being sought

(Peng & Goodrich, 2020; Peng & Swanson, 2022). Here, one must nevertheless be realistic about what can be achieved:

> … there is little prospect that WM training with a small number of tasks will ever have a substantial impact on real-life skills such as those required to enhance educational achievement. Such real-life skills are likely to rely on an extensive array of cognitive routines; too many, probably, to be trained with anything other than real-life experience. (Gathercole et al., 2019: 38)

In respect of intervention for learning difficulties, it is important to sensitize teachers to the need to modify their classroom practice when working with children with memory difficulties. Teachers need to understand reasons for not overloading WM and be advised on how best to help such children devise helpful memorization strategies (Gathercole & Alloway, 2008). While such advice can be beneficial in maximizing the classroom experiences of those with WM problems, it is unlikely that such guidance will be of significant value in resolving the complex difficulties encountered by those with severe reading difficulties (Elliott et al., 2010).

Executive Functions

The role of executive functioning (EF) in academic learning has gained much attention in recent years such that it could appear to some to be "the new IQ" (Elliott & Resing, 2015: 142). EF is generally considered to be a top-down, domain general construct consisting of separable components that are used when one has to concentrate and pay attention in order to complete a task (Diamond, 2013). This can be contrasted with other tasks where a more automatic, instinctive response may be appropriate.

While operational definitions, components, and assessments vary greatly, in part reflecting the rather different foci of neuropsychology and cognitive, developmental, and educational psychology (Cirino et al., 2020; Jacob & Parkinson, 2015), core functions are widely considered to be the ability to inhibit one's actions appropriately (to exercise self-control and regulate inhibitory control), working memory, and cognitive flexibility or task-switching (Miyake et al., 2000).

The relationship of reading disability to working memory and to attentional difficulties has already been considered above. Inhibitory control (IC) concerns the ability to inhibit a dominant response in favor of a subdominant response. Cognitive flexibility, or task-switching, concerns the ability to shift flexibly across differing mental states, rule sets, or operations. In addition to these three core functions, several others have been suggested: Cirino et al. (2018), for example, identify eight EF-related constructs in the literature:

    i. working memory
   ii. inhibition
  iii. shifting
  iv. planning
   v. generative fluency
  vi. self-regulated learning
 vii. metacognition
viii. behavioral regulation

There is burgeoning interest in the relationship between EF and reading although greater emphasis has been placed upon reading comprehension (Butterfuss & Kendeou, 2018; Follmer, 2018). Nevertheless, available evidence suggests a relationship with decoding. Spiegel et al. (2021) undertook a meta-analysis of EF and a wide range of academic outcomes in elementary schoolchildren. Working memory was found to be moderately related to reading accuracy and fluency in both early and late stages of elementary school. At the early elementary school stage, IC and shifting were both significantly related to accuracy but not to fluency. However, in late elementary school, IC and shifting were significantly related to fluency but not to accuracy. Of the three components, working memory was found to be more strongly related to decoding across the elementary school phase, although working memory and IC had a similar relationship with this skill in early elementary school. In reflecting upon these findings, Spiegel and colleagues speculate that IC may act largely as a proxy for general EF and implicitly suggest that shifting may have only limited relevance for reading skill.

A more influential role is reported in a meta-analysis of EF and decoding in children and adolescents (Ober et al., 2020). The three core EF constructs (working memory, task-switching, and IC) were all significantly associated with the two measures of decoding (word reading and non-word reading), with average effect size estimates ranging from 0.28 to 0.34. Daucourt et al. (2018) similarly found IC, working memory, and shifting to be equally valuable predictors of reading disability. In contrast, Al Dahhan et al. (2022) found that, in a comparison study of dyslexic and typical reader groups, impaired EF was associated with poorer performance in reading fluency, but no such difference was found for reading accuracy.

According to Halverson et al. (2021), the relationship between EF and reading disability is less clear than it is for reading more generally. Noting that recent meta-analyses (Follmer, 2018; Jacob & Parkinson, 2015; Ober et al., 2020; Peng et al., 2018) had excluded studies specifically focusing upon struggling readers, Halverson and colleagues addressed this short-fall using four subtests from a computer-based measure of EF, the NIH EXAMINER (Kramer et al., 2014) with fourth- and fifth-grade children scoring below the twenty-fifth percentile on a test of silent reading and comprehension. Findings demonstrated an overall EF-reading correlation of 0.26, with values of 0.31 and 0.32 for EF-single word reading accuracy and EF-reading fluency respectively. These figures were higher than for EF-reading comprehension.

Thompson et al. (2015) examined a large range of potential predictors of dyslexia with children tested annually from the age of 3.5 to 8 years. They found that EF skills only contributed to the best-fitting models at one single time point – at age 4.5. The authors speculated that self-regulatory and attentional skills might be of particular importance at a time when children's readiness for formal schooling might vary (n.b. formal schooling commences in the UK in the year that the child has their fifth birthday). Malone, Pritchard, and Hulme (2022) found that EF at age five was a moderate predictor of word reading skill at age six but it no longer accounted for the variance after controlling for domain specific skills such as phoneme awareness and RAN.

Miciak et al. (2019) examined whether EF was able to predict response to intervention in relation to reading comprehension. No differences in EF between responder and non-responder groups were found when reading ability was controlled, a finding that mirrors the general inability of cognitive measures to predict intervention response uniquely.

When considering the relationship of EF to other skills it is important, as noted above, to be mindful that the processes being tapped often vary substantially across studies. Furthermore, it is difficult to assess the relationship of individual components to other factors. Producing tasks that can isolate and measure separate EF components is problematic as there is often significant overlap with other EFs, and with other non-EF processes related to task performance (Snyder, Miyake, & Hankin, 2015).

An alternative approach is to employ EF behavioral rating scales, typically completed by the child's parents or teachers. Several studies of parental and teacher ratings of dyslexic children have reported EF difficulties (Gioia et al., 2002; Karr et al., 2021; Locascio et al., 2010; Morte-Soriano et al., 2021) with some findings suggesting that such problems may be more salient in school than at home (Karr et al. 2021; Morte-Soriano et al., 2021).

In light of their review of the literature Cirino et al. (2020) observed that while EF was found to be uniquely related to reading performance, its contribution was small and it was only a weak predictor of intervention response. They noted that while many struggling readers appear to experience difficulties that relate closely to EF constructs, for example, self-regulation and organization, there may be a mismatch between measures of EF that consist of cognitive and neuropsychological tests and the type of EF-related academic difficulties observed in real-world settings by practitioners. This distinction is supported by brain activation studies showing that cognitive control areas appeared only to be related to differences in reading ability and reading improvement when they involved reading, rather than cognitive control, tasks (Nugiel et al., 2019; Roe et al., 2018).

In the light of these and other findings, Cirino and colleagues (2020) concluded that there is insufficient evidence to support the assessment of EF either for identifying dyslexia or for informing the nature of reading intervention. This mirrors the stance of Elliott and Resing (2015), Fletcher and Miciak (2017) and Vellutino et al. (2004) in relation to the relevance of assessing cognitive skills for reading disability more generally. However, not dissimilar to the final remarks in the working memory section above, Cirino and colleagues add that their recommendation does not rule out the value of modifying the classroom environment and instructional tasks in ways that reflect sensitivity to children's particular memory, attentional, motivational, and self-regulatory difficulties (see also, Elliott et al., 2010; Fletcher et al., 2019), adding that:

> … perhaps the better question is not how and whether EF skills relate to reading and intervention response, but rather how these domain general skills can be supported and enhanced in the context of high-quality reading intervention. (Cirino et al., 2020: 137)

Auditory and Visual Explanations

During the past decade, there has been a resurgence of interest in the role of underlying auditory and visual factors in reading disability. Rather than directly competing with phonological accounts, these have often been integrated within explanations in which phonological processing is held to operate at "a layer above" more basic processes (Plante, 2012: 259). Several theories suggest that phonological and other proximal reading-related difficulties can be traced back to finer-grained sensory-perceptual deficits involving auditory, visual, or motor processing (Stein, 2019; 2022a; Tallal & Gaab, 2006; Vidyasagar & Pammer, 2010). Whether such processes exert a causal influence upon phonological processing and reading or serve as a marker for an underlying neurological abnormality is still subject to debate. O'Brien and Yeatman (2021) contend that rather than perceiving dyslexia as a consequence of a cascade of impairments emanating from a single "core deficit" (typically a phonological deficit), it is more helpful to consider reading difficulties as explained by a variety of distinct, additive predictors or risk factors that include a range of sensory, cognitive, and linguistic processes.

Auditory Processing

The texture and quality of the child's phonological awareness is likely to be dependent upon their auditory processing; if this is impaired in some way, they are unlikely to be able to reflect appropriately upon the sounds in words that they hear. Such an assumption reflects a bottom-up perspective in which basic auditory processing problems are considered to be causally responsible for phonological deficits (Farmer & Klein, 1995; Klein & Farmer, 1995; Tallal & Gaab, 2006). In contrast, top down explanations (Ramus et al., 2003; White et al., 2006) emphasize the role of higher level linguistic processes. According to such accounts, auditory processing difficulties may be present but these do not impact upon phonological processing and thus do not play a causal role in reading disability (for a discussion, see Hämäläinen, Salminen, & Leppänen, 2013).

On the basis of earlier work showing that children with specific language impairment experienced greater difficulty in tasks of auditory sensitivity, Tallal (1980) examined whether such problems might also be a feature of those with reading disability. This proved to be the case with a positive correlation being found between auditory processing and reading. Tallal hypothesized that deficits in auditory processing affected speech perception, which in turn impacted upon the development of phonological awareness and, ultimately, the acquisition of reading skills.

A variety of different auditory tasks have been employed in reading research, many focusing upon the processing of short sounds and fast transitions involving a "rapid" or "temporal" deficit (Tallal, 1980; Tallal & Gaab, 2006). One measure (a time order judgement "repetition test") involves familiarizing participants with two distinct sounds and then asking them to state the order in which these are presented. The time interval between the two sounds indicates whether the task assesses rapid or slow auditory processing. Tallal's conclusions that difficulties centered upon the perception of rapid tones were subsequently challenged on the grounds that she failed to check adequately that the problems she studied were specific to the temporal domain. However, several studies of dyslexics have reported rapid auditory processing deficits involving both speech and non-speech stimuli (Hämäläinen, Salminen, & Leppänen, 2013; Hornickel & Kraus, 2013; Mascheretti et al., 2018), although the evidence concerning non-speech stimuli is less persuasive (Gu & Bi, 2020).

Goswami and her colleagues (Corriveau et al., 2010; Goswami, 2002, 2019) argue that the rapid processing hypothesis offers an insufficient account of the auditory difficulties that are encountered by those with reading disabilities. According to her temporal sampling theory, it may be more appropriate to focus upon the perception of auditory signals underpinning speech rhythm, tempo, and stress that are linked to slow brain oscillations (Di Liberto et al., 2018; Leong et al., 2017; Lizarazu, Lallier, et al., 2021). These impairments are likely to lead to difficulties in drawing upon prosodic cues[17] that appear to be valuable in helping the child develop phonological awareness and early reading skills (Beattie & Manis, 2014; Goodman, Libenson, & Wade-Woolley, 2010; Holliman, Wood, & Sheehy, 2010). One important element of rhythmic sensitivity is *rise time*, which refers to the rate of change of the amplitude of sounds (corresponding to the beats of syllables in the speech stream). In speech, rise time incorporates changes in frequency, duration and intensity – factors that are important for prosodic prominence. Rise time sensitivity appears to be a predictor of phonological awareness in children (Corriveau et al., 2010; Goswami, 2022; Plakas et al., 2013).

Impaired performance on auditory measures has been repeatedly found for dyslexic groups (Goswami, 2015; Mandke et al., 2022) although high levels of inter-study variability in effect sizes have been observed, perhaps because of differences in the nature of the tasks involved (Witton et al., 2020). Studies of young infants (Kalashnikova, Goswami, & Burnham, 2018) and preschoolers (Law, Wouters, & Ghesquière, 2017) at family risk of dyslexia are more likely to show impaired rise time discrimination. Significant correlations between auditory processing, phonological, and language skills have been reported (Goswami, Gerson, & Astruc, 2010; Goswami et al., 2002; Stein, 2008; Walker et al., 2006), although it should be noted that other studies have failed to detect a relationship (Halliday & Bishop, 2006; Nittrouer, 1999; White et al., 2006).

---

[17] Prosodic cues involve the grouping, rhythm, and prominence of the elements of speech, ranging from subparts of the syllable to the phrase (Pierrehumbert, 2003).

One common criticism of auditory processing explanations in relation to reading disability relates to the lack of universality of this problem in dyslexic children (Calcus et al., 2016; Meilleur et al. 2020). Ramus (2003) suggests an overall aggregate of 39 percent for samples of those with reading disabilities. Roughly similar figures of, "… about a third" are provided by Boets, Wouters et al. (2007: 1614) and between 22–36 percent (Wright & Conlon, 2009), although this latter estimate concerns single measures of either auditory or visual sensory processes. McArthur and Hogben (2012) note findings within the range 20–50 percent whereas Stein (2012) reports estimates ranging from 10 to 70 percent. There appears to be some evidence that auditory processing deficits may be less prevalent in some languages other than English (Georgiou et al., 2010, 2012; Goswami et al., 2011; Surányi et al., 2009).

Recognition that auditory processing deficits cannot explain all cases should not directly lead to the conclusion that it cannot explain any of them (Stein, 2008). As is noted above, a similar criticism can equally be applied to the phonological deficit hypothesis (Boets, Ghesquière et al., 2007). Certainly, if one accepts a multiple risk factor account of reading disability, the fact that a risk factor affects some, but not others, should not be seen as theoretically problematic although the large variations between different samples does pose an empirical challenge (McArthur et al., 2008). Another challenge stems from the finding that some normal readers also demonstrate significant auditory and speech perception problems (Halliday & Bishop, 2006; Landerl & Willburger, 2010). It is unclear whether this suggests a limited role for lower-level sensory processing in the acquisition of reading skills or, alternatively, that some children find ways to compensate for such difficulties (Boets, Ghesquière, et al., 2007).

The nature of the data obtained from studies is often such that it is difficult to claim that poor performance on auditory tasks is necessarily caused by a perceptual deficit rather than inattention, working memory or other executive control difficulties (Calcus et al., 2016; O'Brien et al., 2018; Schulte-Körne & Bruder, 2010; Snowling et al., 2018; Snowling & Hulme, 2021). It appears likely that there is not one unitary perceptual deficit but rather, several contrasting reasons for poor performance on auditory tasks.

Noting that children with reading disabilities appear to have problems processing simple speech sounds, but not analogous non-speech sounds, some have suggested that the auditory deficit is specific to speech (Mody, Studdert-Kennedy, & Brady, 1997; Schulte-Körne et al., 1998). However, inconsistencies in findings have proven to be a problem across different speech processing studies (McArthur et al., 2008) and there continues to be debate as to whether phonological problems typically found in poor readers are a product of a general auditory problem or of more specific speech perception deficits (Schulte-Körne & Bruder, 2010; Vandermosten et al., 2010; Zhang & McBride-Chang, 2010).

According to some speech scientists, studies of reading have often placed too great an emphasis upon only one unit of speech – the "tyranny of the phoneme" (Peterson & Pennington, 2012: 1997) and, indeed, even determining in linguistics exactly what is meant by the term "phoneme" is not straightforward (Dresher, 2011). In reality, discrete elements of speech do not map directly onto phonemes, and accumulated evidence now suggests that auditory deficits in poor readers operate across the broader speech stream (Johnson et al., 2011). The long-term implications of this finding are that clinical interventions may need to focus upon helping children to recognize auditory structure at all levels rather than just that of the phoneme.

An alternative theory suggests that dyslexia is not the product of a fundamental weakness in auditory perception but is caused by difficulties in learning about and adapting to featural consistency in auditory stimuli (Ahissar, 2007; Banai & Ahissar, 2010). Puzzled by their observations that struggling readers seemed to perform more poorly than controls in auditory processing tasks, such as two-tone frequency discrimination, only when the same stimuli were used repeatedly, Ahissar and colleagues have suggested that individuals with dyslexia may experience particular difficulty in drawing upon stimulus regularities to help them in these tasks. Their experimental studies led them to hypothesize that when participants are repeatedly presented with the same stimulus (e.g., an auditory tone) alongside others that differ, the former operates as a perceptual anchor providing an internal reference point that facilitates future processing. When asked to make discriminations, participants implicitly draw upon this stored information, so reducing the requirement to undertake explicit computations on each occasion. Ahissar (2007) found that the performance of a dyslexic sample on an auditory discrimination task was highly correlated with phonological memory scores when the same reference tone was utilized, but this was not the case when different tones were used. In this latter variant of the procedure, creating an internal reference would have been of no value in reducing task demands. A series of subsequent studies has supported the suggestion that dyslexic participants make poorer use of stimulus regularities in both speech and nonlinguistic (e.g., simple two-tone frequency discrimination tasks) contexts (Daikhin, Raviv, & Ahissar, 2017; Kimel & Ahissar, 2020) and this is likely to affect the quality of how they categorize sounds (Banai & Ahissar, 2018).

The original anchoring hypothesis has been linked to findings demonstrating impaired speech perception in dyslexia (Gabay & Holt, 2021; Noordenbos & Serniclaes, 2015; Perrachione et al., 2016). According to the principle of categorical speech perception (Liberman et al., 1957), individuals need to be able to recognize a speech sound as fitting in a particular category even though its acoustic manifestation will vary somewhat by speaker or location. Different speech sounds are grouped together in categories with distinct and consistent boundaries between these and other perceived categories. Small acoustic changes should not be noticeable within any particular category but they need to be able to induce a clear perceptual differentiation between categories. Reduced sensitivity to acoustic stimuli results in more rapid decay of their specific memory trace resulting in difficulties in adapting to, or rapidly learning about, featural consistency in auditory stimuli. This results in weaker categorical representations that impact negatively upon reading development.

Ozernov-Palchik, Beach et al. (2022) sought to investigate the extent to which auditory problems in dyslexic children and adults reflected a basic weakness in auditory perception or difficulties in categorical perception. Auditory perceptual deficits were found for both (nonlinguistic) tones and for speech, with these being more pronounced in the children's group. However, adaptation deficits were found to be specific only to the linguistic stimuli; adaptation of nonlinguistic stimuli was significant across all three (typical, and adult and child dyslexic) groups. This finding challenges Ahissar et al.'s (2006) anchoring hypothesis, adding to an already inconsistent set of findings on this issue (Gu & Bi, 2020). Ozernov-Palchik and colleagues also considered the relationship between auditory processing and phonological deficits in dyslexia. In the light of the study findings, it was concluded that while auditory and speech adaptation deficits and phonological deficits are both more common in dyslexia, they do not share a causal relationship.

Studies examining the anchoring hypothesis in dyslexia have largely focused upon the auditory modality, with little examination of the visual modality (but cf. Beattie, Lu, & Manis, 2011). Shulver and Badcock (2021) undertook a systematic review and meta-analysis of seven published studies (together with an additional unpublished paper by Badcock) investigating the relationship between perceptual anchoring (involving both auditory and visual tasks) and dyslexia. A moderate perceptual anchoring deficit was found in dyslexic groups relative to typical reading controls although with significant variability in effect sizes across the studies. However, the authors noted a number of methodological concerns in the included studies (e.g., small sample sizes and questionable perceptual tasks).

While the anchoring hypothesis offers promise for increasing our understanding of complex factors involved in the development of reading, research in this area is still at a rudimentary stage with undetermined implications for educational assessment and intervention. Additionally, the great majority of studies providing supportive findings have concerned Hebrew speakers and these results have not been consistently replicated elsewhere (Ozernov-Palchik, Beach et al., 2022) leading to calls for further such studies involving other languages (Fletcher et al., 2019).

Methodological difficulties, such as the appropriateness and reliability of the tasks employed, the use of correlational designs, and the lack of statistical power that results from small sample sizes, have rendered it difficult to establish causality (Haegens & Golumbic, 2018; Protopapas, 2014; Snowling et al., 2018). Intervention studies could offer valuable information here particularly if auditory training programs could be shown to improve reading. While it has been shown that auditory training interventions can improve sensitivity in infant pre-readers (Van Herck et al., 2022) and lead to gains in phonological awareness at both the rhyme and phoneme levels (Thomson, Leong, & Goswami, 2013), there is currently insufficient evidence to conclude that these will lead to significantly improved reading performance.

McTigue et al. (2020) provide an overview of a large body of research studies evaluating the use of a digital learning program developed in Finland and implemented in more than twenty countries. Given findings concerning the likely relationship between the inefficient processing of speech sounds and reading disability, the Graphogame is designed to support the acquisition of decoding by training letter–sound correspondences and basic reading skills. Although their review reported that there was some evidence of subsequent sublexical skill gains, these did not transfer significantly to improved word reading skill. Evidence about the difficulties of achieving far transfer is also provided by Jakoby et al. (2019) in a study of auditory frequency training with an unselected group of adults. It was found that while the intervention improved performance in the trained tasks, there was no evidence of gains on untrained tasks that also rely on auditory discrimination, or to linguistic tasks. An alternative approach attracting growing interest involves rhythmic training through music (Bonacina et al., 2015; Cancer & Antonietti, 2022; Flaugnacco et al., 2015; Habib, 2021; Schön & Tillmann, 2015) although the evidence in support of subsequent, meaningful academic gains is limited (Sala & Gobet, 2020b).

The direction of any causal relationship between reading skill and various underlying processes has been questioned throughout this chapter. It is conceivable that skilled readers might develop superior auditory skills as a result of the strengths of their phonological prowess (Talcott et al., 2002; Pennington, 2009) or that the relationship is reciprocal rather than unidirectional (Studdert-Kennedy & Mody, 1995). One study (Johnson et al., 2009) tested children (most of whom had a speech disorder) at age five and eight years and found that phonological awareness at age five appeared to be a stronger predictor of auditory processing at age eight than the reverse. However, in a three-year longitudinal study of young children Goswami et al. (2021) found that while measures of auditory sensitivity predicted phonological awareness, there was no reciprocal effect of phonological upon auditory factors. Evidence for the presence of auditory processing difficulties at the earliest stages of infancy has been reported in a series of Finnish studies undertaken by the influential Jyväskylä *Longitudinal Study of Dyslexia* research team. This project is the longest in the world to include children with a familial risk for dyslexia from birth. It aims to identify dyslexia's early precursors, and thus its roots, by comparing the early development of children born with a familial risk for dyslexia to that of matched controls.

Using brain event-related potentials measurement, it was shown that a proportion of struggling readers was affected by auditory-processing deficits from birth. Auditory processing was measured using both speech and nonlinguistic stimuli a few days after birth, at six months, in kindergarten, and at 6.5 years and 9.5 years. In summarizing the research team's series of published findings, Lohvansu et al. (2021) report that very early auditory and speech perception differed between children at (familial) risk or not at risk of dyslexia. Difficulties in auditory perception appeared not to be directly associated with reading problems but, rather, with impaired performance on commonly identified cognitive precursors to reading difficulty. Although not suggesting a direct link to any specific core deficit, they conclude that basic-level deficits may have cascading effects that alter interactions within and between networks which may subsequently affect the development of later developing functions important for reading, such as phonological awareness, rapid naming, and letter knowledge. A subsequent study of a small sample of newborn infants, involving members of the Jyväskylä team and others (Virtala et al., 2023), found weaker reduced speech sound (vowel) discrimination on the part of those at familial risk of dyslexia.

Evidence for the presence of various auditory processing deficits in children and adults with reading disability is persuasive. However, it seems unlikely that auditory processing can serve as more than a partial explanation and there continues to be doubt as to the proportion of poor readers who encounter such problems, a lack of clarity about the developmental trajectory of auditory processing skills during infancy and childhood, and uncertainty as to the precise nature of any causal relationship between auditory problems and reading disability. Finally, while it appears that training programs may be able to help to improve the auditory task performance of children with such deficits, there is insufficient evidence to conclude that gains will lead to improved reading levels.

Visual Processing and Visual Attention

Given that reading requires precise visual recognition of letter strings prior to conversion to their sounds via grapheme–phoneme mapping (Share, 1995), it is unsurprising that visual deficits have long been held to be causes of dyslexia by researchers (Grainger, Dufau, & Ziegler, 2016; Werth, 2019; 2021a) teachers (Washburn et al., 2017), and the lay public (Macdonald et al., 2017). Although a variety of visual processing problems have been shown to have greater presence in those with reading disability, a consistent difficulty has been to establish causality or to draw upon this work to develop effective interventions.

The perceived role of visual-perceptual factors in dyslexia was significantly undermined by Vellutino, who provided a detailed critique of flawed methodologies in the existing literature alongside findings from his own carefully controlled experimental studies (Vellutino, 1979, 1987; Vellutino et al., 2004). These showed that deficits in a range of visual processes such as visualization, visual perception, visual memory, and visual sequencing did not appear to be causally responsible for reading disability.

In the light of this and various other research findings, the American Academy of Pediatrics published a *Joint Statement – Learning Disabilities, Dyslexia, and Vision* expressing the view that:

> … there is inadequate scientific evidence to support the view that subtle eye or visual problems, including abnormal focusing, jerky eye movements, misaligned or crossed eyes, binocular dysfunction, visual-motor dysfunction, visual perceptual difficulties, or hypothetical difficulties with laterality … cause learning disabilities. Statistically, children with dyslexia or related learning disabilities have the same visual function and ocular health as children without such conditions. (American Academy of Pediatrics et al., 2009: 842)

However, while it is still generally accepted that reading disability generally has a strong linguistic component, increasingly sophisticated theories and research approaches (O'Brien & Yeatman, 2021; Yeatman & White, 2021) have led to a resurgence of interest in the role of visual factors (Kristjánsson & Sigurðardóttir, 2023; Vidyasagar, 2019).

i. The Magnocellular Deficit Hypothesis

One prominent theory suggests that the origins of dyslexia can be traced to the magnocellular system (Gori et al., 2016a; Livingstone et al., 1991; Stein, 2019; Werth, 2021a). Magnocellular neurones (essentially, those with a large cell body) are found in all areas of the brain and are instrumental in visual, auditory, and motor functioning (Stein, 2019). While temporal processing difficulties involving auditory, motor, and visual information have been associated with the magnocellular theory of dyslexia (Livingstone et al., 1991; Ronconi, Melcher, & Franchin, 2020; Stein, 2019; Stein, Talcott, & Walsh, 2000) it is visual processing that has arguably been of greatest interest to reading researchers. Here, an important distinction is made between the magnocellular visual pathway which comprises large cells responsible for detecting contrast, motion, and rapid changes in the visual field, and the parvocellular pathway that consists of small cells sensitive to fine spatial detail.

In relation to visual processing the focus of the theory concerns the dorsal pathway which is largely made up of magnocells that are important for timing visual events and detecting motion. Magnocellular deficits have been put forward as an explanation for poorer performance on a range of visual tasks, and in relation to reading, it has been suggested that magnocellular dysfunction could affect contrast sensitivity, the positional encoding of letters in a word, deficits that affect eye movement control, and sluggishness in attentional control (see Stein, 2019, for a detailed outline of the theory and recent supportive research).

Obtaining a clear picture from research studies has been complicated by overlap in the various terms employed. These are listed in Skottun and Skoyles (2008), for example, as:

> "rate processing problems" (Habib, 2000), problems in "temporal processing" (Au & Lovegrove, 2001; Farmer & Klein, 1995; Habib, 2000; Stein & Walsh, 1997), deficits in "temporal perception (temporal acuity)" (Talcott et al., 1998), "transient processing defects" (Stein & Walsh, 1997), or reduced sensitivity to "dynamic stimuli" (Stein & Talcott, 1999). (Skottun & Skoyles, 2008: 666)

Further complication has resulted from the different tests employed to investigate such deficits. These include measures of temporal contrast sensitivity, visual persistence, discrimination of stimulus sequences, temporal acuity, and coherent motion perception. Temporal contrast sensitivity concerns the ability to detect particular stimuli that change over time. Visual persistence refers to the brief continuation of neural activity after a given stimulus has been suddenly terminated. Discrimination of stimulus sequences involves identifying differences in the order of (rapid) presentation of the same stimuli. Temporal acuity involves making judgements about the gaps of time between stimuli presented consecutively (or sometimes simultaneously). Finally, coherent motion perception tests typically involve perception of the direction of movement of a series of dots. Some of the dots move around the computer screen at the same speed in the same direction; others move in a random fashion. The coherent motion threshold can be determined by varying the proportion of coherently moving dots until the direction in which they are moving is identified (see Skottun & Skoyles, 2008: 667–670, for greater description of each of these tests). A meta-analysis of thirty-five studies of motion perception in dyslexia (Benassi et al., 2010) found a moderate mean effect size (d = 0.68), for between group differences (dyslexic versus normal readers) but a small mean effect size (d = 0.18) for the correlational studies.

The reason for this apparent discrepancy is unclear but may reflect the use of continuous measures which may reduce the effect size. More recent support for a relationship between motion perception and dyslexia has been found in several studies (Ebrahimi et al., 2022; Gori et al. 2016a; Manning et al., 2022). In a study of unselected children in two schools, aged from six to eleven years, Piotrowska and Willis (2019) found a global motion perception deficit in 16 percent of the sample. However, this deficit was found to be a weak predictor of reading performance, less influential than a range of other factors including phonological awareness. This finding led the authors to express doubt that motion tasks in isolation would prove sufficiently sensitive to be a reliable indicator of dyslexia.

One set of criticisms has focused upon methodological concerns, in particular the difficulty of generating appropriate behavioral assessments that can isolate magnocellular from other forms of functioning (Amitay et al., 2003; Skottun, 2011, 2015, 2016). Skottun and Skoyles (2006a, 2006b) argue that some tests (visual persistence, coherent motion) are poorly suited for assessing magnocellular sensitivity and contend that more sound measures (temporal contrast sensitivity, temporal acuity) have not consistently supported the theory (see also, Skottun, 2016). While some comparative studies of normal and poor readers have shown that a proportion of those with reading disability tend to demonstrate poor contrast sensitivity (Laycock, Crewther, & Crewther, 2012; Pellicano & Gibson, 2008; Wang et al., 2010), several others have failed to substantiate such findings (Gross-Glenn et al., 1995; Johannes et al., 1996; Skottun, 2000; Spinelli et al., 2002). Schulte-Körne and Bruder's (2010) review of relevant studies of those with dyslexia reported an inconsistent role for contrast sensitivity (deemed by Skottun & Skoyles, 2010a to be the most direct and reliable means of differentiating between magnocellular and parvocellular sensitivities) although it found stronger evidence for rapid motion deficits. Skottun (2015) contends that there is little research evidence for contrast sensitivity deficits of a kind indicative of a magnocellular deficiency in connection with dyslexia and that while a high proportion of studies have found evidence of motion perception abnormalities, this is not sufficient to validate the magnocellular hypothesis as key to dyslexia (see also Manning et al., 2022).

The current picture is one of contrasting and confusing findings. Variability across experimental methods, and the use of small and oftentimes very different samples that might potentially include other co-morbid conditions, have rendered synthesis across research studies problematic (Schulte-Körne & Bruder, 2010). While some poor readers show evidence of visual deficits, these do not appear to be specific to magnocellular dysfunction (Amitay et al., 2002; Ramus, Rosen, et al., 2003). Furthermore, a significant proportion of those who appear to have magnocellular deficits are able to develop adequate reading skills (Skoyles & Skottun, 2004). Stein (2019) accepts this finding but argues that this does not rule out the possibility that such deficits (perhaps alongside weaker auditory temporal processing) can significantly contribute to the development of dyslexia for some individuals. Vidyasagar and Pammer (2010) support the argument that dyslexia may be primarily caused by a visual deficit but argue that the visual problem should not be seen as being wholly restricted to the magnocellular pathway (see Conlon et al., 2012 for a similar suggestion). However, in a study of children with dyslexia, McLean and colleagues (2011) found significant deficits in magnocellular, but not parvocellular temporal resolution, compared with controls, although the association with reading ability was relatively weak. Adding to this complex picture, Wright, Conlon, and Dyck (2012) found that differences between children with dyslexia and controls on a visual search task did not appear to be explained by a magnocellular deficit. Perhaps the most appropriate conclusion is that provided by Skottun and Skoyles, for whom the evidence for magnocellular deficits in dyslexia is "modest" (Skottun & Skoyles, 2010b: 2229).

The problem of relating the hypothesized problems of the magnocellular system to reading difficulties has also been raised (Skottun & Skoyles, 2008, 2010a). The theory seeks to explain how confusion may occur when scanning arrays of words but does not provide a satisfactory account of failure to decode single words in isolation, a task widely seen as the core problem of dyslexia. While a variety of hypotheses as to how magnocellular deficits may ultimately lead to impaired reading have been proposed, there remains insufficient evidence to justify any causal assertions (although see Gori et al., 2016a) and it is possible that any relationship between magnocellular function and reading is mediated by reading experience (Goswami, 2015; Olulade, Napoliello, & Eden, 2013; but cf. Joo, Donnelly, & Yeatman, 2017).

Stein (2008, 2019) has responded to criticisms by arguing that opposition to the magnocellular theory is in part fueled by the mistaken belief that it challenges the view that dyslexics' main difficulties are phonological, rather than visual. He accepts that most (but not all) poor readers demonstrate phonological deficits but contends that phonological theory is set at too high a cognitive level to offer a meaningful explanation of *why* dyslexic children struggle to decode text. Visual input leads to recognition of the structure of words and the understanding that these can be broken down into separate phonemes. Where magnocellular difficulties are present it is not surprising, he contends, that phonemic awareness may be impaired as a result. Stein's logic is based on a belief that there exists both dyslexic and non-dyslexic poor readers, that members of both of these groups will often present with phonological problems, but it is only the dyslexic children who will have the sorts of underlying processing difficulties that are explained by magnocellular theory. However, he also concludes that impaired visual magnocellular function, "… is neither a sufficient, nor a necessary cause of dyslexia, and therefore cannot be advanced as its sole cause. But it probably makes an important contribution in many dyslexics" (Stein, 2019: 71).

The magnocellular theory remains highly controversial although more recently it has been embraced within some theories of visual attention (Ebrahimi et al., 2022; Goswami, 2015; Peters et al., 2021). Others consider this to be unhelpful, arguing that understanding of the role of visual attention in dyslexia would be greater if this were decoupled from magnocellular explanations (Fletcher et al. 2019). Given the strong differences of opinion within the reading research literature, and the sparse number of high-quality dyslexia-related intervention trials derived from the theory, it is perhaps unsurprising that magnocellular theory has yet to become widely influential.

ii. Visual Stress and Scotopic Sensitivity

Some poor readers report that they find the visual aspects of reading physically unpleasant because of glare caused by light reflected from reading materials. This can result in a variety of symptoms such as physical discomfort (e.g., sore eyes, headaches) or visual-perceptual distortions and illusions and difficulties in seeing text clearly (Singleton, 2009a). This condition is variously known as visual stress (Singleton, 2009a), visual discomfort (Conlon et al., 1999; 2012), scotopic sensitivity, and Meares-Irlen syndrome (Irlen, 1991), with claims that its incidence may apply to approximately 20 percent of the general population (Jeanes et al., 1997; Kriss & Evans, 2005). More strikingly, the Irlen Institute has estimated that visual stress may cause problems in as many as 46 percent of those with reading and learning problems (Perceptual Development Corporation, 1998). The theory is highly controversial and has little support from leading medical or health organizations.[18]

Visual stress may be a real phenomenon affecting some good and poor readers but it is highly unlikely to explain the problems of those who present with complex decoding difficulties (Wilkins, 1995; Saksida et al., 2016). Nevertheless, it may add to the difficulties experienced by those with reading disability. Poor readers often struggle with automatic recognition of words and may need to direct greater attention to the physical characteristics of letters. Such difficulties could be exacerbated by any susceptibility to visual stress (Singleton, 2009a). Visual discomfort could reduce the child's willingness to practice reading and, as a result, increase the gap with other readers (the well-known "Matthew effect"). This notwithstanding, and despite anecdotal reports and personal testimonies, there is little significant evidence that the standard tools used to address the problem of visual stress – colored lenses or overlays – are effective means of tackling complex reading difficulties (Griffiths et al., 2016; Miyasaka et al., 2019; Suttle, Lawrenson, & Conway, 2018).

iii. Visual Attention

In considering the role of vision in reading disability, some researchers choose to focus upon low-level perceptual factors (as measured, for example, by motion or frequency detection tasks) while others place greater emphasis upon higher-level mechanisms of visual attention (Facoetti, Franceschini, &

---

[18] See, for example, the 2018 Position Statement from the Royal Australian and New Zealand College of Ophthalmologists, which contends that there is no scientific evidence that Irlen syndrome exists: https://bit.ly/3uqNS2O; accessed November 17, 2023.

Gori, 2019; Provazza et al., 2019; Franceschini et al., 2017; Gori & Facoetti, 2015; Gori et al., 2016b; White, Boynton, & Yeatman, 2019).

> Visual attention represents the mechanism for selecting relevant information within one of the most complex and cluttered environments there is: written text. This both enables prioritization of the stimuli to be processed and permits filtering of those stimuli that are irrelevant …. Written text provides a large number of stimuli to be processed, stimuli that compete for processing resources, and spatial attention enhances this selection by offering better processing, similar to a concentrated spotlight. (Gavril, Roșan, & Szamosközi, 2021: 388)

In their meta-analysis of childhood studies examining various forms of visual attention and reading, Gavril, Roșan, and Szamosközi (2021) reported evidence for a strong and significant relationship which tended to be stronger in languages with an opaque, rather than a transparent, orthography. It was found that the association increased with age, from preliteracy to mature reading possibly because of differences in attentional maturation between strong and weak readers as they develop reading skills. Positive results for the role of visual attention were also reported in a critical review of the literature by Perry and Long (2022) although it was generally found to be only a small predictor and it was noted that many of the reviewed studies failed to control for phonological effects.

One explanation for the auditory and visual temporal deficits observed by dyslexia researchers is that these may be partially explained by sluggish attentional shifting (SAS) (Hari & Renvall, 2001; Franceschini et al., 2018). Hari and Renvall (2001) suggest that SAS could have the effect of distorting the perception of rapid speech streams which, in turn, could hamper the development of phonological representations. This process has sometimes been studied using the "attentional blink" task which examines the disruptive influence of processing one target upon the processing of a second target when they are in close temporal proximity to one other. In relation to vision, there is evidence that performance on attentional blink tasks involving rapid serial visual presentation of stimuli is comparatively weaker in those with reading difficulties (McLean et al., 2010; Badcock & Kidd, 2015) although the nature of any possible causal relationship is unclear.

A popular means of examining sluggish attention is by means of the inhibition of return (IOR) task. Inhibition of return concerns a process that discourages perseverative orienting towards previously attended locations – an inclination to which poor readers are seemingly less resistant. The IOR task typically measures reaction times to stimuli presented on a computer screen following the presentation of a cue. The stimuli are variously located in an expected or unexpected spatial position based upon the preceding cue. The duration between the initial presentation of the cue and the appearance of the subsequent target, either in a correct or incorrect position, can be varied and reactions measured. Those who show less benefit from the priming of the cue are considered to have sluggish attentional shifting (Franceschini et al., 2018). Using a similar approach, Fu et al. (2019) found no reliable inhibitory effect in their small sample of fifteen dyslexic Chinese children, suggesting that these children experienced greater difficulty in disengaging attention (see also Ding et al., 2016).

Support for the sluggish attention hypothesis was provided by findings from a three-year longitudinal study in which ninety-six pre-reading children received a battery of measures in kindergarten and were subsequently followed up in Grades 1 and 2 (Franceschini et al., 2012). In addition to tests of phonemic awareness and rapid naming, the children were given two visuospatial tasks, one a serial search (marking every occurrence of a given symbol across five rows), the other involving a spatial cueing task in which the children had to select the correct orientation of a shape briefly presented (100 ms) to the left or right of a central fixation point. In a subsequent condition, the children's attention was either drawn to that side of a computer screen where the target symbol was subsequently to be presented or, alternatively to the opposite side. In such a task, performance is typically improved where the child's attention is drawn to the side where the image will appear and rendered poorer in cases where their attention is pulled away to the wrong side. Those who scored poorly on the visuospatial tasks subsequently became the weakest readers. On the visual search task, those who were to become poorer readers made twice as many errors. Interestingly, on the cueing task, those who were to become poorer readers only performed worse in cases where the cues were valid. Where there were no cues, or the cues prompted attention to the wrong side of the screen, a cueing effect was not significant. The researchers concluded that visuospatial skills were independent predictors of future reading difficulty, and problems were a consequence of a deficit in attentional orientation rather than an impairment in peripheral vision.

Most studies of visual deficits in poor readers examine children after literacy problems have already emerged, and it is conceivable therefore that any observed poor performance on visual measures is a consequence of their reading difficulties. The strength of Franceschini et al.'s (2012) investigation was that the assessments were undertaken before the children learned to read. However, we should not conclude that a causal link was demonstrated. The data were correlational, of modest size, and 40 percent of those with visual difficulties did not develop reading problems over the three-year period. Moreover, visual problems were also demonstrated by some children who later became sound readers.

Another form of visual attention problem, the visual attention span deficit hypothesis (Bosse, Tainturier, & Valdois, 2007; Lobier, Zoubrinetzky, & Valdois, 2012; Valdois, 2022) has arguably become the mechanism most examined in reading disability, particularly with respect to the use of the Visual Attention Span (VAS) task (Perry & Long, 2022). According to this hypothesis, the dyslexic individual is often limited in the number of letter string elements that can be processed simultaneously. This attentional, rather than perceptual, impairment may be unrelated to that of sluggish attentional processing (Lallier, Donnadieu, et al., 2010; Lallier, Tainturier, et al., 2010). Essentially one can distinguish between the visual attention span deficit hypothesis which focuses upon potential "… deficits in the allocation of attention across letter or symbol strings, limiting the number of elements that can be processed in parallel during reading" (Bosse, Tainturier, & Valdois, 2007: 200) and the sluggish attentional processing hypothesis in which some poor readers have difficulty in shifting their attention from one location to the next in an array.

Proponents of the visual attention span theory have been more resolute than others working in the field of visual processing and attention in attesting that such difficulty may be unrelated to phonological problems (Valdois, 2022). Studies that have examined this relationship have produced inconsistent findings with some indicating that visual attention span difficulties make an independent contribution to reading over and above phonological processes (Bosse, Tainturier, & Valdois, 2007; Chen, Zheng, & Ho, 2019; Van den Boer, Van Bergen, & de Jong, 2015; Zoubrinetzky et al., 2016).

Significant visual attention span differences have been found in group comparisons of children with and without reading disabilities (Saksida et al., 2016), with greater effect sizes for alphabetic, when compared with logographic, languages reported in a recent meta-analysis (Tang et al., 2023). However, despite this general picture, some researchers have failed to find a discrepancy (Banfi et al., 2018). One possible explanation for this may be that, as noted above, a significant visual attention span problem is often found in only a small proportion of poor readers; approximately around one third of the dysexic groups. Zoubrinetzky et al. (2016), for example, found that 32 percent of their dyslexic group demonstrated an isolated visual attention span deficit and a further 11 percent showed a double deficit which included phoneme awareness difficulties. A further

27 percent were found to have an isolated phoneme awareness deficit, and 30 percent showed neither of these two deficits. In a study of dyslexic adolescents, Bazen et al. (2020) found that 31 percent had a visual attention span weakness while 63 percent had a RAN weakness. For phonological weaknesses there was a split where 60 percent of those diagnosed at an early age demonstrated this problem, while this was found only in just over half this number (32%) in those diagnosed later in their school careers. Valdois et al. (2021) found 37.3 percent with a visual attention span deficit in a large sample of dyslexic children with approximately half of this group exhibiting this as a unique disorder. In contrast, Saksida et al. (2016) found that while 28 percent of their dyslexic sample presented with a visual attention span deficit, this was rarely unique and most also showed a phonological deficit.

Proponents for a direct relationship between visual attention and phonological processing note that deficits appear to be more significant for verbal (letters and digits) than nonverbal (symbols) material when these modalities are employed in exactly the same experimental conditions (Cirino et al., 2022; Ziegler, Pech-Georgel et al., 2010; Tang et al., 2023; see also Collis, Kohnen, & Kinoshita, 2013, for a similar finding from a study with adults). Ziegler and colleagues suggest that while such findings may be explained by visual recognition processes, it is more likely that the underlying problem stems from the fact that digits and letters, but not symbols, map onto phonological codes, and it is the link between visual and phonological codes that is the key problem of dyslexia. They conclude that what appears at first to be a visual impairment in processing letters and digits may not actually be the case, and if visual impairments are only obtained for verbal material, phonology can be put, "… back in the front row" (Ziegler, Pech-Georgel et al., 2010: F12). However, as a counter to this position, Romani and colleagues (2011) found a difference between dyslexic and normal readers on a task of symbol matching that did not require naming. It appears that evidence is accumulating against the argument that there is a strong phonological basis for the visual attention problems found in those with dyslexia, with support for such independence emerging from experiments (Lobier, Zoubrinetzky, & Valdois, 2012; Valdois, Lassus-Sangosse, & Lobier, 2012), case studies (Dubois et al., 2010; Valdois et al., 2011), and brain function studies (Peyrin et al., 2011, 2012) (see Lobier & Valdois, 2015, for a review).

To date, there is insufficient evidence to determine the nature of any causal relationship, including the possibility of a reciprocal relationship where visual attention also is improved by reading experience (Goswami,

2015; Kermani, Verghese, & Vidyasagar, 2018). A potentially helpful way to investigate this issue is to examine whether training programs designed to improve visual attention span could also boost the reading performance of children with reading problems. Zoubrinetzky et al. (2019) studied the effects of two training programs designed to improve phonological skills and visual attention span respectively. The participants were forty-three French dyslexic children. The group was split into two with both sub-groups receiving both programs consecutively, albeit in a different order. It was found that both programs resulted in improved performance in the skills they were each designed to address but also, crucially, both also resulted in improved reading. However, there was no control group and the authors noted the need to examine long-term reading progress to ascertain whether initial gains were sustained. A further study has reported reading gains from visual attention span training with a group of dyslexic Chinese children (Zhao et al., 2019).

Another factor that may contribute to visual problems affecting reading, closely linked to sluggish attentional shifting and impaired visual attention span, is abnormal crowding (see Gori & Facoetti, 2015, for a review). Crowding in the reading context refers to the negative influence of nearby letter contours upon visual discrimination. Features unrelated to the target may be integrated in error thus rendering letter discrimination more problematic. While there is persuasive evidence that a subset of poor readers experience crowding difficulties, there is disagreement as to whether crowding and selective attention are part of a common mechanism or whether crowding is primarily a visual processing phenomenon that exacerbates attentional problems (Joo et al., 2018).

One way of addressing issues of role and of cause and effect is to examine the effect of interventions that reduce the impact of crowding. Several studies have demonstrated that artificially increasing the space between letters and words can result in improvement in reading performance (see Joo et al., 2018, for a discussion). In two studies, the effects were found for half (Spinelli et al., 2002) and two thirds (Martelli et al., 2009) of their respective dyslexic samples, a finding that led these authors to conclude that the causal role of crowding applied to some, but not all of those, with dyslexia. Zorzi and colleagues (2012) similarly found that increasing letter spacing improved both reading accuracy and speed for their dyslexic sample, all of whom had normal, or corrected-to-normal, visual acuity. Increasing letter spacing failed to improve the performance of younger reading-level controls, a finding that suggests that the deficits observed could not be held to be a consequence of a lack of reading experience. Perea et al. (2012)

found gains in word and text reading for both normal and dyslexic readers when the gap between letters was widened, although these were substantially larger for the poor reader group. This finding applied to words of six letters but not to those comprised of four letters. Several studies have found reading gains (usually relating to reading speed) for dyslexic groups when letter or text spacing is increased (Bertoni et al., 2019; Stagg & Kiss, 2021; Joo et al., 2018) although introducing wider spacing may be deleterious for skilled adult readers (Korinth, Gerstenberger, & Fiebach, 2020) and improvements from increased spacing or the use of "dyslexia-friendly" fonts such as *Dyslexie* have not been consistently found (Galliussi et al. 2020; Kuster et al., 2018).

Schneps et al. (2013) found that shortening the lines of text on an electronic screen could improve reading speed and comprehension in high school students with dyslexia. The crowding effect has also been found when differently oriented geometric shapes have been used; Moores and colleagues (2011) found that crowding led to far greater deterioration in visual discrimination performance for a dyslexic group than for controls. However, while consistent with an attentional explanation, these authors concluded that existing theoretical accounts of visual attention in dyslexia were insufficient to explain all of their findings.

Perry and Long (2022) criticize many visual attention studies for failing to include phonological awareness (PA) or rapid automatized naming (RAN) as covariates. However, such a design was employed in a study of four visual attention paradigms involving ninety students at high risk of reading disorder (Cirino et al., 2022). The study employed a VAS task, an IOR task, two attentional blink tasks and a paper and pencil visual search task. Phonological awareness was assessed using an Elision subtest.[19] RAN covered four conditions (letters, numbers, colors, and objects). Scores from one of the visual attention measures, the VAS task using letter targets, explained approximately 6 percent of the variance in single word reading once PA, RAN, and age had been controlled for. However, there was no significant effect for reading fluency. A finding that the VAS measure failed to predict reading when nonalphanumeric stimuli were employed, echoes that reported by Ziegler, Bertrand, et al. (2010), leading the authors to recommend further studies to explore the relationship between VAS and phonology. No significant relationships to reading were found for the other visual attention measures, with little statistical association between

[19] This measure involves saying a word orally (e.g., "clap") to the child and then asking them to remove a given sound (e.g., the /k/ sound) and then say what is left ("lap").

the different visual attention tasks. The authors suggested that there may be variability in the way that different visual attentional processes affect struggling readers but expressed little confidence that these would have important implications for intervention.

While recent research in attention has tended to focus upon either auditory or visual processing, it is possible that difficulties apply to both of these in combination (Virsu, Lahti-Nuuttila, & Laasonen, 2003). A cross-sensory deficit of attention would be problematic for the segmentation of both auditory and visual inputs in the form of speech and letter strings respectively. Few studies have examined this in the same dyslexic sample. However, in a study of Italian children comparing those with decoding difficulties with controls, and subsequently, with another group containing slow but accurate decoders, Facoetti and colleagues (2009) found that only those with poor phonological decoding skills demonstrated a temporal multisensory deficit of attention. Individual case analysis confirmed that this finding was not attributable to the presence of a small number of atypical cases in the poor decoder group. Individual differences in multisensory attention accounted for 31 percent of unique variance in nonword reading performance of all the poor readers in the study (both the poor decoders and the slow readers) after controlling for age, IQ, and phonological skills. In a study of young dyslexic adults with phonological awareness deficits, Lallier, Tainturier, et al. (2010) found correlations in visual and auditory processing which appeared to support the suggestion that attentional shifting speed has to be synchronized between visual and auditory modalities in order to develop fluent reading (Breznitz & Misra, 2003).

It has been claimed that specially designed action video games may be able to help readers better allocate their attention across time and space (Pasqualotto et al., 2022). Employing these tools as targeted interventions, a series of studies emanating from a cluster of Italian researchers have produced encouraging findings for both Italian (Bertoni et al., 2019, 2021; Franceschini et al., 2013, 2015) and English poor readers (Franceschini, Trevisan et al., 2017; Peters et al., 2021). It has also been suggested that this approach may help to prevent reading difficulties in young children Gori et al. (2016b, but cf. Łuniewska et al., 2018). Should reported gains be replicated across research teams and orthographies, utilizing larger samples and more rigorous designs (Bavelier & Green, 2019), the proposition that visual training based upon action video games could be a valuable adjunct to more traditional forms of remediation (Facoetti, Franceschini, & Gori, 2019) would be greatly strengthened.

While supportive of the position that visual problems are influential in dyslexia, Werth (2021b) is of the opinion that the primary difficulty concerns eye movement strategy rather than reduced visual attention. According to this account, poor reading occurs when eye movements (saccades) take place too rapidly and fixation times are insufficient for all the letters in the relevant word or word segments to be recognized. To address this problem, Werth trialed a computer-guided reading aloud approach with sixty dyslexic children. The program subdivided the text into segments which consisted of no more letters than the children could simultaneously recognize. It then indicated the location in the segments to which their gaze should be directed, how long the gaze should be directed to each segment, which reading saccades the children should execute, and when the children should pronounce the segments aloud. Despite there being no prior training program, Werth found that the children's rate of reading mistakes immediately dropped by almost 70 percent, and claimed that this was, "… the highest effect size that has ever been measured in a reading therapy" (Werth, 2021b: 12). JothiPrabha, Bhargavi, and Rani (2023) contend that while dyslexia is not primarily a visual disorder, erratic eye movements can often be observed in dyslexics while reading, in part because poor language processing and short-term memory lead to shorter saccades and longer fixation times. For this reason, they claim that measures of eye movements may serve to indicate the severity of dyslexia. How this would improve upon information obtained from the direct use of reading tests, however, is not made clear.

The empirical literature on the relation of visual attention to reading is complex, inconsistent, and difficult to summarize. Nevertheless, evidence does seem to be mounting from both behavioral (Franceschini et al., 2022) and neuroimaging research (Taran et al., 2022) that supports the suggestion that a proportion of those who struggle with reading have visual attention problems that have significantly contributed to their difficulties, with some evidence that the relationship may be stronger for opaque orthographies (Gavril, Roşan, & Szamosközi, 2021). However, not only is there confusion about which visual attention processes are most significant, there is also much disagreement as to their relationship to phonological processing (and, indeed, to short-term memory; see Bogon et al., 2014; Stefanac et al., 2019).

At one extreme some believe that any observed relationship with reading disability is purely a statistical artefact and of little importance once one controls for language; at the other extreme are those who contend that phonological deficits are fundamentally a consequence of difficul-ties of visual attention (Vidyasagar, 2019). In line with the shift towards multifactorial understandings, it seems likely that a wide range of visual factors can play a minor, but significant, role in reading disability.

Psycho-Motor Processing

That there is a statistical relationship between motor skills and cognitive development is largely undisputed, with poor gross motor skills found in some studies of those with learning disabilities (Westendorp et al., 2011). There is also some evidence for the presence of poor fine motor skills in those with reading difficulties (Obeid et al., 2022). Such a difficulty may impact upon handwriting (Gosse & Van Reybroeck, 2020; Kandel et al., 2017; Pagliarini et al., 2015), although it has been suggested that poor handwrit-ing in those with dyslexia is not fundamentally the result of an underlying motor problem (Martínez-García et al., 2021). Either way, handwriting is a process that helps young children to recognize letters (James, 2017) and weaknesses in this respect, together with evidence of poorer copying strat-egies for dyslexic children (Blampain, Gosse, & Van Reybroeck, 2021), are likely to add to otherwise existing reading difficulties.

The prevalence of motor impairments in dyslexic samples has var-ied greatly across studies with the majority reporting such difficulties in between 30 and 65 percent of cases (Chaix et al., 2007; Kaplan et al., 1998; Ramus et al., 2003). These differences are likely, in part, to reflect different methods of assessment and cut-off points.

Given this statistical association, it is not surprising that there has been a search for possible causal factors in dyslexia. Several theories have been put forward to explain the prevalence of tactile (Laasonen, Service, & Virsu, 2001) and motor (Ramus, 2003) difficulties in dyslexic groups with the most influential theory being that of the delayed neural commitment framework (Nicolson & Fawcett, 2006, 2019; Stoodley & Stein, 2011). According to this theory, cerebellar dysfunction results in a failure to con-struct key neural networks that subsequently make it difficult to achieve sound automaticity of various skills (e.g., rapid naming or information processing) that are important for reading acquisition. A core component of the theory is that for those with dyslexia, automaticity difficulties can be found across a broad range of domains, including motor skills (Nicolson & Fawcett, 1990). Nicolson and Fawcett's argument is not that motor problems act as causal factors in reading disability but, rather, that these signify underlying cerebellar impairments. It is important to note that, as indicated above, the cerebellar theory operates at a neural-systems, rather than the cognitive, level. Thus, rather than competing with theories such as that of a phonological deficit, the theory seeks to explain reasons why cognitive-level difficulties arise. This explanation is controversial and while it is accepted by some that cerebellar dysfunction may be implicated for a proportion of poor readers, there is a lack of clarity about the mechanisms involved, acknowledgement of the continuing absence of direct evidence to support the theory (Nicolson & Fawcett, 2019), and recognition that impaired cerebellar function is unlikely to be the primary cause of dyslexia (Marchand-Krynski et al., 2018; Stoodley & Stein, 2011, 2013).

The relationship of motor difficulties to dyslexia is highly contested with some reporting group differences between dyslexic and typical readers (Fawcett, Nicolson, & Maclagan, 2001; Ramus, Pidgeon, & Frith, 2003; Wolff et al., 1995) and others failing to find these (Kronbichler, Hutzler, & Wimmer, 2002; Savage et al., 2005; White et al., 2006). Chaix and colleagues (2007), for example, found no direct causal relationship between reading performance and motor scores in a large sample of children who had attended a clinic for language and learning disabilities. Carroll, Solity, and Shapiro (2016) used a variety of sensorimotor and cognitive measures with a large sample of unselected children at entry to school. The children's reading ability was tested two, three and four years later and poor readers were subsequently identified. Measures of motor skills and balance using the Dyslexia Early Screening Test (Nicolson & Fawcett, 2004) were not significantly related to later literacy.

Several studies examining balance and postural stability have found that poor readers have greater difficulty in maintaining stability than controls (Fawcett & Nicolson, 1999; Getchell et al., 2007) although this appears to be less evident in the case of adults (Loras et al., 2014; Stoodley et al., 2006). It has been suggested that this problem may have a basis in the relationship between sensory (visual) and motor (postural) control systems (Barela et al., 2011; Sela, 2012), perhaps because of difficulties in integrating proprioceptive signals (Laprevotte et al., 2021; Quercia et al., 2011). Nevertheless, the overall picture concerning balance and stability is far from clear, particularly as similar problems can be found for a number of developmental disorders. A meta-analysis of fifteen studies examining balance in dyslexic and control samples (Rochelle & Talcott, 2006) produced an overall effect of 0.64, but there were very large differences between the various studies. Furthermore, the differences in reading scores between the dyslexic and control groups did not appear to be significantly associated with the effect sizes. The authors concluded that that the relationship between dyslexia and poor balance was most likely influenced by variables other than reading skill.

Despite their comorbidity, the evidence for a causal relationship between motor impairment and reading skills is generally regarded as weak (Rochelle & Talcott, 2006). In a detailed review, Savage (2004) concluded that the evidence base for the significance of motor deficits, in general, and Nicolson and Fawcett's automaticity model, in particular, was mixed, adding that improved research designs with better sampling and measurement were required. Particularly valuable would be the deployment of longitudinal studies that could consider associations between automaticity in pre-readers and subsequent literacy and cognitive performance.

Given that motor control difficulties are evident across a wide range of neurodevelopmental disorders such as ADHD, autism spectrum disorder, and language disorders in addition to a primary diagnosis of developmental coordination disorder (Elliott & Place, 2021), it may be helpful to see these as symptoms of often overlapping dimensions of disability risk (Loras et al. 2014; Marchand-Krynski et al., 2018). Given the extant state of knowledge, reading disability and motor disorders can be considered to be different conditions resulting from both independent and shared risk factors (Downing & Caravolas, 2020). At the current time, there is little evidence that assessments of motor functioning can meaningfully guide diagnosis of, or intervention for, reading disability.

Cognitive Level Explanations and Educational Intervention

> The search for deeper or more general explanations has led to multiple potential causes at the cognitive, perceptual, and neural levels. Much of this can be characterized as a reductionist approach to explanation. Terms ground in behavioral explanations (lack of phonemic awareness, poor rapid naming) are abandoned as causal terms: first in favor of terms of cognitive theory (poor phonological representations, slow memory access and retrieval); then in psychophysical terms (poor rise sensitivity, poor temporal dynamics sensitivity); then in large-grain neuroanatomy terms … and then to genetic, biochemical, and fine-grain explanations.
>
> (Perfetti & Harris, 2019: 40)

As this chapter has demonstrated, there continues to be considerable disagreement about the nature, role, and relevance of underlying cognitive and perceptual processes in dyslexia. Given the multifactorial nature of reading disability, with multiple levels of description, multiple weaknesses, and multiple causes (Perfetti, Pugh, & Verhoeven, 2019), it is unsurprising that the development of a shared understanding that can meaningfully inform educational intervention has proven to be elusive.

Professional practice is not helped by the expression of confident, yet misleading, assertions that are commonly found in the field of dyslexia. The lay public, and indeed, many educationalists and clinicians, might be greatly surprised to learn of the tenuous relationship between the vast body of accumulated research findings concerning underlying cognitive and perceptual processes, and current knowledge about how best to help those who struggle to learn to read. While it is possible to find isolated experimental studies where an intervention has produced a promising finding, we must be cautious of any over-ambitious claims that may result from this. Other than phonological awareness training for very young children (and even here, significant doubts continue as to the long-term benefits of interventions that address a phonological deficit [Olson, 2011]), there is no substantial evidence that identifying and directly addressing any of the specific cognitive and perceptual processes that have been highlighted in the dyslexia literature leads to significant and sustained gains in the decoding abilities of those who struggle to learn to read. Specifically, studies of rapid naming, short-term and working memory, executive functions, magnocellular functioning, motor processing, auditory processing, visual processing, and attention have yet to meaningfully inform the design of targeted reading-related interventions that have proven to be effective for significant numbers of poor readers over time.

The above observations, of course, should not be perceived as representing a demeaning of such work. Increasing our understanding of the influence of key cognitive processes underlying all forms of reading difficulty, and ultimately deriving sound multifactorial causal models, are outcomes that may well assist our efforts to develop more powerful forms of intervention, particularly for that small group of "treatment resisters" for whom our current best evidence-based practices continue to fail. At the current time, leading researchers in each of these fields are actively turning their attention to the production of training studies that can improve deficient processes and, as a consequence, help to overcome reading disability. Despite these laudable intentions, it needs to be clearly communicated to education practitioners, clinicians, students and their families, and the lay public, that research in these domains offers possible promise for the future rather than secure knowledge with direct and immediate applications for practice.

Finally, our difficulties in developing a universal science of reading are compounded by the predominance of studies involving the English language. This situation has improved somewhat since Share's (2008) criticism of the distorting effect of this idiosyncratic "outlier" orthography, yet the imbalance continues (Share, 2021b). Future research needs to generate theoretical and computational models of reading that can draw upon and reflect the world's diverse languages and writing systems (Blasi et al., 2022; Huettig & Ferreira, 2022; Lachmann & Bergström, 2023).

CHAPTER 3

The Neurobiological Bases of Reading Disability

Introduction

During the last fifty years, research has unquestionably demonstrated that reading disabilities/dyslexia, however defined or debated, are connected to the human brain and the human genome. The word "connected," however, is broad and means, rather non-specifically, that these entities are associated or related in some respect. The origin and nature of these associations, perhaps surprisingly, continue to be not fully understood. In this context, four questions can be asked. Specifically, are these associations:

- *hierarchical?* i.e., assume a clear order (e.g., the genome – brain – reading behavior);
- *causal?* i.e., variability in reading performance is caused by variability in the brain and the genome;
- *strong or weak?* i.e., variability in reading behavior is reliably predicted by variability in the brain and the genome;
- *permanent or malleable?* i.e., can the strength of association be altered?

As the literature on these associations grows, to distinguish these entities from other ones (some relevant and some not), researchers have coined two terms that will be used in this chapter: "reading brain" – the human brain as it is engaged in reading and reading-related processes (Wolf, 2007), and "reading genome" – the elements of the human genome that are thought to substantiate reading. These entities constitute both univariate (genome–brain, brain–reading, genome–brain) and multivariate (genome–brain–reading, both linear and nonlinear) associations.

This chapter contains many technical terms that may be unfamiliar to non-specialists. Due to space restrictions and narrative coherence, descriptions and definitions of many of these terms have not been provided. However, helpful information about these terms is readily available from both the published sources referenced in this chapter and the Internet.

The Reading Brain

The first part of this chapter discusses both postmortem and *in vivo* investigations of the brain's morphology and function. It will draw upon studies aimed at understanding the brain machinery behind reading at different stages, including prior to the mastery of reading or upon completion of the acquisition of reading. The chapter will also compare the brains of typical readers with those who experience difficulties and examine the brains of poor readers both before and after attempts have been made to remediate their difficulties.

Researchers have been able to build upon early brain anatomy findings obtained from postmortem studies of individuals with reading difficulties thanks to the utilization of a variety of imaging tools such as magnetic resonance imaging (MRI), both functional (fMRI) and structural MRI, diffusion tensor imaging (DTI), magnetic resonance spectroscopy (MRS), positron emission tomography (PET), electroencephalography (EEG), magnetoencephalography (MEG), functional near-infrared spectroscopy (fNIRS), and transcranial magnetic stimulation (TMS). The essence of the brain imaging technologies that appeared in the twentieth century and mushroomed in the twenty-first concerns employing an interaction between brain tissue and various types of energy (e.g., electromagnetic, particle radiation) and interpreting the resulting records, rather than physical incision, to depict information about the structure and function of the brain. Collectively, these data are used to generate both structural and functional brain maps which then can be compared in:

a. individuals at different stages of their lifespan;
b. at pre- and post-intervention;
c. in groups of individuals differentiated by a particular condition (e.g., patients and controls); and
d. while participants are engaged in different tasks.

Structural maps include white matter, made up of large bundles or tracts of myelinated axons that connect regions of the brain, and gray matter, made up of neuronal cell bodies, vasculature, and bone tissue as judged by their physical properties such as density or nuclear resonance characteristics. Functional maps show levels of activity as captured by metabolism, blood flow, chemical composition, absorption, electrical activity. These maps capture both the location of the activation in the brain (e.g., via fMRI and PET) and its timing (e.g., via EEG and MEG) and enable the generation of hypotheses about how the brain masters and performs reading.

Regarding studies of reading disability, as well as studies of illiterate people and adult or later life new readers, this technology has permitted investigations of:

a. the structural and functional peculiarities of the "reading brain" (i.e., what and where in the brain activity occurs when a person reads);
b. the age and developmental aspects of the "reading brain," sampling it before, during, and after the acquisition of reading skills;
c. the brain functioning of individuals with reading difficulties compared to typical readers, and;
d. the impact of remedial interventions aimed at improving the function of the "reading brain" for those experiencing difficulties.

Today's consensual view of reading avers that it takes place in a complex neuronal network comprised of left tempo-parietal, occipito-temporal, and inferior frontal regions (Jobard, Crivello, & Tzourio-Mazoyer, 2003; Richlan, Kronbichler, & Wimmer, 2009, 2011), as well as right frontotemporal areas and cerebellum (Martin et al., 2015) and deeper structures of the brain (Hancock, Richlan, & Hoeft, 2017). Specifically, the network includes the brain areas shown in Figure 3.1:

• left inferior frontal (anterior component region, recruiting, partially, Brodmann areas, BA, 44, 45, 47, and 6);
• posterior dorsal (temporo-parietal [or parieto-temporal] region incorporating the angular and supramarginal gyri and the posterior superior temporal gyrus);
• posterior ventral (ventral occipito-temporal or posterior inferior temporal regions incorporating fusiform and inferior temporal gyri);
• subcortical structures such as the basal ganglia, thalamus, and cerebellum.

Simplifying somewhat the picture of mapped reading componential processes on brain regions or vice versa, Seidenberg (2017) described the reading brain as engaging temporo-parietal areas for audition and phonology, the occipito-temporal areas for spelling and orthography, interior frontal areas for speech planning, production, and lexical interpretation, and subcortical structures, namely basal ganglia, thalamus, cerebellum, for generalized learning. Although the reading brain machinery is more complex than this, the localization of the reading brain helps us to understand why such a distributed network is needed to process, from a visual to a meaningful object, a single word, such as *cat*, engaging the triangle of phonology, orthography, and semantics (Fletcher et al., 2019).

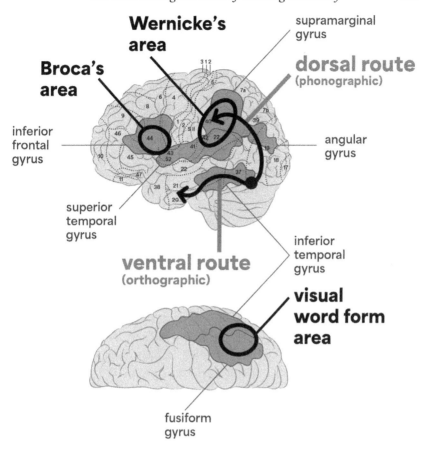

Figure 3.1   Two proposed systems supporting reading in the brain
The dorsal phonographic route and the ventral orthographic route
(Brodmann's map is superimposed).

Early sublexical processing, characteristic of early stages of reading acquisition that require effort, takes a higher route through the brain from the back (where visual processing occurs) forward. The route that travels through the middle temporal and inferior parietal regions is indirect and inefficient for accessing meaning at any kind of speed. However, it is the only way a nonskilled reader can make sense of print as words. The ventral or lower system for reading, which is lexical, develops almost simultaneously in the left occipitotemporal region. It takes advantage of an existing evolutionary system for visual processing, including faces and objects (Vogel, Petersen, & Schlaggar, 2014; Vogel et al., 2012). When a beginning reader starts making sense of words as forms, the ventral system for reading organizes as a rapid orthographic processor. This processor is based in part on the statistical properties of letters and letter combinations. These properties are consistent with connectionist models, in particular, the triangle model (Dehaene et al., 2015; Seidenberg, 2005), and similarly need to develop via learning through exposure to print (Dehaene, 2009; Seidenberg, 2017; Wolf, 2007). The ventral system needs to be functionally restructured to acquire reading as its function; this restructuring requires a considerable amount of exposure. This exposure is timed: it cannot be too early (as other foundational representations in the brain should be formed) or too late (as the system does not get optimally adapted). Importantly, the dorsal system coordinates orthographic mapping input to phonological and semantic properties of written words (Xu et al., 2001), whereas the ventral system is more lexically mediated and efficient (Booth et al., 2001).

Meta-analytic reviews have resulted in widespread agreement that there is a general pattern of activation of the network that differentiates skilled and poor readers, such that the former group engage areas of the left-side of the brain more than the latter, and the latter activates right-side regions more than the former (Cattinelli et al., 2013; Maisog et al., 2008; Martin, Kronbichler, & Richlan, 2016; Martin et al., 2015; Paulesu, Danelli, & Berlingeri, 2014; Pollack, Luk, & Christodoulou, 2015; Richlan, Kronbichler, & Wimmer, 2009, 2011; Taylor, Rastle, & Davis, 2013). Yet, there is uncertainty about the possible mechanisms of this disruption, and it is possible that these areas are affected in their functionality or, alternatively, that they endure deranged information transfer. Multiple hypotheses regarding these mechanisms exist. For example, with regard to the first mechanism, it has been hypothesized that the insula, as a possible binding element between the posterior and frontal language areas, does not function adequately in individuals with dyslexia (Paulesu et al., 1996). In relation to the second mechanism, it has been suggested that dyslexia may result from a "functional disruption" of the two (dorsal and ventral) posterior network areas (Horwitz, Rumsey, & Donohue, 1998; Ligges & Blanz, 2007; Martin et al., 2015; Pugh et al., 2000; Shaywitz et al., 2007). There are more recent hypotheses, but none of these have been widely accepted just yet.

As discussed in Chapter 2, reading is now understood as a complex componential process. In line with this understanding, there is growing evidence that a variety of brain areas, individually and in combination, differentially support distinct components of reading (Katzir, Misra, & Poldrack, 2005; Vigneau et al., 2006). For example, phonological processing is thought to be carried out by superior temporal regions serving grapheme–phoneme mapping processes and inferior frontal regions serving as phonological rehearsal systems (Fiez et al., 2006; Jobard, Crivello, & Tzourio-Mazoyer, 2003; Łuniewska et al., 2019; Vandermosten et al., 2020). As studies accumulate, even greater differentiation both by age and subcomponents appears to be warranted. Thus, neural activity in the left superior temporal gyrus has been viewed as being closely associated with the quality of phonological representations, and neural activity in the left inferior frontal gyrus, as associated with the efficiency of phonological access (Hagoort & Indefrey, 2014). Such findings have permitted hypothesis formulation concerning the relationship between fine-grain developmental changes in patterns of brain activation and maturation in the skill of reading (Wang et al., 2023). The left inferior temporo-occipital gyrus/ fusiform gyrus has been associated with rapid visual word recognition (Brambati et al., 2004; Brem et al., 2020; Brown et al., 2001; Kronbichler et al., 2008; Lochy, Van Reybroeck, & Rossion, 2016; Shaywitz et al., 2002; Silani et al., 2005; Simos et al., 2002; Turkeltaub et al., 2002), although its specificity to real words has been challenged as it also seems to be involved with the decoding of pseudowords (Jobard, Crivello, & Tzourio-Mazoyer, 2003; Liu et al., 2021). However, it appears that its functional significance might differ for typical and atypical readers (Brem et al., 2020; Wimmer et al., 2010). Finally, there is a line of work grounding in the brain the automaticity of reading (Joo et al., 2021), which is the hallmark of skilled reading. It has been argued that skilled reading is substantiated by coactivation in the networks for spoken and written language (McCandliss, Cohen, & Dehaene, 2003; Price, 2012).

To summarize, more than fifty years of modern research into the brain machinery underpinning reading, both typical and disordered (Grigorenko et al., 2020), have led to a widely accepted multicomponential neural reading pathway. This is characterized by partial specificity to various psychological aspects of reading (i.e., routing specific components of reading, such as phonological processing and word identification, through different anatomical structures in the brain). It has also highlighted dominant activation in the left hemisphere in typically developing individuals and pointed to the apparent failure for some people to establish the functional left hemisphere network that is essential to support skilled reading (Fletcher et al., 2019). In comparison, poor readers tend to hypoactivate the pathway in the left hemisphere when reading and hyperactivate it in the right hemisphere. There is also a developmental or time-based differentiation of brain involvement, with the effortful sublexical processing being localized to a dorsal (higher) route through the brain from the back of the brain (where visual processing occurs), forward through the middle temporal and inferior parietal regions, and the lexical processing being localized to the ventral (lower) system in the left occipito-temporal region. Finally, a relatively recent stream of studies points to the importance of subcortical structures for reading; it is not only the newest evolutionary portions of the brain that support reading; the older structures, such as basal ganglia and cerebellum (see for details below) are also engaged.

What follows below is a capsule overview of what we consider to be the most notable landmarks of the field of the neurobiology of reading with regard to the dyslexia debate. We are not attempting to provide a comprehensive overview of the field; we are threading through its rich texture to highlight observations that we deem relevant to the existence of dyslexia as a distinct diagnostic category. We comment on both historical and contemporary research to stress the continuity of some, and discontinuity of other, ideas on the structure and function of the "reading brain" and "reading genome."

Postmortem Studies

As noted in Chapter 1, ideas connecting severe reading difficulty to brain functioning (or, more specifically, to unknown brain lesions) were expressed as early as the late nineteenth century (Berlin, 1887; Hinshelwood, 1895). To briefly recap, Berlin (1887) was the first to hypothesize that reading disability originated from some kind of brain lesion. Hinshelwood (1895) stated that the left occipital and parietal lobes were most likely to be the sources of such a lesion. Pringle Morgan (1896) hypothesized the involvement of the angular gyrus located in the posterior part of the inferior parietal lobule, and Hinshelwood (1902) substantiated this hypothesis through an autopsy completed upon a patient he had followed for many years. These early ideas were further developed by Samuel Orton (Orton, 1937), who argued that, given the complexity of reading, brain bases should be thought of as beyond the angular gyrus or even the parietal and occipital lobes to other areas of the brain, primarily in the left hemisphere. Orton (1937) accordingly posited the poor cerebral dominance hypothesis. Although, Orton's specific theory was not generally confirmed, he certainly offered many insightful ideas that have proven to be relevant to the growing understanding of reading in general and reading disability in particular.

The insights of these early clinicians remained mostly just ideas for many decades until the first systematic pieces of evidence started to accumulate.

Thus, Drake (1968) presented an autopsy case of a boy with reading disability who died from a brain hemorrhage caused by a vascular malformation and whose brain contained a series of deviant brain formations in the cortical gyri of the left inferior parietal lobe. These malformations included ectopias – small areas of abnormally placed neurons originating from cortical dysgenesis – in the subcortical white matter of the brain. Capitalizing on Orton's idea and observations from autopsies of "100 adult human brains, obtained at postmortem, and free of significant pathology," Geschwind and Levitsky (1968: 186) stressed the asymmetry of the planum temporale (an associative auditory area located on the upper surface of the superior temporal gyrus, posterior to Heschl's gyrus), which is considered to be important for the formation of language lateralization (Galaburda, 1993; Shapleske, Rossell, & Woodruff, 1999); this structure was larger and longer on the left than on the right in 65 percent of the analyzed brains. Geschwind's disciples (Galaburda et al., 1985) merged both of these observations in postmortem studies of individuals with dyslexia and have reported the symmetry of planum temporale (Galaburda et al., 1985; Humphreys, Kaufmann, & Galaburda, 1990) and the presence of ectopias in the auditory cortex (Galaburda & Kemper, 1979), the lateral (Livingstone et al., 1991) and medial geniculate nuclei (Galaburda, Menard, & Rosen, 1994) of the thalamus, the primary visual cortex (Jenner, Rosen, & Galaburda, 1999), and the cerebellum (Finch, Nicolson, & Fawcett, 2002). Moreover, researchers have reported qualitative differences in some neurons seen in individuals with reading disability as compared to those of normal readers. For example, in various structures of the thalamus, neurons of poor readers have been reported to be smaller, more variable in size and shape, and more disorganized (Galaburda, Schrott, & Sherman, 1996; Livingstone et al., 1991). Of interest is that there have been reports of gender differences in the distributions of ectopias. For example, the brains of poor female readers were reported to have fewer and differently located micro-cortical malformations (Humphreys, Kaufmann, & Galaburda, 1990).

These observations, although collected on small samples of postmortem brain tissue from an individual with a historical diagnosis of dyslexia and the presence of concordant evidence from genetic studies of reading disability, substantiated the hypothesis that reading disability is, at least partially, related to prenatal dysgeneses of the brain caused by deviations in the process of neuronal migration, resulting in the failure of neurons to reach their normal targets. Such dysgeneses, in turn, could be caused by a variety of events, such as ischemic injuries triggered by autoimmune damage of vessel walls, which result in micro-injuries of the cortex, scars, and disrupted blood flow (Galaburda, Schrott, & Sherman, 1996). Importantly, the hypothesis of wronged neuronal migration and its deriva-tives, although central to the field for a while (Galaburda et al., 2006), has been questioned (Guidi et al., 2018). Similarly, researchers have challenged the lack of asymmetry hypothesis (Livingstone et al., 1991) and, in contrast, have provided evidence of an exaggerated leftward asymmetry (Leonard, as cited in Lim & Helpern, 2002). Moreover, when all available planum tem-porale studies were considered, only five reported symmetry or rightward asymmetry of the structure in poor readers (Ramus et al., 2018).

In summary, the field of neuroscience of the "reading brain" started with a handful of postmortem brain studies and, over a period of more than a century, has blossomed into a number of sophisticated, busy, and engaging subfields. Early studies were characterized by many methodo-logical weaknesses (e.g., participants were not well characterized behav-iorally; they and their brains were quite heterogeneous, and the sample sizes were small – typically, from one to only a few donated specimens from individuals with reading disability). Yet, regardless of their many drawbacks and failures to replicate, these studies were revolutionary in their main presumption – all hypothesizing that the root of reading in general, and reading disability in particular, is in the brain. Importantly, though, for the dyslexia debate, these studies do not reveal a brain signa-ture specific to dyslexia and different from any other presentation of poor reading skills.

Studies of Anatomical Structure

Findings from early postmortem studies were a helpful platform to launch the neuroscience of reading when *in vivo* techniques such as anatomi-cal MRI (aMRI) became available. These newer techniques were able to visualize brain structure by examining measures such as gross as well as voxel-by-voxel regional volumes or densities (voxel-based morphometry [VBM]), cortical surface area and thickness, and diffusion tensor imaging (DTI) of white matter structure. The main questions that were asked by this family of studies centered on *what structures* in the brain are engaged in the task of reading and which aspects of these structures matter most.

The use of imaging studies of the "reading brain" *in vivo* has gener-ally confirmed the results of early postmortem studies; they indicated the presence of a number of abnormalities in various brain structures in individuals with reading disability. Summaries of these (Leonard et al., 2001; Ramus et al., 2018) highlight the presence of differences in both global and local brain measurements. At the global level, for example, there may be lower total brain volume and total cortical surface, and reduced whole-brain gyrification. At the local level, examples include a marked rightward cerebral asymmetry, marked leftward asymmetry of the anterior lobe of the cerebellum, combined leftward asymmetry of the planum and posterior ascending ramus of the Sylvian fissure, and a large duplication of Heschl's gyrus. Various abnormalities have been reported in the planum temporale, corpus callosum, and cerebellum. It is important to note that some of these observations do not replicate consistently, possibly due to differences in sample size, age, and quality control over factors such as motion during data acquisition. However, it is clear that there are some anatomic group differences when the brains of individuals with and without reading disabilities are compared, and these cannot be ignored.

i.   Anatomical Magnetic Resonance Imaging (aMRI)

Planum temporale. A substantial body of research has extended findings from postmortem studies of the planum temporale. Individuals with reading disability, as a group, tend to demonstrate less leftward and more rightward asymmetry (Hynd et al., 1990; Larsen et al., 1990; Rumsey et al., 1997). Yet, not all studies indicate the presence of symmetry or divergent asymmetry (Heiervang et al., 2000). Moreover, there are reports that whereas the right planum temporale may be similar, the left one can be smaller in individuals with reading disability compared to typical readers (Hugdahl et al., 2003). There have also been reports of extreme leftward asymmetry of the planum temporale (Chiarello et al., 2006). Deviations from the patterns of symmetry and asymmetry have been observed in samples of individuals with reading disability not only for the planum temporale but also for a variety of brain structures and areas (Duara et al., 1991; Habib et al., 1995; Kushch et al., 1993). In order to consider different sources of variance that could explain these inconsistencies, researchers have sometimes stratified the results. Thus, a deviant asymmetry of planum temporale might, in fact, be present but limited to boys (Altarelli et al., 2014) and children at family risk for dyslexia (Vanderauwera et al., 2016). Yet, as the meaning and function of the potential impact of a deviant planum temporale asymmetry has not been understood, neither has the heterogeneous pattern of the relevant results.

Corpus callosum. Relatively few MRI studies have compared the size and shape or structure of the corpus callosum between individuals with and without reading disability. These studies are, at least in part, driven by the assumption that the processing of phonological stimuli requires the transfer of information across this brain structure (Badzakova-Trajkov, Hamm, & Waldie, 2005). While defective callosal transfer has been reported in poor readers (Fabbro et al., 2001), findings from other studies have proven to be contradictory (Beaton, 1997). Specifically, some researchers have reported a larger corpus callosum in poor readers (Duara et al., 1991; Robichon & Habib, 1998; Rumsey et al., 1996), whereas others have found it to be smaller (Hynd et al., 1995; Larsen, Hoien, & Odegaard, 1992; von Plessen et al., 2002), or have observed no differences (Casanova et al., 2004). Commenting on the discordancy of the results obtained with different methods of neuroimaging, in particular, on the evidence of a larger corpus callosum and its structural white matter anomalies (Dougherty et al., 2007; Frye et al., 2008; Hasan et al., 2012; Sihvonen et al., 2021), Kershner (2019) suggested that the accelerated or shortened period of plasticity of the structure as manifested in the early onset of myelination might result in poor prospects of reading acquisition.

Cerebellum. Similar types of comparison between poor and typical readers have focused on differences in the cerebellum. Here, results appear to be convergent (Casanova et al., 2004; Eckert et al., 2003; Kronbichler et al., 2008; Leonard et al., 2001; Middleton & Strick, 1997; Schmahmann & Pandya, 1997), although some studies do not support the cerebellar abnormality in reading disability (Ashburn et al., 2020). The consensus is that for those with reading disability, the right anterior lobes of the cerebellum, the bilateral pars triangularis, and total brain volume are often smaller (Eckert et al., 2003) and demonstrate gray matter volume reduction (Eckert et al., 2005). Moreover, children with reading disability can demonstrate smaller rightward cerebellar hemisphere asymmetry (Kibby et al., 2008). Given the critical role of the cerebellum in the reading network (Hoeft et al., 2011; Kujala et al., 2007; Stoodley & Stein, 2013) and the reported differences in its functional connectivity with the right parietal cortex in poor compared to typical readers (H. Li et al., 2020), its structural abnormalities appear to be highly relevant for understanding the role of the cerebellum in the acquisition of reading in general, and poor reading in particular. Although there are clues as to how the cerebellum might contribute to early reading prior to, and at the stage of, acquisition (Nicolson, Fawcett, & Dean, 2001a, 2001b), and longitudinally (Borchers et al., 2019; Bruckert et al., 2019), there are still important details to uncover the general role of the cerebellum and the specific contributions of its lobules to mastery, automatization, and maintenance of reading as a skill (Li, Kepinska, et al., 2021).

ii. Voxel- and Surface-Based Morphometry

Voxel-based morphometry (VBM) (Ashburner & Friston, 2000), and surface-based morphometry (SBM) (Dale, Fischl, & Sereno, 1999; Fischl, Sereno, & Dale, 1999), are methods of estimating the indices of cortical morphology, chiefly using the data generated by T1-weighted MRI (Goto et al., 2022). VBM is an approach that permits an examination of structural changes in the gray matter (i.e., the amount of the brain mass generated by the neuronal bodies, neuropil, glial cells, and capillaries) and cerebrospinal fluid areas in the context of the entire brain, and also on a voxel-by-voxel basis (Mechelli et al., 2005). Decreased gray matter may reflect a regional decrease in neuronal number or neuropil (Selemon & Goldman-Rakic, 1999). Increased gray matter may reflect the classification of dyslaminations and ectopias of gray matter (Barkovich & Kuzniecky, 2000). VBM is automated and, given its relevant ease of use, has been widely used, with about 100 studies involving individuals with reading difficulties.

Although the results found are quite divergent, they have consistently shown some alterations, both increased and decreased gray matter volume in poor readers. Specifically, alterations have been reported in:

- the left posterior temporal and temporo-parietal regions (Brown et al., 2001);
- the occipito-temporal regions bilaterally (Kronbichler et al., 2008);
- left temporal lobe and the frontal area; left parietal region (Hoeft, Meyler, et al., 2007);
- bilateral fusiform gyrus, the bilateral anterior cerebellum, and the right supramarginal gyrus (Kronbichler et al., 2008);
- both temporal lobes, specifically in the left temporal lobe, in the middle and inferior temporal gyri (Steinbrink et al., 2008; Vinckenbosch, Robichon, & Eliez, 2005);
- bilaterally in the planum temporale, inferior temporal cortex, and cerebellar nuclei (Brambati et al., 2004);
- the left temporal lobe and bilaterally in the temporoparietooccipital juncture, but also the frontal lobe, the caudate, the thalamus, and the cerebellum (Brown et al., 2001);
- the left semilunar lobule of the cerebellum (Eckert et al., 2003);
- the middle frontal gyrus (Xia et al., 2016);
- the right cerebellar anterior lobe, right and left pars triangularis, the left and right lingual gyri, the left inferior parietal lobule, and the cerebellum (Eckert et al., 2005);
- and the right posterior superior parietal lobule, the precuneus, and the right supplementary motor area (Menghini et al., 2008).

However, it is important to note that meta-analytic reviews have reported limited consistency of findings across studies (Eckert et al., 2016; Jednoróg et al., 2015; Liloia et al., 2022; Linkersdörfer et al., 2012; McGrath & Stoodley, 2019; Richlan, Kronbichler, & Wimmer, 2013). There are many design, measurement, and analytical reasons (Ramus et al., 2018) that might explain this lack of convergency. Importantly, there is evidence that gray matter differences might be largely a product of reading experience (Krafnick et al., 2014). Thus, once again, what is apparent is that there is consistent evidence of structural differences that differentiate the brains of struggling readers, if not consistently unidimensionally, then definitely multidimensionally.

Surface-based morphometry is used for the estimation of cortex volume, cortical mantle thickness, and folding across sulci or gyrification (Mills & Tamnes, 2014). The group of studies assessing these parameters is newer and, therefore, not as voluminous as the gray matter volume studies discussed above. Yet, there is a convergence of results indicating a reduction in cortical thickness in language and reading areas in children (Clark et al., 2014; Williams et al., 2018) and adults (Kujala et al., 2021) with reading difficulties. Yet, other studies (Altarelli et al., 2013; Frye et al., 2010; Ma et al., 2015) have produced somewhat incongruent results. Although gyrification studies are limited in number, they are, at least at this point, consistent in their observation of increased gyrification in children with reading difficulties, although specific localizations of these differences vary, covering the left occipito-temporal and left temporo-parietal regions (Im et al., 2016), the left inferior occipito-temporal and left anterior and superior frontal cortices (Williams et al., 2018), and the left lateral temporal and middle frontal regions (Caverzasi et al., 2018). Importantly, although these brain indicators differentiated typical and poor readers, there have been no attempts to appraise whether they will differentiate individuals who might be deemed to have dyslexia from any other poor readers.

iii.   Diffusion Tensor Imaging

Diffusion tensor imaging (DTI) is an MRI technique that permits the visualization (tractography) and characterization of the axonal (white matter) organization of the brain. DTI can provide unique information about the integrity of white matter formations (anisotropy) and connectivity (fiber tracking) in the human brain (Feldman et al., 2010). DTI also permits the derivation of quantitative indicators displaying underlying tissue properties (i.e., mean diffusivity and fractional anisotropy); these indicators can be used to determine both markers for typical and atypical brain maturation (Lim & Helpern, 2002).

DTI is a relatively recent methodological development that has not been widely used in the field of reading disabilities. However, relevant studies are now increasingly being reported (Vandermosten, Boets, Wouters, et al., 2012). DTI has been used both to reveal and access the connection between individual differences in the microstructure of white matter and individual differences in various reading indicators. In general, such studies have shown an association between lower anisotropy coherence and lower performance scores on various reading-related tasks both in typical and disabled readers (Beaulieu et al., 2005; Christodoulou et al., 2017; Deutsch et al., 2005; Hoeft et al., 2011; Klingberg et al., 1999; Niogi & McCandliss, 2006). Specifically, white matter alterations in left-lateralized language areas, particularly in the arcuate fasciculus (a bundle of axons that connects the temporal cortex and inferior parietal cortex to locations in the frontal lobe in general and Broca's and Wernicke's areas in particular), have been reliably observed in children (Langer et al., 2017) and adults (Vandermosten, Boets, Poelmans, et al., 2012) with reading disability. The arcuate connects the back of the reading network (mapping language sounds onto their written counterparts) to the frontal regions (reading fluency and comprehension). However, findings have been somewhat inconsistent; for example, in one study (Andrews et al., 2010), a positive association was registered between fractional anisotropy of the corpus callosum and reading and reading-related scores, although in another study (Dougherty et al., 2007), the relationship proved negative. When originally subjected to meta-analysis (Vandermosten, Boets, Wouters, et al., 2012), these studies pointed to decreased fractional anisotropy around the left temporo-parietal junction of poor readers. However, the most recent meta-analysis with enhanced methodology failed to replicate these findings and reported no reliable group differences in white matter (Moreau et al., 2018).

In addition to highlighting sources of the group differences between typical and atypical readers, DTI studies have delineated major white matter pathways that appear to be important in the acquisition of reading skills: the superior corona radiata, the corpus callosum (Hasan et al., 2012), and the superior longitudinal fasciculus (Ben-Shachar, Dougherty, & Wandell, 2007). In more recent studies, it has become customary to analyze fractional anisotropy, not only averaged across an entire tract (as sampled above) but all along the tract length, focusing on limited portions of the track and recording group differences locally, even if there is no signal across the track globally (Wang et al., 2017). There have also been attempts to combine tractography with region-of-interest analyses to identify specific hot spots in the brain that might drive the correlations between fractional anisotropy and specific reading skills. For example, one study has associated single-word identification scores with indicators of fractional anisotropy of the superior corona radiata (Beaulieu et al., 2005). Though interesting, this finding has been challenged (Keller & Just, 2009; Yeatman et al., 2009); yet this brain structure continues to be featured in the literature, stressing its role in typical and atypical reading acquisition (Cui et al., 2016; Lebel et al., 2019).

Importantly, white matter development and myelination appear to be experience-sensitive; the requirements can change as specific tracks are used at high(er) frequencies and intensity (Fields, 2008; Mattson, 2002). In this context, of particular interest is a study in which micro changes in the white matter (specifically, significantly increased fractional anisotropy in a region of the left anterior centrum semiovale) were documented in poor readers aged between 8 and 10 years, whose phonological decoding skills had improved after 100 hours of intensive remedial instruction (Keller & Just, 2009). Similarly, white matter changes associated with receiving reading intervention have been reported by various intervention studies (Gebauer et al., 2012; Hofstetter, Friedmann, & Assaf, 2017).

In brief, DTI studies generally demonstrate lower fractional anisotropy values in left temporo-parietal and frontal areas in poor readers. The localization of these regions is being debated, with most studies pointing to the left superior longitudinal fasciculus and corona radiata and rather fewer to the posterior part of the corpus callosum or to more ventral tracts such as the inferior longitudinal fasciculus or the inferior fronto-occipital fasciculus (Vandermosten, Boets, Wouters, et al., 2012). Interpreting DTI findings, Gabrieli (2009) has suggested that in the case of reading disability, there is a lack of balance in the white-matter pathways supporting reading; in fact, they appear to project too weakly within the primary reading network (thus, hypoactivation of the left hemisphere components of the network) and too strongly between hemispheres (thus, hyperactivation of the right hemisphere components of the network). As this technique is still relatively new, glaring differences in its application and a lack of common standards might explain the variability of the results today. Moreover, fractional anisotropy has recently been criticized with regard to its accuracy in presenting diffusion and a different indicator, quantitative anisotropy, has been preferentially featured (Yeh et al., 2016). As a result of these methodological issues, rigorous meta-analyses integrating sufficiently comparable data are not available. Thus, the question of the reproducibility of the reported findings is still open. Yet, despite related theoretical, methodological, and implementational difficulties, the emerging picture from this area of work indicates that reading disability is a neurodevelopmental condition that involves the detachment of brain structure and function. Furthermore, there is growing evidence that the growth of reading skills is accompanied by substantial alterations of white track tractography (Cheema & Cummine, 2018); these changes might serve as indicators and biological bases of the emergence of the "reading brain." Importantly, although there is strengthening evidence for the white-matter differentiation of "reading" and "nonreading" (or deficiently reading) brains, there is currently no evidence for subtyping "nonreading" brains into dyslexia- and non-dyslexia brains.

Studies of Brain Function

Functional imaging is a type of brain imaging aimed at detecting or registering changes in metabolism, blood flow, or regional chemical composition. In contrast to structural or anatomical imaging, as discussed above, functional imaging shows changes in the brain in real-time when it is not doing anything or when it is engaged in specific cognitive activities such as reading. There are multiple types of functional imaging, and only some of them can be discussed here. Although they are based on different technologies and different assumptions, these methods explore two key questions:

1. *how* brain structures support reading and;
2. *how* different cognitive processes that contribute to reading are enacted by the brain.

Reading researchers are interested in functional imaging because it can provide valuable data to inform debates about theories of reading disability. This includes factors related to phonological, visual, and cerebellar theories, which, among others, were sampled in Chapter 2 and will be considered here only briefly. We will also make references to integrative theories, such as dual-route theory (Coltheart et al., 2001) and connectionist theory (Plaut et al., 1996). It is noteworthy, however, to acknowledge both the important and organizing role of other theories, in studies of brain functioning, such as the multiple route model (Grainger et al., 2012) and the grain size hypothesis (Ziegler & Goswami, 2005).

As noted in Chapter 2, the major thrust of *phonological theories* of reading disability is that the central deficit is related to both the quality of, and access to, phonemic information (Ramus, 2004) as it is processed by and stored in the left superior temporal and inferior frontal cortex, or perhaps even in the whole temporoparietal region including the posterior superior temporal and the inferior parietal region (Bach et al., 2010; Dufor et al., 2007; Jobard, Crivello, & Tzourio-Mazoyer, 2003). Specifically, numerous studies have pointed to an impairment of left posterior brain systems that are known to be involved in the cross-modal integration of auditory and visual information and, thus, affect the realization of connections between occipito-temporal and temporo-parietal circuits (Shaywitz & Shaywitz, 2008). When poor readers perform phonological tasks, these posterior systems often exhibit reduced or absent activation. These deficient patterns of activation could either be genuine, that is, first-order deficits, or derivative, that is, second-order deficits resulting from impairments in auditory processing, which could thwart the acquisition of the phoneme–grapheme maps that are essential for the development of accurate and efficient reading skills (Stein, 2023). Relatedly, as the brain needs to learn how to link graphemes to phonemes, it is important to understand when this learning is unfolding in the brain. There is some evidence that the neural bases of reading, specifically its grapho-phonological route, have already begun to be shaped in the left hemisphere in early childhood (5–7 years of age) in typically developing children (Mathur, Schultz, & Wang, 2020; Weiss, Cweigenberg, & Booth, 2018) with a delay, and primarily bilaterally, in children with later-emerging reading difficulties (Yamada et al., 2011). Importantly, phonology-related brain indicators have been argued to be, at maximum, a better predictor of reading skills than behavioral measures (Maurer et al., 2009; Wang, Joanisse, & Booth, 2020) or, at minimum, are able to increase predictive power when combined with behavioral measures (Kuhl et al., 2020; Wang et al., 2021), both concurrently and longitudinally.

As discussed at length in Chapter 2, the central assumption of one of the most popular visual theories of reading disabilities (Stein, 2022a) rests on the presupposition of the existence of low-level visual disorders related to deficiencies in the thalamic magnocellular system (Stein, 2019). These are manifested as increased thresholds for the detection of low contrast, low spatial, or higher temporal frequencies, poor sensitivity to visual motion, and jeopardized capacity for directing attention, performing eye movements, and conducting a visual search and visual segregation (Livingstone et al., 1991; Lovegrove et al., 1980; Ronconi, Melcher, & Franchin, 2020; Stein & Walsh, 1997). With regard to the magnocellular and other visual deficit theories of dyslexia (Lawton, 2016; Taskov & Dushanova, 2020; Vidyasagar, 2019), studies of different aspects of visual processing in reading have pointed to the involvement, for primary lower-level deficits, of the retina, the thalamus (lateral geniculate nuclei), the primary visual cortex, dorsal visual areas which receive magnocellular inputs (Demb, Boynton, Best, et al., 1998; Demb, Boynton, & Heeger, 1998; Pegado et al., 2014); and, for secondary higher-level deficits, of the inferior-temporal cortex, angular or supramarginal gyri and inferior frontal gyrus (Hoeft, Meyler et al., 2007; Horowitz-Kraus et al., 2014; Paulesu et al., 2001; Pugh et al., 2000; Taran et al., 2022).

The main idea underlying the *cerebellar hypothesis* is that dyslexia is a type of general learning disorder that is characterized by impaired automatization of sensory-motor procedures critical to reading but also to writing (Nicolson, Fawcett, & Dean, 2001a, 2001b). The neuronal substrate of these impairments is related to abnormal structure and function in the lateral cerebellum (Doyon et al., 2002), as discussed above. A current reincarnation of the cerebellar deficit hypothesis is the "Delayed Neural Commitment" framework (Nicolson & Fawcett, 2019). It proposes that the root of the slower acquisition of reading skills in children with dyslexia is that the assembly of the neural networks that are needed to enable the acquisition of reading takes longer.

While the theories sampled above focus either specifically on reading componental process (e.g., phonological processing) or an anatomical structure (e.g., cerebellum), there is a conversion of evidence on the triangle network substantiating reading in the brain discussed above. The operation of this network (Figure 3.1) is captured by two theories. The first one, the dual-route model, exists in multiple versions (Castles & Coltheart, 1993; Dehaene, 2009), which assert the engagement in reading of two distinct neural processing pathways; these interchangeably "do the work" depending on which one is activated in response to what kind of processing of the written information is needed. Thus, the dorsal sublexical system is responsible for decoding; it is largely phonological and critical for processing novel words. The ventral lexical system is responsible for word identification based on its orthographic patterns; it is largely semantic and critical for processing familiar words. The sublexical system takes time and effort; the lexical system is instantaneous. The more experienced the reader is, the more reliant he or she is on the lexical route and the less on the sublexical rule. The underlying mechanism for the second (connectionist) model is singular (not dual), and the driving force of the network is the exposure to words and text (Seidenberg, Farry-Thorn, & Zevin, 2022). Ongoing training and feedback activate different orthographical patterns and mark them by computational rules that continually change throughout the lifespan. The network continues to learn by exposure to a visual representation, encoding the pronunciation of the word, and receiving feedback on the accuracy of this pronunciation, enhancing the connections between different "sides" of the triangle – orthography, phonology, and semantics.

Functional brain studies of the "reading brain" are intimately related to structural approaches by extending the *what* (i.e., what anatomical structures) question to that of *how* (i.e., how these structures realize reading) as well as to cognitive theories of reading disabilities. This is achieved by probing the cognitive processes theorized to be important for reading disabilities through specific experimental tasks and by targeting specific brain regions thought to be substrates for these processes, or by exploring the activity of the whole brain.

i.   Positron Emission Tomography

Results using positron emission tomography (PET) methodology support the view that the patterns of activation of the brains of poor readers are different to those of typically developing readers. PET registers processes associated with the metabolism and distribution of positron-emitting radionuclide-labeled probes *in vivo*. For example, studies of those with reading disability have reported hypoactivation in the left temporo-parietal region (Rumsey et al., 1992), the left insula (Paulesu et al., 1996), the left occipito-temporal area (McCrory et al., 2005), and the frontal and parietal left hemisphere regions (Dufor et al., 2007). Of note also is a finding that when the right frontal cortex was activated, the activated regions were larger than for controls (Dufor et al., 2007). Compared to MRI and spectroscopy, PET, with its sensitivity, spatial resolution, and time efficiency, is deemed significantly more advantageous (Z. Tan et al., 2022) for the quantification of various parameters (e.g., glucose metabolic rate, protein synthesis rate, gene expression, enzyme activity, and receptor density) related to specific biochemical pathways operating in the brain. However, it is currently not widely used in studies of the reading brain due to its relative expense, its use of radiation and other markers, and the limited availability of expertise.

ii.   Functional Magnetic Resonance Imaging

Functional magnetic resonance imaging (fMRI) is a specialized subtype of MRI used to assess changes in blood flow associated with brain neural activity. Since the early 1990s, fMRI has come to dominate the brain mapping field in general, and the field of reading in particular, due to its relatively low invasiveness, relatively high availability, absence of radiation exposure, and the lack of any need to inject special tracking chemicals.

fMRI has been employed in a variety of studies of reading. First, it has been utilized to evaluate hypotheses concerning the cortical machinery substantiating typical reading (Schlaggar & McCandliss, 2007) and reading acquisition (Dehaene et al., 2015). Importantly, as the technological and methodological sophistication of fMRI grows, so does the field's capacity to refine the precision of the brain reading maps (Caffarra et al., 2021). Second, it has been used to compare this machinery in typical and poor readers to elucidate the specificity of processing reading stimuli in reading disability (Corina et al., 2001; Eden et al., 1996; Georgiewa et al., 1999; Hoeft et al., 2006; Temple et al., 2001). Third, it has been used as a source of information about brain plasticity. This has been evaluated with regard to:

a. normative developmental changes throughout the process of reading acquisition in different languages (Chyl et al., 2021; Feng et al., 2022; Nathaniel et al., 2022);
b. comparative studies of literate and illiterate adults in alphabetic and nonalphabetic orthographies (Brice et al., 2021; Hervais-Adelman et al., 2022; Rueckl et al., 2015), and;
c. changes that result from the introduction of specialized intervention programs (Perdue et al., 2022).

Whereas studies in groups (a) and (b) have constantly been expanding to languages "other than English", correcting the early Anglocentricity of the field (Share, 2008) and differentiating orthography-general and -specific changes in the brain during reading acquisition, studies in group (c) are still predominantly English-based, and the vast majority of studies focus on monolinguals, which are estimated to be less than half of the world population (Grosjean, 2021).

Importantly, the applications of fMRI in the field of reading can be subdivided into studies that focus specifically on reading-related processes and those that focus on more general cognitive processes that are known to be related to reading. The former studies emerged earlier and dominated related literature in the early twenty-first century. The latter studies have emerged fairly recently and are currently a "new wave" in the field.

fMRI studies specifically focusing on reading-related processes initially focused on normative development. Thus, the approach has been utilized in studies of literate adults to register and specify the involvement of the superior temporal cortex (superior temporal gyrus/superior temporal sulcus) and auditory cortex (Heschl sulcus/planum temporale) in the integration of letters and speech sounds (Hervais-Adelman et al., 2022; Raij, Uutela, &

Hari, 2000; Rueckl et al., 2015; van Atteveldt et al., 2004). These findings have been informed by studies that have included adults with reading disability who were hypothesized to differ from controls in letter–sound integration (Blau et al., 2009; Holloway et al., 2015). Consistent with this, the results demonstrated that poor readers under-activate the superior temporal gyrus for the integration of passively presented letter–speech sound stimuli. Behaviorally, this reduced integration was directly associated with reduced auditory processing of speech sounds, which, in turn, was associated with poorer performance on phonological tasks (Blau et al., 2009). Congruent phonological and visual representations complement each other, forming the basis for the effectiveness and efficiency of visual word recognition (Kast et al., 2011; Raij, Uutela, & Hari, 2000). Findings from pediatric studies substantiate these observations demonstrating that for children with reading disability, there is evidence of hypoactivation in the perisylvian cortex and occipito-temporal gyri (Cao et al., 2006; Shaywitz et al., 2002; Temple et al., 2001), and, more specifically, the planum temporale/Heschl sulcus and the superior temporal sulcus (Blau et al., 2010). This is coupled with, in many but not all instances, deviant patterns of activation in the frontal cortex (Gabrieli, 2009; Maisog et al., 2008). Furthermore, a whole-brain analysis (Blau et al., 2010) of unisensory visual and auditory group differences revealed diminished unisensory responses to letters in the fusiform gyrus in children with reading disabilities, as well as reduced activity for processing speech sounds in the anterior superior temporal gyrus, planum temporale/Heschl sulcus and superior temporal sulcus. These effects are statistically significant and substantial; indicators of the neural integration of letters and speech sounds in the planum temporale/Heschl sulcus, and indicators of the neural response to letters in the fusiform gyrus collectively explained almost 40 percent of the variance in the reading performance of participating children. Moreover, in a longitudinal study of children in first and second grades, it was observed that audiovisual integration processing of letters from the pre-reading to the early reading stage was substantiated by increased activation in the left superior temporal gyrus, inferior frontal gyrus, and ventral occipitotemporal cortex (Karipidis et al., 2021). Consequently, dysfunction in integrating orthographic (letter) and phonological (sound) information into a unified audiovisual gestalt has been identified as an essential contributor to reading difficulties both in alphabetic (Blau et al., 2010; McNorgan, Randazzo-Wagner, & Booth, 2013; van Atteveldt et al., 2004) and logographic (Yang et al., 2020) languages.

There are currently hundreds of fMRI studies of reading, the majority of which, unless published by the same group, do not overlap much in terms of their theoretical platforms, their characterization of groups of typical and poor readers, their experimental tasks, and their analytical tools. Nevertheless, regardless of their methodological and theoretical differences, studies of both children and adults provide consistent evidence that individuals with reading difficulties, however this term is defined and quantified, possess a deficient functional profile of the left posterior brain system. The essence of this deficiency is unclear but could be reflective of disruptions in either the structure of, or the connections between, the dorsal and ventral (see Figure 3.1) routes for reading (Brunswick et al., 1999; Démonet, Taylor, & Chaix, 2004; Helenius et al., 1999; Paulesu et al., 2001; Salmelin et al., 1996; Shaywitz et al., 1998; Simos, Breier, Fletcher, et al., 2000; Simos, Breier, Wheless, et al., 2000). Of note is that, as a group, individuals with reading disability are characterized by a shift in the pattern of activities which, in conjunction with specific characteristics of a given study, can be defined as overbalanced towards the more anterior left regions or right temporal and perisylvian regions of the brain (Brunswick et al., 1999; Démonet, Taylor, & Chaix, 2004; Georgiewa et al., 2002; Shaywitz et al., 2002; Shaywitz et al., 1998; Simos, Breier, Fletcher, et al., 2000). Although the general definition of the brain system underlying reading appears to be solid, there is an ongoing desire to differentiate the system with regard to multiple conditionals, such as reading single words versus reading sentences (Acunzo, Low, & Fairhall, 2022) and reading word and pseudowords (Ekert et al., 2021).

The mosaic of findings from these studies has been summarized in a number of meta-analyses. Although there is convergence on the importance of the occipito-temporal and temporo-parietal regions, the specifics of the roles of the inferior frontal gyrus and the angular gyrus are still being questioned, as the evidence for the involvement of these structures is much less consistent (Fletcher et al., 2019). One issue is that it is unclear whether and when the inferior frontal gyrus is under- or over-activated in poor readers. Even more ambiguous is the role of the angular gyrus in reading. Here we present a summary of major highlights from these studies. The most robust finding for an early meta-analysis of PET and fMRI studies with adults categorized as dyslexic and typical (Maisog et al., 2008) concerned evidence of reduced activation in the left occipito-temporal region, specifically the fusiform gyrus (the visual form area). The next meta-analysis (Richlan, Kronbichler, & Wimmer, 2011) included both adults and children with and without reading disability. Across all ages, struggling readers once again, demonstrated reduced activation in the left occipito-temporal region, among other observations. A subsequent meta-analytic study (Paulesu, Danelli, & Berlingeri, 2014) supported the previous summative results (Maisog et al., 2008) regarding evidence of underactivation in the ventral left occipito-temporal and dorsal left temporo-parietal regions in individuals with dyslexia. Pollack, Luk, and Christodoulou's (2015) meta-analysis reported different spatial patterns of activation for typical and atypical reader groups. Specifically, although the typical readers showed activation in the left hemisphere network (left frontal and temporal lobe components), those with reading disability demonstrated more bilateral patterns for these structures. Martin and colleagues (Martin, Kronbichler, & Richlan, 2016) considered the generalizability of these observations to various types of orthographies, namely opaque or deep and transparent or shallow (see below for more detail). Importantly, although the engagement of reading-related anatomical structures was constant across the two groups of languages, underactivation was greater in the opaque orthographies. Generalizing from these summative reflections on the field, there is convincing evidence of a failure to establish the effective and efficient left hemisphere network which serves as the brain foundation of reading. There is also convincing evidence that the faulty network can originate from multiple causes, acting individually and in accord.

There is a "new wave" of studies that have begun to expand beyond a focus on reading-related regions of the brain to other brain networks. Instead of focusing on domain-specific regions associated with language, this research focuses on the organization and function of domain-general functional brain networks, that is, the so-called control regions that are recruited independently of task or modality and involve a widespread network including the lateral prefrontal cortex, anterior insula/frontal operculum, posterior parietal cortex, and dorsal anterior cingulate cortex/ pre-supplementary motor area (Dosenbach et al., 2008; Duncan, 2010; Power & Petersen, 2013). Recent studies have demonstrated that:

1. the characteristics of the engagement of these networks correlated with performance on reading tasks (Jolles et al., 2020);
2. reading-related change over time also involves changes in these nonreading networks, possibly related to the maturation of controlled attention, or reflecting a change in effort or motivation over time (Aboud, Barquero, & Cutting, 2018; Hoeft et al., 2011; Nugiel et al., 2019).

Importantly, as noted by Church, Grigorenko, and Fletcher (2021), the engagement of these additional brain regions in the reading process varies with regard to the type of reading task being studied; thus, reading comprehension tasks appear to be more likely than other reading tasks to engage the brain's cognitive control regions (Aboud et al., 2016; Meyler et al., 2007; Patael et al., 2018; Roe et al., 2018). Moreover (Church, Grigorenko, & Fletcher, 2021), differences in the engagement of these nonreading networks between struggling and non-struggling readers, or in struggling readers over time, are apparent only during reading tasks; cognitive control tasks that do not require reading do not differentiate good and poor readers (Nugiel et al., 2019; Roe et al., 2018).

The discussion above has focused primarily on the task-based approach when brain activation and functional connectivity of the various brain structures are evaluated while participants complete reading or reading-related tasks. Although burgeoning in the late twentieth and early twenty-first centuries, task-based functional neuroimaging work has slowed down somewhat, in part because there is no consensus regarding the types of tasks that are optimal for characterizing brain networks for reading and, correspondingly, an understanding of possible biases introduced by different tasks. Thus, observations of group differences in task-based fMRI findings can be confounded with behavioral differences in performance on the task utilized; this, in turn, makes it difficult to differentiate between the cause and effect of these differences or the mechanisms that account for group differences (Cross et al., 2021). A promising alternative to task-based assessment is evaluating functional networks while participants are in a resting state. As it is task-free, the neuroimaging data cannot be influenced by any particular task demands, differences in task performance, or differences in cognitive processing strategies. Resting-state (task-free) functional connectivity (RSFC) is an fMRI technique used to evaluate temporal correlations in the low-frequency fluctuations (<0.1 Hz) in the blood oxygenation-level-dependent (BOLD) signal of functionally related brain areas (Biswal et al., 1995); it is advantageous for the examination of neural networks implicated in reading across ages as it is thought to be organized in a way that reflects the brain's functional networks (Fox & Raichle, 2007). It is assumed that functionally related regions tend to be temporally positively correlated, whereas the unrelated regions tend to have weakly or negatively correlated BOLD in terms of their spontaneous BOLD activity. RSFC has been used in the field of reading for a relatively short period. The main observation from this research is that networks of functional connectivity align closely between task-based and task-free fMRI data (Cross et al., 2021; Koyama et al., 2010). Another important conclusion pertains to RSFC-based differences between typical and poor readers. In general, as observed (Cross et al., 2021) in individuals with reading disabilities, RSFC is characterized by reduced connectivity between:

1. the left and right inferior frontal gyri (Farris et al., 2011);
2. the left intraparietal sulcus and left middle frontal gyrus (Finn et al., 2014; Koyama et al., 2013); and
3. the left inferior gyrus and left posterior temporal areas including the fusiform gyrus, and inferior, middle, and superior temporal gyri (Schurz et al., 2015).

Individuals with reading difficulties have also demonstrated differences in connectivity among other brain networks, including decreased RSFC from visual networks to executive function and attention networks (Horowitz-Kraus et al., 2015) and increased RSFC between regions associated with reading and areas of the default mode network, particularly the precuneus (Schurz et al., 2015). Importantly, the results suggest that although reading subskills rely to some extent on shared functional networks, there are also distinct functional connections supporting different components of reading ability in children (Cross et al., 2021). More specifically, as per this study, RSFC from the left thalamus to the right fusiform gyrus positively correlated with performance on sight word reading, reading comprehension, and rapid naming tasks, indicating that this functional network contributes to the performance of all these reading skills. In contrast, specific RSFC-task associations were registered for phonemic decoding, that is, decoding efficiency was uniquely related to increased RSFC from the left precentral gyrus to bilateral parietal and frontal regions. Negative RSFC-behavior associations were also registered for decoding efficiency, rapid naming, and reading comprehension tasks; this might be related to the functional segregation of attentional networks and reading-related regions, which occurs along with the improvement of reading skills.

It is important to note that the overwhelming majority of fMRI studies of reading disabilities draw upon and support the phonological deficit hypothesis. Studies that are underpinned by theoretical approaches that assume the presence of visual magnocellular deficit or auditory rate processing and cerebellar deficiencies are few, especially among children. It is also important to note that fMRI technology and the data acquired with this technology have permitted the generation of new theories, such as the neural noise hypothesis (Hancock, Pugh, & Hoeft, 2017). According to this theory, an excessive amount of neural noise (i.e., stochastic variability in the neural response to repeated presentations of the same stimulus) impairs the power of neurons and their assemblies to stabilize and maintain consistent patterns of activity, challenging the formation and maintenance of representations. Although of interest due to its capacity to provide a single umbrella for highly heterogeneous types of deficits present in a specific reading disability, this theory is far from being explored in detail experimentally, and when it has, it has been questioned (Y. Tan et al., 2022). There is also a growing line of research focusing on the emergence of the reading brain developmentally and its assembly from the areas of the brain that are functionally polynomial. Thus, it has been observed that specific brain responses to printed words are absent prior to the acquisition of reading but become first registrable and then more pronounced in beginning readers (Feng et al., 2022). Although these responses are spread throughout the brain (see Figure 3.1), of particular developmental interest are the sectors of the ventral visual cortex that become specialized for words and faces, differentiating both the anatomy of this part of the brain and its functional connectivity, with its visual word form area extending connections to the left-hemispheric spoken language areas, and the fusiform face area to the contralateral region and the amygdalae. These and many other observations form the foundation of the view that reading acquisition occurs through the recycling of a pre-existing but plastic circuit, whose functional specificity arises, in part, through the patterns of its connectivity to other areas of the brain.

Finally, a remarkable accumulation of data since the beginning of the twenty-first century, especially within the last decade, has permitted the formulation of classification and diagnostic approaches based on complex statistical models, both theory-driven, whether frequentist-based or Bayesian (Siegelman et al., 2021; Yan, Perkins, & Cao, 2021), and theory-free, using machine learning approaches (Cui et al., 2016).

iii. Electrophysiological Studies

Studies utilizing electroencephalograms (EEG) permit the gathering of important details by investigating the temporal dimension of cognitive processes as they unfold while dealing with printed symbols. In this context, the spectrum of electroencephalograms has been studied and compared topographically with regard to the mean amplitude in each of five EEG bands (delta, theta, alpha, slow beta, and fast beta) between groups of individuals with reading disabilities and controls. It has been reported that multiple patterns of activity at multiple regions distinguish individuals with and without reading disability. Thus, children with reading problems show increased slow activity (delta and theta) in the frontal and right temporal regions (Arns et al., 2007). Typical readers demonstrated greater theta and beta activation at the left frontal site, while individuals with reading disability showed more right-lateralized activation (Spironelli, Penolazzi, & Angrilli, 2008).

One type of EEG study, event-related potentials (ERP), separately and in combination with fMRI studies, has offered insight into the timing and utilization of various brain structures during the process of reading (Duncan et al., 1994). Most ERP studies are devoted to electrophysiological events (i.e., specific EEG components) such as P300, N400, or mismatch negativity (MMN) that are considered to be informative for understanding the time distribution of the brain response to print. These studies are voluminous and often diverse in their findings. However, they appear to be rather convergent with regard to the following two observations. Patterns of brain activation in individuals with reading disability are characterized by a different time course of network activation compared to normal readers (Grünling et al., 2004; Ligges et al., 2010; Zhang, Riecke, & Bonte, 2021). Moreover, it has been observed that the network activation in the reading disability group is more diffused, while that of the controls is more focused in the dorsal and ventral brain areas.

To illustrate, consider research on the MMN (or mismatch field, MMF, when measured with magnetoencephalography, see below) which has been studied in the context of reading in a variety of languages and with multiple types of participants of different ages (from infancy to late adulthood), with individuals with familial risk for reading difficulties, and with individuals with different developmental disorders, including reading difficulties (Volkmer & Schulte-Körne, 2018). The neural response to a change in repetitive stimulation, that is, the mismatch response, is considered to be a hallmark of central auditory processing; it is conditioned not only by novel (deviant) input but also on a sensory memory trace of the preceding "standard" stimulus (Näätänen, 2001). It has been suggested that individuals with a specific reading disability have a deficit in implicit memory that limits their perceptual learning in repetitive contexts (Jaffe-Dax, Kimel, & Ahissar, 2018; Vicari et al., 2005; Vicari et al., 2003). Reading impairments and familial risk for this have been variously associated with reduced amplitude, later onset, and differential scalp topography of the MMN, although there is a significant amount of variation in the observed associations (Gu & Bi, 2020). When meta-analyzed, the group differences between those with and without reading difficulties are not present in MMN response amplitudes to nonspeech stimuli, but there is a significantly reduced MMN in such individuals in studies that have used speech stimuli (Gu & Bi, 2020). In order to partially resolve the resulting heterogeneity and contribute to the field's understanding of the MMN-reading association, Norton and colleagues (2021) worked with English-speaking kindergarten children oversampled for risk for reading failure, who completed assessments of phonological awareness and rapid automatized naming, and a speech-syllable MMN paradigm. They examined how early and late MMN mean amplitude and laterality were related to these established behavioral predictors of reading skills. They reported that late MMN amplitude was significantly greater in children with typical, compared to low, phonological awareness. In contrast, the laterality of the early and late MMN was significantly different in children with low versus the typical skill of rapid sequential naming. The authors interpreted these findings as suggestive that the amplitude of the MMN may relate to phonological representations and the ability to manipulate them, whereas MMN laterality may reflect differences in brain processes that support the automaticity needed for reading (Norton et al., 2021).

iv.   Magnetoencephalography

Similar to those using EEG and ERP, magnetoencephalography (MEG) studies are able to provide insight into the temporal resolution of brain activity, substantiating reading and reading-related processes. MEG methodologically excels ERP because it permits a reliable distinction between sources in the left and right auditory cortices and the separation of functionally distinct processes that may indicate different levels of maturation in the developing brain (Hämäläinen et al., 1993). MEG studies (e.g., Destokya et al., 2022; Lizarazu, Lallier, et al., 2021; Lizarazu, Scotto di Covella, et al., 2021; Mittag et al., 2021; Nora et al., 2021; Paul et al., 2006; Salmelin et al., 1996; Simos et al., 2011; Thiede et al., 2020; Vourkas et al., 2011) have also demonstrated that poor readers utilize a different pathway while processing printed and spoken stimuli which, compared to controls, is altered. For reading, this involves:

a.   the activated brain structures (in comparison with controls, poor readers activate structures in the right hemisphere more often, and in the left hemisphere less often);

b.   the intensity of activation (poor readers demonstrate hypoactivation in the structures of the left hemisphere and hyperactivation in the structures of the right hemisphere);

c.   the time course of the activation;

and, for speech, this involves:

d. poor brain-speech synchronization (poor readers demonstrate over/ under-synchronization to speech over/under-taxing the brain while processing speech).

Regarding the latter, MEG-based technology is particularly popular for interrogating the temporal sampling (TS) theory (Goswami, 2015). This theory has been developed to summarize a diverse literature on reading acquisition and provide a coherent sensory, neural, and developmental framework to explain how phonological representations for words arise from automatic sensory and neural processes that are active from infancy, but its verification by empirical studies has produced contradictory observations (Lizarazu, Scotto di Covella, et al., 2021).

Different MEG-based event-related field (ERF) components have been identified to reflect the stages of phonological, morphological, semantic, and syntactic processes in adults and, to some extent, in children. For example, using repetitive auditory stimuli, Beach and colleagues (2022) registered MMF to study mechanisms of neural adaption in typical and disabled adult readers. In concert with the ERP findings, it appears that individuals with reading difficulties are unable to efficiently accumulate and integrate short-term statistical regularities to improve performance while reducing neural processing costs. With regard to morphological processing, MEG studies in English, testing adults and using single words with different morphological complexity, have demonstrated that the early visual N170 response is sensitive to the morphological structure of words (Solomyak & Marantz, 2010; Zweig & Pylkkänen, 2009). Furthermore, ERF responses during visual processing of derivational word forms in comparison to non-derived words in French-speaking (Cavalli et al., 2016) and English-speaking (Solomyak & Marantz, 2010) adults have revealed brain activity differences at 350 ms. Similarly, the important role of derivational morphology has been demonstrated in the early phases of learning to read in both typical and dyslexic children, with no significant group differences registered (Louleli et al., 2022).

v. **Magnetic Resonance Spectroscopy**

Magnetic resonance spectroscopy (MRS) is a noninvasive diagnostic technique that allows the measurement of biochemical changes in the brain in response to an event (e.g., the development of a tumor) or biochemical differences between groups. This technique utilizes the same machinery as conventional MRI (see above) and involves a series of tests that are added to the MRI scan to characterize the chemical metabolism in a particular area of the brain by analyzing the distribution of hydrogen ions (protons). Currently, MRS allows the reliable measurement of such metabolites as amino acids, lipids, lactate, alanine, N-acetyl aspartate, choline, creatine, and myoinositol. To illustrate, for individuals with reading disability, biochemical differences (lower ratios, compared to controls, of choline-containing compounds to N-acetylaspartate) have been found in the left temporoparietal lobe and in the right cerebellum (Rae et al., 1998). In contrast, a different study reported a group of individuals with reading disability who had a lower N-acetylaspartate/choline ratio in the right cerebellar hemisphere along with a higher choline/creatine ratio in the left cerebellar hemisphere (Laycock et al., 2008). There has also been a report of a greater area of elevated brain lactate in the left anterior region (Richards et al., 1999). Similarly, phosphorus-MRS also showed that the phosphomonoester peak area was significantly elevated in a group of individuals with dyslexia, as evidenced by higher phosphomonoester/total phosphorus ratios (Richardson et al., 1997). In addition to group comparisons, there are studies where a correlation is sought between reading skills and metabolite concentration. These studies are very few, yet the published research seems to point to a negative correlation between phonological skills and choline concentration levels in a left temporo-parietal region and negative correlations between phonological skills and choline concentration levels as well as glutamate levels in the medial occipital region, respectively (Bruno et al., 2013; Pugh et al., 2014). These findings are consistent with the hypothesis of an abnormal membrane phospholipid metabolism in individuals with dyslexia (Rae et al., 1998). In short, reading disability appears to be associated with particularities of brain metabolism, but its specific signature has yet to be reliably established. In general, MRS is a technology that permits evaluating *in vivo* the concentration of neurometabolites in specific brain regions. It is rarely used, and yet, there is enough evidence to state that the turnover of metabolites is connected to reading and that it differs in individuals with and without reading difficulties.

vi.   Functional Near Infrared Spectroscopy (fNIRS)

Functional near-infrared spectroscopy, or fNIRS, is a method of neuroimaging that offers a view of brain functioning that is based on blood oxygenation that does not require a large immobile scanner. This optical imaging technique detects changes in how hemoglobin absorbs near-infrared light, typically at wavelengths between 750 and 1,200 nanometers. Specifically, it enables the recording of changes in the concentrations of oxygenated and deoxygenated hemoglobin; such changes are considered to reflect neural activity. Importantly, fNIRS is minimally sensitive to motion, and therefore brain activity in naturalistic, reciprocal, real-time interaction can be more easily examined. This makes the approach highly valuable for studies involving children.

fNIRS has been steadily gaining popularity in the field for use in studies of reading acquisition (Jasińska et al., 2020) and group-comparison studies of typical and impaired readers focusing on specific reading-related processes (Gao et al., 2022; Marks et al., 2022). For example, Marks and colleagues (2022) worked with English-speaking children aged 6–11 years who completed standard literacy assessments as well as an auditory morphological awareness task during fNIRS, which included root (e.g., *PERSON* + al) and derivational (e.g., quick + *LY*) morphology. The results pointed to the multifaceted natures of morphological processing in the brain areas associated both with phonological and semantic processes, as well as those implicated in segmentation and word analyses. Specifically, whole-word, root morpheme, and derivational affix processing all recruited bilateral auditory language processing regions, namely the inferior frontal gyrus and superior temporal gyrus, and demonstrated relative deactivation of posterior brain regions. Interestingly, the two morphological awareness conditions both revealed greater engagement in several hubs of the semantic system (Binder et al., 2009) compared to the whole-word processing control. The authors (Marks et al., 2022: 376) reported differential patterns of activation while processing different morphological structures. Thus, processing free roots triggered greater left temporal activity than whole words, especially in the left middle temporal gyrus, a region previously associated with lexical or semantic retrieval (Binder et al., 2009). Roots also incurred greater activation in the left inferior frontal gyrus and anterior superior temporal gyrus. The inferior frontal gyrus has previously been linked to phonological, semantic, and syntactic processing (Vigneau et al., 2006). More specifically, the ventral aspect of the inferior frontal gyrus (BA 47) is typically associated with complex semantic retrieval analyses, and the more dorsal aspect of the left inferior frontal gyrus (BA 44 and 45) region is typically associated with both phonological (Ip et al., 2019) and morpho-syntactic (Kovelman, Baker, & Petitto, 2008; Skeide & Friederici, 2016) language processes. Activity in the anterior superior temporal gyrus has been previously connected to syntactic complexity (Brennan et al., 2012). It is noteworthy that Arredondo and colleagues (2015) similarly reported inferior frontal gyrus and anterior superior temporal gyrus activation during a morphological judgement task with children. To summarize, the free root morpheme condition relied on brain regions associated with both phono-logical and semantic processes, as well as those implicated in segmentation and word analysis, extending the field's observations on the complexity of the representation in the brain of reading-related componential processes and subprocesses.

fNIRS has also been used for the purpose of understanding the neural underpinnings of learning from storybooks. Piazza et al. (2021) recorded the neural activity of preschool-aged children during joint book reading with an adult experimenter. The researchers observed synchronized neural activity between the child participants during shared book reading and found that neural synchrony between the children in parietal channels was significantly correlated with both the learning of individual words and the overall learning of story content. Specifically, the closer each child's neural time series was to the signature pattern (especially in the parie-tal cortex), the better they learned new words introduced throughout the story. Thus, this study offers insight into the importance of joint book reading with an adult as the processing of modeling an ideal neural signa-ture for learning new words. These results are substantiated by evidence indicating that richer shared reading experience in infants conditions the developing brain by strengthening predictive signals and, in turn, by stim-ulating expressive vocabulary acquisition (Wang, Tzeng, & Aslin, 2022). In bilingual children, this triggered significant changes to early bilingual prefrontal cortex function for cognitive control language processing (C. Li et al., 2020). Finally, and importantly, fNIRS is relatively mobile and per-mits researchers to conduct their studies in schools, thus enabling greater participation than when they are reliant upon volunteers visiting MRI research centers.

Training and Intervention Studies

Imaging approaches have been employed to examine the impact of vari-ous interventions to remediate reading disabilities on brain functioning. During the early twenty-first century, fMRI, MEG, and EEG methodolo-gies have all been used to track changes in the patterns of brain activation and to correlate these changes with those occurring at the behavioral level. For example, fMRI has been used to track changes in the patterns of brain activation and to correlate these changes with those occurring at the behav-ioral level (Aylward et al., 2003; Farris et al., 2016; Gebauer et al., 2012; Heim et al., 2015; Horowitz-Kraus et al., 2014; Lovett et al., 2017; Nugiel et al., 2019; Odegard et al., 2008; Partanen, Siegel, & Giaschi, 2019; Richards et al., 2007; Richards, Aylward, Berninger, et al., 2006; Richards, Aylward, Field, et al., 2006; Roe et al., 2018), as have MEG (Simos et al., 2002; Simos et al., 2007), and EEG (Molfese, Fletcher, & Denton, 2013; Bedo et al., 2021; Okumura, Kita, & Inagaki, 2017). Specifically, these studies have tracked the cerebral correlates of linguistic performance sampled through various reading-related componential processes longitudinally by assessing them prior to, after, and in some cases, during training protocols. This literature has been systematically reviewed, and the intervention impact on the brain has been meta-analyzed (Barquero, Davis, & Cutting, 2014; Perdue et al., 2022); although the former analysis captured some convergence in the studies published at that time while the latter did not.

All these fMRI studies have shown consistent behavioral improvement in reading and reading-related skills with significant plastic reorganization reported in the typical reading network, namely, the left temporoparietal-occipital regions (Aylward et al., 2003; Shaywitz et al., 2004; Simos et al., 2002; Temple et al., 2003), the left anterior brain regions, such as the left inferior frontal gyri (Richards & Berninger, 2008; Richards et al., 2000), as well as increased activation in the right hemisphere, most consistently in the inferior frontal gyrus (Partanen, Siegel, & Giaschi, 2019; Temple et al., 2003) and subcortical regions. Similarly, the reading intervention has also been associated with changes in functional and structural connectivity in the brain (Horowitz-Kraus et al., 2014; Richards et al., 2016; Richards et al., 2017). Finally, there is evidence that intervention is associated with structural brain changes, although the corresponding literature is quite limited, with regard to research into both white (Davis et al., 2010; Huber et al., 2018; Richards et al., 2018) and gray matter structure (Krafnick et al., 2011; Romeo et al., 2018).

To illustrate, in a recent study, Partanen and colleagues (2019) examined changes in brain activation related to school-based intervention with a printed word rhyming task and a spelling judgement task. Children with poor reading skills showed greater activation following school-based intervention than at pre-intervention scanning during the printed word rhyming task in the bilateral insula and the inferior frontal gyrus. In addition, compared to typical readers, there was greater activation in the right parietal cortex for easy (more frequent) words, and activation in that region was positively associated with improvement in nonword decoding. No effects were observed during the spelling judgement task. Thus, the skills gained in this intervention appeared to primarily affect phonological skills and associated neural circuitry and may not generalize to orthographic knowledge and recognition of irregularly spelled words.

The literature has shown that progress resulting from interventions geared to improving the accuracy and fluency of reading can be coupled with cortical plastic reorganization (Penolazzi et al., 2010; Shaywitz & Shaywitz, 2008; Temple et al., 2003; Tressoldi, Lonciari, & Vio, 2000), although the magnitude and sustainability of these changes are not yet clear. Moreover, we have yet to determine whether the observed behavior changes are due to cortical reorganization or whether indicators of such organization are merely correlates of these behavioral changes that are driven by something else. Importantly, in combination with longitudinal imaging studies, intervention studies provide insights into the windows of natural plasticity for reading and reading intervention and stress the importance of early intervention in the first years of primary school (Phan et al., 2021).

A primary focus of current research is upon gaining greater understanding of the meaning and labeling of changes in the brain that are associated with, or generated by, evidence-based reading interventions. To date, such changes remain unclear and further empirical research on a significantly larger scale is needed (Perdue et al., 2022). Two putative mechanisms by which individuals improve at the neurobiological level have been labeled "compensation" and "normalization." Compensation concerns adjustment for dysfunction of the left-hemisphere reading system with increased activation during reading-related tasks in regions associated with domain-general cognitive processing, including right hemisphere and frontal and subcortical structures (D'Mello & Gabrieli, 2018). To help overcome reading difficulties, compensation might rely (or overly rely) on one or a combination of cognitive processes such as working memory, attention, articulatory mechanisms, and declarative memory (D'Mello & Gabrieli, 2018). In contrast, normalization is signified by increased activation in the "typical" reading network, which is thought to indicate engagement of typical reading strategies via phonological decoding and/or rapid word recognition (Barquero, Davis, & Cutting, 2014; D'Mello & Gabrieli, 2018).

An alternative perspective emphasizes the systemic adjustment of the reading brain. This implies the retuning of the connections among brain regions leading to an enhancement of some and a reduction of others (Cheema et al., 2021; Richards et al., 2016). This conception involves moving away from describing intervention-related brain changes as "normalized" or "compensatory," and instead aiming to characterize the complex interaction of cognitive systems that support improvement in reading (Perdue et al., 2022). Here, the reading brain is seen as a complex self-regulating structure composed of distributed and interactive cognitive, linguistic, and sensory systems that adjust to the challenge of acquiring new skills in general and reading in particular.

Noninvasive Brain Stimulation Techniques

Noninvasive brain stimulation (NIBS) techniques have become increasingly popular across numerous disciplines. These techniques include both transcranial magnetic stimulation (TMS), and transcranial electrical stimulation, for example, transcranial direct current stimulation (tDCS), transcranial random noise stimulation (tRNS), and transcranial alternating current stimulation (tACS) (Vosskuhl, Strüber, & Herrmann, 2018). NIBS are used either in conjunction with various forms of functional neuroimaging to advance the current knowledge about neural networks (Hartwigsen, 2018) and to map neuroplastic after-effects of N intervention (Begemann et al., 2020; Bergmann & Hartwigsen, 2021) or as a neuromodulatory treatment for a wide range of neuropsychiatric and neurological disorders (Schulz, Gerloff, & Hummel, 2013). There are numerous NIBS methods; although not discussed here, there are a number of relevant reviews (Antal et al., 2022; Salehinejad et al., 2022; Vosskuhl, Strüber, & Herrmann, 2018). The following methods, TMS, tDCS, and tACS, are particularly relevant to the literature on reading (see also Chapter 4).

Transcranial magnetic stimulation (TMS) relies on the production of a brief electric high-current pulse through a magnetic coil through which TMS generates a high-intensity magnetic field that causes electrical currents in the underlying brain tissue and thus elicits action potentials in neuronal axons, the release of neurotransmitters at terminal synapses, and hence modulates brain activity (Bestmann, 2008). TMS is used primarily with adults. Studies with children and adolescents use transcranial direct current stimulation (tDCS), which produces weak electrical currents through two electrodes placed on the scalp for a duration of up to thirty minutes, modulating the resting membrane potential of cortical neurons, which either increases or decreases the likelihood of spontaneous or task-evoked neuronal firing (Nitsche & Paulus, 2011). Such modulation may alter neuronal activity and behavior, leading to improvements or deteriorations in task performance. Whereas anodal tDCS (the anode placed over a region of interest) is commonly thought to increase brain activation, cathodal tDCS (the cathode placed over a region of interest) is expected to decrease brain activation in the targeted area. These changes in brain activation are thought to, in turn, map onto the respective behavioral consequences (Krause et al., 2013), although given the overall low focality of tDCS, direct structure–function relationships are hard to establish, especially with respect to the induced behavioral changes (Seibt et al., 2015). Aside from TMS and tDCS, more recent NIBS approaches include the application of alternating currents at fixed frequencies (transcranial alternating current stimulation [tACS]) or random frequencies (transcranial random noise stimulation [tRNS]). Both techniques can be used to entrain or modulate specific neuronal oscillations in the brain, although these methods have not yet been applied widely.

It has been argued that NIBS procedures provide a unique opportunity to make valuable contributions to our understanding of the neurobiology of reading (Turker & Hartwigsen, 2021). While the corresponding empirical literature is relatively sparse, several useful reviews of the literature have been produced (Cancer & Antonietti, 2018; Turker & Hartwigsen, 2022; van den Noort, Struys, & Bosch, 2015; Wilcox et al., 2020). According to Turker and Hartwigsen's review (2022), only one study (Costanzo et al., 2013), had used TMS in adults with dyslexia. More recently, the literature has grown remarkably (Battisti et al., 2022; Lazzaro, 2021a; Lazzaro et al., 2021b; Mirahadi et al., 2023; Rios et al., 2018). Of the remaining fifteen experimental studies reviewed by Turker and Hartwigsen (2022) that met the eligibility criteria, fourteen used transcranial electrical stimulation: tDCS (Costanzo et al., 2016) or tACS (Rufener et al., 2019). As already noted earlier tDCS is generally deemed to be more appropriate than TMS for children and adolescents. The majority of these studies focused on stimulating the left temporo-parietal cortex before providing different reading tasks (e.g., word reading, pseudoword reading, and text reading). The driving assumption behind studies is that this particular brain area is typically found to be under-activated in poor readers, and anodal stimulation might increase the responsiveness of this region to reading instruction. The authors of the review did not offer a definitive conclusion, claiming that it was too early to judge the efficacy of NIBS given the state of the field and methodological shortcomings in many of studies involved, although they did indicate that initial results were promising.

Cross-Linguistic Imaging

It is important to note that many of the neuroimaging studies conducted so far have been carried out with middle-class participants of European descent. Neuroimaging research overall has only recently focused on diversifying its samples to include lower-income participants, who often vary in their educational attainment, and thus more broadly encompass a range of reading (Garcini et al., 2022). Similarly, the overwhelming majority of the studies that contain data on the brain bases of reading disability have been carried out using alphabetic languages and, even then, only a small number of European languages. In other words, our current views of which parts of the brain do what when a person reads, is based primarily on individuals who are native speakers and readers of a European alphabetic language. In the last portion of the brain section of this chapter, we shall briefly comment on the question: Are the biological bases for reading disabilities/dyslexia "the same or different" across different languages? Here this question is reformulated so that it applies to the brain foundation of reading disability in different languages.

As data from different languages accumulate, different theories have developed about the etiology, emergence, manifestation, and prognosis of reading disabilities around the world (Share, 2008; Ziegler, Bertrand, et al., 2010). These theories capture different levels of the complex theoretical representations of reading disability. Thus, with regard to the brain foundation of this problem, there are theories that presume that individuals with reading disability have the same type of brain abnormality irrespective of the properties of the orthographic systems of particular languages (Paulesu et al., 2001; Silani et al., 2005). This presumption, however, has been challenged as inaccurate and misleading (Hadzibeganovic et al., 2011) for two chief reasons. First, there are now multiple layers of data illustrating the presence of differences in how a given writing system connects print to spoken language (Goswami, 2002; Perfetti, Liu, & Tan, 2005; Price & Mechelli, 2005; Schlaggar & McCandliss, 2007; Siok et al., 2004). Second, even within a single orthographic system, there are many different types of reading difficulties which, however defined, appear to differ behaviorally, cognitively, and perhaps, anatomically (Kochunov et al., 2003), and are assumed to reflect different "neural impairments" (Hadzibeganovic et al., 2011: 1314).

Currently, it is not possible to answer this question definitively. Seminal work by Paulesu and colleagues (2001) used positron emission tomography to study differences between Italian, French, and English typical readers and those with reading disability. Reduced activation was found in the same brain areas in those with reading problems in these languages when compared to typical readers. Based on these results, a universal biological foundation of reading disability was hypothesized, and it was suggested that the same remediation programs should have similar effects across all three languages. This hypothesis has been largely supported, demonstrating a biological unity of dyslexia in alphabetic languages (Paulesu et al., 2001; Richlan, 2014, 2020), even if their orthographic depth is different and leads to the variations of the degree or spatial extent in the dysfunctional regions. However, as the number of studies in various languages keeps growing, more detailed analyses become possible. For example, a meta-analysis (Martin, Kronbichler, & Richlan, 2016) divided studies in several European languages into two groups based on their orthographic depth – the degree to which the grapheme–phoneme mapping of the language is based on a one-to-one or one-to-many correspondence (Frost, Katz, & Bentin, 1987; Seymour, Aro, & Erskine, 2003). The two orthographic groupings were: shallow (Finnish, Greek, Italian, Spanish, German, Norwegian, Icelandic), and deep (French, Danish, English). The results indicated an important differentiation of the existing findings by the orthographic depth and age of participants of the left temporo-parietal cortex in reading together with a subtler parcellation of occipito-temporal areas according to a rostro-caudal gradient (see Martin, Kronbichler, & Richlan, 2016: 2683, for related images). When considered together, the findings support the unified brain-based platform of reading difficulties, although specific orthography-based differences were also observed. In other words, the ongoing accumulation of data in multiple languages preserves the general notion that the biological machinery of reading acquisition, and related difficulties, have both language-general and language-specific features.

This notion of generality and commonality of reading brains across multiple writing systems needs to be verified, preferably in as many languages as possible. As mentioned above, brain imaging studies in a variety of non-West European languages, both alphabetic and non-alphabetic, have begun to mushroom. For example, several studies have been conducted with readers of Chinese, a logographic language. In one study it was found (Siok et al., 2004) that Chinese readers (without reading disability) appear to recruit a network of brain areas known to be utilized in response to increased visual attention; this is what is needed when logographic words are being processed. Interestingly, those with reading disability demonstrated reduced activation in visual attention areas but not in those areas implicated in reading disabilities for alphabetic languages (Cao et al., 2017; Liu et al., 2012; Siok et al., 2009; Yang et al., 2020). These findings, then, directly contradict both parts of the hypothesis put forward by Paulesu and colleagues – it appears that the brain machinery supporting skilled and poor reading may differ in different languages and, moreover, remediation of reading disability might require different intervention programs in logographic versus alphabetic languages. However, other research (Feng et al., 2020; Hu et al., 2010) has generated results more consistent with the logic and findings of Paulesu and his colleagues. A recent meta-analysis (Li

& Bi, 2022) examined activation abnormalities in children with difficulties mastering reading in Chinese (ten studies) and alphabetic (twenty-two studies) writing systems. The results revealed system-common and specific features. Specifically, all children with reading difficulties manifested a universal attention-related dysfunction with hypoactivation in the left inferior frontal cortex and the anterior cingulate cortex. Children learning to read in alphabetic languages additionally demonstrated hypoactivation in the left occipito-temporo-parietal regions. In contrast, children learning to read in Chinese showed specific hyperactivation in the right postcentral gyrus, the left rectus, and the right middle temporal gyrus. Clearly, these findings are of interest and challenge the field to gain an understanding of how and why such differences emerge.

Finally, yet another burgeoning area of inquiry concerns the neural correlates of reading in two or more languages, where the central question is whether these are the same or different for reading in the first (L1) and second (L2) languages and any subsequent languages. A meta-analysis of bilingual studies (Li, Zhang, & Ding, 2021) revealed that compared to L1, the left inferior parietal lobule tended to show greater activation during L2 processing. Results indicated that whereas the brain machinery substantiating reading acquisition in L1 seems to be universal, the mastery of reading in L2 is associated with brain organization that is more specific to different languages.

Brain Studies: A Summary

Current brain-based understandings of reading and reading disabilities have been derived from multiple sources of information, both structural (as evident from postmortem and *in vivo* studies) and functional (as evident from developmental, experimental, and intervention studies) brain research.

Early postmortem and subsequent structural imaging studies of reading disability have converged to suggest the presence of various small alterations in the structure of the brains of poor readers. The causes of these alterations are not clear, but it has been hypothesized that these are related to the early stages of brain maturation and development (Galaburda et al., 2006; Kershner, 2019). Extensive research into the brain structures and functions that support typical and disordered reading has converged on the recognition of a reading brain network that is assembled of left-hemisphere regions whose patterns of neural activation vary in response to specific task demands (Price, 2012). As indicated above, this network includes various areas of the brain in occipito-temporal, temporo-parietal, and frontal regions. In mature reading, these regions work in concert, although each demonstrates a bias towards supporting a particular reading-related componential process such as visual word processing, phonological mapping, and derivation of meaning. The reading brain is assembled gradually, coupled with the accumulation of gray and white matter volume and the acquisition of reading as a holistic skill resting on the foundation of its componential processes (Hoeft, Ueno, et al., 2007). Reading-related cortical regions are connected through multiple white-matter tracts, also specializing in various componential processes (Cross et al., 2021; Saygin et al., 2016), whose strength of connectivity increases with age (Yeatman et al., 2012). In fact, there is evidence that both structural and functional aberration of the reading network precedes literacy acquisition and remains challenged in poor readers (Kuhl et al., 2020). Specifically, its major components, residing in the occipito-temporal and temporo-parietal regions, demonstrate under- or hypoactivation. This is a persistent source of group difference in both children and adults with reading difficulties when compared to typical readers (Hoeft et al., 2006; Hoeft, Meyler, et al., 2007; Pugh et al., 2001; Shaywitz et al., 2004; Shaywitz et al., 2002; Temple et al., 2001), although some studies have registered differing effects (Richlan, Kronbichler, & Wimmer, 2009). Importantly, the left inferior frontal lobe appears to be increasingly engaged or hyper-activated (Hancock, Richlan, & Hoeft, 2017; Hoeft, Meyler, et al., 2007) or demonstrating misplaced activation (Temple et al., 2001) within this region when reading is a challenge. These functional brain differences among groups of typical and atypical readers are also reflected in differences in brain structure. Structural differences include reduced gray matter in the parietotemporal region (Brown et al., 2001; Silani et al., 2005; Vinckenbosch, Robichon, & Eliez, 2005) and white matter alterations in the left temporo-parietal region in poor readers (Klingberg et al., 2000). The engagement of imaging technologies with high temporal resolution (EEG, MEG, fNIRS) has demonstrated the disruption of neural processing of rapid auditory stimuli in poor readers, indicated the particular importance of the parieto-temporal region in reading disability, and showed that dysfunction in posterior cortical regions leads to compensation in frontal lobe systems. Differences in brain electrical activation considered to be characteristic of typical readers and those with reading disability can be traced, at least in part, to as early as six months of age (Leppanen & Lyytinen, 1997) and perhaps even earlier (Leppänen et al., 2010).

Language involves a highly complex system of cognitive processes that engage most of the cortex. Reading is a cognitive system that is closely related to language but has links to other systems in the brain (e.g., visual) and its own brain representation and pathways. Both language (Angrilli et al., 2003; Angrilli & Spironelli, 2005; Spironelli, Angrilli, & Pertile, 2008) and reading (Aylward et al., 2003; Shaywitz et al., 2004; Temple et al., 2003) are highly plastic and thus can be reorganized in both adults and children throughout normal development, but also in response to systematic interventions (e.g., schooling) and events such as acquired lesions. As is discussed in Chapter 4, the acquisition of reading, however, is distinctly different from that of language; the development of reading skills requires the presence of multiple prerequisite skills and at least a decade of practice to ensure the automatization of the visual associative areas that are closely connected to the linguistic regions developed early for spoken language (i.e., left temporal and frontal cortices). From an evolutionary viewpoint, the left occipito-temporal junction is the main candidate connecting anterior linguistic speech areas and posterior visual cortices. It is, perhaps, particularly interesting that current evidence in the literature consistently shows functional aberrations in this particular region for those with reading disability regardless of their age (Brunswick et al., 1999; Helenius et al., 1999; Maurer et al., 2007; Paulesu et al., 2001; Penolazzi, Spironelli, & Angrilli, 2008; Penolazzi et al., 2006; Shaywitz & Shaywitz, 2005, 2008; Spironelli & Angrilli, 2006; Spironelli, Penolazzi, & Angrilli, 2008). Notably, this system seems to be the first to come online during the acquisition of reading (Brem et al., 2010).

What does neuroimaging research bring to the dyslexia debate? First and foremost, this work provides confirmation of the existence of a complex biological phenomenon that underlies, at the level of the brain, the cognitive and behavioral manifestations of reading disability. However, to what extent can extant knowledge in this field assist in the differential diagnosis and intervention of a dyslexic subgroup?

Brain studies of reading and reading disabilities can be roughly subdivided into four categories. Studies in the first (and still most voluminous, although pediatric studies are catching up) category focus on typical reading in adults and attempt to understand how the "reading brain" does its job. The unequivocal conclusion from these studies is that the brain's involvement is systematic, consistently engaging specific pathways of information processing and automatizing processes as much as possible. Through these studies, the field has identified "where reading happens" in the brain and has defined how literate and illiterate brains differ.

Studies in the second category examine the process of reading acquisition and the emergence of the "reading brain" developmentally. These studies are conducted either cross-sectionally, looking at readers of different ages and stages of skill mastery, or longitudinally, following the same cohort of children as they acquire the skill of reading. The indisputable conclusion from this work is that the brain enters the stage of reading acquisition functionally different from its exit at the stage of fluent reading (Dehaene et al., 2015). So, the brain changes while reading is being mastered, and then the brain maintains these newly acquired features so that a skilled reader does not have to re-learn this skill every time he or she encounters print in L1 or L2 (or any other additional languages). Another accepted conclusion is that the "action" is focused on the left-hemispheric processing that differentiates both beginning and accomplished and typical and impaired readers. Importantly, challenged left-hemispheric processing has also been observed in developmental language disorder (Whitehouse & Bishop, 2008), suggesting either common etiological roots, similar brain phenotypes, or both for these developmental disorders. Finally, it appears that such aberrant left frontal processing occurs in infancy before native phoneme skills, and mapping phonemes with visual information such as graphemes or characters, are acquired, signaling a risk for reading difficulties before print is systematically encountered (Langer et al., 2017; Ozernov-Palchik et al., 2019; Wang et al., 2017; Yu et al., 2018).

The third category of studies includes those in which the structural and functional properties of the "reading brain" of typical readers are compared to those of individuals with reading disability. Such work would appear to be most valuable for resolving the dyslexia debate, yet, paradoxically, it offers comparatively little at the current time. The reason for this is that, for these studies to take place, the "target group" to be compared to typical readers has to be defined, and this assumes the existence of a category of reading disabilities (or dyslexia) that can be reliably and validly identified. Unfortunately, the neuroscience literature of reading contains as many definitions of these terms as the cognitive and educational literature and the particular definition that is employed by each study largely depends on researcher preference. This is a hugely important issue for resolving the dyslexia debate, but one, perhaps, that is less important for neuroscience researchers. The field, no doubt, appreciates this difficulty, as many brain imaging studies conceive reading and reading-related traits as continuous (Jasińska et al., 2020; Nugiel et al., 2019; Roe et al., 2018; Rueckl et al., 2015).

Unlike studies where a reading-disabled group needs to be identified before comparison with typical readers, the fourth category of brain studies has greater potential to contribute to the resolution of the dyslexia debate. This category includes brain imaging studies that are conducted alongside behavior intervention studies. Although still relatively few in number but rapidly growing in mass, this type of study has the potential to contribute to the debate by accessing whether and how the mechanisms of the brain respond to a given intervention and whether behavioral outcomes are the same or different for individuals with, for example, decoding difficulties as compared to those with other reading problems. The hope is that researchers can bring portable devices to school, where teaching and learning reading happen, and record brain activity during reading acquisition *in vivo* (Bevilacqua et al., 2019; Davidesco et al., 2021; Dikker et al., 2017, 2020). This will surely help to reduce concerns about the artificiality of a situation where children are asked to perform rather specific tasks, where the complexity of real reading is decomposed to its ingredients, where they are confronted by a strange noisy machine, and where, when reading, they are immobilized for a significant period of time. Such an approach should be able to produce a large amount of relatively inexpensive real-time data that are much more ecologically valid. While, by definition, the data are likely to be much noisier than those presented in this chapter, they offer the promise of being more relevant for examining the process of reading acquisition.

As this section has sought to demonstrate, research into the "reading brain" has contributed substantially to our understanding of reading and reading difficulties. However, it is important that we should not stray beyond the limits of our present knowledge and assume that findings from this field of research can currently inform diagnosis or intervention for those with reading disability. At present, we cannot use the understandings gleaned from neuroscience to help resolve the dyslexia debate. What we can say is that the reading system in the brain seems to be reliably established and is universal for typical reading and all types of reading disabilities, although we are far from understanding its emergence and functioning.

At the current time, such work cannot enable us to identify members of a dyslexic subsample from a larger pool of poor decoders in particular, or identify poor readers in general. Furthermore, there are no brain-based measures that can identify a subset of poor readers for whom a particular form of intervention would be demonstrably preferential. While neuroscience offers a potentially powerful contribution to future work with struggling readers, it has not yet enabled a resolution to the conceptual, definitional, and diagnostic dilemmas that are outlined in Chapter 1 or the problems of how best to structure targeted interventions that are discussed in Chapter 4. Looking to the future, recent attempts have been made to translate global knowledge concerning biological factors into discussions of specific cases (Thomas et al., 2023), although no connection to intervention at an individualized level has yet been established.

Genetic Bases of Typical and Atypical Reading

> Genetics and dyslexia,
> A topic that's not so easy-a,
> The genes that we inherit,
> Can make reading quite a merit.
>
> Dyslexia is a condition,
> That affects many a person,
> It makes reading quite a task,
> And can be quite a mask.
>
> But genetics can help us see,
> What makes dyslexia be,
> It's not just one gene that's to blame,
> But many that play the game.
>
> So if you're feeling down,
> And your reading is not so sound,
> Just remember that genetics play a role,
> And you're not alone in this goal.

This mini-poem was written by Bing, an AI living on Skype, in response to a request to generate a piece of poetry on genetics and dyslexia. It took less than a minute in which it had learned about both genes and dyslexia and how they interact. Bing's task was revised slightly, and it was asked to write about genes and reading disorders. This is what it subsequently generated:

> Genes and reading disorder,
> A topic that's hard to order,
> The genes that we inherit,
> Can make reading quite a merit.
>
> Reading disorder is a condition,
> That affects many a person,
> It makes reading quite a task,
> And can be quite a mask.

But genes can help us see,
What makes reading disorder be,
It's not just one gene that's to blame,
But many that play the game.

So if you're feeling down,
And your reading is not so sound,
Just remember that genes play a role,
And you're not alone in this goal.

Clearly, the databases that Bing screened in a split second provided no reason for it to differentiate dyslexia and reading disorder, at least in relation to the genetic bases of these (or this?) condition(s). Prior to providing a capsule review of the quantitative and molecular genetic studies of typical and atypical reading, it is important to acknowledge that the related literature is quite large and, therefore, cannot be represented here fully. Thus, the following might reflect a selection bias in the sampling of the literature. Yet, there are specific aspects of the field that are important to highlight. First, the currently unfolding inquiry into the genetic bases of reading difficulties has set up a historical context that is still relevant for ongoing research. Second, research since the 1980s has continued to develop in two directions, namely quantitative and molecular genetics, although with greatly intensified complexity concerning both questions and methods. Finally, as is the case with neuroimaging research, the investigative terrain has been dominated by studies of readers of the English language, with some work in other European languages, although this is now changing.

Historical Context

Since the early clinical investigations of the late nineteenth century, reading disability has been considered to be a condition whose emergence involves hereditary factors (Hinshelwood, 1907; Pringle Morgan, 1896; Stephenson, 1907; Thomas, 1905). However, our understanding of the impact of these factors, and the genetic machinery behind them, has changed significantly in more recent times.

As noted throughout this book, it is widely accepted that reading involves a complex system of cognitive processes supported by multiple areas of the brain forming a particular functional system known as the "reading brain" (Pugh & McCardle, 2009; Seidenberg, Cooper Borkenhagen, & Kearns, 2020; Wolf, 2007). The current view asserts that this system is established under the influence of complex genetic machinery, the "reading genome." This brain system can be "broken" or challenged in more than one way;

thus, there is no "single" route to reading disability (Pernet et al., 2009). Similarly, it is likely that multiple types and numbers of deficiencies in the genetic machinery can lead to the emergence of such a malfunctioning brain system (Grigorenko, 2009). Importantly, considerations of the "reading brain" and the "reading genome" do not involve the mooted presence of a special entity that is necessary or sufficient for the mastery of reading. On the contrary, there are prolonged and engaged discussions substantiating the notion that both the "reading genome" and "reading brain" are emergent epiphenomena that result from the re-utilization of the components of the genome and the brain to aid the new functionality required for reading. In other words, *Homo sapiens* did not generate a specialized biological organ for reading; they used what they already had to add this new skill to their repertoire of proficiencies (Grigorenko, 2023; Markov, Kharitonova, & Grigorenko, 2023).

Quantitative-Genetic Studies

It is important to recognize that researchers currently have only a rudimentary understanding of the components of the genetic machinery substantiating reading or how these components operate. First, it should be noted that, when studying the genetics of reading, it is assumed that the reading skills of sampled groups cannot be wholly explained by the extent and quality of reading experience or instruction that members of these groups have received. Second, reading skills (e.g., reading accuracy and reading speed) and reading-related processes (e.g., phonemic awareness, phonological decoding, lexical retrieval – see Chapter 2) are continuously distributed in the general population regardless of the language involved (e.g., Zoccolotti et al., 2009). In other words, in any language and in any population, there are individuals who vary in their capacity to manipulate phonemes, in their speed of reading single words, and in their capacity to comprehend printed text. When examining the nature of individual differences in reading and other reading-related performance, it has been established that a substantial portion of these differences can be attributed to variations in their genetic endowments (i.e., the genomes of individuals characterized by these differences) and that these variations can be estimated. These estimates are obtained through so-called "genetically informed designs," which involve various combinations of blood relatives, ranging from mono- and di-zygotic twin pairs to sibships and nuclear and extended families. Juxtaposing theoretical expectations regarding what should be expected for shared genes and environments for various types of relatives, correlations between these various types of relatives can be decomposed to estimate the heritability – the ratio of genetic variance to the total trait variance – of a trait of interest in a sample (or population) of interest. This family of genetically informed designs permits the evaluation of contributions to the total trait variance of genetic (A^2) and environmental (shared by relatives, C^2, and unique to each person, E^2) variance components.

Importantly, estimates of the magnitude of heritability vary:

a.   across the life span (Byrne et al., 2009);
b.   for different languages (Samuelsson et al., 2008);
c.   for different societal groups (Friend, DeFries, & Olson, 2008); and
d.   for different classroom environments (Taylor et al., 2010).

They are also derived from different types of relatives – twins (Erbeli, Hart, & Taylor, 2018; Olson, 2006; Petrill et al., 2006), biological (Erbeli, Hart, & Taylor, 2019; Lohvansuu et al., 2021; Raskind et al., 2000; van Bergen et al., 2012), and adopted (Kirkpatrick et al., 2011) families.

Numerous statistical techniques have been developed to estimate heritability coefficients using both behavioral data and the known degree of genetic relatedness (Elston & Johnson, 2008). Each of these techniques has its own strengths and weaknesses; correspondingly, they are often used in combination so that estimation precision can be maximized.

Differences in performance have been attributed to differences in the genome at an average of 41–74 percent (Grigorenko, 2004), although systematic fluctuations in these estimates have been observed (DeFries, Fulker, & LaBuda, 1987; Gayán & Olson, 1999). Although genetic influences appear to be present in virtually any componential process related to reading, there is some variation with regard to specific processes. Thus, estimates are found in the 50–80 percent range for various indicators of phonological processing (Byrne et al., 2009; Byrne et al., 2002), 60–87 percent for various indicators of orthographic processing (Gayán & Olson, 2001, 2003), and 60–67 percent for semantic processing or reading comprehension (Betjemann et al., 2008; Harlaar, Dale, & Plomin, 2007; Keenan et al., 2006; Petrill et al., 2007). Moreover, these estimates tend to be lower when they are obtained earlier in the child's development, for example, among preschoolers or in early grades (e.g., Byrne et al., 2009). They also tend to vary depending on the language in which they are obtained and the specific characteristics of reading for which they are obtained, suggesting that there is tremendous variation in how genetic factors manifest themselves in the different languages in which reading is acquired (e.g., Naples et al., 2009). In addition, these estimates tend to diverge depending on the characteristics of the sample from which they were obtained, for example, SES, ethnicity, and quality of schooling (e.g., Taylor et al., 2010).

Having obtained heritability estimates for many (if not all) reading-related processes, researchers have sought to understand the role of other cognitive skills on both cross-sectional and longitudinal representations of reading-related skills. Recently there has been much interest regarding the role of soft skills such as mindset and grit in academic achievement (see Chapter 4 for discussion of reading interventions involving mindset). Using a twin sample (Martinez et al., 2022) examined the relationship between both grit and mindset on current, future, and change in reading comprehension performance. While the study's focus was upon reading comprehension rather than decoding, three conclusions from this study are of interest. First, there was very limited relation between either mindset or grit with concurrent reading ability or any change in reading performance over time. Second, twin modeling suggested little to no common genetic or environmental influences between mindset and grit to reading ability. Third, the best predictor of future reading performance was the child's previous reading score. The study's findings suggest that, even if claims that mindset and grit have a role in raising general educational achievement are valid, they may be less important or effective constructs for guiding reading performance interventions.

The extensive and vibrant field of heritability studies of reading and reading-related processes has provided opportunities for various systematic reviews on literacy (Asbury & Plomin, 2013; Asbury & Wai, 2020; Kovas, Haworth, Dale, & Plomin, 2007; Little, Haughbrook, & Hart, 2017; Olson et al., 2014) and meta-analyses on reading-related skills (Andreola et al., 2021), reading comprehension (Little, Haughbrook, & Hart, 2017), and school achievement (de Zeeuw, de Geus, & Boomsma, 2015). De Zeeuw, de Geus, and Boomsma's (2015) analysis offers a general landscape of heritability estimates for skills that contextualize those for reading-related skills. Specifically, using data from up to 5330 MZ and 7084 DZ twin pairs offered estimates of heritability for various aspects of reading grouped together (73%), reading comprehension (49%), mathematics (57%), spelling (44%), language (64%), and educational achievement (66%). Importantly, the magnitude of genetic effects varied between countries. Thus, heritability estimates were observed to be consistently high in the Netherlands but rather more variable for the USA and the UK. Thus, it appears that genetic variation is an important contributor to individual differences in educational achievement, with some indication of an interaction by country. This country-based landscape of differing heritability estimates was ostensibly explained by specific differences in education systems (e.g., the ways education is funded and whether an educational system has, or does not have, a core curriculum) as well as by general societal differences (e.g., different facets of equality and inequality). Similar to the International Longitudinal Twin Study, increased intensity and uniformity of literacy instruction, in particular, and the homogeneity of society, in general, (e.g., in the Netherlands) appeared to be associated with increased heritability estimates.

A meta-analysis by Andreola et al. (2021) sought to synthesize the results of quantitative genetic research on reading-related componential phenotypes (e.g., general reading, letter-word knowledge, phonological decoding, reading comprehension, spelling, phonological awareness, rapid automatized naming). This involved forty-nine twin studies spanning 4.1–18.5 years of age, with a total sample size of more than 38,000 individuals. Using the traditional ACE model, where A stands for additive genetic effects, C stands for shared environment, and E stands for non-shared environment, the researchers reported that the causal architecture across these components corresponded to the following: $A^2 > E^2 > C^2$. Heritability estimates were 66 percent for general reading, 62 percent for letter-word knowledge, 68 percent for phonological decoding, 68 percent for reading comprehension, 80 percent for spelling, 52 percent for phonological awareness, and 46 percent for rapid automatized naming. The researchers also completed a moderator analysis that indicated that sex and spoken language did not impact the heritability of any reading-related skills. However, school grade levels moderated the heritability of general reading, reading comprehension, and phonological awareness. It is important to note that, although previously common and conducted as stand-alone investigations, heritability estimates that were previously obtained from quantitative-genetic studies are embedded in molecular-genetic studies.

Importantly, the last decade of heritability research has registered the shared genetic liability for reading disorder with other neurodevelopmental difficulties such as language disorder (Snowling et al., 2020), learning and attention disorders (Daucourt et al., 2020), and emotional difficulties, although the literature is not always convergent (Hendren et al., 2018; Whitehouse, Spector, & Cherkas, 2009; Willcutt & Pennington, 2000).

Genetic influences appear to be of even greater magnitude when one considers reading disability, rather than normative reading performance. When selecting samples of poor readers (e.g., Deffenbacher et al., 2004), variation is often limited, as relatives of poor readers often demonstrate similarly depressed levels of performance. Such studies typically result in higher heritability estimates.

Some researchers employ a statistical approach known as "relative risk" estimates. These indicate the probability that a relative of someone with reading disability may also experience this problem. These estimates are then compared to estimates of the general population risk. Estimating the population risk is not an easy task as there is much variation in the literature as to cut-off points. Despite this caveat, relative risk statistics suggest that the prevalence of reading disabilities among relatives of those with this difficulty is substantially higher than the general population estimates. Relative risk statistics are obtained from samples that include families of individuals with reading impairment (i.e., families of so-called probands with the disability). Multiple family constellations can be used in these studies: sibling or cousin units (i.e., pairs or larger groupings), nuclear families, and extended families. As is the case with heritability estimates, no particular method is preferred, and samples that include different groupings of relatives are characterized by specific advantages and disadvantages; correspondingly, multiple approaches are typically employed to maximize the accuracy and precision of findings.

As indicated at the beginning of this section, estimates of heritability and relative risk, if high, are indicative of the presence of a substantial genetic component underpinning difficulties related to reading acquisition. However, the important task of translating these estimates into specific molecular mechanisms has proven difficult. In fact, when it became possible to not only estimate, but also measure, the genetic component of phenotype variability by sampling the human genome experimentally, it became evident that quantitative heritability estimates were substantially higher than those generated via the molecular-genetic method. In fact, this difficulty was so common in studies of complex human traits, it was labeled the "missing heritability problem" (Maher, 2008). Thus, percentages offered by the studies above suggest that genetic factors play a large role in the differences found between individuals in reading performance and related componential processes. Yet, genome-wide association studies (GWAS), which quantify (i.e., estimate the explained percentage variance) and qualify (i.e., localize this variance to particular genetic polymorphisms) actual differences in DNA between individuals, suggest that genes exhibit minimal influence on behavioral differences between individuals, typically 1 percent–5 percent for any given reading-related activity. So, what is going on? Where is the missing heritability?

Molecular-Genetic Studies

To understand and rectify the problem of missing heritability, it is important to understand the landscape of molecular-genetic studies, also known as "wet" studies. These are laboratory-based studies where relative similarity is evaluated molecularly, in contrast to heritability studies where similarity is estimated. Molecular-genetic studies permit the discovery of the molecular machinery underlying variability in the acquisition of reading. Despite substantial evidence in the literature that genetic factors are important for understanding individual differences in reading acquisition and reading performance, their specific role continues to be unclear although the field's knowledge and appreciation of the complexity of these factors has been increasing. Unlike relative risk studies, in which only behavioral characterization of the probands and their family members takes place, molecular-genetic (molecular) studies require the collection of biological specimens (typically either blood or saliva) from which DNA can be extracted. Molecular-genetic studies consist of one of two major types (both types can be further subdivided into subtypes), depending on the participants they engage, namely genetically unrelated cases or probands and matched controls or family units such as siblings or nuclear and extended families), and the type of genetic entity they target (i.e., specific genes, specific genetic regions, or the whole genome).

The very first molecular-genetic study of reading disability and related processes was a whole-genome linkage scan completed with a number of extended families of individuals with reading difficulties (Smith et al., 1983). A typical protocol for these studies is that families in which an individual has reading disability are approached, and members are asked for permission to be evaluated behaviorally (i.e., complete a number of reading and reading-related tasks) and to donate a biological specimen (i.e., blood or saliva or some other specimen from DNA can be extracted). The agenda, once again, is to correlate the similarities in performance on various assessments to similarities in the structural variation in the genome, only with this approach, the genetic similarities are not estimated, as previously in quantitative-genetic studies of heritability, but measured using special molecular-genetic (i.e., genotyping and sequencing) and statistical (e.g., linkage and association analyses and machine learning) techniques. For such studies, family units can include a variety of relatives (e.g., siblings, parent-offspring, cousins, aunts, and uncles) and family sizes (e.g., a pair, a nuclear family, and extended family). Illustrations of different types of samples used in molecular-genetic studies of reading disabilities can be found in Grigorenko (2005, 2022).

Smith and colleagues' ground-breaking study (1983) took the form of a whole-genome scan, although, at this time, very few markers were available, and those that were used, were protein markers (technology at that time was insufficient for work with DNA markers). Since then, much has changed, including an abundance of polymorphic DNA markers, the cost of genotyping and sequencing, and computer capacity. Such changes have shaped the lay of the land so much that dozens of genome-wide screens for reading disability have since been reported. Modern studies are drastically different from the 1983 study, both technologically (hundreds of thousands or even millions of markers are now used) and in relation to sample-size (hundreds of individuals are now recruited to make sure that such studies are adequately powered).

Some studies have focused on particular, selected regions of the genome. The decision concerning which regions to select will typically result from a previous whole-genome scan or a theoretical hypothesis capitalizing on a particular aspect of reading disability (Skiba et al., 2011). There are also other bases on which decisions can be made. For example, some researchers have selected their candidate regions on the basis of a known chromosomal aberration. For example, in Denmark, all newborns are screened for macro-chromosomal changes (e.g., large rearrangements). Some commercial genetics laboratories, such as the Baylor Genetics Laboratory, a collaboration between Baylor Medical College and a Japanese company, complete diagnostic tests for a large number of various referrals. Databases can then be used to inform decisions about who should be screened for reading disability/dyslexia (Buonincontri et al., 2011; Fliedner et al., 2020, respectively). The hypothesis here is that a gene affected by such an aberration in a proband experiencing reading disability is somehow related to the disability.

Although different accounts exist, the literature (Figure 3.2) has referenced about twenty (Schumacher et al., 2007) potential genetic susceptibility loci, which mark locations in the genome that have been "statistically linked" to reading disability. It is important to note that these regions are typically large, by genomic standards, and may contain more than one, and sometimes hundreds of genes. The literature also makes reference to various genes (Grigorenko, 2022; Grigorenko & Naples, 2009; Kere, 2014; Mascheretti et al., 2017; Peterson & Pennington, 2012), so-called candidate genes for reading disability, that is, genes that, being located within the susceptibility loci, might actually be the specific genes whose altered function is associated with the emergence of reading disability. None of these has been either fully accepted or fully rejected by the research

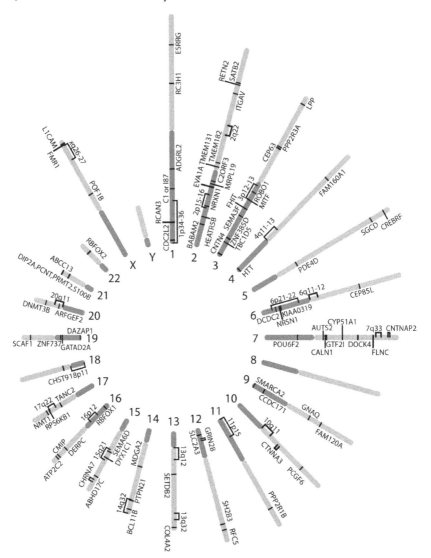

Figure 3.2 Linkage and association signals
Linkage signals are shown in square brackets and signify the regions of particular chromosomes that have been linked to specific reading disabilities. Association signals are shown by locations on the gene, although far from all of their markers in a particular gene have been shown to be associated with the phenotype of interest. Importantly, the "reading genes" seem to reside pretty much on all chromosomes of the genome, except chromosomes 8 and Y, and, at least so far, justify the usage of the metaphor of the "reading genome."

community, although their overall standing has been challenged by recent failures to identify them as related to variation in reading skills in recent large-scale studies (Doust et al., 2022; Eising et al., 2022; Gialluisi et al., 2021; Price, Wigg, Eising, et al., 2022). Some of these genes have been identified through rare cases of families in which reading disorder appears to be transmitted as a single-gene disorder (Carrion-Castillo et al., 2021; de Kovel et al., 2004; Einarsdottir et al., 2015; Fagerheim et al., 1999; Grimm et al., 2020; Nopola-Hemmi et al., 2001). Other genes have been identified through multi-family studies demonstrating that reading disability and its componential processes are genetically heterogeneous and likely involve the influence of variation in multiple genes (e.g., Cardon et al., 1994, 1995; Field et al., 2013; Fisher et al., 2002; Grigorenko et al., 1997; Grigorenko et al., 2001; Igo et al., 2006; Nöthen et al., 1999).

There is ongoing debate regarding the specificity of the impact of genes related to reading disorders. The issue here is whether the hypothesized candidate genes for these are sources of the specific genetic variation that accounts for individual differences in reading and reading-related processes only, or whether these genes have a broader impact on other types of learning (i.e., learning math) and other cognitive processes. In an attempt to address this issue, the so-called "generalist gene hypothesis" (Plomin & Kovas, 2005) contends that genes that affect one area of learning, such as reading performance, are largely the same genes that affect other abilities (and disabilities). Such a position is still open to debate although multiple candidate genes for reading disability have been identified as associated with other neurodevelopmental disorders (Price et al., 2020).

As noted above, approximately twenty different genomic regions are currently considered to be harboring candidate genes for reading disabilities, although this figure is likely to grow (Rubenstein et al., 2011). In attempts to interrogate these regions while looking at specific signals, several candidate genes have been identified for reading disability. Early studies identified six candidates that are being evaluated as causal genes for reading disabilities/dyslexia (*DYX1C1/EKN1*, now known as *DNAAF4, KIAA0319, DCDC2, ROBO1, MRPL2*, and *C2orf3*). Independent attempts to replicate these findings have resulted in both positive outcomes (Bates et al., 2007; Cope et al., 2012; Eicher et al., 2015; Gabel et al., 2010; Mascheretti et al., 2014; Massinen et al., 2016; Riva et al., 2015; Sun et al., 2014; Tran et al., 2014) and negative ones (Bellini et al., 2005; Cope et al., 2004; de Kovel et al., 2008; Marino et al., 2005; Petryshen et al., 2000; Scerri et al., 2004; Scerri et al., 2017; Sharma et al., 2020; Szalkowski et al., 2013). Unsurprisingly, therefore, meta-analyses have been unable to report a conclusive result. (Deng, Zhao, & Zuo, 2019; Grigorenko, 2005; Schumacher et al., 2007; Shao et al., 2016; Tran et al., 2013; Zhong et al., 2013; Zou et al., 2012). Importantly, most of these studies included only small samples that accordingly, resulted in low statistical power. More genes are being reported as putative additions to the earlier list of candidates, in part, because of the availability of larger samples that can offer increased statistical power (Buonincontri et al., 2011; Doust et al., 2022; Eising et al., 2022; Ercan-Sencicek et al., 2012; Newbury et al., 2011; Price, Wigg, Eising, et al., 2022; Scerri et al., 2010).

With technological advancement and the price drop for genotyping, the field has moved away from linkage family studies towards case-control or unselected sample association studies. These genome-wide association studies (GWAS) are a more powerful approach for examining complex traits in which effect sizes of individual risk introduced by single genetic variants are small. Importantly, none of the "original" candidate genes have been found to be associated with reading disability with monolingual GWAS (Eicher et al., 2013; Field et al., 2013; Gialluisi et al., 2014; Luciano et al., 2013; Meaburn et al., 2008; Roeske et al., 2011; Truong et al., 2019) or in large multilingual samples (Becker et al., 2014; Gialluisi et al., 2020; Gialluisi et al., 2019). However, is should be noted that early monolingual reading disability GWAS were underpowered, and the variants with the strongest associations to this difficulty (e.g., in genes *RBFOX2, ABCC13, ZNF385D, COL4A2,* and *FGF18)* did not survive corrections for multiple comparisons and related interrogations (Eicher et al., 2013; Field et al., 2013; Gialluisi et al., 2014; Luciano et al., 2013); thus, only suggestive associations with reading disability and reading-related traits were identified. More recently, however, GWAS for reading disability, reading performance, and various reading-related tasks have begun to yield results with genome-wide statistical significance, generating signals of single-nucleotide polymorphism (SNP)-based analysis at p ~ 10^{-8} (Doust et al., 2022; Eising et al., 2022) and gene-based analysis at p ~ 10^{-6} (Gialluisi et al., 2021; Price et al., 2020). Figure 3.2 captures the "old" (region-based) and "new" (gene-specific) candidate genes and their locations in the genome. At the current time, there is mixed evidence for the involvement of each of these genes, and findings have proven difficult to interpret in a systematic fashion.

As is evident from Figure 3.2, the following observations can be made. First, various genes associated with typical and challenged reading and reading-related processes are distributed throughout the genome. In fact, so far, there is only one chromosome that has not been added to the "reading genome" – chromosome Y, colloquially known as the "gene desert"

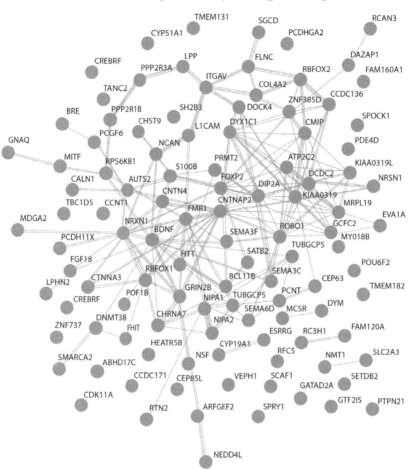

Figure 3.3   Connection network of dyslexia candidate genes
The STRING drawing capitalizes on the relevant information currently available in the field regarding the connections between proteins produced by the genes involved in the various aspects of reading and reading disorders. What is evident here is that these genes do not form a comprehensive genetic system that uniquely and comprehensively substantiates reading.

(Quintana-Murci & Fellous, 2001). Second, given the variety of genes involved, there is no obvious clustering of these candidates either by gene family or by gene function. A graphical representation of the associations of all types presented in the literature recovered a limited network of connections (see Figure 3.3). Based on these observations, there is no reason to suggest that human genome evolution developed in order to substantiate reading as an exceptionally human skill. The human genome, just like the human brain, has developed into a "reading genome" by utilizing existing material and reassembling the present structure into a new functional system with new properties. Currently, there is no clear understanding of how this assembly happened evolutionarily or how it happens in each individual. There are, however, various hypotheses regarding the connections between these genes.

Thus, some of these strong and not-so-strong candidate genes (*KIAA0319, KIAA0319L, DCDC2, DNAAF4,* and *ROBO1*) have been functionally linked to each other, as all have been implicated in neuronal migration – a relocation of neurons in the brain so they form appropriate spatial relationships and cluster in interactive units. Just as neuronal migration hypotheses have featured in brain studies of reading disability, these have also been tested in model organism studies. In other words, the genes previously associated with reading and reading-related components have been studied through their orthologs (i.e., genes in different species that have evolved from a common ancestral gene by speciation; typically, orthologs retain the same function during the course of evolution) in model organisms (Levecque et al., 2009; Taipale et al., 2003; Velayos-Baeza et al., 2007).

A number of knockdown[20] experiments with *Kiaa0319, Kiaa0319l, Dcdc2,* and *Dnaaf4* have been undertaken in the developing brains of mice or rats. Genetic manipulations were undertaken to reduce target gene expression, and consequently, most neural cells did not migrate as expected from the lower ventricular zone to the higher cortical plate but, instead, remained in the ventricular or intermediate zones. These events demonstrated disrupted neuronal migration, although different patterns were demonstrated for different genes, (Burbridge et al., 2008; Gonda et al., 2013; Meng et al., 2005; Paracchini et al., 2006; Platt et al., 2013; Wang et al., 2006).

In turn, a number of gene overexpression experiments have led to the manifestation of neural phenotypes, including aberrant neurite outgrowth for *Dcdc2* (Massinen et al., 2011), delayed radial migration (Martinez-Garay et al., 2017), and altered axon growth and regeneration (Franquinho et al., 2017) for *Kiaa0319*. Unfortunately, subsequent independent knockout experiments[21] failed to replicate the findings (Franquinho et al., 2017; Guidi et al., 2017; Guidi et al., 2018; Rendall et al., 2017; Wang et al., 2011). Critically, although cortical abnormalities

[20] A gene knockdown is a technique whereby the expression of one or more of an organism's genes is reduced.
[21] A gene knockout involves the total removal or permanent deactivation of a gene.

have been observed with knockdown of the rat orthologs of *Dnaaf4* (Wang et al., 2006), *Kiaa0319* (Paracchini et al., 2006), or *Dcdc2* (Meng et al., 2005), this is not observed in knockout mice (Martinez-Garay et al., 2017; Rendall et al., 2017; Wang et al., 2011), and the cortical migration hypothesis remains unproven (Guidi et al., 2018). Although both human and model organism data on neuronal migration remain inconclusive, the hypothesis per se appeals, and as soon as there is even limited evidence in its support, it resurfaces in the literature, generating new candidate genes (Price, Wigg, Eising, et al., 2022; Price et al., 2020). Alternative hypotheses connecting candidate genes for reading disorders have suggested that these genes have a role in ciliogenesis (Massinen et al., 2011; Schueler et al., 2015; Tarkar et al., 2013), synaptic transmission (Che et al., 2016), or axonal growth (Franquinho et al., 2017), leading to consideration of additional pathogenesis pathways for reading difficulties. However, none of these hypotheses have yet been sufficiently verified.

While we have some robust knowledge of the genetic bases of dyslexia, there continue to be many areas of uncertainty. We can be sure that individual differences in reading performance are partially, and very likely, substantially, genetic. Moreover, the relationship between reading and the genome appears to be stronger as the individual develops from early childhood to early adulthood. At the current time, however, there is a dearth of genetically-informed studies of reading for older populations. Most of what is known about the genetics of typical and atypical reading has been derived from individuals younger than 18 years of age who are of European descent and who speak English. This situation has been changing, albeit slowly. In their attempt to quantify and qualify the distribution of studies of typical and atypical reading, Verhoeven and Perfetti (2021) offered a broad grouping of languages and writing systems: Asian (Chinese, Japanese, Korean, Kannada), West Semitic (Arabic, Hebrew), Romance (Italian, French, Spanish), Germanic (German, Dutch, English), Slavic (Czech, Slovak, Russian), Greek, Finnish, and Turkish. These languages represent the major writing systems, namely the syllabic, morpho-syllabic, alphasyllabic, abjad, and alphabetic. Needless to say, the current distribution of studies across various languages is highly skewed, as there is not enough research in representative languages to carry out a comprehensive analysis of the universals and particulars of the genetic underpinnings of reading acquisition within and across different language groups. The presence of European samples and languages (Dutch, Finnish, French, German, Hungarian, Italian) is increasing, and there is also relevant research in Hindi and Chinese-speaking samples, but the mass of work to compare and contrast the universality and specificity of genetic signatures has not been reached (Grigorenko, 2022).

There are many reasons why our knowledge concerning the genetics of reading is still rudimentary. First and foremost, reading and reading-related processes are complex in structure and, most likely, are complex in their genetic sources (Smith, 2007). Second, developmental models of reading acquisition assume the involvement of both the formation and engagement of multiple psychological representations (Grigorenko & Naples, 2008) – phonological, orthographical, morphological, and others (see Chapter 2). These representations permit the holistic process of reading to emerge. Although corresponding multivariate models of reading are commonly found in the behavioral literature (Wagner & Torgesen, 1987), they are less prevalent in the genetic literature on reading. Although studies utilizing complex quantitative models of reading have been published, they are still in the minority (Davis et al., 2014; Gialluisi et al., 2021; Gialluisi et al., 2019). Third, environmental risk factors play an important role in the development of reading disability and these appear to have an interactional relationship with genes (i.e., a bioecological gene by environment interaction). For example, while an association between the heritability of dyslexia and the level of parental education has been found – the higher the level of education, the greater the heritability (Friend, DeFries, & Olson, 2008; Rosenberg et al., 2012) – it is not yet known which environmental factors play a mediating role in this (Grigorenko, 2012). Fourth, it appears that not only do many genes underlie individual differences in reading and its components, these also typically involve only small-to-moderate effect sizes, (Meaburn et al., 2008). Reading is best described as a system of the related variables that quantify these components (Grigorenko, 2007). In order to identify the relevant genes, studies require large numbers of individuals who are homogeneous genetically (e.g., individuals with similar ancestry) and well-characterized behaviorally with multivariate phenotypes. Unfortunately, accessing samples on the required scale has been a challenge although recently, collaborations between various research consortia have enabled different genetic datasets to be brought together and combined (Doust et al., 2022; Eising et al., 2022; Gialluisi et al., 2021; Price, Wigg, Eising, et al., 2022).

With this greater ability to build large samples, the missing heritability problem appears to be potentially solvable. For example, a recent powerful study (n ~ up to 33,959 participants) has revealed robust SNP heritability (13–26%) for all of the analyzed behavioral traits (Eising et al., 2022). This is still much lower than the meta-analyzed quantitative-genetic estimates, but it is substantially higher than previously reported SNP heritability from GWAS conducted on a smaller scale. Finally, it is important to recognize that even large-scale (or very large-scale) GWAS projects generate only statistical associations with reading and reading-related processes. In order to determine biological relevance, observed statistical associations require corroboration of the variants and haplotypes of interest in other reading-disabled sample sets, or functional studies in an appropriate cell model (Weirauch et al., 2014).

The notion that the genetic machinery that supports typical and atypical reading is complex and substantiated by small contributions from multiple genes, and multiple polymorphic sites within these genes, accords with the general landscape of the field of the genetics of complex human traits. Reflecting and informing such understandings is the use of polygenetic risk scores (PRS); these are scores that predict the risk for a trait or disorder (Wray et al., 2018). Such scores can be assigned to specific individuals, assuming that their genetic data are available. They can also be constructed for specific disorders and specific populations. For example, a PRS for educational attainment has been constructed on a large (~1,100,000 people) sample of individuals (Lee et al., 2018). One PRS study compared educational attainment with reading efficiency and comprehension. It was found that educational attainment accounted for 2.1 percent (at the age of 7) (Gialluisi et al., 2019) and 5.1 percent (at the age of 14) (Selzam et al., 2017) of the genetic variance in the reading measures. Yet another possible utilization of PRS is for understanding the familial transmission of reading and other academic skills (Axelrud et al., 2023). Although far from recovering all of the "missing heritability," the use of PRS can help rescue some of it.

The last two decades of genetic and genomic research have led to an explosion of studies implicating a great variety of different types of structural variation in the genome that are related to the origin and manifestation of various developmental disabilities (Miller et al., 2010). These types of structural variation range from large to small genomic events of different natures – deletions, insertions, spatial alterations (e.g., translocations and inversions), and the presence or absence of transposable elements (1000 Genomes Project Consortium, 2010; Gonzaga-Jauregui, Lupski, & Gibbs, 2012; Stankiewicz & Lupski, 2010).[22] The importance of considering these (and perhaps other) types of variation has been demonstrated for

---

[22] A transposable element is a DNA sequence that can change its relative position (self-transpose).

autism spectrum disorder (O'Roak et al., 2011; Sanders et al., 2011; Sanders et al., 2012), various developmental delays (Cooper et al., 2011), intellectual disabilities (Lu et al., 2007), ADHD (Lionel et al., 2011), and a number of specific genomic syndromes (Jalal et al., 2003; Roberts et al., 2004) many of which are associated with different types of learning disability. Although DNA structural variations are present in individuals without reading difficulties, individuals with various neurodevelopmental and neuropsychiatric disorders appear to present with structural variation in their genomes to a higher degree (e.g., more variants are observed) or have variations of a particular type (e.g., deletions and insertions of larger size are observed), or at particular crucial locations (e.g., the deletion at 22q11.2 results in a well-known genomic condition, DiGeorge syndrome, one facet of which is the presentation of learning problems).

Different types of structural variation have been implicated in the manifestation of various reading difficulties (including reading comprehension), and through analysis of these, several candidate genes have been identified, *ROBO1* (Hannula-Jouppi et al., 2005), *DNAAF4* (Taipale et al., 2003), and *SEMA6D* (Ercan-Sencicek et al., 2012). All of these genes have been detected through studies of isolated families (Taipale et al., 2003) or even of individual cases (Ercan-Sencicek et al., 2012). Systematic explorations of the importance of different types of structural variation in the field of reading have been few and, so far, have only concerned large events, that is, insertions and deletions larger than 1 Megabase (Girirajan et al., 2011). Yet, it is important to stress that large structural variants of this kind are relatively rare (e.g., <1% of the general population), and the underlying assumption here is that their identification will provide a clue for subsequent studies of the gene(s) affected by this structural alteration, or the pathways involved. It is especially relevant to investigations of the genetic bases of complex traits such as reading abilities or disabilities. The idea is that once a rare variant is identified and associated with a particular trait (e.g., reading), it is necessary to investigate common variants in the gene or region that is impacted by this rare variant. Of particular interest here are population-based evaluations of structural variation in well-characterized cohorts of specific ancestry. For example, in an investigation of a large Icelandic cohort of ~100,000 people, large deletions/insertions at the long arm of chromosome 15 were observed to be associated with indicators of typical and atypical reading (Ulfarsson et al., 2017).

Along with the enhanced understanding of the role of structural variation in the genome, ongoing exploration into other mechanisms might prove to be relevant to our understanding of the genetics of typical and atypical reading. Some of these will now be briefly discussed.

First, it is important to note that reading skills are acquired within a developmental context. Behavior-genetic studies of typical and atypical reading and related phenotypes have indicated the presence of developmental heterogeneity in corresponding genetic bases (Byrne et al., 2009; Petrill et al., 2010). Specifically, when multiple time points of the same reading-related phenotype have been considered, results have indicated the presence of time-general and time-specific genetic factors that have contributed to the additive genetic component of phenotypic variance (Harlaar, Dale, & Plomin, 2007). Outcomes of this type have been reported for such reading-related phenotypes as phonetic-phonological processes (Coventry et al., 2011), orthographic processes (Byrne et al., 2008), and vocabulary (Hart et al., 2009). Thus, the impact of specific genetic risk factors should be investigated longitudinally. It is even more important to track, at the genetic/genomic level, the impact of effective behavioral interventions.

Second, there are molecular entities, both within the DNA and separate from it, that have been found to affect DNA functioning and its products. Current estimates of protein-coding genes suggest ~21,000, or 1.5 percent of the human genome (Clamp et al., 2007). However, as our accuracy in detailing the sequence of the genome has increased, it has become clear that genes constitute a minority compared with other types of DNA structures, for example, functional conserved non-coding elements (CNEs). These are sequences within the DNA that do not code for proteins but serve other important functions. Substantial data from studies have led to the suggestion that the differentiation of species may be driven more by variation in CNEs than by changes in proteins (Lander, 2011). It may be important, therefore, to broaden the search for the genetic bases of reading beyond protein-coding genes. The role of CNEs in reading might be directly related to the role of transposable elements, as many of the CNEs appear to be structurally derived from these (Bejerano et al., 2006). Importantly, the human genome contains arrays of CNEs termed genomic regulatory blocks (GRBs); these can be utilized to detect genes under long-range developmental regulation (Vitsios et al., 2021). Interestingly, polymorphisms associated with neurodevelopmental disorders in various GWAS projects have been found to be overrepresented in GRBs. The GRB model may prove to be a powerful tool for connecting these significantly associated polymorphisms to their correct target genes under long-range regulation, thus connecting them to genes to which they are functionally, rather than geographically related (Barešić et al., 2020). Although such analyses have not been carried out for reading disability or other learning disorders, they might help to link the signals in the "reading genome" (see Figure 3.2) to a coherent functional hypothesis.

Finally, another mechanism worthy of exploration in developmental and interventionally oriented research is the epigenetic (or epigenomic) regulation of the genome. This concerns heritable events in genome transcription that are traceable through changes in gene expression yet are *not* caused by structural changes in DNA. In other words, what is synthesized by a particular DNA fragment may not be directly caused by changes in the DNA sequence. It has been observed that functionally active domains/components of the genome are characterized by specific epigenetic marks, that is, the presence of particular molecules (Lander, 2011) that may influence the transcription process. These marks can be recorded, catalogued, and assembled in developmental (skill acquisition) and intervention (skill reconstruction) epigenomic maps. Although the question of the tissue- and cell-specificity of these marks remains open, it has been shown (Thompson et al., 2013) that cells from saliva and blood provide a great deal of information indicating epigenomic maps that differentiate behavioral groups (Naumova et al., 2012) or that correlate with behavioral traits (Essex et al., 2013). There is no reason to believe that epigenomic studies will not prove to be equally, if not more useful, for typical and atypical reading as for other complex behavioral traits. For example, DNA methylation molecular signatures obtained in a sample of individuals aged 8–19 reflected the early life social determinants of lifelong disparities in health and cognition, and were associated with their performance on a range of cognitive and academic tests, including processing speed, general executive function, perceptual reasoning, verbal comprehension, reading, and math (Raffington et al., 2023).

Genome Studies: A Summary

In recent years, there has been substantial growth in our understanding of the role of genes and the genome in reading and reading disability. While it has been clearly established that reading is partially and substantially controlled by genes, there continues to be only limited knowledge and understanding of the role genetic factors play in reading acquisition. A proliferation of inconsistent and contrasting findings, together with recognition of the role of a bioecological gene in environmental interactions, have both added to the complexity of this field. Recognition of such complexity, however, represents an important counter to over-simplistic and unrealistic expectations that a simple genetic account could materialize.

As Bing, the Skype AI, pointed out,

Just remember that genes play a role,
And you're not alone in this goal.

Scientists spread across the world, speaking many different languages, are making consistent progress in understanding how the human genome develops into a reading genome, phylogenetically and ontogenetically. Most of the work continues to be focused on gaining understanding of structural variation in the genome, but other interesting ideas are being explored. Many ideas are being discussed but none of them, to the best of our knowledge, involve an attempt to differentiate the genetics of dyslexia from the genetics of reading disability, other reading difficulties or other neurodevelopmental disorders. Indeed, the consensus is that the genetic bases of typical and atypical reading are common (Erbeli, Rice, & Paracchini, 2022) and reading disorders share their genetic background with other neurodevelopmental disorders (Georgitsi et al., 2021).

Thus, it is important to note that existing knowledge in the field of genetics cannot support the position of those who seek to identify dyslexia as a diagnosable condition discrete from other reading problems. Currently, we are unable to progress beyond a recognition that reading disabilities have a genetic component (or even a rudimentary understanding of some possible specifics of these components), to construct a knowledge base capable of informing differential diagnosis and individualized forms of intervention that could ideally commence even before the infant starts school. Such practice may be possible one day, but we are still far from this stage.

The Promise of Neurobiology for Resolving the Dyslexia Debate

Advances in the neuroscience and genetics of reading and reading disabilities over the first quarter of the twenty-first century have been substantial. As this chapter has shown, we have gained far greater insight into the biological bases of reading and reading disability. In part this is a consequence of having access to larger samples and more sophisticated technology for our investigations. However, this progress underscores the amazing complexity of the genome-brain mechanisms in turning the genome into the "reading genome" and the brain into the "reading brain." Comprehending this complexity requires understanding and appreciation of the inappropriateness of simple explanations or recommendations. In both fields of study, knowledge accumulation is rapid, but there are very few examples where this can be employed to inform interventions for individuals with reading difficulties and their families. Such translation is the field's next challenge, one that will sit alongside the task of cracking the code of how the human genome turns into the "reading genome" and the human brain turns into the "reading brain."

Finally, in concluding this chapter, we wish to explicitly address a misunderstanding that has been observed in the literature since the publication of *The Dyslexia Debate* in 2014. As we stated in that book, and repeatedly in this one, by no means do we deny the existence of biologically rooted reading disability. On the contrary, we wholeheartedly recognize the existence and the importance of the biological causality behind complex reading difficulties; in fact, we have been studying them and contributing to the field. However, in relation to the dyslexia debate, the fundamental issue is that there is no evidence for a biological signature (brain and/or genome-based) that differentiates dyslexia from any, or all, other reading difficulties. And, if there is one, it has yet to be discovered!

CHAPTER 4

Assessment, Instruction, and Intervention

Introduction

In examining how assessment, instruction, and intervention relate to the dyslexia debate, it is necessary to explore the following questions:

a. Which general approaches to the teaching of reading are likely to minimize the incidence and severity of reading disability?
b. How can we best identify young children at risk of reading disability and prevent later problems?
c. What can be done to help those who fail to respond to initial interventions?
d. What is specialist dyslexia teaching, and is this particularly effective for a subgroup of poor readers designated as dyslexic?

Which General Approaches to the Teaching of Reading Are Likely to Minimize the Incidence and Severity of Reading Disability?

The Reading Wars and the Science of Reading

Reading disability is the product of a multifactorial combination of genetic and environmental risk and resilience factors. One important contributory component will be the quality of the reading instruction that children experience. Skilful classroom assessment and teaching should reduce the proportion who struggle with reading and thus enable resources available for specialized intervention to be used to maximum effect.

Sadly, a lack of consensus about how best to teach reading continues. Indeed, a long history of fierce controversy, sometimes described as the "great debate" (Chall, 1996) or the "reading wars," has more recently been energized by the vigorous promotion of approaches subsumed under the heading of the Science of Reading (SoR), a term deemed to be the "hottest" topic by leading literacy experts in 2022 (Grote-Garcia & Ortlieb,

2023). Interest surged following publication of Seidenberg's (2017) book, *Language at the Speed of Sight: How we read, why so many can't, and what can be done about it?* This text, drawing largely upon research developments in the cognitive sciences and neuroscience made a series of influential claims about how reading should and should not be taught. These were subsequently picked up and widely publicized to practitioners, policymakers, and the lay public via traditional publishing (Hanford, 2018), radio and television, and social media outlets.

While drawing upon cutting edge research in the basic sciences, the fundamental issues underpinning the debate over the SoR reflect broader value-laden historical disputes between traditionalist and progressive approaches to education. In the traditionalist reading camp are those who emphasize bottom-up approaches dominated by phonics, defined as:

> … an approach to, or type of, reading instruction that is intended to promote the discovery of the alphabetic principle, the correspondences between phonemes and graphemes, and phonological decoding. (Scarborough & Brady, 2002: 326)

In contrast, the progressives, with a heritage stretching back to Deweyian-inspired child-centered approaches (Pearson, 2004) were conceived as those who advocate top-down "whole language" approaches in which an emphasis upon textual meaning has primacy. For this latter group:

> … phonics is regarded as the polar opposite of whole language; it is rigid, authoritarian and fanatically concerned with the acquisition of skills such as spelling. Phonics is seen as deeply anti-democratic, and its critics, defenders of whole language, find it inconsistent with the abstract values of progressive education. (Anderson, 2000: 5)

Underpinning the debate were clear differences between the camps as to the extent to which reading was seen as a natural process. Advocates of the whole language approach tended to argue that children learn to read naturally even in the absence of explicit or systematic instruction.

> Why do people create and learn written language? They need it! How do they learn it? The same way they learn oral language, by using it in authentic literacy events that meet their needs. Often children have trouble learning written language in school. It's not because it's harder than learning oral language, or learned differently. It's because we've made it hard by trying to make it easy. (Goodman, 1986: 24)

Goodman contended that the use of structured skills-based approaches, largely divorced from any meaningful context, was inadvisable. This argument, widely espoused by advocates of the whole language approach, failed to reflect contemporary scientific understandings in which reading, unlike speech, is not naturally acquired (Liberman, 1999; Perfetti, 1991; Share, 1995, 1999; Stanovich, 2000; Tunmer & Nicholson, 2011). Language, an evolved behavior that developed from the origins of humanity, is very different from literacy, a cultural invention that has only featured in the past few millennia (Pennington & Olson, 2005). Steven Pinker, the celebrated neuroscientist notes:

> Language is a human instinct, but written language is not. Language is found in all societies, present and past …. All healthy children master their own language without lessons or corrections. When children are thrown together without a usable language, they invent one of their own. Compare all this with writing. Writing systems have been invented a small number of times in history …. Until recently, most children never learned to read or write; even with today's universal education, many children struggle and fail. A group of children is no more likely to invent an alphabet than it is to invent the internal combustion engine.
>
> Children are wired for sound, but print is an optional accessory that must be painstakingly bolted on. This basic fact about human nature should be the starting point for any discussion of how to teach our children to read and write. (Pinker, 1998: ix)

The debate as to whether children learn better with an initial method that emphasizes meaning, or one that stresses learning the code, stretches back to the nineteenth century (Chall, 1996; Snow & Juel, 2005) and is closely associated with the rising and waning influence of a diverse range of interest groups (Song & Miskel, 2002). Following a trip to Europe, Horace Mann, Secretary of the Massachusetts Board of Education sought to introduce practices he observed in the teaching of reading. This involved replacing the existing approach involving the bottom-up teaching of sounds and letters by an emphasis upon top-down word learning. At a lecture to the American Institute of Instruction in 1841, Mann disparagingly described letters and words as "… skeleton-shaped, bloodless, ghostly apparitions" such that it was "… no wonder that the children look and feel so death-like, when compelled to face them" (cited in Adams, 1990: 22).

Whole word sight reading became the dominant methodology in the USA from the 1920s until the 1960s. However, in a highly influential text, *Why Johnny Can't Read,* Flesch (1955) attacked the "look and say" whole word approach on the grounds that a lack of skill in phonics limited children's ability to read books that did not contain the carefully controlled vocabularies that were being used.

Supported by a broad spectrum of US conservative interest groups (Burnett, 1998), phonics gained influence throughout the 1960s and 70s at the same time that the growth of child-centered education approaches in England was taking reading instruction in the other direction (see Solity, 2022, for a detailed account of the history of reading instruction in England). By the 1980s, whole language approaches, fueled by the seminal writing of Smith (1971) and Goodman (1965, 1969, 1970), and backed by the vigorous support of university education departments and professional associations for teachers of English, had regained their former influence in the USA, mirroring a largely similar position in the UK. The dominant picture was one whereby reading was primarily a linguistic, rather than a perceptual, process (Pearson, 2004) and phonics, taught minimally, if at all, should be incidentally taught according to the child's needs, primarily when problems in reading text were encountered.

By emphasizing the communicative function of written language (Stahl & Miller, 1989) the whole language approach proved popular with class-room teachers on both sides of the Atlantic. Its use of bright and appealing children's literature – so-called "real books" – compared favorably with the often visually and linguistically sterile texts that were typically used as basal readers. In contrast, phonics approaches were seen to be taking meaning and context out of reading and replacing these with lists and drills that reduced children's interest and motivation. However, amongst all the polemic, the need to achieve balance was overlooked, and in some cases, whole language proponents seemed to concentrate on increasing children's interest in reading rather than on how to make them better readers. Zane (2005), for example, cites a teacher survey in which respondents tended to see research into motivation to read as more important than conducting scientific investigations into how best to improve reading comprehension.

Whole language approaches also played out differently in terms of teacher identity. Unlike the heavy prescription and structure of phonics instruction, these emphasized teacher professionalism and autonomy (Snow & Juel, 2005). Goodman (1992) claimed that as a result of this pedagogical shift teachers were regaining confidence in their professional evaluations of themselves and their pupils. Unfortunately, appeals to teacher professionalism often took place in a climate that was antagonistic to scientific research approaches and dismissive of notions of objectivity.

During the 1990s, the debate became particularly polarized and often heated on both sides of the Atlantic (Chall, 2000). As Calfee and Norman (1998) remarked, "A battle is raging" (p. 244). In the UK, the Government's Department of Education and Science refused to publish its sponsored teacher training package, *Language in the National Curriculum,* to the outrage of many teacher education departments partly because, allegedly, "… it didn't bang on sufficiently about phonics" (Goddard, 1991: 32).

By the turn of the century, the pendulum was swinging away from the whole language camp. A range of factors was involved in the demise of this previously dominant approach, several of which were primarily ideological. Particularly relevant was the widespread political and in some quarters, professional, mistrust of the qualitative, interpretivist research tradition, with its embrace of individual classroom ethnographies and teacher action research. In its place:

> … a new brand of experimental work began to appear … with great emphasis placed on "reliable, replicable research", large samples, random assignment of treatment to teachers/and or schools, and tried and true outcome measures. It finds its aegis in the experimental rhetoric of science and medicine and in the laboratory research that has examined reading as a perceptual process. (Pearson, 2004: 225)

This trend was clearly evident in the convening of a National Reading Panel in the USA in 1997 that was charged to provide a scientific review of reading research. Its heavy quantitative focus (utilizing meta-analytic techniques wherever possible) and the exclusion of non-experimental studies (e.g., ethnographic studies of students learning to read) clearly reflected the decline in influence of the interpretivist tradition.

The subsequent National Reading Panel Report (2000) considered research undertaken in five key areas between 1966 and 1997: alphabetics, fluency, comprehension, teacher education, and technology. In the alphabetics section the Panel gave close attention to instruction in phonemic/phonological awareness, as this, together with letter knowledge, appeared to be the best predictor of children's early reading progress. The results of a meta-analysis of fifty-two studies that satisfied the Panel's demanding scientific criteria were described as "impressive." Findings showed that incorporating phonemic awareness training in instruction improved children's reading significantly more than programs that did not use such an approach. The Report also indicated that systematic phonics instruction enhanced children's ability to learn to read and noted that this was more effective than instruction that taught little or no phonics. While the impact of phonics was strongest in the early years, it also proved beneficial for older students who struggled to learn to read. However, echoing a conclusion from another major review produced two years earlier by the National Research Council (Snow, Burns, & Griffin, 1998), it was

emphasized that a balanced approach to the teaching of reading was necessary; one in which phonemic awareness training and phonics instruction
were important components.

Prior to the publication of Seidenberg's book (2017) there had long
been frustration on the part of many in the traditionalist camp, particularly in the USA, that despite the strong case for structured phonic approaches to the teaching of reading, teacher training institutions
and school leaders were continuing to emphasize approaches that were
unhelpful for children, particularly those at risk of reading disability.

The emergence of the SoR movement, emphasizing cognitive science and neuroscience, not only reignited the reading wars, it took the
dispute far beyond academic and professional deliberation, to anxious
parents despairing over their children's reading struggles, and to policymakers concerned about the levels of reading performance in public
schools. For advocates of the SoR, the introduction of research findings
from neuroscience, highly persuasive to non-expert audiences (Weisberg
et al., 2008) offered a particularly significant contribution. However, one
could argue that, for the purposes of instruction, findings from neuroscience have largely been used to justify existing practices, particularly the
importance of teaching explicit phonics, the value of which had already
been consistently demonstrated following direct examination of instructional outcomes (Shanahan, 2020).

Arguments about the value of instructional practices informed by the
SoR reflect broader debates within educational research and practice
about the role of cultural and contextual influences. Yaden, Reinking,
and Smagorinsky (2021), for example, argue that a false binary between
nature (represented by the SoR) and nurture has resulted in undue focus
upon "… individualistic, biological, cognitive or neurological orientations
to understanding mental functions in reading isolated from environmental influences" (p. S120). This approach, they contend, has neglected the
influence of learning to read, and broader social and cultural experiences,
upon brain development. Mirroring critiques articulated in the reading
wars over many decades, these authors criticize the SoR movement for
promoting a narrow and monolithic conception of science, underesti-
mating the importance of environmental influences, promoting experimental designs and replicability as the gold standard while minimizing
other investigatory methods, and dismissing other understandings of the
reading process as unscientific and therefore not valuable for informing
educational practice. Hence, the emerging debate is less concerned with
the relative value and status of scientific versus non-scientific approaches

than differing understandings about which research approaches should be described as scientific (or unscientific).

> The future science of reading cannot be limited to a single perspective drawn from the findings of a largely white, Western view of neurology, development, and pedagogy. It cannot be limited to discrete levels of language (orthography, phonology, and semantics) without accounting for the reciprocal relations between other dimensions of language-in-use: discourse, pragmatics, rhetoric, and the culture it maintains and conveys. It demands both culturally and cognitively responsive instruction, continuous improvement that is done with and for those who it is meant to serve. This depends on a two-way flow of evidence where teachers and students take their positions as co-inquirers: remaking, reimagining, and re-mediating education for everyone. (Gabriel, 2020b: 18)

How can findings in basic science research be best translated into the complex understandings that are necessary for effective implementation across different educational contexts (Seidenberg, Cooper Borkenhagen, & Kearns, 2020)? Phonics is a case in point here; Seidenberg and his colleagues note that support for this approach follows logically from scientific studies showing that the important integration of orthography and phonology is much weaker in poor readers. However, how best to deliver phonics teaching in practice is under-researched and far from fully understood (Castles, Rastle, & Nation, 2018; Solity, 2022). The science of reading does not deal significantly with the science of teaching and has little to say about instructional craft. This is a longstanding dilemma and the intellectual forebears of the scientific approach have often been criticized for their limited knowledge and understanding of educational practices, and for underemphasizing the important role of teacher agency and judgement. Without significant attention to the reality of classroom contexts it is unlikely that any new instructional practices can be widely implemented in ways that prove to be effective (Paige et al., 2021).

The SoR has offered particular challenge to instructional approaches that emphasize a studied focus upon contextual factors when reading. Chief amongst these is the three-cueing system associated with the work of Goodman (1967) whose description of the reading process as a "psycholinguistic guessing game" reflected a view of the skilled reader as one who drew upon contextual clues and background knowledge to enable the identification of words. On this basis, teachers were trained to undertake "miscue analysis" in which the child's oral reading errors were classified on the basis of semantic, syntactic, or graphophonic cues. This information could then be used to help children to become more skilled in the guessing process.

Over many decades, research studies have established that prediction on the basis of contextual information as a means of facilitating word identification has been over-emphasized (Adams, 1990; Gough, 1983; Snow & Juel, 2005). By focusing upon alternative cues, and guessing what seems to fit into the text, attention is taken away from the important tasks of building letter–sound connections, and developing automatic word recognition skills, that are so crucial to proficient reading (Ehri, 2020). Contrastingly, contextual cues are more likely to be relied upon by poorer readers who need to find ways to compensate for their poor decoding skills (Stanovich, 1980; Tunmer & Chapman, 2003). As Pressley (2006) observed:

> … perhaps the most disturbing conclusion that comes from this research is that teaching children to decode by giving primacy to semantic-contextual and syntactic-contextual cues over graphemic–phonemic cues is equivalent to teaching them to read the way weak readers read! (Pressley, 2006: 164)

This does not mean that readers should never be encouraged to use other sources of information, particularly the sentence context, when they encounter problems with text. What matters is that such information is used in combination with the decodable aspects of the word such that this will help them to remember the word when they encounter it in the future (Scanlon & Anderson, 2020). In making this point, Scanlon and Anderson emphasize that this is not an either/or issue, but rather, one of prioritization. For these authors, it is crucial that readers are encouraged to closely examine the alphabetic information in the word; otherwise, they are unlikely to be able to store it in memory and eventually be able to read it effortlessly. However, particularly in opaque languages like English, a wholesale reliance on graphophonic information is likely to undermine the reader's ability to self-check for inaccurate pronunciation and impair fluent reading.

The primary difficulty in the reading wars stems from a longstanding divide in which each camp has historically viewed the other with little sympathy, if not contempt. Too often in the past, those who espoused whole language approaches held and presented structured, systematic phonics approaches in a negative light, seeking to reject or marginalize their use. The tedious and decontextualized drills of the past may have been far from ideal for motivating young readers, yet, in the shift towards "authenticity," balance was sacrificed and the advantages of structured instruction in basic skills were often overlooked (Pearson, 2004). For those at risk of reading disability, the historical rejection of systematic skills instruction by the more extreme advocates of the whole language movement has been particularly unhelpful. On the other hand, some advocates for phonics have been guilty of over-emphasizing the contribution of this approach to the point that other key components of reading instruction have been marginalized or ignored. It is not difficult to conclude that both of these extreme positions are unhelpful. A considerably more difficult issue is how to achieve appropriate weighting of these elements in real world contexts, with typically developing readers and with others who are likely to require more individualized approaches (Connor & Morrison, 2016). It is to be hoped that some systemic advances will result as research begins to grapple not only with what works, but also what works for whom, under what conditions (Petscher et al., 2020; Shanahan, 2021; Siegelman et al., 2022).

The disinterested observer might well remark that surely what is needed in the reading wars is a greater sense of balance between different camps. However, balance is a rather slippery concept and as Calfee and Norman (1998) observe, neither side has argued for an unbalanced position; instead, each group criticizes the other for holding extreme views. The search for a more nuanced approach has been compromised by the promotion of the term "balanced literacy" largely by those whose position was weakened by scientific developments at the end of the twentieth century, a time when some believed that the reading wars were drawing to a close. At this time, there was renewed hope that new insights offered opportunities for a shared understanding. Such optimism was reflected in a report produced for a British Government working group (Literacy Task Force, 1997):

> There have been few more vigorous educational controversies in the last decade than the one over how literacy, and in particular reading, should be taught. Opposing sides in the national debate have vociferously proclaimed their loyalty to "phonics" or "real books". But while this often shallow debate has raged, research and the understanding of "best practice" have moved on. (Literacy Task Force, 1997: 14)

To advocates of the SoR, the ready adoption of balanced literacy approaches failed to mark the end of the reading wars. It was perceived (sometimes accurately) that the term was introduced to serve as a smokescreen that could enable opponents to bypass the increasingly persuasive evidence for phonics and continue with the whole language approach largely as before. While "balanced literacy" is an attractive concept, the difficulty of developing and delivering an effective instructional approach on this basis created a vacuum that was unsurprisingly filled by existing practices:

> Incorporating phonics in a serious way requires addressing some tough
> questions: how to teach it, how much is enough, how much is too much,
> how to integrate it with reading and literacy. Balanced literacy provided lit-
> tle guidance for teachers who thought that phonics was a cause of poor read-
> ing and did not know how to teach it …. For educators opposed to phonics,
> only a nod in that direction was required for curricula and practices to be
> marketable as a "balanced" program. (Seidenberg, 2017: 266–267)

In the heat of the reading wars it has sometimes been overlooked that
approaches to the teaching of reading may not be uniformly appropriate for all levels of ability. Those with reading difficulties, irrespective of
their individual biological and environmental circumstances, are more
likely than others to be undermined by whole language approaches that
neglect explicit instruction of letter–sound relationships (Juel & Minden-
Cupp, 2000; Stanovich, 2000; Tunmer & Nicholson, 2011; Tunmer &
Prochnow, 2009). They are less able than their normally achieving peers
to discover letter–sound patterns as a consequence of reading, and thus
require more explicit teaching (Calfee & Drum, 1986). Such instruction
should not leave essential skills and knowledge to be discovered by the
child on their own (Torgesen, 2004).

While "attention to small units in early reading instruction is helpful
for all children, harmful for none, and crucial for some" (Snow & Juel,
2005: 518) a very high level of structured intervention may not be necessary or, indeed, ideal for all (Arrow & Tunmer, 2012). Thus, in a comparative study of stronger and weaker readers, Juel and Minden-Cupp
(2000) found that first-grade children with limited reading skills made
more progress in classrooms where there was greater emphasis upon word
recognition instruction. In contrast, those with stronger skills benefited
more from a literature-rich environment with rather less emphasis upon
basic decoding. Similarly, in a study of first graders, Connor, Morrison,
and Katch (2004) found that an emphasis upon the explicit teaching of
decoding skills was beneficial for those children with low initial decoding
skills but had no effect for those with high initial scores. Underlying the
importance of this debate for reading-disabled children, the influence of
classroom instruction, positive or negative, was greater for those with poor
decoding skills and weaker vocabulary than for those with strengths in
these areas. Thus, the suggestion that a standard balanced approach is suitable for all children is over-simplistic and potentially misleading. Instead,
the available evidence suggests that the particular emphasis of differing
instructional strategies in any given context should be adjusted to reflect
students' differing skill levels and particular areas of reading difficulty

(Burns, Young, et al., 2022; Connor et al., 2009; Connor, 2011; Connor & Morrison, 2016; Ehri, 2020; Szadokierski, Burns, & McComas, 2017).

Irrespective of the child's reading skills, it is now widely accepted that a systematic phonics approach generally leads to superior reading skills when compared with a non-phonics or nonsystematic phonics approach in both opaque (Brooks, 2022; Ehri et al., 2001) and transparent (de Graaff et al., 2009) languages (but cf. Bowers, 2020, and a response by Fletcher, Savage, & Vaughn, 2021; Brooks, 2023). Nevertheless, and perhaps because of contested positions, the evidential claims for phonics (and which type of phonics approach should be employed; Solity, 2022) are sometimes overstated by advocates and policymakers (Wyse & Bradbury, 2022). This may lead to cynicism and continuing reluctance on the part of some teachers to embrace such approaches.

The value of providing explicit phonics instruction in a systematic fashion is clear although this should only be part of the instructional story (Castles, Rastle, & Nation, 2018). Evidence that teachers need to look to a balanced approach in which phonics instruction is but one important element was provided in a research synthesis of reading programs for children in the elementary grades (Slavin et al., 2009). Beginning reading programs that were found to be effective or promising had a strong focus on teaching phonics and phonemic awareness (see Rehfeld et al., 2022; Rice et al., 2022), for reviews demonstrating the efficacy of phonemic awareness training. Helpful guidance to practitioners on phonemic awareness training is provided by Rice, Erbeli, and Wijekumar (2023), although also see Clemens et al. (2021) advocating caution in the use of "advanced" phonemic awareness training, particularly should this take away from time engaging with print.

Researchers have also cautioned against a disproportionate emphasis on both phonics and phonemic awareness as these, in isolation, are unlikely to prove sufficient for achieving positive reading gains. Rather, teachers should address the key components of linguistic awareness – phonological, orthographic, and morphological – that are important for reading development (Berninger et al., 2010; Colenbrander et al., 2022; Lyster et al., 2021). Furthermore, phonics should not be taught in a narrow, decontextualized fashion. Teachers need to root such instruction within a broad-based literacy curriculum that includes sight-word recognition, fluency, vocabulary, spelling, oral and written comprehension (Bianco et al., 2010), and reading for meaning and writing (Brooks, 2022; Wyse & Bradbury, 2022). Their emphasis should be differentiated on the basis of student strengths and weaknesses (Fletcher et al., 2019).

The appropriate question to ask of a twenty-first century science of teaching is not the superiority of phonics versus alternative reading methods, including whole language and balanced literacy, but how best to combine different components of evidence-based reading instruction into an integrated and customized approach that addresses the learning needs of each child. (Fletcher, Savage, & Vaughn, 2021: 1249)

How Can We Best Identify Young Children at Risk of Reading Disability and Prevent Later Problems?

Identification of Those at Risk of Reading Disability

Reading is not a natural process and no brain systems have evolved for the purpose of reading. To become a reader, the individual needs to repurpose and reorganize existing visual and language processing neural circuits. Over a period of years these become integrated into an increasingly sophisticated system that enables skilful reading. Where this process does not happen effectively, the child begins to fall behind and their ability to recognize patterns of letters automatically is hindered. Reading becomes a challenging and unrewarding task with concomitant negative effects upon the child's motivation and agency (Vaughn & Fletcher, 2021). The need to intervene as early as possible has been highlighted by growing awareness of the greater plasticity of the brain, particularly during early development (Gilmore, Knickmeyer, & Gao, 2018; Yeatman, 2022a) but also by research showing that word reading interventions commencing after kindergarten and first grade tend to be less effective (Wanzek et al., 2016; Lovett et al., 2017). Not only does the struggling reader start to fall behind their peers, but they are also likely to find it increasingly difficult to establish the necessary neural systems later in their lives. For children at risk of reading disability, the provision of high-quality whole class instruction may prove insufficient. Some will require closer monitoring leading, where necessary, to supplementary intervention. This may need to continue for several years as gains are not necessarily sustained over time, a phenomenon sometimes referred to as "fade-out" (Bailey et al., 2020; Middleton et al., 2022; Slavin et al. 2011; Sokolowski & Peters, 2022).

For the reasons outlined above, early ascertainment of risk, together with early intervention, are preferable to traditional "wait to fail" approaches where children with reading disability are typically not identified until later grades. The lengthy process of initial inaction, followed by referral, assessment, and finally, a diagnosis, is likely to conclude at a point when the best time for intervention has already passed; an unfortunate situation that has been termed the "dyslexia paradox" (Ozernov-Palichik & Gaab, 2016).

As discussed in Chapter 1, RTI involving MTSS typically, but not exclusively, consisting of three levels, has been widely promoted and adopted in the USA and in several other countries as a means to provide as early and as swift a response as possible (National Center for Response to Intervention, 2010). While RTI approaches were principally designed to identify children who were failing to respond to instruction, screening from a very young age is now recognized as an essential component.

At the level of primary intervention (Tier 1), high-quality literacy instruction provided by classroom teachers is fundamental (Al Otaiba, Allor, et al., 2019). Sound teacher expertise from the first years of schooling is essential, given that teacher content knowledge of early language and literacy skills has been shown to be related to the development of students' foundational reading skills (Porter et al., 2023).

It is important that classroom teachers can quickly become alert to those children who are finding it difficult to acquire early reading skills (Clemens et al., 2023). The awareness that the skilled teacher gains from repeated interactions with their students should be complemented by more systematic screening and close monitoring of subsequent progress. A reading inventory may be employed to assess the child's reading related skills in greater detail and identify areas requiring more explicit instruction (Fletcher, Savage, & Vaughn, 2021). It is anticipated that Tier 1 provision of this kind will be sufficient for the majority of children identified as at risk, particularly those whose problems stem predominantly from a less rich language experience early in life (Catts & Hogan, 2021). For those who continue to make inadequate progress, secondary intervention (Tier 2) is provided by the classroom teacher, a trained teaching assistant supervised by the classteacher or by a specialist reading teacher. Such assistance may take the form of supplemental small-group instruction, involving more explicit instruction, scaffolding, and practice alongside regular and systematic monitoring of the child's progress. Here further short probes involving timed word or passage reading can provide valuable information to teachers (Fuchs et al., 2021). For the small proportion of children who continue to experience difficulty, tertiary intervention (Tier 3) provides more intensive small group or individual instruction with a significant emphasis upon ongoing assessment, feedback and monitoring. In practice, the distinction between tiers 2 and 3 is often one more of degree than of kind, with the major differences between them usually being the intensity of the intervention and the precision of the measurements (Reschly, 2005).

This can include special education which further adds to the complexity of the model (Sayeski, Reno, & Thoele, 2022). Fletcher et al. (2019) suggest that, of those children who are involved in a three tier model, one might anticipate 75–90 percent being situated at Level 1, 10–25 percent at Level 2, and 2–10 percent at Level 3. The process for a given individual does not need progression through each tier in turn and in a small number of cases, screening might indicate that the child's needs would be better served if they were directly assigned to a Tier 2 or Tier 3 intervention (Al Otaiba et al., 2014; Bouton et al., 2018).

Despite its emphasis upon universal screening and close monitoring, the growth of the RTI approach has not dispelled concerns that many children who are likely to develop a reading disability are failing to be identified or adequately supported. These appear to be well founded in a significant number of cases, particularly in those schools where low literacy performance is the norm rather than the exception (Odegard, Hutchings, et al., 2021). Growing pressure from worried parents that schools are not meeting the literacy needs of their children has resulted in a vociferous and powerful dyslexia lobby that has had some success in campaigning for more effective direct instruction in basic skills and special programs for identified dyslexic children. In the United States, such advocacy has resulted in dyslexia legislation being introduced in most states with more than forty requiring some form of screening (Vaughn & Fletcher, 2021).

Calls for dyslexia screening by influential political and advocacy groups have more recently gained the attention of UK policymakers. However, reflecting the principal concern of the present text, the issue of how exactly the term dyslexia should be operationalized is rarely considered or debated in detail. In many cases, the term dyslexia is employed to refer to a persistent difficult in reading and spelling, a conception that perhaps maps closely on to Dyslexia 1 (a synonym for reading disability) and 3 (persistent intractability to high-quality reading intervention) as described in Chapter 1. Researchers and commentators may occasionally differentiate between dyslexia and reading difficulties although typically they fail to operationalize these terms, merely referring back to existing definitions, which fail to clarify the nature of the distinction. Burns, VanDerHeyden, et al. (2022), for example, examine the ability of various literacy screening tools to predict dyslexia, employing a composite measure of phonological awareness as the principal dyslexia criterion. They justify this by referring to the emphasis upon phonology expressed in the International Dyslexia Association's definition of dyslexia. However, using a measure incorporating items such as letter naming and word and nonword reading as a predictor of a dyslexic condition that is itself operationalized by phonological awareness, illustrates the confusions and misunderstandings that abound.

Ascertaining risk status in respect of reading disability for very young children is not a straightforward enterprise. All screening assessments should have high sensitivity (true positives detected by the screening tool) and high specificity (true negatives that are detected by the screening tool). In similar vein, assessors try to minimize decisions that children are at risk when they are not (false positives) and that children are not at risk when, in actuality, they are (false negatives). The proportion of true and false positives and negatives will be a function of the cut-off point used for screening, but these are essentially arbitrary given that reading skill is dimensional rather than categorical. The more lenient the cut-off, the more likely that an increased number of positive cases, both true and false, will be identified. False negatives can result in at-risk children failing to receive the additional intervention that they require (Jenkins, Hudson, & Johnson, 2007). In contrast, high levels of false positives can result in the inappropriate use of scarce resources and take teachers away from the key task of providing instruction (Castro-Villareal, Rodriguez, & Moore, 2014; Catts et al., 2009). While the desire to achieve high sensitivity values may have often led to high false-positive rates, this is generally considered to be less of a problem than missing those who need help (Burns, VanDerHeyden, et al., 2022 Vaughn & Fletcher, 2021) and it is possible that even wrongly identified kindergarten children may still benefit from specialized interventions (Scanlon et al., 2005). Moreover, interventions focusing upon emergent literacy skills in kindergarten and first grade often need to be less intensive than in the later years and thus, are relatively inexpensive.

Where US states have mandated screening, almost all require screening in kindergarten (Odegard et al., 2024). However, predicting future reading disability can be difficult before children have had sufficient experience of literacy-based activities. At this age, literacy experience and instruction can have a significant influence upon performance on the measures of letter knowledge and phonological awareness that are typically found in screening assessments (Catts et al., 2009). Furthermore, predictors vary in their ability to identify future reading difficulties for children of different ages. For example, letter naming fluency is a powerful predictor of word reading accuracy and fluency at the end of first grade but afterwards this declines significantly (Catts et al., 2015). With increased interest in the use of new statistical approaches to evaluate multivariate screening assessments (Petscher & Koon, 2020) screening for skills that are often in rapid development can be likened to hitting a moving target (Speece, 2005). It is important to note in this respect that screening cannot be purely an early years' initiative. A significant proportion of children in kindergarten and Grade 1 who are progressing appropriately in the development of early literacy skills, such as phonemic segmentation and knowledge of letter sounds and names (variables that predict response to reading intervention in kindergarten; Hagan-Burke et al., 2013), later demonstrate reading problems, particularly around third or fourth grade (Catts et al., 2012; Leach, Scarborough, & Rescorla, 2003; Lipka, Lesaux, & Siegel, 2006; O'Connor et al., 2005) when a greater proportion of multisyllabic words is being introduced. Subsequently, a gradual shift from learning to read to reading to learn results in greater demands involving greater use of technical vocabulary and unfamiliar text structures (Gutiérrez et al., 2022).

An alternative option that is increasingly being advocated by RTI advocates is to avoid making screening decisions on the basis of a one-off measure and, instead, utilize multistage assessment.[23] Given the arbitrary and problematic nature of thresholds and cut-off scores for continuous normally distributed scores, which are prone to measurement error, it is invidious to treat, as different, students who may score very similarly but are just narrowly situated on one side or the other of any single decision point. Accordingly, decisions should not be made on the basis of a single assessment or screening score but should involve multiple measures and data points and, where possible, the use of confidence intervals and clinical or educational judgement.

Assessment on the basis of progress is not without its methodological problems, particularly when used with very young children. Some infants may not have sufficient cognitive, linguistic, or attentional maturity to respond to the tasks in ways that will reveal their true potential. For others, significant gains may be made in kindergarten that cannot be sustained in later years, particularly where the home environment is suboptimal (Kieffer, 2012). Al Otaiba and colleagues (2011) found that a good response on a variety of language and literacy measures in kindergarten, across a diverse range of schools, was not a good predictor of first-grade performance. They suggested that this was probably because low scoring children tended to have more room for growth when entering kindergarten than their more advantaged peers. Such gains may mask the true extent of some

---

[23] RTI assessment should also involve examination of children's progress in performance over time, although this issue has received far less researcher attention than has screening, perhaps because the latter tends to be easier and less expensive to conduct (Fuchs & Vaughn, 2012).

children's difficulties and, as a result, a need for specialized support in first grade may not be recognized.

There are many measures available for screening young children at risk of reading disability. These can be divided into those that directly address underlying reading skills and others, often purporting to identify underlying dyslexia, that introduce other, supposedly related, skills. Those of the former approach tend to include measures of phonemic awareness, letter naming fluency, concepts about print, word reading and oral language fluency (Compton et al., 2010). Arguably, the most common screening tool in the USA is the *Dynamic Indicators of Basic Early Literacy Skills, DIBELS* (Good & Kaminski, 2003).

DIBELS was originally designed to measure progress over time for children from kindergarten to sixth grade but is also used within RTI models of practice as a screening tool to identify children who may be at risk of reading disabilities. This tool initially consisted of seven measures, five of which directly address underlying decoding skills: phonological awareness (fluency in identifying initial sounds of given words and segmenting the phonemes in a word), knowledge of the alphabetic principle (fluency in letter naming and nonsense word reading) and oral reading fluency of connected text. Reported reliabilities are sound (Good et al., 2004), although concern has been expressed about the equivalencies of some of the reading passages. If these differ in demand, it is possible that the particular passage selected at a given measurement point might affect perceptions as to whether a child's performance has changed substantially, for the better or the worse (Scanlon, 2011). Zumeta, Compton, and Fuchs (2012), for example, found that, for low achieving first-grade children, a measure with a broad range of high-frequency words appeared to be a better predictor than one using a more narrowly sampled list. Since its inception, DIBELS has been regularly revised and updated, and is currently operating a seventh edition, *DIBELS Next*.

Catts and colleagues (2009) surveyed findings from *DIBELS* screening in relation to progress for more than eighteen thousand children enrolled in the Florida *Reading First* program. They found significant floor effects that obscured individual differences between those at the lower end of the distribution, and poor predictability. These difficulties were not tied to a particular grade level but were a feature of initial administrations of the measures. Predictability improved as further administrations took place, although problems remained with the initial sound and phoneme segmentation tasks. Noting that other measures of phonological awareness (e.g., the *Comprehensive Test of Phonological Processing*, Wagner, Torgesen, &

Rashotte, 1999; and the *Phonological Awareness Test*, Robertson & Salter, 1997) also show floor effects at the beginning of kindergarten, the authors emphasized the importance of not only selecting the correct screening instrument but also ensuring that this is administered at the right time. While delaying the assessment may help, this leaves open the possibility that identification of children at risk of reading disability will also be delayed.

An evaluation of the predictive accuracy and psychometric adequacy of the sixth edition of *DIBELS* (Smolkowski & Cummings, 2016) proved to be largely positive although, similar to Catts et al. (2009), doubts were expressed about the predictive validity of the phoneme segmentation task. Interestingly, in a large meta-analysis of children in Grades K, 1 or 2, phoneme segmentation scores also had a weaker overall correlation with relatively advanced reading outcomes compared with measures of alphabetic knowledge (i.e., letter names and sounds) (January & Klingbeil, 2020).

As noted above, dyslexia screening tests can be divided into those situations where the term operates as a synonym for reading disability (Dyslexia 1 and 3) (e.g., Fletcher et al., 2019; Barnes & Peltier, 2022) and others where dyslexia is considered to be a separate, discrete condition (Dyslexia 2 and 4) (e.g., Burns, VanDerHeyden et al., 2022). Barnes and Peltier (2022) lament what they consider to be misunderstandings of these terms such that some US states screen for risk of dyslexia and word-level reading disability as if they were differing conditions.

In New Zealand, an assessment protocol for schools, *Three Steps in Screening for Dyslexia* (New Zealand Ministry of Education, 2021) has been evaluated by Sleeman and colleagues (2022b). Their examination of the use of this tool with children aged 8–10 years identified a number of technical difficulties which led them to offer a series of recommendations for modification. However, these authors failed to challenge a screening approach for dyslexia that appears to be highly questionable for the following reasons:

a. the tool appears to conceive of screening in a very different way to contemporary understandings where the predominant emphasis is upon identifying children at risk of future reading disability. This should take place as early as possible; the children in the study had already reached an age where the introduction of targeted intervention is far from ideal;

b. the spurious use of "language comprehension" as a means of determining which poor readers should be termed dyslexic is problematic; conceptually, technically, practically and equitably (see Chapter 1 for discussion);

c. the assessment procedure is very time-consuming, and asking teachers effectively to diagnose dyslexia takes time away from instruction. Identifying those who are struggling with reading can be undertaken with short reading and spelling assessments.

Dyslexia screeners that seek to differentiate dyslexia from reading disability tend to include a wider range of items. In its twelve subtests, for example, the Dyslexia Early Screening Test (2nd edition) (DEST; Nicolson & Fawcett, 2004), designed for children aged 4.5 to 6.5 years, includes measures of rapid naming, memory, shape copying, postural stability, and bead threading.

Fine and gross motor skills of various kinds often feature in dyslexia checklists although their role in screening and diagnosis has long been contentious (see Chapter 2). According to Crombie and Reid (2009), early identification of future literacy difficulties can be made from observations of very young children, with early pointers including a "… lack of coordination and sequencing skills as the baby struggles to learn to crawl (or simply does not bother to crawl)" (p. 72). However, despite its appeal, the evidence base for the predictive validity of motor assessment in relation to reading disability is weak (Barth et al., 2010). Although the DEST authors claim that postural stability is "… one of the best predictors of resistance to remediation" (Nicolson & Fawcett, 2004: 15), Barth and colleagues (2010) found little evidence to link performance on either of the two motor subtests to reading proficiency or to children's response to intervention; the most powerful predictors proved to be phonological awareness and rapid naming of letters. Simpson, and Everatt (2005) found that some DEST subtests; sound order (a measure of auditory perception), rapid naming (of familiar outline pictures), and knowledge of lower case letter names, proved to be better predictors of reading and spelling performance than the total score. Carroll, Solity, and Shapiro (2016) similarly found that for entrants to school aged between 4 and 5, the rapid naming subtest from the DEST, and a measure of letter naming, were unique predictors of later literacy difficulties. The DEST's motor skill and balance measures proved not to be closely related to subsequent literacy performance. Employing two measures of fine motor skill (bead threading and line drawing) from the Movement ABC (Henderson, Sugden, & Barnett, 2007), Malone, Pritchard, and Hulme (2022) sought to ascertain the extent to which performance at age 5 predicted word-level decoding skills a year later. While a weak correlation was found, fine motor performance failed to account for variance in reading after controlling for domain-specific predictors of early reading skill such as phoneme awareness, letter sound knowledge, and RAN.

Given the high numbers of children who may be potentially at risk of reading failure (Odegard et al., 2021), and concerns that complex and resource-heavy RTI systems are not succeeding in identifying and individualizing children's needs, screening approaches need to be brief yet maintain sound levels of predictive reliability and validity. Fletcher, Francis et al. (2021) summarized findings from a long-running research program in Texas that sought to develop and evaluate short (3–5-minute) teacher-administered screening tools geared to predict those children at risk of reading difficulties (word reading and reading comprehension). The program was guided by five challenges:

a. creating a short measure that could be administered in 3–5 minutes but could maintain a false negative rate below 10 percent;
b. predicting future reading achievement prior to the introduction of formal reading instruction;
c. identifying when the tasks in the screening measure would be maximally predictive
d. exploring whether similar or reduced false positive and false negative rates could be achieved with an even briefer assessment;
e. ensuring that there was no gender, ethnic, or age bias in the predictions.

The data reported in the paper were gathered in 1992–96. Children were assessed in the middle and at the end of kindergarten, at the beginning and end of first grade and at the beginning of second grade. Measures covered phonological processing, rapid naming, knowledge of letter names and sounds, vocabulary, and single word reading. Outcome assessments were undertaken at the end of first and second grade using word reading and reading comprehension tests.

For the kindergarten children, letter–sound naming and phonological awareness were consistently found to be the best predictors. However, by the beginning of first grade, letter–sound knowledge had reached a performance ceiling for many, so this measure was only retained for those for those who had not attended kindergarten. At this stage, phonological awareness and simple word reading were most predictive; however, by the end of first grade, only word reading was a necessary predictor. The authors emphasize that while other elements such as rapid naming and vocabulary were predictive, they did not offer additional information that could improve decision-making (see also Kim & Petscher, 2023, for a similar finding for vocabulary). However, they noted that other studies have indicated unique contributions from measures of language (e.g., Catts et al., 2015). There were no indications of age or gender effects. No bias in prediction was found for gender or ethnicity. This latter finding is particularly important given evidence for lower screening identification of students of color in the USA (Odegard et al., 2020) and immigrant groups in Europe (e.g., Verpalen, de Vijver, & Backus, 2018).

In addition to examining absolute performance at any given time, the growth trajectory of children's early reading skills is likely to provide valuable additional information that can inform practice. Clemens et al. (2023) examined the progress of 426 ethnically and linguistically diverse children considered to be at risk for reading difficulties at the start of kindergarten. The children's early reading skill development was assessed during the year using seven measures: letter–name fluency, letter–sound fluency, phoneme segmentation fluency, word reading fluency, decodable word reading, nonsense word fluency, and a computer adaptive early literacy test. At the end of kindergarten and first grade, the children were given standardized tests of word reading, pseudoword decoding, and oral reading. Growth in letter–sound fluency during the fall was found to be most strongly related to later word reading skills. During the subsequent spring, progress in word reading fluency took over as the strongest predictor. These findings appeared to be equally applicable to emergent bilingual children, although, here, interpretive caution was recommended. Emphasizing the importance of monitoring the progress of basic reading skills in kindergarten, the authors concluded that measures of letter–sound fluency and word reading fluency, undertaken during fall and spring respectively, may be powerful indicators of any need to intensify preventive interventions.

Kim and Petscher (2023) have suggested that simple spelling measures may also help to predict subsequent reading difficulties. They showed that a researcher-designed spelling task, undertaken in kindergarten, was able to improve the accuracy of reading performance predictions in Grade 1 when employed in combination with measures of letter identification and word reading.

Fletcher, Francis et al. (2021) note that legislation has often required school authorities to use multiple measures for screening (Petscher et al., 2019). They caution that not only does this place too great a burden upon practitioners, the introduction of additional variables that are less powerful predictors may result in reduced accuracy (VanderHeyden, Burns, & Bonifay, 2018). In addition, too much data may confuse practitioners, particularly if they lack sufficient knowledge about how to use it effectively.

Findings from two large-scale evaluations in the USA (Balu et al., 2015; Cordray et al., 2012), for example, found screening to be unhelpful because school staff did not use the data obtained to inform action, perhaps because they felt insufficiently trained to be able to base their practice on the assessment data generated (Al Otaiba, Baker, et al., 2019).

It is also important that contextual factors are not overlooked. In seeking to identify methods and measures that can be used to predict subsequent reading disability it is easy to forget that a significant variable will be the classroom environment, involving such elements as the influence of classmates, the nature of the curriculum, and the nature and expression of individual teacher skill.

Finally, there are other professionals who can assist in the identification of potential problems. Concerted attempts are being made to raise awareness on the part of social workers (Schelbe et al., 2021) and pediatricians (Tridas et al., 2023; Sanfilippo et al., 2020) about how they might assist in the identification of children who may need special help with reading, particularly those living in socially disadvantaged circumstances. Educators need to be aware of the challenges that are more likely to confront children from disadvantaged environments but acting on recommendations that a range of environment and sociocultural factors should be included in screening procedures (e.g., Gaab & Petscher, 2022) could prove problematic. This would be likely to render screening measures overly complex and burdensome and lead them to be less impactful for teacher action. Simple screening using key predictors for all children is preferable, but such measures should operate alongside heightened awareness that reading difficulties often fail to be identified and treated in children from minority ethnic groups or those who live in poverty (Odegard et al., 2020). The individual learning needs of children who have been subjected to various types of adversity should not be ignored, but, given current understandings, there is a risk that emphasis upon such factors within the screening process could reduce the "unexpected" nature of the reading problem and thus impact the likelihood of a dyslexia diagnosis with the resource benefits that often follow this label (see Chapter 1 for relevant discussion).

Reading Interventions in the Early Years

The goal of secondary intervention is that struggling readers will be enabled to catch up with their peers. Crucially, explicit instruction needs to be provided as early as possible, preferably before the end of second grade.

While the precise balance of activities needs to be tailored to the particular strengths and weaknesses of the child, key elements should include:

- phonemic awareness
- phonics
- spelling/writing
- fluency
- vocabulary
- comprehension

A vast raft of studies utilizing structured approaches to intervention have generally produced positive outcomes showing that young children at risk of reading disability can be helped to make significant gains in basic reading skills (but cf. Suggate, 2016, for a less positive conclusion). In a series of intervention studies, Vellutino and colleagues (Scanlon et al., 2005; Vellutino, Scanlon, & Jaccard, 2003; Vellutino, Scanlon, & Lyon, 2000; Vellutino et al., 1996; Vellutino, Scanlon, & Tanzman, 1998) repeatedly demonstrated this powerful effect. In their 1996 study (Vellutino et al., 1996), daily one-to-one tutoring was provided to first-grade children scoring below the fifteenth percentile on measures of word and pseudoword reading. Those who failed to make adequate progress received further help in second grade. The total amount of assistance ranged from thirty-five to sixty-five hours. It was found that 67.1 percent of the tutored children could be brought to within the average range of reading ability in just one semester of remediation and most could maintain this level of functioning when reassessed at the end of the fourth grade.

Vellutino, Scanlon and their colleagues (Scanlon et al., 2005; 2008) have also examined interventions in kindergarten for children at risk of reading difficulty. It was found that small group instruction, with a heavy emphasis upon the development of phonological processing skills (two 30-minute sessions each week throughout the school year, and continued in first grade), reduced the number of children who qualified as poor readers in first grade (Scanlon et al., 2005). Moreover, this intervention reduced the number of children who were still struggling with reading at the end of first grade (treatment resisters). Indeed, at the end of first grade, none of the children who had received the kindergarten intervention, plus a first-grade programme emphasizing the development of phonological skills, obtained a standard score below 85 on the Basic Skills subtest of the Woodcock Reading Mastery Test (WRMT-R; Woodcock, 1987). In the light of their findings, the authors suggested that a powerful means of reducing treatment resistance is to provide modest amounts of small-group intervention in kindergarten before early differences in literacy skills are exacerbated by subsequent failure to profit from classroom instruction. This should be followed up in first grade by an intensive intervention with a particular focus upon the development of phonological skills.

Systematic reviews and meta-analyses are being increasingly employed across the social sciences as means to obtain an integrative picture of findings from studies in particular areas that can often prove to be contradictory (Sharpe & Poets, 2020). Unsurprisingly, such approaches have been widely employed to yield an estimate of the effectiveness of interventions for reading disability. While such analyses are useful, we must recognize that comparison across studies is rendered problematic by differences in the operationalization of terms such as at risk and inadequate responder, changes in norms in standardized tests over time, the nature of control and comparison groups, varying levels of participant attrition, the experience and skill of personnel in operating standardized interventions, differences in readiness to measure and account for fidelity of implementation, the tendency for publication bias, and frequent findings of low statistical power (Calvi et al., 2023; King et al., 2023). Dahl-Leonard et al. (2023) examined the level of fidelity reporting for 51 reading intervention studies in grades K-5 for students with, or at risk of, dyslexia. While 75 percent of the studies reported some fidelity data this tended to focus upon the dosage and adherence to the program. As was similarly found in an earlier exercise by Capin et al. (2018), very little information was provided about other important aspects of fidelity such as quality, responsiveness, and differentiation (see Dane & Schneider, 1998, for delineation of these components).

Most systematic reviews and meta-analytic studies of reading disability have focused upon the potential contribution of phonics-based approaches. A positive finding was reported in an analysis of one-to-one tutoring programs for struggling readers (Slavin et al., 2011) where an overall effect size (ES) of 0.39 was found. Those schemes with less emphasis upon phonics (e.g., *Reading Recovery*; Clay, 1985) tended to report smaller effect sizes (mean = 0.23) than studies with an explicit and systematic approach to phonics (0.56). This finding is particularly relevant to young children as the contribution of phonics tends to be less powerful for older struggling readers (Flynn, Zheng, & Swanson, 2012). A more recent *Reading Recovery* study involving more than 17,000 third and fourth-grade children (May et al., 2023) found that state test results for reading and English language arts were both statistically significant and substantially negative. Students who participated in *Reading Recovery* in first grade had third and fourth grade state test scores in reading (ELA) that were, on average, 0.19 to 0.43

standard deviations (about one-half to one full grade level) below the state test scores of similar students who did not participate in the program. For a detailed account of issues surrounding *Reading Recovery* and the role played by phonics in this program, see Chapman and Tunmer (2019b).

Wanzek and her colleagues have undertaken a number of meta-analyses and reviews of interventions for elementary schoolchildren. Wanzek and Vaughn (2007) examined intervention studies involving students enrolled in kindergarten through to third grade that had been conducted between 1995 and 2005. Their focus was upon extensive interventions (involving more than 100 sessions), aspects that had not been specifically examined in previous syntheses (Foorman, 2003; McCardle & Chhabra, 2004; Pressley, 2006). For the purposes of this investigation, extensive interventions were defined as those occurring for 100 sessions or more. Interestingly, it could be questioned whether there was disagreement as to whether the interventions were really operating at Tier 2 (Fletcher et al., 2019) or more closely resembled those at Tier 3. At Tier 2, additional instruction is typically provided for children for whom core Tier 1 provision appears to be insufficient although where the boundaries should lie between this and Tier 3 is not always clear.

A further noteworthy aspect of Wanzek and Vaughn's meta-analysis was their desire to focus upon the relative contributions of standardized and individualized approaches. Standardized approaches are those where instruction is provided in a relatively uniform fashion to all the students, but with some adjustments to ensure appropriateness of challenge to those of differing ability levels. Individualized approaches involve more of a problem-solving approach in which children's skills are assessed, the nature of the form of intervention for each child is determined individually, close monitoring of progress is conducted, and in the light of regular feedback, the nature of the intervention is amended. In practice, the authors were unable to locate any extensive intervention studies utilizing an individualized approach and, as a result, their synthesis compared approaches categorized as high versus low standardization. Low standardization lessons were those with less clear prescription where teachers had more freedom to modify their approach in the light of emerging student needs. Eighteen studies met the criteria for inclusion in the synthesis.

Wanzek and Vaughn (2007) reported mean effect sizes ranging from 0.34 to 0.56 on measures of foundational reading skills after the provision of extensive intervention. It was found that higher effect sizes were associated with early intervention (beginning in first grade) and smaller group sizes. No difference was found between high and low standardization groups. While this finding is based upon a relatively small number of studies, it is consonant with outcomes reported by Mathes et al. (2005) and by Vaughn et al. (2011) in the case of struggling middle school students. Mathes and colleagues found only one difference between more and less standardized approaches; in this case the former group scored rather more highly on a measure of word attack. However, as these researchers noted, while there may be scope for teacher choice about which approach to use, this does not mean that the content of supplementary instruction is unimportant. In comparing two very different approaches (behavioral versus cognitive-apprenticeship) that proved to be equally effective, they point out that both:

> … provided for instruction in key reading skills, balanced with opportunities to apply reading and writing skills in connected text, and they both provided students with explicit instruction and practice in skills related to phonemic awareness, decoding, fluent word recognition and text processing, and spelling. Likewise, both approaches provided instruction in comprehension strategies applied to connected text. (Mathes et al., 2005: 179)

An update to this meta-analysis was produced by Wanzek et al. (2018). As before, the focus was upon intensive reading interventions for children in grades K-3 in which there were more than 100 sessions. Most of the interventions took place daily or four times per week, were commonly of 30-minute duration, and operated in one-to-one or small group situations. Twenty-five studies met the study criteria and the subsequent analysis produced a mean effect size of 0.39 which was lowered to 0.28 when correction for publication bias was undertaken. More than 90 percent of the effect sizes involved were taken from standardized measures which added to researcher confidence about the findings.

Wanzek and colleagues (2016) also carried out a meta-analysis of less extensive Tier 2 reading interventions involving 72 studies for children in Grades K-3 who were considered to have, or be at risk of, reading difficulties. Unlike the more intensive interventions discussed above, work with the majority of children in the early years has a strong preventative element with a focus upon early identification of those at risk of reading failure and implementation of a relatively brief intervention to try to enable the children to get back on track. Feedback from this can then be used to identify those children who will require more substantial input.

Wanzek and her colleagues identified 72 studies; 37 experimental, 30 quasi-experimental, and a further five where allocation to treatment and comparison groups was unclear. Nineteen studies examined interventions in kindergarten only, 27 in first grade only, two in third grade only, and

17 operated across multiple grades. The number of intervention sessions ranged from 15 to 99 sessions over 4–32 weeks. The mean effect size for the 63 studies that used standardized measures of reading was 0.49, indicating a moderate positive effect of intervention on children's foundational reading skills such as phonemic awareness, decoding, word recognition, and text reading fluency. In the 33 studies that used non-standardized measures, the effect size was 0.62. Effect sizes using the standardized measures were higher in kindergarten (0.54) and first grade (0.50) than in second and third grade (0.40).

The meta-analysis also examined the potential effects of a number of moderator variables. Variance was not significantly explained by instructional group size, the type of intervention provided, the total number of hours of intervention, or who had implemented the intervention. However, the authors noted that sample sizes may have resulted in insufficient statistical power in some cases. A further lesson was that, particularly for the youngest children, there may be little difference in immediate effects irrespective of whether the intervention focuses solely upon foundational reading skills or alternatively, takes the form of a multicomponent intervention that includes work on comprehension and language. This finding, relating to practice in the early years, can be contrasted with the emphasis upon multicomponent intervention that is considered to be best practice for children in the upper elementary and secondary grades. While group size (1:1, 2–3 or 4–5 students) within a set of Tier 2 interventions was not shown to be a key moderator, interventions with small group sizes appeared to be more effective than those comprising larger numbers of children.

Gersten et al. (2020) undertook a meta-analysis of reading interventions for children in grades 1–3. Similar to Wanzek et al. (2016) the focus was upon less intense Tier 2 interventions although, in this analysis, Tier 3 interventions were specifically excluded. Particular emphasis was placed upon including only those studies that demonstrated high methodological rigor. Thirty-three studies were reviewed in total, with two thirds conducted in Grade 1. The authors reported an overall mean effect size on reading outcomes of 0.39 and effect sizes of 0.41 for word reading, 0.32 for comprehension and 0.31 for fluency. Interventions with an emphasis upon phonological or phonemic awareness were associated with significantly smaller effects than those that addressed encoding or writing (although see Kilpatrick & O'Brien, 2019, advocating the positive effects of phonemic training). In the light of their findings, Gersten and colleagues raise the question as to whether focusing upon these pre-reading skills, once children have started to learn how to decode, might take time and focus away from the task of building proficiency in decoding.

Several potential moderator variables were considered for further examination, for example, whether interventions were conducted by teachers or other personnel, and whether these were delivered one-to-one or in small groups of 2–5 children. Differences were largely found not to be statistically significant although there was some evidence to suggest that one-to-one may be more productive for children in first grade.

Despite a degree of overlap in the selected studies, the effect sizes reported by Gersten et al. (2020) are somewhat lower than those reported by Wanzek et al. (2016). The authors suggest that this seeming discrepancy might be explained by their requirement that selected studies should have highly rigorous methodological standards, and their exclusion of kindergarten interventions.

Austin, Vaughn, and McClelland (2017) carried out a systematic review of students with reading difficulties in grades K–3 who had responded inadequately at Tier 2 and subsequently been provided with a Tier 3 intervention. This was a narrative study and no overall effect size was generated. Twelve studies met the inclusion criteria although none involved Tier 3 work in kindergarten. In general, the results were encouraging, demonstrating that such interventions could result in significant gains in reading when compared with controls (although the difficulty of selecting comparison/control groups in such studies was noted). However, and consistent with the earlier literature, the children were largely unable to catch up with their higher performing peers. The authors noted that while expecting such an outcome was unrealistic, the interventions could still have a positive effect upon the children's academic performance. Similar to Wanzek et al. (2016), outcomes were not affected by group size, the implementer of the program, the type of the intervention (researcher or commercially based, scripted or unscripted) and the amount of intervention (dosage). Indeed, the authors noted that some of the Tier 3 interventions with greater dosage failed to produce significant results whereas some of the much shorter interventions were shown to be effective.

In an overarching "review of reviews," Al Otaiba, McMaster, et al. (2022) summarized findings across the reviews and meta-analyses discussed above alongside some additional studies. Generally positive moderate effects for interventions focusing upon foundational reading skills were found. As has generally been reported in the literature, the impact of interventions upon reading comprehension was more modest. No differential effects were found on the basis of the children's initial skills, their risk status or the nature of the person undertaking the intervention. Insufficient research has been conducted to evaluate the comparative effects of standardized or more individualized interventions.

Two further meta-analytic reviews have been reported since the publication of Al Otaiba, McMaster, et al.'s (2022) analysis of analyses. Neitzel et al. (2022) undertook a review of 65 studies of 51 interventions for struggling readers ranging from kindergarten to Grade 6. These were all published between 1990 and 2020. For the purposes of the analysis, the notion of a struggling reader was rather broad and included children reading at a higher level than would typically be considered to be indicative of reading disability/dyslexia. The study also differed somewhat from many of the other meta-analyses in that its focus was largely upon the effects of different types of program rather than specific variables of interest.

The authors reported a statistically significant effect size of 0.23 across all of the interventions although, as is often the case, significant heterogeneity was found across the studies. A mean effect of 0.31 was found for whole class Tier 1 approaches although this was not statistically significant. One-to-one tuition was found to deliver significantly higher effect sizes than one-to-small group provision, with a mean effect size of 0.41 found for the former when this was provided to children in Tier 3. It appeared not to matter greatly whether the tutors were teachers, teaching assistants, or paid volunteers although the mean effect size was considerably lower for unpaid volunteers. In their concluding remarks, Neitzel et al. (2022) emphasized the powerful effects of all forms of tutoring, although they recognized that further understanding was needed as to how best to deliver such provision in an efficacious and cost-effective fashion.

Hall et al.'s (2022) meta-analysis focused upon the effects of reading intervention for children with, or at risk for, dyslexia in Grades K–5. The authors argued that their study differed from other recent meta-analyses on the grounds that it focused more narrowly upon a dyslexia-specific group rather than children with broader reading and language difficulties. In line with a Dyslexia 1 conception, dyslexia was defined as, "... the lower part of a continuous distribution of word reading and spelling skill" (2022: 286). To qualify for inclusion, the studies had to involve children who scored below the twenty-fifth percentile, or who were in a participant group with a mean score below the sixteenth percentile on a standardized measure of word reading, spelling, or skills deemed to be foundational to word reading such as phonics knowledge or phonological awareness. The final meta-analysis included fifty-three studies that had been conducted during the period 1980–2020.

The meta-analysis found a mean effect size of 0.33 across combined outcomes. Effects on word reading/spelling (0.34) and phonological awareness (0.44) were higher than on text reading (0.25) and reading comprehension (0.26). Although substantial heterogeneity was found across effect sizes in relation to instructional differences, only dosage and the inclusion of a spelling component were statistically significant moderators. It was found that for every hour of additional instruction, the effect size tended to increase by 0.002. Studies where spelling instruction had been added to word reading instruction showed larger effects than reading instruction alone (0.37 versus 0.23). Including a phonological component to the instruction resulted in a higher effect size but this was not statistically significant. Providing morphology or vocabulary instruction in combination with word reading instruction yielded similar effects to word reading interventions that did not include these components. Multisensory components were not shown to increase effect size. Interventions with one-to-one instruction resulted in a higher effect size than those involving small groups, although this was not statistically significant. Although this outcome is similar to those reported by both Gersten et al. (2020) and Wanzek et al. (2016), it contrasts with Neitzel et al. (2022) who found that significantly higher effects were obtained for one-to-one tuition.

In comparing their findings with those of other recent meta-analyses, Hall et al. (2022) comment upon the general similarities that emerged. Taken overall, the analyses suggest that there is little difference in the effectiveness of commonly employed instruction programs designed for children with reading difficulties.

What Can Be Done to Help Those Who Fail to Respond to Initial Interventions?

Intervention programs for older struggling readers have proven to be considerably less successful than those operating for young children (Scammacca et al., 2015; Wanzek et al., 2013). Indeed, an already dispiriting picture has become even less positive in recent times with consistent evidence of declining effect sizes as more rigorous research designs are utilized (Fletcher et al., 2019; Scammacca et al., 2016). Smaller effect sizes are typically associated with larger sample sizes, and the average sample size in reading intervention studies conducted between 2010–2014 is three times the size of those in the preceding decade (Scammacca et al., 2016). Other possible explanatory factors are the increasing use of standardized, rather than experimenter-generated, outcome measures, and greater reliance upon randomized, rather than quasi-experimental, designs (Cheung & Slavin, 2016). Non-standardized outcome measures are more likely to be closely aligned to the aims of the specific interventions and, accordingly, tend to provide higher effect sizes than traditional assessments (Swanson, Hoskyn, & Lee, 1999). A further explanatory factor may be the reduced use of control groups offering no parallel remedial intervention; these have largely been replaced by business-as-usual reading intervention controls The additional instruction offered to children in these groups, if of sound quality, will make it harder for experimental groups to demonstrate superior gains (Fletcher et al., 2019).

Scammacca et al.'s (2007) original meta-analytic review of instruction for struggling readers across grades 4–12 included thirty-one studies undertaken between 1980 and 2004. When measures of decoding, fluency and comprehension were included together an overall effect size of 0.95 was found. However, when only standardized measures were examined, the resultant effect size of 0.42 was considerably smaller. Differences in effect sizes between research and teacher implemented interventions were notable. In particular, an overall effect-size of 0.21 for teacher implemented interventions using standardized measures raised many questions about generalization and transfer. Scammacca et al. (2015) subsequently extended the meta-analysis period to 2011. The mean effect size on reading outcomes across all studies was considerably lower than before (0.49), with a much smaller effect of 0.13 when standardized tests only were employed. The difference between the two overall mean scores for the 1980–2004 and 2005–2011 groups of studies was statistically significant. For both meta-analyses, the effect of intervention upon reading fluency was considerably lower than for reading comprehension. While researcher-led (versus teacher-led) interventions resulted in a higher mean effect size when all studies were included, no differences were found when only the 2005–2011 studies were examined. Scammacca et al.'s (2015) study included all the outputs in Wanzek et al.'s (2013) examination of the effect of reading interventions of seventy-five sessions or more to students in grades 4–12. Wanzek and colleagues found effect sizes of 0.10 for reading comprehension, 0.15 for word reading and 0.16 for fluency. Longer interventions were associated with smaller effect sizes, a rather surprising outcome given that disappointing trial results in dyslexia research often lead to recommendations that interventions need to be more extensive.

Flynn, Zheng, and Swanson (2012) undertook a selective meta-analysis of ten intervention studies involving reading-disabled students in grades 5–9. Using standardized reading tests as outcome measures, the mean effect size was 0.42, the same score as that reported by Scammacca et al. (2007) for standardized tests. Note, however, that these scores are considerably higher than the effect size of 0.21 for such measures reported in Scammacca et al.'s (2015) follow-up analysis. It is possible that, in part, this drop reflects the exclusion of older students from the later analysis.

Extending an earlier synthesis (Wanzek et al., 2010), Donegan and Wanzek (2021) examined findings from experimental and quasi-experimental research studies of interventions for struggling readers primarily in grades 4 and 5. These covered the period 1988–2019. The primary outcomes were foundational reading (decoding accuracy and reading fluency) and reading comprehension. Mean effect sizes reported were 0.22 for foundational reading and 0.21 for comprehension although when standardized outcomes only were included, effect sizes ranged from 0.09 for foundational reading to 0.13 for reading comprehension. As found in other recent meta-analyses, effect sizes were lower for more recent studies although this was only the case for reading comprehension. In addition to reasons already noted above that might explain this trend, the authors observed that the average level of reading performance at pretest was higher for the students included in the later studies, possibly because the students had already been receiving higher quality intervention in their schools (see also Lemons et al., 2014, for discussion of this phenomenon).

Boucher et al. (2023) undertook a meta-analysis of twenty-two intervention studies for students in grades 3–12 with significant reading difficulties (i.e., with standard scores of 80 or below on a standardized pretest measure of word reading). The findings demonstrated how difficult it continues to be to help those with the greatest difficulties to make meaningful progress. An overall effect size of 0.14 was found for reading interventions although there was considerable heterogeneity in effect sizes across the included studies. While performance on pseudoword reading was statistically significant, with an effect size of 0.38, there were no statistically significant overall intervention effects on a range of other reading skill domains including word identification, word identification fluency, and text reading fluency. The researchers observe that while the overall impact of the interventions studied was statistically significant, the modest overall effect size and the lack of impact upon real word reading performance suggest that their actual impact appears to be relatively minimal. As noted above, meta-analyses and systematic reviews have largely been unable to identify moderator variables that can meaningfully explain variation in effect sizes (Al Otaiba, McMaster et al., 2022; Scammacca et al., 2016; Donegan & Wanzek, 2021). Grade level, participants' learning disability status, the numbers of hours of intervention, and teacher versus researcher implementation have all tended to show no meaningful effects. In contrast, Boucher et al.'s (2023) meta-analysis found that of several aspects of dosage (including, total hours, total weeks, group size, number and frequency of sessions), only total hours of intervention moderated the effects of intervention.

Consideration of effectiveness needs to include the thorny issue of maintenance of performance although few intervention studies have included a long-term follow-up evaluation (Daniel, Capin, & Steinle, 2021; Gersten et al., 2020). As already noted, some young children can initially make sound progress after an intervention but drop back in third grade and in subsequent years (Vellutino et al., 2008), a period of time when reading demands increase significantly. Torgesen (2005) reflected upon the difficulties encountered by some children engaged in an intensive intervention for fourth grade students with severe reading disabilities (Torgesen et al., 2001). While the results were seen to be "very impressive" (Hulme & Snowling, 2009: 87), a significant proportion (between a third and a half) were unable to score within the normal range (a standard score of 90 or above) on a test of reading accuracy. Furthermore, the gains made could not be sustained by all; over the following two years, approximately one quarter of the sample lost most of the standard score gains they had achieved. Just over half of the sample succeeded in sustaining or improving their gains once the intervention had been completed. Improving reading fluency was also a challenge for most of the students and although many showed signs of improvement, their standard scores failed to increase. Student factors that seemed most important for predicting progress after the intervention were teachers' ratings of attentional behaviors, receptive language, and socioeconomic status.

The ability to read text fluently is important for skilled reading because this can enable decoding to become a largely automatic process and thus free cognitive resources to focus upon higher-order meaning-related text processing. Unsurprisingly, students with reading difficulties are more likely to struggle with fluent oral reading than their peers (Tindal et al., 2016). Fluency has a strong relationship to reading comprehension, although how this might apply to intervention varies somewhat according to children's age and reading ability (O'Connor, 2018) as the strength of the association can decline in adolescence (Wexler et al., 2008; Steinle, Stevens, & Vaughn, 2022). Somewhat neglected in studies of English, where the primary focus is typically upon reading accuracy (Share, 2008) this skill is often central in transparent languages where letter–sound decoding is less problematic and reading rate is typically a primary concern for teachers.

Unfortunately, reading fluency has proven difficult to remediate and, as noted by the meta-analytic and system reviews above, gains in alphabetic decoding do not necessarily lead to improved fluency or reading comprehension (Moats & Foorman, 1997; Torgesen, Rashotte, & Alexander, 2001). Older students who have struggled with reading for many years typically read less than normal readers and, given the established relationship between reading volume and reading proficiency (Allington & McGill-Franzen, 2021), their reduced exposure to print (Cunningham & Stanovich, 1998; Pfost, Dörfler, & Artelt, 2012) is likely to reduce the number of words that can be read automatically (Ehri, 2002; Share & Stanovich, 1995), an example of the "Matthew Effect" (Stanovich, 1986). Thus weak readers will continue to struggle to "catch up" with their classmates and even significant gains in word reading skills may still be insufficient to enable them to read as fluently as their peers (Torgesen, 2005; Torgesen, Rashotte, & Alexander, 2001).

Some fluency interventions have focused upon repeated reading, a technique that requires the student to read the same passage of text multiple times in order to reach a specified fluency criterion. Typically, a partner will sit alongside the reader and provide immediate support and feedback. Some studies include "listening passage preview" a process where a more proficient reader models fluent reading. Studies suggest that these activities can improve oral reading fluency (Kim et al., 2017; Morgan, Sideridis, & Hua. 2012; Stevens, Walker, & Vaughn, 2017; Wu, Stratton, & Gadke, 2020), although concern has been expressed that gains are not easily generalizable and do not transfer readily to other texts (Lee & Yoon, 2017) or have much impact upon reading comprehension (Wexler et al., 2008).

An alternative approach, non-repetitive reading, involves similar supportive practice but here students are asked to read a series of different passages rather than one repeatedly. This may involve wide reading, where students undertake single readings of multiple texts under the guidance and supervision of a peer or adult tutor, or independent reading, which involves greater student choice of texts and silent rather than oral reading. By substantially increasing reading volume, non-repetitive reading provides opportunities to encounter a large number of new words which should help with word recognition, fluency and automaticity (Mol & Bus, 2011). The value of silent reading for promoting reading outcomes in children has yet to be confirmed by existing research studies, many of which are considered to be methodologically weak (Erbeli & Rice, 2022).

A meta-analysis of non-repetitive reading fluency interventions for students with reading difficulties between 1987 and 2017 (Zimmerman, Reed, & Aloe, 2021) identified eight studies. The groups ranged from second to twelfth grade although here only two studies included adolescents. Seven of the eight studies implemented a form of wide reading although the nature and length of the interventions varied. The remaining study (Coward, 2015) employed independent interventions. Across the eight studies, the mean effect size for reading fluency improvement was 0.105 although large variation across studies and large confidence intervals rendered it difficult to draw firm conclusions about the effectiveness of the approach. The mean effect size for reading comprehension was a slightly larger 0.239 but the difference between the outcomes was not significant. As for fluency, effect sizes varied quite considerably across the studies and relatively wide confidence intervals compounded the difficulty of drawing conclusions.

While direct comparison between non-repetitive and repeated reading intervention was not part of the study design, Zimmerman and colleagues noted that six of the studies in the meta-analysis also had a repeated reading component. Little difference in the range of effect sizes was found between the two approaches. The authors tentatively concluded that non-repetitive reading appears to be a "plausible" means of intervening with students with reading difficulties, adding the need for further research to identify which components might prove to be most effective. Given the limited effectiveness of such approaches, however, improved fluency may be better achieved by an initial focus upon decoding related skills followed by targeted speed and automaticity (Metsala & David, 2022).

Steinle, Stevens, and Vaughn (2022) undertook a systematic review of fluency intervention research for struggling readers in grades 6–12 during the period 2006 to 2019. Seventeen studies examining reading fluency and comprehension outcomes were included. Repeated reading was found to be the most commonly employed approach. The review found inconsistency in the impact upon reading fluency across the studies and there was little evidence of improved reading comprehension. The authors concluded that the evidence did not support claims that repeated reading interventions can improve fluency in children in the secondary grades. In their advice to practitioners, they suggest that wide reading approaches may be preferable to repeated reading as these may help build vocabulary and background knowledge. This is little more than speculation, however, and it was acknowledged that the field remains unsure of the best practices for improving reading fluency in older struggling readers, in part, because of methodological weaknesses in research studies (Naveenkumar et al., 2022; Calvi et al. 2023).

Building upon their theoretical work, Wolf and colleagues have developed an approach to the development of children's reading fluency and comprehension that draws upon several linguistic systems. Their RAVE-O (Retrieval, Automaticity, Vocabulary, Elaboration and Orthography) program (Wolf, Miller, & Donnelly, 2000) is based upon the premise that the more the child understands about a word (i.e., in relation to phonemes, orthographic patterns, semantic meanings, syntactic uses, and morphological roots and affixes; see also Berninger et al., 2008, 2010) the more speedily it will be decoded, retrieved and comprehended. In addition to focusing upon identified core words each week, and relating these to each of the various linguistic systems in a connected fashion, RAVE-O places an emphasis upon a variety of metacognitive strategies geared to helping children segment words into common orthographic and morphological units. A multi-site intervention (one hour daily for seventy days) in which RAVE-O was combined with another program focusing upon letter–sound knowledge and blending skills (Phonological Analysis and Blending; PHAB) (Gallagher & Frederickson, 1995) and utilizing direct instruction approaches, resulted in significant gains in a variety of reading skills compared with control programs.

Further research is needed to help understand the effects of different elements of multiple component interventions in relation to differing levels of student need and local capacity (Scammacca et al., 2007). While this approach would seem to be one that offers promise, the appropriate balance of activities is difficult to determine and, with some notable exceptions, guidance in the research literature has often focused more upon the need for intensive, individualized approaches than specifics about the balance of content.

Shaywitz, Morris, and Shaywitz (2008) observe that no intervention program is appropriate for all struggling readers. For these authors, there is a need to focus upon contextual or procedural factors as well as the particular content of intervention programs. In this respect, greater understanding is required in relation to instructional intensity, program fidelity, teacher skills, program focus, and the influence of student-related variables such as prior experience and current abilities (see also, Foorman et al., 2008).

Estimates of the proportion of those poor readers who continue to struggle despite receiving high-quality intervention vary, although a figure of between 4–6 percent of the school population is commonly cited (Kamps et al., 2008; Mathes & Denton, 2002; Mathes et al., 2005).

Vaughn and Roberts (2007) offer a more optimistic estimate in which less than 10 percent of the 20–30 percent of children who require supplemental, research-based instruction are deemed likely to make little or no substantial progress. Scanlon and colleagues (2005) suggest a slightly higher figure of 15–20 percent of remediated readers. In a randomized controlled trial intervention involving individual and small group input, approximately one quarter of the participants failed to respond to the intervention (Hatcher et al., 2006). Singleton's (2009b) review concludes that between 1.5 and 3 percent of children are likely to require further help after the provision of secondary intervention. Torgesen (2004) has suggested that if all children were given the most effective interventions when needed, the incidence of early reading difficulties might range from 1.6–6 percent of the total population. Of course, this would leave a particularly intransigent group of treatment resisters for whom meaningful progress would be hard to achieve (Torgesen, 2005).

Response to Intervention programs can result in young children moving rapidly through to high level (Tier 3) provision within the first years of schooling rather than having to wait many years for such assistance. Given a lack of success at the earlier Tier 2 phase, a more individualized program, albeit still focusing primarily upon the development of decoding skills, may be called for. Employing a randomized controlled trial, Denton et al. (2013) examined the operation of a Tier 3 intervention with second-graders. The intervention was provided to groups of two or three students a day in 45-minute sessions over a six-month period. Instruction was based upon a structured program, *Responsive Reading Instruction* (Denton & Hocker, 2006) and, where appropriate, an additional fluency program, *Read Naturally* (Ihnot et al., 2001). Staff providing the intervention were encouraged to use the programs' evidence-based instructional activities in a flexible fashion tailored to individual student needs. Compared with controls who received typical school instruction, children in the intervention group made significantly greater progress on measures of word identification, phonemic decoding, word reading fluency, and a measure of sentence and paragraph reading comprehension. However, statistically significant differences between the groups were not found for pseudoword reading, text reading fluency, and comprehension of extended passages of text. While these findings are promising, severe problems remained for many of the children, particularly in respect of reading fluency and reading comprehension. Furthermore, a statistically significant difference was not found between the control and intervention groups in respect of the proportion who demonstrated the benchmark level of performance considered to represent an adequate response to intervention. In general, those who were inadequate responders to the Tier 3 intervention demonstrated greater impairments on a range of language measures that had been evident prior to an earlier Tier 2 intervention.

In many ways, identifying and addressing the precise nature of reading-related difficulties in adolescents is more complex than for younger children. Where an RTI model operates, there may be a need for some students to progress directly to a more intensive third tier intervention (Compton, Gilbert, et al., 2012; Fuchs, Fuchs, & Compton, 2012; Vaughn & Fletcher, 2012), although, as noted earlier, this strategy is also increasingly being advocated for young children. Rather than using poor responsiveness to intervention to determine the level and intensity of support needed, as tends to be the case for younger children, it may be more appropriate to base decisions upon the child's current performance on measures of reading accuracy, fluency and comprehension (Daniel et al., 2022). It has also been suggested that the ability to estimate a poor reader's educational prognosis accurately would be useful in guiding decisions about tier level and different instructional methods but, to date, predictive capability of this kind is rudimentary (Middleton et al., 2022).

It is unclear whether standardized programs are more helpful than individualized interventions; meta-analyses and systematic reviews have not offered a clear resolution to this issue. In their review of a century of reading intervention, Scammacca et al. (2016) argue for a greater focus upon individualized instruction, with flexible approaches that respond to individual student need, particularly for those who are not responding adequately to existing interventions. However, large-scale reviews have generally found that individualized interventions have tended to be less successful than standardized approaches, perhaps because teachers have found the complexities involved difficult to manage (Al Otaiba, McMaster, et al., 2022). Donegan and Wanzek's (2021) review of grade 4 and 5 interventions also led to the conclusion that standardized approaches tend to be more effective, although it was recognized that individualized practices vary greatly and may be employed more often with students experiencing greatest difficulty.

The use of individualized approaches also poses difficulty for researchers for whom standardization and consistency of instructional input are desirable when conducting randomized control trial studies. However, whether a standardized, individualized, or hybrid approach (Russell-Freudenthal, Zaru, & Al Otaiba, 2023) is utilized, it is important to be aware of, and respond to, both differing and changing needs at this stage: some students will continue to experience significant word-reading difficulties that require help at the letter–sound level, while others will have few problems with single-syllable words but struggle with those which are multisyllabic (Archer, Gleason, & Vachon, 2003). For this latter group, more advanced word study involving a variety of word analysis skills will typically be more appropriate (Curtis, 2004; Roberts et al., 2008).

As children move into middle childhood, the importance of reading fluency and comprehension increases. Some children who had appeared to be making adequate progress in the early grades may begin to struggle as a new set of demands is placed upon them. At this stage, children are required to draw upon ideas and words that are likely to be outside of their everyday experience (Chall, 1996). Greater focus will be placed upon understanding and analysing a range of texts and genres that will require the child to draw upon wider vocabulary and concept knowledge. For those who continue to struggle with basic reading skills, such activities will prove particularly demanding (Goldman, Snow, & Vaughn, 2016; Hebert et al., 2016).

> Older students with reading difficulties may need instruction in any of a range of reading components from beginning phonics skills to decoding multi-syllabic words and practicing reading for fluency, depending on their degree of development and corresponding areas of need. In addition, many students benefit from multiple opportunities to read text aloud and to engage in activities that involve reading fluency …. Even older students who require instruction in the basic elements of decoding and word-level reading should not be precluded from receiving instruction in vocabulary, concept development, and reading comprehension. (Vaughn et al., 2008: 339)

Motivation to read is a problem for many poor readers, particularly during adolescence. A history of struggle and embarrassment is often compounded by classroom environments in which reading material becomes increasingly more complex. Teacher awareness about the importance of fostering motivation to read may be lower than for educators in early years' settings (Roberts et al., 2008; Wilmot et al., 2022). Older students with difficulties can have reduced belief in their ability to overcome their reading difficulties and may seek to protect themselves from potential public humiliation by appearing to be unmotivated and dismissive of the value of schoolwork (Covington, 1992). It is for such reasons that interventions need to be designed in ways that can engage and motivate older students. This can be a challenging task, in part because, as has been highlighted by proponents of the whole language approach, the highly structured nature of phonics teaching is not easily rendered intrinsically appealing.

One popular approach to fostering achievement motivation is to encourage a growth mindset whereby a belief is inculcated in the child that intelligence and academic ability are malleable, rather than fixed. Meaningful progress is associated with hard work, the deployment of effective strategies, and the positive support of others. While initial enthusiasm for this approach has been tempered by some disappointing trial results (Li & Bates, 2019; Sisk et al., 2018; Wanzek et al., 2021), the heterogeneous nature of findings across individuals and contexts has led to greater focus upon when and how such approaches might prove most helpful, and what might be important moderating variables (Donegan et al., 2023; Yeager & Dweck, 2020).

Several studies have examined the impact of mindset-related motivational interventions on the reading achievement of poor readers. Lovett et al. (2021) trialed the inclusion of such components within their existing reading intervention program. Described as North America's longest continuing reading research program (Fletcher et al., 2019), it is currently known as the Phonological and Strategy Training (PHAST) reading program (Lovett, Barron, & Frijters, 2013). Designed for children with severe reading difficulties, in different phases of schooling, the program offers two core strands, direct instruction in phonologically-based skills, and a dialogue-based approach to strategy instruction geared to build decoding and word identification accuracy. Lovett and colleagues carried out an intervention study (2021) with children in grades 6, 7 and 8 in schools located in Toronto and Atlanta. The PHAST program was adapted for this age group and each of the two experimental groups received an additional PHAST component focusing upon either reading comprehension or reading fluency. Active treatment controls were children in the same schools with the same degree of reading impairment who received their schools' usual small group remedial reading instruction. All involved were expected to receive small group (1:4–1:8) instruction for 45–60 minutes daily, four or five days a week, amounting to a total of 125 hours. The motivational components sought to tackle the deleterious consequences of the children's history of reading struggle. These were integrated into the daily inputs and sought to enhance reading self-efficacy, reorient negative motivational perspectives (e.g., unproductive attributions for reading success and failure), encourage peer group support in the learning process, and increase positive reading experiences.

Outcomes were assessed at the end of the intervention with a one-year follow-up. Immediately afterwards, all three groups of children demonstrated improvement, although greater gains were found for the two intervention groups than for controls on eight of the sixteen measured outcomes. Effect sizes for growth over time between the PHAST and the control groups were 0.78 for nonword decoding, 0.56 for single word reading, and 0.36 for passage comprehension. In relation to the motivational component, the PHAST groups similarly showed greater gains on a self-report measure of perceived reading competence. Somewhat unexpectedly, no significant differences on the measures were found at any time between the PHAST Fluency and PHAST Comprehension groups. Follow-up assessment a year later included only the experimental groups (for ethical reasons). Increased performance was found for several outcomes including word identification, reading fluency, passage comprehension, and spelling. However, decreases were found for word attack and sense of competence.

Given that the PHAST initiative was compared with reading remediation provided by special education teachers in the schools with similarly sized groups and for the same duration, the results appear encouraging, and largely exceed findings reported in Scammacca et al.'s (2015) meta-analysis. However, more disappointingly, the thorny problem of maintaining student motivation persisted. Despite continuing to make reading progress, the PHAST children registered a decline in their sense of competence a year later. A relevant question, not posed by the research team, is whether the positive response at the end of the intervention was accurate or, in part, an artefact resulting from the suggestibility of subconscious priming messages delivered during the program. Noting that the attributional profiles of struggling readers can vary significantly (Tsujimoto et al., 2018, 2019), Lovett and colleagues recommended that motivational and self-evaluative work should continue long-term for those who struggle in these respects.

Despite some modestly encouraging findings from a number of other studies operating in a variety of different phases of schooling (see, Al Otaiba, Wanzek, et al., 2022 for a review) the extent to which mindset-related interventions can help tackle reading difficulties remains unclear. However, it is possible that the development of a positive mindset is influenced not primarily by immediate classroom experiences but by the messages that students receive from their family, school, and wider community. As such, educators may find that individualized interventions programs prove less powerful than those which address children's broader experiences (Stanley et al., 2023).

It has often been assumed that fidelity of implementation of structured reading programs is a critical component of success, and there is some supportive evidence for this (e.g., Benner et al., 2011) particularly for struggling readers (Boardman et al., 2016; Capin et al., 2022). Nevertheless, there may be times when procedures need to be amended. Although programs should normally operate in ways that have been empirically verified, a degree of flexibility may sometimes be required in order to accommodate the needs of particular settings and diverse student populations (Harn, Parisi, & Stoolmiller, 2013).

Our continuing inability to find practical ways to help all those with the greatest problems, beyond advocating "more of the same" represents a significant concern. Although the overall picture supports arguments for the provision of intensive reading interventions over an extended period of many years, it is not clear exactly how the interventions can be rendered more powerful. Taking a lead from findings with younger children, researchers have been largely confined to speculating upon the possible benefits of more intensive and more prolonged forms of intervention for older students (Vaughn, Roberts, et al., 2019). For example, in reflecting upon the modest gains achieved following a lengthy intervention with Grade 6 students (Vaughn et al., 2010) involving more than 100 hours of instruction per child, two of the authors (Vaughn & Fletcher, 2010) were unable to offer further guidance other than to emphasize the need to focus resources and intensity upon those students (estimated to be 2–5%) who prove to be most resistant to evidence-based practices. Vaughn and colleagues (2019) suggest that intensification may involve several components: introducing longer-term interventions, reducing group size, individualizing intervention programs according to student need, offering reading instruction more widely across the curriculum, and providing supplementary reading inputs after school or during the summer vacation. However, reviews of research findings have generally been unable to demonstrate that either increasing the time of interventions, or reducing instructional group size (both commonly considered to be ways of increasing intensity) are effective for students whose reading problems persist into fourth grade and beyond. While recognizing the seeming inability of longer interventions and smaller group sizes to impact favorably upon older struggling readers in general and citing findings from a number of studies (Donegan, Wanzek, & Al Otaiba, 2020; Miciak, Roberts, et al. 2018; Sanchez & O'Connor, 2015), Donegan and Wanzek (2021) suggest that these may be of greater benefit to those with the most severe reading difficulties.

D. Fuchs et al. (2013) question whether quantitative approaches to increasing intervention intensity (i.e., increasing time and/or duration or reducing group size) will prove to be sufficient when students have already failed to progress following earlier, similar interventions. Instead, they argue for an approach to increased intensity that is qualitatively, rather than quantitatively, different. This might involve making changes to the curriculum, instructional approaches, teaching personnel (e.g., the use of a peer rather than a teacher), forms of feedback, and motivational drivers. To inform and evaluate these modifications, this approach uses an ongoing process of data-driven hypothesis testing termed "data-based individualization." This involves ascertaining, in the light of data systematically gathered over several time points, what works best for a given individual who appears not to be responding to particular instructional approaches. Meta-analyses of relevant studies have been encouraging, although effect sizes were found to be higher for students with intensive learning needs across a range of content areas (Jung et al., 2018) than for those termed as struggling readers (Filderman et al., 2018). For the approach to work most effectively, educators need to acquire a range of high-level skills, be provided with appropriate training, and have ongoing access to high-quality professional and technological support (Filderman et al., 2022; L. S. Fuchs et al., 2021; Russell-Freudenthal, Zaru, & Al Otaiba, 2023).

Given the high numbers of struggling readers, it would be helpful to determine whether specialized reading interventions for children with reading disabilities are only likely to be successful if undertaken by qualified teachers. Fortunately, as noted above, recent meta-analytic reviews suggest that this is not necessarily the case (see also, Jones, Erchul, & Geraghty, 2021). However, it is unclear whether this applies equally to those children with particularly severe difficulties. Vadasy and colleagues (2008), for example, found that paraeducators were able to provide effective supplemental code-oriented intervention to first-grade children with reading scores initially in the bottom quartile. However, they observed that, for those children who fail to respond to this level of intervention, more differentiated instruction from highly skilled teaching staff may be necessary. One of the benefits of using paraeducators in the early stages is that this may free up specialist time for those children who subsequently need more intensive, individualized assistance. Most likely, it is the level of expertise of the professional concerned that is important, not whether or not the instructor is a qualified teacher. Introducing additional, yet insufficiently skilled, personnel is unlikely to be helpful as it has been shown that the use of poorly trained or ineffective classroom aides can be deleterious to the progress of those with learning difficulties (Rubie-Davies et al., 2010; Webster, Russell, & Blatchford, 2015). In the USA, tertiary level interventions are sometimes undertaken by specially trained staff brought in from outside the school although it has been argued that this is unnecessary where school staff have appropriate training and sufficient resources (Kamps et al., 2008).

Finally, the debate as to whether children with reading and other learning disabilities are better catered for in fully inclusive or in resource room settings continues (McLeskey & Waldron, 2011). It seems that it is not the physical location of the provision that is critical but the appropriate utilization of mainstream and specialist teacher skills.[24] In mainstream classrooms it has been found that while the quality of general education is often sound, it is difficult to provide the individualized and structured programming that can address the learning-disabled child's specific needs (McLeskey & Waldron, 2011) and at the same time ensure that the other students in the classroom are working productively (Denton, 2012). Education in resource settings has frequently been criticized for being undemanding, insufficiently tailored to individual needs, lacking accountability, and associated with reduced student engagement (Moody et al., 2000).

What Is Specialist Dyslexia Teaching and Is This Particularly Effective for a Subgroup of Poor Readers Designated as Dyslexic?

Undoubtably there are different types of struggling readers in the higher grades. Yet there exists almost no evidence that any particular approach is better than any other for different profiles of hard-to-remediate older readers. Nor is there evidence of whether different combinations of approaches, or different weightings of approaches, lead to better long-term outcomes.

(Lovett et al., 2021: 674)

The origins of many popular intervention approaches for children with reading disability can be traced back to the work of Samuel Orton in the 1930s, which successfully challenged the dominant view held in medical circles that severe reading difficulties were caused by permanent brain damage that could not be remediated. Although his emphasis on hemispheric difficulties as the underlying cause of reading disability has been superseded by more recent scientific advances, his multisensory teaching approach (influenced by the kinesthetic approach of Fernald; Fernald & Keller, 1921), is still widely employed today.

Orton worked with an educator, Anna Gillingham, to develop the highly structured Orton-Gillingham multisensory teaching method (Gillingham

---

[24] It is skills rather than solely information that are essential here as sound teacher knowledge of language and literacy constructs will not necessarily be applied in their practice (Parrila et al., 2023).

& Stillman, 1997) that underpins many present-day programs (Stevens et al., 2021). While the sequence of activities differs from one variant of the approach to another, the key elements are as follows:

a.   Individual letters are paired with their sounds using a Visual-Auditory-Kinesthetic-Tactile (VAKT) procedure that involves tracing the letter while saying its name and sound.[25]
b.   Repetition is stressed as a means of gaining mastery between letters and sounds. The technique of overlearning involves constant repetition in order that newly acquired skills become automatized and readily recalled when needed.
c.   Letters are blended together to enable the child to read words and sentences.
d.   Spelling is advanced by means of dictation.
e.   Short stories which contain the taught sounds are read. More complex texts are subsequently tackled.

In a review of specialist approaches to dyslexia teaching, Singleton (2009b) highlighted common features as outlined by Townend (2000) and Thomson (1990). Townend emphasized the following elements, which, with the exception of the multisensory component, are strongly supported by research evidence:

a.   a structured approach involving small steps
b.   a multisensory approach
c.   reinforcement of learned skills with an emphasis upon automatization
d.   an emphasis upon the learning of skills rather than facts
e.   developing metacognitive approaches in which students reflect upon appropriate strategies for use in particular circumstances

The Orton-Gillingham (OG) approach, incorporating most of these components, has been widely promoted by dyslexia associations, dyslexia advocates, and specialist dyslexia teachers (Boardman, 2020; Clemens & Vaughn, 2023; Stevens et al., 2021), although critics have questioned its theoretical grounds, scientific rationale, and claims for its empirical support (Johnston & Scanlon, 2021; Schlesinger & Gray, 2017).

---

[25] Teaching both letter names and sounds to early readers has proven controversial (Adams, 1990). More recently, this approach has received some empirical support although explicit instruction in letter sounds is considered to be the more important element for children with poor phonological abilities (Piasta & Wagner, 2010).

In the USA, significant parental pressure has been placed upon school districts to provide specific branded programs that use this approach, although attempts to use legal routes to achieve this end have proven largely unsuccessful (Sayeski & Zirkel, 2021). Key reasons for this are the lack of strong supportive evidence and recognition that many aspects of these programs, included in the guidelines for effective reading and instruction produced by the National Reading Panel (Ehri et al., 2001), are often already part of schools' existing provision. An important issue, therefore, is whether OG "… the calling card of many private schools" (Sayeski & Zirkel, 2021: 484) or its branded equivalents, can be clearly shown to be more effective than other structured reading interventions. To date this has not proven to be the case and research evaluations have generally concluded that there is little evidence to support claims about the additional value of OG or its branded equivalents (Ritchey & Goeke, 2006; Wanzek & Roberts, 2012; What Works Clearinghouse, 2010).

The National Reading Panel (2000) review found only four studies using the OG approach that had sufficient methodological rigour for inclusion. Only two of these demonstrated positive effect sizes. Consistent with this finding, a more recent meta-analysis of OG studies with students with, or at risk for, reading disabilities Stevens et al. (2021) found that while OG interventions scored higher than other forms of intervention in improving foundational reading skills (phonological awareness, phonics, fluency, and spelling) or vocabulary or comprehension, the differences were not statistically significant. It should be noted that concern has been expressed in the literature about the quality of many of these studies (Sayeski & Hurford, 2022). On the basis of the findings from their meta-analysis, Stevens et al. (2021) concluded that these:

> … raise concerns about legislation mandating OG. The findings from this synthesis suggest "promise" but not confidence or evidence-based effects … (Stevens et al., 2021: 441)

Few research studies have specifically evaluated the utility of the multisensory element of the OG approach and whether this particular component adds value to explicit and systematic phonics-based instruction. Evaluations have largely taken the form of case studies (Riccio, Sullivan, & Cohen, 2010) and while many have been positive (Fernald & Keller, 1921; Strauss & Lehtinen, 1947), high-quality research evidence for the additional benefits of the multisensory component within a broader structured phonological approach is sparse and not overly convincing (Al Otaiba, Rouse, & Baker, 2018; Solari, Petscher, & Hall, 2021; Petscher et al., 2020). A meta-analysis of reading interventions for children with dyslexia (Hall et al., 2022) found no advantage for multisensory approaches, leading the authors to suggest that, on the basis of their findings, practitioners should not opt for multisensory interventions over other evidence-based interventions.

An added complexity is that there is little consensus about how the "multisensory" term is defined and operationalized (Fletcher et al., 2019). Beyond recommending the simultaneous use of auditory, visual, tactile and kinesthetic learning experiences, it is unclear how such a combination might best work in practice (Stevens et al., 2021). It is sometimes overlooked that these elements are commonly found in everyday classroom contexts; thus, in some ways, differences between OG and other instructional practices may not be substantial. One (auditory) component, reading aloud, is found in almost all initial reading approaches, although another element, silent reading, described as an ideovisual component (Watkins, 1922) has not thrived (Brooks, 1984).

In summary, there is insufficient scientific evidence to support claims that a multisensory approach is more effective than other structured phonological-based approaches that do not include a strong multisensory component (Petscher et al., 2020).

It is possible that the strengths of programs such as OG lie in their use of an intense, explicit, and systematic approach to instruction, and explicit attention to the structure of language, focused upon the particular needs of individual students. In considering this issue, Fletcher et al. (2019) argue that these are important characteristics of sound reading instruction that are not specific to children with reading disability, although struggling readers are likely to require greater intensity, time on task, and differentiation than their peers. For Fletcher et al. (2019) instruction should involve the explicit use of phonics as part of a multicomponent, integrated program that includes all aspects of literacy (phonics, sight-word recognition, spelling, reading fluency, vocabulary knowledge, and reading comprehension). Here the balance should be determined by individual strengths and weaknesses. In such cases, the specific program is likely to be less important than how well it is delivered.

Research evidence does not currently support legislative mandates that schools train teachers in the delivery of or provide students with branded or unbranded OG instruction (or reading instruction that employs a multisensory-specific component). Issues about the primacy of particular intervention programs should not be conflated with the importance of providing explicit, systematic, evidence-based instruction to students with word-level reading difficulties and the vital role of teacher training to effect this.

The Use of Computers and Assistive Technology

Computers and other electronic devices have the potential both to help remediate reading difficulties and to provide assistance to those for whom reading
and writing continues to be a significant struggle despite being in receipt of
intensive, high-quality educational interventions (Wood et al., 2018).

Unfortunately, information and communications technology (ICT) has
largely failed to help to assist the development of reading skills of those
with reading disability significantly. Slavin and colleagues' (2011) review
of interventions for struggling readers reported that computer-assisted
instruction had minimal effects upon reading achievement. More than a
decade later, a follow-up meta-analysis by Slavin's team (Neitzel et al.,
2022) suggested that the situation is little improved. Here a non-significant
effect size of 0.09 was found for technology-supported adaptive instruction for struggling readers at Tier 2. Such a picture echoes that resulting
from a review of secondary (Grades 6–12) reading programs (Baye et al.,
2019). It is possible that children who struggle academically may respond
better to tutors who are more able to motivate and respond in productive
ways to their unique dispositions and changing circumstances.

As discussed in Chapter 2, researchers emphasizing the problems of
visual attention for reading difficulties have reported findings suggesting
that play with commercially available action video games can improve
the attention and reading performance of Italian dyslexic children. It is
unclear, however, whether such interventions will have significant long-
term impact and, if so, whether this will apply equally to languages with
more opaque orthographies.

Complementary and Alternative Approaches to Treatment

The field of dyslexia, as for other developmental disorders, has been subject
to claims of effectiveness for a variety of alternative non curriculum-based
interventions (Jacobson, Foxx, & Mulick, 2005). Typically, these are promoted as tackling underlying physical or cognitive problems that lead to
academic or behavioral difficulties. These alternative therapies, sometimes
touted as miracle cures, can receive significant media attention and may be
attractive to parents and professionals who are eager to discover any program that may help seemingly intractable difficulties (Bull, 2009; Favell,
2005; Stephenson, 2009). However, rigorous scientific studies of such
interventions have been unable to demonstrate significant efficacy in relation to learning difficulties, and the volume of claims as to the effectiveness
of many of these appears to have receded in recent years.

Perceptual-Motor Training

Given evidence of statistical associations between motor proficiency and academic performance in reading and math (Macdonald et al., 2018), some have suggested that provision of more opportunities for physical exercise, or specific psychomotor training exercises, might result in academic gains. A long tradition of perceptual-motor developing training has sought to improve cognitive functioning in children with developmental disorders. In relation to children with poor neurological functioning, the work of Doman and Delacato (Delacato, 1959, 1963; Doman & Delacato, 1968) and Ayres (1963, 1979) has been highly influential. However, much of this early work and its later variants (e.g., Blythe, 1992) has been criticized for relying on testimonials, case studies, and emotional appeal, rather than upon rigorous peer-reviewed scientific examination (American Academy of Pediatrics, 1982; Balow, 1996, 1971; Fawcett & Reid, 2009; Holm, 1983; Silver, 1987). In addition to criticisms of their low scientific rigour, published studies have failed to yield promising findings. Kavale and Mattson's (1983) meta-analysis of 180 studies of perceptual-motor programs, for example, found no important effect sizes for academic skills and, indeed, only a small effect (0.17) for perceptual-motor skills themselves.

After a period of reduced influence in the 1980s (Hallahan & Mercer, 2001), perceptual-motor skills training regained a degree of popularity at the beginning of the new millennium, in part because of its supposed association with developing insights and understandings about brain functioning. Of the various kinesthetic initiatives for children with learning difficulties, perhaps the most prominent in recent years was the DORE programme (also known as the *Dyslexia, Dyspraxia, Attention Treatment Program; DDAT*) (Dore & Brookes, 2006). This was based upon the notion of cerebellar developmental delay as the primary cause of dyslexia (Nicolson, Fawcett, & Dean, 2001a, 2001b). Intervention involved the child undertaking a series of physical exercises for approximately ten minutes, twice daily. Although claims for the success of the program largely relied upon personal testimony, two highly controversial publications in a specialist dyslexia journal (Reynolds & Nicolson, 2007; Reynolds, Nicolson, & Hambly, 2003), in which results from a UK primary school intervention were reported, drew much ire from the scientific community. These reports testified to the success of the intervention with one of the authors stating on BBC Radio that "… it's the closest thing to a cure that I have ever seen" (cited in Rack et al., 2007: 98). The program had earlier received significant publicity after it was described on a television news item in 2002 as a "breakthrough in the treatment of dyslexia."[26]

Despite initial enthusiasm, a series of research papers subsequently identified serious design flaws in the study (Bishop, 2007; McArthur, 2007; Rack, 2003; Rack et al., 2007; Snowling & Hulme, 2003), criticisms that were not abated by the response of the original authors (Nicolson & Reynolds, 2007). Among a lengthy list of problems, perhaps the two most influential were a failure to compare sufficiently the subsequent performance of the control group, and questions about the true weaknesses of the children in the study; the pretest performance of the treated group indicated that many did not have a significant reading problem at the outset. In reviewing the relevant literature Bishop (2007) concluded that one should be sceptical of claims that the intervention improves any skills other than those that are trained in the exercises.

An alternative movement-based approach to the enhancement of children's academic skills was pioneered by McPhillips and colleagues in Northern Ireland. This work was derived from interventions that sought to remediate abnormal primary reflexes (Blythe, 1992; Goddard Blythe, 2005; Goddard Blythe et al., 2022). Cognizant of the poor quality of previous evaluations in this field, McPhillips and his team endeavoured to undertake more rigorous, scientific evaluations (although criticism of the approach used for assessing children's reflexes was offered by Hyatt, Stephenson, & Carter, 2009).

Of particular interest to McPhillips and his team was the asymmetrical tonic neck reflex, with persistence of this into the school years having been found to be associated with literacy difficulties (McPhillips & Jordan-Black, 2007). Higher levels of persistent primitive reflex response have also been found in children with developmental language disorder (Matuszkiewicz & Gałkowski, 2021). However, McPhillips and colleagues acknowledged that not all children with reading and spelling problems demonstrate persistent reflexes and some children with clinically high levels of persistent reflex are good readers.

In an attempt to reduce the proportion of children with academic difficulties, McPhillips devised the *Primary Movement Programme* which involved children undertaking a series of movements that are designed to mimic the early reflex movements of the foetus. The exercises were hypothesized to stimulate the major motor centers in the brain including

[26] "A miracle cure?" *Tonight with Trevor McDonald*, ITV, January 21, 2002.

the cerebellum. Research findings from two intervention studies undertaken by this team (McPhillips, Hepper, & Mulhern, 2000) indicated gains in reading and mathematics although there was no suggestion that such interventions could help children overcome severe reading disabilities. In reviewing this work, Hyatt, Stephenson, and Carter (2009) noted that reported gains were modest and concluded that the approach was no more likely to be successful in remediating reading disabilities than earlier perceptual-motor programs.

The perceived viability of perceptual-motor programs has persisted, buoyed by the allure and promise of neuroscience. Although growing awareness that the supposed basis for these may bear little relationship to current understandings of brain functioning (Howard-Jones, 2014), some teachers retain a belief in the value of motor-perception training for the improvement of literacy skills (Hughes, Sullivan, & Gilmore, 2020; Ruiz-Martin et al., 2022).

More than four decades ago, Kavale and Mattson (1983) sought to explain the longevity of a tradition that has signally failed to deliver success. In so doing, they commented upon "remarkable" resistance to the weight of evidence against the approach, in part, a consequence of its "deep historical roots and strong clinical tradition" (1983: 172).

> Process training has always made the phoenix look like a bedraggled sparrow. You cannot kill it. It simply bides its time in exile after being dislodged by one of history's periodic attacks upon it, and then returns, wearing disguises or carrying new *noms de plume,* as it were, but consisting of the same old ideas, doing business much in the same old way. (Mann, 1979: 539)

Visual Interventions

With the resurgence of interest in visual aspects of reading disability, an increasing number of possible interventions have been proposed, and, less frequently, developed, piloted and evaluated (e.g., Bucci, 2021; Caldani et al., 2020; Werth, 2021b). Despite some encouraging findings (Peters et al., 2019), methodological concerns such as small sample sizes, insufficient consideration of long-term effects and possible publication bias are such that further robust evidence will be necessary to justify the introduction of any large-scale vision-based initiatives.

A particularly controversial form of visual intervention for reading problems relates to scotopic sensitivity syndrome (also known as Meares-Irlen syndrome). Treatment typically involves the use of individually prescribed colored lenses designed to reduce visual stress and so increase reading speed. While such lenses have been widely promoted as a "cure" for dyslexia, leading advocates of this technology such as Wilkins (2003, 2021) and Singleton (Singleton, 2009a, 2009b, 2012) have emphasized that resolving the primary problems of reading disability is not an appropriate aim for such treatments. For Wilkins, colored filters are not a treatment for dyslexia, but they may help to address "... the visual discomfort and anomalous perceptual effects that sometimes accompany the condition" (Wilkins, 2021: 78). For Singleton, visual stress is often likely to be comorbid with dyslexia; these difficulties having a multiplicative detrimental effect upon reading performance. Those who struggle with reading may be more susceptible to visual stress, perhaps because they typically need to focus upon the visual components of the text more than skilled readers do (Shovman & Ahissar, 2006). Accordingly, Wilkins and Singleton both contend that those who are susceptible to visual stress (whether reading-disabled or not) can be helped to make the reading process less uncomfortable and this outcome could lead to gains in reading speed.

Research has failed to show a clear causal relationship between the use of colored lenses or overlays and meaningful reading gains in children (or university students; Henderson, Tsogka, & Snowling, 2013) with reading difficulties. A small number of laboratory studies using overlays have reported increased reading speeds (Razuk et al., 2018; Guimarães et al., 2020; but cf. Denton & Meindl, 2016 for an opposing finding). Unfortunately, attempts to evaluate the effectiveness of colored lenses and overlays have not been helped by poor design and methodological flaws (Albon, Adi, & Hyde, 2008; Hyatt, Stephenson & Carter, 2009; Suttle, Lawrenson, & Conway, 2018; Zane, 2005). Particular concerns include the use of anecdotal reports, poor controls, failure to determine equivalence of groups at the pre-test phase, potential researcher bias, inappropriate measurement metrics and statistical analyses, and likely placebo effects.

In seeking to provide an overview of available evidence, Suttle, Lawrenson, and Conway (2018) examined four published systematic reviews of relevant studies (Albon, Adi, & Hyde, 2008; Evans & Allen, 2016; Galuschka et al., 2014; Griffiths et al., 2016). Three of the reviews concluded that the quality of the evidence was not sufficient to support the use of colored overlays or lenses for treating reading difficulty. The fourth review (Evans & Allen, 2016) acknowledged the poor quality of many of their included studies but nevertheless concluded that the evidence suggested that such equipment might alleviate symptoms in people with visual stress. Note that Evans and Allen's more optimistic conclusion relates to a condition that, similar to Wilkins (Wilkins, 2021; Wilkins & Evans, 2022), is considered to be distinct from dyslexia.

In the light of their review of reviews, Suttle, Lawrenson, and Conway (2018) concluded that the available evidence is insufficiently reliable to adjudge that colored filters are effective for alleviating either reading difficulty or visual discomfort. In their opinion, until and unless reliable evidence to demonstrate effectiveness is made available, such a form of treatment should not be recommended.

In 2009, a joint statement was provided on dyslexia and vision by a group of US medical associations: the American Academy of Pediatrics, Section on Ophthalmology, the Council on Children with Disabilities, the American Academy of Ophthalmology, the American Association for Pediatric Ophthalmology and Strabismus and the American Association of Certified Orthoptists (2009). This stated that various forms of vision therapy for dyslexia were not supported by the available evidence. The statement resulted in a rebuttal by an optometrist, Lack (2010), which fiercely criticized the statement's "… false, confusing and contradictory statements" (p. 540). The debate served to highlight ongoing professional disagreements between medical (opthalmologists) and other vision professionals (optometrists) about the appropriateness of vision-based interventions for learning disabilities.

The American Academy of Pediatrics' 2009 statement was subsequently updated in a joint technical report produced by these same medical academies (Handler et al., 2011). Taking a similar stance as before, the report endorsed the view that various forms of vision therapy for dyslexics had not been scientifically validated:

> Scientific evidence does not support the claims that visual training, muscle exercises, ocular pursuit-and tracking exercises, behavioral/perceptual vision therapy, training glasses, prisms, and colored lenses and filters are effective direct or indirect treatments for learning disabilities. There is no evidence that children who participate in vision therapy are more responsive to educational instruction than those who do not participate. The reported benefits of vision therapy, including nonspecific gains in reading ability, can often be explained by the placebo effect, increased time and attention given to students who are poor readers, maturation changes, or the traditional remedial techniques with which they are usually combined. (Handler et al., 2011: e847)

As discussed in Chapter 2 and earlier in this chapter, recent advances in understanding the potential role of visual attention in reading disability has led to interest in possible forms of visual intervention ranging from computer-controlled spacing of text to the use of action video games. At the current time, however, there is an insufficiently strong evidence base to recommend the adoption of such approaches as primary treatments.

Dietary and Chemical Interventions

Scientific findings concerning the efficacy of various dietary or chemical approaches to reading disability have not provided evidential support for their use.

There is some evidence to suggest a correlation between fatty acid levels and reading performance (Borasio et al., 2022; Richardson et al., 2000), although whether this has implications for intervention is unclear. Stein (2018, 2019, 2022a, 2022b) has long argued that supplementing the diet of dyslexic children with unsaturated fatty acid dietary supplementation (docosahexaenoic acid) can often, "sometimes dramatically" (Stein, 2018: 9), help them to improve their reading.

Confident assertions of this kind have yet to be supported by a program of rigorous research. Studies that have been cited to support claims that fatty acid supplements may help those with dyslexia (Cyhlarova et al., 2007; Richardson, 2006; Richardson & Montgomery, 2005) have been criticized for their poor research design, the use of correlational data, and a lack of clear focus on the development of reading skills. In an attempt to remedy these weaknesses, an experimental study (Kairaluoma et al., 2008) sought to ascertain the effects of fatty acid supplements upon the reading skills of dyslexic children. After a period of treatment, gains on a variety of measures of reading and spelling were made by both intervention and control (placebo) groups and parents reported that their children's reading skills had improved. Tellingly, however, no differences were found between the two groups on any of the measures, indicating that it was not the nature of the supplement itself that could explain any improvements. While some have argued for the benefits of supplements for all children, a study using omega-3 supplementation with a mainstream school population (A. Kirby et al., 2010) found no gains in reading ability. Richardson et al. (2012) found a small positive effect upon poor readers, evidence supporting the use of fatty acids as a means of remediating complex reading difficulties, yet there appear to be no significant replications to substantiate this finding.

In summary, there is a lack of robust research evidence that the provision of dietary supplements will improve reading performance for those with dyslexia. Given the potentially powerful commercial impact that successful outcomes would generate, the continuing absence of these in the scientific literature is hardly suggestive of its likely potential.

Some interest has been voiced in the use of medication to enhance reading. Piracetam, a cyclic derivative of gamma-aminobutyric acid, has been proposed as a nootropic (a so-called "brain-booster") that can enhance reading and spelling performance. However, Wilsher and Taylor (1994) were unable to find a significant effect and, given the possibility of side-effects, it was concluded that the risks seemed higher than any possible benefits.

A number of studies have examined the effects of treatments for children diagnosed with comorbid ADHD and reading difficulties (Denton et al., 2020; Dvorsky et al., 2021; Froehlich et al., 2018; Tannock et al., 2018). In general, it has been found that disorder-specific treatments are most appropriate for treating such children. Outside of this particular grouping, there is no significant evidence to suggest that medications designed for attentional problems (e.g., methylphenidate) are valuable for the treatment of reading disability.

Auditory Interventions

Given the possibility that auditory processing deficits have a negative influence upon the development of reading skill, there is understandable interest in the possibility that auditory interventions may be able to help tackle reading disability. Most recently, the work of Goswami and her colleagues (e.g., 2022), discussed in Chapter 2, has yielded significant new insights, yet it is important to recognize that this extensive body of work has yet to lead to validated interventions for reading disability.

The possible use of auditory training for reading disability stretches back to the twentieth century. Initial studies examining the effectiveness of a computer-based auditory training program used with children with language impairments (Merzenich et al., 1996; Tallal et al., 1996) led to claims that such an approach could be valuable, although there was some strong opposition from Tallal's former colleagues at the Haskins lab, internationally renowned for its pioneering work in speech, language, and reading (Mody, Studdert-Kennedy, & Brady, 1997). In the light of Tallal's work, a commercial product, *Fast ForWord,* consisting of a suite of computer programs, was launched in 1997. The programs involve the auditory presentation of acoustically modified speech that is initially slowed down and gradually modified as the child becomes more skilled on various tasks. This product, geared to improve both language and reading skills, proved to be popular, having been used over the subsequent decade with more than 570,000 children in the USA alone (What Works Clearinghouse, 2007). The program involves a significant commitment on the part of participants who are required to spend 30 to 100 minutes a day, five days a week, for four to sixteen weeks. Interestingly, the claims on websites that have promoted the *Fast ForWord* approach, often drawing upon findings from its publisher's "… privately conducted and non-peer reviewed studies" (Scientific Learning Corporation, 1999; 2003; Strong et al., 2011), have not been generally supported by independent, peer-reviewed studies published in the scientific literature (Olson, 2011).

Strong and colleagues (2011) undertook a systematic meta-analysis of six studies, taken from a larger pool of thirteen, all of which met appropriate scientific criteria. They found that when compared with untreated or alternative treatment controls, there was no evidence for the effectiveness of *Fast ForWord* for the treatment of either reading or language. In addition, the only study in the meta-analysis that included a measure of auditory temporal processing (Gillam et al., 2008) failed to result in significant gains on the auditory processing task for the *Fast ForWord* intervention group. On the basis of their review, Strong and colleagues concluded that their findings cast considerable doubt on the claims that *Fast ForWord* training can remediate auditory processing problems, or that this intervention offers significant benefits for reading and language development.

One of the criticisms of meta-analytic approaches is that their inclusion solely of those studies with high-quality scientific designs can result in the discarding of other investigations that may provide contrasting findings. Strong and colleagues (2011), for example, included only six studies in their meta-analysis from thirteen that were identified as potentially appropriate. To address the possibility that this might underestimate meaningful effects, Stevenson (2011) considered the seven studies that had been excluded. He noted that, of these, only one study (Troia & Whitney, 2003), excluded because of the absence of baseline group equivalence, showed any evidence of significant gains for the program, and this was in just one of the four measures employed. Stevenson also remarked upon the potential for publication bias whereby studies with negative findings tend to be less likely to be published in peer-reviewed journals. However, as is pointed out, the conundrum here is that the inclusion of studies without positive outcomes would only have served to reduce the overall effect size reported in the meta-analysis.

McArthur (2009) reviewed the evidence from six studies of auditory training programs that included a focus upon either nonspeech sounds or simple speech sounds. She concluded that such programs appeared to help increase performance on auditory tasks of those with marked deficits but had little effect upon the literacy performance of poor readers.

In the light of findings suggesting poorer rhythmic ability for some dyslexic children (Bégel et al., 2022) some growing interest in the potential role of rhythmic training has been expressed (Flaugnacco et al., 2015; Habib et al., 2016). However, the application of this research to intervention is still at a rudimentary stage (Groß et al., 2022) and currently there is insufficient evidence that any form of auditory training is an effective means of tackling severe reading difficulties.

Neurofeedback

The use of various forms of biofeedback for those with a variety of developmental difficulties, including reading disability, has persisted for a long time (Tansey, 1991) but the effect of this approach upon reading accuracy has not proven persuasive. In a single blind study with dyslexic adults, Liddle, Jackson, and Jackson (2005) provided feedback from each participant's cardiac cycle. Comparison with controls indicated no subsequent gains for reading accuracy although there was a small, but significant effect for reading speed.

Two studies have claimed that neurofeedback (a particular form of biofeedback that provides feedback directly on brain activity) can assist poor readers (Thornton & Carmody, 2005; Walker & Norman, 2006), although sample sizes were very small and neither study employed a control group. Breteler et al. (2010) conducted what they claimed to be the only randomized controlled treatment neurofeedback study with dyslexics but failed to find an improvement in reading. Gains were found in spelling for the experimental group, most likely, according to the authors, because of improved attention. However, it should be noted that group sizes were small (n = 10, experimental and n = 9, control) and there was no attempt to measure whether the gains observed were maintained for any period once the experiment was completed. Although it has been suggested that advances in quantitative EEG techniques may lead to improved neurofeedback interpretations and interventions (Walker, 2010), practitioners will currently need to look elsewhere. Breteler et al.'s conclusion that "Neurofeedback can make an important contribution to the treatment of dyslexia" (2010: 10) would, many years later, still be best understood as an aspiration rather than as an established finding.

It is notable that there has been a dearth of studies examining the potential of biofeedback for treating reading disability during the past decade (Darling, Benore, & Webster, 2020). This suggests that researchers in the field have largely concluded that this is not a promising approach.

Transcranial Stimulation

Greater understanding of brain structure and functioning in children with learning difficulties has resulted in attention being given to the potential of targeted electrical brain stimulation (van Bueren, Kroesbergen, & Cohen Kadosh, 2022). The nature and use of this approach as a means to study brain functioning and improve cognitive performance is considered in Chapter 3. Related discussion in this present section is focused primarily upon available evidence for its possible value as an intervention for reading disability.

As discussed in Chapter 3, transcranial direct current stimulation (tDCS) is a non-invasive technique that involves the delivery of weak electrical currents through electrodes placed on the scalp. It is considered to be a safe procedure for children and young people (Buchanan et al., 2021). An alternative approach (transcranial magnetic stimulation, TMS) tends to be less frequently employed with children and adolescents (Turker & Hartwigsten, 2022). Both approaches have been used in treatments designed to improve cognitive functioning in those with various brain disorders such as in schizophrenia, depression, dementia, Parkinson's disease, stroke, traumatic brain injury, and multiple sclerosis. A recent meta-analytic review (Begemann et al., 2020) of eighty-two studies reported small but statistically significant effects upon working memory and attention that did not differ substantially across the type of brain disorder. Results for executive functioning, processing speed, verbal fluency, verbal learning, and social cognition were not significant.

Turker and Hartwigsen (2022) conducted a systematic review of fifteen studies involving the use of transcranial stimulation with children and adults with reading difficulties. They concluded that the use of this approach, undertaken alongside reading interventions, had the potential to result in long-lasting improvements. However, where gains were found, these tended to vary across studies in relation to different aspects of reading. Rios et al. (2018), for example, found that the use of tDCS with a sample of Brazilian children with dyslexia led to increased reading performance for pseudowords, but not for single word reading. A study with Italian children (Battisti et al., 2022), published after the systematic review, found a statistically significant improvement in nonword reading speed but not for reading accuracy or for speed in reading passages of text, or lists of high and low frequency words. Mirahadi et al. (2022) offer a plausible explanation for a broadly similar finding in relation to the effects of tDCS upon Iranian dyslexic children's reading of nonword versus low and high frequency words.

While offering some beguiling possibilities, it is important to guard against unrealistic claims about the potential of this approach. The evidence to date is hardly persuasive; many studies have methodological problems, in particular, the use of small sample sizes, treatment effects are modest, and results are inconsistent across differing reading tasks. Few longitudinal studies have been conducted and, where this has occurred, results have been mixed. This form of treatment is still in its infancy and it is far from clear what might be the most suitable tDCS protocols for different populations. In conclusion, while it is conceivable that one or more forms of cranial stimulation may help predispose the brain to respond more effectively to teaching, the extent to which any of these have any long-term value for improving reading skill in those with reading disability is currently unclear.

The Allure of Complementary Treatment Approaches – Concluding Remarks

In seeking help for intractable forms of reading disability, families may turn to alternative or complementary therapies despite an absence of evidence that these are effective (Snowling, 2010). In popularizing these alternative approaches, there has been an over-reliance upon personal testimonials, anecdotes, and in-house studies; sources which are often associated with pseudoscientific thinking (Hyatt, Stephenson & Carter, 2009; Park, 2003). Greenspan (2005) highlights several factors that can lead to gullibility and credulity in respect of treatment fads, and stresses the need for professional service providers to maintain a strongly scientific approach to the validation of new approaches:

> Obviously science advances in sometimes unexpected ways, and a blind and knee-jerk skepticism can sometimes cause legitimate advances to be resisted and delayed. But the dangers of an unwarranted belief are much greater than the dangers of unwarranted skepticism, and a central tenet of the scientific method is to be skeptical of new claims until they are demonstrated, replicated, and hopefully, explained. (Greenspan, 2005: 137)

This situation is compounded by the possibility that studies that report large effect sizes for treatment efficacy are providing an overestimate. A misleading result is particularly likely to occur where small participant samples are used and there are small true effects. Small samples will result in low statistical power that makes it difficult to distinguish between true and false positive results (Szűcs & Ioannidis, 2020; Toffalini et al., 2021).

Given the continuing difficulties in finding effective means to help those with severe reading disability, a strong temptation to look elsewhere will persist. For this reason, anxious parents (and professionals) need to be helped to understand that alternative approaches have yet to be proven effective. Despite periodic claims for the success of various forms of non-educational intervention, it has yet to be shown that positive outcomes found in laboratory studies can be replicated in controlled studies in field settings and, importantly, demonstrate that any initial gains will lead to meaningful educational progress over time. Until scientific findings suggest otherwise, our best option is to continue to focus upon the search for the most efficacious intensive and systematic approaches to reading instruction. These are most likely to involve phonologically-based reading interventions that are embedded within the context of a broad and balanced literacy curriculum.

> There are many systematic approaches to improving reading outcomes for students with dyslexia, but the most common characteristic of effective programs is the use of explicit instruction in phonics. (Clemens & Vaughn, 2023: 184)

As regards future inquiry, the field will need to conduct further investigations to ascertain whether effective interventions for reading disability need to be amended or timed differently when the individual presents with one or more other comorbid disorders (Moll, 2022).

The Pedagogic Value of a Diagnosis of Dyslexia

Given widespread recognition of the need for early intervention for all children with reading difficulties, one can question whether it is helpful to differentiate between two distinct groups of poor decoders – those deemed to be dyslexic and others who are considered not to be dyslexic. To justify such a stance, we would need to demonstrate that each of these groups requires different forms of intervention and that, if so, the two groupings could be reliably identified. Both of these preconditions are problematic (Miciak & Fletcher, 2020).

In relation to intervention in the early years, seeking to identify children who are deemed to be dyslexic and distinct from other poor readers appears to have little practical relevance for instruction:

We currently have no scientific evidence that effective prevention of reading difficulties in students with dyslexia depends on accurate differential
diagnosis of the disorder in kindergarten or first grade. What *is* critical is
that difficulties learning to read are identified as early as possible, and that
intensive and well-targeted interventions be provided to students who are
lagging behind, no matter what the cause. (Torgesen, Foorman, & Wagner
(n.d.): 5, emphasis original)

The situation for older students is broadly similar. For example, in a
UK web-based discussion between special needs teachers on the topic of
dyslexia (SENCO-Forum, 2005), it was widely reported that referral to
specialist agencies by school personnel was largely motivated by a desire
for advice on how best to help the child's reading. Unfortunately, guidance subsequently received from specialist assessors tended to offer little
that added to practices that were already in widespread use. Vellutino
et al. (2004) criticized clinicians' reports for often having little prescrip-
tive value for educational or remedial planning. These authors argued
that clinicians should concern themselves less with the use of psychometric tests for the purposes of categorical labeling and, instead, devote
their energies to providing guidance to educators to help with the implementation of appropriate remedial interventions tailored to each child's
individual needs.

The ways in which a diagnosis of dyslexia might lead to differential
forms of intervention was an issue specifically explored by the UK House
of Commons Science and Technology Committee (2009). In taking oral
evidence from those advocating the need for such a diagnosis, repeated
attempts were made by the Chair to ascertain how provision for such a
group would be "different" to that of other poor readers (2009: Evidence
28–29, Questions 97–102). The Select Committee, seemingly unconvinced
by the claims of some expert witnesses, subsequently concluded that it was
not useful from an educational point of view to differentiate between the
dyslexic child and other poor readers:

There is no convincing evidence that if a child with dyslexia is not labelled
as dyslexic, but receives full support for his or her reading difficulty, that
the child will do any worse than a child who is labelled as dyslexic and
then receives specialist help. That is because the techniques to teach a child
diagnosed with dyslexia to read are exactly the same as the techniques used
to teach any other struggling reader. There is a further danger that an over-
emphasis on dyslexia may disadvantage other children with profound reading difficulties. (House of Commons Science and Technology Committee,
2009: Evidence 28)

Clearly, it is important to differentiate between children who have decoding difficulties and accurate and fluent readers who struggle with other reading-related problems such as spelling and comprehension. It is also helpful to identify those with adequate reading skills but whose progress is hampered by low motivation or a lack of enthusiasm for reading (Morgan & Fuchs, 2007). In undertaking clinical assessment, the assessor will also wish to ascertain whether there are other co-occurring difficulties (e.g., language impairment, attentional difficulties) the provision for which may need to be incorporated into intervention programs.

Despite beliefs to the contrary on the part of some practitioners, it is largely impossible to differentiate between two etiologically distinct groups – those whose poor reading and reading-related skills are a result of inherent neurobiological deficits, and others whose difficulties are a consequence of impoverished learning experiences at home and at school. Where such distinctions have been drawn, they have had little utility for guiding instruction (although family outreach work may prove additionally helpful where domestic circumstances are disadvantageous; Foorman et al., 2002; Schelbe et al., 2021).

It has been suggested that differentiating between different subtypes of dyslexia may have value in guiding intervention. One widely employed distinction is between phonological dyslexia, in which nonword reading is particularly impaired, and surface dyslexia, where exception (irregular) word reading is problematic. While awareness of individual differences in these areas may help to guide intervention, research has shown that evidence for the stability of the surface subtype is weak (Fletcher et al., 2019) and differentiating between the two subtypes has little prognostic value (Peterson et al., 2014). It is possible that more complex reading-disabled subgroupings, drawing upon multifactorial models and using advanced data-analytic techniques, will one day help to guide differential instruction (Lorusso & Toraldo, 2023) but this is a goal for the future rather than a present-day reality.

Perhaps the key message from this chapter in relation to the dyslexia debate is that categorical labeling *within* the population of children with decoding difficulties offers little guidance for intervention:

> If we want to identify children with problems in reading, then identified problems in reading should serve as the basis for identification. There is no need to distinguish between "reading disability" and "poor reading". One need only identify problems in reading and treat them accordingly. (Sternberg & Grigorenko, 2002b: 82)

In a "thought experiment," Brooks (2015) questions what it would take to rebut the main conclusion of *The Dyslexia Debate*. He concludes that the field (scientists, practitioners, policymakers) would need to agree upon and adopt a stable definition of dyslexia which enabled reliable identification and differentiation of struggling readers into dyslexic (DSR) and non-dyslexic (NDSR) groups. Interventions would then need to be devised that clearly differed for the two groups. A series of randomized control trials could then examine whether there is an aptitude × treatment interaction that consistently show the DSR approach to be more effective for the DSR group and the contrasting NDSR approach more effective for the NDSR group. At the current time, such a body of work has not been reported (Miciak & Fletcher, 2020) and, given that there appears to be no clear rationale upon which to base contrasting programs, it seems highly unlikely that this will happen in the conceivable future.

CHAPTER 5

Dyslexia
The Power of the Label

Introduction

At the age of 22, William Carter gained national prominence in the UK in 2021 for an uplifting account of his academic journey from the bottom streams at school to his award of a First Class Honours degree at Bristol University. He won multiple public awards for his achievements and was subsequently awarded a Fulbright Scholarship to study for a PhD at the University of California, Berkeley. In press accounts he described how he was mocked at primary school for his inability to read and was even asked by one of his secondary school teachers whether he was "retarded."[27] He believed that his skin color and adverse socioeconomic circumstances were seen by some as explanatory factors and struggled to cope with consequential feelings of alienation. William reported many years of feeling stupid and "a second-class learner" and of often encountering difficulty in participating in his lessons. Such experiences led to feelings of loneliness and isolation and growing school attendance problems. However, once he received a dyslexia diagnosis at secondary school, a "life-changing" moment, he began to get additional assistance, including support from in-class teaching assistants and his grades improved rapidly.[28] At the age of eighteen he gained some of the best public examination results ever achieved at his school. According to William, "Fundamentally, dyslexia made me who I am today."[29]

William's story, powerful and uplifting, perfectly illustrates many of the key issues and challenges that lie behind the dyslexia debate. It tells the story of a child, seemingly written off as stupid by teachers and school administrators who had failed to recognize his potential. After years of

---

[27] "Dyslexic student recounts escape from classroom of the damned," *The Times*, March 6, 2021.
[28] "Fundamentally, dyslexia made me who I am today," *Epigram*, March 3, 2021. https://bit.ly/3NisIuo; accessed December 8, 2023.
[29] www.bbc.co.uk/news/uk-england-bristol-56249776; accessed July 6, 2022.

struggle, he was seen by a specialist who determined that the problem was dyslexia, a condition unrecognized by the professionals who had worked with him over the previous decade. At last, he had an explanation for his difficulties. Following the diagnosis, teaching and resourcing appropriate for a child with dyslexia were soon made available, teacher expectations rose, and he subsequently reframed his self-perceptions in ways that provided him with greater agency, efficacy, and positivity. A life-changing transformation was the consequence.

The desire to know why we have a medical or learning problem is universal and William's experience strikes a familiar chord. Many personal accounts in the literature and on social media have described a dyslexia diagnosis as a positive experience that helped the individual to understand why they were struggling (Camilleri, Chetcuti, & Falzon, 2020; Wilmot et al., 2022). In turn, this typically leads to powerful feelings of relief and enhanced self-esteem (Glazzard, 2010; Ingesson, 2007; Leitão et al., 2017).

As an example of an individual's triumph over adversity, no one could fail to respond positively to William's story. However, when one situates the issues involved within a broader systemic consideration, a number of troubling questions emerge:

- William's deep-seated reading problems had long been known to his teachers. On what basis was the dyslexia diagnosis made and what new insights resulted from the conferral of this label?
- In what ways did the diagnosis affect the nature of instruction he subsequently received to help him address his literacy difficulties and his more general learning needs?
- Why was supportive provision, such as access to teaching assistants, provided only after the diagnosis?
- Should a diagnosis of dyslexia be a catalytic determinant of how a struggling reader is understood and supported by educational professionals?
- Did the diagnosis offset negative understandings and expectations of William based upon race and social class? If so, is taking this route an appropriate means to remedy what is undeniably an unacceptable situation?
- Ultimately, is William's story really about the powerful role of judgements of intelligence in determining which children struggling with their learning have the greatest potential and thus deemed to be most "worthy" of additional time, attention, and resources?

These questions map closely onto many of the issues and concerns expressed in this book. In particular, they reveal how a seemingly benign and helpful process for an individual may, at a systemic level, support misunderstandings, misattributions, and false beliefs, and help to sustain unjust, divisive, and inequitable responses to genuine need.

Given the slipperiness and inconsistency of dyslexia's diagnostic criteria, the reality that a diagnosis cannot meaningfully differentiate dyslexic (DSRs) from other "garden-variety" poor decoders (NDSRs), the lack of any relationship between this distinction and differing approaches to intervention, the negative attributional risks to economically disadvantaged groups, and the inequalities and inequities in resourcing, Elliott and Grigorenko (2014) concluded *The Dyslexia Debate* by calling for discontinuation of the label. In its place, the use of the term "reading disability" (based upon normative performance on appropriate reading tests) was recommended when referring to a difficulty in accurately and fluently decoding text.

This recommendation brought strong responses from academics, practitioners, parents, and politicians, both supportive and oppositional. A number of UK educational (school) psychology services began to search for ways to close the DSR/NDSR divide by addressing children's reading difficulties irrespective as to whether or not dyslexia had been proposed or diagnosed. This stance was heavily criticized by two peers in the House of Lords[30] with the resultant political fallout leading some psychologists working in this way effectively to be silenced by their employers.[31]

The argument that all struggling readers should be identified and appropriately supported from an early age according to their particular individual needs and abilities, is socially, educationally, and ethically incontrovertible. However, less attractive to many critics was the concomitant recommendation that, as a consequence, individual assessment would no longer need to be geared to the identification and diagnosis of a comparatively small proportion of poor readers who would be labeled as dyslexic.

The dyslexia debate, like so many issues in education, is not neutral and value-free but, instead, reflects a myriad of differing political and social agendas that apply both to those who experience difficulties and those who provide services to help them. In understanding the arguments and positions involved it is important to recognize the differing perspectives, needs, interests, and agendas of diverse stakeholders. Geneticists, neuroscientists, medical practitioners, academic cognitive psychologists, clinical

---

[30] https://bit.ly/3QMrI2C; accessed November 17, 2023.
[31] https://bit.ly/3sCZOy2; accessed November 17, 2023.

psychologists, neuropsychologists, school and educational psychologists, speech and language therapists, education researchers, mainstream teachers, special education teachers, literacy specialists, education consultants and trainers, social workers, lobby and advocacy groups, and, of course, struggling readers and their families, have each appropriated the dyslexia label, ascribing to it different meanings and utilizing it in different ways.

The interest of medical practitioners in assessing and diagnosing dyslexia is likely to grow in the foreseeable future, especially should medical insurance for the treatment of dyslexia become more readily available (Al Dahhan et al., 2021). The attractions of medicalizing reading difficulty for the purposes of insurance are significant (Braaten, 2020; Moll et al., 2022). Sanfilippo and colleagues (2019) advised pediatricians to look for an early risk of dyslexia and recommended that the medical community should become involved in national conversations about this condition. In similar vein, Youman and Mather (2015) noted a proposal for the state of Kansas which would have required schools to accept a dyslexia diagnosis from a licensed psychologist, physician, or psychiatrist, and provide services accordingly. While it is self-evidently important to ensure that struggling learners do not have an underlying medical condition or infirmity (e.g., a sensory impairment), it should be understood that reading disability/dyslexia is essentially an educational problem requiring an educational solution. Although audiologists, physical therapists, optometrists, and pharmacists can have a contributory role in supporting struggling learners, such professions do not have measures that can be employed to diagnose or treat dyslexia or, indeed, other specific learning disabilities (Grigorenko et al., 2020). Unsurprisingly, however, the field is beset by a variety of underlying personal and professional tensions and rivalries:

> The definition of dyslexia, and the assessment and classification of literacy difficulties are discursive spaces for ongoing resistance, challenges and contestation, because they are key aspects in the construction of social and personal identities associated with dyslexia … they are central to the professional practice/discourse surrounding dyslexia because of their inextricable links to professional identity, power relationships and the access to resources. (Soler, 2010: 190–191)

Many arguments, personal, professional, and scientific, have been put forward to refute the challenges to the formal process of dyslexia diagnosis that were expressed in *The Dyslexia Debate* and the recommendations that followed. Areas of rebuttal commonly offered are concerned with:

- learner empowerment and exculpation;
- gaining access to finite resources;

- the perceived failure of teachers, schools, and school systems;
- meeting the needs of adult learners in further and higher education;
- neurodiversity, disability, and the dyslexic identity;
- other arguments offered for retention of the label.

Each of these areas is considered below.

Learner Empowerment and Exculpation

A commonly cited benefit of a dyslexia diagnosis is that it can reduce feelings of shame or guilt (Burden, 2008) by reassuring learners that they are not stupid or lazy – that their literacy problem is not their fault (Snowling, 2019).

> Knowing that his dyslexia is a respectable neurological diagnosis, and not another word for laziness or stupidity can transform a child's self-image. (Stein, 2012: 189)

Negative attitudes and actions towards those with reading difficulties have long been problematic. The following two quotations, produced more than a century apart, raise very similar concerns:

> It is a matter of the highest importance to recognise as early as possible the true nature of this defect, when it is met with in a child. It may prevent much waste of valuable time and may save the child from suffering and cruel treatment. When a child manifests great difficulty in learning to read and is unable to keep up in progress with its fellows, the cause is generally assigned to stupidity or laziness, and no systematised method is directed to the training of such a child. (Hinshelwood, 1902; cited in Shaywitz, 2005: 21–22)
>
> Parents of students with dyslexia continually face challenges within our educational system, experiencing frustration, disappointment, and anger due to a lack of understanding about dyslexia. All too often students with dyslexia are misdiagnosed, misunderstood, or just plain ignored. As a result, their skills and abilities often are overlooked. These students begin to doubt themselves and their abilities; they feel stupid, lazy, and worthless. This lack of knowledge about dyslexia often means schools do not provide the necessary identification, instruction, intervention, and accommodations that students with dyslexia need to succeed. From the time a student's dyslexia is first identified … it is essential that educators understand the potential of our students when given appropriate instruction and accommodations. (Steinberg & Andrist, 2012, n.p.)

Personal testimonies, such as William Carter's, have shown how receipt of the label can exert a powerful, often empowering effect, upon struggling readers and their families (Riddick, 2010; Wilmot et al., 2022). It can help to assuage the negativity that has been so often experienced, a negativity that stems from the belief that those who struggle to learn to read are less intelligent than their peers.

However, since the demise of the now discredited IQ-reading discrepancy criterion, there are no grounds to suggest that a dyslexia diagnosis is indicative of higher intellectual functioning. Indeed, despite occasionally sending mixed messages about creativity and various intellectual strengths, leading dyslexia associations now explicitly state that dyslexia occurs across the intellectual spectrum. While it might be argued that little harm results from the continuance of such misperceptions on the grounds that these engender greater positivity and agency, such a view is dangerously flawed. In what is principally a zero-sum game scenario, the use of the dyslexia label in this way has significant, often unrecognized, ramifications (Worthy et al., 2017). By championing the superior intellectual abilities of people diagnosed dyslexic, a "dyslexic" versus "stupid poor reader" binary is maintained in public consciousness.

> The ways in which dyslexia has recently emerged and been constructed in popular discourse and legislation are strikingly similar to those of LD [learning disability], as dyslexia is often described as unexpected and is conflated with intelligence and creativity. The current use of the term sets up artificial, and arguably discriminatory, distinctions between students who are considered intelligent but with specific reading challenges and those considered to have global learning difficulties. (Worthy et al., 2021: 8)

For NDSRs, the outcome may be an increased likelihood of lowered expectations and reduced teacher efforts to raise these children's academic performance. The potential for such pernicious, largely hidden, deleterious consequences is typically overlooked in the celebratory, powerful, personal anecdotes in media stories and, indeed, are rarely identified in the scientific or professional literatures.

Stories in popular culture regularly reference the "gift" of dyslexia, portrayed as above-average abilities and positive dispositions and motivations that lead to high levels of success in life (Davis, 1997; Eide & Eide, 2011; Kirby, 2019). Alexander-Passe (2016) cites a study of UK millionaires, for example, that reported that 40 percent were dyslexic. Here it was stated that people with dyslexia "... don't do failure, they redefine it. Failure for them is a learning experience that will enable them to be even better. If the fall over, they just come straight back up again" (Alexander-Passe, 2016: 3).

In similar vein, Franks and Frederick (2013) provide a list of positive and negative dyslexic characteristics. Positive factors listed are: a proficient verbal communicator, innovative, resilient/determined, logical problem solver, intuitive/insightful/curious, strong global/spatial skills, excellent mechanical skills, conceptual /3D thinker, expert delegator. Negative factors are low self/ esteem efficacy, low level literacy skills, poor executive functioning skills, social isolation, and an external locus of control. These authors contend that, given this mix of strengths and weaknesses and a tendency to dislike imposed structure, it is unsurprising that many dyslexic people gravitate towards self-employed entrepreneurship (Logan & Martin, 2012).

As noted in Chapter 1, such accounts have a popularity and resonance that are largely undimmed by the absence of scientific support (Chamberlain et al., 2018; Erbeli, Peng & Rice, 2022; Gilger, Allen, & Castillo, 2016; Majeed, Hartanto, & Tan, 2021; Martinelli, Camilleri & Fenech, 2018; Seidenberg, 2017) and such messages are rarely challenged by dyslexia lobby groups (Johnston & Scanlon, 2021). Research does not support the suggestion that success is based on dyslexia's pre-existing compensatory gifts (Logan, 2009; Marazzi, 2011). Rather than demonstrating superior creative and visuospatial abilities, the achievements of high-performing adults with dyslexia, whether contemporary or famous figures from the past, appear to depend more upon personality and motivational factors (Erbeli, Peng, & Rice, 2022; Łockiewicz, Bogdanowicz, & Bogdanowicz, 2014).

Selecting a small proportion of dyslexic high achievers and generalizing from their experiences distorts the fact that struggling readers do not as a group present with exceptionally high skills or abilities. Indeed, as discussed in Chapter 1, many struggle cognitively, emotionally, behaviorally, and vocationally. It has been estimated, for example, that dyslexia is far more common amongst incarcerated offenders than across the general population and US legislation now requires federal prison inmates to be screened for dyslexia (First Step Act of 2018). However, it would be no more appropriate to suggest that dyslexia is associated with a delinquent disposition or traits than to accept the claim that it confers positive gifts. It is more likely that a history of reading difficulty will influence the ways that individuals build and capitalize on their particular strengths, weaknesses, opportunities, and networks. Becoming a successful entrepreneur, an artist, or an offender, may, in part, be attributable to one's experience of a reading disability.

A second common theme concerns the power of the diagnosis in removing perceived culpability for one's reading difficulties. While any reduction of guilt and shame in struggling learners is obviously desirable, it is hard to identify how the diagnosis would enable any meaningful apportionment of personal responsibility or blame. The understanding that dyslexia has a biological origin (although see the discussion regarding genes versus environment in Chapter 1) may reassure the diagnosed individual that the difficulty is not their fault (Snowling, 2019). However, as a thought experiment, would the individual be more blameworthy even if it could be shown (which it cannot) that their problem was wholly a consequence of adverse environmental factors?

A widely perceived value of a dyslexia diagnosis is that it can confer a level of moral value by helping to negate the suggestion that the individual's literacy difficulties are a consequence of laziness (Gwernan-Jones & Burden, 2010). However, any suggestion that, for other children, severe developmental difficulty in learning to read is caused by indolence or a lack of interest, rather than having a biological etiology, is a gross and misleading oversimplification, and the belief that any such distinction can be accurately determined by a diagnostic assessment, is unsustainable.

Children clearly differ in the extent to which they are eager to expend energy to tackle their reading difficulties. For many, the difficulty of making and sustaining demonstrable progress leads to low self-efficacy and a sense of frustration that is likely to reduce the enjoyment of reading (van Bergen et al., 2022). Negative experiences, self-perceptions and attributions can reduce any hope that hard work and persistence will ultimately pay off. As the poor reader becomes increasingly self-conscious and concerned about peer reaction, self-protective mechanisms, such as procrastination or significant withdrawal of effort, may be employed in a protective attempt to counter external perceptions of low intellectual ability (Covington, 1992). Such behavior may be interpreted by observers as laziness, an understanding that carries with it greater personal culpability than more neutral terms such as demotivation or disengagement.

The relationship between motivation and reading ability is complex and multi-layered (Lackaye & Margalit, 2006; Morgan, Fuchs, et al., 2008) although it seems that motivational problems are more likely to be a consequence than a cause of reading difficulty (Hebbecker, Förster, & Souvignier, 2019; Toste et al., 2020). Over-simplistic conceptions, whereby a dyslexia diagnosis is seen as a means of exculpation, are unlikely to help our understanding of the interactions between interest, agency, self-concept, self-efficacy, and engagement that are likely to impact upon reading behavior.

In arguing for the maintenance of the dyslexia label, Snowling (2015) draws a distinction between science and personal experience:

> … it is rare to find a person with an affected family member who does not want to use the label. Negative consequences of labelling include stigmatisation and self-fulfilling prophecy. In the case of dyslexia, the efforts of at least 50 years of scientific research have removed any stigma which

is attached, and rather than being an obstacle to progress, the label can offer hope to the child who is affected, coupled with increased (rather than declining) motivation. (Snowling, 2015: 20)

While Snowling's words may well be true, they fail to acknowledge or address the system-wide repercussions of using dyslexia diagnoses to address the needs of struggling readers. The recommendations of Camilleri, Chetcuti, and Falson (2020) following in-depth interviews with Maltese high school students demonstrate this problem:

> … it is very important to diagnose students as early on as possible and also make teachers and educators aware of the characteristics of dyslexia so that they can avoid labelling students as lazy and stupid. (Camilleri, Chetcuti, & Falson, 2020: 370)

This, of course, begs the question, discussed earlier, as to whether it is acceptable that laziness and stupidity can be deemed to be appropriate attributions to explain the difficulties of (supposedly) non-dyslexic children who struggle to learn to read.

Malchow (2014) contends that the term dyslexia:

> … offers a common understanding in classrooms across America that reading difficulties are not easily explained by laziness or low intelligence. Instead they may lie in a neurodevelopmental condition that effective methods can address. (Malchow, 2014)

While Malchow's reference to reading difficulties here, used interchangeably with the term dyslexia, seems to closely mirror the position that we present in this book, further examination of his article offers a different picture. Writing in his capacity as President-Elect of the International Dyslexia Association, this was principally a refutation of the key proposals in *The Dyslexia Debate*. In this account, he offered vigorous support for existing approaches and practices while ignoring the problems we had raised about adequate operationalization, differential diagnosis, and educational inequity.

Receipt of a dyslexia diagnosis is not always positive; it can sometimes be perceived to be stigmatizing (Gibby-Leversuch, Hartwell, & Wright, 2021). Some researchers have questioned whether categorization as dyslexic necessarily succeeds in raising students' academic self-beliefs and aspirations (Knight, 2021) or their teachers' beliefs about their capacity to help (Gibbs & Elliott, 2015; Knight, 2021).

It has been argued that teachers may find the notion of the dyslexic child as one who is intellectually able to be helpful. They may consider that this will assist them in determining how best to provide appropriate learning activities and in understanding the particular frustrations these children may encounter (Regan & Woods, 2000). Such a perspective needs to be challenged as not only is this view based on a misguided IQ discrepancy model, it could also readily result in inappropriate estimates of these and other poor readers' abilities.

Teachers need to have a sound understanding of the intellectual functioning and potential of every struggling reader; otherwise, there is a significant risk that they might pitch the academic challenge too low or too high. However, intellectual functioning and word reading are more appropriately treated as independent processes.

Gaining Access to Finite Resources

In public education systems there will always be greater demand for resources and services than are available. Consequently, difficult decisions must be made about who will gain access to these and who will be denied. One way of managing this is to create a highly bureaucratic diagnostic process that can operate as a bottleneck to exclude some otherwise needy students. For those who struggle to develop reading skills, a problem encountered on a huge scale, the requirement for a formal dyslexia diagnosis serves such a function. Those who can gain access to a clinical assessment, with the high likelihood of a dyslexia diagnosis, may receive additional resources and support that are inaccessible to peers with similar or greater reading abilities. In the UK, for example, it is not uncommon for parents of children with a dyslexia diagnosis to subsequently seek, and receive, state funding for highly expensive forms of day or residential special education. Where local authorities are not prepared to fund such requests, Government appointed tribunals may be asked to investigate subsequent appeals by means of a formal hearing. If persuaded, these can support parental wishes by mandating the local authority (school district) to provide the necessary funding. Such expenditure will reduce the resources available for the operation of adequate services to other children. Often the losers here are children from socially disadvantaged families who, for various reasons, are less likely to seek or obtain help for their children's learning difficulties (Leavett, Nash, & Snowling, 2014).

It would be churlish to criticize any parent for actively seeking the diagnosis. In addition to gaining access to additional resources and support, the diagnosis can help to overcome parental frustration and leave the family feeling more optimistic about the future (Denton et al., 2022). However, as noted above, these benefits come at a cost to others in ways that are not immediately obvious. Given the vast number of students who struggle with reading, the needs of the majority are unlikely to be resolved by maintaining dyslexia as a distinct and diagnosable problem separate from reading disability. Indeed, it is something of a paradox that successful appeals to legislators for increased dyslexia testing and specialist teaching may reduce political pressure to recognize and provide for the needs of all poor readers. Dyslexia lobbyists are often vociferous in their calls for more dyslexia testing and resourcing, but they tend to be less supportive of the suggestion that the term should be employed to describe and cater for all poor readers. To do so reduces a competitive advantage for available resources. Perhaps this is why those who question traditional diagnostic procedures that are largely based upon cognitive test scores have been criticized on the spurious grounds that they are seeking to reduce resourcing for those with dyslexia (Brooks, 2015).

The medicalisation of academic underperformance has had significant implications for the creation and maintenance of social and educational inequality. Disability critical race scholars such as Annamma, Connor, and Ferri (2013) have questioned the neutrality of disability labels and how factors such as race, class, privilege, and power affect student experiences in school. Although the additional support offered by special education services can prove beneficial to students (Schwartz, Hopkins, & Stiefel, 2021), it can also lead to exclusion from peers, reduced access to appropriately challenging content, and provide little benefit to already marginalized or disadvantaged groups. Within a hierarchy of educational disability some categories enjoy a higher social status and these tend to lead to more beneficial services (Fish, 2019). A diagnosis of specific learning difficulty (SLD), including dyslexia, typically offers a higher-status categorization than one that relates to intellectual or emotional-behavioral functioning. Such a label is desirable for families because it "… allows elites to maintain access to important symbolic and cultural capital" (Fish, 2022a: 3), "… a category of privilege for the privileged" (Blanchett, 2010). Similarly, Sleeter criticizes the Learning Disabilities (LD) category as one "… created by white middle class parents in an effort to differentiate their children from low-achieving, low-income, and minority children" (Sleeter, 1987: 210).

Suhr and Johnson (2022) reflect upon the increase in the receipt of educational accommodations in the United States and growing disparity in who receives them. Similar to the authors above, they note that levels of diagnosis for conditions such as LD and ADHD, and subsequent provision of high-stakes test accommodations, are much higher for students from high-performing schools in wealthier communities. In their opinion, the increasing medicalization of learning difficulties has resulted in the tendency of psychologists to over-pathologise the difficulties that many learners encounter in daily life.

In his case study of a privileged school in Sweden, Holmqvist (2020) speaks critically of a process of "consecrating medicalization" which aids the already more privileged to obtain a dyslexic label and all the benefits that accrue from this, while effectively excluding others. In addition to resourcing, labels may influence teacher attributions for undesirable classroom behavior that will color their understandings and sympathies (Fish, 2022a, 2022b). Unsurprisingly, perhaps, the existence of racial differences in access to higher versus lower status disability labels is a common phenomenon in the USA (Blanchett, 2010; Fish, 2019, 2022a, 2022b; Saatcioglu & Skrtic, 2019; Cruz et al., 2023). Dyslexia appears less likely to be diagnosed and treated in the case of children from minority backgrounds or who live in poverty (Odegard et al., 2020; Schelbe et al., 2021). In their study of nearly 8,000 second-grade children in one state that was using a universal dyslexia screening measure, Odegard et al. (2020) found African American students to be half as likely as White students to be identified with dyslexia and thus be provided with appropriate instruction as mandated by the state legislation.

Odegard et al. (2024) note that inequity of provision for socially disadvantaged children with learning disabilities is, in part, a consequence of the use of exclusionary criteria for specific learning disability that rule out from a diagnosis those children whose learning problems are, "… primarily the result of … environmental, cultural, or economic disadvantage" (US Department of Education, 2004). If one is poor and cannot read, it is often assumed that the reason is poverty; such reasoning helps to explain why schools with a high proportion of economically disadvantaged children tend to under-identify dyslexia. In schools where a high proportion of children are struggling with reading, an individual's difficulty is more likely to appear to be the norm rather than exceptional. In their analysis of practice in one US state, Odegard and his colleagues found that the higher the proportion of children in any given school who scored below the state screener benchmark for reading and spelling, the greater the likelihood was that the school would report no risk of reading problems for that group. It is unsurprising, yet problematic, that a struggling reader is less likely to stand out as "exceptional" or be deemed to have an "unexpected" reading difficulty in schools where many others present with similar problems.

This is not solely a USA phenomenon. In the UK, Knight and Crick (2021) used secondary data from the UK Millenium Cohort Study to examine which eleven-year-olds were identified as dyslexic by their teachers. Socioeconomic class and parental income were both found to be significant predictors of the label (together with gender and season of birth). While the data were unable to indicate which children had received a formal diagnosis from a qualified assessor, the authors concluded that additional resources and accommodations appeared not to be fairly allocated, leading them to question "… the reliability, validity and moral integrity of the allocation of the dyslexia label across current education systems in the UK" (Knight & Crick, 2021: 1).

Chapman and Tunmer (2015) identified similar problems in their submission to an enquiry undertaken by the New Zealand Education and Science Select Committee. They observed that the use of the dyslexia label in their country excluded some children with literacy difficulties who, because of their social, economic, and ethnic background, were denied the diagnosis and resources that follow. The term dyslexia was held to be particularly disadvantageous for indigenous Maori and Pasifika students whose needs were not being adequately catered for as "… definitions of dyslexia favour middle class children in higher decile schools" (Chapman & Tunmer, 2015: paragraph 8.1).

The Perceived Failure of Teachers, Schools, and School Systems

William Carter's story tells of the life-changing transformation that followed his diagnosis. Specialist intervention and resourcing replaced an inadequate educational diet and pre-existing low teacher expectations were subsequently raised. A picture is presented here of a poorly performing education system.

Concerns about the perceived failings of public school teachers in tackling dyslexia are a common theme in social media. Some commentators attribute this to poor professional training, lamenting the "ignorance, complacency and resistance" (Hurford et al., 2016: 1) of teacher educators. Such criticisms reflect long-standing concerns that teacher educators' allegiance to whole language approaches to the teaching of reading have led them to eschew structured phonics instruction (Seidenberg, 2017). Such perceptions appear to be justified, at least in the United States, where a study of 693 undergraduate and graduate teacher training programs undertaken by the National Council on Teacher Quality (Ellis et al., 2023) found that only 25 percent of courses covered all the core elements of what was described as "scientifically based reading instruction" (phonemic awareness, phonics, reading fluency, vocabulary, and reading comprehension). Additionally, 40 percent of these programs advocated practices, such as three-cueing strategies, that have been heavily criticized by the science of reading movement.

Rather more questionable are criticisms concerning the perceived failure of teacher educators to prepare teachers to differentiate sufficiently between DSRs and NDSRs (Hurford et al., 2016; Toste, 2016). In the light of a survey of teachers, for example, Washburn et al. (2017) were critical of teacher educators because "… teachers had accurate understandings when asked about reading disability but misconceptions when asked about dyslexia" (2017: 169). Given the analysis provided in this book, it is hardly surprising that this flawed distinction has confused teachers.

The understandings of teacher educators can vary significantly. Worthy et al. (2018a) interviewed twenty-five literacy teacher educators in Texas about dyslexia and dyslexia legislation. Five respondents (20%) produced accounts that closely mapped onto those which are typically promoted by dyslexia lobby groups and backed by the law in Texas. Dyslexia was understood by them as a distinct disability primarily experienced by creative and intelligent individuals. In their opinion, intervention should incorporate phonics and multisensory approaches provided by a specialist with dyslexia-specific expertise and training. The majority of the other interviewees (80%), held a very different position They did not consider dyslexia to be different from other forms of reading disability and expressed concerns about imprecise and inconsistent identification procedures. These professionals were largely critical of recent dyslexia legislation and reported frustration about authoritative presentations on the topic provided by those who, in their opinion, lacked an appropriate educational background or expertise.

Parental concerns that the potential of their children may be undermined by a failure on the part of schools to recognize, understand, and address reading difficulties effectively may often be valid, and, as such, their efforts to obtain more productive instruction for their children are laudable. Parental pressure, ably coordinated by advocacy groups, has led to the creation of dyslexia legislation in nearly every state in the USA. This outcome can be seen as an understandable response to an educational system that has seemingly failed to provide adequate reading instruction from an early age (Odegard et al., 2024).

In her study of policy narratives and testimonials in the USA, Gabriel (2020a) describes a scenario in which the perceived failure of public schools to cater for the individual needs of dyslexic children is contrasted with a privatized assessment and intervention industry that, it is believed, offers greater understanding and superior instructional solutions. Gabriel noted a common picture, provided by parents, that involved years of struggle to get help for their child. In most of these cases, the eventual diagnosis of their child's dyslexia was considered to be the turning point in their lives. For Gabriel, such accounts provide a form of "conversion narrative" in which the privately funded expert is lionized for getting to the heart of a problem that is unrecognized or ignored by a poorly serving educational establishment.

There are few who would doubt the merits of pressurizing policymakers to address shortfalls in provision for reading difficulties. However, the nature and focus of such pressure becomes problematic where a distinction is drawn between widespread reading difficulty, portrayed as a societal problem, and dyslexia, framed "... as a personal tragedy exacerbated by schools that neither identify nor specifically address it" (Gabriel, 2020a: 311). In the case of dyslexia, highly specialist programs (often brand-named), differing from the school's usual (typically unbranded) offering, are often deemed to be necessary.

> The use of conversion narratives, rather than scientific or economic arguments signals a move away from accountability era ideas about evidence-based practices or standard protocols for identifying and remediating reading difficulties among all school children. Brand-name programs sold by for-profit companies are discursively constructed as religions unto themselves, with educators and families publicly declaring allegiance, attributing miraculous turnarounds to their methods, and describing the moment of diagnosis/training in the same terms as a moment of conversion or enlightenment. (Gabriel, 2020a: 332)

Gabriel argues that little emphasis is placed in such accounts upon the need for school systems to address systemic failings or inadequacies; instead, the particular needs of dyslexic children are prioritized over and above those of other poor readers. As a response to such criticism, some have called for greater numbers of dyslexic poor readers to be identified, assessed, diagnosed, and treated. For all practical purposes, however, given the numbers and costs involved, channeling intervention through an expansion of traditional diagnostic routes is an unworkable, unrealistic, and unnecessary strategy.

Worthy et al. (2018a, 2018b) draw upon Bakhtin's (1981) theorizing about how humans deal with opposing viewpoints. Here, a contrast is offered between internally persuasive and authoritative discourse. Whereas the former involves the consideration, questioning, and challenging of different perspectives, the exploration of ideas, and the negotiation of meaning, authoritative discourse involves statements of fact offered from positions of authority. It is static, inflexible and not open to questioning or interpretation. According to Worthy and her colleagues, dyslexia legislation in the USA has "institutionally sanctioned" (Brantlinger, 1997: 509) an authoritative discourse promoted by "… a closed circle of dyslexia advocacy organizations associated with intervention, training, and certification" (Worthy et al., 2018b: 378). This discourse largely excludes public school teachers and teacher educators on the grounds that such personnel often lack the knowledge and skills to teach dyslexic students (see also Rosheim & Tamte, 2022 in relation to similar issues reported by literacy specialists operating within school districts).

A vast industry geared to providing assessments, diagnoses, and treatments has developed to address the Manichaean divide between the perceived lack of professional expertise in state school systems and the much greater competence of independent dyslexia specialists. There are many reasons why this supposed distinction has gained and maintained traction. The largely positive response of those who are informed that they "have dyslexia" means that the diagnosis is rarely questioned in publicly disseminated personal accounts (Gabriel, 2020a). However, while presented as unbiased, the livelihoods of private providers are dependent upon customer satisfaction, and professionals can be placed under significant pressure by families to provide a desired label (Sternberg & Grigorenko, 1999). Dyslexia is not a difficult diagnosis at which to arrive given that most struggling readers will present with symptoms of one kind or another that can be cited as indicators of the condition, particularly when some assessors employ a wide proliferation of measures. Even in questionable cases, the doubts of parents and adult clients can be assuaged by the use of terminology such as "mild dyslexia" or "dyslexia-like symptoms." Staff in schools, even if unpersuaded, can be reluctant to question a diagnosis provided by independent assessors. Seeking to avoid conflict and potential litigation, and believing that they may be deemed to lack expert authority and knowledge, it may be easier to quietly acquiesce than incur parental displeasure. For teaching staff with responsibility for managing and providing instruction to children with learning difficulties, there may also be a recognition that dyslexia diagnoses can be a means to press school managers for additional resources (SENCo Forum, 2005).

Meeting the Needs of Adult Learners in Further and Higher Education

The use of dyslexia diagnoses for adult learners has been particularly prevalent in UK universities and colleges as these can help students access additional resources and other forms of additional support, including a

Disabled Students' Allowance. Students with a recognized disability are eligible for a full Needs Assessment which typically results in recommendations both for the student concerned and for their academic institution. The latter can be provided with a list of "reasonable adjustments" which may include additional time in examinations, additional tutorial time, alternative forms of assessment, and the ability to signal to the markers of the student's work that they have particular difficulties with literacy. While assistance of this kind is often perceived as desirable, its effectiveness has yet to be demonstrated by high-quality research (Beck, 2022; Dobson Waters & Torgerson, 2021).

The ready availability of government funded resources to support diagnosed dyslexic students in UK universities at the beginning of the present century may partially explain the rise in the number of those with a formal diagnosis of dyslexia, or self-identifying, from 1.2 percent of the student body in 2000 to 5 percent in 2016 (Ryder & Norwich, 2018). Recognizing that controls over expenditure were needed, the Government placed responsibility for meeting the needs of disabled students (and the associated costs involved) onto the institutions themselves in the hope that this might put the brake on the rising levels of diagnosed disability. Prior to this, specialist personnel based in university disability services had responsibility for identifying the nature of any learning disability and resources necessary for their students but the costs of providing these largely fell to central Government. With the broadening of dyslexia's conceptual frame of reference in adult education, the largely positive response of the students concerned, and the lack of any financial brake on the host institution, such a situation offered a recipe for the untethered expansion of costs.

Calls for the increased recognition of dyslexia in the USA have largely reflected parental concern about children's unmet literacy needs (Odegard et al., 2021) with attention primarily focused upon the school sector. Published work on dyslexia in the college sector in the USA is comparatively rare. Indeed, Gabriel and Kelley (2021) reported that no studies of students with dyslexia diagnoses had been conducted in the USA within the past decade.

As noted above, a diagnosis of dyslexia can often offer more to students than just additional resources and accommodations. For some, it offers the opportunity to:

> … escape from accusations of moral and intellectual inferiority which appear still to be connected to people who struggle with particular culturally valued performances like reading, writing, memorising and expressing academic ideas quickly and articulately. (Cameron & Billington, 2015: 1237)

It is understandable why the dyslexic label and identity may be prized by university students experiencing difficulties in their learning. However, for some, the benefits can be tempered by concern that they may be perceived as engaging in chicanery in order to obtain undeserved help, or that the worth of their degree may be devalued (Cameron & Billington, 2015). Some university or college lecturers can be less than sympathetic, in part because of concerns that special assistance may not be fair for other students (Madriaga et al., 2010; Riddell & Weedon, 2006; Ryder & Norwich, 2019) or that some benefiting from help are merely playing the system. Problems arising from the potential for feigned deficits on the part of those seeking accommodations, and how any irregularities might be identified, are rarely expressed in the scientific literature although these issues are examined by Harrison and Edwards (2010), Hurtubise et al. (2017), van den Boer, de Bree, and de Jong, (2018), and Weis and Droder (2019).

Diagnostic practices involving dyslexia in the college and university sector appear to lack a strong scientific basis and findings from research studies published in leading research journals often appear to have been attenuated or ignored. Indeed, analyses such as those presented in *The Dyslexia Debate* have been criticized for drawing too heavily upon psychological science and not attending sufficiently to the experiences of people deemed to have dyslexia (Cameron & Billington, 2015).

Cameron (2021) offers a case study of Beth, a student whose dyslexia diagnosis was later "taken away." The case study describes the severe disappointment caused by the subsequent removal of specialist tutoring and other forms of support, and the loss of a sense of camaraderie shared with other students who had also been diagnosed dyslexic. Beth believed that she may have completed some of the psychometric subtests too quickly, and performed too well, leaving her to ponder whether she would have been wiser to have been less committed and to have underperformed. According to Cameron the decision to remove Beth's dyslexia label, for whatever reason, failed to take into consideration its social and educational impact: "… it was not only the dyslexia she had had which had been taken but also any future possibility of dyslexia, and its accompanying 'forgiveness'" (Cameron, 2021: 13). For Cameron, scientific analyses and understandings about dyslexia are important, but these should be considered alongside sociological examinations of the way that such labels affect people's lives. She concludes:

> In education, overly narrow access to legitimizing labels can support a hierarchy of human value which … is both harmful and avoidable …. A redrawing of the educational landscape to foreground an understanding of

> special educational needs as socially constructed and relational may enable
> some escape from the potential pitfalls of a solely scientific understanding
> of difference and distress. (Cameron, 2021: 13)

There is a curious circular logic in how common understandings of dyslexia in university students have been derived. These have largely been based on the presence of particular cognitive deficits that are more frequently observed in struggling readers. These typically include low processing speed, poor working memory, weak rapid naming, together with attentional, organizational, and self-regulatory difficulties. A diagnosis of dyslexia is often made where there appear to be deficits in one or more of these areas, even if the student's literacy skills are not unduly problematic at the time of assessment (Ryder & Norwich, 2018).

A number of research studies have asked professionally diagnosed or self-diagnosed dyslexic adults about the difficulties they encounter in their learning. On the basis of self-reports from volunteer adult respondents recruited online, Protopapa and Smith-Spark (2022) noted, for example, that those with "dyslexia-related traits" reported more attentional lapses and memory failures. This led the authors to conclude that deficits in dyslexia are not limited to reading and spelling difficulties. Here, issues of comorbidity and causality appear to have become conflated.

Gabriel and Kelley (2021) interviewed nineteen students with dyslexia labels at a US university. Perhaps the most striking finding was that no two participants defined dyslexia the same way and most saw manifestations of dyslexia as varying by the individual. Such heterogeneity reflects findings from other studies where reported difficulties have variously included: expressing ideas orally, memorizing names and facts, remembering sequences, completing other rote memory tasks, problems with telling the time and time-keeping, writing, copying and word retrieval, note taking in lectures, listening, keyboard skills, legible handwriting, producing coursework assignments, retaining the meaning of texts, marshaling facts effectively in examinations, producing disjointed written work due to losing track of sequential information, and using libraries and learning centers (Fuller et al., 2004; Gilroy & Miles, 1996; Klein, 1993; McLoughlin, Fitzgibbon, & Young, 1994; Mortimore & Crozier, 2006; Riddick, Farmer, & Sterling, 1997).

Somewhat surprisingly, many respondents in Gabriel and Kelley's (2021) study saw their ability in reading and writing as relative strengths and expressed greater concern about mathematical difficulties and the significant time it took to complete tasks. Interestingly, there was no reference in the paper to any memory difficulties, an omission that contrasts strongly with commonly held assessor and student understandings in UK higher education settings.

Gabriel and Kelley, note that the participants presented their experience of dyslexia as "… unique and individual as well as bound by conditions and contexts rather than neurological profiles, or text features" (2021: 164). Employing a social constructionist stance (see below for discussion) they call for greater consideration of the perspectives of young adults with direct experience of dyslexia. However, this implies that people's formal diagnosis or self-diagnosis should be uncritically accepted, and understandings in the field about the nature of dyslexia can be deepened by factoring in the symptoms and challenges they report. The strategy is highly questionable; there is a difference between the need to take students' experiences and concerns seriously, and diagnosing a condition on the basis of their subjective opinion. It has been shown that postsecondary students' self-reports of academic disability are often flawed because difficulties of academic functioning commonly experienced by most college students are frequently misinterpreted as indicators of a personal disability (Johnson & Suhr, 2021; Suhr & Johnson, 2022; Weis & Waters, 2023). This "… raises significant concerns regarding the use of self-report as primary evidence for impairment to make accommodation decisions" (Suhr & Johnson, 2022: 255). Such a problem can be compounded by the tendency of some clinicians to endorse the student's belief by erroneously interpreting isolated test scores and discrepancies among test scores as supportive evidence of their disability or impairment. A combination of clinician confirmatory bias and advocacy, together with reduced student effort in their clinical assessment (perhaps fueled by a conscious or subconscious desire to have their self-diagnosis confirmed), can significantly increase the likelihood of a misdiagnosis (Harrison & Sparks, 2022).

Given widespread student misunderstanding about what constitutes atypical problems of academic functioning, the ready acceptance of the difficulties that individuals self-report as symptoms of a clinically diagnosed condition called dyslexia, purely because that is what they independently believe, is highly questionable.

This dilemma is compounded by the widespread belief on the part of both students and assessors that dyslexia is revealed by the presence of various cognitive difficulties, a phenomenon that is particularly endemic in postsecondary education and adult work settings. Although those with a reading disability are statistically more likely to experience a wide variety of epiphenomenal comorbid difficulties, these do not necessarily play a causal role in reading disability (Carroll, Solity, & Shapiro, 2016) and their presence cannot be reverse engineered to diagnose dyslexia. Nevertheless, the requirement for a formal label to trigger disability support in adult education, and the emphasis upon learner identity and agency that has grown out of social constructionist accounts, have stimulated the broadening of the dyslexia construct from a significant and persistent decoding difficulty (as generally understood in the scientific literature) to its growing use as a nebulous, umbrella term that encompasses learning difficulties that range far beyond reading.

All learners will present with a mixture of different cognitive, affective, and conative strengths and weaknesses. Some cognitive deficits are considered to be indicative of dyslexia; others are often less so. This raises a number of questions:

- Are there particular cognitive difficulties that merit the provision of disability accommodation and support, and others which don't?
- How severe do these problems need to be before such assistance is offered?
- Does it matter in practice whether such difficulties are considered to be part of a diagnosable dyslexic condition?
- Is receiving a dyslexia diagnosis the principal (perhaps only) means to gain help and support for problems in these areas?

The problematics behind these questions become clearer once we start to examine specific cognitive processes in turn. For example, given that dyslexia is more closely associated with working memory than long-term memory, are students with working memory deficits, and thus more likely to be labeled dyslexic, more deserving of additional help or accommodation than those who struggle to retain or recall information over long periods of time? If it is considered that working memory should not be prioritized over long-term memory, surely students who find it hard to memorize course material should not be expected to sit public examinations without access to written notes and materials? Others, however, might argue that the ability to retain, recall, and draw upon relevant information is a key component of most academic examinations.

Similarly, should someone who gains a low score on a speed of processing measure, or who experiences organizational or self-regulatory difficulties, both widely considered to be symptoms of dyslexia, be denied access to special accommodations if they present with adequate reading skills? Is a slow processing (or, alternatively, a self-regulatory) component sufficient in itself to obtain a dyslexia diagnosis? Should disability support for those who experience one or both these difficulties be provided irrespective of receipt of a formal dyslexia label?

Thus, returning to the bulleted questions above, is it appropriate that an individual's cognitive difficulties must be linked to a diagnosis of dyslexia (or another neurodiverse label) before various forms of disability support can be provided? If the label is, indeed, an essential prerequisite, is it appropriate for an assessor to seek to identify cognitive symptoms of dyslexia even in cases where the individual's reading is clearly not problematic? In such cases, how difficult would it be for an assessor to find such symptoms?

The untrammelled expansion of the dyslexia construct helps to explain why research studies have repeatedly found practitioner uncertainty and inconsistency about exactly what dyslexia is, and how it should be assessed. Ryder and Norwich (2018), for example, surveyed the perspectives of 118 dyslexia assessors working in the UK higher education (university) sector. Participants were shown a list of deficits that might inform a dyslexia diagnosis and asked to indicate if they were "necessary," "important but not necessary," or "not necessary." The proportion of respondents who identified the following deficits as necessary for the diagnosis are as follows:

- current literacy skills difficulties   70%
- phonological processing difficulties   32%
- working memory difficulties   31%
- processing speed difficulties   28%
- substantial underachievement   39%
- receptive/expressive language difficulties   19%
- spiky profile   60%
- absence of general intellectual impairment   57%
- ability/literacy attainment discrepancy   44%

As can be seen, the responses demonstrated significant inconsistency. The need to ensure an absence of an intellectual impairment was cited by more than half of respondents. It should be noted that the focus in this study was upon students in university settings who would be highly unlikely to have an intellectual disability. Those identifying this category, therefore, were most likely referring to a low IQ; this is reflected by the observation that 44 percent of respondents considered a discrepancy between traditional ability measures and literacy attainment to be necessary. Surprisingly, perhaps, almost a third of respondents did not consider the existence of current difficulties with literacy skills to be essential.

The picture provided from interviews conducted as a second part of this study also indicates disagreement, confusion and uncertainty. Some assessors used the dyslexia label as, "… an umbrella term for a range of imprecisely defined and not very clearly understood learning difficulties" (Ryder & Norwich, 2018: 119). More than a third considered their understanding of the dyslexia construct to be imprecise and 30–50 percent were either unsure or lacked confidence in aspects of their assessment practice and the diagnostic conclusions that resulted. While 43 percent believed that there were no widely agreed criteria that could signal the nature of dyslexia, it was nevertheless still deemed to be diagnosable on the grounds that some respondents, "… conceived of it intuitively as a clinically recognizable 'essence' that defied description" (p. 119). The claim that expert clinicians have a wealth of tacit knowledge that enables them to recognize dyslexia when they see it (Morgan & Klein, 2000) is a common, yet largely unconvincing, response to criticisms about the absence of clear diagnostic criteria.

While a small number (13%) of respondents expressed the opinion that environmental factors such as sociocultural deprivation or poor instruction were in themselves sufficient to cause dyslexia, a substantial proportion considered it necessary to explore whether the student's problems were of environmental origin or because of low intelligence. The presence of either of these factors, would, in their opinion, most likely rule out a diagnosis of dyslexia.

Given the complex, multifactorial nature of learning difficulties, it is understandable that doubts were expressed by the assessors about their ability to adjudicate such issues. A particular concern resulting from such understandings, and echoed elsewhere in this book, is whether a student whose reading difficulty is believed to be biologically-based should be considered more deserving of help than someone whose adverse life experiences have seemingly hampered their academic progress. At some level, this conundrum appears to have been grasped by some of the assessors who admitted that, rather than ruling out some students from help, they would use the label pragmatically to secure the support that they considered to be needed.

In reflecting upon the findings from their study, Ryder and Norwich (2018) state:

> The lack of confidence and resultant inconsistent practice raise important questions about the viability of differential diagnosis, and in the context of disability entitlement, whether such differentiation is ethically acceptable in terms of advancing equality of opportunity. (Ryder & Norwich, 2018: 123)

Some of the difficulties concerning dyslexia assessment in higher and further education stem from the requirement for a formal label prior to accessing disability support. As has been noted, students can present with a variety of cognitive difficulties that impede their learning and academic performance; categorizing these within a single label is not easy. The appropriation of the influential dyslexia construct as a response to this dilemma, its delineation morphing far beyond the term's original conception as a severe reading difficulty, has unfortunately resulted in a widening divide between scientific and practitioner understandings.

Clearly, there are some students in post-secondary settings with a history of reading difficulties that continue to present them with learning challenges. Such students can be provided with strategies to help them manage their learning more effectively (Howard-Gosse, Bergey, & Deacon, 2023). However, such input may be more appropriately offered individually or in groups via the institution's teaching and learning support services. This could be made available to any students experiencing such difficulties. A disability diagnosis should not be necessary to gain access to instructional support of this nature.

Neurodiversity, Disability, and the Dyslexic Identity

Defining "neurodiversity" is not easy as the term is understood and used in many different ways and continues to evolve (Dwyer, 2022; Ne'eman & Pellicano, 2022). At one level it can be used to reflect and celebrate the fact that naturally occurring diversity of mind and brain occurs throughout humanity. However, the term is usually understood in more specific ways; "neurodiversity" operates as a particular theoretical perspective which can be distinguished from a "neurodiversity movement" that advocates for the rights and wellbeing of "neurodivergent" people (Walker, 2014). In this latter usage, a distinction is drawn between those termed as neurotypical and others, the neurodiverse or the neurominority, who experience developmental challenges. The neurodiverse activist movement originated in the field of autism (Singer, 1999), but has since incorporated a range of neurodevelopmental conditions such as dyslexia, autistic spectrum disorder, dyspraxia (developmental coordination disorder), and attention deficit (with or without hyperactivity) disorder. In neurodiverse understandings of dyslexia, it is seldom that the condition is limited "merely" to reading; rather, accounts in the academic literature and in social media usually reflect a Dyslexia 4 perspective (see Chapter 1).

The concept of neurodiversity sits easily with those who believe that dyslexia is signaled by the presence of various strengths and weaknesses, although this within-person perspective operates more problematically within a social model of disability (Dwyer, 2022). Reflecting a view that dyslexic brains are qualitatively different, reference can commonly be found to the "dyslexic difference" or the "dyslexic way of thinking," in which heavy emphasis is placed upon the positive contributions this offers the individual, and society more broadly (Alexander-Passe, 2018). This conception enables people with dyslexia to understand the learning challenges they encounter in ways that encourage greater positivity and an enhanced sense of agency.

On the basis of their study of an online forum, Thompson, Bacon, and Auburn (2015) differentiated between three different dyslexic identities: learning-disabled, differently-enabled, and societally-disabled. They found that those who saw themselves as differently-abled tended to hold more positive conceptions of themselves and their difficulties; in some cases, this has been expressed as "dyslexic pride" (Burden, 2005: 81). Arguing that the more adaptive perspective is one where differences are regarded as variations of normal, rather than different forms of abnormal, Thompson, Bacon, and Auburn (2015) questioned whether it might be possible to help people change their self-perceptions from learning disabled to differently enabled.

Unfortunately, as is discussed earlier in this chapter, there is an absence of evidence to support claims that the experience of a complex reading disability involves a different way of thinking or that it confers positive advantages. While widely promoted in the media and by some dyslexia lobby groups[32] such a notion appears to amount to little more than wishful thinking. Indeed, not all who promote neurodiverse conceptions are persuaded of the value of emphasizing strengths in this way as this stance may have potentially counterproductive sociopolitical implications (Fletcher-Watson, 2022).

Often closely associated with neurodiverse perspectives, the socio-constructionist/social model of disability operates from a very different perspective to that of the medical model. Arising from concerns that there needs to be a political platform to advocate for, and secure the rights of, those with disabilities (Lang, 2001), and reflecting perspectives drawn from Foucauldian and Marxist perspectives (Foucault, 1989; Campbell, 2011), social constructionist perspectives de-emphasize individual deficits and instead, focus upon disabling barriers in education and the workplace that lead to discrimination, inequality, and social alienation. Studies in this tradition are concerned to investigate the experiences of those who do not fit normative beliefs and assumptions, examine how these can adversely impact formal and informal judgements about individual capabilities and potential, and highlight the deleterious consequences that may result.

---

[32] See, for example, www.madebydyslexia.org; accessed November 26, 2023.

There are several theoretical variations of the social model, some of which have been criticized for focusing too greatly upon structural factors and placing insufficient emphasis upon individuals' lived experience of their disabling environment (Crow, 1994; Hughes & Paterson, 1997). Dwyer (2022) distinguishes between the "strong" social model whereby disability is wholly a consequence of society's responses to an individual's "impairments" and an alternative understanding that accepts the argument that some difficulties will have a biological origin.

Naturally occurring diversity can be considered through the lens of both biomedical and socio-constructionist/social models of disability although those who emphasize neurodiverse accounts typically reject the dominant medical model and only some accept social models of disability. Dwyer (2022) proposes that the neurodiverse approach should take the middle ground between the social and medical models. The picture is complex in the case of dyslexia as some who describe themselves as neurodiverse base this on their clinically derived dyslexia diagnosis. In determining the appropriateness of this label for a given individual, diagnosticians typically adhere to the operation of a medical model of assessment in which cognitive and academic tests are routinely employed. Further complication stems from the sorts of arguments deemed necessary to gain political recognition and funding. In this respect, dyslexia advocacy groups have largely lobbied for support by contending that dyslexia is a biologically-based difficulty experienced by those whose brains function in an atypical fashion. Such an argument does not sit easily with the contention that disability is caused by society (Kirby, 2018; 2019; Kirby & Snowling, 2022).

From a socio constructionist perspective, debate about the meaning and use of the terms "disability" and "impairment" can become highly complex (Shakespeare, 2013). For some, these are inappropriate medical constructs that provide negative connotations of learners. Others disagree and some argue that while "impairment" can be criticized for offering pejorative connotations of a functional limitation, "disability" is less problematic. For those who hold this opinion, "disability" can operate as a valuable construct when it is framed in a way that challenges dominant deficit perspectives (Hanebutt, & Mueller, 2021) and enables critical analysis of the limiting of opportunities caused by the inability of society to reduce social and physical barriers (Bunbury, 2019; Lang, 2001).[33]

---

[33] While beyond the scope of the present text, a valuable examination of conceptions of disability within the field of critical disability studies is provided by Vehmas and Watson (2014).

Currently, argumentation about language is perhaps fiercest in the field of autism where attempts to restrict, or even censor, the use of terms such as "risk," "disorder," "deficit," "symptoms," "comorbid," and "prevention," to be replaced by "more neutral terminology" (Natri et al., 2023: 673), are held to be presenting serious difficulties for scientists seeking to describe research findings and clinical realities (Singer et al., 2023).

Some leading promoters of the social model (e.g., Macdonald, 2010, 2019; Macdonald & Deacon, 2019; Riddick, 2001, 2010) have not been averse to the consideration of dyslexia as an impairment on the grounds that this may help struggling learners to obtain additional support to overcome disabling or discriminatory barriers. Macdonald and Deacon (2019), for example, advise that where schools dismiss a parental belief that their child may have dyslexia, assessment by an educational (school) psychologist can be obtained via a referral from their family doctor. The seeming contradiction here between theory and espoused practice likely reflects pragmatic recognition that, despite qualified support for the social model from some governmental agencies, disability legislation still largely adheres to the medical model (Bunbury, 2019; Cruz et al., 2023).

Collinson (2020) challenges normative assumptions about literacy that lead to "Othering" and discrimination. He rejects the use of the term dyslexia, together with synonyms such as specific learning disability, learning disability, or reading disability, on the grounds that these suggest that those who do not fit within expected norms have some form of disorder, deficit or impairment. In pointing to those who wish to retain the dyslexia label, he cites not only dyslexia charities who provide diagnoses, and the "dyslexia industry who claim the ability to cure or remediate dyslexia," but also dyslexics themselves who "… might self-oppress and cling to the concept of dyslexia long after any utility has faded" (2020: 1005). Collinson states that while he rejects the value of dyslexia as a concept, he is not rejecting the existence of dyslexic people; indeed, he considers himself to be dyslexic. However, his dyslexic identity arises from his self-perception as one who has been, "… Othered and discriminated against by normative literacy" (2020: 1005).

As this brief section illustrates, the dyslexic identity can be manifested in many different ways. The following fictional statements, designed to reflect participants' comments commonly found in the literature, are provided to illustrate views reflecting traditional biomedical, neurodiverse, and "strong" social model understandings:

- I thought I had a problem but was surprised to learn that I had dyslexia when this was eventually diagnosed by a specialist assessor.

- I always thought I was dyslexic but it was only when I was tested that this was confirmed.
- I am a neurodiverse learner and, rather than being a disabling condition, my dyslexia represents a difference that I celebrate.
- Although being diagnosed with dyslexia got me additional help, the real problem rests with the failure of the education system to provide greater support for people like me who have complex reading difficulties.
- Although being diagnosed with dyslexia got me additional help, the real problem rests with the failure of the education system to provide greater support for neurodiverse people like me who experience a wide range of cognitive strengths and challenges.
- Although being diagnosed with dyslexia got me additional help, the real problem rests with the failure of schools to teach reading effectively.
- Although being diagnosed with dyslexia got me additional help, the real problem rests with the failure of an educational system that, through a range of poor practices, unnecessarily causes students to experience difficulties with their learning.
- Normative views as to what is an appropriate level of literacy performance have created an "Other" group of less skilled readers (irrespective as to whether dyslexia or another synonymous term is employed) that is marginalized and discriminated against.

Social models of disability have helped to increase our understanding that wholly within-person accounts of learning difficulty are insufficient. The quality of the educational environment also needs close consideration in order to ensure that learning problems do not arise or are sustained unnecessarily. In applying this principle to the dyslexia debate, we would argue that the primary focus should be switched from the provision of help and support targeted upon the diagnosed few to the creation of teaching and learning environments designed to cater for the literacy needs of all students. This involves providing high-quality, evidence-based instruction to all children from an early age, and identifying, addressing, and monitoring individual needs as necessary. With such a system in place, a dyslexia diagnosis would no longer be a necessary means to access support. However, widespread acceptance of this position may be easier to achieve in principle than in practice. Rather paradoxically, those who espouse social models of disability may be no more inclined to dispense with their dyslexic identities, and the targeted support that follows the label, than those who, operating within a medical model, remain committed to dyslexia diagnoses based upon cognitive testing.

Other Arguments Offered for Retention of the Label

Following the publication of *The Dyslexia Debate,* a number of other arguments have been put forward to justify the retention of the label (Elliott, 2020).

Dyslexia as a Meaningful Construct Has Been Evidenced by Findings from Genetics and Neuroscience

In considering the validity of this argument, it is first necessary to ascertain whether or not dyslexia is being employed in this context as a synonym for reading disability, as is the case for most scientific studies (Lopes et al., 2020). If so, the argument that there appears to be a strong biological component holds true. Unfortunately, this understanding is often employed to justify the continuation of a clinical distinction between DSRs and NDSRs. Nicolson (2005), for example, misleadingly states that:

> The fact that 50 per cent of the variance in dyslexia is genetic means that dyslexia does have a clear and distinct basis. (Nicolson, 2005: 658)

As outlined in Chapter 3, there is little doubt that reading disability has a substantial heritable component, ranging from moderate to high (Fletcher et al., 2019; Paracchini, 2022). However, as is also discussed earlier, the complex relationship of biology and environment, considered in increasingly sophisticated multifactorial models, has shown that a binary distinction in which dyslexia is essentially "biological" and "garden-variety" poor reading is "environmental" is misleading.

Neuroscience has offered valuable insights into structural and functional differences in the brains of struggling and typical readers. However as is the case for studies in both genetics and cognitive science, participants in neuroscientific studies of dyslexia are typically selected on the basis of their low-scores on reading tests, not on the basis of criteria that could meaningfully differentiate them from other poor readers.

Understandings are rendered more complex by the complexities of neuroscience where dyslexia research is frequently characterized by "… distortions, simplifications and misrepresentations" (Worthy et al., 2019: 314). Beguiling references to brain scans (Weisberg, Taylor, & Hopkins, 2015) and the brightly colored pictures of brain activation can be highly persuasive and reduce critical faculties (Bowers, 2016a, 2016b; Howard-Jones,

2014; Satel & Lilienfeld, 2013). Indeed, the term "neuroseduction" has been coined to describe the ways by which such images can increase the likelihood that one will be persuaded by explanations or conclusions unjustified by the facts (Berent & Platt, 2021; Fernandez-Duque, 2017; Schwartz et al., 2016; Fernandez-Duque et al., 2015; Weisberg, Taylor, & Hopkins, 2015).

Notwithstanding the considerable methodological difficulties and complexities involved in neuroscience (Protopapas & Parrila, 2018; Ramus et al., 2018), misunderstandings also persist about its current clinical utility. Despite the caution expressed by leading neuroscientists that the employment of brain imaging for the purpose of differential assessment and individualized intervention is an aspiration for the future (Kearns et al., 2019; Norton, Beach & Gabrieli, 2015; Ozernov-Palchik & Gaab, 2016; Sand & Bolger, 2019) that may ultimately "… be proven to be unfeasible" (Ozernov-Palchik, Yul, et al., 2016: 52), some advocates remain ignorant of, or are unwilling to acknowledge, this crucial point. Such reticence is not helped by scholars who confidently provide misleading messages in education journals about current knowledge in neuroscience. Green (2022), for example, a university researcher who reports that she testified to the Montana state legislature in support of its Dyslexia Bill, incorrectly claims that "Contemporary studies have shown that there is a demonstrated difference between the brains of proficient readers, poor readers, and those with dyslexia" (Green, 2022: 76). Misleading claims such as this can be seized upon by practitioners to justify the continuation of a DSR/NSDR distinction.

It is salutary to note that, despite the sometimes overblown claims for the pedagogical contributions of neuroscience, the key approaches to instruction, as advocated by leading dyslexia advocacy groups, have changed little over the past century (Gabriel, 2020a).

Dyslexia's Conceptual Problems Are Not Unique and Will Ultimately Be Resolved

Some researchers acknowledge the conceptual and diagnostic weaknesses of the dyslexia construct but justify its usage on the grounds that such flaws are equally true for many other developmental and psychiatric disorders (e.g., Cutting, 2014; Snowling, 2015; Kirby & Snowling, 2022). However, the basis for a diagnosis of dyslexia is rather different to those for other clinical categories such as ADHD, obsessive compulsive disorder, or clinical depression. Despite heterogeneity within (Sonuga-Barke, 2016) and overlap between (Rutter & Pickles, 2016) diagnostic categories in psychiatry, and some subjectivity in their interpretation by clinicians (Regier et al., 2013), psychiatric manuals such as DSM-5 (APA, 2013) offer explicit criteria that guide diagnosis.

This is not the case for dyslexia – other than when the term is used as synonymous with reading disability (i.e., a Dyslexia 1 conception). There are no clear and consistent criteria that can consistently enable differentiation of DSRs from NDSRs. Dyslexia symptoms found in sometimes lengthy checklists are typically features of all poor readers and arbitrarily selecting a few items from such lists results in inconsistent usage and interpretation of the label. It was for these reasons (see Chapter 1) that the dyslexia term was initially dropped as a diagnostic term in initial drafts of DSM-5.

When pressed on the issue of absent or inappropriate diagnostic criteria, some have countered by arguing that the dyslexia construct differentiates accurate and fluent reading from reading comprehension. This point is, at best, an unintended distraction, and at worst, sophistry, as it sidesteps the fact that while reading comprehension is related to poor word recognition, it is not central to the dyslexia debate.

Another argument for the retention of the dyslexia label is that, despite its existing conceptual flaws, we should continue its use while working towards its improved definition and operationalization. Cutting (2014), for example, notes:

> Science needs to evolve so that we can make distinctions between various types of reading difficulties, and the dyslexia label, along with the broader reading disability term, pushes us to keep propelling science forward. (Cutting, 2014: 1252)

Ramus (2014) takes a similar stance arguing that the current "absence of evidence will not last forever" (2014: 374). Such a view of ongoing conceptual refinement and precision neatly reflects the scientific model. However, research scientists, many renowned as experts in the field of dyslexia, may be less cognizant of how this plays out in contemporary policy and practice and in public understanding. The literature has consistently shown that education professionals across the world are confused by the term's widely differing usage, believing that individuals with dyslexia require reading instruction that is different to that for NDSRs (Elbeheri & Siang, 2023; Mather, White, & Youman, 2020). Such uncertainty, sometimes exacerbated by the vaunted recondite expertise of dyslexia specialists, reduces the confidence and ability of teachers, psychologists, and other professionals to identify problems, advise, and intervene appropriately (Dymock

& Nicholson, 2022; White, Mather, & Kirkpatrick, 2020; Worthy et al., 2016; Worthy, Svrcek, et al., 2018).

The quest for increased scientific precision, while laudable, can become problematic when an ill-defined and variously understood construct crosses from the sphere of academic consideration to the domain of professional activity and is then used as the basis for real-life decisions about individuals, and for guiding educational and social policy. Unfortunately, when applied to practice, the caution, uncertainty and nuance that should accompany scholarly analysis can be replaced by unhelpful oversimplification, misrepresentation and the misplaced certainty of authoritative discourse.

Fallacies of Relevance

Arguments for maintaining dyslexia as a clinical term can have a spurious relevance to reasoned and logical debate. In this respect, Elliott (2020) describes various fallacies such as: straw man, *ad hominem, ad verecundiam, ad populum*, and arguments from ignorance (Sternberg, 2004).

i.   Straw Man and *ad hominem* Fallacies

A rhetorical device, known as a "straw man" argument, involves offering a misleading account of an adversary's argument or position and then critiquing its weaknesses. By covertly replacing an opponent's proposition by another it enables the illusion of having refuted it. In the process, the seeming proponent can be portrayed as foolish or mendacious. In responding to *The Dyslexia Debate*, some critics have claimed that the authors' premise was that dyslexia does not exist (Stein, 2023). Citing the very real problems of large numbers of children who struggle with reading, critics can then point out that this problem cannot all be the fault of poor teaching or a lack of motivation; thus, dyslexia surely exists. Underpinning this line of argument is the implicit suggestion that those who question the existence of the condition are inured to the significant challenges that confront struggling readers. This *reductio ad absurdum* reframing of our position lays the ground for its easy rebuttal.

Given the multiple understandings of what is meant by the term dyslexia, arguments about whether "it" exists are meaningless and largely serve as a distraction. This point has repeatedly been made clear in our writings:

> … the primary issue is not whether biologically based reading difficulties exist (the answer is an unequivocal "yes"), but rather how we should best

understand and address literacy problems across clinical, educational, occupational, and social policy contexts. Essentially, the dyslexia debate centers
upon the extent to which the dyslexia construct operates as a rigorous scientific construct that adds to our capacity to help those who struggle to learn
to read. (Elliott & Grigorenko, 2014: 4)

> … the key question is not whether dyslexia exists but whether the wide-
> spread use of the dyslexia label demonstrates scientific validity and practical
> utility … of course, complex reading difficulties, typically occurring along-
> side one or more of a wide range of comorbid difficulties, clearly do exist.
> (Gibbs & Elliott, 2020: 487)

Other criticisms have been made of our observation that those with
greater socioeconomic advantage are more likely to seek, and be able to
obtain, a dyslexia diagnosis. This claim is indisputable, representing a
phenomenon evident since Victorian times (Kirby, 2020a, 2020b; Kirby
& Snowling, 2022). Middle-class parents typically have access to specialized cultural capital and financial resources that provide them with greater
ability to act as advocates for their reading disabled children (Nevill,
Savage, & Forsey, 2023). Socially advantaged children with learning difficulties tend to gain greater access to specialist assessments and resources
than their similarly performing peers (Sternberg & Grigorenko, 1999),
particularly when the former attend schools in affluent neighborhoods
where educational standards are high and a reading difficulty is more
likely to appear exceptional (Odegard et al., 2020). The particular *ad
hominem* device employed in this case, known as "appeal to motive,"
addresses, not the accuracy of this statement but the motivations of the
proposer. Presenting different explanations of this socioeconomic phenomenon as all making the same point, results in the conflation of those
who seek to explain parental behavior in an uncritical light with others
who are more dismissive. Kirby (2020a) illustrates this point in the following extract:

> … dyslexia is an invention of, or at least especially favoured by, over-
> concerned parents. Thus for Elliott & Grigorenko (2014, p. 579): "Some
> parents believe that [by being labelled 'dyslexic'] their child will be treated
> more sympathetically by teachers, and expectations of their intellectual and
> academic potential will be higher". For Liddle (2014), less delicately: "dys-
> lexia has been the crutch upon which middle-class parents support them-
> selves when they discover that their children are actually dense … contrary
> to their expectations" (p. 21). (Kirby, 2020a: 480)

Again, conflating different arguments, Kirby states that while some parents seek the label for "self-interested" reasons, the "cynicism of such a

minority" (2020a: 483) should not lead to the rejection of dyslexia's scientific validity. He adds that the history of concerned parents should not be seen as "a sinister plot to acquire undeserved funding, but a necessary reaction to the absence of state support for reading difficulties" (2020a: 484).

Presenting parents who worry about their children's reading and who seek a dyslexia label as being "overconcerned" is unfair and unhelpful. Evidence demonstrating the widespread problems of instructional delivery to struggling readers has shown that their concerns are often justified (Odegard et al., 2021). In our opinion, the vast majority of parents who seek the diagnosis recognize that their children are genuinely struggling and are eager to find some way to remedy this. Reference to a "sinister plot" to obtain undeserved resources is little more than unhelpful rhetoric. Gibbs and Elliott (2020) state:

> A primary driver of the dyslexia diagnosis industry of assessment, diagnosis and dyslexia-special interventions stems from parental anxiety that their child's needs may be being overlooked and, as a result, they will not receive the specialist instruction needed. Where a child is deemed by education services not to require additional intervention, where reading instruction is not being successfully implemented, or where progress is not being made despite sound provision, concerned parents may, understandably, explore alternative routes to secure assistance. (Gibbs & Elliott, 2020: 495)

Our writings have repeatedly and explicitly stated that we do not suggest, or accept, the demonization of parents (middle-class or otherwise) who are trying to help their struggling children. Neither do we criticize those parents who believe that a dyslexia label may lead their struggling child to be perceived more positively by teachers and others. Unfortunately, and for various reasons, reports have sometimes offered a gross distortion of our argument that parents may be rightly fearful that their children's reading difficulties could result in the underestimation of their intellectual abilities.

A further *ad hominem* tactic has involved presenting us as academic researchers ignorant of, and indifferent to, the concerns of "the real world." In responding to the arguments raised in *The Dyslexia Debate*, Malchow (2014) highlighted what he contended are our (seemingly unrealistic) standards for a scientific definition, and cautioned that:

> … in their pursuit of a more perfect definition, Drs. Elliott and Grigorenko overlook real world consequences for people who actually live with the condition they would rename. … those who tamper with commonly understood language do so at their peril (n.p.). (Malchow, 2014: n.p.)

In drawing together several of the themes listed above, Malchow criticizes what he considers to be our search for a "more perfect" definition. In referencing "academic speculation," he implicitly suggests that a combination of scholarly pedantry and naivety, on our part, has led to claims by others that are based upon misunderstandings of our core arguments, with potentially negative consequences for struggling readers and their families. To argue, however, that dyslexia (or any such constructs) should not be forensically examined and debated because of the risk that one's arguments and conclusions may be misrepresented or misunderstood is redolent of a cancel culture and wholly unacceptable.

The imperative to challenge *ad hominem* attacks of this kind should not stem from any requirement to protect the personal sensitivities of academics but, rather, to ensure that rational and relevant debate is encouraged rather than stymied. While the criticisms noted above fail to hold up to scrutiny, they can still be highly influential. For often desperate parents, seeking ways to help their struggling children, the seeming dismissal of the core reading problem as non-existent, alongside reported criticisms that they are overconcerned, cynical, selfish, or in denial about their children's true abilities, will surely fuel anger and antipathy and lead to outright dismissal of other more complex and nuanced critiques. Professionals in schools and clinics will similarly be alienated by seeming disregard for the concerns of those with whom they work on a daily basis. Portraying us as arrogant and lofty academics, detached from everyday life, and insensitive to the concerns of children and their families, is a tactically shrewd yet dubious strategy. It serves to disparage and dismiss those who challenge dyslexia orthodoxies, and distracts scientific and public debate away from the core issues. As a rhetorical device, *ad hominem* challenge can prove persuasive, yet it represents a fallacious approach to debate that undermines scientific progress and hinders the development of positive practice.

ii. *ad verecundiam* Arguments

These typically involve deference to higher authorities that lead us to accept (or reject) assertions because they are associated with individuals who have achieved high status, prestige, or respect. They are regularly employed by advocacy groups who reference the biographies of historical figures and personal testimonies of well-known celebrities who, it is contended, have struggled with dyslexia. Accounts of their exceptional achievements serve as means to raise awareness of the condition and suggest that success can be achieved, in part, because of compensatory gifts. Such accounts implicitly offer a version of dyslexia that can be of benefit to society as a whole

(Gabriel, 2020a). As illustrated in the case of William, above, the experiences of dyslexic high-achievers (Gerber & Raskind, 2013), often diagnosed later in their lives having seemingly not had their difficulties recognized at school, are used to legitimate, sustain, and promote the notion that this "hidden" condition may not be spotted unless expert testing is undertaken.

Although this approach can act as a powerful means of influencing public perception, the problem with *ad verecundiam* arguments is that the appeal is to an authority that typically lacks scientific expertise or credibility (Sternberg, 2004).

iii.   *ad populum* Arguments

These take the form that if "everyone" thinks something is correct, then it must surely be so. In relation to dyslexia, public understandings have resulted in an ever-expanding construct that, somewhat paradoxically, manages to incorporate widely divergent, and potentially dissonant, perspectives. With so much information widely available on the internet, and so many proclaimed experts, it seems that "everyone knows" what dyslexia is, with formal diagnoses usually accepted uncritically. Unfortunately, public conversations about dyslexia policy and practice are often dominated by those with limited expertise or experience in the field of literacy, and authoritative statements about what has been proven to work are often "disingenuous and inaccurate" (Worthy et al., 2021: 20). Rarely referencing sociopolitical considerations, popular conceptions of dyslexia on the internet appear to largely exclude those outside of dominant, privileged groups (Annamma, Connor, & Ferri, 2013; Worthy et al., 2021). In the case of dyslexia policy and practice, it appears that *ad populum* arguments largely involve the opinions of only one sector of society.

iv.   Arguments from Ignorance

These suggest that a phenomenon should be considered to be true because it has not been shown to be false. While accepting our argument that research has yet to identify forms of intervention that differ meaningfully for DSRs and NDSRs, Ramus (2014) contends that the field should continue to differentiate between these categories because such a distinction may be helpful in the future. Citing visual and visual-attentional deficits that have been found to be more common in poor readers, Ramus argues that research may one day identify approaches for such groupings that are more helpful than standard reading interventions.

Seeking to identify potential aptitude × treatment interactions that can guide alternative forms of intervention for different kinds of learners is a worthy aim of scientific research, and Ramus's call for further work to this end is justified. However, there is a difference between developing multi-factorial models that may one day inform differential forms of intervention and the use of these (or, indeed, unitary models) to arrive at a DSR/NDSR binary. A further complication is that, because of the methodological complexities involved, studies applying prospective multifactorial models to educational settings have tended to focus upon cognitive processes and have found it difficult to include other component factors such as genetic risk and environmental influence (Middleton et al., 2022; Odegard, Farris, & Washington, 2022). In order to move beyond over-simplistic "core deficit thinking" we shall require substantial change in the way that we design and analyse our research studies (Astle & Fletcher-Watson, 2020; Wagner et al., 2023).

It may one day be possible to identify a more precise and educationally meaningful binary DSR/NDSR distinction. However, as we develop increasingly sophisticated methods of data analysis, with all the future promise of developments in Artificial Intelligence, it seems more likely that we may one day be capable of identifying a variety of complex subtypes of reading disability that demonstrably benefit from different types of reading intervention. Using sub-groupings of this kind may prove to be a workable means of dealing with the practical and methodological challenges of providing fully personalized approaches (Lorusso & Toraldo, 2023). Given a scenario in which there are several clusters of poor readers, each requiring a different form of intervention, a simple binary conception of the dyslexic/non-dyslexic poor reader would not be sufficient or relevant.

While we can speculate on a potentially exciting future for the reduction of reading disability, we should not lose sight of the imperative that ongoing clinical and educational practice should operate on the basis of current evidence.

The Realities of the Dyslexia Debate: Meeting the Needs of All Struggling Readers

Given the continuing absence of clear criteria, the reality that a dyslexia diagnosis cannot meaningfully differentiate DSRs from NDSRs, the lack of any relationship between such a distinction and effective forms of intervention, and the lack of equity in resourcing that so often results, it is hardly surprising that in *The Dyslexia Debate* we called for discontinuation of the label. In its place, it was recommended that the term "reading disability" (based upon normative performance on appropriate reading tests) should be used to describe the central problem of all who struggle to decode text. Although the term "disability" can sometimes be unattractive to educationalists (e.g., Serry & Hammond, 2015) this enables the establishment of a contrast with "reading difficulty," a superordinate construct that includes problems both of word recognition and reading comprehension.

Many arguments have been put forward to justify the continued use of the dyslexia label, some of which can be persuasive. It has been claimed that without this the desire for a term that can help the person understand their problem will not be easily met; they will doubt themselves, and fail to recognize their strengths and their potential; they will no longer be empowered by the notion that it is not their fault that reading is so difficult; children will be written off by their teachers as stupid or lazy; they will experience greater shame and guilt; they will continue to struggle silently in classrooms with teachers ill-equipped to identify or intervene; teacher education will continue to fail to deliver appropriate training on the teaching of reading; the design and establishment of specialist interventions for those with dyslexia will be hindered; the public's (and therefore, policymakers') interest in tackling reading difficulties will be reduced; legislation to protect dyslexic children will be undone; additional resources from government, district and local education administrations will be harder to secure; parents will have reduced opportunity to press the school for the recognition and support required by their child; support for those who experience a range of learning difficulties in adult education will be reduced; growing recognition of neurodiversity, where difference rather than deficit is emphasized, will be reversed; positive compensations, including the sense and camaraderie of a shared condition, that result from one's embrace of a dyslexic identity will be lost; professional status resulting from possession of a dyslexia specialism will be diminished, research grants and other significant funding to study dyslexia from the perspective of a wide range of academic disciplines will largely disappear; the prominence of dyslexia scholars, dyslexia assessors, dyslexia institutes and other research centers, specialist dyslexia journals and publications, dyslexia advocacy groups, special schools for those with dyslexia, dyslexia training centers and licensed programs, dyslexia aids and other educational materials, and dyslexia merchandise, will decline.

There can be no doubt that such concerns offer a powerful testament to the excellent and inspirational work that has proven valuable for many people. However, in our opinion, contemporary understandings of dyslexia and its treatment need to change. Psychological and educational science, supported by work in genetics and neuroscience, has guided our current understanding of reading disability as the product of multiple, heterogeneous risk and resilience factors. Research has shown that simplistic biological/environmental binary explanations are no longer tenable, yet this knowledge has yet to filter through to mass practitioner and lay understandings. Sociological and socio-constructionist perspectives have challenged the traditional medical model and helped us to become more cognizant of issues of equity, equality, and identity. They have shown how many struggling readers are excluded from a dyslexia diagnosis, not only because they lack the means to gain access to formal assessment, but also because the diagnostic criteria employed often operate to their disfavor.

In our final chapter, we will present conclusions based upon our review of the literature and offer a series of recommendations.

CHAPTER 6

Conclusions and Recommendations

In reflecting upon developments in the literature since the publication of *The Dyslexia Debate* in 2014, we have been struck by the observation that, despite the production of a vast body of new research across a wealth of disciplines, the fundamental issues remain essentially unchanged. Perhaps this should not have been too surprising as many of the criticisms listed in the present text have been voiced since the late nineteenth century. However, concern about how these issues relate to social and educational inequity is a relatively modern phenomenon.

It has been argued that criticism of the term's continuing ambiguity, "… overlooks the greater specificity that has been brought to the term since the Victorian era" (Kirby & Snowling, 2022: 173). However, despite a huge volume of work, it continues to be impossible to identify a dyslexic subgroup of poor readers or, alternatively, a much broader group of struggling dyslexic learners, in a consistent, coherent, and meaningful fashion that is acceptable to the broad scientific and professional community.

A key area of development during the past decade has been a steadily growing awareness of the multifactorial, heterogeneous nature of reading disability. Researchers and practitioners are now more cognizant that risk factors are probabilistic rather than deterministic, and that biological and environmental risk and resilience factors operate in conjunction, often reciprocally (Cheesman et al., 2020; Plomin et al., 2013), to increase or decrease the likelihood that an individual will encounter reading problems.

Although traditional ways of diagnosing dyslexia as a condition distinct from garden-variety poor reading cannot be justified, the search for specific causal factors that can supposedly reveal the presence of an underlying dyslexic condition persists in some quarters. The list of possible candidates has changed over time and includes: visual processing deficits, IQ-reading discrepancy, patterns of cognitive strengths and weaknesses, and problems relating to executive functioning, working memory, rapid naming, and phonological awareness. For many practitioners, evidence of phonological problems is still considered to be a necessary criterion for a dyslexia diagnosis. In Denmark, for example, dyslexia diagnosis is based solely upon phonological coding performance (Ottosen et al., 2022). However, as discussed in Chapter 2, this is highly questionable. Indeed, while evidence indicates that the origin of reading difficulties is primarily linguistic, there are increasingly strong arguments for a visual attention component for some individuals.

Family history and specific environmental context may offer helpful insights into an individual's personal circumstances (although, for opposing views on the diagnostic value of family history, see Pennington, McGrath, & Peterson, 2019; Ferrer et al., 2022). Greater understanding of the contributory role of environmental factors to reading disability should assist in maximizing the effectiveness of early screening and also encourage additional community-based approaches to intervention that are not bounded by school-based instruction.

It has been suggested that a formal diagnosis of dyslexia should be based upon the individual's resistance to high-quality educational intervention (Dyslexia 3). Miciak and Fletcher's (2020) hybrid model contains three components: low achievement in accurate and fluent reading and spelling, poor response to generally effective instruction, and consideration of other factors such as sensory impairment or ADHD, that might necessitate other forms of specialized intervention. This framework appears to be consonant with the views of other leading researchers who have emphasized dyslexia's early onset, persistence, and the importance of identifying and addressing co-occurring difficulties independently of its diagnosis (Snowling, Hulme, & Nation, 2020).

Miciak and Fletcher's approach is unlikely to prove universally popular with diagnosticians, parents, or adult clients. Firstly, their focus upon low achievement in specific areas of reading and spelling is likely to be unacceptable to those who consider the nature and scope of the dyslexic condition to be narrower (Dyslexia 2) or broader (Dyslexia 4). Secondly, it runs counter to the desire of many parents and teachers for the early application of this diagnostic label. Thirdly, there continue to be difficulties in identifying appropriate measures of adequate versus inadequate response (Hendricks & Fuchs, 2020). Finally, it largely dispenses with an assessment approach that currently maintains a substantial dyslexia industry.

Achieving the effective deployment of Miciak and Fletcher's model in educational systems will be difficult as, to operate most appropriately, a sound RTI and MTSS system (or an equivalent) needs to be in place. Notwithstanding the challenge of the measurement complications that abound, the greatest difficulty here is establishing effective instructional and monitoring systems that can operate successfully at scale (see Allington, 2019). Despite the scientific merit of Miciak and Fletcher's model, and the promise of RTI/MTSS, there are likely to be too many competing personal and professional perspectives, interests, and agendas for their conception of dyslexia to gain and retain widespread purchase.

> … no matter how noble the intention, these labels do not stand still. They are pushed into a world of competing discursive constructions and ideological common sense which fragment and hijack intended meanings. (Cameron & Billington, 2017: 1369)

From a medical model perspective, a key purpose of diagnosis is that it should help to determine the nature of appropriate treatment. Although it has been repeatedly shown that no particular reading intervention is more appropriate for a DSR than for a NDSR (reading at the same level), practitioner recognition, and full acceptance of the practical implications that result from this, have been slow.

The "science of reading" movement has reassured reading disability specialists, many teachers, and the wider public, of the value of structured approaches and the important role of phonics, for all developing readers. Others have argued that "balance" has been lost and, while a persuasive case for phonics has been made, this approach should not dominate and children should still be taught to draw upon contextual information in the text when confronted by an unknown word. Thus, while seemingly more nuanced, the reading wars (and associated disputes about what should be considered as scientific evidence) have continued.

We maintain that our conclusion in *The Dyslexia Debate* in 2014 – that the dyslexia construct is unhelpful and should be discontinued – would appear to be still valid because:

i. reading disability and dyslexia are generally treated as a synonymous condition by most scientific researchers;
ii. this problem is a consequence of multiple genetic and environmental factors that, in combination, impact the individual in many different ways;
iii. there appear to be no clear criteria to differentiate DSRs from NDSRs reading at similar levels;
iv. there is no intervention that is more or less appropriate for DSRs than for NDSRs reading at similar levels;
v. there is no educational, ethical, or moral basis for providing additional resources to those diagnosed with dyslexia while witholding these from other poor readers reading at similar levels.

As we noted at the time, our perspective was one that had been voiced many times before. Indeed, half a century ago, a UK Government Committee Report on the teaching of reading in schools (Department of Education & Science, 1975) had offered very similar criticisms. The Committee commented upon a:

> ... group of children who experience a difficulty in learning to read that cannot be accounted for by limited ability or by emotional or extraneous factors. The term dyslexic is commonly applied to these children. We believe that this term serves little useful purpose other than to draw attention to the fact that the problem of these children can be chronic and severe. *It is not susceptible to precise operational definition; nor does it indicate any clearly defined course of treatment.* (Department of Education & Science, 1975: 268, emphasis added)

The Committee's views had been heavily influenced by findings from a large-scale epidemiological study on the Isle of Wight, England. Reflecting upon this work, one of the study's lead researchers (Yule, 1976) commented:

> The era of applying the label dyslexic is rapidly drawing to a close. The label has served its function in drawing attention to children who have great difficulty in mastering the arts of reading, writing, and spelling but its continued use invokes emotions which often prevent rational discussion and scientific investigation. (Yule, 1976: 166)

Despite the perspicacity of his analysis, Yule's prediction failed, most likely because the label met the psychological, social, political, and emotional needs and desires of so many stakeholders. However, we hoped that the extensive review in *The Dyslexia Debate*, operating across genetics, neuroscience, psychology, and education literatures, would prompt the field to consider the issue from a detached, disinterested, scientific perspective. We argued that the promotion of dyslexia diagnosis as a means to meet individual needs had produced unanticipated iatrogenic effects that undermined equitable and effective educational practice. In our opinion, these were so problematic and irredeemable the label should be discontinued and replaced by the term *reading disability*, operationalized by performance on relatively straightforward reading measures. This more neutral term, we contended, would increase the likelihood that all struggling readers would be identified and helped at an early age.

However, we were not blind to the power of this label, one so rooted in everyday discourse that any articulation of theoretical and ethical concerns about its use might still be insufficient to reduce its hold (Reason & Stothard, 2013). We noted Kamhi's (2004), description of dyslexia as a classic example of a *meme,* a unit of cultural transmission, complementary to genetic transmission, whereby ideas and behaviors are passed on from one person to another (Blackmore, 1999; Dawkins, 1976). The meme's ability to survive by means of replication does not depend upon whether it is true, useful, or even potentially harmful. What is crucial is that it is "… easy to understand, remember, and communicate to others" (Kamhi, 2004: 106), characteristics that apply readily to everyday conceptions of dyslexia. The fact that such understandings are often impoverished, misleading, or incorrect has little bearing upon the dyslexia meme's capacity for survival as:

> … an unfortunate consequence of … selection forces is that successful memes typically provide superficially plausible answers for complex questions. (Kamhi, 2004: 105)

We argued that researchers, educationalists, and clinicians should not abdicate their responsibility to challenge the application of constructs lacking in scientific precision and rigor to professional and practitioner contexts. We accurately predicted that some proponents might respond by arguing that the adoption of a truly scientific approach should involve further examination and analysis that might ultimately result in the establishment of a more rigorous understanding and deployment of the construct. However, we countered this by cautioning that the power of the dyslexia meme might prove too powerful for scientific refinement of this kind.

Although the conceptual and operational difficulties raised in *The Dyslexia Debate* are fundamentally unchanged, merely repeating our former recommendations is unlikely to prove productive in the evolution of policy or practice. Belief perseverance often occurs even when individuals are provided with new information that disaffirms or contradicts strongly held beliefs (Anderson, 2007). This explains why evidence-based arguments can have limited impact upon policy and practice, and public understanding and trust. Content on the internet, and communications via social media, have transformed notions of expertise and evidence. For example, the advocacy group *Made by Dyslexia* (see Chapter 1) has proudly announced on its website[34] that as a result of its campaign, "Dyslexic Thinking" can now by listed as a "vital skill" on the profiles of LinkedIn's 810+ million members.

Seemingly authoritative pronouncements are often targeted at, or sought by, partisan consumers who, displaying confirmation bias (Nickerson,

---

[34] www.madebydyslexia.org; accessed May 30, 2023.

1998), and a desire to avoid high levels of complexity (Gorman & Gorman, 2021), are eager to have their existing views confirmed. Highly questionable assertions, fallacies of relevance, even "fake news," may be readily accepted if this material accords with the needs and desires of recipients. Growing freedoms for individuals to self-identify their own personal characteristics (e.g., gender and ethnicity) have been paralleled by a belief in some quarters that those who wish to identify as dyslexic should have the right to do so. How such a stance can be reconciled with decision-making about supportive educational resource allocation is unclear (Kirby & Snowling, 2022).

In offering revised recommendations, we seek to establish some common ground with those who have expressed alternative views – an important first step in reconciling opposing positions. We recognize the meaningfulness of some of the arguments that have been put forward for retaining the use of the construct and have sought to accommodate these in our proposal.

The Way Forward?

We recommend that:

   i.   Dyslexia should be used solely to reference a severe and persistent difficulty in accurate and fluent word reading in the individual's first language.
   ii. The use of dyslexia as a term synonymous with a medical diagnosis, with symptoms and an underlying cause, should be discontinued.
   iii. It should no longer be considered appropriate to divide struggling readers into diagnosable dyslexic and non-dyslexic categories.
   iv. It should be recognized that some reading difficulties are primarily a consequence of intellectual disability and severe sensory impairment (i.e., hearing or vision). Such difficulties are likely to require modified approaches to the teaching of reading.
   v.   The assessment of reading difficulties should focus primarily upon relevant literacy skills and how these can best be enhanced.
   vi. Given the probabilistic, multifactorial nature of reading difficulty, the use of the term dyslexia should carry no assumptions as to etiology in respect of any individual reader.
   vii. Co-occurring comorbidities should be acknowledged, where appropriate, but these should not be seen to be indicative of an underlying dyslexic condition.

   viii. The expanded understanding of the dyslexia construct, spreading far beyond reading disability, should be discontinued.

    ix. Where required by national or regional education systems, formal labeling of difficulty in academic areas should employ broad classificatory terms such as learning disability or specific learning disability. This should specify the particular areas of difficulty encountered by the individual (accurate and fluent word reading, reading comprehension, spelling, math etc.).

     x. Professional training of educators should focus upon the prevention of, recognition of, and intervention for, literacy difficulties (including problems of word recognition/decoding).

    xi. The notion that those hitherto diagnosed as dyslexic require a different instructional approach to that appropriate for other struggling readers should be actively dispelled.

As indicated in the points listed above, we recommend that the term dyslexia be used to describe a severe and persistent difficulty with accurate and fluent reading but, crucially, this should no longer take the form of a diagnosed, categorical label. Instead, "dyslexia" would return to its Greek etymological roots as a descriptor of poor word recognition/decoding. This view involves an evolutionary transition from its former use as, "… some entity that *causes* poor reading to a simple" "… *name* for poor reading" (Protopapas, 2019: 8). Requiring no specific causal explanation, this usage sits easily within current multifactorial understandings. There would be no need for any diagnostic cut-off point, although, as noted below, formal education systems might still need to base resourcing decisions on the severity and persistence of the individual's reading difficulty.

The notion that highly skilled diagnosticians are well placed to determine which struggling readers have a neurodevelopmental disorder and which others do not (Lachmann et al., 2022) is superficially attractive. However, even if this assertion were valid, which we doubt for the majority of cases, the practicalities involved would be daunting. Given that as many as one in five children are considered to have reading difficulties, the costs of undertaking such assessments would be overwhelming and only a very small proportion of such children could ever be included. Even at the level of current practice, diagnostic procedures are resource heavy and would often be better employed for the assessment of language and literacy skills that can inform targeted intervention (Vellutino et al., 2004). As noted by Snowling, Hulme, and Nation (2020) "… elaborate comprehensive assessments are not required to identify a child as in need of reading intervention" (p. 508). Assessment of underlying cognitive processes such as phonological awareness, RAN, processing speed, working memory and language skills may offer some additional insights in respect of a particular struggling reader (Mather & Schneider, 2023), but such information cannot and should not be used to diagnose, categorize or label an individual's particular learning disability (Peterson et al., 2018).

Reframing dyslexia, as is suggested, would significantly increase the number of struggling readers understood to have a severe problem that requires systematic intervention. Obviating the need for a formal diagnosis it would meet the widely held desire for a descriptive term for children's reading difficulties (Snowling, 2015). As long as classroom professionals are adequately trained, and appropriately supported by specialists, (a clear imperative in any educational system) children struggling with dyslexia, as well as those experiencing other, closely related, literacy difficulties (e.g., spelling, reading comprehension, and expressive writing), should be easily identified for the purposes of monitoring and intervention. Given sufficient levels of resourcing, appropriate intervention could be immediately provided without any need to wait for a label. Inappropriate and unhelpful notions that compound and fuel inequity, such as dyslexia being a hidden or unexpected condition that needs to be diagnosed by an expert assessor, would no longer have purchase or credibility. The literacy needs of those with severe sensory or intellectual difficulties, and second language learners with weak proficiency in the language concerned, would be identified and addressed as appropriate. The expansion of the dyslexia construct to its use as an umbrella term reaching far beyond the realm of literacy would be halted.

We are optimistic that our proposal could build upon, rather than diminish, the positive progress that has been made following intensive reading-related lobbying. For example, preventive approaches to dyslexia in the early years, featuring widely in recent state legislation in the USA, and increasingly in other countries, are generally concerned to address the needs of any child struggling with reading and reading related skills. Rather than attempting a form of DSR/NDSR differentiation, these initiatives appear to operate largely from a Dyslexia 1 understanding that would in no way be undermined by our proposal (see also Catts & Petscher, 2022, for a broadly similar conclusion).

As noted in the preceding chapter, a common argument for the maintenance of a dyslexia diagnosis is that this can help the child dispel inappropriate attributions that they are stupid or lazy, that they are somehow culpable for their difficulty. While this message can indeed be helpful for the individual concerned, it also reinforces potentially negative messages about those children deemed to be NDSRs. What is required is a widening of this more benign understanding. Thus, professional training and public communications should clearly, forcefully, and repeatedly emphasize that there is no relationship between intelligence and difficulty with accurate or fluent reading (dyslexia) and no assumptions should be made about an individual's intellectual or creative abilities or potential on the basis of their word reading skills. While emphasizing that literacy difficulties should never be considered to be the child's fault, it should be noted that struggling readers can become reluctant to apply themselves when provided with reading support activities. However, it should be explained and understood that problems of motivation and engagement are typically a consequence, rather than a cause, of a significant reading difficulty that, to the individual concerned, may seem impossible to overcome and a source of public embarrassment. Mechanisms of self-worth protection such as withdrawal, avoidance, disengagement, and disparagement of reading are understandable reactions given the shame and frustration that can be experienced (Covington, 1992).

Our proposal should present few conceptual challenges to reading researchers as the majority already operate from the understanding that dyslexia and reading disability are synonymous concepts (Lopes et al., 2020). Indeed, wider consensus about the term, and its successful decoupling from diagnostic labeling, may offer reassurance to researchers that their work will not be misrepresented or misunderstood. The ongoing search for effective interventions for struggling readers would continue unhindered. Indeed, dispensing with the DSR/NDSR binary and recognizing the heterogeneity of factors underpinning poor reading should help in the search for powerful aptitude treatment interactions that can inform more bespoke forms of intervention.

In Chapter 5 we noted the power of the dyslexia term with legislators and policymakers. Largely resulting from effective lobbying by advocacy groups, there has been legislative transformation in the USA, alongside significant policy developments in many other countries (Elbeheri & Siang, 2023). Acceptance of our recommendations would reduce the existing highly problematic variability in the definition and use of "dyslexia" in legislation (Chapman & Tunmer, 2019a; Gearin et al., 2022). It would also highlight the size and scale of the problem of literacy underachievement and, most likely add to, rather than reduce, political pressure to act. Here, the significant skill, drive and influence of dyslexia lobby groups could be utilized to promote the development and maintenance of effective evidence-based, system-wide interventions.

In many countries, formal labels are required prerequisites for special education and funding. Where this is the case, we believe it preferable to employ a generic label such as learning disability or specific learning disability or learning disorder, terms which can then be supplemented by reference to specific areas of difficulty, for example, word recognition, reading comprehension, expressive writing, spelling or math. DSM-5 (APA, 2013) has a broadly similar taxonomic approach but the late addition of dyslexia as a "signifier," following fierce advocacy, muddied the waters in unhelpful ways. Difficult resourcing decisions, which are likely to vary from one educational system to another, would be best made on the basis of the severity of the specific problem and its persistence following intervention (Catts & Petscher, 2022; Dombrowski, Kamphaus, & Reynolds, 2004).

As noted earlier, a common argument for maintaining dyslexia diagnoses is that these are a requirement of the "system": without the label, additional help for poor readers cannot always be accessed. Both this original problem and the espoused response are unsatisfactory. Researchers and professionals should be calling upon policymakers and legislators to amend laws and practices in the light of emerging scientific understanding. Where this is unforthcoming, it is their responsibility to offer constructive challenge, rather than passive accommodation, to existing procedures.

Our recommendation for a reformulation of the use of the dyslexia construct should not present a professional threat to the majority of those involved in clinical work. We believe that detailed clinical assessment can still have a valuable role (Protopapas, 2019) but the primary focus of such work should be assessment for intervention rather than assessment for diagnosis. An assessment of a child with a history of reading difficulty would no longer seek to ascertain whether he or she should be diagnosed as dyslexic. Instead, the principal aim would be to identify the best ways to effect academic progress in the light of the child's unique circumstances. In addition to a detailed assessment of core and underpinning language and literacy skills (Tunmer & Hoover, 2019), examination might also include other cognitive, affective, and conative processes (with basic checks of hearing and vision having already been undertaken). Until research can offer new insights, cognitive assessment should not be concerned with identifying process deficits to be remediated in order to improve reading. Rather, its primary purpose should be to provide a picture of functioning geared to help teachers (and parents) offer individualized instruction and appropriate levels of support and challenge.

Although an assessment of intellectual functioning is largely irrelevant in determining the nature or content of specialist word reading instruction, it can occasionally help ensure appropriate challenge in relation to decisions about broader curricular material and related tasks (Elliott & Resing, 2015). Severe literacy difficulties, and their long-term effects on personal motivation and agency, can sometimes mask a student's intellectual abilities and lead to low teacher expectations and insufficient challenge across school subjects. Two children with very similar reading difficulties, and requiring similar forms of reading instruction, may differ greatly in the nature of instruction they should receive in math, science, the humanities, and the arts. Some may experience little difficulty in grasping and tackling complex ideas and problems. Here teachers need to provide challenging learning activities that, as far as possible, are unconstrained by the child's literacy difficulties. Others may struggle to understand even basic academic content. These children are more likely to profit from tasks that employ a less complex, step by step sequential structure, and require higher levels of teacher direction, scaffolding, and support.

Identification of a working memory difficulty might result in advice to teachers that they should avoid the use of lengthy or complex oral instructions and restrict the cognitive load of classroom tasks provided to the child (Gathercole & Alloway, 2008). In the case of significant attentional problems, the student might need to be seated in a classroom location where distractions are minimized, or provided with a structured behavioral system that provides consistent reminders about the need to complete particular tasks (Willcutt & Petrill, 2023). Findings from examination of the child's self-concept, self-efficacy beliefs, and self-worth protective strategies may inform recommendations geared to increase motivation and engagement. Such a focus may help address the long-term challenges of reading disability to emotional wellbeing, educational, and vocational success, and a prosperous adult life (Maughan, Rutter, & Yule, 2020; McLaughlin, Speirs, & Shenassa, 2014).

The vast majority of struggling readers are unlikely to gain access to detailed educational or clinical assessments of this kind. Given the valuable information and insights that can result, some of which are noted in the preceding paragraphs, this is an unfortunate reality. However, as the dyslexia/non-dyslexia binary disappears, and the focus of professional assessment becomes increasingly geared to advising on intervention, it is to be hoped that greater teacher expertise, derived in partnership with reading specialists, will be readily applied to other poor readers with similar profiles and needs (Kulesz et al., 2023).

Our proposals should help to reduce the uncertainties and discomfort about dyslexia that have been widely reported by teachers, teacher trainers, school psychologists, and other professionals. It should dispel "some of the mystery" surrounding dyslexia (Catts & Petscher, 2022: 172) and remove the concomitant distractions of determining which poor readers are dyslexic, whether such students require a different kind of intervention to other poor readers, and what its nature should be. Professional training for educators would highlight the multifactorial nature of reading problems and emphasize the current limitation of etiological considerations for guiding educational practice. The primary focus of training would be upon heightening teacher skills in identifying and catering for all struggling readers from an early age, in the process reducing any likelihood that children's SES and ethnicity will blind schools to need (Fish, 2022b).

As diagnostic hurdles are removed, the troubling sense of social injustice and inequity that can cause some education professionals to appear dismissive when the possibility of dyslexia is raised by parents should fade. Rather than rejecting a parental suggestion of this kind, it will be possible to accept the term as a description of a significant difficulty with reading. Similarly, with increased professional understanding, skill, confidence, and sense of purpose it is to be hoped that the disregard sometimes expressed towards those working in public schools (Gabriel, 2020a) will decline to be replaced by increased levels of mutual respect, trust, and partnership.

The withdrawal of dyslexia as a diagnosed label would help to resolve some of the problems that have been raised by those who advocate socio-constructionist and neurodiverse perspectives (Fletcher-Watson, 2022). It should appeal to those who eschew the medical model of disability and help to maintain a particular focus on the quality of the educational environment (Cruz et al., 2023). It would be consistent with critiques of approaches that yield discrete categorical diagnoses (Astle et al., 2022) and be consonant with emerging data-driven transdiagnostic approaches to the identification of neurodevelopmental difficulties that are now beginning to be introduced to clinical settings (Boulton et al., 2021; Finlay-Jones et al., 2019).

Within adult education settings, a variety of conceptual and practical problems resulting from the expansion of the construct's purview need to be urgently addressed. While not opposed to the provision of learning support to students who experience various cognitive difficulties, we believe that such decisions should be decoupled from considerations of accommodation and support for reading disability. The return of dyslexia to its original conceptualization may be the first step in unravelling the minefield that has resulted from the incorporation of a multitude of cognitive, affective, and conative elements into dyslexia disability frameworks. Ensuring that dyslexia is no longer employed as an umbrella label may also have the helpful effect of encouraging universities to replace systems of individual support, dependent upon the recommendations of assessor gatekeepers, with more widely accessible open-access support, training, and workshops, and, in appropriate cases, individual assessment and mentoring (Kelly & Erwin, 2022).

While we believe that our proposal addresses most of the arguments for dyslexia summarized at the end of the previous chapter, we recognize that it will nevertheless prove contentious. Although dyslexia lobbyists have called for more extensive dyslexia assessment, the broadening of the term to encompass the difficulties of a much larger group of struggling readers may be perceived as potentially weakening current levels of political and social influence. Despite the personal, social, and economic benefits that would accrue from successfully tackling reading disability (Moll, Georgii, Tunder, & Schulte-Körne, 2022) legislators and policymakers may blanche at the resource implications involved. Clinicians whose expertise resides in the use of psychometric testing may be discomfited by a change of emphasis, one recommended in a seminal paper by Vellutino et al. (2004), in which the primary purpose of assessment is to inform and advise upon the operation of tailored reading instruction. Specialist dyslexia teachers and assessors, whose sense of professional pride and status is often closely associated with the term, may view the proposal as blurring their knowledge and expertise with that of other practitioners. Those adult learners who hold to a Dyslexia 4 conceptualization, may object to the return of the term dyslexia to its etymological origins and the discontinuation of its use as a formal diagnosis. Those for whom a conferred dyslexic identity, operationalized by reference to a wide range of strengths and weaknesses, adds to their sense of well-being may also remain unpersuaded.

Current usage of the term dyslexia meets a variety of personal needs and it is likely that many will wish to maintain the status quo. As a former President of the International Dyslexia Association stated in response to the publication of *The Dyslexia Debate*:

> We believe that "dyslexia" is a beautiful word. True, it describes a category of learning disorders. But it also describes a community, a body of knowledge, a category of law, a more positive sense of self, and a belief about the progress we can achieve together. (Malchow, 2014)

Our revised position reflects a decade of reflection on multiple positions voiced in the dyslexia debate. While in no doubt that scientific developments since this time have reinforced and strengthened our earlier position, we recognize that a fragmented field continues to be weakened, somewhat paradoxically, by both misplaced certainty and large-scale uncertainty. Social, political, and technological changes resulting in the explosive power of social media, issues of personal identity, the growth in the use of accommodations for disabled students, increasing commercial interest in special education, a reduction in the esteem in which scientific research is held, and constraints placed upon education budgets, have all rendered it more difficult to achieve consensus. New forms of influence, persuasion, and political power are exercised by well-organized, highly net-worked, peer-driven groups channeled and influenced by "stewards" and "super-participants" (Timms & Heimans, 2018). Computer algorithms direct information, views, and arguments to like-minded others, creating "echo chambers" in which only one side is legitimized, or even voiced (Shafik, 2017). The views of "people like me" can engender greater weight and trust than those with many years of professional or academic experi-ence. Through their use of formal channels of communication, recondite language, and professional distance, experts in the sciences and the social sciences have not always helped the public to navigate, differentiate, or impartially weigh up the merits of the mass of information that is now so readily accessible.

We seek to offer a simple and practical solution to a longstanding prob-lem that we hope will be readily understandable, if not uniformly attrac-tive, to researchers, practitioners, policymakers, those directly affected by literacy difficulties, and the wider lay public. We remain adamant that traditional methods of diagnosing dyslexia that exclude large numbers of people are inequitable, lack scientific credibility, represent an inefficient use of resources and expertise, and must be discontinued. We recognize the imperative to identify and meet the needs of all struggling readers as early and as speedily as possible. Scientific progress in genetics, neurosci-ence, and psychology may one day enable us to develop differing and more powerful forms of intervention tied to particular groupings, but until such a time arrives, we must rely upon existing knowledge to address a signifi-cant problem:

> Collectively, we must acknowledge that the most fundamental problem we face is not dyslexia. The most fundamental problem is one we all share – the majority of children in the US are not proficient readers, and the vast majority of these children struggle with basic reading skills. (Odegard et al., 2021: 58)

By advocating for the term dyslexia to be used solely to describe a partic-ular phenomenon – difficulty with accurate and fluent reading – we seek to ensure that higher levels of intellectual, professional, and political focus and energy are expended. In so doing, many of the concerns expressed in response to the publication of *The Dyslexia Debate* and our subsequent writings can be assuaged – at least, for now. In time, science may help us to draw upon genetics, brain imaging, environmental influences, lifestyle, and personal strengths and weaknesses to develop a system of "precision education" that will cater for individual differences in poor readers (Yeatman, 2022b). Sadly, such a scenario is little more than an aspiration for the long-term future, whereas the recommendations that are offered here serve as guidance for the present.

It is likely that there will continue to be many for whom the broadening of the concept of dyslexia, and its removal as a diagnostic term, will be anathema. Big business is unlikely to welcome a proposal that may impact predictions of rapid growth in the "Dyslexia Treatment Market" (Future Market Insights, 2022; Market Research Intellect, 2023). In its Preview, the Future Market Insights Report states that:

> The global dyslexia treatment market is anticipated to touch a market worth US$ 8061.5 Million in 2032, increasing from US$ 4096.1 Million in 2022. (Market Research Intellect, 2023)

"Key players" listed on the websites promoting these reports are almost exclusively pharmaceutical and healthcare companies.

As for education practitioners, clinicians, and reading disability researchers, some may persist with the argument that current diagnostic practices should be maintained until our knowledge and understanding are substantially advanced and, until that time arrives, the dyslexia debate is an unnecessary distraction that can be ignored; we disagree. While Wheldall, Castles, and Nayton (2014) make the valuable point that the terms used to describe those who struggle with reading are less important than ensuring that they get the right support, the inescapable reality is that the two are inextricably linked.

References

1000 Genomes Project Consortium. (2010). A map of human genome variation from population-scale sequencing. *Nature, 467,* 1061–1073.

Aaron, P. G., Joshi, R. M., Ayotollah, M., et al. (1999). Decoding and sight-word naming: Are they independent components of word recognition skill? *Reading and Writing, 11,* 89–127.

Aboud, K. S., Bailey, S. K., Petrill, S. A., & Cutting, L. E. (2016). Comprehending text versus reading words in young readers with varying reading ability: Distinct patterns of functional connectivity from common processing hubs. *Developmental Science, 19,* 632–656.

Aboud, K. S., Barquero, L. A., & Cutting, L. E. (2018). Prefrontal mediation of the reading network predicts intervention response in dyslexia. *Cortex, 101,* 96–106.

Ackerman, B. P., Izard, C. E., Kobak, R., Brown, E. D., & Smith, C. (2007). Relation between reading problems and internalizing behavior in school for preadolescent children from economically disadvantaged families. *Child Development, 78*(2), 581–596.

Ackerman, P. T., Holloway, C. A., Youngdahl, P. L., & Dykman, R. A. (2001). The double-deficit theory of reading disability does not fit all. *Learning Disabilities Research & Practice, 16,* 152–160.

Acunzo, D. J., Low, D. M., & Fairhall, S. L. (2022). Deep neural networks reveal topic-level representations of sentences in medial prefrontal cortex, lateral anterior temporal lobe, precuneus, and angular gyrus. *Neuroimage, 251,* 119005.

Adams, M. J. (1990). *Beginning to Read: Thinking and Learning about Print.* Cambridge, MA: MIT Press.

Adlof, S. M. (2020). Promoting reading achievement in children with developmental language disorders: What can we learn from research on specific language impairment and dyslexia? *Journal of Speech, Language, and Hearing Research, 63*(10), 3277–3292.

Adlof, S. M., & Hogan, T. P. (2018). Understanding dyslexia in the context of developmental language disorders. *Language, Speech, and Hearing Services in Schools, 49*(4), 762–773.

Adlof, S. M., Catts, H. W., & Lee, J. (2010). Kindergarten predictors of second versus eighth grade reading comprehension impairments. *Journal of Learning Disabilities, 43*(4), 332–345.

Ahissar, M. (2007). Dyslexia and the anchoring-deficit hypothesis. *Trends in Cognitive Sciences, 11*, 458–465.

Ahissar, M., Lubin, Y., Putter-Katz, H., & Banai, K. (2006). Dyslexia and the failure to form a perceptual anchor. *Nature Neuroscience, 9*, 1558–1564.

Al Dahhan, N. Z., Halverson, K., Peek, C. P., et al. (2022). Dissociating executive function and ADHD influences on reading ability in children with dyslexia. *Cortex, 153*, 126–142.

Al Dahhan, N. Z., Mesite, L., Feller, M. J., & Christodoulou, J. A. (2021). Identifying reading disabilities: A survey of practitioners. *Learning Disability Quarterly, 44*(4), 235–247.

Al Otaiba, S., Allor, J. H., Baker, K., et al. (2019). Teaching phonemic awareness and word reading skills: Focusing on explicit and systematic approaches. *Perspectives on Language and Literacy, 45*(3), 11–16.

Al Otaiba, S., Baker, K., Lan, P., et al. (2019). Elementary teachers' knowledge of response to intervention implementation: A preliminary factor analysis. *Annals of Dyslexia, 69*(1), 34–53.

Al Otaiba, S., Connor, C. M., Folsom, J. S., et al. (2014). To wait in tier 1 or intervene immediately: A randomized experiment examining first-grade response to intervention in reading. *Exceptional Children, 81*(1), 11–27.

Al Otaiba, S., Folsom, S. J., Schatschneider, C., et al. (2011). Predicting first-grade reading performance from kindergarten response to Tier 1 instruction. *Exceptional Children, 77*, 453–470.

Al Otaiba, S., McMaster, K., Wanzek, J., & Zaru, M. W. (2022). What we know and need to know about literacy interventions for elementary students with reading difficulties and disabilities, including dyslexia. *Reading Research Quarterly, 58*(2), 313–332.

Al Otaiba, S., Rouse, A., & Baker, K. (2018). Elementary grade intervention approaches to treat specific learning disabilities, including dyslexia. *Language, Speech, and Hearing Services in Schools, 49*(4), 829–842.

Al Otaiba, S., Russell-Freudenthal, D., & Zaru, M. W. (2024). Effective instruction and intervention for word-level reading for students with and at-risk for learning disabilities. In C. Okolo, N. Patton-Terry, & L. Cutting (eds.), *Handbook of Learning Disabilities*. 3rd edition. New York: Guilford Press.

Al Otaiba, S., Wanzek, J., Zaru, M., et al. (2022). Reading achievement and growth mindset of students with reading difficulties or reading disabilities: Contemporary research and implications for research and practice. In C. J. Lemons, S. R. Powell, K. L. Lane, & T. C. Aceves (eds.), *Handbook of Special Education Research, Volume II: Research-Based Practices and Intervention Innovations* (pp. 31–42). New York: Routledge.

Albon, E., Adi, Y., & Hyde, C. (2008). *The Effectiveness and Cost-Effectiveness of Colored Filters for Reading Disability: Systematic Review*. Birmingham, AL: University of Birmingham Department of Public Health and Epidemiology.

Alexander-Passe, N. (2015). The dyslexia experience: Difference, disclosure, labelling, discrimination and stigma. *Asia Pacific Journal of Developmental Differences, 2*(2), 202–233.

Alexander-Passe, N. (2016). The school's role in creating successful and unsuccessful dyslexics. *Journal of Psychology and Psychotherapy, 6*(238), 1–13.

Alexander-Passe, N. (2018). Should "developmental dyslexia" be understood as a disability or a difference? *Asia Pacific Journal of Developmental Differences, 5*(2), 247–271.

Allington, R. L. (2019). The hidden push for phonics legislation. *Tennessee Literacy Journal, 1*(1), 7–20.

Allington, R. L., & McGill-Franzen, A. M. (2021). Reading volume and reading achievement: A review of recent research. *Reading Research Quarterly, 56,* S231–S238.

Alloway, T. P. (2007). *Automated Working Memory Assessment (AWMA).* London: Harcourt Assessment.

Alloway, T. P., Gathercole, S. E., Kirkwood, H. J., & Elliott, J. G. (2009). The cognitive and behavioral characteristics of children with low working memory. *Child Development, 80,* 606–621.

Alloway, T. P., Gathercole, S. E., & Pickering, S. J. (2006). Verbal and visuospatial short-term and working memory in children: Are they separable? *Child Development, 77*(6), 1698–1716.

Alt, M., Fox, A., Levy, R., et al. (2021). Phonological working memory and central executive function differ in children with typical development and dyslexia. *Dyslexia, 28*(1), 20–39.

Altarelli, I., Leroy, F., Monzalvo, K., et al. (2014). Planum temporale asymmetry in developmental dyslexia: Revisiting an old question. *Human Brain Mapping, 35,* 5717–5735.

Altarelli, I., Monzalvo, K., Iannuzzi, S., et al. (2013). A functionally guided approach to the morphometry of occipitotemporal regions in developmental dyslexia: Evidence for differential effects in boys and girls. *Journal of Neuroscience, 33,* 11296–11301.

American Academy of Pediatrics. (1982). The doman-delacato treatment of neurologically handicapped children: A policy statement by the American Academy of Pediatrics. *Pediatrics, 70,* 810–812.

American Academy of Pediatrics (Section on Ophthalmology & Council on Children with Disabilities, Ophthalmology, American Academy of Ophthalmology, American Association for Pediatric Ophthalmology and Strabismus, & American Association of Certified Orthoptists). (2009). Learning disabilities, dyslexia, and vision. *Pediatrics, 124,* 837–844.

American Educational Research Association (AERA), American Psychological Association (APA), & National Council on Measurement in Education (NCME). (2014). *Educational and Psychological Testing.* AERA.

American Psychiatric Association (APA). (2013). *Diagnostic and Statistical Manual of Mental Disorders, 5th edition.* (DSM-5). Arlington, VA: American Psychiatric Association.

Amitay, S., Ben-Yehudah, G., Banai, K., & Ahissar, M. (2002). Disabled readers suffer from visual and auditory impairments but not from a specific magnocellular deficit. *Brain, 125,* 2272–2285.

Amitay, S., Ben-Yehudah, G., Banai, K., & Ahissar, M. (2003). Visual magnocellular deficits in dyslexia: Reply to the Editor. *Brain, 126*, e3.

Amland, T., Lervåg, A., & Melby-Lervåg, M. (2021). Comorbidity between math and reading problems: Is phonological processing a mutual factor? *Frontiers in Human Neuroscience, 14*, 577304, 592.

Amtmann, D., Abbott, R. D., & Berninger, V. W. (2007). Mixture growth models of RAN and RAS row by row: Insight into the reading system at work over time. *Reading and Writing, 20*, 785–813.

Anderson, C. A. (2007). Belief perseverance. In R. F. Baumeister, & K. D. Vohs (eds.), *Encyclopedia of Social Psychology* (pp. 109–110). Thousand Oaks, CA: Sage.

Anderson, K. (2000, June 18th). The reading wars: Understanding the debate over how best to teach children to read. *Los Angeles Times Book Review*. Available at SSRN: https://ssrn.com/abstract=935776.

Anderson, N. J., Rozenman, M., Pennington, B. F., Willcutt, E. G., & McGrath, L. M. (2023). Compounding effects of domain-general cognitive weaknesses and word reading difficulties on anxiety symptoms in youth. *Journal of Learning Disabilities, 56*(5), 343–358.

Andreola, C., Mascheretti, S., Belotti, R., et al. (2021). The heritability of reading and reading-related neurocognitive components: A multi-level meta-analysis. *Neuroscience & Biobehavioral Reviews, 121*, 175–200.

Andrews, J. S., Ben-Shachar, M., Yeatman, J. D., et al. (2010). Reading performance correlates with white-matter properties in preterm and term children. *Developmental Medicine & Child Neurology, 52*, 505–506.

Angrilli, A., Elbert, T., Cusumano, S., Stegagno, L., & Rockstroh, B. (2003). Temporal dynamics of linguistic processes are reorganized in aphasics' cortex: An EEG mapping study. *Neuroimage, 20*, 657–666.

Angrilli, A., & Spironelli, C. (2005). Cortical plasticity of language measured by EEG in a case of anomic aphasia. *Brain and Language, 95*, 32–33.

Annamma, S. A., Connor, D., & Ferri, B. (2013). Dis/ability critical race studies (DisCrit): Theorizing at the intersections of race and dis/ability. *Race Ethnicity and Education, 16*(1), 1–31.

Antal, A., Luber, B., Brem, A. K., et al. (2022). Non-invasive brain stimulation and neuroenhancement. *Clinical Neurophysiology Practice, 7*, 146–165.

Araújo, S., & Faísca, L. (2019). A meta-analytic review of naming-speed deficits in developmental dyslexia. *Scientific Studies of Reading, 23*(5), 349–368.

Araújo, S., Reis, A., Petersson, K. M., & Faísca, L. (2015). Rapid automatized naming and reading performance: A meta-analysis. *Journal of Educational Psychology, 107*(3), 868–883.

Archer, A. L., Gleason, M. M., & Vachon, V. L. (2003). Decoding and fluency: Foundation skills for struggling older readers. *Learning Disability Quarterly, 26*, 89–101.

Arnett, A. B., Pennington, B. F., Peterson, R. L. et al. (2017). Explaining the sex difference in dyslexia. *Journal of Child Psychology and Psychiatry, 58*, 719–727

Arnoutse, C., van Leeuwe, J., & Verhoeven, L. (2005). Early literacy from a longitudinal perspective. *Educational Review and Research, 11*, 253–275.

Arns, M., Peters, S., Breteler, R., & Verhoeven, L. (2007). Different brain activation patterns in dyslexic children: Evidence from EEG power and coherence patterns for the double-deficit theory of dyslexia. *Journal of Integrative Neuroscience, 6*, 175–190.

Aro, T., Eklund, K., Eloranta, A. K., Ahonen, T., & Rescorla, L. (2022). Learning disabilities elevate children's risk for behavioral-emotional problems: Differences between LD types, genders, and contexts. *Journal of Learning Disabilities, 55*(6), 465–481.

Arredondo, M. M., Ip, K. I., Shih Ju Hsu, L., Tardif, T., & Kovelman, I. (2015). Brain bases of morphological processing in young children. *Human Brain Mapping, 36*, 2890–2900.

Arrow, A. W., & Tunmer, W. E. (2012). Contemporary reading acquisition theory: The conceptual basis for differentiated reading instruction. In S. Suggate, & E. Reese (eds.), *Contemporary Debates in Childhood Education and Development* (pp. 241–249). London: Routledge.

Asbury, K., & Plomin, R. (2013). *G Is for Genes: The Impact of Genes on Education and Achievement*. Chichester: Wiley-Blackwell.

Asbury, K., & Wai, J. (2020). Viewing education policy through a genetic lens. *Journal of School Choice, 14*(2), 301–315.

Asghar, Z. B., Siriwardena, A. N., Elfes, C., et al. (2018). Performance of candidates disclosing dyslexia with other candidates in a UK medical licensing examination: Cross-sectional study. *Postgraduate Medical Journal, 94*(1110), 198–203.

Asghar, Z. B., Williams, N., Denney, M., & Siriwardena, A. N. (2019). Performance in candidates declaring versus those not declaring dyslexia in a licensing clinical examination. *Medical Education, 53*(12), 1243–1252.

Ashburn, S. M., Flowers, D. L., Napoliello, E. M., & Eden, G. F. (2020). Cerebellar function in children with and without dyslexia during single word processing. *Human Brain Mapping, 41*(1), 120–138.

Ashburner, J., & Friston, K. J. (2000). Voxel-based morphometry – The methods. *Neuroimage, 11*, 805–821.

Ashton, C. (1996). In defence of discrepancy definitions of specific learning difficulties. *Educational Psychology in Practice, 12*, 131–140.

Ashton, C. (1997). SpLD, discrepancies and dyslexia: A response to Solity and the Stanoviches. *Educational Psychology in Practice, 13*, 9–11.

Astle, D. E., Bathelt, J., CALM Team, & Holmes, J. (2019). Remapping the cognitive and neural profiles of children who struggle at school. *Developmental Science, 22*, e12747.

Astle, D. E., & Fletcher-Watson, S. (2020). Beyond the core-deficit hypothesis in developmental disorders. *Current Directions in Psychological Science, 29*(5), 431–437.

Astle, D. E., Holmes, J., Kievit, R., & Gathercole, S. E. (2022). Annual Research Review: The transdiagnostic revolution in neurodevelopmental disorders. *Journal of Child Psychology and Psychiatry, 63*(4), 397–417.

Au, A., & Lovegrove, B. (2001). Temporal processing ability in above average and average readers. *Perception & Psychophysics, 63*, 148–155.

Austin, C. R., Vaughn, S., & McClelland, A. M. (2017). Intensive reading interventions for inadequate responders in grades K–3: A synthesis. *Learning Disability Quarterly*, *40*(4), 191–210.

Axelrud, L. K., Hoffmann, M. S., Vosberg, D. E., et al. (2023). Disentangling the influences of parental genetics on offspring's cognition, education, and psychopathology via genetic and phenotypic pathways. *Journal of Child Psychology and Psychiatry*, *64*, 408–416.

Aylward, E., Richards, T., Berninger, V., et al. (2003). Instructional treatment associated with changes in brain activation in children with dyslexia. *Neurology*, *61*, 212–219.

Ayres, A. J. (1963). The development of perceptual-motor abilities: A theoretical basis for treatment of dysfunction. *American Journal of Occupational Therapy*, *17*, 221–225.

Ayres, A. J. (1979). *Sensory Integration and the Child*. Los Angeles: Western Psychological Services.

Bach, S., Brandeis, D., Hofstetter, C., et al. (2010). Early emergence of deviant frontal fMRI activity for phonological processes in poor beginning readers. *Neuroimage*, *53*, 682–693.

Badcock, N. A., & Kidd, J. C. (2015). Temporal variability predicts the magnitude of between-group attentional blink differences in developmental dyslexia: A meta-analysis. *PeerJ*, *3*, e746.

Baddeley, A. D. (2000). The episodic buffer: A new component of working memory? *Trends in Cognitive Sciences*, *4*, 417–422.

Baddeley, A. D., & Hitch, G. (1974). Working memory. In G. Bower (ed.), *The Psychology of Learning and Motivation: Vol. 8* (pp. 47–90). New York: Academic Press.

Badian, N. A. (1997). Dyslexia and the double deficit hypothesis. *Annals of Dyslexia*, *47*, 69–87.

Badzakova-Trajkov, G., Hamm, J. P., & Waldie, K. E. (2005). The effects of redundant stimuli on visuospatial processing in developmental dyslexia. *Neuropsychologia*, *43*, 473–478.

Bailey, D. H., Duncan, G. J., Cunha, F., Foorman, B. R., & Yeager, D. S. (2020). Persistence and fade-out of educational-intervention effects: Mechanisms and potential solutions. *Psychological Science in the Public Interest*, *21*(2), 55–97.

Bakhtin, M. (1981). *The Dialogic Imagination: Four Essays*. Translated by C. Emerson & M. Holquist. Austin: University of Texas Press.

Balow, B. (1971). Perceptual-motor activities in the treatment of severe reading disability. *The Reading Teacher*, *24*, 513–525.

Balow, B. (1996). Perceptual-motor activities in the treatment of severe reading disability. *The Reading Teacher*, *50*, 88–97.

Balu, R., Zhu, P., Doolittle, F., et al. (2015). *Evaluation of Response to Intervention Practices for Elementary Reading (NCEE 2016-4000)*. Washington, DC: US Department of Education, Institute of Education Sciences.

Banai, K., & Ahissar, M. (2004). Poor frequency discrimination probes dyslexics with particularly impaired working memory. *Audiology & Neurotology*, *9*, 328–340.

Banai, K., & Ahissar, M. (2010). On the importance of anchoring and the consequences of its impairment in dyslexia. *Dyslexia, 16,* 240–257.

Banai, K., & Ahissar, M. (2018). Poor sensitivity to sound statistics impairs the acquisition of speech categories in dyslexia. *Language, Cognition and Neuroscience, 33*(3), 321–332.

Banfi, C., Kemény, F., Gangl, M., et al. (2018). Visual attention span performance in German-speaking children with differential reading and spelling profiles: No evidence of group differences. *PLoS One, 13*(6), e0198903.

Barela, J. A., Dias, J. L., Godoi, D., Viana, A. R., & de Freitas, P. B. (2011). Postural control and automaticity in dyslexic children: The relationship between visual information and body sway. *Research in Developmental Disabilities, 32,* 1814–1821.

Barešić, A., Nash, A. J., Dahoun, T., Howes, O., & Lenhard, B. (2020). Understanding the genetics of neuropsychiatric disorders: The potential role of genomic regulatory blocks. *Molecular Psychiatry, 25,* 6–18.

Barkley, R. A. (2015). *Attention-Deficit Hyperactivity Disorder: A Handbook for Diagnosis and Treatment.* 4th edition. New York: Guilford Press.

Barkovich, A. J., & Kuzniecky, R. I. (2000). Gray matter heterotopia. *Neurology, 55,* 1603–1608.

Barnes, Z., & Peltier, T. (2022). Translating the science of reading screening into practice: Policies and their implications. *Perspectives on Language and Literacy, 48*(1), 42–48

Barquero, L. A., Davis, N., & Cutting, L. E. (2014). Neuroimaging of reading intervention: A systematic review and activation likelihood estimate meta-analysis. *PLoS ONE, 9,* e83668.

Barrett, C. A., Burns, M. K., Maki, K. E. et al. (2022). Language used in school psychological evaluation reports as predictors of SLD identification within a response to intervention model. *School Psychology, 37*(2), 107–118.

Barth, A. E., Denton, C. A., Stuebing, K. K., et al. (2010). A test of the cerebellar hypothesis of dyslexia in adequate and inadequate responders to reading intervention. *Journal of International Neuropsychological Society, 16,* 526–536.

Bates, T. C., Luciano, M., Castles, A., et al. (2007). Replication of reported linkages for dyslexia and spelling and suggestive evidence for novel regions on chromosomes 4 and 17. *European Journal of Human Genetics, 15,* 194–203.

Battisti, A., Lazzaro, G., Costanzo, F., et al. (2022). Effects of a short and intensive transcranial direct current stimulation treatment in children and adolescents with developmental dyslexia: A crossover clinical trial. *Frontiers in Psychology, 13.*

Bavelier, D., & Green, C. S. (2019). Enhancing attentional control: Lessons from action video games. *Neuron, 104*(1), 147–163.

Baye, A., Inns, A., Lake, C., & Slavin, R. E. (2019). A synthesis of quantitative research on reading programs for secondary students. *Reading Research Quarterly, 54*(2), 133–166.

Bazen, L., van den Boer, M., de Jong, P. F., & de Bree, E. H. (2020). Early and late diagnosed dyslexia in secondary school: Performance on literacy skills and cognitive correlates. *Dyslexia, 26*(4), 359–376.

Beach, S. D., Ozernov-Palchik, O., May, S. C., et al. (2022). The neural representation of a repeated standard stimulus in syslexia. *Frontiers of Human Neuroscience, 16*, 823627.

Beaton, A. A. (1997). The relation of planum temporale asymmetry and morphology of the corpus callosum to handedness, gender, and dyslexia: A review of the evidence. *Brain and Language, 60*, 255–322.

Beattie, R. L., Lu, Z. L., & Manis, F. R. (2011). Dyslexic adults can learn from repeated stimulus presentation but have difficulties in excluding external noise. *PloS one, 6*(11), e27893.

Beattie, R. L., & Manis, F. R. (2014). The relationship between prosodic perception, phonological awareness and vocabulary in emergent literacy. *Journal of Research in Reading, 37*(2), 119–137.

Beaujean, A. A., Benson, N. F., McGill, R. J., & Dombrowski, S. C. (2018). A misuse of IQ scores: Using the dual discrepancy/consistency model for identifying specific learning disabilities. *Journal of Intelligence, 6*(3), 36.

Beaulieu, C., Plewes, C., Paulson, L. A., Roy, D., Snook, L., Concha, L., & Phillips, L. (2005). Imaging brain connectivity in children with diverse reading ability. *Neuroimage, 25*(4), 1266–1271.

Beck, S. (2022). Evaluating the use of reasonable adjustment plans for students with a specific learning difficulty. *British Journal of Special Education, 49*(3), 399–419.

Becker, J., Czamara, D., Scerri, T. S., et al. (2014). Genetic analysis of dyslexia candidate genes in the European cross-linguistic NeuroDys cohort. *European Journal of Human Genetics, 22*, 675–680.

Becker, N., Vasconcelos, M., Oliveira, V., et al. (2017). Genetic and environmental risk factors for developmental dyslexia in children: Systematic review of the last decade. *Developmental Neuropsychology, 42*(7–8), 423–445.

Bedo, N., Ender-Fox, D., Chow, J., Siegel, L., Ribary, U., & Ward, L. M. (2021). Effects of a phonological intervention on EEG connectivity dynamics in dyslexic children. In J. Glazzard, & S. Stones (eds.), *Dyslexia IntechOpen.* www.intechopen.com/chapters/75089. Accessed December 3, 2023.

Bégel, V., Dalla Bella, S., Devignes, Q., et al. (2022). Rhythm as an independent determinant of developmental dyslexia. *Developmental Psychology, 58*(2), 339–358.

Begemann, M. J., Brand, B. A., Ćurčić-Blake, B., Aleman, A., & Sommer, I. E. (2020). Efficacy of non-invasive brain stimulation on cognitive functioning in brain disorders: A meta-analysis. *Psychological Medicine, 50*(15), 2465–2486.

Bejerano, G., Lowe, C. B., Ahituv, N., et al. (2006). A distal enhancer and an ultraconserved exon are derived from a novel retroposon. *Nature, 441*, 87–90.

Bellini, G., Bravaccio, C., Calamoneri, F., et al. (2005). No evidence for association between dyslexia and *DYX1C1* functional variants in a group of children and adolescents from Southern Italy. *Journal of Molecular Neuroscience, 27*, 311–314.

Benassi, M., Simonelli, L., Giovagnoli, S., & Bolzani, R. (2010). Coherence motion perception in developmental dyslexia: A meta-analysis of behavioral studies. *Dyslexia, 16*, 341–357

Benner, G. J., Nelson, J. R., Stage, S. A., & Ralston, N. C. (2011). The influence of fidelity of implementation on the reading outcomes of middle school students experiencing reading difficulties. *Remedial and Special Education, 32,* 79–88.

Ben-Shachar, M., Dougherty, R. F., & Wandell, B. A. (2007). White matter pathways in reading. *Current Opinion in Neurobiology, 17,* 258–270.

Benson, N. F., Floyd, R. G., Kranzler, J. H., et al. (2019). Test use and assessment practices of school psychologists in the United States: Findings from the 2017 National Survey. *Journal of School Psychology, 72,* 29–48.

Benson, N. F., Maki, K. E., Floyd, R. G., et al. (2020). A national survey of school psychologists' practices in identifying specific learning disabilities. *School Psychology, 35*(2), 146–157.

Benton, A. L., & Pearl, D. (eds.). (1978). *Dyslexia: An Appraisal of Current Knowledge.* New York: Oxford University Press.

Berent, I, Vaknin-Nusbaum, V., Balaban, E., & Galaburda, A. M. (2012). Dyslexia impairs speech recognition but can spare phonological competence. *PLoS ONE, 7*(9), e44875.

Berent, I., & Platt, M. (2021). Public misconceptions about dyslexia: The role of intuitive psychology. *PloS ONE, 16*(12), e0259019.

Bergmann, T. O., & Hartwigsen, G. (2021). Inferring causality from noninvasive brain stimulation in cognitive neuroscience. *Journal of Cognitive Neuroscience, 33,* 195–225.

Berkeley, S., Scanlon, D., Bailey, T. R., Sutton, J. C., & Sacco, D. M. (2020). A snapshot of RTI implementation a decade later: New picture, same story. *Journal of Learning Disabilities, 53*(5), 332–342.

Berlin, R. (1887). *Eine besondre Art der Wortblindheit* [A particular kind of word-blindness]. Verlag von J. F. Beckmann.

Berninger, V. W., Abbott, R. D., Nagy, W., & Carlisle, J. (2010). Growth in phonological, orthographic, and morphological awareness in grades 1 to 6. *Journal of Psycholinguistic Research, 39,* 141–163.

Berninger, V. W., Raskind, W., Richards, T., Abbott, R., & Stock, P. (2008). A multidisciplinary approach to understanding developmental dyslexia within working-memory architecture: Genotypes, phenotypes, brain, and instruction. *Developmental Neuropsychology, 33,* 707–744.

Bertoni, S., Franceschini, S., Puccio, G., et al. (2021). Action video games enhance attentional control and phonological decoding in children with developmental dyslexia. *Brain Sciences, 11*(2), 171.

Bertoni, S., Franceschini, S., Ronconi, L., Gori, S., & Facoetti, A. (2019). Is excessive visual crowding causally linked to developmental dyslexia? *Neuropsychologia, 130,* 107–117.

Bestmann, S. (2008). The physiological basis of transcranial magnetic stimulation. *Trends in Cognitive Sciences,* 81–83.

Betjemann, R. S., Willcutt, E. G., Olson, R. K., et al. (2008). Word reading and reading comprehension: Stability, overlap and independence. *Reading and Writing, 21,* 539–558.

Bevilacqua, D., Davidesco, I., Wan, L., et al. (2019). Brain-to-brain synchrony and learning outcomes vary by student-teacher dynamics: Evidence from a real-world classroom electroencephalography study. *Journal of Cognitive Neuroscience, 31*, 401–411.

Bianco, M., Bressoux, P., Doyen, A., et al. (2010). Early training in oral comprehension and phonological skills: Results of a three-year longitudinal study. *Scientific Studies of Reading, 14*, 211–246.

Binder, J. R., Desai, R. H., Graves, W. W., & Conant, L. L. (2009). Where is the semantic system? A critical review and meta-analysis of 120 functional neuroimaging studies. *Cerebral Cortex, 19*, 2767–2796.

Bishop, D. V. M. (2006). Dyslexia: What's the problem?. *Developmental Science, 9*, 256–257.

Bishop, D. V. M. (2007). Curing dyslexia and ADHD by training motor coordination: Miracle or myth? *Journal of Paediatrics and Child Health, 43*, 653–655.

Bishop, D. V. M., Mcdonald, D., Bird, S., & Hayiou-Thomas, M. E. (2009). Children who read accurately despite language impairment: Who are they and how do they do it? *Child Development, 80*, 593–605.

Bishop D. V. M., Snowling, M. J., Thompson, P. A., & Greenhalgh, T. (2017). Phase 2 of CATALISE: A multinational and multidisciplinary Delphi consensus study of problems with language development: Terminology. *Journal of Child Psychology and Psychiatry, 58*, 1068–1080.

Biswal, B., Zerrin Yetkin, F., Haughton, V. M., & Hyde, J. S. (1995). Functional connectivity in the motor cortex of resting human brain using echo-planar MRI *Magnetic Resonance in Medicine, 34*, 537–541.

Blackmore, S. (1999). *The Meme Machine*. Oxford: Oxford University Press.

Blampain, E., Gosse, C., & Van Reybroeck, M. (2021). Copying skills in children with and without dyslexia. *Reading and Writing, 34*(4), 859–885.

Blanchett, W. J. (2010). Telling it like it is: The role of race, class, & culture in the perpetuation of learning disability as a privileged category for the white middle class. *Disability Studies Quarterly, 30*(2).

Blasi, D. E., Henrich, J., Adamou, E., Kemmerer, D., & Majid, A. (2022). Over-reliance on English hinders cognitive science. *Trends in Cognitive Sciences, 26*(12), 1153–1170.

Blau, V., Reithler, J., van Atteveldt, N., et al. (2010). Deviant processing of letters and speech sounds as proximate cause of reading failure: A functional magnetic resonance imaging study of dyslexic children. *Brain, 133*, 868–879.

Blau, V., van Atteveldt, N., Ekkebus, M., Goebel, R., & Blomert, L. (2009). Reduced neural integration of letters and speech sounds links phonological and reading deficits in adult dyslexia. *Current Biology, 19*, 503–508.

Blythe, P. (1992). *A Physical Approach to Resolving Specific Learning Difficulties*. Chester: Institute for Neuro-Physiological Psychology.

Boardman, A. G., Vaughn, S., Buckley, P., et al. (2016). Collaborative strategic reading for students with learning disabilities in upper elementary classrooms. *Exceptional Children, 82*(4), 409–427.

Boardman, K. (2020). An exploration of teachers' perceptions and the value of multisensory teaching and learning: A perspective on the influence of Specialist Dyslexia Training in England. *Education 3–13, 48*(7), 795–806.

Boets, B. (2014). Dyslexia: Reconciling controversies within an integrative developmental perspective. *Trends in Cognitive Sciences, 18*(10), 501–503.

Boets, B., De Smedt, B., Cleuren, L., et al. (2010). Towards a further characterization of phonological and literacy problems in Dutch-speaking children with dyslexia. *British Journal of Developmental Psychology, 28*, 5–31.

Boets, B., Ghesquière, P., van Wieringen, A., & Wouters, J. (2007). Speech perception in preschoolers at family risk for dyslexia: Relations with low-level auditory processing and phonological ability. *Brain and Language, 101*, 19–30.

Boets, B., Op de Beeck, H. P., Vandermosten, M., et al. (2013). Intact but less accessible phonetic representations in adults with dyslexia. *Science, 342*(6163), 1251–1254.

Boets, B., Wouters, J., van Wieringen, A., & Ghesquière, P. (2007). Auditory processing, speech perception and phonological ability in preschool children at high-risk of dyslexia: A longitudinal study of the auditory temporal processing theory. *Neuropsychologia, 45*, 1608–1620.

Bogaerts, L., Szmalec, A., De Maeyer, M., Page, M. P., & Duyck, W. (2016). The involvement of long-term serial-order memory in reading development: A longitudinal study. *Journal of Experimental Child Psychology, 145*, 139–156.

Bogaerts, L., Szmalec, A., Hachmann, W. M., Page, M. P., & Duyck, W. (2015). Linking memory and language: Evidence for a serial-order learning impairment in dyslexia. *Research in Developmental Disabilities, 43*, 106–122.

Bogon, J., Finke, K., Schulte-Körne, G., et al. (2014). Parameter-based assessment of disturbed and intact components of visual attention in children with developmental dyslexia. *Developmental Science, 17*(5), 697–713.

Bonacina, S., Cancer, A., Lanzi, P. L., Lorusso, M. L., & Antonietti, A. (2015). Improving reading skills in students with dyslexia: The efficacy of a sublexical training with rhythmic background. *Frontiers in Psychology, 6*, 1510.

Booth, J. N., Boyle, J. M., & Kelly, S. W. (2014). The relationship between inhibition and working memory in predicting children's reading difficulties. *Journal of Research in Reading, 37*(1), 84–101.

Booth, J. R., Burman, D. D., Santen, F. W. V., et al. (2001). The development of specialized brain systems in reading and oral language. *Child Neuropsychology, 7*, 119–141.

Borasio, F., Syren, M. L., Turolo, S., et al. (2022). Direct and indirect effects of blood levels of Omega-3 and Omega-6 fatty acids on reading and writing (dis) abilities. *Brain Sciences, 12*(2), 169.

Borchers, L. R., Bruckert, L., Dodson, C. K., et al. (2019). Microstructural properties of white matter pathways in relation to subsequent reading abilities in children: A longitudinal analysis. *Brain Structure and Function, 224*, 891–905.

Bosse, M. L., Tainturier, M. J., & Valdois, S. (2007). Developmental dyslexia: The visual attention span deficit hypothesis. *Cognition, 104*, 198–230.

Boucher, A. N., Bhat, B. H., Clemens, N. H., Vaughn, S., & O'Donnell, K. (2023). Reading interventions for students in Grades 3–12 with significant word reading difficulties. *Journal of Learning Disabilities.* https://doi.org/10.1177/00222194231207556

Boulton, K. A., Coghill, D., Silove, N., et al. (2021). A national harmonised data collection network for neurodevelopmental disorders: A transdiagnostic assessment protocol for neurodevelopment, mental health, functioning and well-being. *JCPP Advances, 1*(4), e12048.

Bouton, B., McConnell, J. R., Barquero, L. A., Gilbert, J. K., & Compton, D. L. (2018). Upside-down response to intervention: A quasi-experimental study. *Learning Disabilities Research & Practice, 33*(4), 229–236.

Bowers, J. S. (2016a). The practical and principled problems with educational neuroscience. *Psychological Review, 123*(5), 600.

Bowers, J. S. (2016b). Psychology, not educational neuroscience, is the way forward for improving educational outcomes for all children: Reply to Gabrieli (2016) and Howard-Jones et al. (2016). *Psychological Review, 123*(5), 628–635

Bowers, J. S. (2020). Reconsidering the evidence that systematic phonics is more effective than alternative methods of reading instruction. *Educational Psychology Review, 32*(3), 681–705.

Bowers, P. G., Sunseth, K., & Golden, J. (1999). The route between rapid naming and reading progress. *Scientific Studies of Reading, 3*, 31–53.

Bowers, P. G., & Wolf, M. (1993). Theoretical links among naming speed, precise timing mechanisms and orthographic skill in dyslexia. *Reading and Writing, 5*, 69–85.

Braaten, E. (2020). *Playing the insurance game: When is testing covered?* MGH Clay Center for Young Heathy Minds. https://bit.ly/3GwAXPD. Accessed August 28, 2022.

Bradley, L., & Bryant, P. E. (1983). Categorizing sounds and learning to read – A causal connection. *Nature, 301*, 419–421.

Brady, S. (2019). The 2003 IDA definition of dyslexia: A call for changes. *Perspectives on Language and Literacy, 45*(1), 15–21.

Brambati, S. M., Termine, C., Ruffino, M., et al. (2004). Regional reductions of gray matter volume in familial dyslexia. *Neurology, 63*, 742–745.

Bramlett, R. K., Murphy, J. J., Johnson, J., & Wallingsford, L. (2002). Contemporary practices in school psychology: A national survey of roles and referral problems. *Psychology in the Schools, 39*, 327–335.

Brandenburg, J., Klesczewski, J., Fischbach, A., et al. (2015). Working memory in children with learning disabilities in reading versus spelling: Searching for overlapping and specific cognitive factors. *Journal of Learning Disabilities, 48*(6), 622–634.

Brantlinger, E. (1997). Using ideology: Cases of nonrecognition of the politics of research and practice in special education. *Review of Educational Research, 67*, 425–459.

Brem, S., Bach, S., Kucian, K., et al. (2010). Brain sensitivity to print emerges when children learn letter–speech sound correspondences. *Proceedings of the National Academy of Sciences, 107*, 7939–7944.

Brem, S., Maurer, U., Kronbichler, M., et al. (2020). Visual word form processing deficits driven by severity of reading impairments in children with developmental dyslexia. *Scientific Reports, 10,* 18728.

Brennan, J., Nir, Y., Hasson, U., et al. (2012). Syntactic structure building in the anterior temporal lobe during natural story listening. *Brain and Language, 120,* 163–173.

Breteler, M. H. M., Arns, M., Peters, S., Giepmans, I., & Verhoeven, J. (2010). Improvements in spelling after QEEG-based neurofeedback in dyslexia: A randomized controlled treatment study. *Applied Psychophysiological Biofeedback, 35,* 5–11.

Breznitz, Z., & Misra, M. (2003). Speed of processing of the visual–orthographic and auditory–phonological systems in adult dyslexics: The contribution of "asynchrony" to word recognition deficits. *Brain and Language, 85,* 486–502.

Brice, H., Frost, S. J., Bick, A. S., et al. (2021). Tracking second language immersion across time: Evidence from a bi-directional longitudinal cross-linguistic fMRI study. *Neuropsychologia, 154,* 107796.

Brimo, K., Dinkler, L., Gillberg, C., et al. (2021). The co-occurrence of neurodevelopmental problems in dyslexia. *Dyslexia, 27*(3), 277–293.

British Psychological Society. (1999). *Dyslexia, Literacy and Psychological Assessment: Report by a Working Party of the Division of Educational and Child Psychology of the British Psychological Society.* Leicester: British Psychological Society.

Brooks, G. (1984). The teaching of silent reading to beginners. In G. Brooks, & A. K. Pugh (eds.), *Studies in the History of Reading* (pp. 85–96). Reading: Centre for the Teaching of Reading, University of Reading and UK Reading Association.

Brooks, G. (2015). A response to Elliott. *The Psychology of Education Review, 39*(1), 17–19.

Brooks, G. (2022). Current debates over the teaching of phonics. *Oxford Research Encyclopedia of Education.* Published online, July 18, 2022.

Brooks, G. (2023). Disputing recent attempts to reject the evidence in favour of systematic phonics instruction. *Review of Education, 11*(2), e3408.

Brown, W. E., Eliez, S., Menon, V., et al. (2001). Preliminary evidence of widespread morphological variations of the brain in dyslexia. *Neurology, 56,* 781–783.

Brown Waesche, J. S., Schatschneider, C., Maner, J. K., Ahmed, Y., & Wagner, R. K. (2011). Examining agreement and longitudinal stability among traditional and RTI-based definitions of reading disability using the affected-status agreement statistic. *Journal of Learning Disabilities, 44,* 296–307.

Bruckert, L., Borchers, L. R., Dodson, C. K., et al. (2019). White matter plasticity in reading-related pathways differs in children born preterm and at term: A longitudinal analysis. *Frontiers in Human Neuroscience, 13.*

Bruno, J. L., Lu, Z. L., & Manis, F. R. (2013). Phonological processing is uniquely associated with neuro-metabolic concentration. *Neuroimage, 67,* 175–181.

Brunswick, N., McCrory, E., Price, C. J., Frith, C. D., & Frith, U. (1999). Explicit and implicit processing of words and pseudowords by adult developmental dyslexics: A search for Wernicke's Wortschatz? *Brain, 122,* 1901–1917.

Bryant, P. E., Maclean, L., Bradley, L., & Crossland, J. (1990). Rhyme and alliteration, phoneme detection, and learning to read. *Developmental Psychology*, *26*, 429–438.

Bucci, M. P. (2021). Visual training could be useful for improving reading capabilities in dyslexia. *Applied Neuropsychology: Child*, *10*(3), 199–208.

Buchanan, D. M., Bogdanowicz, T., Khanna, N., et al. (2021). Systematic review on the safety and tolerability of transcranial direct current stimulation in children and adolescents. *Brain Sciences*, *11*(2), 212.

Buckingham, J., Wheldall, K., & Beaman-Wheldall, R. (2013). Why poor children are more likely to become poor readers: The school years. *Australian Journal of Education*, *57*(3), 190–213.

Bull, L. (2009). Survey of complementary and alternative therapies used by children with specific learning difficulties (dyslexia). *International Journal of Language & Communication Disorders*, *44*(2), 224–235.

Bunbury, S. (2019). Unconscious bias and the medical model: How the social model may hold the key to transformative thinking about disability discrimination. *International Journal of Discrimination and the Law*, *19*(1), 26–47.

Buonincontri, R., Bache, I., Silahtaroglu, A., et al. (2011). A cohort of balanced reciprocal translocations associated with dyslexia: Identification of two putative candidate genes at DYX1. *Behavior Genetics*, *41*, 125–133.

Burbridge, T. J., Wang, Y., Volz, A. J., et al. (2008). Postnatal analysis of the effect of embryonic knockdown and overexpression of candidate dyslexia susceptibility gene homolog Dcdc2 in the rat. *Neuroscience*, *152*(3), 723–733.

Burden, R. L. (2005). *Dyslexia and Self-Concept*. London: Whurr.

Burden, R. L. (2008). Is dyslexia necessarily associated with negative feelings of self-worth? A review and implications for future research. *Dyslexia*, *14*, 188–196.

Burenkova, O. V., Naumova, O. Y., & Grigorenko, E. L. (2021). Stress in the onset and aggravation of learning disabilities. *Developmental Review*, *61*, 100968.

Burgoyne, K., Lervåg, A., Malone, C., & Hulme, C. (2019). Speech difficulties at school entry are a significant risk factor for later reading difficulties. *Early Childhood Research Quarterly*, *49*, 40–48.

Burnett, J. R., (1998). Phonics controversy in Texas. Radio broadcast, October 19. National Public Radio.

Burns, M. K., Petersen-Brown, S., Haegele, K., et al. (2016). Meta-analysis of academic interventions derived from neuropsychological data. *School Psychology Quarterly*, *31*(1), 28–42.

Burns, M. K., VanDerHeyden, A. M., Duesenberg-Marshall, M. D., et al. (2022). Decision accuracy of commonly used dyslexia screeners among students who are potentially at-risk for reading difficulties. *Learning Disability Quarterly*, *46*(4), 306–316.

Burns, M. K., Young, H., McCollom, E. M., Stevens, M. A., & Izumi, J. T. (2022). Predicting intervention effects with preintervention measures of decoding: Evidence for a skill-by-treatment interaction with kindergarten and first-grade students. *Learning Disability Quarterly*, *45*(4), 320–330.

Burt, C. (1937). *The Backward Child*. London: University of London Press.

Butterfuss, R., & Kendeou, P. (2018). The role of executive functions in reading comprehension. *Educational Psychology Review*, *30*(3), 801–826.

Byrne, B., Coventry, W., Olson, R., et al. (2008). A behaviour-genetic analysis of orthographic learning, spelling and decoding. *Journal of Research in Reading*, *31*, 8–21.

Byrne, B., Coventry, W. L., Olson, R. K., et al. (2009). Genetic and environmental influences on aspects of literacy and language in early childhood: Continuity and change from preschool to Grade 2. *Journal of Neurolinguistics*, *22*, 219–236.

Byrne, B., Delaland, C., Fielding-Barnsley, R., & Quain, P. (2002). Longitudinal twins study of early reading development in three countries: Preliminary results. *Annals of Dyslexia*, *52*, 49–73.

Cabbage, K. L., Farquharson, K., Iuzzini-Seigel, J., Zuk, J., & Hogan, T. P. (2018). Exploring the overlap between dyslexia and speech sound production deficits. *Language, Speech, and Hearing Services in Schools*, *49*(4), 774–786.

Caffarra, S., Karipidis, I., Yablonski, M., & Yeatman, J. D. (2021). Anatomy and physiology of word-selective visual cortex: From visual features to lexical processing. *Brain Structure and Function*, *226*, 3051–3065.

Caglar-Ryeng, Ø., Eklund, K., & Nergård-Nilssen, T. (2020). The effects of book exposure and reading interest on oral language skills of children with and without a familial risk of dyslexia. *Dyslexia*, *26*(4), 394–410.

Cain, K., Oakhill, J., & Bryant, P. (2004). Children's reading comprehension ability: Concurrent prediction by working memory, verbal ability, and component skills. *Journal of Educational Psychology*, *96*(1), 31.

Calcus, A., Lorenzi, C., Collet, G., Colin, C., & Kolinsky, R. (2016). Is there a relationship between speech identification in noise and categorical perception in children with dyslexia? *Journal of Speech, Language, and Hearing Research*, *59*(4), 835–852.

Caldani, S., Gerard, C. L., Peyre, H., & Bucci, M. P. (2020). Visual attentional training improves reading capabilities in children with dyslexia: An eye tracker study during a reading task. *Brain Sciences*, *10*(8), 558.

Calfee, R. C., & Drum, P. (1986). Research on teaching reading. In M. C. Whittock (ed.), *Handbook of Research on Teaching* (pp. 804–849). New York: Macmillan.

Calfee, R. C., & Norman, K. A. (1998). Psychological perspectives on the early reading wars: The case of phonological awareness. *Teachers College Record*, *100*, 242–274.

Calvi, M., Vieira, A. P. A., Georgiou, G., & Parrila, R. (2023). Systematic review on quality indicators of randomised controlled trial reading intervention studies for students in years 7–12. *Australasian Journal of Special and Inclusive Education*, 1–12.

Cameron, H. (2021). "It's been taken away": An experience of a disappearing dyslexia diagnosis. *International Journal of Inclusive Education*, 1–15.

Cameron, H., & Billington, T. (2015). The discursive construction of dyslexia by students in higher education as a moral and intellectual good. *Disability & Society*, *30*(8), 1225–1240.

Cameron, H., & Billington, T. (2017). "Just deal with it": Neoliberalism in dyslexic students' talk about dyslexia and learning at university. *Studies in Higher Education*, *42*(8), 1358–1372.

Camilleri, S., Chetcuti, D., & Falzon, R. (2020). "They labelled me ignorant": The role of neuroscience to support students with a profile of dyslexia. In A. El-Baz, & J. Suri (eds.), *Neurological Disorders and Imaging Physics: Vol. 5: Applications in Dyslexia, Epilepsy and Parkinson's* (pp. 356–389). Bristol: IOP Publishing Ltd.

Campbell, T. (2011). From Aphasia to Dyslexia, a fragment of a genealogy: An analysis of the formation of a "Medical Diagnosis." *Health Sociology Review*, *20*(4), 450–461.

Cancer, A., & Antonietti, A. (2018). tDCS modulatory effect on reading processes: A review of studies on typical readers and individuals with dyslexia. *Frontiers in Behavioral Neuroscience*, *12*, 162.

Cancer, A., & Antonietti, A. (2022). Music-based and auditory-based interventions for reading difficulties: A literature review. *Heliyon*, e09293.

Cao, F., Bitan, T., Chou, T. L., Burman, D. D., & Booth, J. R. (2006). Deficient orthographic and phonological representations in children with dyslexia revealed by brain activation patterns. *Journal of Child Psychology and Psychiatry*, *47*, 1041–1050.

Cao, F., Yan, X., Wang, Z., et al. (2017). Neural signatures of phonological deficits in Chinese developmental dyslexia. *Neuroimage*, *146*, 301–311.

Capin, P., Roberts, G., Clemens, N. H., & Vaughn, S. (2022). When treatment adherence matters: Interactions among treatment adherence, instructional quality, and student characteristics on reading outcomes. *Reading Research Quarterly*, *57*(2), 753–774.

Capin, P., Walker, M. A., Vaughn, S., & Wanzek, J. (2018). Examining how treatment fidelity is supported, measured, and reported in K–3 reading intervention research. *Educational Psychology Review*, *30*, 885–919.

Caravolas, M., Lervåg, A., Mousikou, P., et al. (2012). Common patterns of prediction of literacy development in different alphabetic orthographies. *Psychological Science*, *23*(6), 678–686.

Cardon, L. R., Smith, S. D., Fulker, D. W., et al. (1994). Quantitative trait locus for reading disability on chromosome 6. *Science*, *226*, 276–279.

Cardon, L. R., Smith, S. D., Fulker, D. W., et al. (1995). Quantitative trait locus for reading disability: Correction. *Science*, *268*, 1553.

Carrion-Castillo, A., Estruch, S. B., Maassen, B., et al. (2021). Whole-genome sequencing identifies functional noncoding variation in SEMA3C that cosegregates with dyslexia in a multigenerational family. *Human Genetics*, *140*, 1183–1200.

Carroll, J. M., Maughan, B., Goodman, R., & Meltzer, H. (2005). Literacy difficulties and psychiatric disorders: Evidence for comorbidity. *Journal of Child Psychology and Psychiatry*, *46*(5), 524–532.

Carroll, J. M., Snowling, M. J., Stevenson, J., & Hulme, C. (2003). The development of phonological awareness in preschool children. *Developmental Psychology*, *39*, 913–923.

Carroll, J. M., Solity, J., & Shapiro, L. R. (2016). Predicting dyslexia using pre-reading skills: The role of sensorimotor and cognitive abilities. *Journal of Child Psychology and Psychiatry, 57*(6), 750–758.

Casanova, M. F., Araque, J., Giedd, J., & Rumsey, J. M. (2004). Reduced brain size and gyrification in the brains of dyslexic patients. *Journal of Child Neurology, 19*, 275–281.

Cassar, M., Trieman, R., Moats, L., Pollo, T. C., & Kessler, B. (2005). How do the spellings of children with dyslexia compare with those of nondyslexic children? *Reading and Writing: An Interdisciplinary Journal, 18*, 27–49.

Cassidy, J., Grote-Garcia, S., & Ortlieb, E. (2022). What's hot in 2021: Beyond the science of reading. *Literacy Research and Instruction, 61*(1), 1–17.

Cassidy, L., Reggio, K., Shaywitz, B. A., Holahan, J. M., & Shaywitz, S. E. (2021). Dyslexia in incarcerated men and women: A new perspective on reading disability in the prison population. *Journal of Correctional Education, 72*(2), 61–81.

Castles, A., & Coltheart, M. (1993). Varieties of developmental dyslexia. *Cognition, 47*, 149–180.

Castles, A., Rastle, K., & Nation, K. (2018). Ending the reading wars: Reading acquisition from novice to expert. *Psychological Science in the Public Interest, 19*(1), 5–51.

Castro-Villareal, F., Rodriguez, B. J., & Moore, S. (2014). Teachers' perceptions and attitudes about response to intervention (RTI) in their schools: A qualitative analysis. *Teaching and Teacher Education, 40*, 104–112.

Cattinelli, I., Borghese, N. A., Gallucci, M., & Paulesu, E. (2013). Reading the reading brain: A new meta-analysis of functional imaging data on reading. *Journal of Neurolinguistics, 26*, 214–238.

Catts, H. W. (2021). Commentary: The critical role of oral language deficits in reading disorders: Reflections on Snowling and Hulme (2021). *Journal of Child Psychology and Psychiatry, 62*(5), 654–656.

Catts, H. W., Adlof, S. M., Hogan, T. P., & Weismer, S. E. (2005). Are specific language impairment and dyslexia distinct disorders? *Journal of Speech Language and Hearing Research, 48*, 1378–1396.

Catts, H. W., Compton, D., Tomblin, J. B., & Bridges, M. S. (2012). Prevalence and nature of late-emerging poor readers. *Journal of Educational Psychology, 104*(1), 166.

Catts, H. W., Gillispie, M., Leonard, L., Kail, R. V., & Miller, C. A. (2002). The role of speed of processing, rapid naming, and phonological awareness in reading achievement. *Journal of Learning Disabilities, 35*, 509–524.

Catts, H. W., & Hogan, T. (2021). Dyslexia: An ounce of prevention is better than a pound of diagnosis. *The Reading League Journal, 2*, 6–13.

Catts, H. W., McIlraith, A., Bridges, M. S., & Nielsen, D. C. (2017). Viewing a phonological deficit within a multifactorial model of dyslexia. *Reading and Writing, 30*(3), 613–629.

Catts, H. W., Nielsen, D. C., Bridges, M. S., Liu, Y. S., & Bontempo, D. E. (2015). Early identification of reading disabilities within an RTI framework. *Journal of Learning Disabilities, 48*(3), 281–297.

Catts, H. W., & Petscher, Y. (2022). A cumulative risk and resilience model of dyslexia. *Journal of Learning Disabilities, 55*(3), 171–184.

Catts, H. W., Petscher, Y., Schatschneider, C., Bridges, M. S., & Mendoza, K. (2009). Floor effects associated with universal screening and their impact on the early identification of reading disabilities. *Journal of Learning Disabilities, 42*, 163–176.

Catts, H. W., Terry, N. P., Lonigan, C. J., et al. (2024). Revisiting the definition of dyslexia. *Annals of Dyslexia*, 1–21.

Cavalli, E., Colé, P., Badier, J. M., et al. (2016). Spatiotemporal dynamics of morphological processing in visual word recognition. *Journal of Cognitive Neuroscience, 28*, 1228–1242.

Cavalli, E., Duncan, L. G., Elbro, C., El Ahmadi, A., & Colé, P. (2017). Phonemic—Morphemic dissociation in university students with dyslexia: An index of reading compensation? *Annals of Dyslexia, 67*(1), 63–84.

Caverzasi, E., Mandelli, M. L., Hoeft, F., et al. (2018). Abnormal age-related cortical folding and neurite morphology in children with developmental dyslexia. *NeuroImage: Clinical, 18*, 814–821.

Cederlöf, M., Maughan, B., Larsson, H., D'Onofrio, B. M., & Plomin, R. (2017). Reading problems and major mental disorders – Co-occurrences and familial overlaps in a Swedish nationwide cohort. *Journal of Psychiatric Research, 91*, 124–129.

Chaix, Y., Albaret, J., Brassard, C., et al. (2007). Motor impairment in dyslexia: The influence of attention disorders. *European Journal of Paediatric Neurology, 11*, 368–374.

Chall, J. S. (1996). *Learning to Read: The great debate.* 3rd edition. Orlando, FL: Harcourt Brace.

Chall, J. S. (2000). *The Academic Achievement Challenge.* New York: Guilford Press.

Chamberlain, R., Brunswick, N., Siev, J., & McManus, I. C. (2018). Meta-analytic findings reveal lower means but higher variances in visuospatial ability in dyslexia. *British Journal of Psychology, 109*(4), 897–916.

Chapman, J. W., & Tunmer, W. E. (2015). *Submission on the Inquiry into the identification and support for students with the significant challenges of dyslexia, dyspraxia, and autism spectrum disorders in primary and secondary schools.* (Presented to the New Zealand Education and Science Select Committee).

Chapman, J. W., & Tunmer, W. E. (2019a). Dyslexia and equity: A more inclusive approach to reading difficulties. *LDA Bulletin, 51*(2 & 3), 28–32.

Chapman, J. W., & Tunmer, W. E. (2019b). Reading Recovery's unrecovered learners: Characteristics and issues. *Review of Education, 7*(2), 237–265.

Charlton, C. T., Sabey, C. V., Young, E. L., & Moulton, S. E. (2020). Interpreting critical incidents in implementing a multi-tiered system of supports through an active implementation framework. *Exceptionality, 28*(3), 161–175.

Che, A., Truong, D. T., Fitch, R. H., & LoTurco, J. J. (2016). Mutation of the dyslexia-associated gene Dcdc2 enhances glutamatergic synaptic transmission between layer 4 neurons in mouse meocortex. *Cerebral Cortex, 26*, 3705–3718.

Cheema, K., & Cummine, J. (2018). The relationship between white matter and reading acquisition, refinement and maintenance. *Developmental Neuroscience, 40*, 209–222.

Cheema, K., Ostevik, A. V., Westover, L., Hodgetts, W. E., & Cummine, J. (2021). Resting-state networks and reading in adults with and without reading impairments. *Journal of Neurolinguistics, 60*, 101016.

Cheesman, R., Hunjan, A., Coleman, J. R., et al. (2020). Comparison of adopted and nonadopted individuals reveals gene–environment interplay for education in the UK Biobank. *Psychological Science, 31*(5), 582–591.

Chen, N. T., Zheng, M., & Ho, C. S. H. (2019). Examining the visual attention span deficit hypothesis in Chinese developmental dyslexia. *Reading and Writing, 32*(3), 639–662.

Cheung, A. C., & Slavin, R. E. (2016). How methodological features affect effect sizes in education. *Educational Researcher, 45*(5), 283–292.

Cheung, C. H., Wood, A. C., Paloyelis, Y., et al. (2012). Aetiology for the covariation between combined type ADHD and reading difficulties in a family study: The role of IQ. *Journal of Child Psychology and Psychiatry, 53*(8), 864–873.

Chiappe, P., Stringer, R., Siegel, L. S., & Stanovich, K. E. (2002). Why the timing deficit hypothesis does not explain reading disability in adults. *Reading and Writing, 15*, 73–107.

Chiarello, C., Lombardino, L. J., Kacinik, N. A., Otto, R., & Leonard, C. M. (2006). Neuroanatomical and behavioral asymmetry in an adult compensated dyslexic. *Brain and Language, 98*, 169–181.

Chirkina, G. V., & Grigorenko, E. L. (2014). Tracking citations: A science detective story. *Journal of Learning Disabilities, 47*(4), 366–373.

Christodoulou, J. A., Murtagh, J., Cyr, A., et al. (2017). Relation of white-matter microstructure to reading ability and disability in beginning readers. *Neuropsychology, 31*, 508–515.

Christopher, M. E., Miyake, A., Keenan, J. M., et al. (2012). Predicting word reading and comprehension with executive function and speed measures across development: A latent variable analysis. *Journal of Experimental Psychology: General, 141*(3), 470–488.

Church, J. A., Grigorenko, E. L., & Fletcher, J. M. (2021). The role of neural and genetic processes in learning to read and specific reading disabilities: Implications for instruction. *Reading Research Quarterly. 58*(2), 203–219.

Chyl, K., Kossowski, B., Wang, S., et al. (2021). The brain signature of emerging reading in two contrasting languages. *Neuroimage, 225*, 117503.

Cirino, P. T., Ahmed, Y., Miciak, J., et al. (2018). A framework for executive function in the late elementary years. *Neuropsychology, 32*(2), 176.

Cirino, P. T., Barnes, M. A., Roberts, G., Miciak, J., & Gioia, A. (2022). Visual attention and reading: A test of their relation across paradigms. *Journal of Experimental Child Psychology, 214*, 105289.

Cirino, P. T., Church, J. A., Miciak, J., & Fletcher, J. M. (2020). The role of executive functions in reading development, reading disability, and intervention response. In E. Grigorenko, Y. Shtyrov, & P. McCardle (eds.), *All about Language: Science, Theory, and Practice* (pp. 126–140). Baltimore: Paul H. Brookes Publishing Co.

Clamp, M., Fry, B., Kamal, M., et al. (2007). Distinguishing protein-coding and noncoding genes in the human genome. *PNAS, 104*, 19428–19433.

Clark, K. A., Helland, T., Specht, K., et al. (2014). Neuroanatomical precursors of dyslexia identified from pre-reading through to age 11. *Brain, 137*, 3136–3141.

Clay, M. M. (1985). *The Early Detection of Reading Difficulties*. 3rd edition. Portsmouth, NH: Heinemann.

Clayton, F. J., West, G., Sears, C., Hulme, C., & Lervåg, A. (2020). A longitudinal study of early reading development: Letter–sound knowledge, phoneme awareness and RAN, but not letter–sound integration, predict variations in reading development. *Scientific Studies of Reading, 24*(2), 91–107.

Clemens, N. H., Lee, K., Liu, X., Boucher, A., Al Otaiba, S., & Simmons, L. (2023). The relations of kindergarten early literacy skill trajectories on common progress monitoring measures to subsequent word reading skills for students at risk for reading difficulties. *Journal of Educational Psychology, 115*(8), 1045–1106.

Clemens, N. H., Solari, E., Kearns, et al. (2021). They say you can do phonemic awareness instruction "in the dark," but should you? A critical evaluation of the trend toward advanced phonemic awareness training. *PsyArXiv*. https://doi.org/10.31234/osf.io/ajxbv

Clemens, N. H., & Vaughn, S. (2023). Understandings and misunderstandings about dyslexia: Introduction to the special issue. *Reading Research Quarterly, 58*(2), 181–187.

Cohen-Mimran, R., & Sapir, S. (2007). Deficits in working memory in young adults with reading disabilities. *Journal of Communication Disorders, 40*(2), 168–183.

Colenbrander, D., Kohnen, S., Beyersmann, E., et al. (2022). Teaching children to read irregular words: A comparison of three instructional methods. *Scientific Studies of Reading, 26*(6), 545–564.

Collinson, C. (2020). Ordinary language use and the social construction of dyslexia. *Disability & Society, 35*(6), 993–1006.

Collis, N. L., Kohnen, S., & Kinoshita, S. (2013): The role of visual spatial attention in adult developmental dyslexia. *The Quarterly Journal of Experimental Psychology, 66*(2), 245–260.

Coltheart, M., Rastle, K., Perry, C., Langdon, R., & Ziegler, J. (2001). DRC: A dual route cascaded model of visual word recognition and reading aloud. *Psychological Review, 108*(1), 204–256.

Compton, D. L. (2021). Focusing our view of dyslexia through a multifactorial lens: A commentary. *Learning Disability Quarterly, 44*(3), 225–230.

Compton, D. L., Fuchs, D., Fuchs, L. S., et al. (2010). Selecting at-risk first-grade readers for early intervention: Eliminating false positives and exploring the promise of a two-stage gated screening process. *Journal of Educational Psychology, 102*, 327–340.

Compton, D. L., Gilbert, J. K., Jenkins, J. R., et al. (2012). Accelerating chronically unresponsive children to Tier 3 instruction: What level of data is necessary to ensure selection accuracy? *Journal of Learning Disabilities, 45*, 204–216.

Conlon, E. G. (2012). Visual discomfort and reading. In J. Stein, & Z. Kapoula (eds.), *Visual Aspects of Dyslexia* (pp. 79–90). Oxford: Oxford University Press.

Conlon, E. G., Lilleskaret, G., Wright, C. M., & Power, G. F. (2012). The influence of contrast on coherent motion processing in dyslexia. *Neuropsychologia, 50*, 1672–1681.

Conlon, E. G., Lovegrove, W., Chekaluk, E., & Pattison, P. (1999). Measuring visual discomfort. *Visual Cognition, 6*, 637–663.

Connor, C. M. (2011). Child by instruction interactions: Language and literacy connections. In S. B. Neuman, & D. K. Dickinson (eds.), *Handbook on Early Literacy Research.* 3rd edition. (pp. 256–275). New York: Guilford.

Connor, C. M., & Morrison, F. J. (2016). Individualizing student instruction in reading: Implications for policy and practice. *Policy Insights from the Behavioral and Brain Sciences, 3*(1), 54–61.

Connor, C. M., Morrison, F. J., Fishman, B. J., Schatschneider, C., & Underwood, P. (2007). Algorithm-guided individualized reading instruction. *Science, 315*, 464–465.

Connor, C. M., Morrison, F. J., & Katch, E. L. (2004). Beyond the reading wars: Exploring the effect of child–instruction interaction on growth in early reading. *Scientific Studies of Reading, 8*, 305–336.

Connor, C. M., Piasta, S. B., Fishman, B., et al. (2009). Individualizing student instruction precisely: Effects of child by instruction interactions on first graders' literacy development. *Child Development, 80*, 77–100.

Cooper, G. M., Coe, B. P., Girirajan, S., et al. (2011). A copy number variation morbidity map of developmental delay. *Nature Genetics, 43*, 838–846.

Cope, N., Eicher, J. D., Meng, H., et al. (2012). Variants in the DYX2 locus are associated with altered brain activation in reading-related brain regions in subjects with reading disability. *Neuroimage, 63*, 148–156.

Cope, N., Hill, G., van den Bree, M., et al. (2004). No support for association between dyslexia susceptibility 1 candidate 1 and developmental dyslexia. *Molecular Psychiatry, 10*, 237–238.

Cordray, D., Pion, G., Brandt, C., Molefe, A., & Toby, M. (2012). *The Impact of the Measures of Academic Progress (MAP) Program on Student Reading Achievement. Final Report. NCEE 2013–4000.* National Center for Education Evaluation and Regional Assistance.

Corina, D. P., Richards, T. L., Serafini, S., et al. (2001). fMRI auditory language differences between dyslexic and able reading children. *Neuroreport, 12*, 1195–1201.

Corriveau, K. H., Goswami, U., & Thomson, J. M. (2010). Auditory processing and early literacy skills in a preschool and kindergarten population. *Journal of Learning Disabilities, 43*, 369–382

Costanzo, F., Menghini, D., Caltagirone, C., Oliveri, M., & Vicari, S. (2013). How to improve reading skills in dyslexics: The effect of high frequency rTMS. *Neuropsychologia, 51*, 2953–2959.

Costanzo, F., Varuzza, C., Rossi, S., et al. (2016). Reading changes in children and adolescents with dyslexia after transcranial direct current stimulation. *Neuroreport, 27*, 295–300.

Coventry, W. L., Byrne, B., Olson, R. K., Corley, R., & Samuelsson, S. (2011). Dynamic and static assessment of phonological awareness in preschool: A behavior-genetic study. *Journal of Learning Disabilities, 44*, 322–329.

Covington, M. V. (1992). *Making the Grade: A Self-Worth Perspective on Motivation and School Reform.* New York: Cambridge University Press.

Cowan, N. (2017). The many faces of working memory and short-term storage. *Psychonomic Bulletin & Review, 24*(4), 1158–1170.

Cowan, N., Elliott, E. M., Saults, J. S., et al. (2005). On the capacity of attention: Its estimation and its role in working memory and cognitive aptitudes. *Cognitive Psychology, 51*, 42–100

Coward, S. (2015). *High school readers: A study of sustained silent reading and academic progress* Unpublished doctoral dissertation, Capella University, Minneapolis, MN.

Coyne, M. D., Oldham, A., Dougherty, S. M., et al. (2018). Evaluating the effects of supplemental reading intervention within an MTSS or RTI reading reform initiative using a regression discontinuity design. *Exceptional Children, 84*(4), 350–367.

Critchley, M. (1970). Developmental dyslexia: A constitutional disorder of symbolic perception. *Research Publications – Association for Research in Nervous and Mental Disease, 48*, 266–271.

Crombie, M., & Reid, G. (2009). The role of early identification research: Models from research and practice. In G. Reid (ed.), *The Routledge Companion to Dyslexia* (pp. 71–79). London: Routledge.

Cronbach, L. J. (1975). Beyond the two disciplines of scientific psychology. *American Psychologist, 30*, 116–127.

Cronbach, L. J., & Snow, R. E. (1977). *Aptitudes and Instructional Methods: A Handbook for Research on Interactions.* New York: Irvington.

Cross, A. M., Ramdajal, R., Peters, L., et al. (2021). Resting-state functional connectivity and reading subskills in children. *Neuroimage, 243*, 118529.

Crow, L. (1994). Including all of our lives: Renewing the social model of disability. In C. Barnes, & G. Mercer (eds.), *Exploring the Divide* (pp. 55–72). Leeds: The Disability Press.

Cruz, R. A., Kramarczuk Voulgarides, C. M., Firestone, A. R., McDermott, L., & Feng, Z. (2023). Is Dis-ability a foregone conclusion? Research and policy solutions to disproportionality. *Review of Educational Research*, 00346543231212935.

Cui, Z., Xia, Z., Su, M., Shu, H., & Gong, G. (2016). Disrupted white matter connectivity underlying developmental dyslexia: A machine learning approach. *Human Brain Mapping, 37*, 1443–1458.

Cunningham, A. E., & Stanovich, K. E. (1998). The impact of print exposure on word recognition. In J. L. Metsala, & L. C. Ehri (eds.), *Word Recognition in Beginning Literacy* (pp. 235–262). Mahwah, NJ: Erlbaum.

Cunningham, A. J., Burgess, A. P., Witton, C., Talcott, J. B., & Shapiro, L. R. (2021). Dynamic relationships between phonological memory and reading: A five-year longitudinal study from age 4 to 9. *Developmental Science, 24*(1), e12986.

Curtis, M. (2004). Adolescents who struggle with word identification: Research and practice. In T. L. Jetton, & J. A. Dole (eds.), *Adolescent Literacy Research and Practice* (pp. 119–134). New York: Guilford.

Cutting, L. E. (2014). What is in a word? *Science, 345*(6202), 1252.

Cutting, L. E., & Denckla, M. B. (2001). The relationship of rapid serial naming and word reading in normally developing readers: An exploratory model. *Reading and Writing, 14,* 673–705.

Cyhlarova, E., Bell, J. G., Dick, J. R., et al. (2007). Membrane fatty acids, reading and spelling in dyslexic and non-dyslexic adults. *European Neuropsychopharmacology, 17,* 116–121.

Dahl-Leonard, K., Hall, C., Capin, P., et al. (2023). Examining fidelity reporting within studies of foundational reading interventions for elementary students with or at risk for dyslexia. *Annals of Dyslexia, 73,* 288–313.

Daikhin, L., Raviv, O., & Ahissar, M. (2017). Auditory stimulus processing and task learning are adequate in dyslexia, but benefits from regularities are reduced. *Journal of Speech, Language, and Hearing Research, 60*(2), 471–479.

Dailey, S., & Bergelson, E. (2022). Language input to infants of different socio-economic statuses: A quantitative meta-analysis. *Developmental Science, 25*(3), e13192.

Dale, A. M., Fischl, B., & Sereno, M. I. (1999). Cortical surface-based analysis. I. Segmentation and surface reconstruction. *Neuroimage, 9,* 179–194.

Daley, S. G., & Rappolt-Schlichtmann, G. (2018). Stigma consciousness among adolescents with learning disabilities: Considering individual experiences of being stereotyped. *Learning Disability Quarterly, 41*(4), 200–212.

Dane, A. V., & Schneider, B. H. (1998). Program integrity in primary and early secondary prevention: Are implementation effects out of control? *Clinical Psychology Review, 18,* 23–45.

Daniel, J., Capin, P., & Steinle, P. (2021). A synthesis of the sustainability of remedial reading intervention effects for struggling adolescent readers. *Journal of Learning Disabilities, 54*(3), 170–186.

Daniel, J., Vaughn, S., Roberts, G., & Grills, A. (2022). The importance of baseline word reading skills in examining student response to a multicomponent reading intervention. *Journal of Learning Disabilities, 55*(4), 259–271.

Darling, K. E., Benore, E. R., & Webster, E. E. (2020). Biofeedback in pediatric populations: A systematic review and meta-analysis of treatment outcomes. *Translational Behavioral Medicine, 10*(6), 1436–1449.

Daucourt, M. C., Erbeli, F., Little, C. W., Haughbrook, R., & Hart, S. A. (2020). A meta-analytical review of the genetic and environmental correlations between reading and attention-deficit hyperactivity disorder symptoms and reading and math. *Scientific Studies of Reading, 24,* 23–56.

Daucourt, M. C., Schatschneider, C., Connor, C. M., Al Otaiba, S., & Hart, S. A. (2018). Inhibition, updating working memory, and shifting predict reading disability symptoms in a hybrid model: Project KIDS. *Frontiers in Psychology, 9,* 238.

Davidesco, I., Matuk, C., Bevilacqua, D., Poeppel, D., & Dikker, S. (2021). Neuroscience research in the classroom: Portable brain technologies in education research. *Educational Researcher, 50*, 649–656.

Davis, N., Fan, Q., Compton, D., et al. (2010). Influences of neural pathway integrity on children's response to reading instruction. *Frontiers in Systems Neuroscience, 4*.

Davis, O. S. P., Band, G., Pirinen, M., et al. (2014). The correlation between reading and mathematics ability at age twelve has a substantial genetic component. *Nature Communications, 5*, 4204–4204.

Davis, R. D. (1997). *The Gift of Dyslexia*. London: Souvenir Press.

Davison, K. E., Zuk, J., Mullin, L. J., et al. (2023). Examining shared reading and white matter organization in kindergarten in relation to subsequent language and reading abilities: A longitudinal investigation. *Journal of Cognitive Neuroscience, 35*(2), 259–275.

Dawkins, R. (1976). *The Selfish Gene*. Oxford: Oxford University Press.

De Beer, J., Heerkens, Y., Engels, J., & van der Klink, J. (2022). Factors relevant to work participation from the perspective of adults with developmental dyslexia: A systematic review of qualitative studies. *BMC Public Health, 22*(1), 1–20.

De Clercq-Quaegebeur, M., Casalis, S., Lemaitre, M., et al. (2010). Neuropsychological profile on the WISC-IV of French children with dyslexia. *Journal of Learning Disabilities, 43*, 563–574.

De Clercq-Quaegebeur, M., Casalis, S., Vilette, B., Lemaitre, M. P., & Vallée, L. (2018). Arithmetic abilities in children with developmental dyslexia: Performance on French ZAREKI-R test. *Journal of Learning Disabilities, 51*(3), 236–249.

de Graaff, S. E. H., Bosman, A. M. T., Hasselman, F., & Verhoeven, L. (2009). Benefits of systematic phonics instruction. *Scientific Studies of Reading, 13*, 318–333.

de Jong, P. F. (2023). The validity of WISC-V profiles of strengths and weaknesses. *Journal of Psychoeducational Assessment, 41*(4), 363–379.

de Jong, P. F., & van Bergen, E. (2017). Issues in diagnosing dyslexia. In E. Segers, & P. van den Broek (eds.), *Developmental Perspectives in Written Language and Literacy* (pp. 349–361). Amsterdam: John Benjamins.

de Kovel, C. G. F., Franke, B., Hol, F. A., et al. (2008). Confirmation of dyslexia susceptibility loci on chromosomes 1p and 2p, but not 6p in a Dutch sib-pair collection. *American Journal of Medical Genetics (Neuropsychiatric Genetics), 147B*, 294–300.

de Kovel, C. G. F., Hol, F. A., Heister, J., et al. (2004). Genomewide scan identifies susceptibility locus for dyslexia on Xq27 in an extended Dutch family. *Journal of Medical Genetics, 41*, 652–657.

de la Calle, A. M., Guzmán-Simón, F., García-Jiménez, E., & Aguilar, M. (2021). Precursors of reading performance and double-and triple-deficit risks in Spanish. *Journal of Learning Disabilities, 54*(4), 300–313.

de Weerdt, F., Desoete, A., & Roeyers, H. (2013). Working memory in children with reading disabilities and/or mathematical disabilities. *Journal of Learning Disabilities, 46*(5), 461–472.

de Zeeuw, E. L., de Geus, E. J. C., & Boomsma, D. I. (2015). Meta-analysis of twin studies highlights the importance of genetic variation in primary school educational achievement. *Trends in Neuroscience and Education, 4*(3), 69–76.

Dębska, A., Łuniewska, M., Zubek, J., et al. (2022). The cognitive basis of dyslexia in school-aged children: A multiple case study in a transparent orthography. *Developmental Science, 25*(2), e13173.

Deffenbacher, K. E., Kenyon, J. B., Hoover, D. M., et al. (2004). Refinement of the 6p21.3 quantitative trait locus influencing dyslexia: Linkage and association analyses. *Human Genetics, 115*, 128–138.

DeFries, J. C., Fulker, D. W., & LaBuda, M. C. (1987). Evidence for a genetic aetiology in reading disability of twins. *Nature, 329*, 537–539.

Dehaene, S. (2009). *Reading in the Brain.* New York: Viking.

Dehaene, S., Cohen, L., Morais, J., & Kolinsky, R. (2015). Illiterate to literate: Behavioural and cerebral changes induced by reading acquisition. *Nature Reviews Neuroscience, 16*, 234–244.

Delacato, C. H. (1959). *The Treatment and Prevention of Reading Problems.* Springfield, IL: Thomas.

Delacato, C. H. (1963). *The Diagnosis and Treatment of Speech and Reading Problems.* Springfield, IL: Thomas.

Demb, J. B., Boynton, G. M., Best, M., & Heeger, D. J. (1998). Psychophysical evidence for a magnocellular pathway deficit in dyslexia. *Vision Research, 38*, 1555–1559.

Demb, J. B., Boynton, G. M., & Heeger, D. J. (1998). Functional magnetic resonance imaging of early visual pathways in dyslexia. *Journal of Neuroscience, 18*, 6939–695'.

D'Mello, A. M., & Gabrieli, J. D. E. (2018). Cognitive neuroscience of dyslexia. *Language, Speech, and Hearing Services in Schools, 49*(4), 798–809

Démonet, J.-F., Taylor, M. J., & Chaix, Y. (2004). Developmental dyslexia. *Lancet, 363*, 1451–1460.

Denckla, M. B. (1972). Color-naming deficits in dyslexic boys. *Cortex, 8*(2), 164–176.

Denckla, M., & Rudel, R. (1974). Rapid "automatized" naming of pictured objects, colors, letters and numbers by normal children. *Cortex, 10*, 186–202.

Denckla, M., & Rudel, R. (1976a). Naming of object-drawings by dyslexic and other learning disabled children. *Brain and Language, 3*, 1–15.

Denckla, M., & Rudel, R. (1976b). Rapid "automatized" naming (R.A.N.): Dyslexia differentiated from other learning disabilities. *Neuropsychologia, 14*, 471–479.

Deng, K. G., Zhao, H., & Zuo, P. X. (2019). Association between KIAA0319 SNPs and risk of dyslexia: A meta-analysis. *Journal of Genetics, 98*(1).

Denton, C. A. (2012). Response to intervention for reading difficulties in the primary grades: Some answers and lingering questions. *Journal of Learning Disabilities, 45*(3), 232–243.

Denton, C. A., & Hocker, J. L. (2006). *Responsive Reading Instruction: Flexible Intervention for Struggling Readers in the Early Grades.* Longmont, CO: Sopris West.

Denton, C. A., Tamm, L., Schatschneider, C., & Epstein, J. N. (2020). The effects of ADHD treatment and reading intervention on the fluency and comprehension of children with ADHD and word reading difficulties: A randomized clinical trial. *Scientific Studies of Reading, 24*(1), 72–89.

Denton, C. A., Tolar, T. D., Fletcher, J. M., et al. (2013). Effects of tier 3 intervention for students with persistent reading difficulties and characteristics of inadequate responders. *Journal of Educational Psychology, 105*(3), 633–648.

Denton, K., Coneway, B., Simmons, M., Behl, M., & Shin, M. (2022). Parents' voices matter: A mixed-method study on the dyslexia diagnosis process. *Psychology in the Schools, 59*(11), 2267–2286.

Denton, T. F., & Meindl, J. N. (2016). The effect of colored overlays on reading fluency in individuals with dyslexia. *Behavior Analysis in Practice, 9*(3), 191–198.

Department of Education and Science. (1975). *A Language for Life*. The Bullock Report. London: HMSO.

Destokya, F., Bertels, J., Niesena, M., et al. (2022). The role of reading experience in atypical cortical tracking of speech and speech-in-noise in dyslexia. *Neuroimage, 253*.

Deutsch, G. K., Dougherty, R. F., Bammer, R., et al. (2005). Children's reading performance is correlated with white matter structure measured by diffusion tensor imaging. *Cortex, 41*, 354–363.

Di Folco, C., Guez, A., Peyre, H., & Ramus, F. (2022). Epidemiology of reading disability: A comparison of DSM-5 and ICD-11 criteria. *Scientific Studies of Reading, 26*(4), 337–355.

Di Liberto, G. M., Peter, V., Kalashnikova, M., et al. (2018). Atypical cortical entrainment to speech in the right hemisphere underpins phonemic deficits in dyslexia. *Neuroimage, 175*, 70–79.

Diamond, A. (2013). Executive functions. *Annual Review of Psychology, 64*, 135–168.

Dickman, E. (2017). Do we need a new definition of dyslexia? *The Examiner (International Dyslexia Association), 6*(1).

Dikker, S., Haegens, S., Bevilacqua, D., et al. (2020). Morning brain: Real-world neural evidence that high school class times matter. *Social Cognitive Affective Neuroscience, 15*, 1193–1202.

Dikker, S., Wan, L., Davidesco, I., et al. (2017). Brain-to-brain synchrony tracks real-world dynamic group interactions in the classroom. *Current Biology, 27*, 1375–1380.

Ding, Y., Zhao, J., He, T., et al. (2016). Selective impairments in covert shifts of attention in Chinese dyslexic children. *Dyslexia, 22*(4), 362–378.

Dirks, E., Spyer, G., van Lieshout, E. C., & de Sonneville, L. (2008). Prevalence of combined reading and arithmetic disabilities. *Journal of Learning Disabilities, 41*(5), 460–473.

Dobson Waters, S., & Torgerson, C. J. (2021). Dyslexia in higher education: A systematic review of interventions used to promote learning. *Journal of Further and Higher Education, 45*(2), 226–256.

Doehring, D. G. (1978). The tangled web of behavioral research on developmental dyslexia. In A. L. Benton, & D. Pearl (eds.), *Dyslexia: An Appraisal of Current Knowledge* (pp. 123–137). New York: Oxford University Press.

Doman, G., & Delacato, C. H. (1968). Learning and human achievement: Philosophy and concepts. *Human Potential, 1*, 113–116.

Dombrowski, S. C., Kamphaus, R. W., & Reynolds, C. R. (2004). After the demise of the discrepancy: Proposed learning disabilities diagnostic criteria. *Professional Psychology: Research and Practice, 35*(4), 364.

Dombrowski, S. C., J. McGill, R., Farmer, R. L., Kranzler, J. H., & Canivez, G. L. (2022). Beyond the rhetoric of evidence-based assessment: A framework for critical thinking in clinical practice. *School Psychology Review, 51*(6), 771–784.

Dombrowski, S. C., McGill, R. J., Watkins, M. W., et al. (2022). Will the real theoretical structure of the WISC-V please stand up? Implications for clinical interpretation. *Contemporary School Psychology, 26*(4), 492–503.

Donegan, R. E., & Wanzek, J. (2021). Effects of reading interventions implemented for upper elementary struggling readers: A look at recent research. *Reading and Writing, 34*(8), 1943–1977.

Donegan, R. E., Wanzek, J., & Al Otaiba, S. (2020). Effects of a reading intervention implemented at differing intensities for upper elementary students. *Learning Disabilities Research & Practice, 35*(2), 62–71.

Donegan, R. E., Wanzek, J., Petscher, Y., & Otaiba, S. A. (2023). The impact of student race, sex, and mindset on reading intervention response at the upper elementary level. *The Elementary School Journal, 123*(3), 437–456.

Donolato, E., Cardillo, R., Mammarella, I. C., & Melby-Lervåg, M. (2022). Research review: Language and specific learning disorders in children and their co-occurrence with internalizing and externalizing problems: A systematic review and meta-analysis. *Journal of Child Psychology and Psychiatry, 63*(5), 507–518.

Dore, W., & Brookes, D. (2006). *Dyslexia: The Miracle Cure*. London: Blake.

Dosenbach, N. U., Fair, D. A., Cohen, A. L., Schlaggar, B. L., & Petersen, S. E. (2008). A dual-networks architecture of top-down control. *Trends in Cognitive Sciences, 12*, 99–105.

Downing, C., & Caravolas, M. (2020). Prevalence and cognitive profiles of children with comorbid literacy and motor disorders. *Frontiers in Psychology*, 3347.

Dougherty, R. F., Ben-Shachar, M., Deutsch, G. K., et al. (2007). Temporal-callosal pathway diffusivity predicts phonological skills in children. *Proceedings of the National Academy of Sciences of the United States of America, 104*, 8556–8561.

Doust, C., Fontanillas, P., Eising, E., et al. (2022). Discovery of 42 genome-wide significant loci associated with dyslexia. *Nature Genetics, 54*, 1621–1629.

Doyon, J., Song, A. W., Karni, A., et al. (2002). Experience-dependent changes in cerebellar contributions to motor sequence learning. *Proceedings of the National Academy of Sciences of the United States of America, 99*, 1017–1022.

Drake, W. E. (1968). Clinical and pathological finding in a child with a developmental learning disability. *Journal of Learning Disabilities, 1*, 486–502.

Dresher, B. E. (2011). The phoneme. In M. van Oostendorp, C. J. Ewen, E. Hume, & K. Rice (eds.), *The Blackwell Companion to Phonology: Vol. 1* (pp. 241–266). Oxford: Wiley-Blackwell.

Duara, R., Kushch, A., Gross-Glenn, K., et al. (1991). Neuroanatomic differences between dyslexic and normal readers on magnetic resonance imaging scans. *Archives of Neurology, 48,* 410–416.

Dubois, M., Kyllingsboek, S., Prado, C., et al. (2010). Fractionating the multi-character processing deficit in developmental dyslexia: Evidence from two case studies. *Cortex, 46,* 717–738.

Duff, F. J., Hayiou-Thomas, M. E., & Hulme, C. (2012). Evaluating the effectiveness of a phonologically based reading intervention for struggling readers with varying language profiles. *Reading and Writing, 25,* 621–640.

Duff, F. J., Nation, K., Plunkett, K., & Bishop, D. (2015). Early prediction of language and literacy problems: Is 18 months too early? *PeerJ, 3,* e1098.

Dufor, O., Serniclaes, W., Sprenger-Charolles, L., & Demonet, J. F. (2007). Top-down processes during auditory phoneme categorization in dyslexia: A PET study. *Neuroimage, 34,* 1692–1707.

Duncan, C. C., Rumsey, J. M., Wilkniss, S. M., et al. (1994). Developmental dyslexia and attention dysfunction in adults: Brain potential indices of information processing. *Psychophysiology, 31,* 386–401.

Duncan, J. (2010). The multiple-demand (MD) system of the primate brain: Mental programs for intelligent behaviour. *Trends in Cognitive Sciences, 14,* 172–179.

Dvorsky, M., Tamm, L., Denton, C. A., Epstein, J. N., & Schatschneider, C. (2021). Trajectories of response to treatments in children with ADHD and word reading difficulties. *Research on Child and Adolescent Psychopathology, 49*(8), 1015–1030.

Dwyer, P. (2022). The neurodiversity approach(es): What are they and what do they mean for researchers? *Human Development, 66*(2), 73–92.

Dymock, S., & Nicholson, T. (2022). Dyslexia seen through the eyes of teachers: An exploratory survey. *Reading Research Quarterly, 58*(2), 333–344.

Dyslexia Foundation of New Zealand. (2008). *Dealing with Dyslexia: The Way Forward for New Zealand Educators.* Christchurch, New Zealand: Dyslexia Foundation of New Zealand.

Dyson, H., Best, W., Solity, J., & Hulme, C. (2017). Training mispronunciation correction and word meanings improves children's ability to learn to read words. *Scientific Studies of Reading, 21*(5), 392–407.

Ebrahimi, L., Pouretemad, H., Stein, J., Alizadeh, E., & Khatibi, A. (2022). Enhanced reading abilities is modulated by faster visual spatial attention. *Annals of Dyslexia, 72*(1), 125–146.

Eckert, M. A., Berninger, V. W., Vaden, K. I., Gebregziabher, M., & Tsu, L. (2016). Gray matter features of reading disability: A combined meta-analytic and direct analysis approach. *ENeuro, 3*(1).

Eckert, M. A., Leonard, C. M., Richards, T. L., et al. (2003). Anatomical correlates of dyslexia: Frontal and cerebellar findings. *Brain, 126,* 482–494.

Eckert, M. A., Leonard, C. M., Wilke, M., et al. (2005). Anatomical signatures of dyslexia in children: Unique information from manual and voxel based morphometry brain measures. *Cortex, 41,* 304–315.

Eden, G. F., VanMeter, J. W., Rumsey, J. M., et al. (1996). Abnormal processing of visual motion in dyslexia revealed by functional brain imaging. *Nature, 382,* 66–69.

Edwards, J. (1994). *The Scars of Dyslexia: Eight Case Studies in Emotional Reactions.* London: Continuum.

Ehm, J. H., Schmitterer, A. M., Nagler, T., & Lervåg, A. (2023). The underlying components of growth in decoding and reading comprehension: Findings from a 5-year longitudinal study of German-speaking children. *Scientific Studies of Reading, 27*(4), 311–333.

Ehri, L. C. (1999). Phases of development in learning to read words. In J. Oakhill, & R. Beard (eds.), *Reading Development and the Teaching of Reading: A Psychological Perspective* (pp. 79–108). Oxford: Blackwell.

Ehri, L. C. (2002). Phases of acquisition in learning to read words and implications for teaching. *British Journal of Educational Psychology: Monograph Series, 1,* 7–28.

Ehri, L. C. (2020). The science of learning to read words: A case for systematic phonics instruction. *Reading Research Quarterly, 55,* S45–S60.

Ehri, L. C., Nunes, S. R., Stahl, S. A., & Willows, D. M. (2001). Systematic phonics instruction helps students learn to read: Evidence from the National Reading Panel's meta-analysis. *Review of Educational Research, 71,* 393–447.

Eicher, J. D., Powers, N. R., Miller, L. L., et al. (2013). Genome-wide association study of shared components of reading disability and language impairment. *Genes, Brain and Behavior, 12,* 792–801.

Eicher, J. D., Stein, C. M., Deng, F., et al. (2015). The DYX2 locus and neurochemical signaling genes contribute to speech sound disorder and related neurocognitive domains. *Genes, Brain and Behavior, 14*(4), 377–385.

Eide, B. L., & Eide, F. F. (2011). *The Dyslexic Advantage: Unlocking the Hidden Potential of the Dyslexic Brain.* New York: Hudson Street Press.

Eising, E., Mirza-Schreiber, N., de Zeeuw, E. L., et al. (2022). Genome-wide analyses of individual differences in quantitatively assessed reading- and language-related skills in up to 34,000 people. *Proceedings of the National Academy of Sciences, 119,* e2202764119.

Einarsdottir, E., Svensson, I., Darki, F., et al. (2015). Mutation in CEP63 co-segregating with developmental dyslexia in a Swedish family. *Human Genetics, 134,* 1239–1248.

Eising, E., Mirza-Schreiber, N., de Zeeuw, E. L., et al. (2022). Genome-wide analyses of individual differences in quantitatively assessed reading- and language-related skills in up to 34,000 people. *Proceedings of the National Academy of Sciences, 119,* e2202764119.

Ekert, J. O., Lorca-Puls, D. L., Gajardo-Vidal, A., et al. (2021). A functional dissociation of the left frontal regions that contribute to single word production tasks. *Neuroimage, 245,* 118734.

Elbeheri, G., & Everatt, J. (2009). Dyslexia and IQ: From research to practice. In G. Reid (ed.), *The Routledge Companion to Dyslexia* (pp. 22–32). London: Routledge.

Elbeheri, G., & Siang, L. (eds.). (2023). *The Routledge International Handbook of Dyslexia in Education*. London: Routledge.

Elliott, J. G. (2020). It's time to be scientific about dyslexia. *Reading Research Quarterly*, *55*, S61–S75.

Elliott, J. G., Gathercole, S. E., Alloway, T. P., Kirkwood, H., & Holmes, J. (2010). An evaluation of a classroom-based intervention to help overcome working memory difficulties. *Journal of Cognitive Education and Psychology*, *9*, 227–250.

Elliott, J. G., & Gibbs, S. J. (2008). Does dyslexia exist? *Journal of Philosophy of Education*, *42*(3–4), 475–491.

Elliott, J. G., & Grigorenko, E. L. (2014). *The Dyslexia Debate*. New York: Cambridge University Press.

Elliott, J. G., & Place, M. (2019). Practitioner review: School refusal: Developments in conceptualisation and treatment since 2000. *Journal of Child Psychology and Psychiatry*, *60*(1), 4–15.

Elliott, J. G., & Place, M. (2021). *Children in Difficulty: A Guide to Understanding and Helping*. 4th edition. London: Routledge.

Elliott, J. G., & Resing, W. C. (2015). Can intelligence testing inform educational intervention for children with reading disability? *Journal of Intelligence*, *3*(4), 137–157.

Elliott, J. G., & Resing, W. C. (2019). Extremes of intelligence. In R. J. Sternberg (ed.). *Human Intelligence*, (pp. 317–348). New York: Cambridge University Press.

Ellis, C., Holston, S., Drake, G., Putman, H., Swisher, A., & Peske, H. (2023). *Teacher Prep Review: Strengthening Elementary Reading Instruction*. Washington, DC: National Council on Teacher Quality.

Elston, R. C., & Johnson, W. D. (2008). *Basic Biostatistics for Geneticists and Epidemiologists*. Chichester: Wiley.

Engle, R. W. (2002). Working memory capacity as executive attention. *Current Directions in Psychological Science*, *11*(1), 19–23.

Erbeli, F., Hart, S. A., & Taylor, J. (2018). Longitudinal associations among reading-related skills and reading comprehension: A twin study. *Child Development*, *89*, e480–e493.

Erbeli, F., Hart, S. A., & Taylor, J. (2019). Genetic and environmental influences on achievement outcomes based on family history of learning disabilities status. *Journal of Learning Disabilities*, *52*, 135–145.

Erbeli, F., Peng, P., & Rice, M. (2022). No evidence of creative benefit accompanying dyslexia: A meta-analysis. *Journal of Learning Disabilities*, *55*(3), 242–253.

Erbeli, F., & Rice, M. (2022). Examining the effects of silent independent reading on reading outcomes: A narrative synthesis review from 2000 to 2020. *Reading & Writing Quarterly*, *38*(3), 253–271.

Erbeli, F., Rice, M., & Paracchini, S. (2022). Insights into dyslexia genetics research from the last two decades. *Brain Sciences*, *12*, 27.

Ercan-Sencicek, A. G., Davis Wright, N. R., Sanders, S. S., et al. (2012). A balanced t(10;15) translocation in a male patient with developmental language disorder. *European Journal of Medical Genetics*, *55*, 128–131.

References

Essex, M. J., Boyce, W. T., Hertzman, C., et al. (2013). Epigenetic vestiges of early developmental adversity: Childhood stress exposure and DNA methylation in adolescence. *Child Development, 84*, 58–75.

Evans, B. J., & Allen, P. M. (2016). A systematic review of controlled trials on visual stress using Intuitive Overlays or the Intuitive Colorimeter. *Journal of Optometry, 9*(4), 205–218.

EY (Ernst and Young). (2018). *The Value of Dyslexia: Dyslexic Strengths and the Changing World of Work*. London: EY.

Fabbro, F., Pesenti, S., Facoetti, A., et al. (2001). Callosal transfer in different subtypes of developmental dyslexia. *Cortex, 37*, 65–73.

Facoetti, A., Franceschini, S., & Gori, S. (2019). Role of visual attention in developmental dyslexia. In L. Verhoeven, C. Perfetti, & K. Pugh (eds.), *Developmental Dyslexia across Languages and Writing Systems* (pp. 307–326). Cambridge: Cambridge University Press.

Facoetti, A., Trussardi, A. N., Ruffino, M., et al. (2009). Multisensory spatial attention deficits are predictive of phonological decoding skills in developmental dyslexia. *Journal of Cognitive Neuroscience, 22*, 1011–1025.

Fagerheim, T., Raeymaekers, P., Tonnessen, F. E., et al. (1999). A new gene (DYX3) for dyslexia is located on chromosome 2. *Journal of Medical Genetics, 35*, 664–669.

Farmer, M. E., & Klein, R. M. (1995). The evidence for a temporal processing deficit linked to dyslexia: A review. *Psychonomic Bulletin & Review, 2*, 460–493.

Farmer, R. L., McGill, R. J., Dombrowski, S. C., & Canivez, G. L. (2021). Why questionable assessment practices remain popular in school psychology: Instructional materials as pedagogic vehicles. *Canadian Journal of School Psychology, 36*(2), 98–114.

Farris, E. A., Odegard, T. N., Miller, H. L., et al. (2011). Functional connectivity between the left and right inferior frontal lobes in a small sample of children with and without reading difficulties. *Neurocase, 17*, 425–439.

Farris, E. A., Ring, J., Black, J., Lyon, G. R., & Odegard, T. N. (2016). Predicting growth in word level reading skills in children with developmental dyslexia using an object rhyming functional neuroimaging task. *Developmental Neuropsychology, 41*, 145–161.

Favell, J. E. (2005). Sifting sound practice from snake oil. In J. W. Jacobson, R. M. Foxx, & J. A. Mulick (eds.), *Controversial Therapies for Developmental Disabilities: Fad, Fashion and Science in Professional Practice* (pp. 19–30). Mahwah, NJ: Lawrence Erlbaum.

Fawcett, A. J., & Nicolson, R. I. (1999). Performance of dyslexic children on cerebellar and cognitive tests. *Journal of Motor Behavior, 31*, 68–78.

Fawcett, A. J., Nicolson, R. I., & Maclagan, F. (2001). Cerebellar tests differentiate between groups of poor readers with and without IQ discrepancy. *Journal of Learning Disabilities, 34*(2), 119–135.

Fawcett, A. J., & Reid, G. (2009). Dyslexia and alternative interventions for dyslexia: A critical commentary. In G. Reid (ed.), *The Routledge Companion to Dyslexia* (pp. 157–174). New York: Routledge.

Feldman, H. M., Yeatman, J. D., Lee, E. S., Barde, L. H., & Gaman-Bean, S. (2010). Diffusion tensor imaging: A review for pediatric researchers and clinicians. *Journal of Developmental & Behavioral Pediatrics, 31,* 346–356.

Feldon, D. F., & Litson, K. (2021). Modeling theories and theorizing models: An attempted replication of Miller-Cotto & Byrnes' (2019) comparison of working memory models using ECLS-K Data. *Educational Psychology Review, 33*(4), 1907–1934.

Feng, X., Altarelli, I., Monzalvo, K., et al. (2020). A universal reading network and its modulation by writing system and reading ability in French and Chinese children. *eLife, 9,* e54591.

Feng, X., Monzalvo, K., Dehaene, S., & Dehaene-Lambertz, G. (2022). Evolution of reading and face circuits during the first three years of reading acquisition. *Neuroimage, 259,* 119394.

Fernald, G. M., & Keller, H. (1921). The effect of kinaesthetic factors in the development of word recognition in the case of non-readers. *The Journal of Educational Research, 4,* 355–377.

Fernandez-Duque, D. (2017). Lay theories of the mind/brain relationship and the allure of neuroscience. In C. M. Zedelius, B. Müller, & J. W. Schooler (eds.), *The Science of Lay Theories: How Beliefs Shape Our Cognition, Behavior, and Health* (pp. 207–227). Cham, Switzerland: Springer.

Fernandez-Duque, D., Evans, J., Christian, C., & Hodges, S. D. (2015). Superfluous neuroscience information makes explanations of psychological phenomena more appealing. *Journal of Cognitive Neuroscience, 27*(5), 926–944.

Ferrer, E., Shaywitz, B. A., Holahan, J. M., Marchione, K., & Shaywitz, S. E. (2010). Uncoupling of reading and IQ over time: Empirical evidence for a definition of dyslexia. *Psychological Science, 21,* 93–101.

Ferrer, E., Shaywitz, B. A., Holahan, J. M., & Shaywitz, S. E. (2022). Family history is not useful in screening children for dyslexia. *Journal of Pediatric Neuropsychology, 8*(1), 15–21.

Field, L. L., Shumansky, K., Ryan, J., et al. (2013). Dense-map genome scan for dyslexia supports loci at 4q13, 16p12, 17q22; suggests novel locus at 7q36. *Genes, Brain and Behavior, 12,* 56–69.

Fields, R. D. (2008). White matter matters. *Scientific American, 298,* 42–49.

Fiez, J. A., Tranel, D., Seager-Frerichs, D., & Damasio, H. (2006). Specific reading and phonological processing deficits are associated with damage to the left frontal operculum. *Cortex, 42*(4), 624–643.

Filderman, M. J., Toste, J. R., Didion, L. A., Peng, P., & Clemens, N. H. (2018). Data-based decision making in reading interventions: A synthesis and meta-analysis of the effects for struggling readers. *The Journal of Special Education, 52*(3), 174–187.

Filderman, M. J., Toste, J. R., Didion, L., & Peng, P. (2022). Data literacy training for K–12 teachers: A meta-analysis of the effects on teacher outcomes. *Remedial and Special Education, 43*(5), 328–343.

Finch, A. J., Nicolson, R. I., & Fawcett, A. J. (2002). Evidence for a neuroanatomical difference within the olivo-cerebellar pathway of adults with dyslexia. *Cortex, 38,* 529–539.

Finlay-Jones, A., Varcin, K., Leonard, H., et al. (2019). Very early identification and intervention for infants at risk of neurodevelopmental disorders: A transdiagnostic approach. *Child Development Perspectives, 13*(2), 97–103.

Finn, E. S., Shen, X., Holahan, J. M., et al. (2014). Disruption of functional networks in dyslexia: A whole-brain, data-driven analysis of connectivity. *Biological Psychiatry, 76*, 397–404.

First Step Act of 2018, Pub.L. No. 115-391. (2018). www.congress.gov/115/plaws/pub1391/PLAW-115pub1391.pdf

Fischl, B., Sereno, M. I., & Dale, A. M. (1999). Cortical surface-based analysis. II: Inflation, flattening, and a surface-based coordinate system. *Neuroimage, 9*, 195–207.

Fish, R. E. (2019). Standing out and sorting in: Exploring the role of racial composition in racial disparities in special education. *American Educational Research Journal, 56*(6), 2573–2608.

Fish, R. E. (2022a). Stratified medicalization of schooling difficulties. *Social Science & Medicine*, 115039.

Fish, R. E. (2022b). The role of socioeconomic and ethnic disparities for dyslexia and dyscalculia. In M. A. Skeide (ed.), *The Cambridge Handbook of Dyslexia and Dyscalculia* (pp. 251–262). Cambridge: Cambridge University Press.

Fisher, S. E., Francks, C., Marlow, A. J., et al. (2002). Independent genome-wide scans identify a chromosome 18 quantitative-trait locus influencing dyslexia. *Nature Genetics, 30*, 86–91.

Flanagan, D. P., Costa, M., Palma, K., Leahy, M. A., Alfonso, V. C., & Ortiz, S. O. (2018). Cross-battery assessment, the cross-battery assessment software system, and the assessment–intervention connection. In D. P. Flanagan, & E. M. McDonough (eds.), *Contemporary Intellectual Assessment: Theories, Tests, and Issues* (pp. 731–776). New York: Guilford Press.

Flannery, K. A., Liederman, J., Daly, L., & Schultz, J. (2000). Male prevalence for reading disability is found in a large sample of Black and White children free from ascertainment bias. *Journal of the International Neuropsychological Society, 6*, 433–442.

Flaugnacco, E., Lopez, L., Terribili, C., et al. (2015). Music training increases phonological awareness and reading skills in developmental dyslexia: A randomized control trial. *PloS one, 10*(9), e0138715.

Flesch, R. (1955). *Why Johnny Can't Read and What You Can Do about It.* New York: Harper & Row.

Fletcher, J. M. (2009). Dyslexia: The evolution of a scientific concept. *Journal of the International Neuropsychological Society, 15*(4), 501–508.

Fletcher, J. M., Francis, D. J., Foorman, B. R., & Schatschneider, C. (2021). Early detection of dyslexia risk: Development of brief, teacher-administered screens. *Learning Disability Quarterly, 44*(3), 145–157.

Fletcher, J. M., Lyon, G. R., Fuchs, L. S., & Barnes, M. A. (2007). *Learning Disabilities: From Identification to Intervention.* New York: Guilford Publications.

Fletcher, J. M., Lyon, G. R., Fuchs, L. S., & Barnes, M. A. (2019). *Learning Disabilities: From Identification to Intervention.* 2nd edition. New York: Guilford Press.

Fletcher, J. M., & Miciak, J. (2017). Comprehensive cognitive assessments are not necessary for the identification and treatment of learning disabilities. *Archives of Clinical Neuropsychology, 32*(1), 2–7.

Fletcher, J. M., Morris, R. D., & Lyon, G. R. (2003). Classification and definition of learning disabilities: An integrative perspective. In H. L. Swanson, K. R. Harris, & S. Graham (eds.), *Handbook of Learning Disabilities* (pp. 30–56). New York: Guilford Press.

Fletcher, J. M., Savage, R., & Vaughn, S. (2021). A commentary on Bowers (2020) and the role of phonics instruction in reading. *Educational Psychology Review, 33*(3), 1249–1274.

Fletcher, J. M., Stuebing, K. K., Barth, A. E., et al. (2011). Cognitive correlates of inadequate response to reading intervention. *School Psychology Review, 40*, 3–22.

Fletcher, J. M., Stuebing, K. K., Barth, A. E., Mi et al. (2014). Agreement and coverage of indicators of response to intervention: A multi-method comparison and simulation. *Topics in Language and Learning Disorders, 34*, 74–89.

Fletcher, J. M., Stuebing, K. K., Morris, R. D., & Lyon, G. R. (2013). Classification and definition of learning disabilities: A hybrid model. In H. L. Swanson, K. R. Harris, & S. Graham (eds.), *Handbook of Learning Disabilities*. 2nd edition (pp. 33–50). New York: Guilford Press.

Fletcher, J. M., & Vaughn, S. (2009). Response to intervention: Preventing and remediating academic difficulties. *Child Development Perspectives, 3*, 30–37.

Fletcher-Watson, S. (2022). Transdiagnostic research and the neurodiversity paradigm: Commentary on the transdiagnostic revolution in neurodevelopmental disorders by Astle et al. *Journal of Child Psychology and Psychiatry, 63*(4), 418–420.

Fliedner, A., Kirchner, P., Wiesener, A., et al. (2020). Variants in SCAF4 cause a neurodevelopmental disorder and are associated with impaired mRNA processing. *American Journal of Human Genetics, 107*, 544–554.

Flowers, L., Meyer, M., Lovato, J., Wood, F., & Felton, R. (2001). Does third grade discrepancy status predict the course of reading development? *Annals of Dyslexia, 51*, 49–71.

Flynn, J. M., & Rahbar, M. H. (1994). Prevalence of reading failure in boys compared with girls. *Psychology in the Schools, 31*, 66–70.

Flynn, L. J., Zheng, X., & Swanson, H. L. (2012). Instructing struggling older readers: A selective meta-analysis of intervention research. *Learning Disabilities Research & Practice, 27*(1), 21–32.

Follmer, D. J. (2018). Executive function and reading comprehension: A meta-analytic review. *Educational Psychologist, 53*(1), 42–60.

Foorman, B. R. (2003). *Preventing and Remediating Reading Difficulties: Bringing Science to Scale*. Baltimore, MD: York Press.

Foorman, B. R., Anthony, J., Seals, L., & Mouzaki, A. (2002). Language development and emergent literacy in preschool. *Seminars in Pediatric Neurology, 9*, 172–183.

Foorman, B. R., York, M., Santi, K. L., & Francis, D. (2008). Contextual effects on predicting risk for reading difficulties in first and second grade. *Reading and Writing, 21*, 371–394.

Foucault, M. (1989) *The Birth of the Clinic: An Archaeology of Medical Perception.* London: Routledge.

Fox, M. D., & Raichle, M. E. (2007). Spontaneous fluctuations in brain activity observed with functional magnetic resonance imaging. *Nature Review Neuroscience, 8,* 700–711.

Franceschini, S., Bertoni, S., Puccio, G., et al. (2022). Visuo-spatial attention deficit in children with reading difficulties. *Scientific Reports, 12*(1), 1–10.

Franceschini, S., Bertoni, S., Ronconi, L., et al. (2015). "Shall we play a game?": Improving reading through action video games in developmental dyslexia. *Current Developmental Disorders Reports, 2*(4), 318–329.

Franceschini, S., Gori, S., Ruffino, M., Pedrolli, K., & Facoetti, A. (2012). A causal link between visual spatial attention and reading acquisition. *Current Biology, 22,* 814–819.

Franceschini, S., Gori, S., Ruffino, M., et al. (2013). Action video games make dyslexic children read better. *Current Biology, 23*(6), 462–466.

Franceschini, S., Mascheretti, S., Bertoni, S., et al. (2018). Sluggish dorsally-driven inhibition of return during orthographic processing in adults with dyslexia. *Brain and Language, 179,* 1–10.

Franceschini, S., Trevisan, P., Ronconi, L., et al. (2017). Action video games improve reading abilities and visual-to-auditory attentional shifting in English-speaking children with dyslexia. *Scientific Reports, 7*(1), 1–12.

Francis, D. A., Caruana, N., Hudson, J. L., & McArthur, G. M. (2019). The association between poor reading and internalising problems: A systematic review and meta-analysis. *Clinical Psychology Review, 67,* 45–60.

Francis, D. J., Shaywitz, S. E., Stuebing, K. K., Shaywitz, B. A., & Fletcher, J. M. (1996). Developmental lag versus deficit models of reading disability: A longitudinal individual growth curves analysis. *Journal of Educational Psychology, 88,* 3–17.

Franks, K., & Frederick, H. (2013). Dyslexic and entrepreneur: Typologies, commonalities, and differences. *Journal of Asia Entrepreneurship and Sustainability, 11*(1), 95–115.

Franquinho, F., Nogueira-Rodrigues, J., Duarte, J. M., et al. (2017). The dyslexia-susceptibility protein KIAA0319 inhibits axon growth through Smad2 signaling. *Cerebral Cortex, 27,* 1732–1747.

Friend, A., DeFries, J. C., & Olson, R. K. (2008). Parental education moderates genetic influences on reading disability. *Psychological Science, 19,* 1–7.

Frith, U. (1997). Brain, mind and behaviour in dyslexia. In C. Hulme, & M. J. Snowling (eds.), *Dyslexia: Biology, Cognition, and Intervention* (pp. 1–19). London: Whurr.

Froehlich, T. E., Fogler, J., Barbaresi, W. J., et al. (2018). Using ADHD medications to treat coexisting ADHD and reading disorders: A systematic review. *Clinical Pharmacology & Therapeutics, 104*(4), 619–637.

Frost, R., Katz, L., & Bentin, S. (1987). Strategies for visual word recognition and orthographical depth: A multilingual comparison. *Journal of Experimental Psychology: Human Perception and Performance, 13,* 104–115.

Frye, R. E., Hasan, K., Xue, L., et al. (2008). Splenium microstructure is related to two dimensions of reading skill. *Neuroreport, 19,* 1627–1631.

Frye, R. E., Liederman, J., Malmberg, B., et al. (2010). Surface area accounts for the relation of gray matter volume to reading-related skills and history of dyslexia. *Cerebral Cortex, 20,* 2625–2635.

Fu, W., Zhao, J., Ding, Y., & Wang, Z. (2019). Dyslexic children are sluggish in disengaging spatial attention. *Dyslexia, 25*(2), 158–172.

Fuchs, D., & Fuchs, L. S. (2017). Critique of the national evaluation of response to intervention: A case for simpler frameworks. *Exceptional Children, 83*(3), 255–268.

Fuchs, D., Fuchs, L. S., & Compton, D. L. (2012). Smart RTI: A next generation approach to multilevel prevention. *Exceptional Children, 78*(3), 263–279.

Fuchs, D., McMaster, K. L., Fuchs, L. S., & Al Otaiba, S. (2013). Data-based individualization as a means of providing intensive instruction to students with serious learning disorders. In H. L. Swanson, K. R. Harris, & S. Graham (eds.), *Handbook of Learning Disabilities.* 2nd edition (pp. 526–544). New York: Guilford Press.

Fuchs, L. S., Fuchs, D., Hamlett, C. L., & Stecker, P. M. (2021). Bringing data-based individualization to scale: A call for the next-generation technology of teacher supports. *Journal of Learning Disabilities, 54*(5), 319–333.

Fuchs, L. S., & Vaughn, S. (2012). Responsiveness-to-intervention: A decade later. *Journal of Learning Disabilities, 45*(3), 195–203.

Fuller, M., Healey, M., Bradley, A., & Hall, T. (2004) Barriers to learning: A systematic study of the experience of disabled students in one university. *Studies in Higher Education, 29,* 303–318.

Furnes, B., & Samuelsson, S. (2010). Predicting reading and spelling difficulties in transparent and opaque orthographies: A comparison between Scandinavian and US/Australian children. *Dyslexia, 16,* 119–142.

Furnes, B., Elwér, Å., Samuelsson, S., Olson, R. K., & Byrne, B. (2019). Investigating the double-deficit hypothesis in more and less transparent orthographies: A longitudinal study from preschool to grade 2. *Scientific Studies of Reading, 23*(6), 478–493.

Future Market Insights. (2022). Dyslexia Treatment Market Size, Share, Outlook, Trend and Forecast (www.marketresearchintellect.com) (Rep-GB-5281). Accessed June 1, 2023.

Gaab, N., & Petscher, Y. (2022). Screening for early literacy milestones and reading disabilities: The why, when, whom, how, and where. *Perspectives on Language and Literacy,* 11–18.

Gabay, Y., & Holt, L. L. (2021). Adaptive plasticity under adverse listening conditions is disrupted in developmental dyslexia. *Journal of the International Neuropsychological Society, 27*(1), 12–22.

Gabel, L. A., Gibson, C. J., Gruen, J. R., & LoTurco, J. J. (2010). Progress towards a cellular neurobiology of reading disability. *Neurobiology of Disease, 38,* 173–180.

Gabriel, R. E. (2020a). Converting to privatization: A discourse analysis of dyslexia policy narratives. *American Educational Research Journal, 57*(1), 305–338.

Gabriel, R. E. (2020b). The future of the science of reading. *The Reading Teacher*, *74*(1), 11–18.

Gabriel, R., & Kelley, S. L. (2021) It's about time: Constructing dyslexia in higher education. In J. N. Lester (ed.), *Discursive Psychology and Disability* (pp. 143–168). London: Palgrave Macmillan,

Gabrieli, J. D. (2016). The promise of educational neuroscience: Comment on Bowers (2016). *Psychological Review*, *123*, 613–619.

Gabrieli, J. D. E. (2009). Dyslexia: A new synergy between education and cognitive neuroscience. *Science*, *325*, 280–283.

Galaburda, A. M. (1993). Neuroanatomic basis of developmental dyslexia. *Neurology Clinics*, *11*, 161–173.

Galaburda, A. M., & Kemper, T. L. (1979). Cytoarchitectonic abnormalities in developmental dyslexia: A case study. *Annals of Neurology*, *6*, 94–100.

Galaburda, A. M., LoTurco, J. J., Ramus, F., Fitch, R. H., & Rosen, G. D. (2006). From genes to behavior in developmental dyslexia. *Nature Neuroscience*, *9*, 1213–1217.

Galaburda, A. M., Menard, M. T., & Rosen, G. D. (1994). Evidence for aberrant auditory anatomy in developmental dyslexia. *PNAS*, *91*, 8010–8013.

Galaburda, A. M., Schrott, L. M., & Sherman, G. F. Rosen, G. D., & Denenberg, V. H. (1996). Animal models of developmental dyslexia. In C. H. Chase, G. D. Rosen, & G. F. Sherman (eds.), *Developmental Dyslexia* (pp. 3–14). Baltimore: York Press.

Galaburda, A. M., Sherman, G. F., Rosen, G. D., Aboitiz, F., & Gerschwin, N. (1985). Developmental dyslexia: Four consecutive patients with cortical anomalies. *Annals of Neurology*, *18*, 222–233.

Gallagher, A., & Frederickson, N. 1995. The Phonological Assessment Battery (PhAB): An initial assessment of its theoretical and practical utility. *Educational and Child Psychology*, *12*, 53–67.

Galliussi, J., Perondi, L., Chia, G., Gerbino, W., & Bernardis, P. (2020). Inter-letter spacing, inter-word spacing, and font with dyslexia-friendly features: Testing text readability in people with and without dyslexia. *Annals of Dyslexia*, *70*(1), 141–152.

Galuschka, K., Ise, E., Krick, K., & Schulte-Körne, G. (2014). Effectiveness of treatment approaches for children and adolescents with reading disabilities: A meta-analysis of randomized controlled trials. *PloS one*, *9*(2), e89900.

Gao, F., Wang, R., Armada-da-Silva, P., et al. (2022). How the brain encodes morphological constraints during Chinese word reading: An EEG-fNIRS study. *Cortex*, *154*, 184–196.

Garcini, L. M., Arredondo, M. M., Berry, O., et al. (2022). Increasing diversity in developmental cognitive neuroscience: A roadmap for increasing representation in pediatric neuroimaging research. *Developmental Cognitive Neuroscience*, *58*, 101167.

Gartland, D., & Strosnider, R. (2020). The use of response to intervention to inform special education eligibility decisions for students with specific learning disabilities. *Learning Disability Quarterly*, *43*(4), 195–200.

Gathercole, S. E., & Alloway, T. P. (2008). *Working Memory & Learning: A Practical Guide for Teachers.* London: SAGE.

Gathercole, S. E., Dunning, D. L., Holmes, J., & Norris, D. (2019). Working memory training involves learning new skills. *Journal of Memory and Language, 105*, 19–42.

Gathercole, S. E., Woolgar, F., Kievit, R. A., et al. (2016). How common are WM deficits in children with difficulties in reading and mathematics? *Journal of Applied Research in Memory and Cognition, 5*(4), 384–394.

Gavril, L., Roşan, A., & Szamosközi, Ş. (2021). The role of visual-spatial attention in reading development: A meta-analysis. *Cognitive Neuropsychology, 38*(6), 387–407.

Gayán, J., & Olson, R. K. (1999). Reading disability: Evidence for a genetic etiology. *European Child and Adolescent Psychiatry, 8*, 52–55.

Gayán, J., & Olson, R. K. (2001). Genetic and environmental influences on orthographic and phonological skills in children with reading disabilities. *Developmental Neurology, 20*, 483–507.

Gayán, J., & Olson, R. K. (2003). Genetic and environmental influences on individual differences in printed word recognition. *Journal of Experimental Child Psychology, 84*, 97–123.

Gearin, B., Petscher, Y., Stanley, C., Nelson, N. J., & Fien, H. (2022). Document analysis of state dyslexia legislation suggests likely heterogeneous effects on student and school outcomes. *Learning Disability Quarterly, 45*(4), 267–279.

Gebauer, D., Fink, A., Kargl, R., et al. (2012). Differences in brain function and changes with intervention in children with poor spelling and reading abilities. *PLoS ONE, 7*, e38201.

Georgiewa, P., Rzanny, R., Gaser, C., et al. (2002). Phonological processing in dyslexic children: A study combining functional imaging and event related potentials. *Neuroscience Letters, 318*, 5–8.

Georgiewa, P., Rzanny, R., Hopf, J. M., et al. (1999). fMRI during word processing in dyslexic and normal reading children. *Neuroreport, 10*, 3459–3465.

Georgiou, G. K., Aro, M., Liao, C. H., & Parrila, R. (2016). Modeling the relationship between rapid automatized naming and literacy skills across languages varying in orthographic consistency. *Journal of Experimental Child Psychology, 143*, 48–64.

Georgiou, G. K., Inoue, T., & Parrila, R. (2021). Developmental relations between home literacy environment, reading interest, and reading skills: Evidence from a 3-year longitudinal study. *Child Development, 92*(5), 2053–2068.

Georgiou, G. K., Inoue, T., & Parrila, R. (2023). Are vocabulary and word reading reciprocally related? *Scientific Studies of Reading, 27*(2), 160–168.

Georgiou, G. K., Martinez, D., Vieira, A. P. A., et al. (2022). A meta-analytic review of comprehension deficits in students with dyslexia. *Annals of Dyslexia, 72*(2), 204–248.

Georgiou, G. K., Martinez, D., Vieira, A. P. A., & Guo, K. (2021). Is orthographic knowledge a strength or a weakness in individuals with dyslexia? Evidence from a meta-analysis. *Annals of Dyslexia, 71*(1), 5–27.

Georgiou, G. K., Papadopoulos, T. C., Zarouna, E., & Parrila, R. (2012). Are auditory and visual processing deficits related to developmental dyslexia? *Dyslexia, 18*(2), 110–129.

Georgiou, G. K., & Parrila, R., (2013). Rapid automatized naming and reading: A review. In H. L. Swanson, K. R. Harris, & S. Graham (eds.), *Handbook of Learning Disabilities* (pp. 169–185). New York: Guilford Press.

Georgiou, G. K., Parrila, R., Cui, Y., & Papadopoulos, T. C. (2013). Why is rapid automatized naming related to reading? *Journal of Experimental Child Psychology, 115*(1), 218–225.

Georgiou, G. K., Parrila, R., & Kirby, J. R. (2009). RAN components and reading development from grade 3 to grade 5: What underlies their relationship? *Scientific Studies of Reading, 13,* 508–534.

Georgiou, G. K., Parrila, R., & Papadopoulos, T. C. (2016). The anatomy of the RAN-reading relationship. *Reading and Writing, 29*(9), 1793–1815.

Georgiou, G. K., Protopapas, A., Papadopoulos, T. C., Skaloumbakas, C., & Parrila (2010). Auditory temporal processing and dyslexia in an orthographically consistent language. *Cortex, 46,* 1330–1344.

Georgiou, G. K., Vieira, A. P. A., Rothou, K. M., et al. (2023). A meta-analysis of morphological awareness deficits in developmental dyslexia. *Scientific Studies of Reading, 27*(3), 253–271.

Georgitsi, M., Dermitzakis, I., Soumelidou, E., & Bonti, E. (2021). The polygenic nature and complex genetic architecture of specific learning disorder. *Brain Sciences, 11,* 631.

Gerber, P. J., & Raskind, M. H. (2013). *Leaders, Visionaries, Dreamers: Extraordinary People with Dyslexia and Other Learning Disabilities.* New York: Nova Science.

Gerst, E. H., Cirino, P. T., Macdonald, K. T., et al. (2021). The structure of processing speed in children and its impact on reading. *Journal of Cognition and Development, 22*(1), 84–107.

Gersten, R., Haymond, K., Newman-Gonchar, R., Dimino, J., & Jayanthi, M. (2020). Meta-analysis of the impact of reading interventions for students in the primary grades. *Journal of Research on Educational Effectiveness, 13*(2), 401–427.

Gersten, R., Jayanthi, M., & Dimino, J. (2017). Too much, too soon? Unanswered questions from national response to intervention evaluation. *Exceptional Children, 83*(3), 244–254.

Geschwind, N., & Levitsky, W. (1968). Human brain: Left-right asymmetries in temporal speech region. *Science, 161,* 186–187.

Getchell, N., Pabreja, P., Neeld, K., & Carrio, V. (2007). Comparing children with and without dyslexia on the movement assessment battery for children and the test of gross motor development. *Perceptual and Motor Skills, 105,* 207–214.

Gialluisi, A., Andlauer, T. F. M., Mirza-Schreiber, N., et al. (2020). Genome-wide association study reveals new insights into the heritability and genetic correlates of developmental dyslexia. *Molecular Psychiatry,* 3004–3017.

Gialluisi, A., Andlauer, T. F. M., Mirza-Schreiber, N., et al. (2021). Genome-wide association study reveals new insights into the heritability and genetic correlates of developmental dyslexia. *Molecular Psychiatry, 26,* 3004–3017.

Gialluisi, A., Andlauer, T. F. M., Mirza-Schreiber, N., et al. (2019). Genome-wide association scan identifies new variants associated with a cognitive predictor of dyslexia. *Translational Psychiatry*, *9*, 77.

Gialluisi, A., Newbury, D. F., Wilcutt, E. G., et al. (2014). Genome-wide screening for DNA variants associated with reading and language traits. *Genes, Brain and Behavior*, *13*, 686–701.

Gibbs, S. J., & Elliott, J. G. (2015). The differential effects of labelling: How do "dyslexia" and "reading difficulties" affect teachers' beliefs. *European Journal of Special Needs Education*, *30*(3), 323–337.

Gibbs, S. J., & Elliott, J. G. (2020). The dyslexia debate: Life without the label. *Oxford Review of Education*, *46*(4), 487–500.

Gibby-Leversuch, R., Hartwell, B. K., & Wright, S. (2021). Dyslexia, literacy difficulties and the self-perceptions of children and young people: A systematic review. *Current Psychology*, *40*(11), 5595–5612.

Gilger, J. W., Allen, K., & Castillo, A. (2016). Reading disability and enhanced dynamic spatial reasoning: A review of the literature. *Brain and Cognition*, *105*, 55–65.

Gilger, J. W., Pennington, B. F., & DeFries, J. C. (1992). A twin study of the etiology of comorbidity: Attention deficit-hyperactivity disorder and dyslexia. *Journal of the American Academy of Child and Adolescent Psychiatry*, *31*, 343–348.

Gillam, R. B., Loeb, D. F., Hoffman, L. M., et al. (2008). The efficacy of Fast ForWord language intervention in school-age children with language impairment: A randomized controlled trial. *Journal of Speech, Language, and Hearing Research*, *52*, 97–119.

Gillingham, A., & Stillman, B. W. (1997). *The Gillingham Manual: Remedial Training for Children with Specific Disability in Reading, Spelling, and Penmanship*. 8th edition. Cambridge, MA: Educators Publishing Service.

Gilmore, J. H., Knickmeyer, R. C., & Gao, W. (2018). Imaging structural and functional brain development in early childhood. *Nature Reviews Neuroscience*, *19*(3), 123–137.

Gilroy, D. E., & Miles, T. R. (1996) *Dyslexia at College*. 2nd edition. London: Whurr.

Gioia, G. A., Isquith, P. K., Kenworthy, L., & Barton, R. M. (2002). Profiles of everyday executive function in acquired and developmental disorders. *Child Neuropsychology*, *8*(2), 121–137.

Giovagnoli, S., Mandolesi, L., Magri, S., et al. (2020). Internalizing symptoms in developmental dyslexia: A comparison between primary and secondary school. *Frontiers in Psychology*, *11*, 461.

Girirajan, S., Brkanac, Z., Coe, B. P., et al. (2011). Relative burden of large CNVs on a range of neurodevelopmental phenotypes. *PLOS GENET*, *7*, e1002334.

Gladwell, M. (2013). *David and Goliath: Underdogs, Misfits and the Art of Battling Giants*. New York: Little, Brown and Company.

Glazzard, J. (2010). The impact of dyslexia on pupils' self-esteem. *Support for Learning*, *25*(2), 63–69.

Goddard Blythe, S. (2005). Releasing educational potential through movement: A summary of individual studies carried out using the INPP test battery and developmental exercise programme for use in schools with children with special needs. *Child Care in Practice*, *11*, 415–432.

Goddard Blythe, S., Duncombe, R., Preedy, P., & Gorely, T. (2022). Neuromotor readiness for school: The primitive reflex status of young children at the start and end of their first year at school in the United Kingdom. *Education 3–13*, *50*(5), 654–667.

Goddard, R. (1991). Why LINC matters. *English in Education*, *25*, 32–39.

Goldman, S. R., Snow, C., & Vaughn, S. (2016). Common themes in teaching reading for understanding: Lessons from three projects. *Journal of Adolescent & Adult Literacy*, *60*(3), 255–264.

Gonda, Y., Andrews, W. D., Tabata, H., et al. (2013). Robo1 regulates the migration and laminar distribution of upper-layer pyramidal neurons of the cerebral cortex. *Cerebral Cortex*, *23*, 1495–1508.

Gonzaga-Jauregui, C., Lupski, J. R., & Gibbs, R. A. (2012). Human genome sequencing in health and disease. *Annual Review of Medicine*, *63*, 35–61.

Good, R. H., & Kaminski, R. A. (2003). *Dynamic Indicators of Basic Early Literacy Skills*. Longmont, CO: Sopris West Educational Services.

Good, R. H., Kaminski, R. A., Shinn, M., et al. (2004). *Technical Adequacy and Decision Making Utility of DIBELS*. Technical Report No. 7. Eugene, OR: University of Oregon.

Goodman, I., Libenson, A., & Wade-Woolley, L. (2010). Sensitivity to linguistic stress, phonological awareness and early reading ability in preschoolers. *Journal of Research in Reading*, *33*(2), 113–127.

Goodman, K. S. (1965). A linguistic study of cues and miscues in reading. *Elementary English*, *42*, 639–643.

Goodman, K. S. (1967). Reading: A psycholinguistic guessing game. *Journal of the Reading Specialist*, *6*, 126–135.

Goodman, K. S. (1969). Analysis of oral reading miscues: Applied psycholinguistics. *Reading Research Quarterly*, *5*(1), 9–30.

Goodman, K. S. (1970). Reading: A psycholinguistic guessing game. In H. Singer, & R. B. Ruddell (eds.), *Theoretical Models and Processes of Reading* (pp. 259–272). Newark, DE: International Reading Association.

Goodman, K. S. (1986). *What's Whole in Whole Language?* Portsmouth, NH: Heinemann.

Goodman, K. S. (1992). Why whole language is today's agenda in education. *Language Arts*, *69*, 354–363.

Gordon, P. C., & Hoedemaker, R. S. (2016). Effective scheduling of looking and talking during rapid automatized naming. *Journal of Experimental Psychology: Human Perception and Performance*, *42*(5), 742.

Gori, S., Bertoni, S., Sali, M., et al. (2016b). Dyslexia prevention by action video game training: Behavioural and neurophysiological evidence. *Journal of Vision*, *16*(12), 489.

Gori, S., & Facoetti, A. (2015). How the visual aspects can be crucial in reading acquisition: The intriguing case of crowding and developmental dyslexia. *Journal of Vision*, *15*(1), 8.

Gori, S., Seitz, A. R., Ronconi, L., Franceschini, S., & Facoetti, A. (2016a). Multiple causal links between magnocellular–dorsal pathway deficit and developmental dyslexia. *Cerebral Cortex*, *26*(11), 4356–4369.

Gorman, S. E., & Gorman, J. M. (2021). *Denying to the Grave: Why We Ignore the Science That Will Save Us*. Oxford: Oxford University Press.

Gosse, C., & Van Reybroeck, M. (2020). Do children with dyslexia present a hand-writing deficit? Impact of word orthographic and graphic complexity on handwriting and spelling performance. *Research in Developmental Disabilities*, *97*, 103553.

Goswami, U. (2002). Phonology, reading development and dyslexia: A cross-linguistic perspective. *Annals of Dyslexia*, *52*, 1–23.

Goswami, U. (2015). Sensory theories of developmental dyslexia: Three challenges for research. *Nature Reviews Neuroscience*, *16*(1), 43–54.

Goswami, U. (2019). A neural oscillations perspective on phonological development and phonological processing in developmental dyslexia. *Language and Linguistics Compass*, *13*(5), e12328.

Goswami, U. (2022). Language acquisition and speech rhythm patterns: An auditory neuroscience perspective. *Royal Society Open Science*, *9*(7), 211855.

Goswami, U., Gerson, D., & Astruc, L. (2010). Amplitude envelope perception, phonology and prosodic sensitivity in children with developmental dyslexia. *Reading & Writing*, *23*, 995–1019.

Goswami, U., Huss, M., Mead, N., & Fosker, T. (2021). Auditory sensory processing and phonological development in high IQ and exceptional readers, typically developing readers, and children with dyslexia: A longitudinal study. *Child Development*, *92*(3), 1083–1098.

Goswami, U., Thomson, J., Richardson, U., et al. (2002). Amplitude envelope onsets and developmental dyslexia: A new hypothesis. *Proceedings of the National Academy of Sciences*, *99*(16), 10911–10916.

Goswami, U., Wang, H. L., Cruz, A., et al. (2011). Language-universal sensory deficits in developmental dyslexia: English, Spanish, and Chinese. *Journal of Cognitive Neuroscience*, *23*(2), 325–337.

Gotlieb, R. J., Immordino-Yang, M. H., Gonzalez, E., et al. (2022). Becoming literate: Educational implications of coordinated neuropsychological development of reading and social-emotional functioning among diverse youth. *Literacy Research: Theory, Method, and Practice*, *71*(1), 80–132.

Goto, M., Abe, O., Hagiwara, A., et al. (2022). Advantages of using both voxel- and surface-based morphometry in cortical morphology analysis: A review of various applications. *Magnetic Resonance in Medical Sciences*, *21*, 41–57.

Gough, P. B. (1983). Context, form and interaction. In K. Rayner (ed.), *Eye Movements in Reading: Perceptual and Language Processes* (pp. 203–211). San Diego: Academic Press.

Gough, P. B., & Tunmer, W. E. (1986). Decoding, reading and reading disability. *Remedial and Special Education*, *7*, 6–10.

Grainger, J., Dufau, S., & Ziegler, J. C. (2016). A vision of reading. *Trends in Cognitive Sciences*, *20*(3), 171–179.

Grainger, J., Lété, B., Bertand, D., Dufau, S., & Ziegler, J. C. (2012). Evidence for multiple routes in learning to read. *Cognition*, *123*, 280–292.

Gray, S., Fox, A. B., Green, S., et al. (2019). Working memory profiles of children with dyslexia, developmental language disorder, or both. *Journal of Speech, Language, and Hearing Research*, 62(6), 1839–1858.

Gray, S., Green, S., Alt, M., et al. (2017). The structure of working memory in young children and its relation to intelligence. *Journal of Memory and Language*, 92, 183–201.

Green, E. A. (2022). Continuing the debate: A response to the Literacy Research Association's dyslexia research report. *International Journal of Education and Literacy Studies*, 10(3), 72–79.

Greenspan, S. (2005). Credulity and gullibility among service providers: An attempt to understand why snake oil sells. In J. W. Jacobson, R. M. Foxx, & J. A. Mulick (eds.), *Controversial Therapies for Developmental Disabilities: Fad, Fashion and Science in Professional Practice* (pp. 129–138). Mahwah, NJ: Lawrence Erlbaum.

Gresham, F. M. (2009). Using response to intervention for identification of specific learning disabilities. In A. Akin-Little, S. G. Little, M. A. Bray, & T. J. Kehl (eds.), *Behavioral Interventions in Schools: Evidence-Based Positive Strategies* (pp. 205–220). Washington, DC: American Psychological Association.

Gresham, F. M., & Vellutino, F. R. (2010). What is the role of intelligence in the identification of specific learning disabilities? Issues and clarifications. *Learning Disabilities Research & Practice*, 25(4), 194–206.

Griffiths, P. G., Taylor, R. H., Henderson, L. M., & Barrett, B. T. (2016). The effect of coloured overlays and lenses on reading: A systematic review of the literature. *Ophthalmic and Physiological Optics*, 36(5), 519–544.

Grigorenko, E. L. (2004). Genetic bases of developmental dyslexia: A capsule review of heritability estimates. *Enfance*, 3, 273–287.

Grigorenko, E. L. (2005). A conservative meta-analysis of linkage and linkage-association studies of developmental dyslexia. *Scientific Studies of Reading*, 9, 285–316.

Grigorenko, E. L. (2007). Triangulating developmental dyslexia: Behavior, brain, and genes. In D. Coch, G. Dawson, & K. Fischer (eds.), *Human Behavior and the Developing Brain* (pp. 117–144). New York: Guilford Press.

Grigorenko, E. L. (2009). At the height of fashion: What genetics can teach us about neurodevelopmental disabilities. *Current Opinion in Neurology*, 22, 126–130.

Grigorenko, E. L. (2011). Language-based learning disabilities. In N. Seel (ed.), *Encyclopedia of the Sciences of Learning*. New York: Springer.

Grigorenko, E. L. (2012). Commentary: Translating quantitative genetics into molecular genetics: Decoupling reading disorder and ADHD – Reflections on Greven et al. and Rosenberg et al. *Journal of Child Psychology and Psychiatry*, 53(3), 252–253.

Grigorenko, E. L. (2022). The role of genetic factors in reading and its development across languages and writing systems. *Scientific Studies of Reading*, 26, 96–110.

Grigorenko, E. L. (2023). The never-ending innovativeness of the Wise Man. In D. D. Preiss, J. C. Kaufman, & M. Singer (eds.), *Innovation, Creativity and Change across Cultures*. London: Palgrave Macmillan.

Grigorenko, E. L., Compton, D. L., Fuchs, L. S., et al. (2020). Understanding, educating, and supporting children with specific learning disabilities: 50 years of science and practice. *American Psychologist*, 75(1), 37–51.

Grigorenko, E. L., Hart, L., Hein, S., Kovalenko, J., & Naumova, O. Y. (2019). Improved educational achievement as a path to desistance. *New Directions for Child and Adolescent Development, 2019*(165), 111–135.

Grigorenko, E. L., Macomber, D., Hart, L., et al. (2015). Academic achievement among juvenile detainees. *Journal of Learning Disabilities, 48*(4), 359–368.

Grigorenko, E. L., & Naples, A. (eds.). (2008). *Single-Word Reading: Biological and Behavioral Perspectives.* New York: Lawrence Erlbaum Associates.

Grigorenko, E. L., & Naples, A. J. (2009). The devil is in the details: Decoding the genetics of reading. In P. McCardle, & K. Pugh (eds.), *Helping Children Learn to Read: Current Issues and New Directions in the Integration of Cognition, Neurobiology and Genetics of Reading and Dyslexia* (pp. 133–148). New York: Psychological Press.

Grigorenko, E. L., Wood, F. B., Meyer, M. S., et al. (1997). Susceptibility loci for distinct components of developmental dyslexia on chromosomes 6 and 15. *American Journal of Human Genetics, 60*, 27–39.

Grigorenko, E. L., Wood, F. B., Meyer, M. S., et al. (2001). Linkage studies suggest a possible locus for developmental dyslexia on chromosome 1p. *American Journal of Medical Genetics (Neuropsychiatric Genetics), 105*, 120–129.

Grills, A. E., Fletcher, J. M., Vaughn, S. R., & Bowman, C., 2022. Internalizing symptoms and reading difficulties among early elementary school students. *Child Psychiatry & Human Development*, 1–11.

Grills-Taquechel, A. E., Fletcher, J. M., Vaughn, S. R., & Stuebing, K. K. (2012). Anxiety and reading difficulties in early elementary school: Evidence for unidirectional- or bi-directional relations? *Child Psychiatry & Human Development, 43*, 35–47.

Grimm, T., Garshasbi, M., Puettmann, L., et al. (2020). A novel locus and candidate gene for familial developmental dyslexia on chromosome 4q. *The German Journal for Child and Adolescent Psychiatry and Psychotherapy, 48*, 478–489.

Groß, C., Serrallach, B. L., Möhler, E., et al. (2022). Musical performance in adolescents with ADHD, ADD and dyslexia – Behavioral and neurophysiological aspects. *Brain Sciences, 12*(2), 127.

Grosjean, F. (2021). *Life as a Bilingual.* Cambridge: Cambridge University Press.

Gross-Glenn, K., Skottun, B. C., Glenn, W., et al. (1995). Contrast sensitivity in dyslexia. *Visual Neuroscience, 12*, 153–163.

Grote-Garcia, S., & Ortlieb, E. (2023). What's hot in literacy 2023: The ban on books and diversity measures. *Literacy Research and Instruction*, 1–16.

Grünling, C., Ligges, M., Huonker, R., et al. (2004). Dyslexia: The possible benefit of multimodal integration of fMRI- and EEG-data. *Journal of Neural Transmission, 111*, 951–969.

Gu, C., & Bi, H. Y. (2020). Auditory processing deficit in individuals with dyslexia: A meta-analysis of mismatch negativity. *Neuroscience & Biobehavioral Reviews, 116*, 396–405.

Guidi, L. G., Mattley, J., Martinez-Garay, I., et al. (2017). Knockout mice for dyslexia susceptibility gene homologs KIAA0319 and KIAA0319L have unaffected neuronal migration but display abnormal auditory processing. *Cerebral Cortex*, *27*, 5831–5845.

Guidi, L. G., Velayos-Baeza, A., Martinez-Garay, I., et al. (2018). The neuronal migration hypothesis of dyslexia: A critical evaluation 30 years on. *European Journal of Neuroscience, 48*, 3212–3233.

Guimarães, M. R., Vilhena, D. D. A., Loew, S. J., & Guimarães, R. Q. (2020). Spectral overlays for reading difficulties: Oculomotor function and reading efficiency among children and adolescents with visual stress. *Perceptual and Motor Skills, 127*(2), 490–509.

Gutiérrez, N., Rigobon, V. M., Marencin, N. C., et al. (2022). Early prediction of reading risk in fourth grade: A combined latent class analysis and classification tree approach. *Scientific Studies of Reading*, 1–18.

Gwernan-Jones, R., & Burden, R. L. (2010). Are they just lazy? Student teachers' attitudes about dyslexia. *Dyslexia, 16*, 66–86.

Habib, M. (2000). The neurological basis of developmental dyslexia: An overview and working hypothesis. *Brain, 123*(12), 2373–2399.

Habib, M. (2021). The neurological basis of developmental dyslexia and related disorders: A reappraisal of the temporal hypothesis, twenty years on. *Brain Sciences, 11*(6), 708.

Habib, M., Lardy, C., Desiles, T., et al. (2016). Music and dyslexia: A new musical training method to improve reading and related disorders. *Frontiers in Psychology, 7*, 26.

Habib, M., Robichon, F., Levrier, O., Khalil, R., & Salamon, G. (1995). Diverging asymmetries of temporo-parietal cortical areas: A reappraisal of Geschwind/ Galaburda theory. *Brain and Language, 48*, 238–258.

Hadzibeganovic, T., van den Noort, M., Bosch, P., et al. (2011). Cross-linguistic neuroimaging and dyslexia: A critical view. *Cortex, 46*, 1312–1316.

Haegens, S., & Golumbic, E. Z. (2018). Rhythmic facilitation of sensory processing: A critical review. *Neuroscience & Biobehavioral Reviews, 86*, 150–165.

Haft, S., Greiner de Magalhães, C., & Hoeft, F. (2023). A systematic review of the consequences of stigma and stereotype threat for individuals with specific learning disabilities. *Journal of Learning Disabilities, 56*(3), 193–209.

Hagan-Burke, S., Coyne, M. D., Kwok, O. M., et al. (2013). The effects and inter- actions of student, teacher, and setting variables on reading outcomes for kin- dergarteners receiving supplemental reading intervention. *Journal of Learning Disabilities, 46*(3), 260–277.

Hagoort, P., & Indefrey, P. (2014). The neurobiology of language beyond single words. *Annual Review of Neuroscience, 37*, 347–362.

Hale, J. B., Alfonso, V., Berninger, V., et al. (2010). Critical issues in response to intervention, comprehensive evaluation, and specific learning disabilities eval- uation and intervention: An expert white paper consensus. *Learning Disability Quarterly, 33*, 223–236.

Hale, J. B., & Fiorello, C. A. (2004). *School Neuropsychology: A Practitioner's Handbook*. New York: Guilford Press.

Hale, J. B., Fiorello, C. A., Miller, J. A., et al. (2008). WISC-IV assessment and intervention strategies for children with specific learning difficulties. In A. Prifitera, D. H. Saklofske, & L. G. Weiss (eds.), *WISC-IV Clinical Assessment and Intervention* (pp. 109–171). New York: Elsevier.

Hall, C., Dahl-Leonard, K., Cho, E., et al. (2022). Forty years of reading intervention research for elementary students with or at risk for dyslexia: A systematic review and meta-analysis. *Reading Research Quarterly*, *58*(2), 285–312.

Hallahan, D. P., & Mercer, C. D. (2001). *Learning Disabilities: Historical Perspectives*. Washington, DC: Department of Education, Office of Special Education Programs.

Hallahan, D. P., & Mock, D. R. (2003). A brief history of the field of learning disabilities. In H. L. Swanson, K. R. Harris, & S. Graham (eds.), *Handbook of Learning Disabilities* (pp. 16–29). New York: Guilford Press.

Halliday, L. F., & Bishop, D. V. M. (2006). Is poor frequency modulation detection linked to literacy problems? A comparison of specific reading disability and mild to moderate sensorineural hearing loss. *Brain and Language*, *97*, 200–213.

Halverson, K. K., Derrick, J. L., Medina, L. D., & Cirino P. T. (2021). Executive functioning with the NIH EXAMINER and inference making in struggling readers. *Developmental Neuropsychology*, *46*(3), 213–231.

Hämäläinen, J. A., Salminen, H. K., & Leppänen, P. H. T. (2013). Basic auditory processing deficits in dyslexia: Review of the behavioral, event-related potential/field evidence. *Journal of Learning Disabilities*, *46*(5), 413–427.

Hämäläinen, M., Hari, R., Ilmoniemi, R. J., Knuutila, J., & Lounasmaa, O. V. (1993). Magnetoencephalography: Theory, instrumentation, and applications to noninvasive studies of the working human brain. *Reviews of Modern Physics*, *65*, 413–497.

Hammill, D. D., & Allen, E. A. (2020). A revised discrepancy method for identifying dyslexia. *Journal of Pediatric Neuropsychology*, *6*(1), 27–43.

Hancock, R., Gabrieli, J. D., & Hoeft, F. (2016). Shared temporoparietal dysfunction in dyslexia and typical readers with discrepantly high IQ. *Trends in Neuroscience and Education*, *5*(4), 173–177.

Hancock, R., Pugh, K. R., & Hoeft, F. (2017). Neural noise hypothesis of developmental dyslexia. *Trends in Cognitive Sciences*, *21*, 434–448.

Hancock, R., Richlan, F., & Hoeft, F. (2017). Possible roles for fronto-striatal circuits in reading disorder. *Neuroscience & Biobehavioral Reviews*, *72*, 243–260.

Handler, S. M., Fierson, W. M., the Section of Opthalmology and Council on Children with Disabilities, American Academy of Opthamology, American Association for Pediatric Opthalmology and Strabismus, and American Association of Certified Orthoptists. (2011). Joint technical report – Learning disabilities, dyslexia, and vision. *Pediatrics*, *127*, e818–e856.

Hanebutt, R., & Mueller, C. (2021). Disability Studies, crip theory, and education. In *Oxford Research Encyclopedia of Education*. https://bit.ly/3Gsy01m

Hanford, E. (2018). Why are we still teaching reading the wrong way? *New York Times*. October 26. https://nyti.ms/3T4aFvT

Hannula-Jouppi, K., Kaminen-Ahola, N., Taipale, M., et al. (2005). The axon guidance receptor gene *ROBO1* is a candidate dene for developmental dyslexia. *PLoS*, *1*, e50.

Hari, R., & Renvall, H. (2001). Impaired processing of rapid stimulus sequences in dyslexia. *Trends in Cognitive Sciences*, *5*, 525–532.

Harlaar, N., Dale, P. S., & Plomin, R. (2007). From learning to read to reading to learn: Substantial and stable genetic influence. *Child Development*, *78*, 116–131.

Harn, B., Parisi, D., & Stoolmiller, M. (2013). Balancing fidelity with flexibility and fit: What do we really know about fidelity of implementation in schools? *Exceptional Children*, *79*(2), 181–193.

Harrison, A. G., & Edwards, M. J. (2010). Symptom exaggeration in postsecondary students: Preliminary base rates in a Canadian sample. *Applied Neuropsychology*, *17*(2), 135–143.

Harrison, A. G., & Sparks, R. (2022). Disability diagnoses: Seven sins of clinicians. *Psychological Injury and Law*, *15*(3), 268–286.

Hart, B., & Risley, T. (2003). The early catastrophe. *American Educator*, *27*, 6–9.

Hart, S. A., Petrill, S. A., DeThorne, L. S., et al. (2009). Environmental influences on the longitudinal covariance of expressive vocabulary: Measuring the home literacy environment in a genetically sensitive design. *Journal of Child Psychology and Psychiatry*, *50*, 911–919.

Hartas, D. (2011). Families' social backgrounds matter: Socioeconomic factors, home learning and young children's language, literacy and social outcomes. *British Educational Research Journal*, *37*, 893–914.

Hartwigsen, G. (2018). Flexible redistribution in cognitive networks. *Trends in Cognitive Sciences*, *22*, 687–698.

Hasan, K. M., Molfese, D. L., Walimuni, I. S., et al. (2012). Diffusion tensor quantification and cognitive correlates of the macrostructure and microstructure of the corpus callosum in typically developing and dyslexic children. *NMR in Biomedicine*, *25*(11), 1263–1270.

Hatcher, P. J., Hulme, C., Miles, J. N., et al. (2006). Efficacy of small group reading intervention for beginning readers with reading delay: A randomised controlled trial. *Journal of Child Psychology & Psychiatry*, *47*, 820–827.

Hayiou-Thomas, M. E., Carroll, J. M., Leavett, R., Hulme, C., & Snowling, M. J. (2017). When does speech sound disorder matter for literacy? The role of disordered speech errors, co-occurring language impairment and family risk of dyslexia. *Journal of Child Psychology and Psychiatry*, *58*, 197–205.

Hebbecker, K., Förster, N., & Souvignier, E. (2019). Reciprocal effects between reading achievement and intrinsic and extrinsic reading motivation. *Scientific Studies of Reading*, *23*(5), 419–436.

Hebert, M., Bohaty, J. J., Nelson, J. R., & Brown, J. (2016). The effects of text structure instruction on expository reading comprehension: A meta-analysis. *Journal of Educational Psychology*, *108*(5), 609.

Heiervang, E., Hugdahl, K., Steinmetz, H., et al. (2000). Planum temporale, planum parietale and dichotic listening in dyslexia. *Neuropsychologia, 38,* 1704–1713.

Heim, S., Pape-Neumann, J., van Ermingen-Marbach, M., Brinkhaus, M., & Grande, M. (2015). Shared vs. specific brain activation changes in dyslexia after training of phonology, attention, or reading. *Brain Structure and Function, 220*(4), 2191–2207.

Helenius, P., Tarkiainen, A., Cornelissen, P., Hansen, P., & Salmelin, R. (1999). Dissociation of normal feature analysis and deficient processing of letter-strings in dyslexic adults. *Cerebral Cortex, 9,* 476–483.

Helland, T. (2022). Trends in dyslexia research during the period 1950 to 2020— Theories, definitions, and publications. *Brain Sciences, 12*(10), 1323.

Henderson, L. M., Tsogka, N., & Snowling, M. J. (2013). Questioning the benefits that coloured overlays can have for reading in students with and without dyslexia. *Journal of Research in Special Educational Needs, 13*(1), 57–65.

Henderson, S. E., Sugden, D. A., & Barnett, A. L. (2007). *The Movement Assessment Battery for Children.* Examiner's manual; 2nd edition. London: Pearson Education.

Hendren, R. L., Haft, S. L., Black, J. M., White, N. C., & Hoeft, F. (2018). Recognizing psychiatric comorbidity with reading disorders. *Frontiers in Psychiatry,* 101.

Hendricks E. L., & Fuchs D. (2020). Are individual differences in response to intervention influenced by the methods and measures used to define response? Implications for identifying children with learning disabilities. *Journal of Learning Disabilities, 53,* 428–443.

Herbers, J. E. Cutuli, J. J., Supkoff, L. M., et al. (2012). Early reading skills and academic achievement trajectories of students facing poverty, homelessness, and high residential mobility. *Educational Researcher, 41*(9), 366–374.

Hervais-Adelman, A., Kumar, U., Mishra, R. K., et al. (2022). How does literacy affect speech processing? Not by enhancing cortical responses to speech, but by promoting connectivity of acoustic-phonetic and graphomotor cortices. *The Journal of Neuroscience, 42,* 8826.

Hinshelwood, J. (1895). Word-blindness and visual memory. *Lancet, 146,* 1564–1570.

Hinshelwood, J. (1902). Congenital word-blindness, with reports of two cases. *Ophthalmology Review, 21,* 91–99.

Hinshelwood, J. (1907). Four cases of congenital word-blindness occuring in the same family. *British Medical Journal, 1,* 608–609.

Hinshelwood, J. (1917). *Congenital Word Blindness.* London: H. K. Lewis & Co.

Hitchens, P. (2014). Dyslexia is NOT a disease. It is an excuse for bad teachers. *Mail Online.* March 2. https://bit.ly/3uHX2Z8

Hoeft, F., & Bouhali, F. (2022). Pre-and postnatal environmental effects on learning to read and mathematical learning. In M. A. Skeide (ed.), *The Cambridge Handbook of Dyslexia and Dyscalculia* (pp. 115–250). Cambridge: Cambridge University Press.

Hoeft, F., Hernandez, A., McMillon, G., et al. (2006). Neural basis of dyslexia: A comparison between dyslexic and nondyslexic children equated for reading ability. *Journal of Neuroscience, 26,* 10700–10708.

Hoeft, F., McCandliss, B. D., Black, J. M., et al. (2011). Neural systems predicting long-term outcome in dyslexia. *Proceedings of the National Academy of Sciences of the United States of America*, *108*, 361–366.

Hoeft, F., Meyler, A., Hernandez, A., et al. (2007). Functional and morphometric brain dissociation between dyslexia and reading ability. *Proceedings of the National Academy of Sciences of the United States of America*, *104*, 4234–4239.

Hoeft, F., Ueno, T., Reiss, A. L., et al. (2007). Prediction of children's reading skills using behavioral, functional, and structural neuroimaging measures. *Behavioral Neuroscience*, *121*, 602–613.

Hofstetter, S., Friedmann, N., & Assaf, Y. (2017). Rapid language-related plasticity: Microstructural changes in the cortex after a short session of new word learning. *Brain Structure and Function*, *222*(3), 1231–1241.

Holliman, A. J., Wood, C., & Sheehy, K. (2010). Does speech rhythm sensitivity predict children's reading ability one year later? *Journal of Educational Psychology*, *102*, 356–366.

Holloway, I. D., van Atteveldt, N., Blomert, L., & Ansari, D. (2015). Orthographic dependency in the neural correlates of reading: Evidence from audiovisual integration in English readers. *Cerebral Cortex*, *25*, 1544–1553.

Holm, V. A. (1983). A western version of the Doman-Delacato treatment of patterning for developmental disabilities. *The Western Journal of Medicine*, *139*, 553–556.

Holmqvist, M. (2020). Medical diagnosis of dyslexia in a Swedish elite school: A case of "consecrating medicalization." *British Journal of Sociology*, *71*(2), 366–381.

Hoover, W. A., & Gough, P. B. (1990). The simple view of reading. *Reading and Writing*, *2*, 127–160.

Horbach, J., Mayer, A., Scharke, W., Heim, S., & Günther, T. (2020). Development of behavior problems in children with and without specific learning disorders in reading and spelling from kindergarten to fifth grade. *Scientific Studies of Reading*, *24*(1), 57–71.

Hornickel, J., & Kraus, N. (2013). Unstable representation of sound: A biological marker of dyslexia. *The Journal of Neuroscience*, *33*(8), 3500–3504.

Horowitz-Kraus, T., DiFrancesco, M., Kay, B., Wang, Y., & Holland, S. K. (2015). Increased resting-state functional connectivity of visual- and cognitive-control brain networks after training in children with reading difficulties. *NeuroImage: Clinical*, *8*, 619–630.

Horowitz-Kraus, T., Vannest, J. J., Kadis, D., et al. (2014). Reading acceleration training changes brain circuitry in children with reading difficulties. *Brain and behavior*, *4*, 886–902.

Horwitz, B., Rumsey, J. M., & Donohue, B. C. (1998). Functional connectivity of the angular gyrus in normal reading and dyslexia. *Proceedings of the National Academy of Sciences of the United States of America*, *95*, 8939–8944.

Hoskyn, M., & Swanson, H. L. (2000). Cognitive processing of low achievers and children with reading disabilities: A selective meta-analytic review of the published literature. *School Psychology Review 29*, 102–119.

House of Commons Science and Technology Committee. (2009). *Evidence Check 1: Early Literacy Interventions*. London: The Stationery Office. https://bit.ly/4a4YrJy

Howard-Gosse, A., Bergey, B. W., & Deacon, S. H. (2023). The reading challenges, strategies, and habits of university students with a history of reading difficulties and their relations to academic achievement. *Journal of Learning Disabilities*. https://doi.org/10.1177/00222194231190678

Howard-Jones, P. A. (2014). Neuroscience and education: Myths and messages. *Nature Reviews Neuroscience, 15*(12), 817–824.

Hu, W., Lee, H. L., Zhang, Q., et al. (2010). Developmental dyslexia in Chinese and English populations: Dissociating the effect of dyslexia from language differences. *Brain, 133*, 1694–1706.

Huber, E., Donnelly, P. M., Rokem, A., & Yeatman, J. D. (2018). Rapid and widespread white matter plasticity during an intensive reading intervention. *Nature Communications, 9*, 2260.

Huettig, F., & Ferreira, F. (2022). The myth of normal reading. *Perspectives on Psychological Science, 18*(4), 863–870.

Huettig, F., Lachmann, T., Reis, A., & Petersson, K. M. (2018). Distinguishing cause from effect–many deficits associated with developmental dyslexia may be a consequence of reduced and suboptimal reading experience. *Language, Cognition and Neuroscience, 33*(3), 333–350.

Hugdahl, K., Heiervang, E., Ersland, L., et al. (2003). Significant relation between MR measures of planum temporale area and dichotic processing of syllables in dyslexic children. *Neuropsychologia, 41*, 666–675.

Hughes, B., & Paterson, K. (1997). The social model of disability and the disappearing body: Towards a sociology of impairment. *Disability & Society, 12*(3), 325–340.

Hughes, B., Sullivan, K. A., & Gilmore, L. (2020). Why do teachers believe educational neuromyths? *Trends in Neuroscience and Education, 21*, 100145.

Hulme, C., & Snowling, M. J. (1992). Deficits in output phonology: An explanation of reading failure? *Cognitive Neuropsychology, 9*, 47–72.

Hulme, C., & Snowling, M. J. (2009). *Developmental Disorders of Language Learning and Cognition*. Oxford: Wiley-Blackwell.

Humphreys, P., Kaufmann, W. E., & Galaburda, A. M. (1990). Developmental dyslexia in women: Neuropathological findings in three patients. *Annals of Neurology, 28*, 727–738.

Hurford, D. P., Hurford, J. D., Head, K. L., et al. (2016). The dyslexia dilemma: A history of ignorance, complacency, and resistance in colleges of education. *Journal of Childhood & Developmental Disorders, 2*(3), 1–16.

Hurtubise, J. L., Scavone, A., Sagar, S., & Erdodi, L. A. (2017). Psychometric markers of genuine and feigned neurodevelopmental disorders in the context of applying for academic accommodations. *Psychological Injury and Law, 10*(2), 121–137.

Hutton, J. S., Dudley, J., Horowitz-Kraus, T., DeWitt, T., & Holland, S. K. (2020). Associations between home literacy environment, brain white matter integrity and cognitive abilities in preschool-age children. *Acta Paediatrica, 109,* 1376–1386.

Hyatt, K. J., Stephenson, J., & Carter, M. (2009). A review of three controversial educational practices: Perceptual motor programs, sensory integration, and tinted lenses. *Education and Treatment of Children, 32,* 313–342.

Hynd, G. W., Hall, J., Novey, E. S., et al. (1995). Dyslexia and corpus callosum morphology. *Archives of Neurology, 52,* 32–38.

Hynd, G. W., Semrud-Clikeman, M., Lorys, A. R., Novey, E. S., & Eliopulos, D. (1990). Brain morphology in developmental dyslexia and attention deficit disorder/hyperactivity. *Archives of Neurology, 47,* 919–926.

Ihnot, C., Mastoff, J., Gavin, J., & Hendrickson, L. (2001). *Read Naturally.* Curriculum program. St Paul, MN: Read Naturally.

Igo, R. P. J., Chapman, N. H., Berninger, V. W., et al. (2006). Genomewide scan for real-word reading subphenotypes of dyslexia: Novel chromosome 13 locus and genetic complexity. *American Journal of Medical Genetics (Neuropsychiatric Genetics), 141,* 15–27.

Im, K., Raschle, N. M., Smith, S. A., Ellen Grant, P., & Gaab, N. (2016). Atypical sulcal pattern in children with developmental dyslexia and at-risk kindergarteners. *Cerebral Cortex, 26*(3), 1138–1148.

Ingesson, S. G. (2007). Growing up with dyslexia: Interviews with teenagers and young adults. *School Psychology International, 28*(5), 574–591.

Inoue, T., Georgiou, G. K., & Parrila, R. (2023). The growth trajectories of morphological awareness and its predictors. *Applied Psycholinguistics, 44,* 699–721.

Ip, K. I., Marks, R. A., Hsu, L. S.-J., et al. (2019). Morphological processing in Chinese engages left temporal regions. *Brain and Language, 199,* 104696.

Irlen, H. (1991). *Reading by the Colors: Overcoming Dyslexia and Other Reading Disabilities through the Irlen Method.* New York: Avery.

Jacob, R., & Parkinson, J. (2015). The potential for school-based interventions that target executive function to improve academic achievement: A review. *Review of Educational Research, 85*(4), 512–552.

Jacobson, J. W., Foxx, R. M., & Mulick, J. A. (2005). *Controversial Therapies for Developmental Disabilities: Fad, Fashion and Science in Professional Practice.* Mahwah, NJ: Lawrence Erlbaum.

Jaffe-Dax, S., Kimel, E., & Ahissar, M. (2018). Shorter cortical adaptation in dyslexia is broadly distributed in the superior temporal lobe and includes the primary auditory cortex. *eLife, 7,* e30018.

Jakoby, H., Raviv, O., Jaffe-Dax, S., Lieder, I., & Ahissar, M. (2019). Auditory frequency discrimination is correlated with linguistic skills, but its training does not improve them or other pitch discrimination tasks. *Journal of Experimental Psychology: General, 148*(11), 1953.

Jalal, S. M., Harwood, A. R., Sekhon, G. S., et al. (2003). Utility of subtelomeric fluorescent DNA probes for detection of chromosome anomalies in 425 patients. *Genetics in Medicine, 5,* 28–34.

James, K. H. (2017). The importance of handwriting experience on the development of the literate brain. *Current Directions in Psychological Science, 26*(6), 502–508.

January, S. A. A., & Klingbeil, D. A. (2020). Universal screening in grades K-2: A systematic review and meta-analysis of early reading curriculum-based measures. *Journal of School Psychology, 82*, 103–122.

Jeanes, R., Busby, A., Martin, J., Lewis, E., Stevenson, N., Pointon, D., & Wilkins, A. (1997). Prolonged use of coloured overlays for classroom reading. *British Journal of Psychology, 88*(4), 541–548.

Jednoróg, K., Marchewka, A., Altarelli, I., et al. (2015). How reliable are gray matter disruptions in specific reading disability across multiple countries and languages? Insights from a large-scale voxel-based morphometry study. *Human Brain Mapping, 36*, 1741–1754.

Jenkins, J. R., Hudson, R. F., & Johnson, E. S. (2007). Screening for at-risk readers in a response-to-intervention (RTI) framework. *School Psychology Review, 36*, 582–600.

Jenner, A. R., Rosen, G. D., & Galaburda, A. M. (1999). Neuronal asymmetries in primary visual cortex of dyslexic and nondyslexic brains. *Annals of Neurology, 46*, 189–196.

Jimerson, S. R., Burns, M. K., & VanDerHeyden, A. M. (eds.). (2016). *Handbook of Response to Intervention: The Science and Practice of Multi-tiered Systems of Support.* 2nd edition. New York: Springer Science

Jobard, G., Crivello, F., & Tzourio-Mazoyer, N. (2003). Evaluation of the dual route theory of reading: A metanalysis of 35 neuroimaging studies. *Neuroimage, 20*, 693–712.

Johannes, S., Kussmaul, C. L., Munte, T. F., & Mangun, G. R. (1996). Developmental dyslexia: Passive visual stimulation provides no evidence for a magnocellular processing deficit. *Neuropsychologia, 34*, 1123–1127.

Johnson, E. E., & Suhr, J. (2021). Self-reported functional impairment in college students: Relationship to noncredible reporting, ADHD, psychological disorders, and other psychological factors. *Journal of Clinical and Experimental Neuropsychology, 43*(4), 399–411.

Johnson, E. P., Pennington, B. F., Lowenstein, J. H., & Nittrouer, S. (2011). Sensitivity to structure in the speech signal by children with speech sound disorder and reading disability. *Journal of Communication Disorders, 44*, 294–314.

Johnson, E. S., Humphrey, M., Mellard, D. F., Woods, K., & Swanson, H. L. (2010). Cognitive processing deficits and students with specific learning disabilities: A selective meta-analysis of the literature. *Learning Disability Quarterly, 33*, 3–18.

Johnson, E. S., Jenkins, J. R., Petscher, Y., & Catts, H. W. (2009). How can we improve the accuracy of screening instruments? *Learning Disabilities Research & Practice, 24*, 174–185.

Johnston, P., & Scanlon, D. (2021). An examination of dyslexia research and instruction with policy implications. *Literacy Research: Theory, Method, and Practice, 70*(1), 107–128.

Jolles, D. D., Mennigen, E., Gupta, M. W., et al. (2020). Relationships between intrinsic functional connectivity, cognitive control, and reading achievement across development. *Neuroimage, 221*, 117202.

Jones, B. T., Erchul, W. P., & Geraghty, C. A. (2021). Supplemental reading interventions implemented by paraprofessionals: A meta-analysis. *Psychology in the Schools*, *58*(4), 723–741.

Jones, M. W., Snowling, M. J., & Moll, K. (2016). What automaticity deficit? Activation of lexical information by readers with dyslexia in a rapid automatized naming Stroop-switch task. *Journal of Experimental Psychology: Learning, Memory, and Cognition*, *42*(3), 465.

Joo, S. J., Donnelly, P., & Yeatman, J. (2017). Learning to read does not affect motion processing in dyslexia. *Journal of Vision*, *17*(10), 642–642.

Joo, S. J., Tavabi, K., Caffarra, S., & Yeatman, J. D. (2021). Automaticity in the reading circuitry. *Brain and Language*, *214*, 104906.

Joo, S. J., White, A. L., Strodtman, D. J., & Yeatman, J. D. (2018). Optimizing text for an individual's visual system: The contribution of visual crowding to reading difficulties. *Cortex*, *103*, 291–301.

JothiPrabha, A., Bhargavi, R., & Rani, B. D. (2023). Prediction of dyslexia severity levels from fixation and saccadic eye movement using machine learning. *Biomedical Signal Processing and Control*, *79*, 104094.

Joyce, A., & Breadmore, H. L. (2022). Sleep-disordered breathing and daytime sleepiness predict children's reading ability. *British Journal of Educational Psychology*, *92*(2), 576–593.

Joyner, R. E., & Wagner, R. K. (2020). Co-occurrence of reading disabilities and math disabilities: A meta-analysis. *Scientific Studies of Reading*, *24*(1), 14–22.

Juel, C., & Minden-Cupp, C. (2000). Learning to read words: Linguistic units and instructional strategies. *Reading Research Quarterly*, *35*, 458–492.

Jung, P. G., McMaster, K. L., Kunkel, A. K., Shin, J., & Stecker, P. M. (2018). Effects of data-based individualization for students with intensive learning needs: A meta-analysis. *Learning Disabilities Research & Practice*, *33*(3), 144–155.

Kail, R., & Hall, L. K. (1994). Processing speed, naming speed, and reading. *Developmental Psychology*, *30*, 949–954.

Kairaluoma, L., Närhi, V., Ahonen, T., Westerholm, J., & Aro, M. (2008). Do fatty acids help in overcoming reading difficulties? A double-blind, placebo-controlled study of the effects of eicosapentaenoic acid and carnosine supplementation on children with dyslexia. *Child: Care, Health and Development*, *35*, 112–119.

Kalashnikova, M., Goswami, U., & Burnham, D. (2018). Mothers speak differently to infants at-risk for dyslexia. *Developmental Science*, *21*(1) 1–15.

Kamhi, A. G. (2004). A meme's eye view of speech-language pathology. *Language, Speech, and Hearing Services in Schools*, *35*, 105–111.

Kamps, D., Abbott, M., Greenwood, C., et al. (2008). Effects of small group reading instruction and curriculum differences for students most at risk in kindergarten: Two-year results for secondary- and tertiary-level interventions. *Journal of Learning Disabilities*, *41*, 101–114.

Kandel, S., Lassus-Sangosse, D., Grosjacques, G., & Perret, C. (2017). The impact of developmental dyslexia and dysgraphia on movement production during word writing. *Cognitive Neuropsychology*, *34*(3–4), 219–251.

Kaplan, B. J., Wilson, N. B., Dewey, D., & Crawford, S. G. (1998). DCD may not be a discrete disorder. *Human Movement Science, 17*, 471–490.

Karipidis, I. I., Pleisch, G., Di Pietro, S. V., Fraga-González, G., & Brem, S. (2021). Developmental trajectories of letter and speech sound integration during reading acquisition. *Frontiers in Psychology, 12.*

Karr, J. E., Kibby, M. Y., Jagger-Rickels, A. C., & Garcia-Barrera, M. A. (2021). Sensitivity and specificity of an executive function screener at identifying children with ADHD and reading disability. *Journal of Attention Disorders, 25*(1), 134–140.

Kast, M., Bezzola, L., Jäncke, L., & Meyer, M. (2011). Multi- and unisensory decoding of words and nonwords result in differential brain responses in dyslexic and nondyslexic adults. *Brain and Language, 119*, 136–148.

Katzir, T., Misra, M., & Poldrack, R. A. (2005). Imaging phonology without print: Assessing the neural correlates of phonemic awareness using fMRI. *Neuroimage, 27*, 106–115.

Kaufman, A. S. (1994). *Intelligent Testing with the WISC-III.* New York: Wiley.

Kavale, K. A., & Mattson, P. D. (1983). "One jumped off the balance beam": Meta-analysis of perceptual-motor training. *Journal of Learning Disabilities, 16*, 165–173.

Kearns, D. M., Hancock, R., Hoeft, F., Pugh, K. R., & Frost, S. J. (2019). The neurobiology of dyslexia. *Teaching Exceptional Children, 51*(3), 175–188.

Kearns, D. M., & Fuchs, D. (2013). Does cognitively focused instruction improve the academic performance of low-achieving students? *Exceptional Children, 79*(3), 263–290.

Keenan, J. M., Betjemann, R., Wadsworth, S., DeFries, J., & Olson, R. (2006). Genetic and environmental influences on reading and listening comprehension. *Journal of Research in Reading, 29*, 75–91.

Keller, T. A., & Just, M. A. (2009). Altering cortical connectivity: Remediation-induced changes in the white matter of poor readers. *Neuron, 64*, 624–631.

Kelly, D. R., & Erwin, V. M. (2022). Specific learning difficulty tutors: Direct supports for navigating disabilities and the university environment. *Disability & Society*, 1–24.

Kendell, R. E. (1975). *The Role of Diagnosis in Psychiatry.* Oxford: Blackwell.

Kere, J. (2014). The molecular genetics and neurobiology of developmental dyslexia as model of a complex phenotype. *Biochemical and Biophysical Research Communications, 452*, 236–243.

Kermani, M., Verghese, A., & Vidyasagar, T. R. (2018). Attentional asymmetry between visual hemifields is related to habitual direction of reading and its implications for debate on cause and effects of dyslexia. *Dyslexia, 24*(1), 33–43.

Kershner, J. R. (2019). Neurobiological systems in dyslexia. *Trends in Neuroscience and Education, 14*, 11–24.

Kersting, K. (2004). Debating learning-disability identification. *APA Monitor*, October, 54–55.

Kibby, M. Y., Fancher, J. B., Markanen, R., & Hynd, G. W. (2008). A quantitative magnetic resonance imaging analysis of the cerebellar deficit hypothesis of dyslexia. *Journal of Child Neurology, 23*, 368–380.

Kieffer, M. J. (2012). Before and after third grade: Longitudinal evidence for the shifting role of socioeconomic status in reading growth. *Reading and Writing*, *25*(7), 1725–1746.

Kievit, R. A. (2020). Sensitive periods in cognitive development: A mutualistic perspective. *Current Opinion in Behavioral Sciences*, *36*, 144–149.

Kievit, R. A., Hofman, A. D., & Nation, K. (2019). Mutualistic coupling between vocabulary and reasoning in young children: A replication and extension of the study by Kievit et al. (2017). *Psychological Science*, *30*(8), 1245–1252.

Kilpatrick, D. A., & O'Brien, S. (2019). Effective prevention and intervention for word-level reading difficulties. In D. A. Kilpatrick, R. Malatesha Joshi, & R. K. Wagner (eds.), *Reading Development and Difficulties: Bridging the Gap between Research and Practice* (pp. 179–210). Cham, Switzerland: Springer.

Kim, M. K., Bryant, D. P., Bryant, B. R., & Park, Y. (2017). A synthesis of interventions for improving oral reading fluency of elementary students with learning disabilities. *Preventing School Failure: Alternative Education for Children and Youth*, *61*(2), 116–125.

Kim, Y. S. G., & Petscher, Y. (2023). Do spelling and vocabulary improve classification accuracy of children's reading difficulties over and above word reading? *Reading Research Quarterly*, *58*(2), 240–253

Kim, Y. S. G., Wolters, A., & Lee, J. (2023). Reading and writing relations are not uniform. They differ by the linguistic grain size, developmental phase, and measurement. *Review of Educational Research*. https://doi.org/10.3102/00346543231178830

Kimel, E., & Ahissar, M. (2020). Benefits from morphological regularities in dyslexia are task dependent. *Journal of Experimental Psychology: Learning, Memory, and Cognition*, *46*(1), 155.

King, S., Wang, L., Datchuk, S. M., & Rodgers, D. B. (2023). Meta-analyses of reading intervention studies including students with learning disabilities: A methodological review. *Journal of Learning Disabilities*, *56*(3), 210–224.

Kirby, A., Woodward, A., Jackson, S., Wang, Y., & Crawford, M. A. (2010). A double-blind, placebo-controlled study investigating the effects of omega-3 supplementation in children aged 8–10 years from a mainstream school population. *Research in Developmental Disabilities*, *31*, 718–730.

Kirby, J. R., Georgiou, G. K., Martinussen, R., Parrila, R., Bowers, P., & Landerl, K. (2010). Naming speed and reading: From prediction to instruction. *Reading Research Quarterly*, *45*, 341–362.

Kirby, P. (2018). What's in a name? The history of dyslexia. *History Today*, *64*(12), 20–27.

Kirby, P. (2019). Gift from the gods? Dyslexia, popular culture and the ethics of representation. *Disability & Society*, *34*(9–10), 1573–1594.

Kirby, P. (2020a). Dyslexia debated, then and now: A historical perspective on the dyslexia debate. *Oxford Review of Education*, *46*(4), 472–486.

Kirby, P. (2020b). Literacy, advocacy and agency: The campaign for political recognition of dyslexia in Britain (1962–1997). *Social History of Medicine*, *33*(4), 1306–1326.

Kirby, P., & Snowling, M. J. (2022). *Dyslexia: A History*. London: McGill-Queen's University Press.

Kirk, J., & Reid, G. (2001). An examination of the relationship between dyslexia and offending in young people and the implications for the training system. *Dyslexia, 7*, 77–84.

Kirk, S. A. (1963). Behavioral diagnosis and remediation of learning disabilities. *Conference on exploring problems of the perceptually-handicapped child, 1*, 1–23.

Kirkpatrick, R. M., Legrand, L. S., Iacono, W. G., & McGue, M. (2011). A twin and adoption study of reading achievement: Testing for shared environmental and gene-environment interaction effects. *Learning and Individual Differences, 21*, 368–375.

Kjeldsen, A. C., Saarento-Zaprudin, S. K., & Niemi, P. O. (2019). Kindergarten training in phonological awareness: Fluency and comprehension gains are greatest for readers at risk in Grades 1 through 9. *Journal of Learning Disabilities, 52*(5), 366–382.

Klein, C. (1993) *Diagnosing Dyslexia*. London: Avanti.

Klein, R. M., & Farmer, M. E. (1995). Dyslexia and a temporal processing deficit: A reply to the commentaries. *Psychonomic Bulletin & Review, 2*, 515–526.

Klicpera, C., & Schabmann, A. (1993). Do German-speaking children have a chance to overcome reading and spelling difficulties? A longitudinal survey from the second until the eighth grade. *European Journal of Psychology of Education, 8*, 307–323.

Klingberg, T., Hedehus, M., Temple, E., et al. (2000). Microstructure of temporo-parietal white matter as a basis for reading ability: Evidence from diffusion tensor magnetic resonance imaging. *Neuron, 25*, 493–500.

Klingberg, T., Vaidya, C. J., Gabrieli, J. D., Moseley, M. E., & Hedehus, M. (1999). Myelination and organization of the frontal white matter in children: A diffusion tensor MRI study. *Neuroreport, 10*, 2817–2821.

Knight, C. (2021). The impact of the dyslexia label on academic outlook and aspirations: An analysis using propensity score matching. *British Journal of Educational Psychology, 91*(4), 1110–1126.

Knight, C., & Crick, T. (2021). The assignment and distribution of the dyslexia label: Using the UK Millennium Cohort Study to investigate the socio-demographic predictors of the dyslexia label in England and Wales. *PloS one, 16*(8), e0256114.

Kochunov, P., Fox, P., Lancaster, J., et al. (2003). Localized morphological brain differences between English-speaking Caucasians and Chinese-speaking Asians: New evidence of anatomical plasticity. *Neuroreport, 14*, 961–964.

Korinth, S. P., Gerstenberger, K., & Fiebach, C. J. (2020). Wider letter-spacing facilitates word processing but impairs reading rates of fast readers. *Frontiers in Psychology*, 444.

Kovas, Y., Haworth, C. M., Dale, P. S., & Plomin, R. (2007). The genetic and environmental origins of learning abilities and disabilities in the early school years. *Monographs of the Society for Research in Child Development, 72*(3), 1–144.

Kovas, Y., Haworth, C. M. A., Harlaar, N., Petrill, S. A., Dale, P. S., & Plomin, R. (2007). Overlap and specificity of genetic and environmental influences on mathematics and reading disability in 10-year-old twins. *Journal of Child Psychology and Psychiatry, 48*(9), 914–922.

Kovelman, I., Baker, S. A., & Petitto, L. A. (2008). Bilingual and monolingual brains compared: A functional magnetic resonance imaging investigation of syntactic processing and a possible "neural signature" of bilingualism. *Journal of Cognitive Neuroscience, 20*, 153–169.

Koyama, M. S., Di Martino, A., Kelly, C., et al. (2013). Cortical signatures of dyslexia and remediation: An intrinsic functional connectivity approach. *PLoS ONE, 8*, e55454.

Koyama, M. S., Kelly, C., Shehzad, Z., et al. (2010). Reading networks at rest. *Cerebral Cortex, 20*, 2549–2559.

Krafnick, A. J., Flowers, D. L., Luetje, M. M., Napoliello, E. M., & Eden, G. F. (2014). An investigation into the origin of anatomical differences in dyslexia. *The Journal of Neuroscience, 34*, 901–908.

Krafnick, A. J., Flowers, D. L., Napoliello, E. M., & Eden, G. F. (2011). Gray matter volume changes following reading intervention in dyslexic children. *Neuroimage, 57*, 733–741.

Kramer, J. H., Mungas, D., Possin, K. L., et al. (2014). NIH EXAMINER: Conceptualization and development of an executive function battery. *Journal of the International Neuropsychological Society, 20*(1), 11–19.

Kranzler, J. H., Floyd, R. G., Benson, N., Zaboski, B., & Thibodaux, L. (2016a). Classification agreement analysis of cross-battery assessment in the identification of specific learning disorders in children and youth. *International Journal of School & Educational Psychology, 4*(3), 124–136.

Kranzler, J. H., Floyd, R. G., Benson, N., Zaboski, B., & Thibodaux, L. (2016b). Cross-Battery Assessment pattern of strengths and weaknesses approach to the identification of specific learning disorders: Evidence-based practice or pseudoscience? *International Journal of School & Educational Psychology, 4*(3), 146–157.

Kranzler, J. H., Gilbert, K., Robert, C. R., Floyd, R. G., & Benson, N. F. (2019). Further examination of a critical assumption underlying the dual-discrepancy/consistency approach to specific learning disability identification. *School Psychology Review, 48*(3), 207–221.

Kranzler, J. H., Maki, K. E., Benson, N. F., et al. (2020). How do school psychologists interpret intelligence tests for the identification of specific learning disabilities? *Contemporary School Psychology, 24*, 445–456.

Krause, B., Márquez-Ruiz, J., & Cohen Kadosh, R. (2013). The effect of transcranial direct current stimulation: A role for cortical excitation/inhibition balance? *Frontiers in Human Neuroscience, 7*, 1–4.

Kriss, I., & Evans, B. J. W. (2005). The relationship between dyslexia and Meares-Irlen syndrome. *Journal of Research in Reading, 28*, 350–364.

Kristjánsson A., & Sigurðardóttir, H. M. (2023). The role of visual factors in dyslexia. *Journal of Cognition, 6*(1), 31.

Kronbichler, M., Hutzler, F., & Wimmer, H. (2002). Dyslexia: Verbal impairments in the absence of magnocellular impairments. *Cognitive Neuroscience And Neuropsychology, 13*, 617–620.

Kronbichler, M., Wimmer, H., Staffen, W., et al. (2008). Developmental dyslexia: Gray matter abnormalities in the occipitotemporal cortex. *Human Brain Mapping, 29*, 613–625.

Kudo, M. F., Lussier, C. M., & Swanson, H. L. (2015). Reading disabilities in children: A selective meta-analysis of the cognitive literature. *Research in Developmental Disabilities, 40*, 51–62.

Kuhl, U., Neef, N. E., Kraft, I., et al. (2020). The emergence of dyslexia in the developing brain. *Neuroimage, 211*.

Kujala, J., Pammer, K., Cornelissen, P., et al. (2007). Phase coupling in a cerebro-cerebellar network at 8–13 Hz during reading. *Cerebral Cortex, 17*, 1476–1485.

Kujala, T., Sihvonen, A. J., Thiede, A., et al. (2021). Voxel and surface based whole brain analysis shows reading skill associated grey matter abnormalities in dyslexia. *Scientific Reports, 11*, 10862.

Kulesz, P. A., Roberts, G. J., Francis, D. J., Cirino, P., Walczak, M., & Vaughn, S. (2023). Latent profiles as predictors of response to instruction for students with reading difficulties. *Journal of Educational Psychology.* https://dx.doi .org/10.1037/edu0000832

Kushch, A., Gross-Glenn, K., Jallad, B., et al. (1993). Temporal lobe surface area measurements on MRI in normal and dyslexic readers. *Neuropsychologia, 31*, 811–821.

Kussmaul, L. A. (1877). Disturbances of speech. In H. von Ziemssen (ed.), *Cyclopedia of the Practice of Medicine, Vol. 14.* New York: William Wood and Co.,

Kuster, S. M., van Weerdenburg, M., Gompel, M., & Bosman, A. M. (2018). Dyslexie font does not benefit reading in children with or without dyslexia. *Annals of Dyslexia, 68*(1), 25–42.

Laasonen, M., Service, E., & Virsu, V. (2001). Temporal order and processing acuity of visual, auditory, and tactile perception in developmentally dyslexic young adults. *Cognitive, Affective, & Behavioral Neuroscience, 1*, 394–410.

LaBerge, D., & Samuels, S. J. (1974). Toward a theory of automatic information process in reading. *Cognitive Psychology, 6*(2), 293–323.

Lachmann, T., & Bergström, K. (2023). The multiple-level framework of developmental dyslexia: The long trace from a neurodevelopmental deficit to an impaired cultural technique. *Journal of Cultural Cognitive Science, 7*, 71–93.

Lachmann, T., Bergström, K., Huber, J., & Nuerk, H. C. (2022). Diagnosis of dyslexia and dyscalculia: Challenges and controversies. In M. A. Skeide (ed.), *Cambridge Handbook of Dyslexia and Dyscalculia* (pp. 383–409). Cambridge: Cambridge University Press.

Lack, D. (2010). Another joint statement regarding learning disabilities, dyslexia, and vision – A rebuttal. *Optometry, 81*, 533–543.

Lackaye, T. D., & Margalit, M. (2006). Comparisons of achievement, effort, and self-perceptions among students with learning disabilities and their peers from different achievement groups. *Journal of Learning Disabilities, 39*, 432–446.

Lallier, M., Donnadieu, S., Berger, C., & Valdois, S. (2010). A case study of developmental phonological dyslexia: Is the attentional deficit in the perception of rapid stimuli sequences amodal? *Cortex, 46*, 231–241.

Lallier, M., Tainturier, M., Dering, B., et al. (2010). Behavioral and ERP evidence for amodal sluggish attentional shifting in developmental dyslexia. *Neuropsychologia, 48*, 4125–4135.

Lander, E. S. (2011). Initial impact of the sequencing of the human genome. *Nature, 470*, 187–197.

Landerl, K. (2019). Behavioral precursors of developmental dyslexia. In L. Verhoeven, C. Perfetti, & K. Pugh (eds.), *Developmental Dyslexia across Languages and Writing Systems* (pp. 229–252). Cambridge: Cambridge University Press.

Landerl, K., & Moll, K. (2010). Comorbidity of learning disorders: Prevalence and familial transmission. *Journal of Child Psychology and Psychiatry, 51*, 287–294.

Landerl, K., & Willburger, E. (2010). Temporal processing, attention, and learning disorders. *Learning and Individual Differences, 20*, 393–401.

Landerl, K., & Wimmer, H. (2000). Deficits in phoneme segmentation are not the core problem in dyslexia: Evidence from German and English children. *Applied Psycholinguistics, 21*, 243–262.

Landerl, K., Castles, A., & Parrila, R. (2022). Cognitive precursors of reading: A cross-linguistic perspective. *Scientific Studies of Reading, 26*(2), 111–124.

Landerl, K., Freudenthaler, H. H., Heene, M., et al. (2019). Phonological awareness and rapid automatized naming as longitudinal predictors of reading in five alphabetic orthographies with varying degrees of consistency. *Scientific Studies of Reading, 23*(3), 220–234.

Landerl, K., Ramus, F., Moll, K., et al. (2013). Predictors of developmental dyslexia in European orthographies with varying complexity. *Journal of Child Psychology and Psychiatry, 54*(6), 686–694.

Lang, R. (2001). *The Development and Critique of the Social Model of Disability.* Norwich: Overseas Development Group, University of East Anglia.

Langer, N., Peysakhovich, B., Zuk, J., et al. (2017). White matter alterations in infants at risk for developmental dyslexia. *Cerebral Cortex, 27*, 1027–1036.

Laprevotte, J., Papaxanthis, C., Saltarelli, S., Quercia, P., & Gaveau, J. (2021). Movement detection thresholds reveal proprioceptive impairments in developmental dyslexia. *Scientific Reports, 11*(1), 1–7.

Larsen, J. P., Hoien, T., Lundberg, I., & Odegaard, H. (1990). MRI evaluation of the size and symmetry of the planum temporale in adolescents with developmental dyslexia. *Brain and Language, 39*, 289–301.

Larsen, J. P., Hoien, T., & Odegaard, H. (1992). Magnetic resonance imaging of the corpus callosum in developmental dyslexia. *Cognitive Neuropsychology, 9*, 123–134.

Lavin Venegas, C., N. Nkangu, M., Dufy, M., Fergusson, D., & Spilg, E. (2019). Interventions to improve resilience in physicians who have completed training: A systematic review. *PLoS One, 14*.

Law, J. M., Wouters, J., & Ghesquière, P. (2017). The influences and outcomes of phonological awareness: A study of MA, PA and auditory processing in pre-readers with a family risk of dyslexia. *Developmental Science, 20*(5), e12453.

Lawrence, J. F., A. M. Hagen, J. K. Hwang, G. Lin, and Lervåg, A. (2018). Academic vocabulary and reading comprehension: Exploring the relationships across measures of vocabulary knowledge. *Reading and Writing, 32*(2), 285–306.

Lawton, T. (2016). Improving dorsal stream function in dyslexics by training figure/ground motion discrimination improves attention, reading fluency, and working memory. *Frontiers in Human Neuroscience, 10,* 397.

Laycock, R., Crewther, D. P., & Crewther, S. G. (2012). Abrupt and ramped flicker-defined form shows evidence for a large magnocellular impairment in dyslexia. *Neuropsychologia, 50,* 2107–2113.

Laycock, S. K., Wilkinson, I. D., Wallis, L. I., et al. (2008). Cerebellar volume and cerebellar metabolic characteristics in adults with dyslexia. *Annals of the New York Academy of Sciences, 1145,* 222–236.

Lazzaro, G., Costanzo, F., Varuzza, C., et al. (2021a). Individual differences modulate the effects of tDCS on reading in children and adolescents with dyslexia. *Scientific Studies of Reading, 25*(6), 470–485.

Lazzaro, G., Costanzo, F., Varuzza, C., et al. (2021b). Effects of a short, intensive, multi-session tDCS treatment in developmental dyslexia: Preliminary results of a sham-controlled randomized clinical trial. *Progress in Brain Research, 264,* 191–210.

Lazzaro, G., Varuzza, C., Costanzo, F., et al. (2021c). Memory deficits in children with developmental dyslexia: A reading-level and chronological-age matched design. *Brain Sciences, 11*(1), 40.

Leach, J. M., Scarborough, H. S., & Rescorla, L. (2003). Late-emerging reading disabilities. *Journal of Educational Psychology, 95,* 211–224.

Leavett, R., Nash, H. M., & Snowling, M. J. (2014). Am I dyslexic? Parental self-report of literacy difficulties. *Dyslexia, 20*(4), 297–304.

Lebel, C., Benischek, A., Geeraert, B., et al. (2019). Developmental trajectories of white matter structure in children with and without reading impairments. *Developmental Cognitive Neuroscience, 36,* 100633.

Lee, J. J., Wedow, R., Okbay, A., et al. (2018). Gene discovery and polygenic prediction from a genome-wide association study of educational attainment in 1.1 million individuals. *Nature Genetics, 50,* 1112–1121.

Lee, J., & Yoon, S. Y. (2017). The effects of repeated reading on reading fluency for students with reading disabilities: A meta-analysis. *Journal of Learning Disabilities, 50*(2), 213–224.

Lefèvre, E., Cavalli, E., Colé, P., Law, J. M., & Sprenger-Charolles, L. (2023). Tracking reading skills and reading-related skills in dyslexia before (age 5) and after (ages 10–17) diagnosis. *Annals of Dyslexia,* 1–28.

Leitão, S., Dzidic, P., Claessen, M., et al. (2017). Exploring the impact of living with dyslexia: The perspectives of children and their parents. *International Journal of Speech-language Pathology, 19*(3), 322–334.

Lemons, C. J., Fuchs, D., Gilbert, J. K., & Fuchs, L. S. (2014). Evidence-based practices in a changing world: Reconsidering the counterfactual in education research. *Educational Researcher, 43*(5), 242–252.

Leong, V., Kalashnikova, M., Burnham, D., & Goswami, U. (2017). The temporal modulation structure of infant-directed speech. *Open Mind, 1*(2), 78–90.

Leonard, C. M., Eckert, M. A., Lombardino, L. J., et al. (2001). Anatomical risk factors for phonological dyslexia. *Cerebral Cortex, 11*, 148–157.

Leppanen, P. H., & Lyytinen, H. (1997). Auditory event-related potentials in the study of developmental language-related disorders. *Audiology & Neurotology 2*, 308–340.

Leppänen, P. H. T., Hämäläinen, J. A., Salminen, H. K., et al. (2010). Newborn brain event-related potentials revealing atypical processing of sound frequency and the subsequent association with later literacy skills in children with familial dyslexia. *Cortex, 46*, 1362–1376.

Lervåg, A., & Aukrust, V. G. (2010). Vocabulary knowledge is a critical determinant of the difference in reading comprehension growth between first and second language learners. *Journal of Child Psychology and Psychiatry, 51*(5), 612–620.

Lervåg, A., Bråten, I., & Hulme, C. (2009). The cognitive and linguistic foundations of early reading development: A Norwegian latent variable longitudinal study. *Developmental Psychology, 45*(3), 764.

Lervåg, A., Dolean, D., Tincas, I., & Melby-Lervåg, M. (2019). Socioeconomic background, nonverbal IQ and school absence affects the development of vocabulary and reading comprehension in children living in severe poverty. *Developmental Science, 22*(5), e12858.

Levecque, C., Velayos-Baeza, A., Holloway, Z. G., & Monaco, A. P. (2009). The dyslexia-associated protein KIAA0319 interacts with adaptor protein 2 and follows the classical clathrin-mediated endocytosis pathway. *American Journal of Physiology – Cell Physiology, 297*, C160–C168.

Li, C., Ding, K., Zhang, M., et al. (2020). Effect of picture-book reading with additive audio on bilingual preschoolers' prefrontal activation: A naturalistic functional near-infrared spectroscopy study. *Frontiers of Psychology, 11*, 1939.

Li, H., Booth, J. R., Feng, X., et al. (2020). Functional parcellation of the right cerebellar lobule VI in children with normal or impaired reading. *Neuropsychologia, 148*, 107630.

Li, H., Kepinska, O., Caballero, J. N., et al. (2021). Decoding the role of the cerebellum in the early stages of reading acquisition. *Cortex, 141*, 262–279.

Li, H., Zhang, J., & Ding, G. (2021). Reading across writing systems: A meta-analysis of the neural correlates for first and second language reading. *Bilingualism: Language and Cognition, 24*, 537–548.

Li, Y., & Bates, T. C. (2019). You can't change your basic ability, but you work at things, and that's how we get hard things done: Testing the role of growth mindset on response to setbacks, educational attainment, and cognitive ability. *Journal of Experimental Psychology: General, 148*(9), 1640–1655.

Li, Y., & Bi, H.-Y. (2022). Comparative research on neural dysfunction in children with dyslexia under different writing systems: A meta-analysis study. *Neuroscience & Biobehavioral Reviews, 137*, 104650.

Liberman, A. M. (1999). The reading researcher and the reading teacher need the right theory of speech. *Scientific Studies of Reading, 3*, 95–111.

Liberman, A. M., Harris, K. S., Hoffman, H. S., & Griffith, B. C. (1957). The discrimination of speech sounds within and across phoneme boundaries. *Journal of Experimental Psychology, 54*(5), 358.

Liberman, I. Y., & Shankweiler, D. P. (1985). Phonology and the problems of learning to read and write. *Remedial and Special Education, 6*, 8–17

Liddle, E., Jackson, G., & Jackson, S. (2005). An evaluation of a visual biofeedback intervention in dyslexic adults. *Dyslexia, 11*, 61–77.

Liddle, R. (2014). Children with a severe case of the excuses. *The Spectator.* March 15, 21.

Lidz, C. S., & Elliott, J. G. (eds.). (2000). *Dynamic Assessment: Prevailing Models and Applications.* London: Elsevier.

Ligges, C., & Blanz, B. (2007). Survey of fMRI results regarding a phonological deficit in children and adults with dyslexia: Fundamental deficit or indication of compensation?. *Zeitschrift fur Kinder und Jugendpsychiatrie und Psychotherapie, 35*, 107–115.

Ligges, C., Ungureanu, M., Ligges, M., Blanz, B., & Witte, H. (2010). Understanding the time variant connectivity of the language network in developmental dyslexia: New insights using Granger causality. *Journal of Neural Transmission, 117*, 529–543.

Liloia, D., Crocetta, A., Cauda, F., et al. (2022). Seeking overlapping neuroanatomical alterations between dyslexia and attention-deficit/hyperactivity disorder: A meta-analytic replication study. *Brain Sciences, 12*(10), 1367.

Lim, K. O., & Helpern, J. A. (2002). Neuropsychiatric applications of DTI—a review. *NMR in Biomedicine, 15*, 587–593.

Lin, Y. C., Morgan, P. L., Hillemeier, M., et al. (2013). Reading, mathematics, and behavioral difficulties interrelate: Evidence from a cross-lagged panel design and population-based sample of US upper elementary students. *Behavioral Disorders, 38*(4), 212–227.

Lindgren, M., Jensen, J., Dalteg, A., et al. (2002). Dyslexia and AD/HD among Swedish prison inmates. *Journal of Scandinavian Studies in Criminology and Crime Prevention, 3*(1), 84–95.

Linkersdörfer, J., Lonnemann, J., Lindberg, S., Hasselhorn, M., & Fiebach, C. J. (2012). Grey matter alterations co-localize with functional abnormalities in developmental dyslexia: An ALE meta-analysis. *PLoS ONE, 7*(8), e43122.

Lionel, A. C., Crosbie, J., Barbosa, N., et al. (2011). Rare copy number variation discovery and cross-disorder comparisons identify risk genes for ADHD. *Science Translational Medicine, 3*, 95ra75.

Lipka, O., Lesaux, N. K., & Siegel, L. (2006). Retrospective analyses of the reading development of grade 4 students with reading disabilities: Risk status and profiles over 5 years. *Journal of Learning Disabilities, 39*, 364–378.

Literacy Task Force. (1997). *The Implementation of the National Literacy Strategy.* London: Labour Party.

Little, C. W., & Hart, S. A. (2022). Genetic and environmental influences on learning to read. In M. J. Snowling, C. Hulme, & K. Nation (eds.), *The Science of Reading: A Handbook.* 2nd edition (pp. 515–532). Hoboken, NJ: Wiley.

Little, C. W., Haughbrook, R., & Hart, S. A. (2017). Cross-study differences in the etiology of reading comprehension: A meta-analytical review of twin studies. *Behavior Genetics, 47*(1), 52–76.

Liu, J., Peng, P., Zhao, B., & Luo, L. (2022). Socioeconomic status and academic achievement in primary and secondary education: A meta-analytic review. *Educational Psychology Review, 34*, 2867–2896

Liu, L., Wang, W., You, W., et al. (2012). Similar alterations in brain function for phonological and semantic processing to visual characters in Chinese dyslexia. *Neuropsychologia, 50*, 2224–2232.

Liu, T., Thiebaut de Schotten, M., Altarelli, I., Ramus, F., & Zhao, J. (2021). Maladaptive compensation of right fusiform gyrus in developmental dyslexia: A hub-based white matter network analysis. *Cortex, 145*, 57–66.

Livingston, E. M., Siegel, L. S., & Ribary, U. (2018). Developmental dyslexia: Emotional impact and consequences. *Australian Journal of Learning Difficulties, 23*(2), 107–135.

Livingstone, M. S., Rosen, G. D., Drislane, F. W., & Galaburda, A. M. (1991). Physiological and anatomical evidence for a magnocellular defect in developmental dyslexia. *Proceedings of the National Academy of Sciences of the United States of America, 88*, 7943–7947.

Lizarazu, M., Lallier, M., Bourguignon, M., Carreiras, M., & Molinaro, N. (2021). Impaired neural response to speech edges in dyslexia. *Cortex, 135*, 207–218.

Lizarazu, M., Scotto di Covella, L., van Wassenhove, V., et al. (2021). Neural entrainment to speech and nonspeech in dyslexia: Conceptual replication and extension of previous investigations. *Cortex, 137*, 160–178.

Lobier, M., & Valdois, S. (2015). Visual attention deficits in developmental dyslexia cannot be ascribed solely to poor reading experience. *Nature Reviews Neuroscience, 16*(4), 225.

Lobier, M., Zoubrinetzky, R., & Valdois, S. (2012). The visual attention span deficit in dyslexia is visual and not verbal. *Cortex, 48*(6), 768–773.

Locascio, G., Mahone, E. M., Eason, S. H., & Cutting, L. E. (2010). Executive dysfunction among children with reading comprehension deficits. *Journal of Learning Disabilities, 43*(5), 441–454.

Lochy, A., Van Reybroeck, M., & Rossion, B. (2016). Left cortical specialization for visual letter strings predicts rudimentary knowledge of letter–sound association in preschoolers. *Proceedings of the National Academy of Sciences, 113*, 8544–8549.

Locke, R., Alexander, G., Mann, R., Kibble, S., & Scallan, S. (2017). Doctors with dyslexia: Strategies and support. *The Clinical Teacher, 14*(5), 355–359.

Łockiewicz, M., Bogdanowicz, K. M., & Bogdanowicz, M. (2014). Psychological resources of adults with developmental dyslexia. *Journal of Learning Disabilities, 47*(6), 543–555.

Lockwood, A. B., Benson, N., Farmer, R. L., & Klatka, K. (2022). Test use and assessment practices of school psychology training programs: Findings from a 2020 survey of US faculty. *Psychology in the Schools, 59*(4), 698–725.

Lockwood, A. B., & Farmer, R. L. (2020). The cognitive assessment course: Two decades later. *Psychology in the Schools, 57*(2), 265–283.

Logan, J. (2009). Dyslexic entrepreneurs: The incidence; their coping strategies and their business skills. *Dyslexia, 15*, 328–346.

Logan, J., & Martin, N. (2012). Unusual talent: A study of successful leadership and delegation in entrepreneurs who have dyslexia. *Journal of Inclusive Practice in Further and Higher Education, 4*(1), 55–75.

Lohvansuu, K., Torppa, M., Ahonen, T., et al. (2021). Unveiling the mysteries of dyslexia – Lessons learned from the prospective Jyväskylä longitudinal study of dyslexia. *Brain Sciences, 11*(4), 427.

Lopes, J. A., Gomes, C., Oliveira, C. R., & Elliott, J. G. (2020). Research studies on dyslexia: Participant inclusion and exclusion criteria. *European Journal of Special Needs Education, 35*(5), 587–602.

Loras, H., Sigmundsson, H., Stensdotter, A. K., & Talcott, J. B. (2014). Postural control is not systematically related to reading skills: Implications for the assessment of balance as a risk factor for developmental dyslexia. *PloS one, 9*(6), e98224.

Lorusso, M. L., & Toraldo, A. (2023). Revisiting multifactor models of dyslexia: Do they fit empirical data and what are their implications for intervention? *Brain Sciences, 13*(2), 328.

Louleli, N., Hämäläinen, J. A., Nieminen, L., Parviainen, T., & Leppänen, P. H. T. (2022). Neural correlates of morphological processing and its development from pre-school to the first grade in children with and without familial risk for dyslexia. *Journal of Neurolinguistics, 61*, 101037.

Lovegrove, W. J., Bowling, A., Badcock, D., & Blackwood, M. (1980). Specific reading disability: Differences in contrast sensitivity as a function of spatial frequency. *Science, 210*, 439–440.

Lovett, M. W., Barron, R. W., & Frijters, J. C. (2013). Word identification difficulties in children and adolescents with reading disabilities. In H. L. Swanson, K. R. Harris, & S. Graham (eds.), *Handbook of Learning Disabilities* (pp. 329–360). New York: Guilford Press.

Lovett, M. W., Frijters, J. C., Steinbach, K. A., Sevcik, R. A., & Morris, R. D. (2021). Effective intervention for adolescents with reading disabilities: Combining reading and motivational remediation to improve outcomes. *Journal of Educational Psychology, 113*(4), 656–689.

Lovett, M. W., Frijters, J. C., Wolf, M., et al. (2017). Early intervention for children at risk for reading disabilities: The impact of grade at intervention and individual differences on intervention outcomes. *Journal of Educational Psychology, 109*(7), 889–914.

Lu, X., Shaw, C. A., Patel, A., et al. (2007). Clinical implementation of chromosomal microarray analysis: Summary of 2513 postnatal cases. *PLoS ONE, 2*(3), e327.

Luciano, M., Evans, D. M., Hansell, N. K., et al. (2013). A genome-wide association study for reading and language abilities in two population cohorts. *Genes, Brain and Behavior, 12*, 645–652.

Lundberg, I., Larsman, P., & Strid, A. (2012). Development of phonological awareness during the preschool year: The influence of gender and socioeconomic status. *Reading and Writing, 25*, 305–320.

Łuniewska, M., Chyl, K., Debska, A., et al. (2019). Children with dyslexia and familial risk for dyslexia present atypical development of the neuronal phonological network. *Frontiers in Neuroscience, 13*, 1287.

Łuniewska, M., Chyl, K., Debska, A., et al. (2018). Neither action nor phonological video games make dyslexic children read better. *Scientific Reports*, *8*(1), 1–11.

Lurie, L. A., Hagen, M. P., McLaughlin, K. A., et al. (2021). Mechanisms linking socioeconomic status and academic achievement in early childhood: Cognitive stimulation and language. *Cognitive Development*, *58*, 101045.

Luthar, S. S., Cicchetti, D., & Becker, B. (2000). The construct of resilience: A critical evaluation and guidelines for future work. *Child Development*, *71*(3), 543–562.

Lyon, G. R., Shaywitz, S. E., & Shaywitz, B. A. (2003). A definition of dyslexia. *Annals of Dyslexia*, *53*, 1–14.

Lyster, S. A. H., Snowling, M. J., Hulme, C., & Lervåg, A. O. (2021). Preschool phonological, morphological and semantic skills explain it all: Following reading development through a 9-year period. *Journal of Research in Reading*, *44*(1), 175–188.

Lyytinen, P., Eklund, K., & Lyytinen, H. (2005). Language development and literacy skills in late-talking toddlers with and without familial risk for dyslexia. *Annals of Dyslexia*, *55*(2), 166–192.

Ma, Y., Koyama, M. S., Milham, M. P., et al. (2015). Cortical thickness abnormalities associated with dyslexia, independent of remediation status. *NeuroImage: Clinical*, *7*, 177–186.

Macaruso, P., Locke, J., Smith, S. T., & Powers, S. (1995). Short-term memory and phonological coding in developmental dyslexia. *Journal of Neurolinguistics*, *9*, 135–146.

Macdonald, K. T., Cirino, P. T., Miciak, J., & Grills, A. E. (2021). The role of reading anxiety among struggling readers in fourth and fifth grade. *Reading & Writing Quarterly*, *37*(4), 382–394.

Macdonald, K., Germine, L., Anderson, A., Christodoulou, J., & McGrath, L. M. (2017). Dispelling the myth: Training in education or neuroscience decreases but does not eliminate beliefs in neuromyths. *Frontiers in Psychology*, *8*, 1314.

Macdonald, K., Milne, N., Orr, R., & Pope, R. (2018). Relationships between motor proficiency and academic performance in mathematics and reading in school-aged children and adolescents: A systematic review. *International Journal of Environmental Research and Public Health*, *15*(8), 1603.

Macdonald, S. J. (2019). From "disordered" to "diverse": Defining six sociological frameworks employed in the study of dyslexia in the UK. *Insights into Learning Disabilities*, *16*(1), 1–22.

Macdonald, S. J. (2010). Towards a social reality of dyslexia. *British Journal of Learning Disabilities*, *38*(4), 271–279.

Macdonald, S. J., & Deacon, L. (2019). Twice upon a time: Examining the effect socioeconomic status has on the experience of dyslexia in the United Kingdom. *Dyslexia*, *25*(1), 3–19.

Madriaga, M., Hanson, K., Heaton, C., et al. (2010). Confronting similar challenges? Disabled and non-disabled students' learning and assessment experiences. *Studies in Higher Education*, *35*(6), 647–658.

Maehler, C., & Schuchardt, K. (2009). Working memory in children with learning disabilities: Does intelligence make a difference? *Journal of Intellectual Disability Research*, *53*, 3–10

Maehler, C., & Schuchardt, K. (2011). Working memory in children with learning disabilities: Rethinking the criterion of disability. *International Journal of Disability, Development and Education, 58*(1), 5–17.

Maher, B. (2008). The case of the missing heritability. *Nature, 456*, 18–21.

Maisog, J. M., Einbinder, E. R., Flowers, D. L., Turkeltaub, P. E., & Eden, G. F. (2008). A meta-analysis of functional neuroimaging studies of dyslexia. In G. F. Eden, & D. L. Flowers (eds.), *Learning, Skill Acquisition, Reading, and Dyslexia* (pp. 237–259). Oxford: Wiley-Blackwell.

Majeed, N. M., Hartanto, A., & Tan, J. J. (2021). Developmental dyslexia and creativity: A meta-analysis. *Dyslexia, 27*(2), 187–203.

Maki, K. E., & Adams, S. R. (2019). A current landscape of specific learning disability identification: Training, practices, and implications. *Psychology in the Schools, 56*(1), 18–31.

Maki, K. E., Kranzler, J. H., & Moody, M. E. (2022). Dual discrepancy/consistency pattern of strengths and weaknesses method of specific learning disability identification: Classification accuracy when combining clinical judgment with assessment data. *Journal of School Psychology, 92*, 33–48.

Malchow, H. (2014). IDA responds to the "Dyslexia Debate." https://dyslexiaida.org/dyslexia-debate/

Malone, S. A., Pritchard, V. E., & Hulme, C. (2022). Domain-specific skills, but not fine-motor or executive function, predict later arithmetic and reading in children. *Learning and Individual Differences, 95*, 102141.

Mandke, K., Flanagan, S., Macfarlane, A., et al. (2022). Neural sampling of the speech signal at different timescales by children with dyslexia. *NeuroImage, 253*, 119077.

Mann, L. (1979). *On the Trail of Process*. New York: Grune & Stratton.

Manning, C., Hassall, C. D., Hunt, L. T., et al. (2022). Visual motion and decision-making in dyslexia: Reduced accumulation of sensory evidence and related neural dynamics. *Journal of Neuroscience, 42*(1), 121–134.

Marazzi, C. (2011). Dyslexia and the economy. *Angelaki: Journal of the Theoretical Humanities, 16*(3), 19–32.

Marchand-Krynski, M. È., Bélanger, A. M., Morin-Moncet, O., Beauchamp, M. H., & Leonard, G. (2018). Cognitive predictors of sequential motor impairments in children with dyslexia and/or attention deficit/hyperactivity disorder. *Developmental Neuropsychology, 43*(5), 430–453.

Mareva, S., Akarca, D., CALM team, et al. (2023). Transdiagnostic profiles of behaviour and communication relate to academic and socioemotional functioning and neural white matter organisation. *Journal of Child Psychology and Psychiatry, 64*(2), 217–233.

Marino, C., Giorda, R., Luisa Lorusso, M., et al. (2005). A family-based association study does not support DYX1C1 on 15q21.3 as a candidate gene in developmental dyslexia. *European Journal of Human Genetics, 13*, 491–499.

Market Research Intellect. (2023). Global dyslexia treatment market size by product, by application, by geography, competitive landscape and forecast (Report ID: MRI – 256898). Dyslexia treatment market size, share, outlook, trend and forecast. www.marketresearchintellect.com. Accessed June 1, 2023.

Markov, I., Kharitonova, K., & Grigorenko, E. L. (2023). Language: Its origin and ongoing evolution. *Journal of Intelligence, 11*, 61.

Marks, R. A., Eggleston, R. L., Sun, X., et al. (2022). The neurocognitive basis of morphological processing in typical and impaired readers. *Annals of Dyslexia, 72*, 361–383.

Martelli, M., Di Filippo, G., Spinelli, D., & Zoccolotti, P. (2009). Crowding, reading, and developmental dyslexia. *Journal of Vision, 9*, 1–18.

Martin, A., Kronbichler, M., & Richlan, F. (2016). Dyslexic brain activation abnormalities in deep and shallow orthographies: A meta-analysis of 28 functional neuroimaging studies. *Human Brian Mapping, 37*, 2676–2699.

Martin, A., Schurz, M., Kronbichler, M., & Richlan, F. (2015). Reading in the brain of children and adults: A meta-analysis of 40 functional magnetic resonance imaging studies. *Human Brain Mapping, 36*, 1963–1981.

Martinelli, V., Camilleri, D., & Fenech, D. (2018). Common beliefs and research evidence about dyslexic students' specific skills: Is it time to reassess some of the evidence? *Interdisciplinary Education and Psychology, 2*(2), 4.

Martinez, D., Georgiou, G. K., Inoue, T., Falcón, A., & Parrila, R. (2021). How does rapid automatized naming influence orthographic knowledge? *Journal of Experimental Child Psychology, 204*, 105064.

Martinez, K. M., Holden, L. R., Hart, S. A., & Taylor, J. (2022). Examining mindset and grit in concurrent and future reading comprehension: A twin study. *Developmental Psychology, 58*, 2171–2183.

Martinez-Garay, I., Guidi, L. G., Holloway, Z. G., et al. (2017). Normal radial migration and lamination are maintained in dyslexia-susceptibility candidate gene homolog Kiaa0319 knockout mice. *Brain Structure and Function, 222*, 1367–1384.

Martínez-García, C., Afonso, O., Cuetos, F., & Suárez-Coalla, P. (2021). Handwriting production in Spanish children with dyslexia: Spelling or motor difficulties? *Reading and Writing, 34*(3), 565–593.

Mascheretti, S., De Luca, A., Trezzi, V., et al. (2017). Neurogenetics of developmental dyslexia: From genes to behavior through brain neuroimaging and cognitive and sensorial mechanisms. *Translational Psychiatry, 7*(1), e987–e987.

Mascheretti, S., Gori, S., Trezzi, V., et al. (2018). Visual motion and rapid auditory processing are solid endophenotypes of developmental dyslexia. *Genes, Brain and Behavior, 17*(1), 70–81.

Mascheretti, S., Riva, V., Giorda, R., et al. (2014). KIAA0319 and ROBO1: Evidence on association with reading and pleiotropic effects on language and mathematics abilities in developmental dyslexia. *Journal of Human Genetics, 59*, 189–197.

Massinen, S., Hokkanen, M. E., Matsson, H., et al. (2011). Increased expression of the dyslexia candidate gene DCDC2 affects length and signaling of primary cilia in neurons. *PLoS ONE, 6*, e20580.

Massinen, S., Wang, J., Laivuori, K., et al. (2016). Genomic sequencing of a dyslexia susceptibility haplotype encompassing ROBO1. *Journal of Neurodevelopmental Disorders, 8*, 4.

Masten, A. S. (2001). Ordinary magic: Resilience processes in development. *American Psychologist, 56*(3), 227–238.

Masten, A. S., & Barnes, A. J. (2018). Resilience in children: Developmental perspectives. *Children, 5*(7), 98.

Mather, N., & Schneider, D. (2023). The use of cognitive tests in the assessment of dyslexia. *Journal of Intelligence, 11*(5), 79.

Mather, N., White, J., & Youman, M. (2020). Dyslexia around the world: A snapshot. *Learning Disabilities, 25*(1), 1–17.

Mathes, P. G., & Denton, C. A. (2002). The prevention and identification of reading disability. *Seminars in Pediatric Neurology, 9*, 185–191.

Mathes, P. G., Denton, C. A., Fletcher, J. M., et al. (2005). The effects of theoretically different instruction and student characteristics on the skills of struggling readers. *Reading Research Quarterly, 40*, 148–182.

Mathur, A., Schultz, D., & Wang, Y. (2020). Neural bases of phonological and semantic processing in early childhood. *Brain Connectivity, 10*, 212–223.

Mattson, M. P. (2002). Neurogenetics: White matter matters. *Trends in Neurosciences, 25*, 135–136.

Matuszkiewicz, M., & Gałkowski, T. (2021). Developmental language disorder and uninhibited primitive reflexes in young children. *Journal of Speech, Language, and Hearing Research, 64*(3), 935–948.

Maughan, B., Rutter, M., & Yule, W. (2020). The Isle of Wight studies: The scope and scale of reading difficulties. *Oxford Review of Education, 46*(4), 429–438.

Maurer, U., Brem, S., Bucher, K., et al. (2007). Impaired tuning of a fast occipito-temporal response for print in dyslexic children learning to read. *Brain, 130*(12), 3200–3210.

Maurer, U., Bucher, K., Brem, S., et al. (2009). Neurophysiology in preschool improves behavioral prediction of reading ability throughout primary school. *Biological Psychiatry, 66*, 341–348.

May, H., Blakeney, A., Shrestha, P., Mazal, M., & Kennedy, N. (2023) Long-term impacts of Reading Recovery through 3rd and 4th grade: A regression discontinuity study, *Journal of Research on Educational Effectiveness*, 1–26.

Mayes, S. D., & Calhoun, S. L. (2006). Frequency of reading, math, and writing disabilities in children with clinical disorders. *Learning and Individual Differences, 16*, 145–157.

McArthur, G. M. (2007). Test-retest effects in treatment studies of reading disability: The devil is in the detail. *Dyslexia, 13*, 240–252.

McArthur, G. M. (2009). Auditory processing disorders: Can they be treated? *Current Opinion in Neurology, 22*, 137–143.

McArthur, G. M., Badcock, N. A., Castles, A., & Robidoux, S. (2022). Tracking the relations between children's reading and emotional health across time: Evidence from four large longitudinal studies. *Reading Research Quarterly, 57*(2), 555–585.

McArthur, G. M., Ellis, D., Atkinson, C. M., & Coltheart, M. (2008). Auditory processing deficits in children with reading and language impairments: Can they (and should they) be treated? *Cognition, 107*, 946–977.

McArthur, G. M., Filardi, N., Francis, D. A., Boyes, M. E., & Badcock, N. A. (2020). Self-concept in poor readers: A systematic review and meta-analysis. *PeerJ*, *8*, e8772.

McArthur, G. M., & Hogben, J. H. (2012). Poor auditory task scores in children with specific reading and language difficulties: Some poor scores are more equal than others. *Scientific Studies of Reading*, *16*, 63–89.

McCandliss, B. D., Cohen, L., & Dehaene, S. (2003). The visual word form area: Expertise for reading in the fusiform gyrus. *Trends in Cognitive Sciences*, *7*, 293–299.

McCardle, P., & Chhabra, V. (2004). *The Voice of Evidence in Reading Research*. Baltimore: Paul H. Brookes.

McCrory, E. J., Mechelli, A., Frith, U., & Price, C. J. (2005). More than words: A common neural basis for reading and naming deficits in developmental dyslexia? *Brain*, *128*, 261–267.

McGee, R., Williams, S., Share, D. L., Anderson, J., & Silva, P. A. (1986). The relationship between specific reading retardation, general reading backwardness and behavioral problems in a large sample of Dunedin boys: A longitudinal study from five to eleven years. *Journal of Child Psychology and Psychiatry*, *27*, 597–610.

McGill, R. J., & Busse, R. T. (2017). A rejoinder on the PSW model for SLD identification: Still concerned. *Contemporary School Psychology*, *21*(1), 23–27.

McGill, R. J., Dombrowski, S. C., & Canivez, G. L. (2018). Cognitive profile analysis in school psychology: History, issues, and continued concerns. *Journal of School Psychology*, *71*, 108–121.

McGrath, L. M., Pennington, B. F., Shanahan, M. A., et al. (2011). A multiple deficit model of reading disability and attention-deficit/hyperactivity disorder: Searching for shared cognitive deficits. *Journal of Child Psychology and Psychiatry*, *52*(5), 547–557.

McGrath, L. M., Peterson, R. L., & Pennington, B. F. (2020). The multiple deficit model: Progress, problems, and prospects. *Scientific Studies of Reading*, *24*(1), 7–13.

McGrath, L. M., & Stoodley, C. J. (2019). Are there shared neural correlates between dyslexia and ADHD? A meta-analysis of voxel-based morphometry studies. *Journal of Neurodevelopmental Disorders*, *11*, 31.

McLaughlin, M. J., Speirs, K. E., & Shenassa, E. D. (2014). Reading disability and adult attained education and income: Evidence from a 30-year longitudinal study of a population-based sample. *Journal of Learning Disabilities*, *47*(4), 374–386.

McLean, G. M. T., Castles, A., Coltheart, V., & Stuart, G. W. (2010). No evidence for a prolonged attentional blink in developmental dyslexia. *Cortex*, *46*, 1317–1329.

McLean, G. M. T., Stuart, G. W., Coltheart, V., & Castles, A. (2011). Visual temporal processing in dyslexia and the magnocellular deficit theory: The need for speed? *Journal of Experimental Psychology: Human Perception and Performance*, *37*(6), 1957–1975

McLeskey, J., & Waldron, N. L. (2011). Educational programs for elementary students with learning disabilities: Can they be both effective and inclusive? *Learning Disabilities Research & Practice, 26*(1), 48–57.

McLoughlin, D., Fitzgibbon, G., & Young, V. (1994). *Adult Dyslexia: Assessment, Counselling and Training.* London: Whurr.

McNorgan, C., Randazzo-Wagner, M., & Booth, J. R. (2013). Cross-modal integration in the brain is related to phonological awareness only in typical readers, not in those with reading difficulty. *Frontiers in Human Neuroscience, 7*, 388.

McNulty, M. A. (2003). Dyslexia and the life course. *Journal of Learning Disabilities, 36*(4), 363–381.

McPhillips, M., Hepper, P. G., & Mulhern, G. (2000). Effects of replicating primary-reflex movements on specific reading difficulties in children: A randomised, double-blind, controlled trial. *The Lancet, 355*, 537–541.

McPhillips, M., & Jordan-Black, J. A. (2007). Primary reflex persistence in children with reading difficulties (dyslexia): A cross-sectional study. *Neuropsychologia, 45*, 748–754.

McTigue, E. M., Solheim, O. J., Zimmer, W. K., & Uppstad, P. H. (2020). Critically reviewing GraphoGame across the world: Recommendations and cautions for research and implementation of computer-assisted instruction for word-reading acquisition. *Reading Research Quarterly, 55*(1), 45–73.

McWeeny, S., Choi, S., Choe, J., et al. (2022). Rapid automatized naming (RAN) as a kindergarten predictor of future reading in English: A systematic review and meta-analysis. *Reading Research Quarterly, 57*(4), 1187–1211.

Meaburn, E., Harlaar, N., Craig, I., Schalkwyk, L., & Plomin, R. (2008). Quantitative trait locus association scan of early reading disability and ability using pooled DNA and 100K SNP microarrays in a sample of 5760 children. *Molecular Psychiatry, 13*, 729–740.

Mechelli, A., Price, C. J., Friston, K. J., & Ashburner, J. (2005). Voxel-based morphometry of the human brain: Methods and applications. *Current Methods in Imaging, 1*, 105–113.

Meilleur, A., Foster, N. E., Coll, S. M., Brambati, S. M., & Hyde, K. L. (2020). Unisensory and multisensory temporal processing in autism and dyslexia: A systematic review and meta-analysis. *Neuroscience & Biobehavioral Reviews, 116*, 44–63.

Meisinger, E. B., Breazeale, A. M., & Davis, L. H. (2022). Word-and text-level reading difficulties in students with dyslexia. *Learning Disability Quarterly, 45*(4), 294–305.

Melby-Lervåg, M., & Hulme, C. (2013). Is working memory training effective? A meta-analytic review. *Developmental Psychology, 49*(2), 270.

Melby-Lervåg, M., Lyster, S., & Hulme, C. (2012). Phonological skills and their role in learning to read: A meta-analytic review. *Psychological Bulletin, 138*, 322–352.

Melby-Lervåg, M., Redick, T. S., & Hulme, C. (2016). Working memory training does not improve performance on measures of intelligence or other measures of "far transfer" evidence from a meta-analytic review. *Perspectives on Psychological Science, 11*(4), 512–534.

Meng, H., Smith, S. D., Hager, K., et al. (2005). DCDC2 is associated with reading disability and modulates neuronal development in the brain. *Proceedings of the National Academy of Sciences of the United States of America, 102,* 17053–17058.

Menghini, D., Carlesimo, G. A., Marotta, L., Finzi, A., & Vicari, S. (2010). Developmental dyslexia and explicit long-term memory. *Dyslexia, 16,* 213–225.

Menghini, D., Finzi, A., Carlesimo, G. A., & Vicari, S. (2011). Working memory impairment in children with developmental dyslexia: Is it just a phonological deficit? *Developmental Neuropsychology, 36,* 199–213.

Menghini, D., Hagberg, G. E., Petrosini, L., et al. (2008). Structural correlates of implicit learning deficits in subjects with developmental dyslexia. *Annals of the New York Academy of Sciences, 1145,* 212–221.

Mengisidou, M., & Marshall, C. R. (2019). Deficient explicit access to phonological representations explains phonological fluency difficulties in Greek children with dyslexia and/or developmental language disorder. *Frontiers in Psychology, 10,* 638.

Merz, E. C., Maskus, E. A., Melvin, S. A., He, X., & Noble, K. G. (2020). Socioeconomic disparities in language input are associated with children's language-related brain structure and reading skills. *Child Development, 91,* 846–860

Merzenich, M. M., Jenkins, W. M., Johnston, P., et al. (1996). Temporal processing deficits of language-learning impaired children ameliorated by training. *Science, 271,* 77–81.

Metsala, J. L., & David, M. D. (2022). Improving English reading fluency and comprehension for children with reading fluency disabilities. *Dyslexia, 28*(1), 79–96.

Meyler, A., Keller, T. A., Cherkassky, V. L., et al. (2007). Brain activation during sentence comprehension among good and poor readers. *Cerebral Cortex, 17,* 2780–2787.

Miciak, J., Cirino, P. T., Ahmed, Y., Reid, E., & Vaughn, S. (2019). Executive functions and response to intervention: Identification of students struggling with reading comprehension. *Learning Disability Quarterly, 42*(1), 17–31.

Miciak, J., & Fletcher, J. M. (2020). The critical role of instructional response for identifying dyslexia and other learning disabilities. *Journal of Learning Disabilities, 53*(5), 343–353.

Miciak, J., & Fletcher, J. M. (2023). Specific reading disabilities. In G. G. Brown, T. Z. King, K. Y. Haaland, & B. Crosson (eds.), *APA Handbook of Neuropsychology: Vol. 1: Neurobehavioral Disorders and Conditions: Accepted Science and Open Questions* (pp. 57–80). Washington, DC: American Psychological Association.

Miciak, J., Fletcher, J. M., Stuebing, K. K., Vaughn, S., & Tolar, T. D. (2014). Patterns of cognitive strengths and weaknesses: Identification rates, agreement, and validity for learning disabilities identification. *School Psychology Quarterly 29,* 21–37.

Miciak, J., Roberts, G., Taylor, W. P., et al. (2018). The effects of one versus two years of intensive reading intervention implemented with late elementary struggling readers. *Learning Disabilities Research & Practice, 33*(1), 24–36.

Miciak, J., Taylor, W. P., Stuebing, K. K., & Fletcher, J. M. (2018). Simulation of LD identification accuracy using a pattern of processing strengths and weaknesses method with multiple measures. *Journal of Psychoeducational Assessment, 36*(1), 21–33.

Miciak, J., Williams, J. L., Taylor, W. P., et al. (2016). Do processing patterns of strengths and weaknesses predict differential treatment response? *Journal of Educational Psychology, 108*(6), 898–1011.

Middleton, A. E., Farris, E. A., Ring, J. J., & Odegard, T. N. (2022). Predicting and evaluating treatment response: Evidence toward protracted response patterns for severely impacted students with dyslexia. *Journal of Learning Disabilities, 55*(4), 272–291.

Middleton, F. A., & Strick, P. L. (1997). Cerebellar output channels. *International Review of Neurobiology, 41*, 61–82.

Miller, D. T., Adam, M. P., Aradhya, S., et al. (2010). Consensus statement: Chromosomal microarray is a first-tier clinical diagnostic test for individuals with developmental disabilities or congenital anomalies. *American Journal of Human Genetics, 86*, 749–764.

Miller-Cotto, D., & Byrnes, J. P. (2020). What's the best way to characterize the relationship between working memory and achievement? An initial examination of competing theories. *Journal of Educational Psychology, 112*(5), 1074–1084.

Mills, K. L., & Tamnes, C. K. (2014). Methods and considerations for longitudinal structural brain imaging analysis across development. *Developmental Cognitive Neuroscience, 9*, 172–190.

Mirahadi, S. S., Nitsche, M. A., Pahlavanzadeh, B., et al. (2023). Reading and phonological awareness improvement accomplished by transcranial direct current stimulation combined with phonological awareness training: A randomized controlled trial. *Applied Neuropsychology: Child, 12*, 137–149.

Mittag, M., Larson, E., Clarke, M., Taulu, S., & Kuhl, P. K. (2021). Auditory deficits in infants at risk for dyslexia during a linguistic sensitive period predict future language. *Neuroimage Clinical, 30*, 102578.

Miyake, A., Friedman, N. P., Emerson, M. J., et al. (2000). The unity and diversity of executive functions and their contributions to complex "frontal lobe" tasks: A latent variable analysis. *Cognitive Psychology, 41*(1), 49–100.

Miyasaka, J. D. S., Vieira, R. V. G., Novalo-Goto, E. S., Montagna, E., & Wajnsztejn, R. (2019). Irlen syndrome: Systematic review and level of evidence analysis. *Arquivos de neuro-psiquiatria, 77*, 194–207.

Moats, L. C. (2017). Can prevailing approaches to reading instruction accomplish the goals of RTI. *Perspectives on Language and Literacy, 43*(3), 15–22.

Moats, L. C., & Foorman, B. (1997). Introduction to special issue of SSR: Components of effective reading instruction. *Scientific Studies of Reading, 1*, 187–189.

Mody, M., Studdert-Kennedy, M., & Brady, S. (1997). Speech perception deficits in poor readers: Auditory processing or phonological coding? *Journal of Experimental Child Psychology, 64*, 199–231.

Mol, S. E., & Bus, A. G. (2011). To read or not to read: A meta-analysis of print exposure from infancy to early childhood. *Psychological Bulletin, 137*, 267–296.

Molfese, P. J., Fletcher, J. M., & Denton, C. A. (2013). Adequate versus inadequate response to reading intervention: An event-related potentials assessment. *Developmental Neuropsychology*, *38*(8), 534–549.

Moll, K. (2022). Comorbidity of reading disorders. In M. J. Snowling, C. Hulme, & K. Nation (eds.), *The Science of Reading: A Handbook*. 2nd edition (pp. 439–459). Hoboken, NJ: Wiley.

Moll, K., Fussenegger, B., Willburger, E., & Landerl, K. (2009). RAN is not a measure of orthographic processing. Evidence from the asymmetric German orthography. *Scientific Studies of Reading*, *13*, 1–25.

Moll, K., Georgii, B. J., Tunder, R., & Schulte-Körne, G. (2022). Economic evaluation of dyslexia intervention. *Dyslexia*, *29*(1), 4–21.

Moll, K., Landerl, K., Snowling, M. J., & Schulte-Körne, G. (2019). Understanding comorbidity of learning disorders: Task-dependent estimates of prevalence. *Journal of Child Psychology and Psychiatry*, *60*(3), 286–294.

Moll, K., Loff, A., & Snowling, M. J. (2013). Cognitive endophenotypes of dyslexia. *Scientific Studies of Reading*, *17*(6), 385–397.

Moll, K., Ramus, F., Bartling, J., et al. (2014). Cognitive mechanisms underlying reading and spelling development in five European orthographies. *Learning and Instruction*, *29*, 65–77.

Moody, S., Vaughn, S., Hughes, M., & Fischer, M. (2000). Reading instruction in the resource room: Set up for failure. *Exceptional Children*, *53*, 391–316.

Moreau, D., Stonyer, J. E., McKay, N. S., & Waldie, K. E. (2018). No evidence for systematic white matter correlates of dyslexia: An activation likelihood estimation meta-analysis. *Brain Research*, *1683*, 36–47.

Moores, E., Cassim, R., & Talcott, J. B. (2011). Adults with dyslexia exhibit large effects of crowding, increased dependence on cues, and detrimental effects of distractors in visual search tasks. *Neuropsychologia*, *49*, 3881–3890.

Morgan, E., & Klein, C. (2000). *The Dyslexic Adult*. London: Whurr.

Morgan, P. L., Farkas, G., Tufis, P. A., & Sperling, R. A. (2008). Are reading and behaviour problems risk factors for each other? *Journal of Learning Disabilities*, *41*, 417–436.

Morgan, P. L., & Fuchs, D. (2007). Is there a bidirectional relationship between children's reading skills and reading motivation? *Exceptional Children*, *73*, 165–183.

Morgan, P. L., Fuchs, D., Compton, D. L., Cordray, D. S., & Fuchs, L. S. (2008). Does early reading failure decrease children's reading motivation? *Journal of Learning Disabilities*, *41*, 387–404.

Morgan, P. L., Sideridis, G., & Hua, Y. (2012). Initial and overtime effects of fluency interventions for students with or at risk for disabilities. *The Journal of Special Education*, *46*, 94–116.

Morken, F., Jones, L. Ø., & Helland, W. A. (2021). Disorders of language and literacy in the prison population: A scoping review. *Education Sciences*, *11*(2), 77.

Morris, R. D., Lovett, M. W., Wolf, M., et al. (2012). Multiple-component remediation for developmental reading disabilities: IQ, socioeconomic status, and race as factors in remedial outcome. *Journal of Learning Disabilities*, *45*(2), 99–127.

Morris, R. D., Steubing, K. K., Fletcher, J. M., et al. (1998). Subtypes of reading disability: Variability around a phonological core. *Journal of Educational Psychology*, *90*, 347–373.

Morte-Soriano, M. R., Begeny, J. C., & Soriano-Ferrer, M. (2021). Parent and teacher ratings of behavioral executive functioning for students with dyslexia. *Journal of Learning Disabilities*, *54*(5), 373–387.

Mortimore, T., & Crozier, W. R. (2006). Dyslexia and difficulties with study skills in higher education. *Studies in Higher Education*, *31*(2), 235–251.

Mues, M., Zuk, J., Norton, E., et al. (2021). Clarifying the relationship between early speech-sound production abilities and subsequent reading outcomes. *Mapp. Intimacies*, *10*.

Mugnaini, D., Lassi, S., La Malfa, G., & Albertini, G. (2009). Internalizing correlates of dyslexia. *World Journal of Pediatrics*, *5*, 255–264.

Mundy, I. R., & Hannant, P. (2020). Exploring the phonological profiles of children with reading difficulties: A multiple case study. *Dyslexia*, *26*(4), 411–426.

Mundy, I. R., & Carroll, J. M. (2012). Speech prosody and developmental dyslexia: Reduced phonological awareness in the context of intact phonological representations. *Journal of Cognitive Psychology*, *24*, 560–581.

Näätänen, R. (2001). The perception of speech sounds by the human brain as reflected by the mismatch negativity (MMN) and its magnetic equivalent (MMNm). *Psychophysiology*, *38*, 1–21.

Nag, S. (2022). Dyslexia and the dyslexia-like picture: Supporting all children in primary school. In M. A. Skeide (ed.), *The Cambridge Handbook of Dyslexia and Dyscalculia* (pp. 427–443). Cambridge: Cambridge University Press.

Naglieri, J. A. (2011). The discrepancy/consistency approach to SLD identification using the PASS theory. In D. P. Flanagan, & V. C. Alfonso (eds.), *Essentials of Specific Learning Disability Identification* (pp. 145–172). New York: John Wiley & Sons.

Naglieri, J. A., & Feifer, S. G. (2018). Pattern of strengths and weaknesses made easy: The discrepancy/consistency method. In V. C. Alfonso, & D. P. Flanagan (eds.), *Essentials of Specific Learning Disability Identification* (pp. 431–474). Hoboken, NJ: Wiley.

Naples, A. J., Chang, J. T., Katz, L., & Grigorenko, E. L. (2009). Same or different? Insights into the etiology of phonological awareness and rapid naming. *Biological Psychology*, *80*, 226–239.

Nathaniel, U., Weiss, Y., Barouch, B., Katzir, T., & Bitan, T. (2022). Start shallow and grow deep: The development of a Hebrew reading brain. *Neuropsychologia*, *176*, 108376.

Nation, K., & Snowling, M. (1998). Individual differences in contextual facilitation: Evidence from dyslexia and poor reading comprehension. *Child Development*, *69*(4), 996–1011.

National Center on Response to Intervention. (2010). *Essential Components of RTI: A Closer Look at Response to Intervention*. Washington, DC: US Department of Education, Office of Special Education Programs, National Center on Response to Intervention.

National Early Literacy Panel. (2008). *Developing Early Literacy: Report of the National Early Literacy Panel.* Washington, DC: National Institute for Literacy.

National Reading Panel. (2000). *Teaching Children to Read An Evidence-Based Assessment of the Scientific Literature on Reading and Its Implications for Reading Instruction.* Bethesda, MD: National Institute of Child Health and Human Development.

Natri, H. M., Abubakare, O., Asasumasu, K., et al. (2023). Anti-ableist language is fully compatible with high-quality autism research: Response to Singer et al. (2023). *Autism Research, 16*(4), 673–676.

Naumova, O., Lee, M., Koposov, R., et al. (2012). Differential patterns of whole-genome DNA methylation in institutionalized children and children raised by their biological parents. *Development and Psychopathology, 24*, 143–155.

Naveenkumar, N., Georgiou, G. K., Vieira, A. P. A., Romero, S., & Parrila, R. (2022). A systematic review on quality indicators of randomized control trial reading fluency intervention studies. *Reading & Writing Quarterly, 38*(4), 359–378.

Ne'eman, A., & Pellicano, E. (2022). Neurodiversity as politics. *Human Development, 66*(2), 149–157.

Neitzel, A. J., Lake, C., Pellegrini, M., & Slavin, R. E. (2022). A synthesis of quantitative research on programs for struggling readers in elementary schools. *Reading Research Quarterly, 57*(1), 149–179.

Neuman, S. B., Kaefer, T., & Pinkham, A. M. (2018). A double dose of disadvantage: Language experiences for low-income children in home and school. *Journal of Educational Psychology, 110*(1), 102–118.

Nevill, T., Savage, G. C., & Forsey, M. (2023). It's a diagnosis for the rich: Disability, advocacy and the micro-practices of social reproduction. *British Journal of Sociology of Education, 44*(2), 239–258.

Nevo, E., & Breznitz, Z. (2011). Assessment of working memory components at 6 years of age as predictors of reading achievements a year later. *Journal of Experimental Child Psychology, 109*, 73–90.

New Zealand Ministry of Education. (2021). Three steps in screening for dyslexia. https://bit.ly/47Dord3. Accessed December 3, 2023.

Newbury, D. F., Paracchini, S., Scerri, T. S., et al. (2011). Investigation of dyslexia and SLI risk-variants in reading- and language-impaired subjects. *Behavior Genetics, 41*, 90–104.

Nickerson, R. S. (1998). Confirmation bias: A ubiquitous phenomenon in many guises. *Review of General Psychology, 2*(2), 175–220.

Nicolson, R. I. (2005). Dyslexia: Beyond the myth. *The Psychologist, 18*, 658–659.

Nicolson, R. I., & Fawcett, A. J. (1990). Automaticity: A new framework for dyslexia research? *Cognition, 35*, 159–182.

Nicolson, R. I., & Fawcett, A. J. (2004). *Dyslexia Early Screening Test (DEST).* London: Pearson Education.

Nicolson, R. I., & Fawcett, A. J. (2006). Do cerebellar deficits underlie phonological problems in dyslexia? *Developmental Science, 9*, 259–262; discussion 265–269.

Nicolson, R. I., & Fawcett, A. J. (2007). Procedural learning difficulties: Reuniting the developmental disorders? *Trends in Neurosciences, 30,* 135–141.

Nicolson, R. I., & Fawcett, A. J. (2008). *Dyslexia, Learning, and the Brain.* Cambridge, MA: MIT Press.

Nicolson, R. I., & Fawcett, A. J. (2019). Development of dyslexia: The delayed neural commitment framework. *Frontiers in Behavioral Neuroscience, 13,* 112.

Nicolson, R. I., & Reynolds, D. (2007). Sound design and balanced analyses: Response to Rack and colleagues. *Dyslexia, 13,* 105–109.

Nicolson, R. I., Fawcett, A. J., & Dean, P. (2001a). Developmental dyslexia: The cerebellar deficit hypothesis. *Trends in Neurosciences, 24,* 508–511.

Nicolson, R. I., Fawcett, A. J., & Dean, P. (2001b). Dyslexia, development and the cerebellum. *Trends in Neurosciences, 24,* 515–516.

Niogi, S. N., & McCandliss, B. D. (2006). Left lateralized white matter microstructure accounts for individual differences in reading ability and disability. *Neuropsychologia, 44,* 2178–2188.

Nitsche, M. A., & Paulus, W. (2011). Transcranial direct current stimulation – update 2011. *Restorative Neurology and Neuroscience, 29,* 463–492.

Nittrouer, S. (1999). Do temporal processing deficits cause phonological processing problems? *Journal of Speech, Language, and Hearing Research, 42,* 925–942.

Noordenbos, M. W., & Serniclaes, W. (2015). The categorical perception deficit in dyslexia: A meta-analysis. *Scientific Studies of Reading, 19*(5), 340–359.

Nopola-Hemmi, J., Myllyluoma, B., Haltia, T., et al. (2001). A dominant gene for developmental dyslexia on chromosome 3. *Journal of Medical Genetics, 38,* 658–664.

Nora, A., Renvall, H., Ronimus, M., et al. (2021). Children at risk for dyslexia show deficient left-hemispheric memory representations for new spoken word forms. *Neuroimage, 229,* 117739.

Norton, E. S., Beach, S. D., Eddy, M. D., et al. (2021). ERP Mismatch negativity amplitude and asymmetry reflect phonological and rapid automatized naming skills in English-speaking kindergartners. *Frontiers of Human Neuroscience, 15,* 624617.

Norton, E. S., Beach, S. D., & Gabrieli, J. D. E. (2015). Neurobiology of dyslexia. *Current Opinion in Neurobiology, 30,* 73–78.

Norton, E. S., & Wolf, M. (2012). Rapid automatized naming (RAN) and reading fluency: Implications for understanding and treatment of reading disabilities. *Annual Review of Psychology, 63,* 427–452.

Norwich, B. (2010). Book review of "Developmental disorders of language, learning and cognition" by C. Hulme and M. J. Snowling. *Journal of Research in Special Educational Needs, 10,* 133–135.

Nöthen, M. M., Schulte-Korne, G., Grimm, T., et al. (1999). Genetic linkage analysis with dyslexia: Evidence for linkage of spelling disability to chromosome 15. *European Child & Adolescent Psychiatry, 8,* 56–59.

Nugiel, T., Roe, M. A., Taylor, W. P., et al. (2019). Brain activity in struggling readers before intervention relates to future reading gains. *Cortex, 111,* 286–302.

O'Brien, G. E., McCloy, D. R., Kubota, E. C., & Yeatman, J. D. (2018). Reading ability and phoneme categorization. *Scientific Reports, 8*(1), 1–17.

O'Brien, G. E., & Yeatman, J. D. (2021). Bridging sensory and language theories of dyslexia: Toward a multifactorial model. *Developmental Science, 24*(3), e13039.

O'Connor, R. E. (2018). Reading fluency and students with reading disabilities: How fast is fast enough to promote reading comprehension? *Journal of Learning Disabilities, 51*(2), 124–136.

O'Connor, R. E., Fulmer, D., Harty, K. R., & Bell, K. M. (2005). Layers of reading intervention in kindergarten through third grade: Changes in teaching and student outcomes. *Journal of Learning Disabilities, 38*, 440–455.

Obeid, R., Messina, C. M., Zapparrata, N., Gravelle, C. D., & Brooks, P. J. (2022). Dyslexia and motor skills: A meta-analysis. In *Proceedings of the Annual Meeting of the Cognitive Science Society. Vol. 44.* https://escholarship.org/uc/item/1bj7t64m

Ober, T. M., Brooks, P. J., Homer, B. D., & Rindskopf, D. (2020). Executive functions and decoding in children and adolescents: A meta-analytic investigation. *Educational Psychology Review, 32*(3), 735–763.

Odegard, T. N., Farris, E. A., Middleton, A. E., Oslund, E., & Rimrodt-Frierson, S. (2020). Characteristics of students identified with dyslexia within the context of state legislation. *Journal of Learning Disabilities, 53*(5), 366–379.

Odegard, T. N., Farris, E. A., Middleton, A. E., Rimrodt-Frierson, S., & Washington, J. A. (2024). Trends in dyslexia legislation. In C. Okolo, N. Patton Terry, & L. Cutting (eds.), *Handbook of Learning Disabilities.* 3rd edition. New York: Guilford

Odegard, T. N., Farris, E. A., & Washington, J. A. (2022). Exploring boundary conditions of the listening comprehension-reading comprehension discrepancy index. *Annals of Dyslexia, 72*, 301–323.

Odegard, T. N., Hutchings, T., Farris, E. A., & Oslund, E. L. (2021). External evaluations for dyslexia: Do the data support parent concerns?. *Annals of Dyslexia, 71*(1), 50–59.

Odegard, T. N., Ring, J., Smith, S., Biggan, J., & Black, J. (2008). Differentiating the neural response to intervention in children with developmental dyslexia. *Annals of Dyslexia, 58*, 1–14.

Okumura, Y., Kita, Y., & Inagaki, M. (2017). Pure and short-term phonics-training improves reading and print-specific ERP in English: A case study of a Japanese middle school girl. *Developmental Neuropsychology, 42*(4), 265–275.

Olson, R. K. (1985). Disabled reading processes and cognitive profiles. In D. B. Gray, & J. F. Kavanagh (eds.), *Biobehavioral Measures of Dyslexia* (pp. 215–244). Parkton, MD: York Press.

Olson, R. K. (2011). Evaluation of Fast ForWord Language© effects on language and reading. *Perspectives on Language and Literacy, 37*(1), 11–15.

Olson, R. K. (2006). Genes, environment, and dyslexia. The 2005 Nonnan Geschwind Memorial Lecture. *Annals of Dyslexia, 56*, 205–238.

Olson, R. K. (2011). Genetic and environmental influences on phonological abilities and reading achievement. In S. A. Brady, D. Braze, & C. A. Fowler (eds.), *Explaining Individual Differences in Reading: Theory and Evidence* (pp. 197–216). New York: Psychology Press.

Olson, R. K., Keenan, J. M., Byrne, B., & Samuelsson, S. (2014). Why do children differ in their reading and related skills? *Scientific Studies of Reading, 18*, 38–54.

Olson, R. K., Keenan, J. M., Byrne, B., & Samuelsson, S. (2019). Etiology of developmental dyslexia. In L. Verhoeven, C. Perfetti, & K. Pugh (eds.), *Developmental Dyslexia across Languages and Writing Systems* (pp. 391–412). Cambridge: Cambridge University Press.

Olulade, O. A., Napoliello, E. M., & Eden, G. F. (2013). Abnormal visual motion processing is not a cause of dyslexia. *Neuron, 79*(1), 180–190.

Ordonez Magro, L., Majerus, S., Attout, L., Poncelet, M., Smalle, E. H., & Szmalec, A. (2020). The contribution of serial order short-term memory and long-term learning to reading acquisition: A longitudinal study. *Developmental Psychology, 56*(9), 1671.

Organisation for Economic Co-Operation and Development (OECD). (2015). *The ABC of Gender Equality in Education: Aptitude, Behaviour, Confidence.* Paris: OECD Publishing.

O'Roak, B. J., Deriziotis, P., Lee, C., et al. (2011). Exome sequencing in sporadic autism spectrum disorders identifies severe de novo mutations. *Nature Genetics, 43*, 585–589.

Orton, S. T. (1937). *Reading, Writing, and Speech Problems in Children.* New York: W. W. Norton & Company.

Orton, S. T. (1939). A neurological explanation of the reading disability. *Education Record, 12*, 58–68.

Ottosen, H. F., Bønnerup, K. H., Weed, E., & Parrila, R. (2022). Identifying dyslexia at the university: Assessing phonological coding is not enough. *Annals of Dyslexia, 72*(1), 147–170.

Ozernov-Palchik, O., & Gaab, N. (2016), Tackling the "dyslexia paradox": Reading brain and behavior for early markers of developmental dyslexia. *WIREs Cognitive Science, 7*, 156–176.

Ozernov-Palchik, O., Beach, S. D., Brown, M., et al. (2022). Speech-specific perceptual adaptation deficits in children and adults with dyslexia. *Journal of Experimental Psychology: General, 151*(7), 1556.

Ozernov-Palchik, O., Norton, E. S., Wang, Y., et al. (2019). The relationship between socioeconomic status and white matter microstructure in pre-reading children: A longitudinal investigation. *Human Brain Mapping, 40*, 741–754.

Ozernov-Palchik, O., Sideridis, G. D., Norton, E. S., et al. (2022). On the cusp of predictability: Disruption in the typical association between letter and word identification at critical thresholds of RAN and phonological skills. *Learning and Individual Differences, 97*, 102166.

Ozernov-Palchik, O., Yul, X., Wang, Y., & Gaab, N. (2016). Lessons to be learned: How a comprehensive neurobiological framework of atypical reading development can inform educational practice. *Current Opinion in Behavioral Sciences, 10*, 45–58.

Pace, A., Luo, R., Hirsh-Pasek, K., & Golinkoff, R. M. (2017). Identifying pathways between socioeconomic status and language development. *Annual Review of Linguistics, 3*, 285–308.

Pagliarini, E., Guasti, M. T., Toneatto, C., et al. (2015). Dyslexic children fail to comply with the rhythmic constraints of handwriting. *Human Movement Science, 42*, 161–182.

Paige, D. D., Young, C., Rasinski, T. V., et al. (2021). Teaching reading is more than a science: It's also an art. *Reading Research Quarterly, 56*, S339–S350.

Papadopoulos, T. C., Spanoudis, G. C., & Georgiou, G. K. (2016). How is RAN related to reading fluency? A comprehensive examination of the prominent theoretical accounts. *Frontiers in Psychology, 7*, 1217.

Paracchini, S. (2022). The genetics of dyslexia: Learning from the past to shape the future. In M. J. Snowling, C. Hulme, & K. Nation (eds.), *The Science of Reading: A Handbook*. 2nd edition (pp. 491–514). Oxford: Wiley-Blackwell.

Paracchini, S., Thomas, A., Castro, S., et al. (2006). The chromosome 6p22 haplotype associated with dyslexia reduces the expression of KIAA0319, a novel gene involved in neuronal migration. *Human Molecular Genetics, 15*, 1659–1666.

Park, R. L. (2003). The seven warning signs of bogus science. *Chronicle of Higher Education, 49*, 20–21.

Parrila, R., Dudley, D., Song, S., & Georgiou, G. K. (2020). A meta-analysis of reading-level match dyslexia studies in consistent alphabetic orthographies. *Annals of Dyslexia, 70*(1), 1–26.

Parrila, R., Inoue, T., Dunn, K., Savage, R., & Georgiou, G. (2023). Connecting teachers' language knowledge, perceived ability and instructional practices to Grade 1 students' literacy outcomes. *Reading and Writing: An Interdisciplinary Journal*, 1–29.

Partanen, M., Siegel, L. S., & Giaschi, D. E. (2019). Effect of reading intervention and task difficulty on orthographic and phonological reading systems in the brain. *Neuropsychologia, 130*, 13–25.

Pashler, H., McDaniel, M., Rohrer, D., & Bjork, R. (2008). Learning styles: Concepts and evidence. *Psychological Science in the Public Interest, 9*, 106–119.

Pasqualotto, A., Altarelli, I., De Angeli, A., et al. (2022). Enhancing reading skills through a video game mixing action mechanics and cognitive training. *Nature Human Behaviour, 6*(4), 545–554.

Patael, S. Z., Farris, E. A., Black, J. M., et al. (2018). Brain basis of cognitive resilience: Prefrontal cortex predicts better reading comprehension in relation to decoding. *PLoS ONE, 13*, e0198791.

Paul, I., Bott, C., Heim, S., Eulitz, C., & Elbert, T. (2006). Reduced hemispheric asymmetry of the auditory N260m in dyslexia. *Neuropsychologia, 44*, 785–794.

Paulesu, E., Danelli, L., & Berlingeri, M. (2014). Reading the dyslexic brain: Multiple dysfunctional routes revealed by a new meta-analysis of PET and fMRI activation studies. *Frontiers in Human Neuroscience, 8*.

Paulesu, E., Démonet, J.-F., Fazio, F., et al. (2001). Dyslexia: Cultural diversity and biological unity. *Science, 291*, 2165–2167.

Paulesu, E., Frith, U., Snowling, M., et al. (1996). Is developmental dyslexia a disconnection syndrome? Evidence from PET scanning. *Brain, 119*, 143–157.

Pearson, P. D. (2004). The reading wars. *Education Policy, 18*, 216–252.

Pegado, F., Comerlato, E., Ventura, F. J., et al. (2014). Timing the impact of literacy on visual processing. *Proceedings of the National Academy of Sciences, 111,* E5233–E5242.

Pellicano, E., & Gibson, L. Y. (2008). Investigating the functional integrity of the dorsal visual pathway in autism and dyslexia. *Neuropsychologia, 46*(10), 2593–2596.

Peng, P., Barnes, M., Wang, C., et al. (2018). A meta-analysis on the relation between reading and working memory. *Psychological Bulletin, 144*(1), 48–76.

Peng, P., & Fuchs, D. (2016). A meta-analysis of working memory deficits in children with learning difficulties: Is there a difference between verbal domain and numerical domain? *Journal of Learning Disabilities, 49*(1), 3–20.

Peng, P., Fuchs, D., Fuchs, L. S., et al. (2020). Is "response/no response" too simple a notion for RTI frameworks? Exploring multiple response types with latent profile analysis. *Journal of Learning Disabilities, 53*(6), 454–468.

Peng, P., Fuchs, D., Fuchs, L. S., et al. (2019). A longitudinal analysis of the trajectories and predictors of word reading and reading comprehension development among at-risk readers. *Journal of Learning Disabilities, 52*(3), 195–208.

Peng, P., & Goodrich, J. M. (2020). The cognitive element model of reading instruction. *Reading Research Quarterly, 55,* S77–S88.

Peng, P., & Kievit, R. A. (2020). The development of academic achievement and cognitive abilities: A bidirectional perspective. *Child Development Perspectives, 14*(1), 15–20.

Peng, P., & Swanson, H. L. (2022). The domain-specific approach of working memory training. *Developmental Review, 65,* 101035.

Peng, P., Zhang, Z., Wang, W., et al. (2022). A meta-analytic review of cognition and reading difficulties: Individual differences, moderation, and language mediation mechanisms. *Psychological Bulletin, 148*(3–4), 227.

Pennington, B. F. (2006). From single to multiple deficit models of developmental disorders. *Cognition, 101,* 385–413.

Pennington, B. F. (2009). *Diagnosing Learning Disorders: A Neuropsychological Framework.* 2nd edition. New York: Guilford Press.

Pennington, B. F., & Bishop, D. V. M. (2009). Relations among speech, language, and reading disorders. *Annual Review of Psychology, 60,* 283–306.

Pennington, B. F., Cardoso-Martins, C., Green, P. A., & Lefly, D. L. (2001). Comparing the phonological and double deficit hypotheses for developmental dyslexia. *Reading and Writing, 14,* 707–755.

Pennington, B. F., McGrath, L. M., & Peterson, R. L. (2019). *Diagnosing Learning Disorders: From Science to Practice.* New York: Guilford Publications.

Pennington, B. F., & Olson, R. K. (2005). Genetics of dyslexia. In M. Snowling, & C. Hulme (eds.), *The Science of Reading: A Handbook* (pp. 453–472). Oxford: Blackwell.

Pennington, B. F., Santerre-Lemmon, L., Rosenberg, J., et al. (2012). Individual prediction of dyslexia by single versus multiple deficit models. *Journal of Abnormal Psychology, 121*(1), 212–224.

Penolazzi, B., Spironelli, C., & Angrilli, A. (2008). Delta EEG activity as a marker of dysfunctional linguistic processing in developmental dyslexia. *Psychophysiology, 45,* 1025–1033.

Penolazzi, B., Spironelli, C., Vio, C., & Angrilli, A. (2006). Altered hemispheric asymmetry during word processing in dyslexic children: An event-related potential study. *Neuroreport, 17*, 429–433.

Penolazzi, B., Spironelli, C., Vio, C., & Angrilli, A. (2010). Brain plasticity in developmental dyslexia after phonological treatment: A beta EEG band study. *Behavioural Brain Research, 209*, 179–182.

Perceptual Development Corporation. (1998). Irlen Institute website: Who we help. https://irlen.com/index.php?s=who. Accessed May 14, 2023.

Perea, M., Panadero, V., Moret-Tatay, C., & Gómez, P. (2012). The effects of inter-letter spacing in visual-word recognition: Evidence with young normal readers and developmental dyslexics. *Learning and Instruction, 22,* 420–430.

Perdue, M. V., Mahaffy, K., Vlahcevic, K., et al. (2022). Reading intervention and neuroplasticity: A systematic review and meta-analysis of brain changes associated with reading intervention. *Neuroscience & Biobehavioral Reviews, 132*, 465–494.

Perfetti, C. A., & Harris, L. (2019). Developmental dyslexia in English. In L. Verhoeven, C. Perfetti, & K. Pugh (eds.), *Developmental Dyslexia across Languages and Writing Systems* (pp. 25–49). Cambridge: Cambridge University Press.

Perfetti, C. A. (1991). The psychology, pedagogy and politics of reading. *Psychological Science, 2*, 70–76.

Perfetti, C. A., Liu, Y., & Tan, L. H. (2005). The lexical constituency model: Some implications of research on Chinese for general theories of reading. *Psychological Review, 112*, 43–59.

Perfetti, C. A., Pugh, K., & Verhoeven, L. (2019). Developmental dyslexia across languages and writing systems: The big picture. In L. Verhoeven, C. A. Perfetti, & K. Pugh (eds.), *Developmental Dyslexia across Languages and Writing Systems* (pp. 441–461). Cambridge: Cambridge University Press.

Pernet, C., Andersson, J., Paulesu, E., & Demonet, J. F. (2009). When all hypotheses are right: A multifocal account of dyslexia. *Human Brain Mapping, 30*, 2278–2292.

Perrachione, T. K., Del Tufo, S. N., Winter, R., et al. (2016). Dysfunction of rapid neural adaptation in dyslexia. *Neuron, 92*(6), 1383–1397.

Perry, C., & Long, H. (2022). What is going on with visual attention in reading and dyslexia? A critical review of recent studies. *Brain Sciences, 12*(1), 87.

Peters, L., & Ansari, D. (2019). Are specific learning disorders truly specific, and are they disorders? *Trends in Neuroscience and Education, 17*, 100115.

Peters, J. L., Crewther, S. G., Murphy, M. J., & Bavin, E. L. (2021). Action video game training improves text reading accuracy, rate and comprehension in children with dyslexia: A randomized controlled trial. *Scientific Reports, 11*(1), 1–11.

Peters, J. L., De Losa, L., Bavin, E. L., & Crewther, S. G. (2019). Efficacy of dynamic visuo-attentional interventions for reading in dyslexic and neurotypical children: A systematic review. *Neuroscience & Biobehavioral Reviews, 100*, 58–76.

Peterson, R. L., & Pennington, B. F. (2012). Developmental dyslexia. *The Lancet*, *379*, 1997–2007.

Peterson, R. L., Arnett, A. B., Pennington, B. F., et al. (2018). Literacy acquisition influences children's rapid automatized naming. *Developmental Science*, *21*(3), e12589.

Peterson, R. L., Boada, R., McGrath, L. M., et al. (2017). Cognitive prediction of reading, math, and attention: Shared and unique influences. *Journal of Learning Disabilities*, *50*(4), 408–421.

Peterson, R. L., McGrath, L. M., Willcutt, E. G., et al. (2021). How specific are learning disabilities? *Journal of Learning Disabilities*, *54*(6), 466–483.

Peterson, R. L., & Pennington, B. F. (2012). Developmental dyslexia. *The Lancet*, *379*, 1997–2007.

Peterson, R. L., & Pennington, B. F. (2015). Developmental dyslexia. *Annual Review of Clinical Psychology*, *11*, 283–307.

Peterson, R. L., Pennington, B. F., Olson, R. K., & Wadsworth, S. J. (2014). Longitudinal stability of phonological and surface subtypes of developmental dyslexia. *Scientific Studies of Reading*, *18*(5), 347–362.

Peterson, R. L., Pennington, B. F., Shriberg, L. D., & Boada, R. (2009). What influences literacy outcome in children with speech sound disorder? *Journal of Speech, Language, and Hearing Research*, *52*, 1175–1188.

Petrill, S. A., Deater-Deckard, K., Thompson, L. A., Dethorne, L. S., & Schatschneider, C. (2006). Reading skills in early readers: Genetic and shared environmental influences. *Journal of Learning Disabilities*, *39*, 48–55.

Petrill, S. A., Deater-Deckard, K., Thompson, L. A., et al. (2007). Longitudinal genetic analysis of early reading: The Western Reserve reading project. *Reading and Writing*, *20*, 127–146.

Petrill, S. A., Hart, S. A., Harlaar, N., Logan, J., et al. (2010). Genetic and environmental influences on the growth of early reading skills. *Journal of Child Psychology & Psychiatry & Allied Disciplines*, *51*(6), 660–667.

Petryshen, T. L., Kaplan, B. J., Liu, M. F., & Field, L. L. (2000). Absence of significant linkage between phonological coding dyslexia and chromosome 6p23–21.3, as determined by use of quantitative-trait methods: Confirmation of qualitative analyses. *American Journal of Human Genetics*, *66*, 708–714.

Petscher, Y., & Koon, S. (2020). Moving the needle on evaluating multivariate screening accuracy. *Assessment for Effective Intervention*, *45*(2), 83–94.

Petscher, Y., Cabell, S. Q., Catts, H. W., et al. (2020). How the science of reading informs 21st-century education. *Reading Research Quarterly*, *55*, S267–S282.

Petscher, Y., Fien, H., Stanley, C., Gearin, B., Gaab, N., Fletcher, J. M., & Johnson, E. (2019). *Screening for dyslexia*. Office of Special Education Programs, National Center on Improving Literacy. https://improvingliteracy.org. Accessed December 3, 2023.

Peyrin, C., Démonet, J. F., N'guyen-Morel, M. A., Le Bas, J. F., & Valdois, S. (2011). Superior parietal lobe dysfunction in a homogeneous group of dyslexic children with a visual attention span disorder. *Brain & Language*, *118*, 128–138.

Peyrin, C., Lallier, M., Démonet, J. F., et al. (2012). Neural dissociation of phonological and visual attention span disorders in developmental dyslexia: FMRI evidence from two case reports. *Brain & Language, 120,* 381–394.

Pfost, M., Blatter, K., Artelt, C., Stanat, P., & Schneider, W. (2019). Effects of training phonological awareness on children's reading skills. *Journal of Applied Developmental Psychology, 65,* 101067.

Pfost, M., Dörfler, T., & Artelt, C. (2012). Reading competence development of poor readers in a German elementary school sample: An empirical examination of the Matthew effect model. *Journal of Research in Reading, 35*(4), 411–426.

Pham, A. V. (2016). Differentiating behavioral ratings of inattention, impulsivity, and hyperactivity in children: Effects on reading achievement. *Journal of Attention Disorders, 20*(8), 674–683.

Pham, A. V., & Hasson, R. M. (2014). Verbal and visuospatial working memory as predictors of children's reading ability. *Archives of Clinical Neuropsychology, 29*(5), 467–477.

Phan, T. V., Sima, D., Smeets, D., et al. (2021). Structural brain dynamics across reading development: A longitudinal MRI study from kindergarten to grade 5. *Human Brain Mapping, 42,* 4497–4509.

Piasta, S. B., & Wagner, R. K. (2010). Learning letter names and sounds: Effects of instruction, letter type, and phonological processing skill. *Journal of Experimental Child Psychology, 105,* 324–344.

Piazza, E. A., Cohen, A., Trach, J., & Lew-Williams, C. (2021). Neural synchrony predicts children's learning of novel words. *Cognition, 214,* 104752.

Pierrehumbert, J. (2003). Phonetic diversity, statistical learning and acquisition of phonology. *Language & Speech, 46,* 115–154.

Pinker, S. (1998). Foreword. In D. McGuinness (ed.), *Why Children Can't Read: And what we can do about it.* London: Penguin.

Piotrowska, B., & Willis, A. (2019). Beyond the global motion deficit hypothesis of developmental dyslexia: A cross-sectional study of visual, cognitive, and socioeconomic factors influencing reading ability in children. *Vision Research, 159,* 48–60.

Plakas, A., van Zuijen, T., van Leeuwen, T., Thomson, J. M., & van der Leij, A. (2013). Impaired non-speech auditory processing at a pre-reading age is a risk-factor for dyslexia but not a predictor: An ERP study. *Cortex, 49*(4), 1034–1045.

Plante, E. (2012). Windows into receptive processing. In A. A. Benasich, & R. H. Fitch (eds.), *Developmental Dyslexia: Early Precursors, Neurobehavioral Markers, and Biological Substrates* (pp. 257–274). Baltimore: Paul H. Brookes Publishing.

Platt, M. P., Adler, W. T., Mehlhorn, A. J., et al. (2013). Embryonic disruption of the candidate dyslexia susceptibility gene homolog Kiaa0319-like results in neuronal migration disorders. *Neuroscience, 248,* 585–593.

Plaut, D. C., McClelland, J. L., Seidenberg, M. S., & Patterson, K. (1996). Understanding normal and impaired word reading: Computational principles in quasi-regular domains. *Psychological Review, 103,* 56–115.

Plomin, R., DeFries, J. C., Knopik, V. S., & Neiderhiser, J. M. (2013). *Behavioral Genetics.* 6th edition. New York: Worth Publishers.

Plomin, R., & Kovas, Y. (2005). Generalist genes and learning disabilities. *Psychological Bulletin, 131*, 592–617.

Pollack, C., Luk, G., & Christodoulou, J. A. (2015). A meta-analysis of functional reading systems in typically developing and struggling readers across different alphabetic languages. *Frontiers in Psychology, 6*.

Porter, S. B., Odegard, T. N., Farris, E. A., & Oslund, E. L. (2023). Effects of teacher knowledge of early reading on students' gains in reading foundational skills and comprehension. *Reading and Writing*, 1–17.

Poulsen, M., Juul, H., & Elbro, C. (2015). Multiple mediation analysis of the relationship between rapid naming and reading. *Journal of Research in Reading, 38*(2), 124–140.

Poulsen, M., Protopapas, A., & Juul, H. (2023). How RAN stimulus type and repetition affect RAN's relation with decoding efficiency and reading comprehension. *Reading and Writing*, 1–14.

Powell, D., & Atkinson, L. (2021). Unravelling the links between rapid automatized naming (RAN), phonological awareness, and reading. *Journal of Educational Psychology, 113*(4), 706–718.

Powell, D., Stuart, M., Garwood, H., Quinlan, P., & Stainthorp, R. (2007). An experimental comparison between rival theories of rapid automatised naming (RAN) performance and its relationship to reading. *Journal of Experimental Child Psychology, 98*, 46–68.

Power, J. D., & Petersen, S. E. (2013). Control-related systems in the human brain. *Current Opinion in Neurobiology, 23*, 223–228.

Pressley, M. (2006). *Reading Instruction that Works: The Case for Balanced Teaching*. New York: The Guilford Press.

Preston, J. L., Frost, S. J., Mencl, W. E., et al. (2010). Early and late talkers: School-age language, literacy and neurolinguistic differences. *Brain, 133*(Pt 8), 2185–2195.

Price, C. J. (2012). A review and synthesis of the first 20 years of PET and fMRI studies of heard speech, spoken language and reading. *Neuroimage, 62*, 816–847.

Price, C. J., & Mechelli, A. (2005). Reading and reading disturbance. *Current Opinion in Neurobiology, 15*, 231–238.

Price, K. M., Wigg, K. G., Eising, E., et al. (2022). Hypothesis-driven genome-wide association studies provide novel insights into genetics of reading disabilities. *Translational Psychiatry, 12*(1), 495.

Price, K. M., Wigg, K. G., Feng, Y., et al. (2020). Genome-wide association study of word reading: Overlap with risk genes for neurodevelopmental disorders. *Genes, Brain and Behavior, 19*(6), e12648.

Price, K. M., Wigg, K. G., Misener, V. L., et al. (2022). Language difficulties in school-age children with developmental dyslexia. *Journal of Learning Disabilities, 55*(3), 200–212.

Prifitera, A., & Dersch, J. (1993). Base rates of WISC-III diagnostic subtest patterns among normal, learning disabled and ADHD samples. *Journal of Psychoeducational Assessment, WISC-III Monograph*, 43–55.

Pringle Morgan W. (1896). A case of congenital word blindness. *British Medical Journal, 2*, 1378.

Protopapa, C., & Smith-Spark, J. H. (2022). Self-reported symptoms of developmental dyslexia predict impairments in everyday cognition in adults. *Research in Developmental Disabilities, 128*, 104288.

Protopapas, A. (2014). From temporal processing to developmental language disorders: Mind the gap. *Philosophical Transactions of the Royal Society B: Biological Sciences, 369*(1634), 20130090.

Protopapas, A. (2019). Evolving concepts of dyslexia and their implications for research and remediation. *Frontiers in Psychology, 10*, 2873.

Protopapas, A., Altani, A., & Georgiou, G. K. (2013). Development of serial processing in reading and rapid naming. *Journal of Experimental Child Psychology, 116*(4), 914–929.

Protopapas, A., & Parrila, R. (2018). Is dyslexia a brain disorder? *Brain Sciences, 8*(4), 61.

Protopapas, A., & Parrila, R. (2019). Dyslexia: Still not a neurodevelopmental disorder. *Brain Sciences, 9*, 9.

Provazza, S., Adams, A. M., Giofrè, D., & Roberts, D. J. (2019). Double trouble: Visual and phonological impairments in English dyslexic readers. *Frontiers in Psychology*, 2725.

Pugh, K. R., Frost, S. J., Rothman, D. L., et al. (2014). Glutamate and choline levels predict individual differences in reading ability in emergent readers. *The Journal of Neuroscience, 34*(11), 4082.

Pugh, K. R., & McCardle, P. (eds.). (2009). *How Children Learn to Read: Current Issues and New Directions in the Integration of Cognition, Neurobiology and Genetics of Reading and Dyslexia Research and Practice.* New York: Psychology Press.

Pugh, K. R., Mencl, W. E., Jenner, A. R., et al. (2000). Functional neuroimaging studies of reading and reading disability (developmental dyslexia). *Mental Retardation & Developmental Disabilities Research Reviews, 6*, 207–213.

Pugh, K. R., Mencl, W. E., Jenner, A. R., et al. (2001). Neurobiological studies of reading and reading disability. *Journal of Communication Disorders, 34*, 479–492.

Puglisi, M. L., Hulme, C., Hamilton, L. G., & Snowling, M. J. (2017). The home literacy environment is a correlate, but perhaps not a cause, of variations in children's language and literacy development. *Scientific Studies of Reading, 21*(6), 498–514.

Quercia, P., Demougeot, L., Dos Santos, M. Bonnetblanc, F. (2011). Integration of proprioceptive signals and attentional capacity during postural control are impaired but subject to improvement in dyslexic children. *Experimental Brain Research, 209*(4), 599–608.

Quinn, J. M. (2018). Differential identification of females and males with reading difficulties: A meta-analysis. *Reading and Writing, 31*(5), 1039–1061.

Quinn, J. M., & Wagner, R. K. (2015). Gender differences in reading impairment and in the identification of impaired readers: Results from a large-scale study of at-risk readers. *Journal of Learning Disabilities, 48*(4), 433–445.

Quintana-Murci, L., & Fellous, M. (2001). The human Y chromosome: The biological role of a "functional wasteland." *Journal of Biomedicine and Biotechnology, 1*, 18–24.

Rack, J. P. (2003). The who, what, why and how of intervention programmes: Comments on the DDAT evaluation. *Dyslexia, 9*, 137–139.

Rack, J. P., Snowling, M. J., & Olson, R. K. (1992). The nonword reading deficit in developmental dyslexia – A review. *Reading Research Quarterly, 27*, 28–53.

Rack, J. P., Snowling, M. J., Hulme, C., & Gibbs, S. (2007). No evidence that an exercise-based treatment programme (DDAT) has specific benefits for children with reading difficulties. *Dyslexia, 13*, 97–104.

Raddatz, J., Kuhn, J. T., Holling, H., Moll, K., & Dobel, C. (2017). Comorbidity of arithmetic and reading disorder: Basic number processing and calculation in children with learning impairments. *Journal of Learning Disabilities, 50*(3), 298–308.

Rae, C., Lee, M. A., Dixon, R. M., et al. (1998). Metabolic abnormalities in developmental dyslexia detected by 1H magnetic resonance spectroscopy. *The Lancet, 351*, 1849–1852.

Raffington, L., Tanksley, P. T., Sabhlok, A., et al. (2023). Socially stratified epigenetic profiles are associated with cognitive functioning in children and adolescents. *Psychological Science, 34*, 170–185.

Raij, T., Uutela, K., & Hari, R. (2000). Audiovisual integration of letters in the human brain. *Neuron, 28*, 617–625.

Rakhlin, N., Mourgues, C., Logvinenko, T., Kornev, A. N., & Grigorenko, E. L. (2022). What reading-level match design reveals about specific reading disability in a transparent orthography and how much we can trust it. *Scientific Studies of Reading*, 1–18.

Ramirez, G., Fries, L., Gunderson, E., et al. (2019). Reading anxiety: An early affective impediment to children's success in reading. *Journal of Cognition and Development, 20*(1), 15–34.

Ramus, F. (2003). Developmental dyslexia: Specific phonological deficits or general sensorimotor dysfunction? *Current Opinion in Neurology, 13*, 212–218.

Ramus, F. (2004). Neurobiology of dyslexia: A reinterpretation of the data. *Trends in Neurosciences, 27*, 720–726.

Ramus, F. (2014). Should there really be a "Dyslexia debate"? *Brain, 137*(12), 3371–3374.

Ramus, F., & Ahissar, M. (2012). Developmental dyslexia: The difficulties of interpreting poor performance, and the importance of normal performance. *Cognitive Neuropsychology, 29*(1–2), 104–122

Ramus, F., Altarelli, I., Jednorog, K., Zhao, J., & di Covella, L. S. (2018). Neuroanatomy of developmental dyslexia: Pitfalls and promise. *Neuroscience & Biobehavioral Reviews, 84*, 434–452.

Ramus, F., Pidgeon, E., & Frith, U. (2003). The relationship between motor control and phonology in dyslexic children. *Journal of Child Psychology and Psychiatry and Allied Disciplines, 44*, 712–722.

Ramus, F., Rosen, S., Dakin, S. C., et al. (2003). Theories of developmental dyslexia: Insights from a multiple case study of dyslexic adults. *Brain, 126*, 841–865.

Ramus, F., & Szenkovits, G. (2008). What phonological deficit? *The Quarterly Journal of Experimental Psychology, 61*, 129–141.

Randall, L., & Tyldesley, K. (2016). Evaluating the impact of working memory training programmes on children – A systematic review. *Educational and Child Psychology*, *33*(1), 34–50.

Rashotte, C. A., MacPhee, K., & Torgesen, J. K. (2001). The effectiveness of a group reading instruction program with poor readers in multiple grades. *Learning Disability Quarterly*, *24*, 119–134.

Raskind, W. H., Hsu, L., Berninger, V. W., Thomson, J. B., & Wijsman, E. M. (2000). Familial aggregation of dyslexia phenotypes. *Behavior Genetics*, *30*, 385–396.

Razuk, M., Perrin-Fievez, F., Gerard, C. L., et al. (2018). Effect of colored filters on reading capabilities in dyslexic children. *Research in Developmental Disabilities*, *83*, 1–7.

Reason, R., & Stothard, J. (2013). Is there a place for dyslexia in educational psychology practice? *Debate*, *146*, 8–13.

Redick, T. S., Shipstead, Z., Wiemers, E. A., Melby-Lervåg, M., & Hulme, C. (2015). What's working in working memory training? An educational perspective. *Educational Psychology Review*, *27*(4), 617–633.

Regan, T., & Woods, K. (2000). Teachers' understandings of dyslexia: Implications for educational psychology practice. *Educational Psychology in Practice*, *16*, 333–347.

Regier, D. A., Narrow, W. E., Clarke, D. E., et al. (2013). DSM-5 field trials in the United States and Canada, Part II: Test-retest reliability of selected categorical diagnoses. *American Journal of Psychiatry*, *170*, 59–70

Rehfeld, D. M., Kirkpatrick, M., O'Guinn, N., & Renbarger, R. (2022). A meta-analysis of phonemic awareness instruction provided to children suspected of having a reading disability. *Language, Speech, and Hearing Services in Schools*, *53*(4), 1177–1201.

Reis, A., Araújo, S., Morais, I. S., & Faísca, L. (2020). Reading and reading-related skills in adults with dyslexia from different orthographic systems: A review and meta-analysis. *Annals of Dyslexia*, *70*(3), 339–368.

Rendall, A. R., Tarkar, A., Contreras-Mora, H. M., LoTurco, J. J., & Fitch, R. H. (2017). Deficits in learning and memory in mice with a mutation of the candidate dyslexia susceptibility gene Dyx1c1. *Brain and Language*, *172*, 30–38.

Reschly, D. (2005). Learning disabilities identification: Primary intervention, secondary intervention, and then what? *Journal of Learning Disabilities*, *38*, 510–515.

Reschly, D. J., & Tilley, W. D. (1999). Reform trends and system design alternatives. In D. J. Reschly, W. D. Tilley, & J. P. Grimes (eds.), *Special Education in Transition: Functional Assessment and Noncategorical Programming* (pp. 19–48). Longmont, CO: Sopris West.

Rescorla, L. (2009). Age 17 language and reading outcomes in late-talking toddlers: Support for a dimensional perspective on language delay. *Journal of Speech, Language, and Hearing Research*, *52*(1), 16–30.

Reynolds, C. R., & Shaywitz, S. E. (2009a). Response to intervention: Prevention and remediation, perhaps. Diagnosis, no. *Child Development Perspectives*, *3*, 44–47.

Reynolds, C. R., & Shaywitz, S. E. (2009b). Response to intervention: Ready or not? Or, from wait-to-fail to watch-them-fail. *School Psychology Quarterly*, *24*, 130–145.

Reynolds, D., & Nicolson, R. I. (2007). Follow-up of an exercise-based treatment for children with reading difficulties. *Dyslexia*, *13*, 78–96.

Reynolds, D., Nicolson, R. I., & Hambly, H. (2003). Evaluation of an exercise-based treatment for children with reading difficulties. *Dyslexia*, *9*, 48–71.

Riccio, C. A., Sullivan, J. R., & Cohen, M. J. (2010). *Neuropsychological Assessment and Intervention for Childhood and Adolescent Disorders*. Trenton, NJ: John Wiley and Sons.

Rice, M., & Brooks, G. (2004). *Developmental Dyslexia in Adults: A Research Review*. London: NRDC.

Rice, M., Erbeli, F., Thompson, C. G., Sallese, M. R., & Fogarty, M. (2022). Phonemic awareness: A meta-analysis for planning effective instruction. *Reading Research Quarterly*, *57*(4), 1259–1289.

Rice, M., Erbeli, F., & Wijekumar, K. (2023). Phonemic awareness: Evidence-based instruction for students in need of intervention. *Intervention in School and Clinic*, 1–5.

Richards, T. L., Aylward, E. H., Berninger, V. W., et al. (2006). Individual fMRI activation in orthographic mapping and morpheme mapping after orthographic or morphological spelling treatment in child dyslexics. *Journal of Neurolinguistics*, *19*, 56–86.

Richards, T. L., Aylward, E. H., Field, K. M., et al. (2006). Converging evidence for triple word form theory in children with dyslexia. *Developmental Neuropsychology*, *30*(1), 547–589.

Richards, T. L., & Berninger, V. W. (2008). Abnormal fMRI connectivity in children with dyslexia during a phoneme task: Before but not after treatment. *Journal of Neurolinguistics*, *21*, 294–304.

Richards, T. L., Berninger, V., Winn, W., et al. (2007). Functional MRI activation in children with and without dyslexia during pseudoword aural repeat and visual decode: Before and after treatment. *Neuropsychology*, *21*, 732–741.

Richards, T. L., Berninger, V. W., Yagle, K. J., Abbott, R. D., & Peterson, D. J. (2017). Changes in DTI diffusivity and fMRI connectivity cluster coefficients for students with and without specific learning disabilities in written language: Brain's response to writing instruction. *Journal of Natural Sciences*, *3*.

Richards, T. L., Berninger, V. W., Yagle, K. J., Abbott, R. D., & Peterson, D. (2018). Brain's functional network clustering coefficient changes in response to instruction (RTI) in students with and without reading disabilities: Multi-leveled reading brain's RTI. *Cogent Psychology*, *5*, 1424680.

Richards, T. L., Corina, D. P., Serafini, S., et al. (2000). Effects of a phonologically driven treatment for dyslexia on lactate levels measured by proton MR spectroscopic imaging. *American Journal of Neuroradiology*, *21*, 916–922.

Richards, T. L., Dager, S. R., Corina, D., et al. (1999). Dyslexic children have abnormal brain lactate response to reading-related language tasks. *American Journal of Neuroradiology*, *20*, 1393–1398.

Richards, T. L., Nagy, W., Abbott, R., & Berninger, V. (2016). Brain connectivity associated with cascading levels of language. *Journal of Systems and Integrative Neuroscience, 2*(3).

Richardson, A. J. (2006). Omega-3 fatty acids in ADHD and related neurodevelopmental disorders. *International Review of Psychiatry, 18,* 155–172.

Richardson, A. J., Calvin, C. M., Clisby, C., et al. (2000). Fatty acid deficiency signs predict the severity of reading and related difficulties in dyslexic children. *Prostaglandins, Leukotrienes and Essential Fatty Acids (PLEFA), 63*(1–2), 69–74.

Richardson, A. J., Burton, J. R., Sewell, R. P., Spreckelsen, T. F., & Montgomery, P. (2012). Docosahexaenoic acid for reading, cognition and behavior in children aged 7–9 Years: A randomized, controlled trial (The DOLAB Study). *PLoS ONE 7*(9), e43909.

Richardson, A. J., Cox, I. J., Sargentoni, J., & Puri, B. K. (1997). Abnormal cerebral phospholipid metabolism in dyslexia indicated by phosphorus-31 magnetic resonance spectroscopy. *NMR in Biomedicine, 10,* 309–314.

Richardson, A. J., & Montgomery, P. (2005). The Oxford-Durham study: A randomized, controlled trial of dietary supplementation with fatty acids in children with developmental coordination disorder. *Pediatrics, 115,* 1360–1366.

Richardson, J. (2016). The top 5 things parents should know about the READ Act. International Dyslexia Association. https://dyslexiaida.org/the-top-5-things-parents-should-know-about-the-read-act/. Accessed November 13, 2023.

Richlan, F. (2014). Functional neuroanatomy of developmental dyslexia: The role of orthographic depth. *Frontiers in Human Neuroscience, 8.*

Richlan, F. (2020). The functional neuroanatomy of developmental dyslexia across languages and writing systems. *Frontiers in Psychology, 11,* 155.

Richlan, F., Kronbichler, M., & Wimmer, H. (2009). Functional abnormalities in the dyslexic brain: A quantitative meta-analysis of neuroimaging studies. *Human Brain Mapping, 30,* 3299–3308.

Richlan, F., Kronbichler, M., & Wimmer, H. (2011). Meta-analyzing brain dysfunctions in dyslexic children and adults. *Neuroimage, 56,* 1735–1742.

Richlan, F., Kronbichler, M., & Wimmer, H. (2013). Structural abnormalities in the dyslexic brain: A meta-analysis of voxel-based morphometry studies. *Human Brain Mapping, 34,* 3055–3065.

Riddell, S., & Weedon, E. (2006). What counts as a reasonable adjustment? Dyslexic students and the concept of fair assessment. *International Studies in Sociology of Education, 16*(1), 57–73.

Riddick, B. (2000). An examination of the relationship between labeling and stigmatization with special reference to dyslexia. *Disability and Society, 15,* 653–657.

Riddick, B. (2001). Dyslexia and inclusion: Time for a social model of disability? *International Studies in Sociology of Education, 11,* 223–236.

Riddick, B. (2010). *Living with Dyslexia: The Social and Emotional Consequences of Specific Learning Difficulties/Disabilities.* London: Routledge.

Riddick, B., Farmer, M., & Sterling, C. (1997) *Students and Dyslexia: Growing Up with a Specific Learning Difficulty.* London: Whurr.

Ring, J., & Black, J. L. (2018). The multiple deficit model of dyslexia: What does it mean for identification and intervention? *Annals of Dyslexia, 68*(2), 104–125.

Rios, D. M., Correia Rios, M., Bandeira, I. D., et al. (2018). Impact of transcranial direct current stimulation on reading skills of children and adolescents with dyslexia. *Child Neurology Open, 5*, 2329048X18798255.

Ritchey K. D., & Goeke J. L. (2006). Orton-Gillingham and Orton-Gillingham-based reading instruction: A review of the literature. *The Journal of Special Education, 40*(3), 171–183.

Riva, V., Marino, C., Giorda, R., Molteni, M., & Nobile, M. (2015). The role of DCDC2 genetic variants and low socioeconomic status in vulnerability to attention problems. *European Child & Adolescent Psychiatry, 24*, 309–318.

Roberts, A. E., Cox, G. F., Kimonis, V., Lamb, A., & Irons, M. (2004). Clinical presentation of 13 patients with subtelomeric rearrangements and a review of the literature. *American Journal of Medical Genetics, 128A*, 352–363.

Roberts, G. J., Cho, E., Garwood, J. D., et al. (2020). Reading interventions for students with reading and behavioral difficulties: A meta-analysis and evaluation of co-occurring difficulties. *Educational Psychology Review, 32*(1), 17–47.

Roberts, G., Torgesen, J. K., Boardman, A., & Scammacca, N. (2008). Evidence-based strategies for reading instruction of older students with learning disabilities. *Learning Disabilities Research and Practice, 23*, 63–69.

Robertson, C., & Salter, W. (1997). *The Phonological Awareness Test*. East Moline, IL: LinguiSystems.

Robichon, F., & Habib, M. (1998). Abnormal callosal morphology in male adult dyslexics: Relationships to handedness and phonological abilities. *Brain and Language, 62*, 127–146.

Rochelle, K. S., & Talcott, J. B. (2006). Impaired balance in developmental dyslexia? A meta-analysis of the contending evidence. *Journal of Child Psychology and Psychiatry, 47*, 1159–1166.

Rodgers, B. (1983). The identification and prevalence of specific reading retardation. *British Journal of Educational Psychology, 53*(3), 369–373.

Roe, M. A., Martinez, J. E., Mumford, J. A., et al. (2018). Control engagement during sentence and inhibition fMRI tasks in children with reading difficulties. *Cerebral Cortex, 28*, 3697–3710.

Roeske, D., Ludwig, K. U., Neuhoff, N., et al. (2011). First genome-wide association scan on neurophysiological endophenotypes points to trans-regulation effects on SLC2A3 in dyslexic children. *Molecular Psychiatry, 16*, 97–107.

Romani, C., Tsouknida, E., di Betta, A. M., & Olson, A. (2011). Reduced attentional capacity, but normal processing speed and shifting of attention in developmental dyslexia: Evidence from a serial task. *Cortex, 47*, 715–733.

Romeo, R. R., Christodoulou, J. A., Halverson, K. K., et al. (2018). Socioeconomic status and reading disability: Neuroanatomy and plasticity in response to intervention. *Cerebral Cortex, 28*(7), 2297–2312.

Ronconi, L., Melcher, D., & Franchin, L. (2020). Investigating the role of temporal processing in developmental dyslexia: Evidence for a specific deficit in rapid visual segmentation. *Psychonomic Bulletin & Review, 27*(4), 724–734.

Rose, J. (2009). *Identifying and Teaching Children and Young People with Dyslexia and Literacy Difficulties*. The Rose Report. Nottingham: DCSF Publications.

Rose, L. T., & Rouhani, P. (2012). Influence of verbal working memory depends on vocabulary: Oral reading fluency in adolescents with dyslexia. *Mind, Brain, and Education, 6,* 1–9.

Rosen, V., & Engle, R. W. (1997). Forward and backward serial recall. *Intelligence, 25,* 37–47.

Rosenberg, J., Pennington, B. F., Willcutt, E. G., & Olson, R. K. (2012). Gene by environment interactions influencing reading disability and the inattentive symptom dimension of attention deficit/hyperactivity disorder. *Journal of Child Psychology and Psychiatry, 53*(3), 243–251.

Rosheim, K. M., & Tamte, K. G. (2022). Impact of policy on literacy specialists' work. *Reading Psychology, 43*(8), 576–597.

Rowe, A., Titterington, J., Holmes, J., Henry, L., & Taggart, L. (2019). Interventions targeting working memory in 4–11 year olds within their everyday contexts: A systematic review. *Developmental Review, 52,* 1–23.

Rubenstein, K., Matsushita, M., Berninger, V. W., Raskind, W. H., & Wijsman, E. M. (2011). Genome scan for spelling deficits: Effects of verbal IQ on models of transmission and trait gene localization. *Behavior Genetics, 41,* 31–42.

Rubie-Davies, C. M., Blatchford, P., Webster, R., Koutsoubou, M., & Bassett, P. (2010). Enhancing learning? A comparison of teacher and teaching assistant interactions with pupils. *School Effectiveness and School Improvement, 21,* 429–449.

Rueckl, J. G., Paz-Alonso, P. M., Molfese, P. J., et al. (2015). Universal brain signature of proficient reading: Evidence from four contrasting languages. *Proceedings of the National Academy of Sciences, 112,* 15510–15515.

Rufener, K. S., Krauel, K., Meyer, M., Heinze, H. J., & Zaehle, T. (2019). Transcranial electrical stimulation improves phoneme processing in developmental dyslexia. *Brain Stimulation, 12,* 930–937.

Ruiz-Martin, H., Portero-Tresserra, M., Martínez-Molina, A., & Ferrero, M. (2022). Tenacious educational neuromyths: Prevalence among teachers and an intervention. *Trends in Neuroscience and Education,* 100192.

Rumsey, J. M., Andreason, P., Zametkin, A. J., et al. (1992). Failure to activate the left temporoparietal cortex in dyslexia. An oxygen 15 positron emission tomographic study. *Archives of Neurology, 49,* 527–534.

Rumsey, J. M., Casanova, M., Mannheim, G. B., et al. (1996). Corpus callosum morphology, as measured with MRI, in dyslexic men. *Biological Psychiatry, 39,* 769–775.

Rumsey, J. M., Donohue, B. C., Brady, D. R., et al. (1997). A magnetic resonance imaging study of planum temporale asymmetry in men with developmental dyslexia. *Archives of Neurology, 54,* 1481–1489.

Russell-Freudenthal, D., Zaru, M. W., & Al Otaiba, S. (2023). Early literacy and multi-tiered systems of supports. In S. Cabell, S. Newman, & N. Patton Terry (eds.), *Handbook on the Science of Early Literacy* (pp. 43–59). New York: Guilford Press.

Rutter, M. (1978). Prevalence and types of dyslexia. In A. L. Benton, & D. Pearl (eds.), *Dyslexia: An Appraisal of Current Knowledge* (pp. 5–28). New York: Oxford University Press.

Rutter, M., & Pickles, A. (2016). Annual Research Review: Threats to the validity of child psychiatry and psychology. *Journal of Child Psychology and Psychiatry, 75*(3), 398–416.

Ryder, D., & Norwich, B. (2018). What's in a name? Perspectives of dyslexia assessors working with students in the UK higher education sector. *Dyslexia, 24*(2), 109–127.

Ryder, D., & Norwich, B. (2019). UK higher education lecturers' perspectives of dyslexia, dyslexic students and related disability provision. *Journal of Research in Special Educational Needs, 19*(3), 161–172.

Saatcioglu, A., & Skrtic, T. M. (2019). Categorization by organizations: Manipulation of disability categories in a racially desegregated school district. *American Journal of Sociology, 125*(1), 184–260.

Sadusky, A., Berger, E. P., Reupert, A. E., & Freeman, N. C. (2022). Methods used by psychologists for identifying dyslexia: A systematic review. *Dyslexia, 28*(2), 132–148.

Saksida, A., Iannuzzi, S., Bogliotti, C., et al. (2016). Phonological skills, visual attention span, and visual stress in developmental dyslexia. *Developmental Psychology, 52*(10), 1503.

Sala, G., & Gobet, F. (2020a). Working memory training in typically developing children: A multilevel meta-analysis. *Psychonomic Bulletin & Review, 27*(3), 423–434.

Sala, G., & Gobet, F. (2020b). Cognitive and academic benefits of music training with children: A multilevel meta-analysis. *Memory & Cognition, 48*(8), 1429–1441.

Salehinejad, M. A., Ghanavati, E., Glinski, B., Hallajian, A. H., & Azarkolah, A. (2022). A systematic review of randomized controlled trials on efficacy and safety of transcranial direct current stimulation in major neurodevelopmental disorders: ADHD, autism, and dyslexia. *Brain and Behavior, 12*, e2724.

Salmelin, R., Service, E., Kiesilä, P., Uutela, K., & Salonen, O. (1996). Impaired visual word processing in dyslexia revealed with magnetoencephalography. *Annals of Neurology, 40*, 157–162.

Samuelsson, S., Byrne, B., Olson, R. K., et al. (2008). Response to early literacy instruction in the United States, Australia, and Scandinavia: A behavioral-genetic analysis. *Learning and Individual Differences, 18*, 289–295.

Sanchez, V. M., & O'Connor, R. E. (2015). Building tier 3 intervention for long-term slow growers in grades 3–4: A pilot study. *Learning Disabilities Research & Practice, 30*(4), 171–181.

Sand, L. A., & Bolger, D. J. (2019). The neurobiological strands of developmental dyslexia: What we know and what we don't know. In D. A. Kilpatrick, R. M. Joshi, & R. K. Wagner (eds.), *Reading Development and Difficulties* (pp. 233–270). Cham, Switzerland: Springer.

Sanders, S. J., Ercan-Sencicek, A. G., Hus, V., et al. (2011). Multiple recurrent de novo CNVs, including duplications of the 7q11.23 Williams Syndrome region, are strongly associated with autism. *Neuron, 70*, 863–885.

Sanders, S. J., Murtha, M. T., Gupta, A. R., et al. (2012). De novo mutations revealed by whole-exome sequencing are strongly associated with autism. *Nature, 485*, 237–241.

Sanetti, L. M. H., & Luh, H. J. (2019). Fidelity of implementation in the field of learning disabilities. *Learning Disability Quarterly*, 0731948719851514.

Sanfilippo, J., Ness, M., Petscher, Y., et al. (2020). Reintroducing dyslexia: Early identification and implications for pediatric practice. *Pediatrics, 146*(1), e20193046

Satel, S., & Lilienfeld, S. O. (2013). *Brainwashed: The Seductive Appeal of Mindless Neuroscience*. New York: Basic Books.

Savage, R. S. (2004). Motor skills, automaticity and developmental dyslexia: A review of the research literature. *Reading and Writing, 17*, 301–324.

Savage, R. S., Frederickson, N., Goodwin, R., et al. (2005). Relationships among rapid digit naming, phonological processing, motor automaticity, and speech perception in poor, average, and good readers and spellers. *Journal of Learning Disabilities, 38*, 12–28.

Savage, R. S., Lavers, N., & Pillay, V. (2007). Working memory and reading difficulties: What we know and what we don't know about the relationship. *Educational Psychology Review, 19*, 185–221.

Savitz, R. S., Allen, A. A., & Brown, C. (2021). Variations in RTI literacy implementation in Grades 6–12: A national study. *Literacy Research and Instruction*, 1–24.

Sayeski, K. L., & Hurford, D. P. (2022). A framework for examining reading-related education research and the curious case of Orton-Gillingham. *Learning Disabilities: A Multidisciplinary Journal, 27*(2).

Sayeski, K. L., Reno, E. A., & Thoele, J. M. (2022). Specially designed instruction: Operationalizing the delivery of special education services. *Exceptionality, 31*(3), 198–210.

Sayeski, K. L., & Zirkel, P. A. (2021). Orton-Gillingham and the IDEA: Analysis of the frequency and outcomes of case law. *Annals of Dyslexia, 71*(3), 483–500.

Saygin, Z. M., Osher, D. E., Norton, E. S., et al. (2016). Connectivity precedes function in the development of the visual word form area. *Nature Neuroscience, 19*, 1250–1255.

Scammacca, N. K., Roberts, G. J., Cho, E., et al. (2016). A century of progress: Reading interventions for students in grades 4–12, 1914–2014. *Review of Educational Research, 86*(3), 756–800.

Scammacca, N. K., Roberts, G., Vaughn, S., & Stuebing, K. K. (2015). A meta-analysis of interventions for struggling readers in grades 4–12: 1980–2011. *Journal of Learning Disabilities, 48*(4), 369–390.

Scammacca, N., Roberts, G., Vaughn, S., et al. (2007). *Reading Interventions for Adolescent Struggling Readers: A Meta-Analysis with Implications for Practice*. Portsmouth, NH: RMC Research Corporation Center on Instruction.

Scanlon, D. M. (2011). Response to intervention as an assessment approach. In A. McGill-Franzen, & R. L. Allington (eds.), *Handbook of Reading Disability Research* (pp. 139–148). New York: Routledge.

Scanlon, D. M., & Anderson, K. L. (2020). Using context as an assist in word solving: The contributions of 25 years of research on the interactive strategies approach. *Reading Research Quarterly, 55,* S19–S34.

Scanlon, D. M., Gelzheiser, L. M., Vellutino, F. R., Schatschneider, C., & Sweeney, J. M. (2008). Reducing the incidence of early reading difficulties: Professional development for classroom teachers versus direct interventions for children. *Learning and Individual Differences, 18,* 346–359.

Scanlon, D. M., Vellutino, F. R., Small, S. G., Fanuele, D., & Sweeney, J. M. (2005). Severe reading difficulties: Can they be prevented? A comparison of prevention and intervention approaches. *Exceptionality, 13,* 209–227.

Scarborough, H. S., & Brady, S. A. (2002). Toward a common terminology for talking about speech and reading: A glossary of the "phon" words and some related terms. *Journal of Literacy Research, 34,* 299–336.

Scerri, T. S., Fisher, S. E., Francks, C., et al. (2004). Putative functional alleles of DYX1C1 are not associated with dyslexia susceptibility in a large sample of sibling pairs from the UK. *Journal of Medical Genetics, 41,* 853–857.

Scerri, T. S., Macpherson, E., Martinelli, A., et al. (2017). The DCDC2 deletion is not a risk factor for dyslexia. *Translational Psychiatry, 7,* e1182.

Scerri, T. S., Paracchini, S., Morris, A., et al. (2010). Identification of candidate genes for dyslexia susceptibility on chromosome 18. *PLoS ONE, 5*(10).

Schelbe, L., Pryce, J., Petscher, Y., et al. (2021). Dyslexia in the context of social work: Screening and early intervention. *Families in Society, 103*(3), 269–280.

Schlaggar, B. L., & McCandliss, B. D. (2007). Development of neural systems for reading. *Annual Review of Neuroscience, 30,* 475–503.

Schlesinger, N. W., & Gray, S. (2017). The impact of multisensory instruction on learning letter names and sounds, word reading, and spelling. *Annals of Dyslexia, 67*(3), 219–258.

Schmahmann, J. D., & Pandya, D. N. (1997). The cerebrocerebellar system. *International Review of Neurobiology, 41,* 31–60.

Schmidt, W. H., Burroughs, N. A., Zoido, P., & Houang, R. T. (2015). The role of schooling in perpetuating educational inequality: An international perspective. *Educational Researcher, 44*(7), 371–386.

Schneider, W. J., & Kaufman, A. (2017). Let's not do away with comprehensive cognitive assessments just yet. *Archives of Clinical Neuropsychology, 32,* 8–20.

Schneps, M. H., Thomson, J. M., Chen, C., Sonnert, G., & Pomplun, M. (2013). E-readers are more effective than paper for some with dyslexia. *PloS one, 8*(9), e75634.

Schön, D., & Tillmann, B. (2015). Short-and long-term rhythmic interventions: Perspectives for language rehabilitation. *Annals of the New York Academy of Sciences, 1337*(1), 32–39.

Schueler, M., Braun, D. A., Chandrasekar, G., et al. (2015). DCDC2 mutations cause a renal-hepatic ciliopathy by disrupting Wnt signaling. *American Journal of Human Genetics, 96,* 81–92.

Schulte-Körne, G., & Bruder, J. (2010). Clinical neurophysiology of visual and auditory processing in dyslexia: A review. *Clinical Neurophysiology, 121,* 1794–1809.

Schulte-Körne, G., Deimel, W., Bartling, J., & Remschmidt, H. (1998). Auditory processing and dyslexia: Evidence for a specific speech processing deficit. *Neuroreport*, *9*, 337–340.

Schulz, R., Gerloff, C., & Hummel, F. C. (2013). Non-invasive brain stimulation in neurological diseases. *Neuropharmacology*, *64*, 579–587.

Schumacher, J., Hoffmann, P., Schmal, C., Schulte-Korne, G., & Nothen, M. M. (2007). Genetics of dyslexia: The evolving landscape. *Journal of Medical Genetics*, *44*, 289–297.

Schurz, M., Wimmer, H., Richlan, F., Ludersdorfer, P., Klackl, J., & Kronbichler, M. (2015). Resting-state and task-based functional brain connectivity in developmental dyslexia. *Cerebral Cortex*, *25*(10), 3502–3514.

Schwaighofer, M., Fischer, F., & Bühner, M. (2015) Does working memory training transfer? A meta-analysis including training conditions as moderators. *Educational Psychologist*, *50*(2), 138–166.

Schwartz, A. E., Hopkins, B. G., & Stiefel, L. (2021). The effects of special education on the academic performance of students with learning disabilities. *Journal of Policy Analysis and Management*, *40*(2), 480–520.

Schwartz, S. (2019). Prominent literacy expert denies dyslexia exists; says to "shoot" whoever wrote law on it. *Education Week*. December 11. https://bit.ly/3T9HzLE. Accessed December 3, 2023.

Schwartz, S. J., Lilienfeld, S. O., Meca, A., & Sauvigné, K. C. (2016). The role of neuroscience within psychology: A call for inclusiveness over exclusiveness. *American Psychologist*, *71*(1), 52–70.

Scientific Learning Corporation. (1999). *National Field Trial Results: Results of Fast ForWord Training for Children with Language and Reading Problems*. Berkeley, CA: Scientific Learning Corporation.

Scientific Learning Corporation. (2003). Scientifically based reading research and the Fast ForWord Products: Research implication for effective language and reading intervention. *MAPS for Learning: Research Report*, *7*, 1–7.

Seibt, O., Brunoni, A. R., Huang, Y., & Bikson, M. (2015). The pursuit of DLPFC: Non-neuronavigated methods to target the left dorsolateral prefrontal cortex with symmetric bicephalic transcranial direct current stimulation (tDCS). *Brain Stimulation*, *8*, 590–602.

Seidenberg, M. S. (2005). Connectionist models of word reading. *Current Directions in Psychological Science*, *14*, 238–242.

Seidenberg, M. S. (2017). *Language at the Speed of Sight: How We Read, Why So Many Cannot, and What Can Be Done about It*. New York: Basic Books.

Seidenberg, M. S., Cooper Borkenhagen, M., & Kearns, D. M. (2020). Lost in translation? Challenges in connecting reading science and educational practice. *Reading Research Quarterly*, *55*, S119–S130.

Seidenberg, M. S., Farry-Thorn, M., & Zevin, J. D. (2022). Models of word reading. In M. J. Snowling, C. Hulme, & K. Nation (eds.), *The Science of Reading: A Handbook*. 2nd edition (pp. 36–59). Hoboken, NJ: Wiley.

Sela, I. (2012). The relationships between motor learning, the visual system and dyslexia. reading, writing, mathematics and the developing brain. *Reading,*

Writing, Mathematics and the Developing Brain: Listening to Many Voices, 6, 177–118.

Selemon, L. D., & Goldman-Rakic, P. S. (1999). The reduced neuropil hypothesis: A circuit based model of schizophrenia. *Biological Psychiatry, 45,* 17–25.

Selzam, S., Dale, P. S., Wagner, R. K., et al. (2017). Genome-wide polygenic scores predict reading performance throughout the school years. *Scientific Studies of Reading, 21,* 334–349.

SENCo Forum. (2005). Points of view from the SENCo Forum: Is it dyslexia? *British Journal of Special Education, 32,* 165.

Serry, T. A., & Hammond, L. (2015). What's in a word? Australian experts' knowledge, views and experiences using the term dyslexia. *Australian Journal of Learning Difficulties, 20*(2), 143–161.

Seymour, P. H. K., Aro, M., & Erskine, J. M. (2003). Foundation literacy acquisition in European orthographies. *British Journal of Psychology, 94,* 143–174.

Shafik, N. (2017). Point of view: In experts we trust? – As access to information burgeons, experts are more crucial than ever. *Finance & Development, 54*(3). https://bit.ly/47XrVae. Accessed December 3, 2023.

Shakespeare, T. (2013). *Disability Rights and Wrongs.* 2nd edition. London: Routledge

Shanahan, T. (2020). What constitutes a science of reading instruction? *Reading Research Quarterly, 55*(S1), S235–S247.

Shanahan, T. (2021). A review of the evidence on Tier 1 instruction for readers with dyslexia. *Reading Research Quarterly, 58*(2), 268–284.

Shankweiler, D., & Crain, S. (1986). Language mechanisms and reading disorders: A modular approach. *Cognition, 24,* 139–168.

Shao, S., Niu, Y., Zhang, X., et al. (2016). Opposite associations between individual KIAA0319 polymorphisms and developmental dyslexia risk across populations: A stratified meta-analysis by the study population. *Scientific Reports, 6,* 30454.

Shapleske, J., Rossell, S. L., & Woodruff, P. W. (1999). The planum temporale: A systematic, quantitative review of its structural, functional and clinical significance. *Brain Research Review, 29,* 26–49.

Share, D. L. (1995). Phonological recoding and self-teaching: Sine qua non of reading acquisition. *Cognition, 55,* 151–218.

Share, D. L. (1999). Phonological recoding and orthographic learning: A direct test of the self-teaching hypothesis. *Journal of Experimental Child Psychology, 72,* 95–129.

Share, D. L. (2004). Orthographic learning at a glance: On the time course and developmental onset of self-teaching. *Journal of Experimental Child Psychology, 87,* 267–298.

Share, D. L. (2008). On the anglocentricities of current reading research and practice: The perils of overreliance on an "outlier" orthography. *Psychological Bulletin, 134,* 584–615.

Share, D. L. (2021a). Common misconceptions about the phonological deficit theory of dyslexia. *Brain Sciences, 11*(11), 1510.

Share, D. L. (2021b). Is the science of reading just the science of reading English? *Reading Research Quarterly*, *56*, S391–S402.

Share, D. L., & Stanovich, K. E. (1995). Cognitive processes in early reading development: Accommodating individual differences into a model of acquisition. *Issues in Education*, *1*, 1–57.

Sharma, P., Sagar, R., Deep, R., Mehta, M., & Subbiah, V. (2020). Assessment for familial pattern and association of polymorphisms in KIAA0319 gene with specific reading disorder in children from North India visiting a tertiary care centre: A case-control study. *Dyslexia*, *26*, 104–114.

Sharpe, D., & Poets, S. (2020). Meta-analysis as a response to the replication crisis. *Canadian Psychology*, *61*(4), 377–387.

Shaywitz, B. A., & Shaywitz, S. E. (2020). The American experience: Towards a 21st century definition of dyslexia. *Oxford Review of Education*, *46*(4), 454–471.

Shaywitz, B. A., Shaywitz, S. E., Blachman, B. A., et al. (2004). Development of left occipitotemporal systems for skilled reading in children after a phonologically-based intervention. *Biological Psychiatry*, *55*, 926–933.

Shaywitz, B. A., Shaywitz, S. E., Pugh, K. R., et al. (2002). Disruption of posterior brain systems for reading in children with developmental dyslexia. *Biological Psychiatry*, *52*, 101–110.

Shaywitz, B. A., Skudlarski, P., Holahan, J. M., et al. (2007). Age-related changes in reading systems of dyslexic children. *Annals of Neurology*, *61*, 363–370.

Shaywitz, S. E. (1996). Dyslexia. *Scientific American*, *275*(5), 98–104.

Shaywitz, S. E. (2005). *Overcoming Dyslexia*. New York: Alfred Knopf.

Shaywitz, S. E., Escobar, M. D., Shaywitz, B. A., Fletcher, J. M., & Makuch, R. (1992). Evidence that dyslexia may represent the lower tail of a normal distribution of reading ability. *New England Journal of Medicine*, *326*(3), 145–150.

Shaywitz, S. E., Morris, R., & Shaywitz, B. A. (2008). The education of dyslexic children from childhood to young adulthood. *Annual Review of Psychology*, *59*, 451–475

Shaywitz, S. E., & Shaywitz, B. A. (2005). Dyslexia (specific reading disability). *Biological Psychiatry*, *57*, 1301–1309.

Shaywitz, S. E., & Shaywitz, B. A. (2008). Paying attention to reading: The neurobiology of reading and dyslexia. *Development and Psychopathology*, *20*, 1329–1349.

Shaywitz, S. E., Shaywitz, B. A., Pugh, K. R., et al. (1998). Functional disruption in the organization of the brain for reading in dyslexia. *Proceedings of the National Academy of Sciences*, *95*, 2636–2641.

Shaywitz, S. E., & Shaywitz, J. (2020). *Overcoming Dyslexia*. 2nd edition. London: Sheldon Press.

Shipstead, Z., Redick, T. S., & Engle, R. W. (2012). Is working memory training effective? *Psychological Bulletin*, *138*(4), 628–654.

Shovman, M. M., & Ahissar, M. (2006). Isolating the impact of visual perception on dyslexics' reading ability. *Vision Research*, *46*, 3514–3525.

Shulver, K. D., & Badcock, N. A. (2021). Chasing the anchor: A systematic review and meta-analysis of perceptual anchoring deficits in developmental dyslexia. *Journal of Speech, Language, and Hearing Research*, *64*(8), 3289–3302.

Sideridis, G. D., Simos, P., Mouzaki, A., Stamovlasis, D., & Georgiou, G. K. (2019). Can the relationship between rapid automatized naming and word reading be explained by a catastrophe? Empirical evidence from students with and without reading difficulties. *Journal of Learning Disabilities*, *52*(1), 59–70.

Siegel, L. S., & Ryan, E. B. (1989). The development of working memory in normally achieving and subtypes of learning disabled children. *Child Development*, *60*, 973–980.

Siegel, L. S., Hurford, D. P., Metsala, J., & Odegard, T. N. (2022). The demise of the discrepancy definition of dyslexia: Commentary on Snowling, Hulme, and Nation. *International Journal for Research in Learning Disabilities*, *5*(2), 49–54.

Siegel, L., & Hurford, D. (2019). The case against discrepancy models in the evaluation of dyslexia. *Perspectives of Language and Literacy*, *45*(1), 23–28.

Siegelman, N., Rueckl, J. G., van den Bunt, M., et al. (2022). How you read affects what you gain: Individual differences in the functional organization of the reading system predict intervention gains in children with reading disabilities. *Journal of Educational Psychology*, *114*(4), 855–869.

Siegelman, N., van den Bunt, M. R., Ming Lo, J. C., Rueckl, J. G., & Pugh, K. (2021). Theory-driven classification of reading difficulties from fMRI data using Bayesian latent-mixture models. *Neuroimage*, *242*, 118476.

Sihvonen, A. J., Virtala, P., Thiede, A., Laasonen, M., & Kujala, T. (2021). Structural white matter connectometry of reading and dyslexia. *Neuroimage*, *241*, 118411.

Silani, G., Frith, U., Demonet, J. F., et al. (2005). Brain abnormalities underlying altered activation in dyslexia: A voxel based morphometry study. *Brain*, *128*, 2453–2461.

Silva, S., Faísca, L., Araújo, S., et al. (2016). Too little or too much? Parafoveal preview benefits and parafoveal load costs in dyslexic adults. *Annals of Dyslexia*, *66*(2), 187–201.

Silver, L. B. (1987). A review of the current controversial approaches for treating learning disabilities. *Journal of Learning Disabilities*, *20*, 498–504.

Simons, D. J., Boot, W. R., Charness, N., et al. (2016). Do "brain-training" programs work? *Psychological Science in the Public Interest*, *17*(3), 103–186.

Simos, P. G., Breier, J. I., Fletcher, J. M., et al. (2000). Brain activation profiles in dyslexic children during non-word reading: A magnetic source imaging study. *Neuroscience Letters*, *290*, 61–65.

Simos, P. G., Breier, J. I., Wheless, J. W., Maggio, W. W., Fletcher, J. M., Castillo, E. M., & Papanicolaou, A. C. (2000). Brain mechanisms for reading: The role of the superior temporal gyrus in word and pseudoword naming. *Neuroreport*, *11*, 2443–2447.

Simos, P. G., Fletcher, J. M., Bergman, E., et al. (2002). Dyslexia-specific brain activation profile becomes normal following successful remedial training. *Neurology*, *58*, 1203–1213.

Simos, P. G., Fletcher, J. M., Sarkari, S., et al. (2007). Altering the brain circuits for reading through intervention: A magnetic source imaging study. *Neuropsychology*, *21*, 485–496.

Simos, P. G., Rezaie, R., Fletcher, J. M., et al. (2011). Functional disruption of the brain mechanism for reading: Effects of comorbidity and task difficulty among children with developmental learning problems. *Neuropsychology, 25*, 520–534.

Simos, P. G., Rezaie, R., Papanicolaou, A. C., & Fletcher, J. M. (2014). Does IQ affect the functional brain network involved in pseudoword reading in students with reading disability? A magnetoencephalography study. *Frontiers in Human Neuroscience, 7*, 932.

Simpson, J., & Everatt, J. (2005). Reception class predictors of literacy skills. *British Journal of Educational Psychology, 75*, 171–188.

Singer, A., Lutz, A., Escher, J., & Halladay, A. (2023). A full semantic toolbox is essential for autism research and practice to thrive. *Autism Research, 16*(3), 497–501.

Singer, J. (1999). "Why can't you be normal for once in your life?" From a "problem with no name" to the emergence of a new category of difference. In M. Corker, & S. French (eds.), *Disability Discourse* (pp. 59–70). Buckingham: Open University Press.

Singleton, C. H. (2009a). Visual stress and dyslexia. In G. Reid (ed.), *The Routledge Companion to Dyslexia* (pp. 43–57). New York: Routledge.

Singleton, C. H. (2009b). *Intervention for Dyslexia: A Review of Published Evidence on the Impact of Specialist Dyslexia Teaching*. Hull: University of Hull.

Singleton, C. H. (2012). Visual stress and its relationship to dyslexia. In J. Stein, & Z. Kapoula (eds.), *Visual Aspects of Dyslexia* (pp. 91–110). Oxford: Oxford University Press.

Siok, W. T., Perfetti, C. A., Jin, Z., & Tan, L. H. (2004). Biological abnormality of impaired reading is constrained by culture. *Nature, 431*, 71–76.

Siok, W. T., Spinks, J. A., Jin, Z., & Tan, L. H. (2009). Developmental dyslexia is characterized by the co-existence of visuospatial and phonological disorders in Chinese children. *Current Biology, 19*, R890–R892.

Sisk, V. F., Burgoyne, A. P., Sun, J., Butler, J. L., & Macnamara, B. N. (2018). To what extent and under which circumstances are growth mind-sets important to academic achievement? Two meta-analyses. *Psychological Science, 29*(4), 549–571.

Skeide, M. A., & Friederici, A. D. (2016). The ontogeny of the cortical language network. *Nature Reviews Neuroscience, 17*, 323–332.

Skiba, T., Landi, N., Wagner, R., & Grigorenko, E. L. (2011). In search of the perfect phenotype: An analysis of linkage and association studies of reading and reading-related processes. *Behavior Genetics, 41*, 6–30.

Skottun, B. C. (2000). The magnocellular deficit theory of dyslexia: The evidence from contrast sensitivity. *Vision Research, 40*, 111–127.

Skottun, B. C. (2011). On the use of visual motion perception to assess magnocellular integrity. *Journal of Integrative Neuroscience, 10*(1), 15–32.

Skottun, B. C. (2015). The need to differentiate the magnocellular system from the dorsal stream in connection with dyslexia. *Brain and Cognition, 95*, 62–66.

Skottun, B. C. (2016). A few remarks on the utility of visual motion perception to assess the integrity of the magnocellular system or the dorsal stream. *Cortex, 79*, 155–158.

Skottun, B. C., & Skoyles, J. R. (2006a). Attention, reading and dyslexia. *Clinical & Experimental Optometry, 89*, 241–245.

Skottun, B. C., & Skoyles, J. R. (2006b). Is coherent motion an appropriate test for magnocellular sensitivity? *Brain and Cognition, 61*, 172–180.

Skottun, B. C., & Skoyles, J. R. (2008). Dyslexia and rapid visual processing: A commentary. *Journal of Clinical and Experimental Neuropsychology, 30*, 666–673.

Skottun, B. C., & Skoyles, J. R. (2010a). L- and M-cone ratios and magnocellular sensitivity in reading. *International Journal of Neuroscience, 120*, 241–244.

Skottun, B. C., & Skoyles, J. R. (2010b). Temporal order judgment in dyslexia – Task difficulty or temporal processing deficiency? *Neuropsychologia, 48*, 2226–2229.

Skottun, B. C., & Skoyles, J. R. (2011). Dyslexia, magnocellular integrity and rapidly presented stimuli. *Nature Precedings, 1*–1.

Skoyles, J. R., & Skottun, B. C. (2004). On the prevalence of magnocellular deficits in the visual system of non-dyslexic individuals. *Brain and Language, 88*, 79–82.

Slavin, R. E., Lake, C., Chambers, B., Cheung, A., & Davis, S. (2009). Effective reading programs for the elementary grades: A best-evidence synthesis. *Review of Educational Research, 79*, 1391–1466.

Slavin, R. E., Lake, C., Davis, S., & Madden, N. A. (2011). Effective programs for struggling readers: A best-evidence synthesis. *Educational Research Review, 6*, 1–26.

Sleeman, M., Everatt, J., Arrow, A., & Denston, A. (2022a). The identification and classification of struggling readers based on the simple view of reading. *Dyslexia, 28*(3), 256–275.

Sleeman, M., Everatt, J., Arrow, A., & Denston, A. (2022b). Evaluation of the "Three Steps in Screening for Dyslexia" assessment protocol designed for New Zealand teachers. *New Zealand Journal of Educational Studies, 1*–18.

Sleeter, C. E. (1987). Why is there learning disabilities? A critical analysis of the birth of the field with its social context. In T. Popkewitz (ed.), *The Formation of School Subjects: The Struggle for Creating an American Institution* (pp. 210–237). London: Routledge.

Slomowitz, R. F., Narayan, A. J., Pennington, B. F., et al. (2021). In search of cognitive promotive and protective factors for word reading. *Scientific Studies of Reading, 25*(5), 397–416.

Smalle, E. H., Szmalec, A., Bogaerts, L., et al. (2019). Literacy improves short-term serial recall of spoken verbal but not visuospatial items – Evidence from illiterate and literate adults. *Cognition, 185*, 144–150.

Smith, F. (1971). *Understanding Reading: A Psycholinguistic Analysis of Reading and Learning to Read*. New York: Holt, Rinehart & Winston.

Smith, J. L. M., Nelson, N. J., Smolkowski, K., et al. (2016). Examining the efficacy of a multitiered intervention for at-risk readers in grade 1. *Elementary School Journal, 116*(4), 549–573.

Smith, S. D. (2007). Genes, language development, and language disorders. *Mental Retardation and Developmental Disabilities, 13*, 95–105.

Smith, S. D., Kimberling, W. J., Pennington, B. F., & Lubs, H. A. (1983). Specific reading disability: Identification of an inherited form through linkage analyses. *Science*, *219*, 1345–1347.

Smolkowski, K., & Cummings, K. D. (2016). Evaluation of the DIBELS diagnostic system for the selection of native and proficient English speakers at risk of reading difficulties. *Journal of Psychoeducational Assessment*, *34*(2), 103–118.

Snow, C. E., & Juel, C. (2005). Teaching children to read: What do we know about how to do it? In M. J. Snowling, & C. Hulme (eds.), *The Science of Reading: A Handbook* (pp. 501–520). Oxford: Blackwell.

Snow, C. E., Burns, M. S., & Griffin, P. (1998). *Preventing Reading Difficulties in Young Children*. Washington, DC: National Academy Press.

Snowling, M. J. (2008). Specific disorders and broader phenotypes: The case of dyslexia. *Quarterly Journal of Experimental Psychology*, *61*, 142–156.

Snowling, M. J. (2010). Dyslexia. In C. L. Cooper, J. Field, U. Goswami, R. Jenkins, & B. J. Sahakian (eds.), *Mental Capital and Mental Wellbeing* (pp. 775–783). Oxford: Blackwell.

Snowling, M. J. (2013). Early identification and interventions for dyslexia: A contemporary view. *Journal of Research in Special Educational Needs*, *13*(1), 7–14.

Snowling, M. J. (2015). Open dialogue peer review: A response to Elliott. *The Psychology of Education Review*, *39*(1), 20–21.

Snowling, M. J. (2019). *Dyslexia: A Very Short Introduction*. Oxford: Oxford University Press.

Snowling, M. J., Gooch, D., McArthur, G., & Hulme, C. (2018). Language skills, but not frequency discrimination, predict reading skills in children at risk of dyslexia. *Psychological Science*, *29*, 1270–1282.

Snowling, M. J., Hayiou-Thomas, M. E., Nash, H. M., & Hulme, C. (2020). Dyslexia and developmental language disorder: Comorbid disorders with distinct effects on reading comprehension. *Journal of Child Psychology and Psychiatry*, *61*(6), 672–680.

Snowling, M. J., & Hulme, C. (1994). The development of phonological skills in children. *Philosophical Transactions of the Royal Society B*, *346*, 21–26.

Snowling, M. J., & Hulme, C. (2003). A critique of claims from Reynolds, Nicolson & Hambly (2003) that DDAT is an effective treatment for reading problems: "Lies, damned lies and (inappropriate) statistics." *Dyslexia*, *9*, 1–7.

Snowling, M. J., & Hulme, C. (2021). Annual Research Review: Reading disorders revisited – The critical importance of oral language. *Journal of Child Psychology and Psychiatry*, *62*(5), 635–653.

Snowling, M. J., & Melby-Lervåg, M. (2016). Oral language deficits in familial dyslexia: A meta-analysis and review. *Psychological Bulletin*, *142*(5), 498.

Snowling, M. J., Moll, K., & Hulme, C. (2021). Language difficulties are a shared risk factor for both reading disorder and mathematics disorder. *Journal of Experimental Child Psychology*, *202*, 105009.

Snowling, M. J., Nash, H. M., Gooch, D. C., et al. (2019). Developmental outcomes for children at high risk of dyslexia and children with developmental language disorder. *Child Development*, *90*, e548–e564

Snowling, M. J., Hulme, C., & Nation, K. (2020). Defining and understanding dyslexia: Past present and future. *Oxford Review of Education, 46*(4), 501–513.

Snyder, H. R., Miyake, A., & Hankin, B. L. (2015). Advancing understanding of executive function impairments and psychopathology: Bridging the gap between clinical and cognitive approaches. *Frontiers in Psychology, 6*, 328.

Sokolowski, H. M., & Peters, L. (2022). Persistence and fade-out of responses to reading and mathematical interventions. In M. A. Skeide (ed.), *The Cambridge Handbook of Dyslexia and Dyscalculia* (pp. 362–377). Cambridge: Cambridge University Press.

Solari, E., Petscher, Y., & Hall, C. (2021). What does science say about Orton-Gillingham interventions? An explanation and commentary on the Stevens et al. (2021) meta-analysis. https://doi.org/10.31234/osf.io/mcw82

Soler, J. (2010). Dyslexia lessons: The politics of dyslexia and reading problems. In K. Hall, U. Goswami, C. Harrison, S. Ellis, & J. Soler (eds.), *Interdisciplinary Perspectives on Learning to Read* (pp. 179–192). London: Routledge.

Solity, J. (2022). Instructional Psychology and Teaching Reading: An analysis of the evidence underpinning government policy and practice. *Review of Education, 10*(1), e3349.

Solomyak, O., & Marantz, A. (2010). Evidence for early morphological decomposition in visual word recognition. *Journal of Cognitive Neuroscience, 22*, 2042–2057.

Song, M., & Miskel, C. (2002). *Interest Groups in National Reading Policy: Perceived Influence and Beliefs on Teaching Reading.* Ann Arbor, MI: University of Michigan, Center for the Improvement of Early Reading Achievement.

Song, S., Georgiou, G. K., Su, M., & Hua, S. (2016). How well do phonological awareness and rapid automatized naming correlate with Chinese reading accuracy and fluency? A meta-analysis. *Scientific Studies of Reading, 20*(2), 99–123.

Sonuga-Barke, E. J. S. (2016). Distinguishing between the challenges posed by *surface* and *deep* forms of heterogeneity to diagnostic systems: Do we need a new approach to subtyping of child and adolescent psychiatric disorders? *Journal of Child Psychology and Psychiatry, 57*(1), 1–3.

Soroli, E., Szenkovits, G., & Ramus, F. (2010). Exploring dyslexics' phonological deficit III: Foreign speech perception and production. *Dyslexia, 16*, 318–340.

Spector, J. E. (2005). Instability of double-deficit subtypes among at-risk first grade students. *Reading Psychology, 26*, 285–312.

Speece, D. L. (2005). Hitting the moving target known as reading development: Some thoughts on screening children for secondary interventions. *Journal of Learning Disabilities, 38*, 487–493.

Sperry, D. E., Sperry, L. L., & Miller, P. J. (2019). Reexamining the verbal environments of children from different socioeconomic backgrounds. *Child Development, 90*(4), 1303–1318

Spiegel, J. A., Goodrich, J. M., Morris, B. M., Osborne, C. M., & Lonigan, C. J. (2021). Relations between executive functions and academic outcomes in elementary school children: A meta-analysis. *Psychological Bulletin, 147*(4), 329.

Spinelli, D., De Luca, M., Judica, A., & Zoccolotti, P. (2002). Crowding effects on word identification in developmental dyslexia. *Cortex, 38*, 179–200.

Spironelli, C., & Angrilli, A. (2006). Language lateralization in phonological, semantic and orthographic tasks: A slow evoked potential study. *Behavioural Brain Research*, *175*, 296–304.

Spironelli, C., Angrilli, A., & Pertile, M. (2008). Language plasticity in aphasics after recovery: Evidence from slow evoked potentials. *Neuroimage*, *40*, 912–922.

Spironelli, C., Penolazzi, B., & Angrilli, A. (2008). Dysfunctional hemispheric asymmetry of theta and beta EEG activity during linguistic tasks in developmental dyslexia. *Biological Psychology*, *77*, 123–131.

Sprick, J. T., Bouck, E. C., Berg, T. R., & Coughlin, C. (2020). Attendance and specific learning disability identification: A survey of practicing school psychologists. *Learning Disabilities Research & Practice*, *35*(3), 139–149.

Stagg, S. D., & Kiss, N. (2021). Room to read: The effect of extra-large letter spacing and coloured overlays on reading speed and accuracy in adolescents with dyslexia. *Research in Developmental Disabilities*, *119*, 104065.

Stahl, S. A., & Miller, P. D. (1989). Whole language and language experience approaches for beginning reading: A quantitative research synthesis. *Review of Educational Research*, *59*, 87–116.

Stainthorp, R., Stuart, M., Powell, D., Quinlan, P., & Garwood, H. (2010). Visual processing deficits in children with slow RAN performance. *Scientific Studies of Reading*, *14*, 266–292.

Stankiewicz, P., & Lupski, J. R. (2010). Structural variation in the human genome and its role in disease. *Annual Review of Medicine*, *61*, 437–455.

Stanley, C., Heo, J., Petscher, Y., Al Otaiba, S., & Wanzek, J. (2023). Direct impact of mindset on reading-based outcomes in upper elementary students with reading difficulties. *Frontiers in Education*, 8.

Stanovich, K. E. (1980). Toward an interactive-compensatory model of individual differences in the development of reading fluency. *Reading Research Quarterly*, *16*, 32–71.

Stanovich, K. E. (1986). Matthew effects in reading: Some consequences of individual differences in the acquisition of literacy. *Reading Research Quarterly*, *21*, 360–407.

Stanovich, K. E. (1988). Explaining the differences between the dyslexic and the garden-variety poor reader: The phonological-core variable-difference model. *Journal of Learning Disabilities*, *21*, 590–604.

Stanovich, K. E. (2000). *Progress in Understanding Reading: Scientific Foundations and New Frontiers*. New York: Guilford Press.

Stanovich, K. E. (2005). The future of a mistake: Will discrepancy measurement continue to make the learning disabilities field a pseudoscience? *Learning Disability Quarterly*, *28*, 103–106.

Stanovich, K. E., & Siegel, L. S. (1994). Phenotypic performance profile of children with reading disabilities: A regression-based test of the phonological-core variable-difference model. *Journal of Educational Psychology*, *86*, 24–53.

Stanovich, K. E., & Stanovich, P. J. (1997). Further thoughts on aptitude/achievement discrepancy. *Educational Psychology in Practice*, *13*, 3–8.

Stanovich, K. E., (1991). Discrepancy definitions of reading disability: Has intelligence led us astray? *Reading Research Quarterly, 26,* 7–29.

Steacy, L. M., Kirby, J. R., Parrila, R., & Compton, D. L. (2014). Classification of double deficit groups across time: An analysis of group stability from kindergarten to second grade. *Scientific Studies of Reading, 18*(4), 255–273.

Stefanac, N., Spencer-Smith, M., Brosnan, M., et al. (2019). Visual processing speed as a marker of immaturity in lexical but not sublexical dyslexia. *Cortex, 120,* 567–581.

Stein, J. (2008). The neurobiological basis of dyslexia. In H. Reid, A. Fawcett, F. Manis, & L. Siegel (eds.), *The Sage Handbook of Dyslexia* (pp. 53–76). London: Sage.

Stein, J. (2012). The magnocellular theory of dyslexia. In A. A. Benasich, & R. H. Fitch (eds.), *Developmental Dyslexia: Early Precursors, Neurobehavioral Markers, and Biological Substrates* (pp. 32–45). Baltimore: Paul H. Brookes Publishing.

Stein, J. (2018). What is developmental dyslexia? *Brain Sciences, 8*(2), 26.

Stein, J. (2019). The current status of the magnocellular theory of developmental dyslexia. *Neuropsychologia, 130,* 66–77.

Stein, J. (2022a). The visual basis of reading and reading difficulties. *Frontiers in Neuroscience, 16.*

Stein, J. (2022b). Developmental dyslexia – A useful concept? *Asia Pacific Journal of Developmental Differences, 9*(2), 158–171.

Stein, J. (2023). Theories about developmental dyslexia. *Brain Sciences, 13.*

Stein, J., & Talcott, J. B. (1999). Impaired neuronal timing in developmental dyslexia – The magnocellular hypothesis. *Dyslexia, 5*(2), 59–77.

Stein, J., Talcott, J. B., & Walsh, V. (2000). Controversy about the visual magnocellular deficit in developmental dyslexics. *Trends in Cognitive Science, 4,* 209–211.

Stein, J., & Walsh, V. (1997). To see but not to read: The magnocellular theory of dyslexia. *Trends in Neuroscience, 20,* 147–152.

Steinberg, E., & Andrist, C. G. (2012). Dyslexia comes to Congress: A call to action. International Dyslexia Association. https://dyslexiaida.org. Accessed April 23, 2023.

Steinbrink, C., Vogt, K., Kastrup, A., et al. (2008). The contribution of white and gray matter differences to developmental dyslexia: Insights from DTI and VBM at 3.0 T. *Neuropsychologia, 46,* 3170–3178.

Steinle, P. K., Stevens, E., & Vaughn, S. (2022). Fluency interventions for struggling readers in grades 6 to 12: A research synthesis. *Journal of Learning Disabilities, 55*(1), 3–21.

Stephenson, J. (2009). A case study of unfounded concepts underpinning controversial practices: Lost in "Space Dyslexia." *International Journal of Disability, Development and Education, 56,* 37–47.

Stephenson, S. (1904). Congenital word blindness. *Lancet, 2,* 827–828.

Stephenson, S. (1907). Six cases of congenital word-blindness affecting three generations of one family. *Ophthalmoscope, 5,* 482–484.

Sternberg, R. J. (2021). *Adaptive Intelligence: Surviving and Thriving in Times of Uncertainty.* New York: Cambridge University Press.

Sternberg, R. J., & Grigorenko, E. L. (1999). *Our Labeled Children: What Every Parent and Teacher Needs to Know about Learning Disabilities*. Reading, MA: Perseus Publishing Group.

Sternberg, R. J., & Grigorenko, E. L. (2002a). *Dynamic Testing*. New York: Cambridge University Press.

Sternberg, R. J., & Grigorenko, E. L. (2002b). Difference scores in the identification of children with learning disabilities: It's time to use a different method. *Journal of School Psychology, 40*, 65–83.

Sternberg, R. J. (2004). Four alternative futures for education in the United States: It's our choice. *School Psychology Review, 33*(1), 67–77.

Stevens, E. A., Austin, C., Moore, C., et al. (2021). Current state of the evidence: Examining the effects of Orton-Gillingham reading interventions for students with or at risk for word-level reading disabilities. *Exceptional Children, 87*(4), 397–417.

Stevens, E. A., Walker, M. A., & Vaughn, S. (2017). The effects of reading fluency interventions on the reading fluency and reading comprehension performance of elementary students with learning disabilities: A synthesis of the research from 2001 to 2014. *Journal of Learning Disabilities, 50*(5), 576–590.

Stevenson, J. (2011). Commentary: A contribution to evidence-informed education policy – Reflections on Strong, Torgerson, Torgerson, and Hulme. *Journal of Child Psychology and Psychiatry, 52*, 236–237.

Stoodley, C. J., & Stein, J. F. (2011). The cerebellum and dyslexia. *Cortex, 47*, 101–116.

Stoodley, C. J., & Stein, J. F. (2013). Cerebellar function in developmental dyslexia. *Cerebellum, 12*(2), 267–276.

Stoodley, C. J., Fawcett, A. J., Nicolson, R. I., & Stein, J. F. (2006). Balancing and pointing tasks in dyslexic and control adults. *Dyslexia, 12*, 276–288.

Strauss, A. A., & Lehtinen, L. E. (1947). *Psychopathology and Education of the Brain-Injured Child*. New York: Grune & Stratton.

Strong, G. K., Torgerson, C. J., Torgerson, D., & Hulme, C. (2011). A systematic meta-analytic review of evidence for the effectiveness of the "Fast ForWord" language intervention program. *Journal of Child Psychology and Psychiatry, 52*, 236–237.

Studdert-Kennedy, M., & Mody, M. (1995). Auditory temporal perception deficits in the reading impaired: A critical review of the evidence. *Psychonomic Bulletin and Review, 2*, 508–514.

Stuebing, K. K., Barth, A. E., Molfese, P. J., Weiss, B., & Fletcher, J. M. (2009). IQ is not strongly related to response to reading instruction: A meta-analytic interpretation. *Exceptional Children, 76*, 31–51.

Stuebing, K. K., Fletcher, J. M., Branum-Martin, L., & Francis, D. J. (2012). Evaluation of the technical adequacy of three methods for identifying specific learning disabilities based on cognitive discrepancies. *School Psychology Review, 41*, 3–22.

Stuebing, K. K., Fletcher, J. M., LeDoux, J. M., et al. (2002). Validity of IQ-discrepancy classifications of reading disabilities: A meta-analysis. *American Educational Research Journal, 39*, 469–518.

Stuebing, K. K., Barth, A. E., Trahan, L. H., et al. (2015). Are child cognitive characteristics strong predictors of responses to intervention? A meta-analysis. *Review of Educational Research, 85*(3), 395–429.

Suggate, S. P. (2016). A meta-analysis of the long-term effects of phonemic awareness, phonics, fluency, and reading comprehension interventions. *Journal of Learning Disabilities, 49*(1), 77–96.

Suhr, J. A., & Johnson, E. E. (2022). First do no harm: Ethical issues in pathologizing normal variations in behavior and functioning. *Psychological Injury and Law, 15*(3), 253–267.

Sun, Y., Gao, Y., Zhou, Y., et al. (2014). Association study of developmental dyslexia candidate genes DCDC2 and KIAA0319 in Chinese population. *American Journal of Medical Genetics Part B: Neuropsychiatric Genetics, 165*, 627–634.

Surányi, Z., Csépe, V., Richardson, U., et al. (2009). Sensitivity to rhythmic parameters in dyslexic children: A comparison of Hungarian and English. *Reading and Writing, 22*, 41–56.

Suttle, C. M., Lawrenson, J. G., & Conway, M. L. (2018). Efficacy of coloured overlays and lenses for treating reading difficulty: An overview of systematic reviews. *Clinical and Experimental Optometry, 101*(4), 514–520.

Swanson, H. L. (1999). Reading research for students with LD: A meta-analysis of intervention outcomes. *Journal of Learning Disabilities, 32*, 504–532.

Swanson, H. L., & Hsieh, C.-J. (2009). Reading disabilities in adults: A selective meta-analysis of the literature. *Review of Educational Research, 79*, 1362–1390.

Swanson, H. L., Hoskyn, M., & Lee, C. (1999). *Interventions for Students with Learning Disabilities: A Meta-Analysis of Treatment Outcomes*. New York: Guilford.

Swanson, H. L., Trainin, G., Necoechea, D. M., & Hammill, D. D. (2003). Rapid naming, phonological awareness, and reading: A meta-analysis of the correlation evidence. *Review of Educational Research, 73*, 407–440.

Swanson, H. L., Zheng, X., & Jerman, O. (2009). Working memory, short-term memory, and reading disabilities: A selective meta-analysis of the literature. *Journal of Learning Disabilities, 42*, 260–287.

Szadokierski, I., Burns, M. K., & McComas, J. J. (2017). Predicting intervention effectiveness from reading accuracy and rate measures through the instructional hierarchy: Evidence for a skill-by-treatment interaction. *School Psychology Review, 46*(2), 190–200.

Szalkowski, C. E., Fiondella, C. F., Truong, D. T., et al. (2013). The effects of KIAA0319 knockdown on cortical and subcortical anatomy in male rats. *International Journal of Developmental Neuroscience, 31*(2), 116–122.

Szenkovits, G., & Ramus, F. (2005). Exploring dyslexics' phonological deficit I: Lexical vs. sub-lexical and input vs. output processes. *Dyslexia, 11*, 253–268.

Szenkovits, G., Darma, Q., Darcy, I., & Ramus, F. (2016). Exploring dyslexics' phonological deficit II: Phonological grammar. *First Language, 36*(3), 316–337.

Szűcs, D., & Ioannidis, J. P. (2020). Sample size evolution in neuroimaging research: An evaluation of highly-cited studies (1990–2012) and of latest practices (2017–2018) in high-impact journals. *NeuroImage, 221*, 117164.

Taipale, M., Kaminen, N., Nopola-Hemmi, J., et al. (2003). A candidate gene for developmental dyslexia encodes a nuclear tetratricopeptide repeat domain protein dynamically regulated in brain. *Proceedings of the National Academy of Sciences of the United States of America, 100*, 11553–11558.

Talcott, J. B., Witton, C., Hebb, G. S., et al. (2002). On the relationship between dynamic visual and auditory processing and literacy skills; results from a large primary-school study. *Dyslexia, 8*, 204–225.

Talcott. J. B., Hansen, P. C., Willis-Owen, C., et al. (1998). Visual magnocellular impairment in adult developmental dyslexics. *Neuro-ophthalmology, 20*, 187–201.

Tallal, P. (1980). Auditory temporal perception, phonics, and reading disabilities in children. *Brain and Language, 9*, 182–198.

Tallal, P., & Gaab, N. (2006). Dynamic auditory processing, musical experience and language development. *Trends in Neurosciences, 29*, 382–390.

Tallal, P., Miller, S. L., Bedi, G., et al. (1996). Language comprehension in language-learning impaired children improved with acoustically modified speech. *Science, 271*, 81–84.

Tambyraja, S. R., Farquharson, K., & Justice, L. (2020). Reading risk in children with speech sound disorder: Prevalence, persistence, and predictors. *Journal of Speech, Language, and Hearing Research, 63*(11), 3714–3726.

Tan, Y., Chanoine, V., Cavalli, E., Anton, J. L., & Ziegler, J. C. (2022). Is there evidence for a noisy computation deficit in developmental dyslexia? *Frontiers of Human Neuroscience, 16*, 919465.

Tan, Z., Wei, H., Song, X., et al. (2022). Positron emission tomography in the neuroimaging of autism spectrum disorder: A review. *Frontiers in Neuroscience, 16*.

Tanaka, H., Black, J. M., Hulme, C., et al. (2011). The brain basis of the phonological deficit in dyslexia is independent of IQ. *Psychological Science, 22*(11), 1442–1451.

Tanaka, H., & Hoeft, F. (2017). Time to revisit reading discrepancies in twice exceptional students. *The Examiner*. International Dyslexia Association. https:// bit.ly/47DKP65. Accessed May 29, 2023.

Tang, J., Peng, P., Cha, K., & Zhao, J. (2023). Visual attention span deficits in developmental dyslexia: A meta-analysis. *Research in Developmental Disabilities, 141*, 104590.

Tannock, R., Frijters, J. C., Martinussen, R., et al. (2018). Combined modality intervention for ADHD with comorbid reading disorders: A proof of concept study. *Journal of Learning Disabilities, 51*(1), 55–72.

Tansey, M. (1991). Wechsler (WISC-R) changes following treatment of learning disabilities via EEG biofeedback training in a private practice setting. *Australian Journal of Psychology, 34*, 147–153.

Taran, N., Farah, R., DiFrancesco, M., et al. (2022). The role of visual attention in dyslexia: Behavioral and neurobiological evidence. *Human Brain Mapping, 43*, 1720–1737.

Tarkar, A., Loges, N. T., Slagle, C. E., et al. (2013). DYX1C1 is required for axonemal dynein assembly and ciliary motility [Article]. *Nature Genetics, 45*, 995–1003.

Taskov, T., & Dushanova, J. (2020). Reading-network in developmental dyslexia before and after visual training. *Symmetry*, *12*(11), 1842.

Taylor, J., Roehrig, A. D., Soden Hensler, B., Connor, C. M., & Schatschneider, C. (2010). Teacher quality moderates the genetic effects on early reading. *Science*, *328*, 512–514.

Taylor, J. S. H., Rastle, K., & Davis, M. H. (2013). Can cognitive models explain brain activation during word and pseudoword reading? A meta-analysis of 36 neuroimaging studies. *Psychological Bulletin*, *139*, 766–791.

Taylor, W. P., Miciak, J., Fletcher, J. M., & Francis, D. J. (2017). Cognitive discrepancy models for specific learning disabilities identification: Simulations of psychometric limitations. *Psychological Assessment*, *29*(4), 446–457.

Temple, E., Deutsch, G. K., Poldrack, R. A., et al. (2003). Neural deficits in children with dyslexia ameliorated by behavioral remediation: Evidence from functional MRI. *Proceedings of the National Academy of Sciences of the United States of America*, *100*, 2860–2865.

Temple, E., Poldrack, R. A., Salidis, J., et al. (2001). Disrupted neural responses to phonological and orthographic processing in dyslexic children: An fMRI study. *Neuroreport*, *12*, 299–307.

Theodoridou, D., Christodoulides, P., Zakopoulou, V., & Syrrou, M. (2021). Developmental dyslexia: Environment matters. *Brain Sciences*, *11*(6), 782.

Thiede, A., Glerean, E., Kujala, T., & Parkkonen, L. (2020). Atypical MEG intersubject correlation during listening to continuous natural speech in dyslexia. *Neuroimage*, *216*.

Thomas, C. J. (1905). Congenital "word-blindness" and its treatment. *Ophthalmoscope*, *3*, 380–385.

Thomas, T., Litwin, G., Francis, D. J., & Grigorenko, E. L. (2023). Exploring genetic and neural risk of specific reading disability within a nuclear twin family case study: A translational clinical application. *Journal of Personalized Medicine*, *13*, 156.

Thompson, C., Bacon, A. M., & Auburn, T. (2015). Disabled or differently-enabled? Dyslexic identities in online forum postings. *Disability & Society*, *30*(9), 1328–1344.

Thompson, P. A., Hulme, C., Nash, H. M., et al. (2015). Developmental dyslexia: Predicting individual risk. *Journal of Child Psychology and Psychiatry*, *56*(9), 976–987.

Thompson, T. M., Sharfi, D., Lee, M., et al. (2013). Comparison of whole-genome DNA methylation patterns in whole blood, saliva, and lymphoblastoid cell lines. *Behavior Genetics*, *43*, 168–176.

Thomson, J. M., Leong, V., & Goswami, U. (2013). Auditory processing interventions and developmental dyslexia: A comparison of phonemic and rhythmic approaches. *Reading and Writing*, *26*(2), 139–161.

Thomson, M. (1990). *Developmental Dyslexia*. London: Whurr.

Thomson, M. (2003). Monitoring dyslexics' intelligence and attainments: A follow-up study. *Dyslexia*, *9*, 3–17.

Thomson, M. (2009). *The Psychology of Dyslexia: A Handbook for Teachers*. 2nd edition. Oxford: Wiley-Blackwell.

Thornton, K. E., & Carmody, D. P. (2005). Electroencephalogram biofeedback for reading disability and traumatic brain injury. *Child and Adolescent Psychiatric Clinics of North America, 14*, 137–162.

Timms, H., & Heimans, J. (2018). *New Power*. New York: Doubleday Press.

Tindal, G., Nese, J. F. T., Stevens, J. J., & Alonzo, J. (2016). Growth on oral reading fluency measures as a function of special education and measurement sufficiency. *Remedial and Special Education, 37*, 28–40.

Toffalini, E., Giofrè, D., Pastore, M., et al. (2021). Dyslexia treatment studies: A systematic review and suggestions on testing treatment efficacy with small effects and small samples. *Behavior Research Methods, 53*(5), 1954–1972.

Tønnessen, F. E. (1995) On defining "dyslexia." *Scandinavian Journal of Educational Research, 39*, 139–156.

Tønnessen, F. E. (1997). How can we best define "dyslexia"? *Dyslexia, 3*, 78–92.

Torgesen, J. K. (2004). Lessons learned from research on interventions for students who have difficulty learning to read. In P. McCardle, & V. Chhabra (eds.), *The Voice of Evidence in Reading Research* (pp. 355–382). Baltimore: Brookes.

Torgesen, J. K. (2005). Recent discoveries on remedial interventions for children with dyslexia. In M. J. Snowling, & C. Hulme (eds.), *The Science of Reading: A Handbook* (pp. 521–537). Oxford: Blackwell.

Torgesen, J. K., Alexander, A. W., Wagner, R. K., et al. (2001). Intensive remedial instruction for children with severe reading disabilities: Immediate and long-term outcomes from two instructional approaches. *Journal of Learning Disabilities, 34*, 33–58.

Torgesen, J. K., Rashotte, C. A., & Alexander, A. W. (2001). Principles of fluency instruction in reading: Relationships with established empirical outcomes. In M. Wolf (ed.), *Dyslexia, Fluency, and the Brain* (pp. 333–355). Parkton, MD: York.

Torgesen, J. K., Foorman, B. R., & Wagner, R. K. (no date) Dyslexia: A brief for educators, parents, and legislators in Florida. FCRR Technical Report #8. Florida Center for Reading Research. https://files.eric.ed.gov/fulltext/ED542605.pdf

Torppa, M., Parrila, R., Niemi, P., et al. (2013). The double deficit hypothesis in the transparent Finnish orthography: A longitudinal study from kindergarten to Grade 2. *Reading and Writing: An Interdisciplinary Journal, 26*(8), 1353–1380.

Toste, J. R. (2016). How does the magic happen? Preparing teachers to meet the needs of students with dyslexia. *The Huffington Post.*

Toste, J. R., Didion, L., Peng, P., Filderman, M. J., & McClelland, A. M. (2020). A meta-analytic review of the relations between motivation and reading achievement for K–12 students. *Review of Educational Research, 90*(3), 420–456.

Townend, J. (2000). Phonological awareness and other foundational skills of literacy. In J. Townend, & M. Turner (eds.), *Dyslexia in Practice: A Guide for Teachers* (pp. 1–29). London: Kluwer.

Tran, C., Gagnon, F., Wigg, K. G., et al. (2013). A family-based association analysis and meta-analysis of the reading disabilities candidate gene DYX1C1. *American Journal of Medical Genetics Part B: Neuropsychiatric Genetics, 162*, 146–156.

Tran, C., Wigg, K. G., Zhang, K., et al. (2014). Association of the ROBO1 gene with reading disabilities in a family-based analysis. *Genes, Brain, and Behavior, 13*, 430–438.

Tressoldi, P. E., Lonciari, I., & Vio, C. (2000). Treatment of specific developmental reading disorders, derived from single- and dual-route models. *Journal of Learning Disabilities, 33*, 278–285.

Tridas, E. Q., Petscher, Y., Stanley, C., Sanfillippo, J., & Gaab, N. (2023). *Pediatric early analysis of risk for literacy problems: Draft (PEARL-D).* https://doi.org/10.31219/osf.io/hdxgf

Troia, G. A., & Whitney, S. D. (2003). A close look at the efficacy of Fast ForWord Language for children with academic weaknesses. *Contemporary Educational Psychology, 28*, 465–494.

Truong, D. T., Adams, A. K., Paniagua, S., et al. (2019). Multivariate genome-wide association study of rapid automatised naming and rapid alternating stimulus in Hispanic American and African-American youth. *Journal of Medical Genetics, 56*(8), 557–566.

Tsujimoto, K. C., Boada, R., Gottwald, S., et al. (2019). Causal attribution profiles as a function of reading skills, hyperactivity, and inattention. *Scientific Studies of Reading, 23*(3), 254–272.

Tsujimoto, K. C., Frijters, J. C., Boada, R., et al. (2018). Achievement attributions are associated with specific rather than general learning delays. *Learning and Individual Differences, 64*, 8–21.

Tunmer, W. E. (2008). Recent developments in reading intervention research: Introduction to the special issue. *Reading and Writing: An Interdisciplinary Journal, 21*, 299–316.

Tunmer, W. E. (2011). Foreword. In S. A. Brady, D. Braze, & C. A. Fowler (eds.), *Explaining Individual Differences in Reading: Theory and Evidence* (pp. ix–xiii). New York: Psychology Press.

Tunmer, W. E., & Chapman, J. W. (2003). The reading recovery approach to preventive early intervention. As good as it gets? *Reading Psychology, 24*, 337–360.

Tunmer, W. E., & Greaney, K. (2010). Defining dyslexia. *Journal of Learning Disabilities, 43*, 229–243.

Tunmer, W. E., & Hoover, W. A. (2019). The cognitive foundations of learning to read: A framework for preventing and remediating reading difficulties. *Australian Journal of Learning Difficulties, 24*(1), 75–93.

Tunmer, W. E., & Nicholson, T. (2011). The development and teaching of word recognition skill. In M. L. Kamil, P. D. Pearson, E. B. Moje, & P. Afflerbach (eds.), *Handbook of Reading Research: Vol. 4* (pp. 405–431). London: Routledge.

Tunmer, W. E., & Prochnow, J. E. (2009). Cultural relativism and literacy education: Explicit teaching based on specific learning needs is not deficit theory. In R. Openshaw, & E. Rata (eds.), *Thinking inside the Square: Political and Cultural Conformity in New Zealand* (pp. 154–190). Auckland: Pearson Education.

Tunmer, W. E., Greaney, K. T., & Prochnow, J. E. (2015). Pedagogical constructivism in New Zealand literacy education: A flawed approach to teaching reading. In W. E. Tunmer, & J. W. Chapman (eds.), *Excellence and Equity in Literacy Education* (pp. 121–144). London: Palgrave Macmillan.

Turesky, T. K., Sanfilippo, J., Zuk, J., et al. (2022). Home language and literacy environment and its relationship to socioeconomic status and white matter structure in infancy. *Brain Structure and Function, 227*(8), 2633–2645.

Turkeltaub, P. E., Eden, G. F., Jones, K. M., & Zeffiro, T. A. (2002). Meta-analysis of the functional neuroanatomy of single-word reading: Method and validation. *Neuroimage, 16*, 765–780.

Turker, S., & Hartwigsen, G. (2021). Exploring the neurobiology of reading through non-invasive brain stimulation: A review. *Cortex, 141*, 497–521.

Turker, S., & Hartwigsen, G. (2022). The use of noninvasive brain stimulation techniques to improve reading difficulties in dyslexia: A systematic review. *Human Brain Mapping, 43*(3), 1157–1173.

Ulfarsson, M. O., Walters, G. B., Gustafsson, O., et al. (2017). 15q11.2 CNV affects cognitive, structural and functional correlates of dyslexia and dyscalculia. *Translational Psychiatry, 7*, e1109.

US Department of Education. (2004). *Individuals with Disabilities Education Improvement Act of 2004 (IDEA)*. Washington, DC.

Vadasy, P. F., Sanders, E. A., & Abbott, R. D. (2008). Effects of supplemental early reading intervention at 2-year follow-up: Reading skill growth patterns and predictors. *Scientific Studies of Reading, 12*, 51–89.

Vaessen, A., & Blomert, L. (2010). Long-term cognitive dynamics of fluent reading development. *Journal of Experimental Child Psychology, 105*, 213–231.

Vaessen, A., Gerretsen, P., & Blomert, L. (2009). Naming problems do not reflect a second independent core deficit in dyslexia: Double deficits explored. *Journal of Experimental Child Psychology, 103*, 202–221.

Valdois, S. (2022). The visual-attention span deficit in developmental dyslexia: Review of evidence for a visual-attention-based deficit. *Dyslexia, 28*(4), 397–415.

Valdois, S., Bidet-Ildei, C., Lassus-Sangosse, D., et al. (2011). A visual processing but no phonological disorder in a child with mixed dyslexia. *Cortex, 47*, 1197–1218.

Valdois, S., Lassus-Sangosse, D., & Lobier, M. (2012). Impaired letter-string processing in developmental dyslexia: What visual-to-phonology code mapping disorder? *Dyslexia, 18*, 77–93.

Valdois, S., Reilhac, C., Ginestet, E., & Line Bosse, M. (2021). Varieties of cognitive profiles in poor readers: Evidence for a VAS-impaired subtype. *Journal of Learning Disabilities, 54*(3), 221–233.

van Atteveldt, N., Formisano, E., Goebel, R., & Blomert, L. (2004). Integration of letters and speech sounds in the human brain. *Neuron, 43*, 271–282.

van Bergen, E., de Jong, P. F., Plakas, A., Maassen, B., & van der Leij, A. (2012). Child and parental literacy levels within families with a history of dyslexia. *Journal of Child Psychology and Psychiatry, 53*, 28–36.

van Bergen, E., Hart, S. A., Latvala, A., et al. (2022). Literacy skills seem to fuel literacy enjoyment, rather than vice versa. *Developmental Science*, e13325.

van Bergen, E., Snowling, M. J., de Zeeuw, E. L., et al. (2018). Why do children read more? The influence of reading ability on voluntary reading practices. *Journal of Child Psychology and Psychiatry, 59*(11), 1205–1214.

van Bergen, E., van der Leij, A., & de Jong, P. F. (2014). The intergenerational multiple deficit model and the case of dyslexia. *Frontiers in Human Neuroscience,* 346.

van Bergen, E., van Zuijen, T., Bishop, D., & de Jong, P. F. (2017). Why are home literacy environment and children's reading skills associated? What parental skills reveal. *Reading Research Quarterly, 52*(2), 147–160.

van Bueren, N. E. R., Kroesbergen, E. H., & Cohen Kadosh, R. (2022). Cognitive enhancement and brain stimulation in dyslexia and dyscalculia. In M. A. Skeide (ed.). *The Cambridge Handbook of Dyslexia and Dyscalculia* (pp. 350–361). Cambridge: Cambridge University Press.

van den Boer, M., de Bree, E. H., & de Jong, P. F. (2018). Simulation of dyslexia. How literacy and cognitive skills can help distinguish college students with dyslexia from malingerers. *Plos one, 13*(5), e0196903.

van den Boer, M., Van Bergen, E., & de Jong, P. F. (2015). The specific relation of visual attention span with reading and spelling in Dutch. *Learning and Individual Differences, 39,* 141–149.

van den Noort, M., Struys, E., & Bosch, P. (2015). Transcranial magnetic stimulation research on reading and dyslexia: A new clinical intervention technique for treating dyslexia? *Neuroimmunology and Neuroinflammation, 2,* 145–152.

van Dijk, W., Schatschneider, C., Al Otaiba, S., & Hart, S. (2023). Student behavior ratings and response to Tier 1 reading intervention: Which students do not benefit? *Journal of Research on Educational Effectiveness.* https://doi.org/ 10.1080/19345747.2023.2194894

van Herck, S., Vanden Bempt, F., Economou, M., et al. (2022). Ahead of maturation: Enhanced speech envelope training boosts rise time discrimination in pre-readers at cognitive risk for dyslexia. *Developmental Science, 25*(3), e13186.

van Viersen, S., de Bree, E. H., Zee, M., et al. (2018). Pathways into literacy: The role of early oral language abilities and family risk for dyslexia. *Psychological Science, 29*(3), 418–428.

Vander Stappen, C., Dricot, L., & Van Reybroeck, M. (2020). RAN training in dyslexia: Behavioral and brain correlates. *Neuropsychologia, 146,* 107566.

Vanderauwera, J., Altarelli, I., Vandermosten, M., et al. (2016). Atypical structural asymmetry of the planum temporale is related to family history of dyslexia. *Cerebral Cortex, 28*(1), 63–72.

VanDerHeyden, A. M. (2018). Why do school psychologists cling to ineffective practices? Let's do what works. *School Psychology Forum, 12*(1), 44–52.

VanDerHeyden, A. M., Burns, M. K., & Bonifay, W. (2018). Is more screening better? The relationship between frequent screening, accurate decisions, and reading proficiency. *School Psychology Review, 47*(1), 62–82.

Vandermosten, M., Boets, B., Luts, H., et al. (2010). Adults with dyslexia are impaired in categorizing speech and nonspeech sounds on the basis of temporal cues. *Proceedings of the National Academy of Sciences, 107,* 10389–10394.

Vandermosten, M., Boets, B., Poelmans, H., et al. (2012). A tractography study in dyslexia: Neuroanatomic correlates of orthographic, phonological and speech processing. *Brain, 135*, 935–948.

Vandermosten, M., Boets, B., Wouters, J., & Ghesquière, P. (2012). A qualitative and quantitative review of diffusion tensor imaging studies in reading and dyslexia. *Neuroscience & Biobehavioral Reviews, 36*, 1532–1552.

Vandermosten, M., Correia, J., Vanderauwera, J., et al. (2020). Brain activity patterns of phonemic representations are atypical in beginning readers with family risk for dyslexia. *Developmental Science, 23*(1), e12857.

Vargo, F. E., Grossner, G. S., & Spafford, C. S. (1995). Digit span and other WISC-R scores in the diagnosis of dyslexic children. *Perceptual and Motor Skills, 80*, 1219–1229.

Vaughn, S., & Fletcher, J. M. (2010). Thoughts on rethinking response to intervention with secondary students. *School Psychology Review, 39*, 296–299.

Vaughn, S., & Fletcher, J. M. (2012). Response to intervention with secondary school students with reading difficulties. *Journal of Learning Disabilities, 45*, 244–256.

Vaughn, S., & Fletcher, J. M. (2021). Identifying and teaching students with significant reading problems. *American Educator, 44*(4), 4.

Vaughn, S., & Roberts, G. (2007). Secondary interventions in reading: Providing additional instruction for students at risk. *Teaching Exceptional Children, 39*, 40–46.

Vaughn, S., Cirino, P. T., Wanzek, J., et al. (2010). Response to intervention for middle school students with reading difficulties: Effects of a primary and secondary intervention. *School Psychology Review, 39*, 3–21.

Vaughn, S., Fletcher, J. M., Francis, D. J., et al. (2008). Response to intervention with older students with reading difficulties. *Learning and Individual Differences, 18*, 338–345.

Vaughn, S., Grills, A. E., Capin, P., et al. (2022). Examining the effects of integrating anxiety management instruction within a reading intervention for upper elementary students with reading difficulties. *Journal of Learning Disabilities, 55*(5), 408–426.

Vaughn, S., Martinez, L. R., Williams, K. J., et al. (2019). Efficacy of a high school extensive reading intervention for English learners with reading difficulties. *Journal of Educational Psychology, 111*(3), 373–386.

Vaughn, S., Roberts, G. J., Miciak, J., Taylor, P., & Fletcher, J. M. (2019). Efficacy of a word-and text-based intervention for students with significant reading difficulties. *Journal of Learning Disabilities, 52*(1), 31–44.

Vaughn, S., Wexler, J., Roberts, G., et al. (2011). Effects of individualized and standardized interventions on middle school students with reading disabilities. *Exceptional Children, 77*, 391–407.

Vehmas, S., & Watson, N. (2014). Moral wrongs, disadvantages, and disability: A critique of critical disability studies. *Disability and Society, 29*, 638–650.

Velayos-Baeza, A., Toma, C., Paracchini, S., & Monaco, A. (2007). The dyslexia-associated gene KIAA0319 encodes highly N- and O-glycosylated plasma membrane and secreted isoforms. *Human Molecular Genetics, 17*, 859–871.

Vellutino, F. R. (1979). *Dyslexia: Theory and research.* Cambridge, MA: MIT Press.

Vellutino, F. R. (1987). Dyslexia. *Scientific American, 256,* 34–41.

Vellutino, F. R., Fletcher, J. M., Snowling, M. J., & Scanlon, D. M. (2004). Specific reading disability (dyslexia): What have we learned in the past four decades? *Journal of Child Psychology & Psychiatry, 45,* 2–40.

Vellutino, F. R., Scanlon, D. M., & Jaccard, J. (2003). Toward distinguishing between cognitive and experiential deficits as primary sources of difficulty in learning to read: A two year follow-up of difficult to remediate, readily remediated poor readers. In B. R. Foorman (ed.), *Preventing and Remediating Reading Difficulties: Bringing Science to Scale* (pp. 73–120). Baltimore: York Press.

Vellutino, F. R., Scanlon, D. M., & Lyon, G. R. (2000). Differentiating between difficult-to-remediate and readily remediated poor readers: More evidence against the IQ-achievement discrepancy definition for reading disability. *Journal of Learning Disabilities, 33,* 223–238.

Vellutino, F. R., Scanlon, D. M., & Tanzman, M. S. (1998). The case for early intervention in diagnosing specific reading disability. *Journal of School Psychology, 36,* 367–397.

Vellutino, F. R., Scanlon, D. M., Sipay, E. R., et al. (1996). Cognitive profiles of difficult-to-remediate and readily remediated poor readers: Early intervention as a vehicle for distinguishing between cognitive and experiential deficits as basic causes of specific reading disability. *Journal of Educational Psychology, 88,* 601–638.

Vellutino, F. R., Scanlon, D. M., Zhang, H., & Schatschneider, C. (2008). Using response to kindergarten and first grade intervention to identify children at-risk for long-term reading difficulties. *Reading and Writing, 21,* 437–480.

Verhoeven, L., & Perfetti, C. (2022). Universals in learning to read across languages and writing systems. *Scientific Studies of Reading, 26*(2), 150–164

Verhoeven, L., Perfetti, & Pugh, K. (2019). Developmental dyslexia – A cross linguistic perspective. In C. Perfetti, K. Pugh, & L. Verhoeven (eds.), *Developmental Dyslexia across Languages and Writing Systems* (pp. 1–22). New York: Cambridge University Press.

Verhoeven, L., van Leeuwe, J., & Vermeer, A. (2011). Vocabulary growth and reading development across the elementary school years. *Scientific Studies of Reading, 15*(1), 8–25.

Verpalen, A., Van de Vijver, F., & Backus, A. (2018). Bias in dyslexia screening in a Dutch multicultural population. *Annals of Dyslexia, 68*(1), 43–68.

Vicari, S., Finzi, A., Menghini, D., et al. (2005). Do children with developmental dyslexia have an implicit learning deficit? *Journal of Neurology, Neurosurgery and Psychiatry, 76,* 1392–1397.

Vicari, S., Marotta, L., Menghini, D., Molinari, M., & Petrosini, L. (2003). Implicit learning deficit in children with developmental dyslexia. *Neuropsychologia, 41,* 108–114.

Vidyasagar, T. R. (2019). Visual attention and neural oscillations in reading and dyslexia: Are they possible targets for remediation? *Neuropsychologia, 130,* 59–65.

Vidyasagar, T. R., & Pammer, K. (2010). Dyslexia: A deficit in visuo-spatial attention, not in phonological processing. *Trends in Cognitive Sciences, 14*(2), 57–63.

Vigneau, M., Beaucousin, V., Herve, P. Y., et al. (2006). Meta-analyzing left hemisphere language areas: Phonology, semantics, and sentence processing. *Neuroimage*, *30*, 1414–1432.

Vinckenbosch, E., Robichon, F., & Eliez, S. (2005). Gray matter alteration in dyslexia: Converging evidence from volumetric and voxel-by-voxel MRI analyses. *Neuropsychologia*, *43*, 324–331.

Virsu, V., Lahti-Nuuttila, P., & Laasonen, M. (2003). Crossmodal temporal processing acuity impairment aggravates with age in developmental dyslexia. *Neuroscience Letters*, *336*(3), 151–154.

Virtala, P., Kujala, T., Partanen, E., Hamalainen, J. A., & Winkler, I. (2023). Neural phoneme discrimination in variable speech in newborns; associations with dyslexia risk and later language skills. *Brain and Cognition*, *168*, 105974.

Visser, L., Kalmar, J., Linkersdörfer, J., et al. (2020). Comorbidities between specific learning disorders and psychopathology in elementary school children in Germany. *Frontiers in Psychiatry*, 292.

Vitsios, D., Dhindsa, R. S., Middleton, L., Gussow, A. B., & Petrovski, S. (2021). Prioritizing non-coding regions based on human genomic constraint and sequence context with deep learning. *Nature Communications*, *12*(1), 1504.

Vogel, A., Petersen, S. E., & Schlaggar, B. (2014). The VWFA: It's not just for words anymore. *Frontiers in Human Neuroscience*, 8.

Vogel, A. C., Miezin, F. M., Petersen, S. E., & Schlaggar, B. L. (2012). The putative visual word form area is functionally connected to the dorsal attention network. *Cerebral Cortex*, *22*, 537–549.

Volkmer, S., & Schulte-Körne, G. (2018). Cortical responses to tone and phoneme mismatch as a predictor of dyslexia? A systematic review. *Schizophrenia Research*, *191*, 148–160.

von Plessen, K., Lundervold, A., Duta, N., et al. (2002). Less developed corpus callosum in dyslexic subjects – A structural MRI study. *Neuropsychologia*, *40*, 1035–1044.

Vosskuhl, J., Strüber, D., & Herrmann, C. S. (2018). Non-invasive brain stimulation: A paradigm shift in understanding brain oscillations. *Frontiers in Human Neuroscience*, 12.

Vourkas, M., Micheloyannis, S., Simos, P. G., et al. (2011). Dynamic task-specific brain network connectivity in children with severe reading difficulties. *Neuroscience Letters*, *488*, 123–128.

Vukovic, R. K., & Siegel, L. S. (2006). The double-deficit hypothesis: A comprehensive analysis of the evidence. *Journal of Learning Disabilities*, *39*, 25–47.

Wadsworth, S. J., DeFries, J. C., Willcutt, E. G., Pennington, B. F., & Olson, R. K. (2015). The Colorado longitudinal twin study of reading difficulties and ADHD: Etiologies of comorbidity and stability. *Twin Research and Human Genetics*, *18*, 755–761.

Wadsworth, S. J., Olson, R. K., & DeFries, J. C. (2010). Differential genetic etiology of reading difficulties as a function of IQ: An update. *Behavior Genetics*, *40*, 751–758.

Wagner, R. K. (2008). Rediscovering dyslexia: New approaches for identification and classification. In G. Reid, A. Fawcett, F. Manis, & L. Siegel (eds.), *The Sage Handbook of Dyslexia* (pp. 174–191). London: Sage.

Wagner, R. K., & Lonigan, C. J. (2022). Early identification of children with dyslexia: Variables differentially predict poor reading versus unexpected poor reading. *Reading Research Quarterly, 58*(2), 188–202.

Wagner, R. K., & Muse, A. (2006). Short-term memory deficits in developmental dyslexia. In T. P. Alloway, & S. E. Gathercole (eds.), *Working Memory and Neurodevelopmental Disorders*. New York: Psychology Press.

Wagner, R. K., & Torgesen, J. K. (1987). The nature of phonological processing and its causal role in the acquisition of reading skills. *Psychological Bulletin, 101*, 192–212.

Wagner, R. K., Edwards, A. A., Malkowski, A., et al. (2019). Combining old and new for better understanding and predicting dyslexia. *New Directions for Child and Adolescent Development, 165*, 11–23.

Wagner, R. K., Torgesen, J. K., & Rashotte, C. A. (1999). *Comprehensive Test of Phonological Processing*. Austin: Pro-Ed.

Wagner, R. K., Torgesen, J. K., Rashotte, C. A., et al. (1997). Changing relations between phonological processing abilities and word-level reading as children develop from beginning to skilled readers: A five-year longitudinal study. *Developmental Psychology, 33*, 468–479.

Wagner, R. K., Zirps, F. A., Edwards, A. A., et al. (2020). The prevalence of dyslexia: A new approach to its estimation. *Journal of Learning Disabilities, 53*(5), 354–365.

Wagner, R. K., Moxley, J., Schatschneider, C., & Zirps, F. A. (2023). A bayesian probabilistic framework for the identification of individuals with dyslexia. *Scientific Studies of Reading, 27*(1), 67–81.

Walker, J. E. (2010). Recent advances in quantitative EEG as an aid to diagnosis and as a guide to neurofeedback training for cortical hypofunctions, hyperfunctions, disconnections, and hyperconnections: Improving efficacy in complicated neurological and psychological disorders. *Applied Psychophysiology and Biofeedback, 35*(1), 25–27.

Walker, J. E., & Norman, C. A. (2006). The neurophysiology of dyslexia: A selective review with implications for neurofeedback remediation and results of treatment in twelve consecutive patients. *Journal of Neurotherapy: Investigations in Neuromodulation Neurofeedback and Applied Neuroscience, 10*, 45–55.

Walker, K., Hall, S., Klein, R. G., & Phillips, D. (2006). Development of perceptual correlates of reading performance. *Brain Research, 1124*(1), 126–141.

Walker, N. (2014). Neurodiversity: Some basic terms & definitions. https://neuroqueer.com/neurodiversity-terms-and-definitions. Accessed December 3, 2023.

Wang, J. J., Bi, H. Y., Gao, L. Q., & Wydell, T. N. (2010). The visual magnocellular pathway in Chinese-speaking children with developmental dyslexia. *Neuropsychologia, 48*, 3627–3633.

Wang, J., Joanisse, M. F., & Booth, J. R. (2020). Neural representations of phonology in temporal cortex scaffold longitudinal reading gains in 5- to 7-year-old children. *Neuroimage, 207*, 116359.

Wang, J., Pines, J., Joanisse, M., & Booth, J. R. (2021). Reciprocal relations between reading skill and the neural basis of phonological awareness in 7- to 9-year-old children. *Neuroimage, 236.*

Wang, J., Tong, F., Joanisse, M. F., & Booth, J. R. (2023). A sculpting effect of reading on later representational quality of phonology revealed by multi-voxel pattern analysis in young children. *Brain and Language, 239,* 105252.

Wang, S., Tzeng, O. J. L., & Aslin, R. N. (2022). Predictive brain signals mediate association between shared reading and expressive vocabulary in infants. *PLoS ONE, 17,* e0272438.

Wang, Y., Mauer, M. V., Raney, T., et al. (2017). Development of tract-specific white matter pathways during early reading development in at-risk children and typical controls. *Cerebral Cortex, 27,* 2469–2485.

Wang, Y., Paramasivam, M., Thomas, A., et al. (2006). Dyx1c1 functions in neuronal migration in developing neocortex. *Neuroscience, 143,* 515–522.

Wang, Y., Yin, X., Rosen, G., et al. (2011). Dcdc2 knockout mice display exacerbated developmental disruptions following knockdown of doublecortin. *Neuroscience, 190,* 398–408.

Wanzek, J., Al Otaiba, S., Petscher, Y., et al. (2021). Comparing effects of reading intervention versus reading and mindset intervention for upper elementary students with reading difficulties. *Journal of Learning Disabilities, 54*(3), 203–220.

Wanzek, J., & Roberts, G. (2012). Reading interventions with varying instructional emphases for fourth graders with reading difficulties. *Learning Disability Quarterly, 35*(2), 90–101

Wanzek, J., Stevens, E. A., Williams, K. J., et al. (2018). Current evidence on the effects of intensive early reading interventions. *Journal of Learning Disabilities, 51*(6), 612–624.

Wanzek, J., Vaughn, S. (2007). Research-based implications from extensive early reading interventions. *School Psychology Review, 36*(4), 541–561.

Wanzek, J., Vaughn, S., Scammacca, N. K., et al. (2016) Meta-analyses of the effects of tier 2 type reading interventions in grades K-3. *Educational Psychology Review, 28,* 551–576.

Wanzek, J., Vaughn, S., Scammacca, N. K., et al. (2013). Extensive reading interventions for students with reading difficulties after grade 3. *Review of Educational Research, 83*(2), 163–195.

Wanzek, J., Wexler, J., Vaughn, S., & Ciullo, S. (2010). Reading interventions for struggling readers in the upper elementary grades: A synthesis of 20 years of research. *Reading and Writing, 23,* 889–912.

Wanzek, J., Wood, C., & Schatschneider, C. (2022). Elementary classroom vocabulary experiences. *Remedial and Special Education, 43*(3), 147–159.

Ward, S. B., Ward, T. J., Hatt, C. V., Young, D. L., & Molner, N. R. (1995). The incidence and utility of the ACID, ACIDS and SCAD profiles in a referred population. *Psychology in the Schools, 32,* 267–276.

Washburn, E. K., Mulcahy, C. A., Musante, G., & Joshi, R. (2017). Novice teachers' knowledge of reading-related disabilities and dyslexia. *Learning Disabilities: A Contemporary Journal, 15*(2), 169–191.

Watkins, E. (1922). *How to Teach Silent Reading to Beginners*. Philadelphia and London: Lippincott.

Watkins, M. W. (2000). Cognitive profile analysis: A shared professional myth. *School Psychology Quarterly, 15*, 465–479.

Watkins, M. W., & Canivez, G. L. (2021). Are there cognitive profiles unique to students with learning disabilities? A latent profile analysis of Wechsler Intelligence Scale for Children–fourth edition scores. *School Psychology Review*, 1–13.

Watkins, M. W., Canivez, G. L., Dombrowski, S. C., et al. (2022). Long-term stability of Wechsler Intelligence Scale for Children–fifth edition scores in a clinical sample. *Applied Neuropsychology: Child, 11*(3), 422–428.

Watkins, M. W., Kush, J. C., & Glutting, J. J. (1997). Discriminant and predictive validity of the WISC-III ACID profile among children with learning disabilities. *Psychology in the Schools, 34*, 309–319.

Webster, R., Russell, A., & Blatchford, P. (2015). *Maximising the Impact of Teaching Assistants: Guidance for School Leaders and Teachers*. London: Routledge.

Wechsler, D. (2014). *Wechsler Intelligence Scale for Children, Fifth Edition* (WISC-V). San Antonio, TX: NCS Pearson.

Wegener, S., Beyersmann, E., Wang, H. C., & Castles, A. (2022). Oral vocabulary knowledge and learning to read new words: A theoretical review. *Australian Journal of Learning Difficulties, 27*(2), 253–278.

Weirauch, M. T., Yang, A., Albu, M., et al. (2014). Determination and inference of eukaryotic transcription factor sequence specificity. *Cell, 158*(6), 1431–1443.

Weis, R., & Droder, S. J. (2019). Development and initial validation of a reading-specific performance validity test: The College Assessment of Reading Effort (CARE). *Psychological Injury and Law, 12*(1), 29–41.

Weis, R., & Waters, E. A. (2023). Evidence-based accommodations for postsecondary students with disabilities: Beware the base rate fallacy. *Psychological Injury and Law*, 1–14.

Weisberg, D. S., Keil, F. C., Goodstein, J., Rawson, E., & Gray, J. R. (2008). The seductive allure of neuroscience explanations. *Journal of Cognitive Neuroscience, 20*(3), 470–477.

Weisberg, D. S., Taylor, J. C., & Hopkins, E. J. (2015). Deconstructing the seductive allure of neuroscience explanations, *Judgment and Decision Making, 10*(5), 429–441.

Weiss, Y., Cweigenberg, H. G., & Booth, J. R. (2018). Neural specialization of phonological and semantic processing in young children. *Human Brain Mapping, 39*, 4334–4348.

Werth, R. (2019). What causes dyslexia? Identifying the causes and effective compensatory therapy. *Restorative Neurology and Neuroscience, 37*(6), 591–608.

Werth, R. (2021a). Is developmental dyslexia due to a visual and not a phonological impairment? *Brain Sciences, 11*(10), 1313.

Werth, R. (2021b). Dyslexic readers improve without training when using a computer-guided reading strategy. *Brain Sciences, 11*(5), 526.

West, T. G. (2022). Dyslexic strengths in times of adversity. *Asia Pacific Journal of Developmental Differences, 9*(2), 194–203.

Westendorp, M., Hartman, E., Houwen, S., Smith, J., & Visscher, C. (2011). The relationship between gross motor skills and academic achievement in children with learning disabilities. *Research in Developmental Disabilities, 32,* 2773–2779.

Wexler, J., Vaughn, S., Edmonds, M., & Reutebuch, C. L. (2008). A synthesis of fluency interventions for secondary struggling readers. *Reading and Writing, 21,* 317–347.

What Works Clearinghouse. (2007). Fast ForWord. https://bit.ly/4ap2ssv. Accessed December 8, 2023.

What Works Clearinghouse. (2010). Orton-Gillingham-based strategies (unbranded). US Department of Education, Institute of Education Sciences. https://bit.ly/47FRKM6. Accessed December 3, 2023.

Wheldall, K., Castles, A., & Nayton, M. (2014). Should we dispense with the D word. *Learning Difficulties Australia Bulletin, 46*(1&2), 1–4.

White, A. L., Boynton, G. M., & Yeatman, J. D. (2019). The link between reading ability and visual spatial attention across development. *Cortex, 121,* 44–59.

White, J., Mather, N., & Kirkpatrick, J. (2020). Preservice educators' and noneducators' knowledge and perceptions of responsibility about dyslexia. *Dyslexia, 26*(2), 220–242.

White, S., Milne, E., Rosen, S., et al. (2006). The role of sensorimotor impairments in dyslexia: A multiple case study of dyslexic children. *Developmental Science, 9,* 237–269.

Whitehouse, A. J., & Bishop, D. V. (2008). Cerebral dominance for language function in adults with specific language impairment or autism. *Brain, 131,* 3193–3200.

Whitehouse, A. J., Spector, T. D., & Cherkas, L. F. (2009). No clear genetic influences on the association between dyslexia and anxiety in a population-based sample of female twins. *Dyslexia, 15,* 282–290.

Wilcox, G., Galilee, A., Stamp, J., Makarenko, E., & MacMaster, F. P. (2020). The importance of research on integrating transcranial direct current stimulation (TDCS) with evidence-based reading interventions. *Journal of Pediatric Neuropsychology, 6,* 218–228.

Wilkins, A. (2021). Visual stress: Origins and treatment. *CNS* (6), 74–86.

Wilkins, A. J. (1995). *Visual Stress.* Oxford: Oxford University Press.

Wilkins, A. J. (2003). *Reading through Colour.* London: Wiley.

Wilkins, A. J., & Evans, B. J. (2022). Do coloured filters work? In A. J. Wilkins, & B. J. Evans (eds.), *Vision, Reading Difficulties, and Visual Stress* (pp. 169–193). Cham, Switzerland: Springer Nature.

Willcutt, E. G., & Pennington, B. F. (2000). Psychiatric comorbidity in children and adolescents with reading disability. *Journal of Child Psycholology and Psychiatry, 41,* 1039–1048.

Willcutt, E. G., & Petrill, S. A. (2023). Comorbidity between reading disability and attention-deficit/hyperactivity disorder in a community sample: Implications for academic, social, and neuropsychological functioning. *Mind, Brain, and Education,* 1–10.

Williams, V. J., Juranek, J., Cirino, P., & Fletcher, J. M. (2018). Cortical thickness and local gyrification in children with developmental dyslexia. *Cerebral Cortex*, *28*, 963–973.

Wilmot, A., Pizzey, H., Leitão, S., Hasking, P., & Boyes, M. (2022). Growing up with dyslexia: Child and parent perspectives on school struggles, self-esteem, and mental health. *Dyslexia*, *29*(1), 40–54.

Wilsher, C. R., & Taylor, E. A. (1994). Piracetam in developmental reading disorders: A review. *European Child & Adolescent Psychiatry*, *3*(2), 59–71.

Wimmer, H., Schurz, M., Sturm, D., et al. (2010). A dual-route perspective on poor reading in a regular orthography: An fMRI study. *Cortex*, *46*, 1284–1298.

Witton, C., Swoboda, K., Shapiro, L. R., & Talcott, J. B. (2020). Auditory frequency discrimination in developmental dyslexia: A meta-analysis. *Dyslexia*, *26*(1), 36–51.

Wolf, M. (2007). *Proust and the Squid: The Story and Science of the Reading Brain*. New York: HarperCollins.

Wolf, M., & Bowers, P. G. (1999). The double-deficit hypothesis for the developmental dyslexias. *Journal of Educational Psychology*, *91*, 415–438.

Wolf, M., Bowers, P. G., & Biddle, K. (2000). Naming-speed processes, timing, and reading: A conceptual review. *Journal of Learning Disabilities*, *33*, 387–407.

Wolf, M., Gotlieb, R. J. M., Kim, S. A., et al. (2024). Towards a dynamic, comprehensive conceptualization of dyslexia. *Annals of Dyslexia*, 1–22.

Wolf, M., Miller, L., & Donnelly, K. (2000). Retrieval, Automaticity, Vocabulary Elaboration, Orthography (RAVE-O): A comprehensive, fluency-based reading intervention program. *Journal of Learning Disabilities*, *33*, 375–386.

Wolf, M., O'Rourke, A. G., Gidney, C., et al. (2002). The second deficit: An investigation of the independence of phonological and naming-speed deficits in developmental dyslexia. *Reading & Writing*, *15*, 43–72.

Wolff, P. H., Melngailis, I., Obregon, M., & Bedrosian, M. (1995). Family patterns of developmental dyslexia, Part II: Behavioral phenotypes. *American Journal of Medical Genetics*, *60*, 494–505.

Wolff, U., & Gustafsson, J. E. (2022). Early phonological training preceding kindergarten training: Effects on reading and spelling. *Reading and Writing*, 1–23.

Wood, S. G., Moxley, J. H., Tighe, E. L., & Wagner, R. K. (2018). Does use of text-to-speech and related read-aloud tools improve reading comprehension for students with reading disabilities? A meta-analysis. *Journal of Learning Disabilities*, *51*(1), 73–84.

Woodcock, R. W. (1987). *Woodcock Reading Mastery Tests Revised*. Circle Pines, MN: American Guidance Service.

World Health Organization. (2023) *International Classification of Diseases, 11th Revision*. (ICD-11). https://icd.who.int/en. Accessed December 3, 2023.

Worthy, J., Daly-Lesch, A., Tily, S., Godfrey, V., & Salmerón, C. (2021). A critical evaluation of dyslexia information on the internet. *Journal of Literacy Research*, *53*(1), 5–28.

Worthy, J., DeJulio, S., Svrcek, N., et al. (2016). Teachers' understandings, perspectives, and experiences of dyslexia. *Literacy Research: Theory, Method and Practice*, *65*, 436–453.

Worthy, J., Godfrey, V., Tily, S., Daly-Lesch, A., & Salmerón, C. (2019). Simple answers and quick fixes: Dyslexia and the brain on the internet. *Literacy Research: Theory, Method, and Practice*, *68*(1), 314–333.

Worthy, J., Lammert, C., Long, S. L., Salmerón, C., & Godfrey, V. (2018a). "What if we were committed to giving every individual the services and opportunities they need?" Teacher educators' understandings, perspectives, and practices surrounding dyslexia. *Research in the Teaching of English*, *53*(2), 125–148.

Worthy, J., Salmerón, C., Long, S. L., Lammert, C., & Godfrey, V. (2018b). "Wrestling with the politics and ideology": Teacher educators' responses to dyslexia discourse and legislation. *Literacy Research: Theory, Method, and Practice*, *67*(1), 377–393.

Worthy, J., Svrcek, N., Daly-Lesch, A., & Tily, S. (2018). "We know for a fact": Dyslexia interventionists and the power of authoritative discourse. *Journal of Literacy Research*, *50*(3), 359–382.

Worthy, J., Villarreal, D., Godfrey, V., et al. (2017). A critical analysis of dyslexia legislation in three states. *Literacy Research: Theory, Method, and Practice*, *66*(1), 406–421.

Wray, N. R., Wijmenga, C., Sullivan, P. F., Yang, J., & Visscher, P. M. (2018). Common disease is more complex than implied by the core gene omnigenic model. *Cell*, *173*, 1573–1580.

Wright, C. M., & Conlon, E. G. (2009). Auditory and visual processing in children with dyslexia. *Developmental Neuropsychology*, *34*, 330–355.

Wright, C. M., Conlon, E. G., & Dyck, M. (2012). Visual search deficits are independent of magnocellular deficits in dyslexia. *Annals of Dyslexia*, *62*, 53–69.

Wu, S., Stratton, K. K., & Gadke, D. L. (2020). Maximizing repeated readings: The effects of a multicomponent reading fluency intervention for children with reading difficulties. *Contemporary School Psychology*, *24*(2), 217–227.

Wyse, D., & Bradbury, A. (2022). Reading wars or reading reconciliation? A critical examination of robust research evidence, curriculum policy and teachers' practices for teaching phonics and reading. *Review of Education*, *10*(1), e3314.

Xia, Z., Hoeft, F., Zhang, L., & Shu, H. (2016). Neuroanatomical anomalies of dyslexia: Disambiguating the effects of disorder, performance, and maturation. *Neuropsychologia*, *81*, 68–78.

Xiao, P., Zhu, K., Feng, Y., et al. (2023). Associations between dyslexia and children's mental health: Findings from a follow-up study in China. *Psychiatry Research*, 115188.

Xu, B., Grafman, J., Gaillard, W. D., et al. (2001). Conjoint and extended neural networks for the computation of speech codes: The neural basis of selective impairment in reading sords and pseudowords. *Cerebral Cortex*, *11*, 267–277.

Yaden Jr, D. B., Reinking, D., & Smagorinsky, P. (2021). The trouble with binaries: A perspective on the science of reading. *Reading Research Quarterly*, *56*, S119–S129.

Yamada, Y., Stevens, C., Dow, M., et al. (2011). Emergence of the neural network for reading in five-year-old beginning readers of different levels of pre-literacy abilities: An fMRI study. *Neuroimage, 57*, 704–713.

Yan, X., Perkins, K., & Cao, F. (2021). A hierarchical deficit model of reading disability: Evidence from dynamic causal modelling analysis. *Neuropsychologia, 154*, 107777.

Yang, L., Li, C., Li, X., et al. (2022). Prevalence of developmental dyslexia in primary school children: A systematic review and meta-analysis. *Brain Sciences, 12*(2), 240.

Yang, Y., Yang, Y. H., Li, J., Xu, M., & Bi, H.-Y. (2020). An audiovisual integration deficit underlies reading failure in nontransparent writing systems: An fMRI study of Chinese children with dyslexia. *Journal of Neurolinguistics, 54*, 100884.

Yeager, D. S., & Dweck, C. S. (2020). What can be learned from growth mindset controversies? *American Psychologist, 75*(9), 1269–1284.

Yeatman, J. D. (2022a), Neuroplasticity in response to reading intervention. In M. A. Skeide (ed.), *The Cambridge Handbook of Dyslexia and Dyscalculia* (pp. 202–211). Cambridge: Cambridge University Press.

Yeatman, J. D. (2022b). The neurobiology of literacy. In M. J. Snowling, C. Hulme, & K. Nation (eds.), *The Science of Reading: A Handbook*. 2nd edition (pp. 533–555). Hoboken, NJ: Wiley.

Yeatman, J. D., Ben-Shachar, M., Bammer, R., & Feldman, H. M. (2009). Using diffusion tensor imaging and fiber tracking to characterize diffuse perinatal white matter injury: A case report. *Journal of Child Neurology, 24*, 795–800.

Yeatman, J. D., Dougherty, R. F., Ben-Shachar, M., & Wandell, B. A. (2012). Development of white matter and reading skills. *Proceedings of the National Academy of Sciences, 109*(44), E3045–E3053.

Yeatman, J. D., & White, A. L. (2021). Reading: The confluence of vision and language. *Annual Review of Vision Science, 7*, 487–517

Yeh, F.-C., Vettel, J. M., Singh, A., et al. (2016). Quantifying differences and similarities in whole-brain white matter architecture using local connectome fingerprints. *PLoS Computational Biology, 12*, e1005203.

Youman, M., & Mather, N. (2015). Dyslexia laws in the USA: An update. *Perspectives on Language and Literacy, 41*(4), 10–18.

Younger, R., & Meisinger, E. B. (2020). Group stability and reading profiles of students with dyslexia: A double-deficit perspective. *Learning Disability Quarterly, 45*(4), 239–251.

Yu, X., Zuk, J., & Gaab, N. (2018). What factors facilitate resilience in developmental dyslexia? Examining protective and compensatory mechanisms across the neurodevelopmental trajectory. *Child Development Perspectives, 12*, 240–246.

Yule, W. (1976). Dyslexia. *Psychological Medicine, 6*, 165–167.

Zane, T. (2005). Fads in special education: An overview. In J. W. Jacobson, R. M. Foxx, & J. A. Mulick (eds.), *Controversial Therapies for Developmental Disabilities: Fad, Fashion and Science in Professional Practice* (pp. 175–191). Mahwah, NJ: Lawrence Erlbaum.

Zhang, J., & McBride-Chang, C. (2010). Auditory sensitivity, speech perception, and reading development and impairment. *Educational Psychology Review, 22,* 323–338.

Zhang, M., Riecke, L., & Bonte, M. (2021). Neurophysiological tracking of speech-structure learning in typical and dyslexic readers. *Neuropsychologia, 158,* 107889.

Zhang, S. Z., Inoue, T., Shu, H., & Georgiou, G. K. (2020). How does home literacy environment influence reading comprehension in Chinese? Evidence from a 3-year longitudinal study. *Reading & Writing, 33,* 1745–1767.

Zhang, Z., & Peng, P. (2023) Longitudinal reciprocal relations among reading, executive function, and social-emotional skills: Maybe not for all. *Journal of Educational Psychology, 115*(3), 475–501.

Zhao, J., Liu, H., Li, J., et al. (2019). Improving sentence reading performance in Chinese children with developmental dyslexia by training based on visual attention span. *Scientific Reports, 9*(1), 1–19.

Zhong, R., Yang, B., Tang, H., et al. (2013). Meta-analysis of the association between DCDC2 polymorphisms and risk of dyslexia. *Molecular Neurobiology, 47,* 435–442.

Ziegler, J. C., Bertrand, D., Tóth, D., et al. (2010). Orthographic depth and its impact on universal predictors of reading. *Psychological Science, 21,* 551–559.

Ziegler, J. C., & Goswami, U. (2005). Reading acquisition, developmental dyslexia, and skilled reading across languages: A psycholinguistic grain size theory. *Psychological Bulletin, 131,* 3–29.

Ziegler, J. C., Pech-Georgel, C., Dufau, S., & Grainger, J. (2010). Rapid processing of letters, digits and symbols: What purely visual-attentional deficit in developmental dyslexia? *Developmental Science, 13,* F8–F14.

Zimmermann, L. M., Reed, D. K., & Aloe, A. M. (2021). A meta-analysis of non-repetitive reading fluency interventions for students with reading difficulties. *Remedial and Special Education, 42*(2), 78–93.

Zoccolotti, P. (2022). Success is not the entire story for a scientific theory: The case of the phonological deficit theory of dyslexia. *Brain Sciences, 12*(4), 425.

Zoccolotti, P., De Luca, M., Di Filippo, G., Judica, A., & Martelli, M. (2009). Reading development in an orthographically regular language: Effects of length, frequency, lexicality and global processing ability. *Reading and Writing, 22,* 1053–1079.

Zorzi, M., Barbiero, C., Facoetti, A., et al. (2012). Extra-large letter spacing improves reading in dyslexia. *Proceedings of the National Academy of Sciences, 109,* 11455–11459.

Zoubrinetzky, R., Collet, G., Nguyen-Morel, M. A., Valdois, S., & Serniclaes, W. (2019). Remediation of allophonic perception and visual attention span in developmental dyslexia: A joint assay. *Frontiers in Psychology, 10,* 1502.

Zou, L., Chen, W., Shao, S., et al. (2012). Genetic variant in KIAA0319, but not in DYX1C1, is associated with risk of dyslexia: An integrated meta-analysis. *American Journal of Medical Genetics. Part B, Neuropsychiatric Genetics, 159b,* 970–976.

Zoubrinetzky, R., Collet, G., Serniclaes, W., Nguyen-Morel, M. A., & Valdois, S. (2016). Relationships between categorical perception of phonemes, phoneme awareness, and visual attention span in developmental dyslexia. *PloS one*, *11*(3), e0151015.

Zugarramurdi, C., Fernández, L., Lallier, M., Valle-Lisboa, J. C., & Carreiras, M. (2022). Mind the orthography: Revisiting the contribution of prereading phonological awareness to reading acquisition. *Developmental Psychology*, *58*(6), 1003–1016.

Zumeta, R. O., Compton, D. L., & Fuchs, L. S. (2012). Using word identification fluency to monitor first-grade reading development. *Exceptional Children*, *78*, 201–220.

Zuppardo, L., Serrano, F., Pirrone, C., & Rodriguez-Fuentes, A. (2023). More than words: Anxiety, self-esteem and behavioral problems in children and adolescents with dyslexia. *Learning Disability Quarterly*, *46*(2), 77–91.

Zweig, E., & Pylkkänen, L. (2009). A visual M170 effect of morphological complexity. *Language and Cognitive Processes*, *24*, 412–439.

Index